D1532725

Understanding Directory Services

Beth Sheresh
Doug Sheresh
Systems Research Corporation

SAMS

201 West 103rd St., Indianapolis, Indiana 46290 USA

International Standard Book Number: 0-672-32305-2

Library of Congress Catalog Card Number: 2001094219

Printed in the United States of America

First Printing: December, 2001

04 03 02 01 4 3 2 1

Associate Publisher
Jeff Koch

Acquisitions Editor
William E. Brown

Development Editor
Mark Renfrow

Managing Editor
Matt Purcell

Project Editor
George E. Nedeff

Copy Editor
Linda Seifert

Indexer
Sandy Henselmeier

Proofreader
Wendy Ott

Technical Editor
Marcus Williamson

Team Coordinator
Lynne Williams

Interior Designer
Anne Jones

Cover Designer
Aren Howell

Page Layout
Rebecca Harmon

Contents at a Glance

Contents

About the Authors

Beth Sheresh, CNE, is Systems Research Corporation's lead technologist, with professional experience in network consulting, systems administration, Web development, and technical training course design. Her expertise includes managing technical writing projects, as well as researching, designing, and writing about network technologies. She is currently working on a book series that encourages women to get involved with computers and network technology.

Doug Sheresh, MCSE, is a principal of Systems Research Corporation with professional experience that spans project management, network consulting, technical writing, and all aspects of training course development, design and delivery. His prior writing on technology ranges from developing training on Windows 3.1–95 and contributing to the Windows 95 Resource Kit at Microsoft, as well as co-authoring the *Windows NT Administrators Bible, Option Pack Edition*. More recently, Doug was a core developer of the MOF *Operations Assessment* training for Microsoft Consulting Services.

About the Technical Editor

Marcus Williamson is managing director of Connectotel, the London-based consultancy and software development company that creates solutions for Novell eDirectory and GSM/SMS. From 1990 to 1996 he worked for Novell, latterly as team leader for Novell Consulting, based at Novell Duesseldorf, Germany. Marcus is a contributor to the Novell Research AppNotes and other technical publications, is a regular speaker at Novell's Brainshare events in the U.S. and Europe, and is a sysop on Novell Support Connection forums. Marcus's home page can be found at `www.connectotel.com/marcus`.

Dedication

...for all who teach, and all who seek to learn...

Acknowledgments

"*Poof, it's a book!*"

—Al Valvano, 1999

If it were only that easy, yet any book project requires the effort of a great many people in addition to the authors. A number of people have been integral to the success of this project and we would like to express our appreciation for all their work.

First, we want to give our sincere thanks to William Brown for his commitment to this project and to the development of materials which document core IT technologies, and to commend Mark Renfrow, George Nedeff, Linda Seifert, Wendy Ott, and Sandy Henselmeier at Sams Publishing for their support and efforts to bring the vision of the second edition of *Understanding Directory Services* to fruition.

We also want to extend our deep appreciation to Marcus Williamson for his diligent technical reviews of both the first and second editions, and for his help in refining and improving our explanations of directory service technologies.

The staff of New Riders also has our gratitude for all of its work on the first edition of *Understanding Directory Services*. This team included Al Valvano, Lisa Thibault, Ami Frank Sullivan, Keith Cline, Gina Brown, Alissa Cayton, and Mike LaBonne. We'd also like to thank everyone who did a technical review on all or part of the first edition including Marcus Williamson, Marc Charney, David Stanley, Thomas Willingham, Cory Hendrix, Andrew Mason, and Brian Boston.

We'd also like to extend our ongoing appreciation to Melinda Wynn Klein for her simple yet profound questions.

Dave Kearns deserves thanks for his unwavering dedication to explaining directory services and (repeatedly) providing assistance at key points in the process—sometimes a little help goes a long way, thanks!

Our appreciation also goes to John McGarvey at IBM for his quick review of, and contributions to, our discussion of the SecureWay directory.

Thanks are also due to Dr. Teodor Dumitrescu at Siemens, for his technical review and contributions to the DirX and DirXmetahub sections of this book. His efforts enhance the value of this material, and his assistance is greatly appreciated.

Thanks are also due to Seattle Digital Eve for its ongoing technical support, commentary, and insights. (DigitalEve is an international organization for women in technology `www.digitaleve.org`.)

We'd also like to acknowledge the debt we owe to the many teachers who have helped us along the way. In the course of writing this book, we invoked the names of a couple of our early English teachers repeatedly: Barbara Carlson and Pamela (Ashwood) Keefe, wherever you are, we thank you!

We are grateful that our friends and family are still talking to us after our seclusion while writing this book—you are still talking to us, right?

…and finally, a special thanks to our friend in Australia who shall remain nameless, but who provided us with valuable feedback and perspective on both editions.

Tell Us What You Think!

As the reader of this book, *you* are our most important critic and commentator. We value your opinion and want to know what we're doing right, what we could do better, what areas you'd like to see us publish in, and any other words of wisdom you're willing to pass our way.

As an Associate Publisher for Sams Publishing, I welcome your comments. You can fax, e-mail, or write me directly to let me know what you did or didn't like about this book—as well as what we can do to make our books stronger.

Please note that I cannot help you with technical problems related to the topic of this book, and that due to the high volume of mail I receive, I might not be able to reply to every message.

When you write, please be sure to include this book's title and author as well as your name and phone or fax number. I will carefully review your comments and share them with the author and editors who worked on the book.

Fax:	317-581-4770
E-mail:	`feedback@samspublishing.com`
Mail:	Jeff Koch Associate Publisher Sams Publishing 201 West 103rd Street Indianapolis, IN 46290 USA

Introduction

Understanding Directory Services provides a technical discussion of directory services, starting with basic theory and archetypes, working its way up to the current directory service implementations.

This discussion of directory services is focused on explaining the technologies and operations as objectively as possible. Although most directory books are about specific directory service products, this book provides something a little different: It aims to help you understand how directory services *work*.

Who Should Read This Book

Understanding Directory Services is designed for IT professionals and anyone interested in directory service technologies. If you want to *understand* the subject of directory services, this is the right book for you.

Readers of this book should be familiar with the basics of networking theory and operations, as an understanding of networking concepts and terminology is assumed.

How This Book Is Organized

The book starts with an overview of directory services and their core characteristics, highlighting the key information, distribution, and storage factors. It explores the X.500 standards to help you understand the foundations of directory services. Next, it reviews LDAP, the emerging standard for directory access, and then examines the DNS location services.

The book next discusses the range of directory service products on the market, starting with X.500-based general purpose directories including eTrust, DirX, and Nexor, and then LDAP-based directory products including iPlanet, SecureWay, and OpenLDAP. Following these, the leading directory services for enterprise networks are examined, reviewing the design and operations of eDirectory and Active Directory.

In later chapters, the characteristics of metadirectory technologies are examined, and current metadirectory implementations are reviewed. Then the use of markup languages with directory services is discussed, and the current state of directory markup language standardization is described. Finally, this book documents factors and issues to be assessed in how to evaluate a directory service for your network or e-commerce usage.

The following list gives a brief overview of what you can expect to learn from each chapter:

> Chapter 1: "Introduction to Directory Services"—Explains the big picture of directory services, introduces the types of directory services and describes how they can enhance IT and business operations.

Chapter 2: "Evolution of Directory Services"—Explores the evolving nature of the information the directory contains, and the factors involved in organizing and managing directory information.

Chapter 3: "Storing Directory Information"—Discusses methods of information distribution and storage, and focuses on distributed directory services.

Chapter 4: "X.500: A Model for Directory Services"—Reviews the X.500 standards, which are the archetype for directory services.

Chapter 5: "LDAP: Lightweight Directory Access Protocol"—Describes the LDAP protocol, its growing role in directory access, and more.

Chapter 6: "DNS: The Domain Name System"—Examines DNS from a directory service perspective, noting parallels and differences in structures and operations.

Chapter 7: "X.500 Directory Services"—Identifies X.500-based directory products, and highlights implementation approaches and capabilities.

Chapter 8: "LDAP-Only Directory Services"—Describes the LDAP-based directory products, and identifies similarities and differences between them.

Chapter 9: "eDirectory"—Explains Novell's NDS eDirectory based on the latest version (eDirectory 8.5), and describes the underlying directory architecture and its foundations in X.500.

Chapter 10: "Active Directory"—Examines how Microsoft integrates NT 4, LDAP, and DNS technologies into a directory service that leverages established Windows networks.

Chapter 11: "Metadirectory Services"—Explores the information management issues that metadirectories are designed to address, and characteristics of different types of metadirectory solutions.

Chapter 12: "Directory Markup Languages"—Identifies the designs of XML-based markup languages that map directory schema, objects, and/or operations.

Chapter 13: "Evaluating Directory Services"—Discusses how to evaluate a directory service for use in your network environment, including business considerations.

There is also a companion site to this book available at `www.src.nu/uds`.
Feedback about this book is encouraged and can be sent to `uds@src.nu`.

Conventions Used

In this book, certain typographical conventions have been applied. Command-line entries, directory names, domain names, and directory objects are all highlighted in `monospaced font`.

Pay special attention to the terms that appear in *italic*. These terms are followed by their acronym or abbreviation in parentheses—*Lightweight Directory Access Protocol (LDAP)*, for example. Those acronyms and abbreviations will subsequently be used throughout the book without spelling out the term again, both for the sake of brevity and also to get you used to directory services terminology.

Introduction to Directory Services

CHAPTER

1

...to climb an oak tree, one must first plant an acorn...

IN THIS CHAPTER

Directory services are a powerful technology, and increasingly serving as the foundation for many extremely useful, and sometimes exciting, new services on the corporate network and the Internet. Much as the widespread introduction of networking changed the way that computers interoperate with each other—helping set the stage for the Internet, among other things—directory services are changing the way that people interact with those networked systems.

When networking emerged as a critical new technology, many people found themselves having to select and implement a network with little real understanding of how it all worked. Likewise, many people (sometimes the same ones who were tossed into networking) are now expected to select, design, and implement a directory service with equally little background.

Yet, like networks, directory services are complex and difficult to master. To quote a technical trainer we know, "It makes your brain hurt!"

Directory services are complicated, and comprehensive references on the topic are rare. There are many administrative "how-to" books out there for specific directory products; this is *not* one of them. Rather, the explanations throughout this book revolve around the architectural and technological perspectives of directory services.

This book describes the theory behind directory services, explaining the underlying conceptual models, design characteristics, and methods of managing distributed information. From there, we move on to the (literal) archetype of the directory service: *X.500*. Next, we'll describe the functionality and significance of the *Lightweight Directory Access Protocol (LDAP)* and the *Domain Name System (DNS)*.

There is also a review of the significant directory service implementations; X.500 based general-purpose directories, LDAP-only directories, as well as the NOS directories *eDirectory* and *Active Directory*. The final chapter discusses directory service evaluation dimensions and criteria. Cumulatively, this book provides a comprehensive description of directory service theory, models, operations, technologies, and the current state of directory products.

Cumulatively is an important word here. We designed this book to be read from front to back; early chapters lay the foundation for explanations of the technologies, which in turn are used as a basis for explaining the various types of directory products. Reading it in a linear fashion, especially if you aren't familiar with the topic under discussion, will help your understanding of the subject.

First, it's important to look at the big picture of directory services; thus we need to define a number of terms, explore some possible uses of a directory service, and discuss the functionality a directory service offers. Finally, we'll provide a bit of context for the rest of the book—a brief check on the state of directory services in the wild, so to speak.

What Is a Directory Service?

Directory services are a significant emerging technology; they may not have all the press coverage as the popular "next new thing" but that's largely because no directory-based killer application has hit the radar—yet (but keep an eye on directory-enabled IT provisioning, and directory-based security applications).

For a technology that has been around a long time—the first industry standards for a directory service were published in 1988—directory services have remained quietly in the background. Sure, some businesses have been using them, mainly to manage corporate networks, but directories haven't exactly been taking the world by storm.

Things have been picking up lately; there is an increasing awareness of the value of a directory service, and the directory market seems poised to take off. Vendors are releasing new, and substantially updated, directory products, and applications that take advantage of them. Businesses are deploying directory services to fill a wide range of business needs with implementations providing critical informational support for network and enterprise management, security, messaging, e-commerce, as well as employee and client identity management.

There are even a few directory applications, such as Microsoft's *Passport* service, gaining visibility—even if people aren't talking about the directory part of it much. This isn't surprising, directory services, when done correctly, are often a nearly invisible enabling technology.

Consider some real-life examples of directories in action:

> *You go to your favorite Web site to check the news (local, national, and international—and only the topics you want), read a couple of comics, and check the traffic cameras along your route to the office. The Web server retrieves your cookie, reads a user identification number, and, using that number to identify your directory entry, builds a customized Web page based on the preferences stored in the directory. This directory lookup might be done in a second (literally), or maybe less, providing seamless Web site performance. You pay no attention to the directory service managing this—you just know that you get Dilbert and Doonesbury at the top of your news page, and no sports—and you like that.*

> *You arrive at the office in the morning and turn on your computer. When you log on to the network your e-mail is automatically downloaded, your calendar is updated, and a patch for the latest security hole is applied to your Web browser. In addition, a pop-up message indicates that your reservation for network bandwidth for today's video-conference has been taken care of and the other participants notified. As you work, you are transparently granted access to servers, applications, and other resources as you need them—which sure beats having to remember all those passwords!*

It's your favorite niece's birthday and you want to send her this great book you heard about. Only problem is, you don't remember the title, you only know the name of another book by the same author. You go to your favorite on-line bookseller and search for the other title, click on the link for the author's other books, and there it is—the book you want. You purchase the book, selecting your niece's name from the provided list of shipping addresses. You are notified that the credit card you have on file has expired and must be updated. You are required to provide a password before you can change the credit card information, providing security for personal and financial data. Within just a few minutes, you have a gift-wrapped book on its way to your niece.

In each of these scenarios, directory services provide a critical component of the experience described. Web site personalization solutions, such as those in the first scenario, might store information such as a person's content preferences, a user profile, and a set of personalized links. In the second, a network directory service manages network user, e-mail, and calendar accounts, provides support for a desktop management product, and allows the integration of network infrastructure devices to manage bandwidth usage. The bookstore may use a directory service to support user management, site personalization, and store sensitive information such as credit card numbers; there may well be a second directory handling the catalog data.

A Ubiquitous Management Technology

An increasing number of software products, especially network operating systems, Web services, and distributed applications are relying on a directory service to manage users and security. It is likely that the computer network you use at work daily has numerous "directories" on it, providing a variety of services to users, applications, and so on. Some of these directories may actually be called "directories," although others probably are not. Most likely, you directly access at least one directory as a consumer of the information it contains (such as your e-mail address book). Assuredly, many more work behind the scenes, transparently managing applications, resources, and network security.

A directory can serve as a critical piece of the enterprise information infrastructure, providing secure access to the sensitive information required for your business. Business processes and services are also being increasingly directory-enabled; automated supply chain management and IT provisioning, enhanced partner and customer relationship management, Web site personalization and e-commerce, all these and more rely on directories. A directory can serve as a critical piece of the enterprise information infrastructure, providing secure access to the sensitive information required for your business.

Directory services provide a powerful management technology, supplying logically centralized administration of a physically distributed computing environment. Most networking environments have used some sort of directory service to provide name resolution and facilitate network resource management for a number of years, although the specific capabilities and feature set of these products have varied rather widely. Microsoft only recently added a true directory service (*Active Directory*) to its Windows server product, while Novell has employed a directory service (*eDirectory*, which was previously *Novell Directory Services*) since the early '90s as part of its NetWare operating system.

Over the past decade, a general purpose directory service architecture, X.500, has emerged as the theoretical industry standard for large-scale distributed directory systems. Another standard, the Lightweight Directory Access Protocol, has become the de facto standard method for directory access. Yet what is considered a "directory service" is an evolving set of criteria.

Defining Directory Services

Fundamentally, what a directory service does is securely manage complex systems of interrelated information, and support the widespread distribution and speedy retrieval of that information—*any* information. This information management technology can be applied to a wide range of IT and business operations. The specifics of the information the directory holds, along with the types of services the directory is capable of, are the final determinants of what any given directory implementation can do.

Consider the growing use of directory services on the Internet—where information *is* the point. The information in these directories covers a myriad of subjects; it may be about the site visitor (used to personalize content or support e-commerce), the company (e-mail directory), or the company's product (services, sales, and support information). Although the directory service *product* being used for these applications may be the same, the result is very different.

Directory services provide a powerful management technology, supplying logically centralized administration of a physically distributed computing environment. A directory can serve as a critical piece of the enterprise information infrastructure, providing secure access to the sensitive information required for your business.

In its most general definition, a directory service provides the means to hierarchically organize and manage information, and to retrieve the information by name association. A directory service operates to facilitate access to resources and to ease the administrative burden by providing a unified management view of those resources. A directory must provide secure access to this stored information for users and applications.

Directory services excel in managing the complex information systems of large enterprise operations. A directory service may be employed in a variety of ways—from network management, to a parts classification catalog in support of purchasing operations, to the more complicated real-time information management of the military and its secure messaging needs.

The directory contains a set of entries about people, resources, and services. The specifics of the information in a given directory will vary depending on the purpose of the directory. In a network-centric directory, the objects represent information about the network users, groups, devices, resources, and services. In contrast, a general-purpose directory may contain virtually any set of information (from e-commerce or Web site user management to application data or the information needed to automate the supply chain) so the supported objects will vary widely.

A Directory Service—Piece by Piece

The *schema*—the core data structure that defines all objects that can exist in the directory—internally defines the directory contents. The schema also defines the properties that can be assigned to the object classes, and the syntax for the values of those properties. In addition to defining the directory objects, the schema determines how the directory is structured.

The directory schema can be thought of as the "definition" of the directory, because it defines the essential structure of all directory objects, as well as their possible relationships. The schema information provides rules used to enforce the specified definitions of an object. These definitions are used to specify the directory hierarchy and structure the relationships and interactions between directory objects. The schema effectively defines the directory *namespace*.

In its most generic sense, a namespace can be described as a collection of objects that reside within a common container (an object that can contain other objects) and follow the same naming convention. From a technical perspective, a namespace is a logical and programmatic construct used to define a discrete area containing objects named in compliance with a specified naming model. A namespace is defined by a set of logical rules that determines structural characteristics of the directory (flat or hierarchical, allowable hierarchies, and so on), and determines how objects are named. The directory's objects conform to its naming convention, and can be said to exist within that namespace.

A directory *object*—a data structure with a specified set of attributes and syntax—represents each entry in the directory. Every object definition has a specific set of *attributes* (also referred to as *properties*) each of which is either mandatory or optional. Attributes can hold a variety of information; everything from user account data to security information to graphic images. Each property is constrained to a particular type of syntactical representation—for instance, the telephone number attribute is a numeric string, and so on.

The logical structure of the information in a directory is represented as an inverted tree, commonly referred to as the *Directory Information Tree* (DIT) or the *directory tree*. A directory tree is a hierarchical arrangement of directory objects contained within a contiguous (logically connected) namespace. Certain directory objects are designated as *container* objects; these objects form the nodes of the directory tree and hold the rest of the directory objects. The directory tree provides structure for visually displaying the collection of objects within the tree, as well as to represent a logical hierarchy that can be used to facilitate administration and security management.

The information in the directory is stored in a distributed form generally known as the *Directory Information Base (DIB)*. Because the majority of directory access is for lookups, the DIB is usually optimized for searches, often providing indexes or catalogs. General-purpose directory services sometimes use commercial scalable databases (such as Oracle) for back-end data management, and may even allow for swapping out the data storage mechanism.

The DIB can be subdivided into *partitions* to support large or geographically distributed information systems. Directory services support some form of *replication* (that is, copying) of the DIB to multiple directory servers (usually close to the clients or service that needs the information). Replication provides redundancy for fault tolerance and improved performance. Partitioning the directory also helps improve performance by speeding searches and managing network traffic generated by replication.

A *directory service* also encompasses the services provided to network clients, administrators, directory-enabled applications, and network services. A typical directory provides services that support resource location, user and group management, and may even provide an extension mechanism for application-specific requirements. Directories generally provide robust security services including authentication, access control, PKI certificates management, and sometimes enhancements like encryption, or security tokens (such as smart cards).

The X.500 Standards

In 1988, the first set of X.500 standards was published, defining the architecture and operations of a distributed directory service, initially to support X.400 messaging. X.500 specifies a directory designed to manage large, distributed, and complex information systems by establishing well-defined information, administration, and security models, and methods of information exchange among different directory components.

X.500, directly or indirectly, provides the architectural basis for most current directory services. General-purpose directories are either based on X.500 or LDAP-only—and LDAP is designed to access X.500 directories. The current network-focused directory services are based on X.500 (NDS eDirectory) or LDAP (Active Directory). No matter where in the directory space you look, the influence of X.500 is hard to miss.

> Some aspects of the X.500 specification, such as the information models (which define the directory contents), are widely supported, although other aspects (such as the protocols) are less universally used. We offer a comprehensive examination of X.500 in Chapter 4 "X.500: A Model for Directory Services."

An Example of a Simple Directory

A look at a familiar directory, that of an e-mail application, can show how all this works. While an e-mail directory isn't usually a full-fledged directory service, it can provide a simple example of how the pieces fit together. Most businesses publish an internal directory that lists employees along with their e-mail addresses and perhaps additional information such as job title, phone number, and office location.

In this example, the e-mail address book could be considered a namespace that contains objects (employees) and properties (name, e-mail address, job title, and so on) that describe those objects. The address book namespace follows a specific naming convention (last name, first name) that facilitates identification and location of objects residing within it.

The needs of the messaging application define the schema of the e-mail directory. Because the purpose of this directory is to support e-mail, e-mail addresses are a mandatory property of each user, but job title is probably optional.

Similar to other directory services, e-mail applications use a client/server model that employs server-side and client-side software components to supply the directory functionality. The e-mail directory provides services such as e-mail address lookups and searches to clients, as well as supplying the data needed to support internal operations such as interserver communication. There is likely to be a copy of the directory information on each mail server, and there may well be cached copies of portions of the directory information on client machines acting as local address books.

How Does a Directory Service Work?

At the heart of a directory service lies the architecture for a general-purpose hierarchical information management system, which can be applied to arbitrary sets of complex networking and information systems. Directory services implement a central repository that holds information on a designated set of resources, and provide the means to locate and manage those resources within a distributed computing environment. The directory provides for authentication and access control over the objects represented in the directory.

Directory services operate by using a client/server exchange between an agent that accesses the directory and an agent that provides services to the network client. The server uses software agents to provide directory access and perform the needed lookup and object manipulation tasks. The server agents also provide a means for communication among server software components to allow multiple physical servers to act as one logical directory.

From the client side, a directory is seen as a single entity; queries are submitted to "the directory" and, as long as the query is satisfied, the details of how the directory handles it are not important. This means that even when multiple servers share the load of servicing client requests (as is usually the case), the clients are not aware of it.

Qualities of a Directory Service

Certain characteristics distinguish current directory services from other information management systems, such as relational databases or even earlier directory implementations. Directory services share these qualities:

- **A defined namespace**—Directory services operate in and utilize a *namespace*, essentially a data structure arranged according to a specified naming model. Most directory services use a hierarchical namespace logically arranged in an inverse tree.
- **An extended search capability**—Directory services provide robust search capabilities, allowing searches on individual attributes of objects. This provides a powerful tool for finding network information based on relevant attributes. If you want to find a color printer close to your office, you can search for one, provided the necessary information (printer type, location, and so on) has been entered in the directory.
- **Authentication and access control**—Directory security technologies handle authenticating users and controlling access to directory information.
- **Scales from small to large networks**—A key factor in scalability is the effective distribution of the directory data to multiple servers on the network. A directory service is designed to work as well on an enterprise network connected via WAN and Internet links, as it does on a small LAN.
- **A datastore optimized for reads**—The storage mechanism used for a directory service is usually designed to support an extremely high ratio of read to write operations. It is common for directory product designs to assume that 99 percent of the operations accessing the DIB will be reads (lookups and searches), with relatively few writes (changes and additions).
- **Replicated data**—Directories support replication to make your information system or network more resistant to failure (should a directory server go down) and more accessible to users across geographically distributed networks (by providing local copies of needed data).

- **A distributed information system**—A directory service provides the mechanism to distribute the directory across multiple computers within the network. Partitioning of the directory provides for the physical subdivision of the DIB to support scalability, allow delegation of control, and to speed access to directory information.
- **An extensible schema**—Most directory services support the extension of the directory schema, enabling developers and administrators to extend the native directory object set and implement new and customized directory objects as needed (such as adding a user's photograph to the directory).

What a Directory Service Provides

IT professionals are constantly grappling with information overload, and there's probably nowhere that this is truer than on the corporate network. Consider for a moment the number of managed systems on a typical network; network operating system, applications, messaging, security systems, infrastructure hardware—each of these must manage users, frequently the *same* users. Industry surveys have estimated the number of directories that the average enterprise has, as ranging from 15 to more than 75 "directories" of one kind or another. Surveys of Fortune 1000 companies by Forrester Research in 1997 and Gartner Group in 1998 found those large organizations have
an average of 181 directories. While some of these directories may be little more than an application's list of users, they still require management.

Take the number of directories on the typical enterprise network and multiply that by the number of users who have an account in each directory, or even a subset of them. This represents a staggering array of information to manage. It's not surprising that the management burden would seem, at times, overwhelming.

Given this, it becomes clear that one of the most pressing needs in IT today is for management systems that can consolidate the vast array of resources represented within these many systems. Accordingly, one of the most common uses for a directory service is as a network management

More Than a Database

A directory service is much more than just a database that can handle a large number of entries. It requires tools that streamline management, a client interface that is easy for the consumers of the directory information to use, and, perhaps most importantly, directory-enabled applications that leverage the directory. Without all these, a directory service may become another isolated island of information to manage without ever delivering the potential benefits of a well thought out directory deployment.

mechanism. By integrating the information about all services, systems, and accounts used on the network, directory services can minimize complexity for people trying to access resources on the network.

Directory services can act as much more than network management systems, however, they can also provide critical supportive information services to the enterprise—the directory service becomes a key infrastructure component for business operations. These directories offer one of the strongest incentives for directory deployment, providing the foundation for directory-centric management of the enterprise.

The most fundamental service that a directory provides is storing and retrieving information from the directory. Directory services offer robust search and management capabilities, with powerful, flexible search capabilities that ease retrieval of complex sets of information. The directory must store its information in an organized manner, enabling quick and easy retrieval on demand of any directory information.

Directories must provide security for the information it holds, usually providing highly customizable control of who can view or manipulate the directory information. To control access to the directory, users must be authenticated and thus the directory must store security credentials. X.500 directories are the logical place to store X.509 PKI (Public Key Infrastructure) certificates; for example, the directory can also use the certificates for strong authentication providing a higher level of security than simply passwords.

Applications can also access the directory repository via directory application programming interfaces (APIs), many of which are supported by the current crop of directory products. By providing programmatic access to directory information and functionality, directory vendors offer developers an easy means of directory-enabling applications. One of the more promising areas of directory development is the widespread adoption of LDAP, and thus the LDAP C API, which offers a directory-independent method of programmatic access to directory services.

Directories Managing Personal Information

Directory services are also moving into service provision in the personal arena. One interesting new direction is Internet-based identity and relationship management for individuals. Due to the underlying directory, strong security and a fine degree of control over the display of personal information are provided. For example, tools allow customization of how and when Web forms will be automatically completed, and with what information. This capability may even extend to e-commerce data such as credit card information and PKI certificates.

This style of directory provides a truly portable solution for people who must manage personal, professional, financial, and Web-related information across multiple machines, perhaps even from various locations around the world. The ability to custom manage an increasingly Web-centric personal life makes this style of directory service a powerful personal relationship and information manager. Novell's *digitalme* and Microsoft's *Passport* offer different takes on this sort of directory-based service.

Streamlined Network Administration

To manage any set of resources effectively, you must first have the related information available in a unified and manageable form. A directory service simplifies administration by logically unifying network resources and providing a single point of access. Directory services can integrate information on people (such as network users or e-commerce customers) and resources (network devices, applications, or services, for example) into a single information system.

A directory service can provide the administrator with the ability to "manage the network from any point in the tree." This refers to the ability of a network administrator to access all network resources and management functionality via the directory service. With a unified directory tree and a single point of logon, it's possible to administer the entire network and its resources from any point within the network. Whether the administrator is logged on at their normal workstation, at a satellite office, or even using a dial-up connection from another country, all directory objects and operations are available.

Directory services supply an important administrative capability that can ease the management of network resources distributed in logically or geographically diverse locations. The implementation of a directory service provides administrators with a more detailed information base about network resources, systems, users, and groups. All these resources are accessible through the directory service, providing quicker access to far more information about your network than was possible to obtain from earlier directories.

To compare, many early network implementations required the administrator to be physically present at the server containing the information on the network resources to be managed. It was frequently literally true that this was *the only server* containing this set of resource information, a situation that clearly presented management, as well as reliability and performance issues. On any network with multiple servers, server-based network management presents numerous administrative problems, not the least of which is the required administration time.

Although remote administration tools have been developed which allow management of resources from a secondary (remote) system, they may only provide a subset of the capability needed. Many implementations of remote management tools do not provide access to all network server functionality, but rather are limited to the most commonly used subset of administrative tasks.

Unified Information Repository

Directory services store the information they manage in a unified database of some sort, allowing for simplified data management, a reduction in administrative workload, and improved data quality. When many separate directories exist, there is information about people redundantly stored in multiple places. This duplication of data requires more administrative effort, provides more opportunities for error, and increases the likelihood that the data will be inconsistent. With a directory service all this information is stored in only one place, substantially reducing the data integrity issues.

Consider network management provided by a directory service for just a minute, and look at how this unification works to the benefit of everyone using the network. Initially, NOS directories were server-based and contained information pertaining to local resources only. These earlier, and simpler, directory implementations frequently supplied limited support for browsing or searching the network (to find the resources needed). Although this provided a method for resource location on small networks, it fell short of the more sophisticated directory service required in today's distributed networking environments.

Distributed networks require both a unified means of locating a resource (or range of resources) existing on the network, as well as logical and easy-to-use naming semantics. The unified access to directory content provided by a distributed directory service allows a single user logon to provide access to diverse resources.

Simplified Resource Location

For users and administrators to identify and access network resources, they first must locate those resources. A well-designed directory service using a logical tree structure and intuitive naming can simplify and speed resource location. Multiple methods of accessing the directory, including browsing and searches based on a variety of criteria (such as object name, type, and so on) are provided.

The contents of the directory are presented as objects in an inverted tree, logically ordering the information in a top-down organizational structure. The directory tree unifies the objects representing disparate resources into a single browseable namespace, and leverages the user's understanding of the relative location of entities within the directory to ease location and use of resources.

Even with the enhanced modeling capabilities gained from a directory tree, resources may still be difficult to locate, particularly in a large directory. If there are 10,000 objects in the directory, browsing will be a cumbersome process, no matter how well designed the directory tree.

A centralized directory acts as an easily searchable reference to the contents of the network, simplifying user access to information and resources. The query syntax for directory searches is robust yet simple to use. Most directories offer powerful search capabilities that allow location of objects by arbitrary criteria (everyone whose last name is "Radke," or all color printers in a particular building, for example).

Directory clients usually supply user-friendly search methods by limiting the visible information and translating query language into something a bit easier to understand. Catalogs may also be provided to serve as a fast-search index to network resources.

Resource location is further eased with the use of standardized naming conventions. We've all used networks where each department named its own machines, often based on the personal preferences of the person doing the naming. This has led to groups of computers named after trees, cities in Europe, or (with amazing frequency) cartoon characters. This may be amusing for the people doing the naming—and who *wouldn't* want a computer named "Dogbert"—but it doesn't make it any easier to locate a server if you can't remember which cartoon cat was Disney's.

By comparison, a directory offers a structured naming mechanism that forms the basis for implementation of an enterprisewide naming model. Administrators can designate a standardized naming style that makes object location faster and easier.

Lower Management Overhead

By combining multiple datastores, as is often done when deploying a directory service, you can eliminate the duplication of configuration and management information. And the bottom line is that less duplicated data means fewer duplicated management tasks.

The client configuration information used by the NOS can also be stored in the directory, providing support for roaming users, and supplying a way to recover from client machine failure. In addition, application configuration data for each user can be stored in the directory, further reducing the need to individually configure client machines and applications.

DNS as a Directory Locator

An increasing number of directory services are using DNS to provide location services, supporting directory service operations across enterprisewide WANs as well as the Internet. For example, the latest versions of Windows server platform (Windows.NET or Windows 2000) *requires* the use of DNS to locate directory servers. Microsoft is leveraging the new DNS resource records identifying services, to allow location of LDAP servers. DNS also provides name resolution for the domain portion of an LDAP URL (an LDAP URL is the address form used to access LDAP directories from a Web browser).

This means that a user account could be managed in a single directory, not 5, or 10—or 75—a considerable timesaver. When there are fewer data sources to manage, the likelihood of error is also reduced, further lowering the need for administrator intervention.

You can also reduce the number of help desk calls with a directory service. Consider that one major cause of help desk calls is forgotten passwords; with a directory, password management can be delegated to each user on the network. By doing so, you can offload one of the most common reasons that people call for technical support.

A directory can also reduce configuration problems by providing centralized management of a range of applications and services. When application and network configuration data is handled by the directory service, rather than being distributed across multiple servers (or even client machines), problems are reduced and troubleshooting is easier and faster.

The combined efficiencies can dramatically lower the overall administrative overhead for an enterprise—especially after the directory service has been in place a few years and other directories have been subsumed by it.

Powerful User Management Capabilities

One of the most common uses for a directory service is managing people; whether it's users on a corporate network or customers visiting an e-commerce site, directories *excel* at user management. Using a directory allows the centralization of a person's identity information into a secure location-independent storage mechanism. Any entity that requires user information can query the directory, which maintains the authoritative information on all users.

This centralization of identity information provides additional benefits. The more information the directory stores about any given individual, the broader the range of services that can be performed by the directory for that person.

One common data set being integrated with directory services is human resources details, such as department and work assignment. Administrators can establish profiles that designate a set of actions to be carried out based on these criteria. All the people in the marketing department may require the current version of PowerPoint installed, for example, or the Web developers may all require Internet access. After the involved subsystems are directory-enabled, this type of application or network device configuration can easily be applied based on profiles. In these cases, desktop management software would install PowerPoint onto the client system at logon, and the firewall configured to allow that user unlimited Internet access.

Directory services often have a multilayered approach to management. Many directories allow the assignment of rights to the tree structure itself, applying settings to a container object and thus granting those rights implicitly to any object in that container. This style of rights assignment is generally cumulative, each container can have rights assigned and the totality of the containers above a particular object determine the rights that are granted to it. Additional settings can be applied via group membership or directly to the user object. By using the various levels of management capability wisely, you can substantially streamline directory administration.

Integrated Security Infrastructure

Directory services are acting in critical roles to enable e-commerce, public key infrastructure (PKI) certificates, and support applications that require security services. Most directory services support several security standards and technologies, providing flexible security and access control.

A directory service, at a minimum, supports the operations employed in user authentication and access control. *Authentication* is the mechanism that verifies the identity of the individual user. *Access control* provides differential levels of access to system services and operations.

Some directory services employ an extensible security architecture of some sort, either directly or indirectly. Just about every directory provides support for LDAP, and in turn LDAP supports the *Simple Authentication and Security Layer* (SASL). SASL provides a means by which protocols can specify an authentication and encryption mechanism; options include Kerberos, Secure Sockets Layer (SSL) , Transport Layer Security (TLS) , and custom defined mechanisms.

Even network directory services are incorporating multiple industry security and encryption standards such as X.509 public key certificates and the Kerberos protocol, in addition to the usual network-specific security model.

Cost/Benefit Analysis Of Directory Services

Many sets of criteria for analyzing the cost and benefits of a directory service have been offered by vendors and industry analysts—framed as either *Total Cost of Ownership (TCO)* or *Return on Investment (ROI)*. TCO is a method for determining the cost of owning computers and other IT resources, including equipment, administration, and technical support, as well as end-user actions. ROI, on the other hand, quantifies the benefits of owning a particular technology; for a directory this often includes reduced administrative workload due to fewer redundant tasks, lower demand for tech support, and increased security.

These calculations, although not without value, seem in some ways to miss the point—or at least part of the point. A directory-centric IT strategy can enable new forms of identity management, process automation, and information sharing with a high degree of security. These capabilities can also be extended outside the enterprise, laying the foundation for new forms of business-to-business interactions.

Directory services can also improve security by consolidating and automating management tasks, eliminating redundancy and reducing opportunities for human error. Directories are being used as the information management backbone for commercial automated security and provisioning products as well as home-grown solutions.

Controlled Access to Directory Information

From the obvious things, such as passwords in a network directory, to the less apparent, such as credit card data in an e-commerce directory, most directory services contain a lot of confidential information, which must be protected against unauthorized access. Whatever the specifics, a directory *must* provide security for the information it contains.

As the directory service is storing or retrieving information, it must control access to the information based on the identity of the user. This requires the directory to provide a way to authenticate users as well as to enforce access control on the directory information. As part of every directory storage and retrieval operation, user permissions are compared to access controls on directory information.

Directory vendors generally provide the capability to set directory security at a very granular level, down to the individual property of a directory object. This can be a powerful addition to management capability because it allows selective display of object information, based on the security assigned to the information and the access control rights of the person attempting to view the data. This provides a means to display an object (such as a user) with a subset of its attributes (name, e-mail address, phone) while hiding other properties (salary or other sensitive data) from unauthorized access.

This sort of granularity can be applied to administrative rights as well, providing a means to distribute subsets of administrative tasks while protecting information from unauthorized changes. This means that individuals can access and change some information, such as that related to an e-mail account, while that data is still protected from unauthorized access by others. Yet with this increase in granularity and control comes an increased complexity in management of all these assignable rights.

Directorywide Single Sign-On

Each user on your network typically has an account within the NOS directory and another account for e-mail (at a minimum), each requiring a unique logon name and password. This duplication of logon, and the necessity to remember multiple passwords, leads to one of the more common security concerns in corporate networks today: unsecured passwords. These are usually written down and left stuck to a monitor, in a desk drawer, or somewhere similar.

A directory service provides for a single user logon to access diverse resources in a distributed network. With a single logon, users can access the contents and services of disparate NOS platforms, e-mail, and any directory-enabled application. The distributed access to resources is transparent to the directory user. The client just logs on to any directory server and is granted access to the related resources. The physical location and actual management of the resources is not relevant because it is masked by the directory services.

This integration of access to directory information can result in simplified administration and operation of the network, and can also reduce the security and usability issues associated with multiple passwords.

The advantages of directorywide single sign-on accrue to Internet clients as well; Microsoft's Passport (based in Active Directory) provides single sign-on across a broad range of Microsoft and partner properties. Microsoft has plans in the works to make credit card information available as well to facilitate online shopping.

Reliable High Performance

When examining new technologies, a key consideration for most IT administrators is the impact on the IT infrastructure's performance and reliability. A directory service is a critical part of the infrastructure and, as such, commonly requires 24×7×365 availability. You can't afford for the loss of one server, or even several, to slow or even take down the entire directory.

Two important, although perhaps less obvious, aspects of implementing a directory service are improved network performance and a more robust and fault-tolerant network.

To improve performance and reliability, the directory can be subdivided into *partitions* (subsets of directory information), and *replicas* (a replica is a copy of a partition). Storing the directory information in a partitioned and replicated fashion allows directory operations to take place across multiple servers. This can enhance performance and reliability for all directory operations as well as for applications that rely on it. Each directory service will specify its own methods of partitioning and replicating the directory. These factors require careful consideration in directory planning and deployment.

Scalability

Many things contribute to scalability; a high-performance datastore, powerful distribution mechanisms, and selection of operating platform. A truly robust directory service can scale from a single directory server managing a few hundred network objects to a system using hundreds of directory servers that collectively manage a billion or more directory objects.

The question of scale needs to be considered in the context of the intended use of the directory service—does it have to support 10,000 users on a LAN, or millions of users at an e-commerce site? In both design and implementation, the focus is centered around what the directory is designed to do—how it is supposed to work, the services it provides, and the scale of its operations.

The issue of scale can be expressed in terms of number of objects that can be effectively managed by a given directory service and the number of concurrent users supported. There is quite a bit of variance in scalability between various directory designs. Although network-centric directory products may scale to millions of objects, for example, some X.500 directory services scale to tens or hundreds of millions of objects.

Yet, scalability isn't necessarily fixed along the types of directory service product categories. For example, in its recent evolution from a network directory to a much more general-purpose capability, eDirectory reportedly scales to 1.5 billion objects.

Availability

A directory needs to service large numbers of requests from clients and applications. Consumers of the directory data rely on fast responses to directory queries to provide essential information.

Directory responsiveness can be enhanced by locating copies of directory data to servers close to the client or service that needs the information. Sharing the workload amongst multiple servers holding a given set of directory information, and increasing the number of servers if needed, can also improve directory responsiveness.

Load balancing can be implemented by placing replicas of the same partition on multiple directory servers and directing access to the array of servers to distribute a large workload.

Scalability Means Small, Too

Most of the time when you hear folks talking about scalability they are tossing about some pretty big numbers—millions, tens of millions, sometimes even billions! That's all well and good, but what about the business that's not quite so big? The directory service that is optimal for a large distributed enterprise may be too complex to make it practical for a business with only a thousand or so employees and customers.

The directory that is the right fit for any given situation is a question worth careful consideration. Chapter 13, "Evaluating Directory Services" goes into some detail regarding criteria you might want to consider when looking for a directory service.

To further increase availability of directory information and resources, many directory services use *catalogs*. Directory catalogs contain a subset of the directory contents and are used to provide a fast way to locate information stored in the directory. Catalogs can be distributed around the network, improving response time to directory queries. Proper design and placement of directory catalogs allows for a minimum of network traffic, because most lookup requests can be resolved locally, without referrals to other directory servers for resource location.

Reliability

A critical aspect of a directory service is its capability to function even if one or more servers become unavailable. Directory services supply reliability by enabling you to use multiple directory servers to support each partition of the directory—supplying redundancy in case of server failure.

By replicating the directory to multiple servers, you can guarantee that even if one server becomes unavailable, the entire directory will not become inaccessible. If a single directory server stops functioning, directory service queries will be routed to an available replica (copy) of the directory partition.

Directories can also provide a degree of fault tolerance for applications and services whose configuration and operational data they contain. This support for fault tolerance of network services and functionality can, for instance, redirect application clients to a backup directory server in the event of a primary server failure.

Replication enhances both reliability and performance by providing backup directory servers for redundancy and load balancing. Directory performance can be improved by placing replicas of the appropriate partitions on servers close to the people who will be using that portion of the directory. Authentication to the network and directory queries should take place at the server closest to the user, resulting in minimal network traffic.

Robust Application Development Platform

An important aspect of a directory service is the extent to which it supports the integration of application-specific information. Distributed applications use directory services to identify and connect to network resources and to store application-specific data. A well-designed directory service can provide robust application and programming support for software developers.

Developers can write network applications that leverage existing directory information and operations. Applications can use existing information on network resources, users, and security instead of having to supply their own method of tracking this data. If needed, the directory can also be extended to store application-specific data or supply additional functionality. The ability to leverage a directory for authentication, as well as user and configuration management reduces development costs and speeds time to market for products.

Applications can also use the directory to locate necessary resources and control access to application resources. E-mail services must access user authentication information and mailbox locations, for example, and provide lookup services for addressing outbound mail. A directory service can provide all these services on a networkwide basis.

Applications that use a directory service can provide users with a more personalized application environment, as well as enjoy the benefits that accrue from the integration of directory, network, and application security (eliminating the need for multiple logons, for example).

Application Interfaces to the Directory

Applications commonly use available Application Programming Interfaces (APIs) and protocols to use the directory service operations and to store application-specific configuration data. A directory service must provide APIs to facilitate interaction between the directory and applications that require directory information or services. Applications use the exposed APIs to access the data stored in the directory and use the underlying directory operations.

Most current directory service products provide support for a number of APIs in addition to their proprietary interfaces to their directory data and services. Because LDAP is being widely used, many vendors are adding support for the LDAP C API as well, providing an open API for programmatic directory access.

Directories also commonly support scripting languages such as JavaScript, Perl, and Visual Basic Script, providing easy programmatic access, especially useful for administrative tasks.

Custom Directory Deployments

Every organization has people about whom it needs to manage information; businesses have employees, customers, partners, and vendors; governments have citizens; schools have students; Web sites have visitors. These people interact with many different types of networked systems that provide them a range of services.

Directories excel at managing information about people and there are many useful things you can do with this capability. For example, a directory service can help deliver a highly customized Web site experience, secure services and communications, or provide access control for information and network resources in the enterprise environment.

Extensibility

A directory service needs to be extensible—allowing developers to create extensions that handle objects and functionality not provided by the directory service. This is necessary to allow for the development of custom functionality, and integration of new technologies. A security application, for example, might need the directory to hold photos or encoded biometric data. Similarly, an online directory might need to customize the handling and presentation of query results.

Directory services commonly enable developers to extend the directory in several ways:

- The schema can be extended to implement new objects or properties that contain application-specific values, allowing the directory to store new types of information.
- Directory operations can be extended to provide new functionality; this can be done as an extension to the directory service or dynamically as a control on a single operation.
- Directory management tools are also often designed to be extensible, as a means of providing a framework for managing directory content added via schema extensions as well as implementing new management capabilities.

This approach also has clear advantages for network administrators who reap an important benefit from developer use of directory APIs—the elimination of separate application-specific directories. This helps to reduce unnecessary administrative tasks and cuts down on redundant network management information. As new services are needed, the directory can easily be extended to accommodate the additional functionality, and the administration of complicated operations becomes simpler.

Common Types of Directory Services

There are several basic types of directory services used today, although the lines are blurred between the categories. Each type of product can be categorized by the sorts of objects they contain (scope of content) and the client and management functionality (range of services) they support. We can subdivide directory service implementations currently in use into five types:

- **Networking-focused directories** are designed to support NOS functionality such as user accounts, security, and management of network resources. Early NOS implementations had simple directories, yet as networking platforms evolved they have integrated (to varying degrees) aspects of the directory service technology defined in the X.500 standards.
- **General-purpose directories** commonly provide the widest range of directory services and functionality, and thus support the diverse requirements of an enterprise business as well as the networking environment. The current general-purpose directory products are usually based on the widely accepted X.500 standards, and support standard protocols and services such as LDAP and DNS.

- **Metadirectories** provide a means of managing and integrating information stored in multiple directories. Metadirectories use software agents to collect the data from diverse network and application directories, which are then integrated to varying degrees. Metadirectory operations are characterized by their capability to communicate with diverse directory (and database) implementations, providing functional interoperability with divergent NOS or application namespaces.
- **Application directories** store information about users of a specific application, the types of operations they can perform, and possibly some configuration information as well. The most common use of application directories is for messaging and groupware products. Software agents (programs) are employed to integrate user and application information, and to synchronize directory information across the application platform.
- **Specific-use directories** are designed to store information used for a single purpose, although that purpose can be nearly anything. One example of such a directory is the Domain Name System (DNS), which is used to associate the easy to remember domain names with the difficult to remember IP addresses.

Although each of these directory implementations supports different applications and has different requirements, you will find (as you review the overall structure of directory services and components) that these diverse directory implementations have much in common.

Keep in mind that these are categories of *products*, not definitions of functionality. The reality of the directory market is that there are only two network directory services—Novell's eDirectory and Microsoft's Active Directory—and only one of them is limited to a single operating platform (typically a hallmark of a network directory service). Novell has converted eDirectory, which was originally a NetWare-only service, to a platform-independent general-purpose directory service that, incidentally, can also manage many different network environments.

Network Operating System Directories

One of the most familiar forms of a directory service is those used to manage the network operating system, such as eDirectory or Active Directory. Many enterprises already have a network directory service in place, and as the inevitable adoption of Active Directory by companies committed to Windows NT picks up, those numbers will only increase.

Directory services that are integrated into the network operating systems as management tools can help manage the complex requirements of a distributed network environment. A directory service operates within a network to facilitate access to network resources and to ease network administration and usage by providing a unified organization of network resources. These directories unify and streamline the management of user accounts, speed lookup of network resources, and improve network interoperability and reliability.

A network directory service contains information about network resources and services, including users, workstations, servers, and the services they provide. At a minimum, a network directory contains and manages the following:

- Network resources (servers, printers, services, and so on)
- Network security principals (users and groups)
- Associated network security information

Directory services can provide substantial benefits to network administrators, network users, and the enterprise employing them. By using a network operating system with an integrated directory service, administrators can simplify resource management and facilitate the distribution of administrative tasks while maintaining effective security.

Network users primarily use the directory to locate and access resources, a task at which a NOS-integrated directory service excels. People commonly interact with the directory via client-side applications, Web browsers, and extensions to the NOS user interface.

The deployment of a directory service as a network management mechanism provides the infrastructure for directory-centric enterprise management. Network directory services are increasingly being used by application developers, device manufacturers, and others to provide user management and authentication services. This can be a good thing—every directory-enabled application you can deploy means one less directory for you to manage.

Network directory services are extensible via a scripting language or an administrative application. This capability to extend the NOS directory contents and operations provides a method for developers to integrate application management into network management tools and leverage existing user account and network resource information. Network administrators can also customize the directory to hold additional information required by their organization, such as biometric information, HR data, or ID pictures.

Scalability of Network Directories

As LANs are increasingly linked via WANs and use the Internet as a connectivity backbone, the capability of the network directory to scale to the needs of the enterprise is becoming critical. The distributed services and database management provided by a directory service allows your network to scale from small business LANs to WAN-linked global enterprise networks.

Early NOS directories had a very limited scope, only containing information on users, groups, computers, and devices on the network. These NOS directories (such as those provided in Windows NT 4 and Novell NetWare 3.x), provided limited search functionality or none at all, and did not scale well in enterprise implementations. Although these NOS vendors may refer to their directory storage and service operations as a "directory service," there are substantial differences in scope and functionality between these early NOS directories and current NOS directory services.

By comparison, the current network directory services, eDirectory and Active Directory, are enhanced to contain application-specific information in addition to the information used to manage the users of the network. At this point, network directory services may contain just about any type of information, from the oft-mentioned e-mail accounts to public key certificates.

It is worth noting that while NOS-based directory services are often integrated with, and limited to, a single NOS—Active Directory with Windows 2000, for example—this is not always the case. Novell has ported eDirectory, which was originally tied to NetWare, to every major platform (including Solaris, Linux, NT, Compaq Tru64, and AIX) and provides NOS management functionality for most of these platforms. This provides a means for an enterprise with multiple operating systems to manage all of them from a single directory service, without requiring the presence of any specific platform. Because eDirectory no longer depends on NetWare as the required OS platform, Novell has repositioned it in the marketplace. eDirectory is a mature directory product, which can now run almost anywhere, and is being promoted as a "full-service directory" by Novell. It will be interesting to see how this transition of eDirectory to a more general-purpose directory plays out in the marketplace.

Chapters 9 "eDirectory," and 10, "Active Directory" examine the available network directory services in more depth.

Network Infrastructure Management

Management of network infrastructure devices can also be facilitated with a directory service offering administrators a powerful mechanism for controlling network access, an area of network management that often proves problematic. Vendors of configurable network hardware that currently require separate and complex management tools are working to integrate their products fully into major directory services. Directory Enabled Networking (DEN) is an industry effort that focuses on developing the technology to allow directory services to manage these kinds of network devices. This capability enables control of the network infrastructure, routing, encryption, bandwidth and more, via directory service enforced policies.

Devices that control Internet access, such as firewalls and proxy servers, for example, are one area where directories can help quite a bit. Rather than configuring these devices individually, a laborious task fraught with opportunities for error, directory-enabled infrastructure management is implemented via policy. Access can be easily managed based on group membership (all Web developers need Internet access) or individual need (the VP of marketing Webcasts a speech the first Monday of every month).

General-Purpose Directory Services

A *general-purpose directory* is designed for use in a wide range of implementations and environments. A general-purpose directory service can be applied to just about any business or governmental need. It can be used as a backend for an e-commerce application, manage the property tax system of a regional government, or serve as the backbone for an inventory management system.

A general-purpose directory is usually designed around existing standards for directory services, most notably X.500, although LDAP-only directory products have emerged recently. General-purpose directories are the most flexible of directory implementations and are commonly used to integrate sets of information that might normally reside in different directories and databases. For instance, a general-purpose directory service could manage a single datastore and make it look like an application directory, an e-mail directory, or a network directory depending on the need.

One of the hallmarks of a truly general-purpose directory is its ability to manage huge amounts of data. Directory services in this class scale to the tune of tens, or hundreds, of millions of objects. Admittedly, 10 million directory objects may seem like a lot when you think in raw numbers. It's not such a huge number, however, when the directory information concerns the entire business operation, business partners, clients, and frequently much more.

Examples of general-purpose directory services include eTrust by Computer Associates (previously Open Directory's DXServer), and DirX by Siemens. We will examine some current X.500 directory service offerings in Chapter 7, " X.500 Directory Services."

A *Very* Distributed Directory Service

One of the intended uses of X.500-based directory services is that of a global business white pages. Many businesses are listed in the white pages, providing a centralized point of access to look up business contact information. Because the individual businesses control their own directory namespaces, varying degrees of information are available from each company—some have little information on a subset of staff; others have the listings of the entire staff including addresses, job titles, and sometimes even pictures of employees.

> You may want to explore this directory to gain both a better understanding of the initial intent of X.500 and an appreciation for the complexity of interconnecting (both operationally and administratively) such a service. Dante's NameFLOW-Paradise site at `www.gateway.nameflow.net` provides a public access point to the root of the X.500 tree.

Metadirectories

Enterprises today are using heterogeneous networks, commonly comprised of Windows and/or NetWare-based LANs and Unix servers of some derivation (Sun Solaris, Linux, and others). In this environment, most network administrators have to integrate multiple network directories with messaging directories, application directories, and more. Administrators must then coordinate these directories in the context of thousands (or tens of thousands) of network users and many more servers, workstations, printers, routers, and other resources that comprise the network. The need for integration of disparate directory information is an important factor that makes a clear argument for some combined directory management capabilities.

A metadirectory can integrate multiple directory services (and sometimes other storage structures such as databases) into a unified namespace and provide an integrated and consistent view of many previously isolated resources. To do this, the metadirectory product must address difficult technical issues, including naming and schema discrepancies, data synchronization, and cross-directory security enforcement.

Network administrators will find metadirectory technologies useful for overseeing the management of complex networks and for simplifying user access to corporate network resources. This is particularly true for extensible metadirectory technologies integrated with the network server platform (such as Novell's DirXML). Metadirectory products are also being used as a migration tool and a temporary interoperability measure, and not always as a long-term solution.

Some metadirectory products are standalone directory products (Microsoft Metadirectory Services, for example), while others are integrated with other directory services (such as Novell's DirXML). Still others, like Radiant One Virtual Directory Service by Radiant Logic, are front ends to multiple data sources—providing more of the services and less of the directory (doesn't store directory data).

At the time of writing, a number of metadirectory products are available to support the distributed computing requirements of enterprise networks. A few of these are DirXmetahub from Siemens, DirXML from Novell, iPlanet Directory Server Integration Edition from the Sun|Netscape alliance, and Microsoft Metadirectory Services. Metadirectories are covered in more depth in Chapter 11 "Metadirectory Services."

Application Directories

Another widely used type of directory service is centered on application-specific directories, which are designed to support a very limited set of information and operations. The style of the application supported determines what functionality is provided.

Applications store their configuration and security information in a variety of ways. There may be an actual directory for the application, as well as configuration files on the application server, and configuration data is likely to be stored on the client computer as well.

As application directories span a range of implementations, examining e-mail and instant messaging can highlight some common application directory uses.

E-Mail Directories

Because the messaging directory is the most widely deployed application-specific directory, it merits a closer look to understand what an application directory can and can't do. Messaging directories, at a minimum, contain e-mail account information such as usernames and passwords. Frequently, additional data is supports advanced communication functionality, such as e-mail/fax/voice integration or groupware applications. Messaging directories maintain and synchronize changes to messaging systems, sometimes combined with groupware products.

These messaging products rely on client and server software agents for communicating between individual users and the directory to perform operations such as address lookups. The administrators of messaging directories use product-specific tools to monitor and analyze the messaging flow between the clients and server and to evaluate and manage the application-specific directory database.

E-mail directories are becoming more integrated with those used in scheduling applications, requiring expansion of the related directory and naming conventions to support the additional functionality. Although many different naming formats are used in messaging applications, the explosion in Internet e-mail usage has driven the widespread adoption of the naming convention specified in RFC 822 (for example, `kiernan@mythical.org` or `alexis@netmages.com`).

Early messaging models commonly revolved around either the X.400 specification or proprietary schemes. Yet the X.400 messaging specifications were still lacking in comprehensive directory functionality. The initial concept behind the X.500 standards was to design a fully operational directory model for the telecommunications carriers to provide widespread deployment of a whitepages style directory that would also support X.400 operations. Although most messaging directories use some of the X.500 standards as a conceptual framework, little or no direct interoperation occurs between messaging platforms.

Instant Messaging

Another type of an application-specific directory is that used by a variety of instant messaging services (such as Mirabilis ICQ, AOL Instant Messenger, and others). An instant messaging directory holds not only static information about Internet users (such as their name and e-mail address), but also dynamic attributes such as a logged on user's IP address—this information is used to establish client communication sessions.

Depending on the service, users are allowed to exercise varying degrees of control over the information available in their own listings, such as choosing to hide their directory entry, either from all other users or just specific ones.

The various instant messaging services are competing in a race to gain market share so they each provide unique features. In at least one messaging application, for example, pictures can be associated with directory entries—they are automatically retrieved and displayed during chat sessions.

Specific-Use Directories

Some highly limited directories are in use today, some of which are arguably *not* truly a directory service. These specific-use directories may provide a service (such as name resolution, or verification of security certificates) or public information lists of one sort or another. The specific-use directory is less a product category than a functional one—it generally offers the ability to look up existing information but not modify it, and generally lacks security functionality such as user authentication (a fundamental service for true directory services).

Examples of specific-use directories include the Domain Name System and the publicly accessible information directories available on the Internet (such as InfoSpace, Four11, and so on). These directories allow user access from a Web browser or similar client application. The Internet directories are used for a diverse set of functions, ranging from providing large public directories of e-mail addresses and phone numbers to locating other users for chat.

NOS Directories as Platforms for Directory Applications

As NOS directories become more robust, more application developers are leveraging them to provide the services that application directories have traditionally handled. Existing network resource and account information can be accessed and most directory vendors allow developers to extend the directory schema to support the specific data requirements of the application. This provides an advantage to developers who can just use existing directory functionality instead of creating yet another application-specific database. Network administrators also find this highly preferable to maintaining individual directories for each application in use on the network.

Domain Name System

The *Domain Name System* (DNS) is the most successful and widely used distributed directory available. Although DNS serves a highly specific purpose, primarily performing name-to-IP address resolution for domain host names, it nevertheless is the most scalable directory implementation to be employed in the largest existing distributed network environment (the Internet).

Compared to most other directories, the DNS schema is exceedingly simple, and its scope of content is very limited (containing domain and hostnames and their corresponding IP addresses). Until recently the DNS schema has not been extended much, nor have DNS records been dynamically updateable. With the addition of the *service* (SRV) resource record (initially defined in RFC 2052), however, the schema has been effectively extended to include the identification of hosts that provide specific services (LDAP servers, for example). An SRV resource record is a DNS entry that maps the name of a network service (such as LDAP) to the TCP/IP address of the server providing the specified service.

In addition, the implementation of *Dynamic DNS (DDNS)* now allows the DNS resource records to be dynamically updated to reflect changing server availability and IP addressing. The addition of DDNS is a major step forward in the capabilities of DNS because it allows dynamically assigned IP address/hostnames to be resolved by DNS. As many network environments rely on the *Dynamic Host Configuration Protocol* (DHCP) to supply IP addresses, DDNS can be integrated with DHCP to provide a way to dynamically include *all* network hosts in the DNS database.

For more detailed information on DNS, refer to Chapter 6, "DNS: The Domain Name System."

Is DNS *Really* a Directory Service?

One can take the position that DNS is arguably not truly a *directory service*—it only provides location services for servers, it doesn't provide security services such as authentication or access control, and it doesn't even have user accounts.

One could also, however, make the argument that DNS *is* a directory service; just one with a narrow focus. DNS has many components and functionality that are analogous to those of a directory service. DNS was developed many years ago when many other directory services were similarly simple and limited, and it has filled the need for location services so well there has been little need to change.

DNS is a specific-use directory, although not a directory *service*. It is also becoming an integral part of many, more traditional, directory services. Active Directory *relies* on DNS as its location service, while most other directory products also support some integration with DNS.

Public Directories

Another highly useful way in which specific-use directories are being deployed is as global locator services. These providers are part of an ever-expanding list of companies leveraging directory technology to provide consumers with new services.

Many of these directories provide for the cataloging of a wide range of individual information to assist people in finding other people, or in locating their public key security certificates. Some will provide additional search criteria to enable locating people who are members of professional associations, or alumni of a specific college, for instance. A few examples of this type of directory service include:

- VeriSign
- InfoSpace
- BigFoot
- Four11

Significant restrictions apply to the functionality of most public directories, in that the scope of information is specialized and limited, and the information is not readily changeable by users.

Directory Service Implementations

A directory service provides the perfect platform for innovative management solutions. Directory services can help with many aspects of enterprise management. Many businesses employ directory services to manage at least some portion of their enterprise.

Because directory services are also a development platform, many custom applications are written that leverage their capabilities. With a variety of APIs, readily available SDKs, and *lots* of support for LDAP development, if you can think it up, you can probably develop a directory-enabled version of it.

People are always coming up with new ways to use directories, some of them rather innovative. Consulting firms, some associated with the directory vendors, have developed business solutions integrating enterprise directories and streamlining business operations.

In enterprise environments, directory services are being used for many different purposes. To help you understand how directory services provide key functionality, look at a few categories to demonstrate the range of directory applications.

Automated Provisioning

As directory services come into their own, the first wave of 'killer apps' are appearing; one of the first of these is automated provisioning of corporate resources, IT and otherwise. Directory-enabled automated provisioning demonstrates how a directory service can enable powerful new integrated applications of existing IT systems.

Provisioning is an expensive and time-consuming task fraught with opportunities for mistakes and security breaches. It has also been difficult to automate because of the need to operate on many different systems; network, e-mail, telecommunications, applications, infrastructure devices, and so on. Each of these systems has its own directory, management tools, and methods, and few are compatible with each other, or anything else.

Automated provisioning aims to smooth the process of managing this myriad of critical corporate resources while maintaining the highest possible levels of security. The allocation of corporate resources as varied as network and e-mail accounts, computers, telephone assignments, or the configuration of access rights on devices such as proxy servers or firewalls can be automated.

A directory service is used as the repository for user profiles, security data, and information about managed IT resources. Changes to directory objects can trigger actions in the provisioning software allowing a change to an employee in a human resources directory, for example, to start the process of allocating the resources needed for that employee's new position or assignment. This process can be rolled back with a single action when the person leaves the company, ensuring that all rights are rescinded and accounts are disabled.

By using a directory as its core data repository, provisioning solutions can leverage the inherent strengths of a directory to provide a pervasive solution to one of business's major challenges.

Public Key Infrastructure

One area in which directory services excel is managing public key certificates, something that is becoming increasingly important to all security-conscious businesses. Having strong authentication mechanisms (such as public key technology) are increasingly important to protect the information resources available on the network.

This is an area where the benefits of having a directory service manage such complicated sets of processes and information for you is clear. Take a look now at a complex area of security management—public key certificates—to see how this might work.

Not so long ago, a person had to remember only one or two passwords to use the resources needed to get a job done. All the requisite resources were available on the local network and, in most cases, people seldom communicated with anyone outside of that environment.

Then the Internet came along and everyone started using public channels to communicate, a clear step forward in terms of linking people and companies. However, reality is seldom so straightforward.

If you are sending data across public data channels, as opposed to a private LAN, you need to think about security from a different perspective. One popular method of handling security over the Internet is by using public key certificates. This is a great way to ensure that your data can't be easily compromised, but it requires certificates for each person, maybe more than one—and each certificate may have to be obtained and installed individually on each computer.

It is important to note that certificates are *not* like passwords—you can't memorize them, and they require specific information to be stored in a file somewhere. Those certificates have to be available to the user and other network entities from a number of different physical locations. Clearly, storing certificates somewhere other than the client machine's hard drive is desirable.

Certificate storage and management is one of those places where a directory can help substantially. If you have implemented a directory service on your network, you can store security certificates, either as an attribute of the user they belong to, or as a linked object. The person who needs the certificates no longer has to supply a certificate, it's just there.

This also simplifies management of the certificates because if they need to be renewed, changed, or revoked, they are easily accessible to any directory administrator.

Internet Service Providers

Internet Service Providers (ISP) are an example of a business that can benefit greatly from a directory service. A substantial part of the overhead at an ISP is customer account management; ISPs have a large number of customers and there is an ongoing turnover in that customer base. A directory service could allow a new user account to be created and configured in a minimum of time—something especially useful in an environment with high client turnover.

New functionality such as *Quality of Service* (QoS), which provides bandwidth control, is being provided by directory-enabled devices to enhance network performance for measured network services used by applications such as video on demand. QoS provides an additional revenue stream for ISPs who can provide premium services with guaranteed bandwidth. The level of service allowed, or guaranteed, for a specific person can be set according to criteria such as group membership (for instance, bandwidth can be controlled based on account type).

An ISP is just one business that can significantly reduce the cost of managing clients and create additional revenue with a fully integrated, and thoughtfully designed, directory service.

Web Site Management

Directory services are being used to provide user management for Web sites—such as authentication and user profile information. For example, many Web sites allow people to customize the Web site content to suit their preferences. Web site management that can be provided by a directory includes:

- **User authentication**—Directories are increasingly being used to manage user-authentication for Web sites which support customization. For Web site applications, a directory service provides the needed user authentication and account management service, eliminating the need for the application vendor to develop and manage the user authentication functionality.
- **e-commerce**—Among the critical needs of applications that are going to be delivered across the Internet are scalability and distribution; a large e-commerce site may need to manage hundreds of thousands, or millions, of customers all over the world. By distributing copies of the customer information to strategic locations, you can ensure that client requests are satisfied quickly from a proximate server.
- **Personalization services**—Directories provide an inherently secure, scalable, and distributed means of managing large numbers of users, a critical function for a large Web site. Because of this, many large sites, such as CNN and Yahoo!, have implemented directory services as a means of managing visitor authentication and personalization of site content. Visitors can customize Web sites so that they receive exactly the content they want. At a news site, for example, a person might select several categories of stories, a list of stock tickers, and enter their ZIP code to get local news. These preferences are stored with the user information in a directory. The directory service authenticates the user on site access, and restores the preference information from the user profile.

Government Services

Governments of all sizes are using directory service to build centralized portals for residents, visitors, and businesses. These portals offer government information and provide access to a variety of services. The directory stores security and personalization information for each person using the portal (and eventually perhaps for every resident), allowing customized access to government information from anywhere with Internet access.

Some of the services provided by these government portals include:

- Customized views of the government portal are usually offered; residents are provided information regarding utilities, taxes, and public hearings, while visitors are instead shown a schedule of events, a directory of local hotels and restaurants, and maps of local attractions.

- Secure communications between citizen and government may be provided for, allowing people to contact their elected officials, provide input into public processes like planning, and discuss personal legal business with government employees.
- Residents can conduct online commerce with their local government, making utility payments, paying taxes and court fines, booking facilities, and so on.
- Many municipalities plan on implementing online voting, and it is certain that directory services will serve at the core of these systems. Strong authentication and encryption, provided by the directory, can ensure the privacy and data integrity needed for something as sensitive as voting.

The area of online government services is just getting started; it promises to bring with it many interesting developments. Some deployments are rather modest; many small cities plan to publish information and offer a few services, paying traffic fines via credit card, for example. Other deployments are a bit more ambitious; plans might also include online permitting processes and access to financial accounts such as taxes and unemployment payments. And some governments' plans are truly on a grand-scale; Cap Gemini Ernst and Young recently made a deal with the government of France that represents 35 million eDirectory licenses, enough for the entire country!

Directory-Based Identification Systems

There is a growing call for systems to positively identify people in various business and government contexts. These ID systems need to identify people with relative certainty, requiring the use of security mechanisms such as biometrics. Directory services can support the use of multiple forms of authentication, including biometric measurements, or other security tokens, providing a high degree of security assurance—it's much more difficult, after all, to fake both a password *and* a fingerprint, than faking one or the other.

In its government applications, the identity information needs to be available to a range of agencies, in many locations at all times. Again, a directory service proves well suited—the distribution mechanisms provide access to the same information from any connected system. The ability of a directory to incorporate the use of smart cards and biometrics in a secure distributed identification system, makes it a natural backbone for a security system requiring a high degree of verification.

State of Directory Services

It's probably clear by now that directory services are everywhere; as we've mentioned, industry surveys indicate that the typical enterprise has somewhere between 75–100+ directories. Most corporate network environments include multiple directories for NOS, messaging services, groupware, databases, and other applications, as well as network devices like firewalls and routers.

Although these discrete directories frequently have little in common technically, what they do often share is the information contained within them. A single network user will commonly have an entry in each of the multiple directories, often with pretty much the same information duplicated. As more network services rely on their own directories, the level of redundancy in the stored information is increasing significantly. While there is some movement toward centralizing *all* of this information in a single enterprise directory, nobody is there yet.

There is also substantial movement toward more directory interoperability, fueled in no small part by the explosion of Internet use and the adoption and enhancement of open standards, including X.500, LDAP, and DNS. The most promising development for directory interoperability is the widespread support for LDAP, which has become a standard method for accessing and modifying directory information.

Nevertheless, let's be realistic. When it comes to directories you have a lot of them, you're always going to have a lot of them. True, you will have fewer, but you'll never have just *one*.

Directory services are *not* a one size fits all technology—each business that pursues a directory strategy will come up with a different one. You *should* optimize your directory strategy, however; part of the point of a directory service, after all, is to consolidate data and streamline the management of that data. Understanding the technologies used in directory services will make the process of determining your approach to directories easier.

Evolution of Directory Services

CHAPTER

2

...that which does not evolve loses market share...

IN THIS CHAPTER

This chapter looks at some basic characteristics of directory services and explains the relationship between the desired directory service capability and the resultant directory service design.

The functionality required from directory services has helped shape their design. The increasing need for enhanced directory functionality has spurred the development of more sophisticated directory architecture and mechanisms. Directory information structures have reflected these evolving needs in their approach to information organization, naming, storage, and management.

When examining directory service implementations, it is useful to assess how *need* drives *design*—that is, how what is needed from the directory (focus, scope, capability, and so on) is reflected in the *design* of the directory service (such as in a network directory where it is needed to manage network resources and users, which is reflected in the NOS directory design). From this perspective, each directory service has been designed to fulfill a specific set of requirements within an organization.

The directory service's purpose revolves around the information it manages. The point of implementing a directory service, after all, is to provide and manage access to *information*. The structure of a directory service reflects the nature of the information that the directory is designed to manage.

In the first section of this chapter, the importance of the information that is contained in the directory is addressed, and the political and organizational aspects of directory-based information management are described. Following this, how the overall directory requirements drive the design of a directory service is viewed from several other perspectives:

- **Organization**—How is the directory information organized and named?
- **Storage**—How is the directory information stored?
- **Security**—How is security provided to control access to the information?
- **Administration**—How is the directory service going to be administered?

From each of these perspectives, consider what it means for the design of the directory service. This chapter examines each of these factors and how each of them influences the overall directory design.

An Evolutionary Progression

As an individual vendor's directory products mature, a general progression becomes noticeable: from flat to hierarchical organization, from physical to logical naming, and from centralized to distributed information storage, as well as an increase in the scope of objects managed via the directory.

> This evolution of directory structures is intended to provide more powerful network management capabilities, improve network performance, and provide additional fault tolerance. Yet it also leads to increased complexity and an increasingly steep learning curve for the IT professionals who must master the technology.

Information Characteristics

At the core of a directory service is the structuring of information for distributed storage and retrieval. The specific information set that the directory service is designed to contain has a substantial impact on the construction of the directory service. In the design of a directory service, the information the directory needs to contain and supply, and what the vendor needs the directory service to do will drive the design focus and direct the architecture and technologies employed.

Aspects that need to be considered include the scope and focus of the information, the sensitivity of the content, as well as the relevant regulations. Additionally, issues surrounding ownership and management of the information in the directory often present special challenges.

Scope of Information

Directory services are an information management system, capable of dealing with a wide variety of information, from e-commerce applications and line-of-business operations to critical communications functions and management of enterprise networks. The scope of information that the directory is designed to manage affects its operational capability. For example, if the intended scope is managing generic information systems, a directory will support great flexibility in the creation of objects and attributes and in namespace distribution and design. Conversely, if the scope of the directory is to manage users connected to a specific server, the object and namespace flexibility would be much more limited.

The scope of the information the directory is designed to contain also helps shape the logical organization and presentation methods and defines naming schemes. The scale of the information the directory service will be managing determines the necessary data storage, management, and retrieval capabilities.

As the scope of the directory expands, both numerically and in complexity, more robust and flexible information organization capabilities are needed:

- More directory information equates to more directory entries and requires more sophisticated data management mechanisms.
- The naming model must support the unique identification of the entire scope of information contained in the directory while cognitively and operationally maintaining relationships among information.

- Methods must be defined to support the definition of many types of complex information structures, including abstract information and objects with no real-life analog.
- Issues concerning ownership of information must be dealt with and some sort of distributed control of directory information must be supported. This brings with it a need to organize information to facilitate this distribution and to show relationships between the distributed portions.

Directory Focus

The focus of the directory concerns the kind of functionality it is designed to provide—for example, application directories are designed to provide the specific capabilities needed for the application. The directory for an e-mail application typically contains a set of registered users and provides services such as authentication and address book lookups to clients in addition to the management capabilities provided to the administrator.

Similarly, networking directories are focused on providing and controlling user access to network resources. Network management is the most common focus for directory services. Directory services can provide a critical infrastructure role for enterprise networks by supplying the services required for user authentication and management, directory-enabled applications, network configuration, device management, and content provisioning.

Metadirectories interconnect directories (and possibly databases), and must support the integration of the information in all the connected directories. Meta-directories must also address the security requirements of the underling directory services. Because of this, metadirectories are often the most challenging directories to implement.

Directory services also reach far beyond being a management tool for corporate IT departments. They can support the business infrastructure by managing information related to the company's overall business. In this kind of application, the information set managed by a general-purpose directory service can exceed that used by even the most comprehensive network-centric directory.

An Evolving Focus

The focus of the directories have evolved from specific use to general purpose.

Initially, there were many small-scale directories that did a few things to a limited data set for a specific purpose (e-mail directories, for example).

There are now extremely large-scale directories that do many different things to a seemingly limitless data set, for just about any purpose. And if the directory doesn't do what you want, you can program it so that it will.

Directory Content

The nature of the information that the directory is supposed to contain (such as e-commerce data, content delivery, human resources (HR) data, network management data, e-mail data, and so on) affects the overall directory design. In examining the information managed by a directory service, determine what components the information is actually composed of—does it consist of data about users, financial transactions, e-mail messages, network topology and resources, or enterprisewide information?

Consider the specifics of the information that will be stored in the directory:

- Is the directory service going to contain information on enterprise network users, servers, workstations, and services?
- Will the directory be used to support line-of-business operations, and thus contain detailed information about business operations?
- Will the directory contain personal identifying information (such as birth dates, social security numbers, home addresses, and so on)?
- Will financial information (such as credit card numbers, bank account numbers, transaction data, and so on) be managed in the directory?
- Do you intend to store data that is large in size, like large graphic images?
- Is the directory expected to maintain medical information on users or clients?

Each type of information brings with it different considerations for the overall directory design.

Data Sensitivity

How sensitive is the information contained in, and provided by, the directory service? The answer to this question varies widely depending on context, usage, and other factors. Information sensitivity largely relates to the expected degree of public access to the information. If it is your product catalog, you will want everyone to be able to access the information, yet if it is your HR information, you will want to restrict access to selected HR personnel.

Some data is inherently more sensitive than other data. For example, the name of a released product isn't sensitive, yet the social security number of the CEO is. Financial information is usually considered sensitive, especially account numbers, and thus access to this information (by users or applications) needs to be controlled. Medical information is also sensitive data where access control is required. In the United States, for example, recent regulations governing the management of medical information have come into effect requiring safeguards on medical data. Likewise, many other countries are implementing privacy constraints on obtaining and managing sensitive information.

Other data is only sensitive in some circumstances. Enterprise network information is usually considered sensitive when it comes to external agents such as customers, yet this same information is primarily considered open and available to the company's employees. Thus, the context for the exposure of the information is critical here. It is good if employees know where your network resources are, yet it is not good if customers, competitors, or hackers also have access to this information.

The sensitivity of information, and the environment in which the directory service is supposed to be deployed, affect the security technologies and mechanisms integrated into the directory design. For example, early network directories focused on internal LAN management included simpler authentication and access control methods, whereas directory-enabled e-commerce applications structured to contain financial information in the Internet environment commonly support stronger and more flexible security technologies.

Information Ownership

Important business and political issues are involved in the use of directory services for information management. One of the most important issues is that of ownership and administration of directory information. A core requirement for a highly functional directory service is the capability to distribute the directory information among multiple separate entities, each of which controls its own portion of the namespace.

Depending on the purpose of the directory, this distribution of information ownership is generally one of the following:

- **Totally separate entities**—In a large-scale, distributed directory service, different companies may each own a portion of the total directory service namespace. For example, consider the case of a directory service designed to serve as the consolidated white pages for an entire state. Each local telephone company owns and controls its own portion of the directory namespace, with the directory service also serving to link the different namespaces into a cohesive directory as a whole. This is one of the fundamental aspects of the X.500 design—it is intended to function as a single, logical directory service, yet consists of an interconnected group of globally distributed and locally controlled directory services.
- **Subportions of a single entity**—A single organization may own the entire directory. For example, if the entire scope of the directory service is network management, the information is likely to be controlled by different administrative groups within a single corporation. Frequently, this sharing of information ownership takes a somewhat less complete form than that previously described. A primary administrative group delegates particular management tasks while it ultimately retains control of the entire directory namespace.

- **Sole ownership**—In a limited directory implementation, ownership of the directory namespace may not be shared at all, but lie with a single group. This type of directory implementation tends to be fairly small, serving a single application or server.

Information ownership can be assigned at a highly granular level, usually to the attribute level. The object representing a single user can have many owners of the information it contains. The object itself might belong to the IT department, while specific attributes are controlled by several groups including IT. For example, HR could be responsible for some information (such as manager and job title) while IT controls other data (such as username and password).

A directory service that is designed to support distributed ownership of the directory information must organize the information in a way that both facilitates the distribution of information ownership and clearly maintains the relationships among those distributed portions. The distribution of namespace ownership is best accomplished within a hierarchical directory structure, because the ownership structure can then define the directory tree structure and provide a built-in framework for naming, location, security, and administration.

Management Capability

Simple centralized directories usually consolidate management capabilities around a single server or domain. Administration was relatively simple, yet not scalable to large or distributed environments.

Authoritative Source

Information has an *authoritative source*; that is, the datastore that has the master copy of that specific data. Data obtained from the authoritative source is called *authoritative data*. This authoritative source is always presumed to have the correct information, and supplies its data to clients and other servers (where it is often cached). This cached data may be supplied to clients in response to queries.

Operationally, *owners* of the information are those people who are responsible for maintaining the integrity of the data in the authoritative datastore.

Patience Is a Virtue...

Ownership of the different portions of the directory information may not be easy to negotiate and allocate, even within a single organization. Expect to spend a considerable amount of time and effort in the planning phase of a directory deployment to allow for effective resolution of information ownership issues.

In contrast, distributed and hierarchical directory services are structured to support distributed management of the directory information, enabling delegation of administration. These directories with a hierarchical namespace enable directory administration to be delegated as needed, allowing organizational subdivisions to be locally administered by granting directory administrators the right to manage their portion of the directory.

Especially with larger enterprise directories, this is an important capability because it enables the administrator to subdivide and delegate responsibilities and administration tasks along the same organizational subdivisions that exist within the corporation. As a result, the actual management of the directory information will likely be distributed among multiple (and changing) directory administrators. To have consistent and controlled results, clear policies for managing the directory must be defined.

Regulations and Policies

There is always a range of regulations and policies that apply to information in the directory, and use of the directory information needs to conform to your corporate and legal policies. Your customers, shareholders, and partners alike will require that the confidentiality of their information is protected and controlled.

Existing enterprise policies must be considered, including privacy policies at Web sites and e-commerce applications, network policies, as well as general corporate and HR policies. You also have to consider the general privacy guidelines that your enterprise enforces, and how these need to be reflected in the directory.

In addition, there are likely to be legal and regulatory concerns from a variety of fronts. There are labor laws regarding protection of employee privacy and thus the related information contained in the directory. You must also factor in a myriad of other regulations regarding specific types of information. You may want to consult with legal staff to assess the regulatory requirements on the information stored in the directory. With careful planning, you can effectively build regulatory compliance into the design of your directory service.

Customer Demand

Clients and partners will expect, even demand, protection of their information, especially if that information includes financial, medical, or other sensitive information. This protection is needed to minimize liability of unauthorized disclosure of customer information, as well as to limit exposure to business intelligence gathering efforts.

Your Web sites and e-commerce applications need to provide explicit privacy policies explaining to your clients how you will protect their information, and your directory service must support the stated policies. Your Internet-based communications (such as e-mail, partner sites, Web services, and so forth) will need to supply security measures, such as secure sessions, to ensure private communications.

Company Policy

Every company has corporate policies that apply to verbal and written communications. These policies also specifically limit access to sensitive data (frequently to a "need-to-know" basis). Similarly, the information in the directory needs to be controlled; the same sorts of information management policies apply and for the same reasons.

Yet, with a directory, the context is a little different. Here you are setting access control policies that can affect a range of business operations, from directory-enabled e-commerce or Intranet applications, to internal network management. Company policies regarding control of organization or product information need to be carefully implemented within the directory service to ensure access to information is managed as needed.

Governing Regulations

There is a range of government regulations to consider, from labor law constraints on access to information to general regulations on employee information, as well as topic-specific regulations (such as handling financial information, like salary). Such regulations need to be factored into the policies applied to the directory service, in the form of access controls over sensitive information stored in the directory.

An organization can leverage existing human resources policies in reference to the specifics of the directory service application (what is the directory supposed to do?) when constructing directory information policies. In determining access to information about the enterprise users (the employees, contractors, and so on), the HR department commonly has defined policies for access to sensitive information. HR policies can provide a substantive resource of useful policy information.

Organizing Directory Information

The capabilities required of a directory service, and the scope of the information to be managed, combine to determine the best design for a particular directory implementation. As directory services become more powerful and handle more information, the information structures must change to keep pace with the demands placed on the directory service.

Important aspects of directory information structures revolve around the organization of the information, including the *logical organizational methods*, *naming model*, and the *information and data management mechanisms*. The combination of these describes key aspects of the directory service's capabilities.

The organization of directory information is focused around supporting the directory's scope and requirements in organizing the information, to provide structure for administration, and to enhance security and data management capabilities. Directory information is logically organized into a structure, which allows for consistent naming of objects contained within the directory (referred to as the *namespace*).

Directories can be categorized by the structure of their namespace:

- **Flat namespaces** are those in which all objects are held below a single superior object, as if in a common container. All objects in a flat namespace directory are held in a single logical container.
- **Hierarchical namespaces** provide a means to logically organize the resources in the directory in a treelike hierarchy to facilitate management and access control, enable the distribution of information ownership, support data management, and provide security boundaries.

The rule for how objects are named in the directory is referred to as the *naming model*. The directory naming model supports the need to uniquely identify information by name, maintain relationships between directory information, enforce information ownership, and perhaps even make a context-dependent selection from multiple names for one object. This set of tasks becomes more involved as the set of information managed by the directory grows and the organizational structure of the directory becomes more complex.

Directory services can also be described by the naming model that they use:

- A **physical naming model** dictates that a directory uses actual names of network devices or people to describe objects in the directory. This places a number of constraints on the directory capabilities, which are described in more detail later in this chapter.
- A **logical naming model** uses symbolic names transparently mapped to physical device names. This naming method is flexible enough to support the needs of large, distributed directory services using abstract objects.

The capabilities provided by a hierarchical namespace and logical naming model are some of the important reasons why network administrators praise the availability of robust networking directory services as the means of managing a distributed network.

Namespace Organization: From Flat to Hierarchical

A critical aspect of the directory design is the overall structure of how the directory is logically modeled and presented. In general, directories are either *flat*—holding all directory objects in one large group, or *hierarchical*—modeling the directory into a logical tree of some sort. The directory tree derives its origins from the 1988 X.500 specifications. In the X.500 model of directory services, this hierarchical structure of the directory information is referred to as a *Directory Information Tree (DIT)*.

Directory services implemented in a hierarchical namespace must define general object categories of *container objects* (used for organization) and *leaf objects* (which represent information entities), and define rules that control how they are placed in relationship to each other:

- **Container objects** are used to logically subdivide and structure the directory. Container objects are arranged hierarchically, and may contain other container objects and/or leaf objects.
- **Leaf objects** represent information entities such as services, users, and so on. Leaf objects cannot contain other objects, but may appear to do so because they reference other objects as attribute values, as in the case of groups (which contain a list of users as an attribute of the group object).

The namespace organization reflects the needs (requirements) of the directory service. For example, consider how each of the different types of directories organize its namespace:

- An application directory namespace reflects the purpose of the application; because most applications don't need the benefits of a hierarchical directory tree, applications commonly use a flat namespace.
- A metadirectory namespace is designed to support the integration of the disparate, noncontiguous namespaces of multiple other directories.
- In an e-commerce application, the DIT will reflect the application information and operations requirements.
- A general purpose directory can have the DIT reflect any structure that facilitates the purpose of the implementation.
- Early NOS directories were designed as flat namespaces, reflecting their support for server-based or domain-based directories.

Directories with flat namespaces, such as the NetWare bindery or the Windows NT domain, display all the network resources in a single container along with the users who need access to those resources. These directory namespaces generally contain a relatively small set of directory objects, and were mostly used in early NOS directory implementations and dedicated applications. Although this design can be effective for small network directories or limited applications, it can rapidly become unwieldy as the number of entities that must be managed increases.

Schema Defines Namespace Characteristics

The rules specified in the directory schema determine the structural characteristics of the directory namespace. Information structures in the directory are defined in the schema as objects, attributes, and syntax. The arrangement of objects within the tree is constrained by structure rules, and the attributes assigned to an object are constrained by content rules. The syntax rules determine how information can be entered into attributes.

Most current directory service products employ some sort of a hierarchical model, with at least a nominal capability to model the information as a tree of containers populated with objects (representing the directory resources and users).

In a networking-focused directory service, the DIT is commonly used to reflect a company's internal structure by creating container objects corresponding to business units and other corporate divisions. In a company with multiple locations connected via WAN links, it is common to design the top levels of the DIT along geographic boundaries to facilitate management and control network traffic.

Figure 2.1 shows a simple DIT for a company with two offices (one in the United States, the other in Europe). As you can see, the top layer of the DIT is divided by physical locality with business divisions contained in the appropriate geographic subdivision.

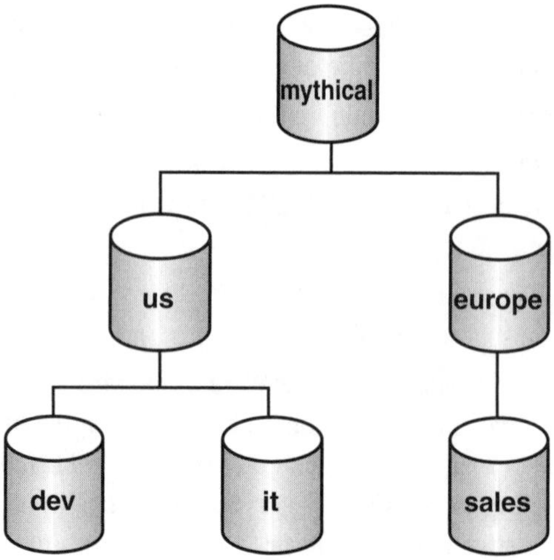

FIGURE 2.1

A hierarchical directory provides a treelike structure for organizing and managing the network.

Hierarchical namespaces also provide the structure for the flow of inherited security rights and administrative privileges. By using the DIT to model the business organization, network administration and security control can be logically assigned and managed within a familiar framework. Likewise, by using the DIT to model a business process, such as an e-commerce application, administration and access control can be logically structured and maintained.

Naming Directory Objects: From Physical to Logical

A fundamental characteristic (and key usability factor) of a directory namespace is the conceptual foundation on which objects in the directory are named. The implications of the naming model a directory is designed on are far reaching, affecting far more than just how object names are assigned. A few less obvious factors in using a particular naming model are

- **Flexibility**—A design that requires every directory entry to have a corresponding real-life object (that is, a printer or file volume) limits the overall flexibility of the directory.
- **Ease of use**—Logical naming models are easier to use because stable, symbolic names based on common language can be employed.
- **Reduction in administration**—Administration for physical naming models is generally more time consuming when compared to a directory using logical names.
- **Stability of network resources**—Using physical device names (physical naming model) requires user configuration updates if the device moves or changes. With a logical naming model, an object's name seldom changes, obviating the need to constantly update network users with a new device name every time a resource is relocated.

To provide a clear example of naming issues, throughout this naming section the focus will be on network directory services, where the objects in the directory describe network resources such as servers, users, printers, and so on. In this environment, the basis for object naming is commonly divided into *physical naming models*, which use network device names, and *logical naming models*, which use symbolic names to represent network resources. To clarify the design and operational differences, the following sections focus on the capabilities and contingencies of physical versus logical naming models as applied in network directory services.

Physical Naming Models

Physical naming models are based on the names of the physical devices attached to the network (commonly, server names). In a physical namespace, shared file and print resources are known and accessed by the name of the specific server and or server/resource location.

Figure 2.2 illustrates the usage of a physical naming model. This example uses a familiar model, the *Universal Naming Convention (UNC),* used by Windows. The `mars` server has two printers attached, `devlaser` and `devinkjet`, and one file share, SRC. As you can see, the printers are known on the network by the combined server and printer names: `\\mars\laser` and `\\mars\inkjet`. Similarly, the `SRC` file share is identified on the network as `\\mars\SRC`.

Clearly, with any network (irrespective of the naming model used) every user has to determine the name of a resource on the network prior to being able to access it. On a small network, with only a few resources, this may be simple—people memorize the names of the resources they use regularly, manually maintain a list, or ask the person at the next desk.

Directories using a physical naming scheme add a layer of complexity, however, in that resources are renamed when they are relocated. Therefore, users are confronted with the requirement of relearning the location (and therefore the name) of a resource whenever the resource is moved to a new location. When the name of the network resource changes when the object is moved, it is said to be a *location-dependent name*.

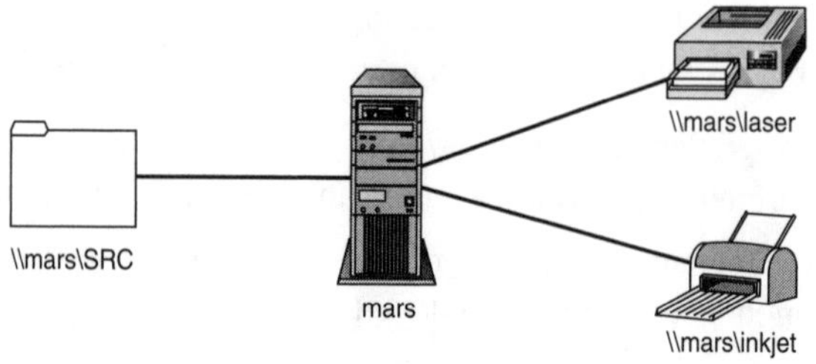

FIGURE 2.2
Physical naming models use actual device names to identify resources on the network.

Now take another look at the server from the preceding example to illustrate the primary shortcoming of location-dependent naming. In Figure 2.3, the `mars` server has become busy enough that the inkjet printer must be moved to another server, `neptune`. As you can see, this means that the printer name changes from `\\mars\inkjet` to `\\neptune\inkjet`, and every reference to that printer must be modified to reflect this change.

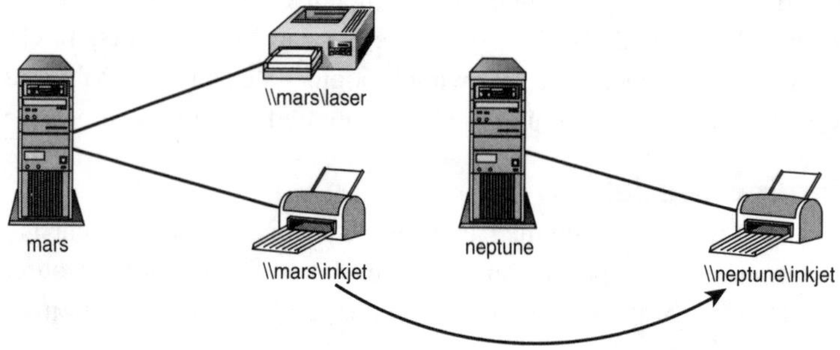

FIGURE 2.3
If directory object names are location-dependent, when a resource moves, its name changes (creating extra work for administrators and confusion for users).

Administrators must not only ensure that network resource names are changed in *every* instance they are referenced (whether by NOS, messaging, applications, or other system components), but must also inform users of all changes that may affect them. Every person and application referencing that printer must now be provided with the new name, and make appropriate configuration changes to reflect the current printer location. This adds considerable overhead to the administration of a large or complex network.

Many types of networks use physical naming models in their directory implementations, including the NetWare bindery and the Windows NT 4 domain models. The NetWare bindery was a server-based directory, with the server name integrally linked to attached resources or users.

Windows NT 4 uses physical names and a flat namespace, yet further organizes resources into *NT domains* (which adds another tier), usually representing a subdivision of the company. Whether implemented as a single-level (server-based) namespace, or as a multitiered (domain-based) namespace, these network directories were implemented as *flat* namespaces (and were not truly hierarchical).

Logical Naming Models

When the scope of the directory is just the physical devices and users on a network, naming can be very simple. When the directory scope expands to more than a small object set, however, naming must be approached from a somewhat different perspective.

The naming models in more powerful directory services must contend with issues such as the following:

- Names must be delinked from physical objects so that abstract objects and information can be represented.
- Names must uniquely identify objects across broad directory namespaces.
- The directory service may need to provide numerous names for the same object depending on requestor or context.

Namespaces that use logical naming models enable you to create a relationship between a physical network device (such as a printer) and a symbolically named directory object that represents that device. Users can then access any network device by using the name of the directory object rather than the physical device name and/or location. The directory is responsible for transparently mapping the logical resource name to the actual physical resource for the client.

Figure 2.4 illustrates the use of a logical naming model on the same resources as in the previous two examples. Because these resources are part of the Development division, the printers are now named `devLaser` and `devInkjet`, and the file share is named `devSRC`. These names no longer designate the physical location of the network resource; they now point to directory objects. The directory maintains the relationship between the logical name used to identify the network resource and the physical location of the resource.

One of the main advantages of using an abstract name to represent network resources is that resource names can remain unchanged, even if the physical locations of resources do not. When the name of a network object remains consistent when the physical location of the resource changes, the naming model is referred to as a *location-independent model*. Location independence simplifies directory management in one critical way: After a resource is named in the directory, there is seldom a need to rename it.

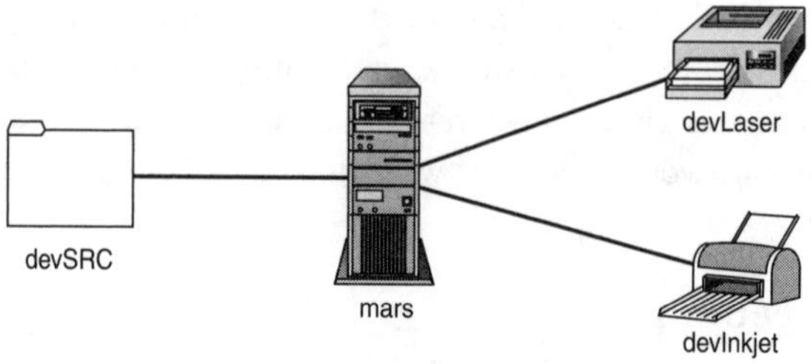

FIGURE 2.4

Logical naming models use symbolic names to identify resources on the network.

Figure 2.5 reexamines the process of moving a printer from one server to another. In this case, the directory entry for `devInkjet` is edited to reflect the new physical location of the printer. Because the name used to identify the printer on the network does not include information regarding its location, moving it does not affect the name by which it is known on the network.

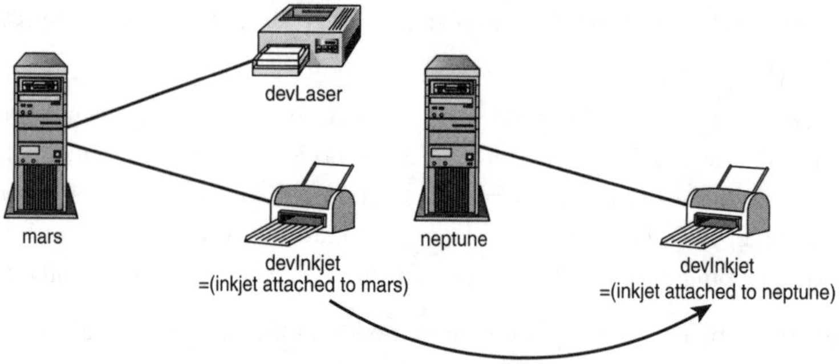

FIGURE 2.5

Location-independent names provide a means for network names to remain the same, even when a resource physically moves.

This approach is clearly advantageous for administrators and users alike. Administrators are required to change the information regarding the printer's physical location in one place only, the directory. Even better, the people and applications that access that printer need not make any configuration changes, nor even necessarily know that the printer is attached to a different server.

If the printer is moved to a different location in the building, another office, for example, the directory can maintain that information as well. By storing the office number of network resources in the directory, users can just check the directory for the printer's room number to locate it. This is useful not only for resources that have moved, but for new employees as well, providing a single location that anyone can check for such data.

Logical naming models do not require a one-to-one relationship of physical resources to directory objects, a feature allowing increased flexibility through the use of objects without a realworld corollary. Because directories using a logical naming model are generally formed as a hierarchical tree, for example, container objects that have no corresponding physical objects can be created solely for structure or to create security boundaries. Other objects can be created to hold specific information, such as application settings, or to provide access to an area of administrative functionality.

Logical naming models provide greater flexibility for network administrators and easier access to resources for network clients. Logical naming models are clearly desirable in a network environment, especially when compared to using physical device names that change and require clients to adjust their resource mappings.

Clearly, physical namespaces are less advantageous than logical namespaces, require more network management, and increase the amount of information a user needs to access available network resources. Conversely, logical naming models reduce administrative overhead and simplify user location of, and access to, network resources.

Common Naming Conventions

To locate information or resources in a directory, every entry included in a directory first must have a name—a way to locate it amongst all the directory contents. One of the key factors in easing location and access to information in a directory is how directory objects are named, variously referred to as the *naming convention*, *naming format*, or *naming model*. The naming convention is the structure that determines the method of naming objects within a directory.

Each directory service uses a specific naming convention, which can be thought of as a particular "style" of naming an object. Each naming convention specifies the number and legality of characters that can be used within names, and the delimiter used to separate the different parts of the name.

All objects in the directory have to be named in accordance with the specified naming model. This naming model is used consistently for all the objects within the directory. For an object to be located within a given directory, the object must have a name that conforms to the designated naming convention.

The naming convention used in a distributed directory environment can make a critical difference in how easily people can identify and find information or resources they need. The naming style can also make a big difference to those who have to manage and support the directory service, providing cognitive organization and logical structure to the entire scope of the information stored and distributed in the directory.

Some naming conventions, notably those rooted in DNS, are nearly universally used and relatively simple to remember. Others, such as those derived from X.500, are more cognitively difficult and, although widely used, can present challenges to the people who must contend with long and complicated name strings. Recently, more directory products are being designed to mask the intricacies of the naming model from the client whenever possible and to provide support for a variety of naming conventions, simplifying a significant aspect of directory usage.

The following section reviews the naming of directory entries (objects) from the perspective of different naming conventions, including X.500, LDAP, NDS, UNC, DNS, and RFC 822 naming. For the purposes of this illustration, the discussion focuses on how a specific person (or her computer, in the case of UNC and DNS naming) would show up in the various directories. These examples assume that the Netmages organization has an employee named Brynna with an account in a number of different directory services and examine how she or her computer (`morgana`) are identified using each naming convention.

X.500 Naming

Many directory implementations provide support for X.500 or X.500-style naming formats. X.500 natively uses a formalized style of designating each directory entry by type, name, and placement in the directory tree.

Each entry in a directory tree has both a local reference called a *Relative Distinguished Name (RDN),* and a fully qualified name referred to as the *Distinguished Name (DN)*. The RDN is just the name of the object paired with the appropriate name type attribute. The DN of a directory entry is constructed of the object's RDN concatenated with the names of its superior objects in the path to the root of the directory tree. Although the RDN is not guaranteed to be unique within the directory, the DN is and thus unambiguously identifies and positions an object within the directory tree.

Each X.500 object class designates a property to serve as its *naming attribute*. For example, the `Common Name` property is frequently designated as the naming attribute for leaf objects, including user objects. The naming attribute also supplies an abbreviation used in the name of each object; in the case of `Common Name`, the abbreviation is `cn`. The abbreviation for the naming attribute is used when forming the X.500 name; therefore, the name is considered *attributed* or *typed*.

In this example, the RDN of the user object would be `cn=brynna`. In X.500, a DN is written starting with the root and continuing down the directory tree to the leafmost object. For a user named Brynna in the Wizards subdivision of the Netmages organization, for example, the RDN is cn=brynna, and the DN is this:

```
o=netmages,ou=wizards,cn=brynna
```

For more detailed information on X.500 naming conventions, refer to Chapter 4, "X.500: A Model for Directory Services."

LDAP Naming

The Lightweight Directory Access Protocol (LDAP) uses the X.500 naming convention referred to as typed naming, where each part of the name is delimited by a comma, and linked to the abbreviation for its name attribute by an equal sign (`cn=brynna`). Yet in LDAP, the order of the components of a DN are written differently. An LDAP DN is written starting with the leafmost object, and continues up the directory tree to the root.

Therefore, although an LDAP DN appears, at first glance, highly similar to an X.500 DN, it is in fact reversed. So the user object referenced in the preceding example would look like this when referenced by an LDAP client:

```
cn=brynna,ou=wizards,o=netmages
```

RFC 2253 describes the mechanism by which X.500 names are converted to LDAP names.

LDAP URL Naming

Directory services that provide access to the directory via Web browsers can support the LDAP URL *naming model*. DNS is used in the LDAP URL resolution for the domain portion of the object's name. LDAP URLs are designed to leverage the existing DNS infrastructure as a means of locating LDAP directory servers for a particular DNS domain (defined in RFC 2255).

A LDAP URL name is constructed in the following form:

```
LDAP://host.domain.tld/path-to-object
```

To continue with the example, with the DNS domain `netmages.org` hosted on `zifnab`, the LDAP URL referencing the same object would be as follows:

```
LDAP://zifnab.netmages.org/cn=brynna,ou=wizards,o=netmages
```

Both these forms of LDAP naming will be discussed in more detail in Chapter 5, "LDAP: Lightweight Directory Access Protocol."

Spaces in X.500 Naming

X.500 names, as well as many naming forms derived from X.500 (such as LDAP), can optionally contain spaces after the comma or other separator characters. Spaces are normally used only to make it easier for people to read the object name and are stripped by the directory when processing the name.

NDS Naming

The Novell Directory Services (NDS) naming model accepts a dot-delimited *typed* or *typeless* derivation of the X.500 naming model. Typeless naming does not use the name attribute, which reduces the amount of data required to specify the object. Like LDAP, NDS naming reverses the X.500 order of the name components when constructing a DN, starting with the leafmost object and proceeding to the root. NDS names can either take the typed form of

```
cn=brynna.ou=wizards.o=netmages
```

or the typeless form

```
brynna.wizards.netmages
```

DNS Naming

Perhaps the most familiar naming format is that used by the Domain Name System (DNS), which is used to locate servers on the Internet (and most other TCP/IP networks). The most basic form of the DNS name is comprised of the organization's domain name, in this case `netmages.org`. Specific servers (hosts) within the domain can be located on a network using DNS resolution by preceding the domain name (`netmages.org`) with the machine name (`morgana`), as shown here:

```
morgana.netmages.org
```

One advantage of DNS and naming schemes based on it, is the widespread and ever-increasing user familiarity with the format. Directories that support DNS names enable administrators to leverage existing user knowledge instead of having to teach a new style of object naming.

E-Mail Naming

Another style of naming familiar to most people is the e-mail name, with a user and domain address separated by the at symbol (@) using an `emailname@domain.tld` format, as shown here:

```
brynna@netmages.org
```

This naming format is specified in RFC 822 and is most commonly employed in e-mail applications. Directories supporting these e-mail names rely on DNS for resolution of the domain portion of the name. The messaging directory service is then responsible for resolving a specific username to an e-mail mailbox and providing delivery information.

UNC Naming

The Universal Naming Convention (UNC) common to the Windows networking platform is designed to specify network server and share locations and uses a `\\server\share` format. To access a share named `docs` on a server named `morgana`, for example, you would use the UNC designation `\\morgana\docs` when connecting.

Multiple Naming Conventions

As has been shown, most networks are designed in such a way that a single user is identified by several names, depending on which location service is being used to find the user. A person can have an e-mail address (`brynna@netmages.org`), another name for identification within an NDS directory (`brynna.wizards.netmages`), and another name used by an LDAP client:

```
LDAP://zifnab.netmages.org/cn=brynna,ou=wizards,o=netmages
```

Although each of these names refers to the same person (Brynna), the format that will be successful in locating her depends on the naming support provided by the directory and client. Clearly the more naming conventions supported by a directory, the more flexible and easy to use it will be.

Storing Directory Information

In the approach to the storage of directory information, you can see how the needs of the directory drive the design of the storage method. Directory information storage methods are determined by scale of information and operational needs such as performance, interconnectivity, reliability, and distribution requirements, factors which all influence the directory service design.

These operational aspects of the directory are particularly relevant in relationship to the data management mechanisms employed by the directory service. These requirements help determine the necessary directory data storage and retrieval mechanisms and physical data distribution and replication methods—factors to be considered when looking at how the capabilities required from a directory service have shaped the overall design and functionality.

Range of Current Storage Methods

As people have demanded higher functionality from directory services, vendors have employed a number of different approaches to issues of data storage and management. Some directory services, such as *eDirectory* and *Active Directory*, incorporate proprietary data management functionality into their directory products. Other directory services, typically the general-purpose style, such as those developed by Computer Associates (*eTrust*), and Siemens (*DirX*), use a relational database that is either directly incorporated or interchangeably plugged in. An emerging approach used by Radiant Logic (*RadiantOne VDS*), described as a "virtual directory service," leverages data from its source storage location without storing the data in a standalone datastore.

Storage: From Centralized to Distributed

As a starting point, a distinction between directory types can be drawn based on whether the directory information is contained as a single datastore on a single server, a single datastore copied to multiple servers, or whether the information can be subdivided and distributed to multiple servers holding distinct portions of the directory database.

The directory information may be stored as:

- A **centralized directory** that holds the entire directory namespace in one datastore on a single server.
- A **centralized and replicated directory** that holds the entire directory namespace in one datastore, yet mandated secondary copies of the directory are stored on additional directory servers to provide reliability and increase availability.
- A **distributed directory** that subdivides the directory namespace it holds, and distributes multiple copies of each subset of directory information throughout the network. These subsets are logically linked into one directory, providing a unified logical interface to all the distributed directory information.

Centralized Directory Information

If all the directory information resides on a single server, the directory service can be considered *centralized*, as opposed to when the directory namespace is distributed among multiple distinct directory servers. The scope of resources controlled by a centralized directory is usually fairly narrow, and may be restricted to the resources directly attached to the single computer containing the directory information.

Network Directory Service Storage

When it comes to network-focused directory products, you can see that these basic characteristics tend to be combined in particular ways:

The NetWare bindery and Windows NT domain are examples of the less-sophisticated directory approaches. These are centralized directories, implemented in a flat namespace, where directory objects directly correspond to users and physical network resources such as servers, printers, and file shares.

More sophisticated directory designs, such as eDirectory and Active Directory, use a more abstract design with a logical naming model, hierarchical structure, and distributed information store. This provides a much more robust and scalable solution than the bindery and domain-style implementations.

A centralized directory, with the sole copy of the directory information contained on a single server, presents some obvious problems for the network administrator. Fault tolerance and performance are both areas deserving special attention when using such a configuration. For example:

- A single copy of the datastore provides no fault tolerance; therefore, if the directory server becomes unavailable, operations that depend on the directory stop functioning. Directories with centralized information require extra diligence on the part of the administrator to ensure regular backups of the directory information.
- There are also performance implications when using a single copy of the directory information. This creates a situation requiring all users to be validated from a single copy of the directory, slowing access for all users and causing delays in directory operations.

Of course, there are also advantages to the simple design of a centralized directory. You can be sure that there will be no data inconsistencies and there is no network traffic associated with maintenance of the directory information. This is a small benefit, however, when contrasted to the liabilities of a single copy of directory information.

A directory that uses a single copy of the directory information may provide adequate performance for small networks or specialized applications, but is generally inadequate for larger networks or large scale line-of-business and e-commerce applications. Centralized directory services also fail to provide the kind of fault tolerance and the performance enhancements possible with a distributed directory design.

Another perspective on whether the directory information can be considered centralized versus distributed is based on whether the information contained in the DIB references information or resources that are attached to (or controlled by) a single server or multiple servers.

An Example of a Simple Centralized Directory

One salient example of a centralized flat directory is the NetWare 3.x bindery. This early implementation of a network directory was maintained on a single server, and required the user to attach individually to every server whose resources the user needed to access.

The NetWare bindery holds information about only one server's resources and is limited to a single copy. Clearly, unless a network is extremely small, with a limited number of users, printers, and so on, this is a rather impractical method of network management.

Centralized and Replicated Directory Information

When a directory database is replicated (that is, copied) to multiple servers, each directory server can handle lookup requests for workstations on its local network, thus reducing response latency and improving directory reliability.

The centralized and replicated directory design does provide some performance benefits, supporting more robust and responsive user authentication and access control, but only the single master database can be added to or modified. The availability of backup directory servers does provide redundancy in case of primary server failure.

A centralized directory for an e-commerce application can provide unified storage of the required business information, and replication of the directory to backup servers can provide reliability and availability. Some directory servers based on LDAP (such as SLAPD) use a centralized and replicated approach to storing directory information.

Some network directories, such as Windows NT 4, are centralized and replicated, implementing one or more backup servers to provide some degree of failover and performance enhancement.

Distributed Directory Information

The use of distributed directory services allows the directory information to be distributed over diverse physical and logical topologies. Multiple directory servers in WAN and LAN environments can share the directory datastore, as well as the lookup and administrative loads for their local network.

The Windows NT Centralized and Replicated Directory

In the Windows NT 4 design, a *primary domain controller* (PDC) supplies a copy of the entire *Security Accounts Manager* (SAM) database to all the *backup domain controllers* (BDCs) within the domain. The BDCs can then take care of some of the network traffic associated with requests from member users, servers, workstations, and remote domains. Additionally, if the NT PDC fails, a BDC can be manually promoted to take over the role of PDC so that full network functionality can be restored.

NT 4 domains are not implicitly integrated and operate as discrete directories. Although trust relationships (allowing interdomain authentication) can be established between NT 4 domain controllers, obviating the need for each user to have an account in every domain's SAM database, administration of a large network still involves significant duplicated overhead when compared to a distributed directory. Although this is better than no redundancy or load balancing at all, it is far from meeting the needs of today's enterprise networks.

The core storage location for directory data is called the *Directory Information Base (DIB)* in the X.500 specifications. In this model, the DIB is distributed across multiple directory servers, each providing authentication services and directory lookups for its portion of the DIB. Queries that request information outside that directory server's part of the DIB are either referred to the correct directory server, or the local directory server obtains the information on behalf of the requesting client.

Distributed directory services can contain many different types of information and are commonly extensible, allowing for new directory object types. The functionality of a truly distributed directory service provides the foundation for new forms of organizing and managing your information, applications, services, and networks.

Most current directories are implemented in a namespace using logical object names and contained in a distributed database of objects structured in a hierarchical tree. Many of these implementations of distributed directory services are derived from the X.500 standards, which specify a number of directory models delimiting the information contained in the directory, and the management of the directory tree. X.500 also defines the structure of the database containing the directory, the protocols and services provided, the directory search model, client and server agents, and the exposed APIs. Because X.500 provides the foundation on which much of current directory services are built, Chapter 4 examines it in depth.

Distributed directories must be designed to address a number of issues regarding multiple server operations, data consistency, fault tolerance, and performance. Partitioning and replication are two important mechanisms used to manage the subdivision and updating of the directory services database. In brief, *partitioning* is the subdividing of the directory, and *replication* is the copying of partition contents to other directory servers. These topics are discussed in the following sections.

Partitioning the Directory Information

A *partition* is a subdivision of the directory. All directories start out as a single partition, and the smaller ones may stay that way. However, this is frequently not an adequate method of managing directory data. Current directory services can hold just about any kind of data, and some of that information may be sizeable. If you decide to have a picture of each employee as an attribute of the employee's user object, for example, and you have 5,000 employees, the DIB will quickly grow quite large.

Partitioning allows different subsets of the directory to exist on different physical computers, for security, administrative, or performance reasons. Subdividing an enterprisewide directory into organizationally or geographically delineated partitions, can allow those subsections of the DIB to be managed by regional administrators, and provides for faster directory lookup services to regional users.

Replicating the Directory Information

In a distributed directory, the contents of the DIB partitions can be copied, or *replicated*, to multiple directory servers. Using replicas of the DIB provides a way to distribute directory service loads across multiple servers to increase performance and improve fault tolerance.

Replication ensures directory service availability by distributing replicas of directory partitions to multiple directory servers; if one replica becomes unavailable, users and applications can still access the directory contents by querying one of the other replicas. Replication can also be used to balance directory traffic loads and speed up directory lookups by distributing the client requests to multiple servers.

Depending on the specific implementation, there may be some limitations on directory functionality when certain replicas are unavailable. If a single master replication scheme is used and the master replica becomes unavailable, for example, people should be able to log on using other replicas, but directory changes may not be possible. Single-master and multi-master replication schemes are discussed in more detail in Chapter 3, "Storing Directory Information."

A distributed directory, in its most basic form, can provide an exact duplicate of the entire DIB to a number of alternate directory servers. This is an example of a single partition with multiple replicas.

More commonly, the directory is partitioned and then replication is performed on a per-partition basis. This allows the data in the directory to be subdivided for security or management purposes and then replicated for performance and fault tolerance.

Searching in a Distributed Directory

When the directory database is distributed, the entire directory may not be held by any one server—a situation that has implications for directory searches. A directory server can only provide information regarding the directory resources that it contains or has the means to locate.

When the DIB is partitioned, directory servers must be capable of resolving user queries within the scope of the portion of the directory (*partition*) contained locally. If the data is not available locally, they must be capable of providing access to other directory servers to continue the search process. To provide this capability, the directory servers must be able to find other directory servers to handle requests outside the scope of the portion of the DIB managed by that server.

To provide this query resolution functionality, the following methods are used:

- **Server-based resolution**—When using *chaining*, a directory server attempts to satisfy queries locally and, if necessary, passes the query to other directory servers. The results from multiple directory servers are compiled and returned to the client as if a single directory server had provided all the returned information.

- **Client-based resolution**—The *referral* process offloads more of the work to the client by only requiring the directory server to fulfill the request as far as possible within the directory partition it holds. After it has done so, the directory server returns the results to the client, along with the names of other directory servers to query. The client must then contact the other servers to complete its directory operation. The use of referrals requires more intelligence on the part of the client software than chaining.
- **Multicasting**—A single request can also be submitted to multiple directory servers at once in a process called *multicasting*. Directory servers that can provide results to the query will do so; servers that cannot will discard the request. Multicasting is not commonly used to make directory queries by most current directory service implementations.

The primary difference among these methods is which software agent is responsible for controlling the process and performing most of the work; chaining is done by directory servers, while referrals require the client to do more of the work. Public directory providers frequently prefer chaining because it ensures a single point of access by all clients into the directory. By contrast, enterprise directories often prefer referrals because they off-load more of the work and control to the client agent. Most directory service implementations support both chaining and referral.

Use of Directory Catalogs

Directory searches on large directories can still be time consuming even when the directory database is distributed and replicated. In an attempt to speed up directory searches, most vendors have provided some type of a catalog (or index) of directory information. A *catalog* usually holds a subset of the data contained in the directory, commonly just the basic identifying information about all objects in the directory and a pointer to the directory server holding the object.

Directory catalogs are not without their trade-offs, however. Catalogs that contain too much data are cumbersome and slow to search, and catalogs that do not contain adequate data to satisfy most queries fail to provide optimal performance. You should also keep in mind that directory catalogs are only as good as their last update. This means that if your directory data changes frequently and your directory updates its catalogs infrequently, searches using the catalogs may return incorrect or incomplete information.

A Common Use of Catalogs

One of the most common implementations of a directory catalog is a sort of "white pages," referencing an index to all (or selected) objects in the directory, enabling users to conduct high-speed searches of the index so that they don't have to search the entire directory.

Securing Directory Information

Because the directory contains sensitive and confidential information about individual users, as well as directory resources, a directory service must control access to the directory and the information it contains. Security is provided differently in various directory services, but is an essential element of all. Each directory service must address basic security factors such as authentication and access control.

The specifics of the security methods selected in the directory design reflect what the directory will be required to do. If the directory is focused on supporting e-commerce applications, it is likely to support a robust set of Internet security standards. Likewise, if the directory is designed as a metadirectory, a robust set of security standards would be supported (as authentication to all external directories is required). Alternatively, if the directory is focused on managing a LAN it may support only a platform specific set of security technologies.

Many proprietary security models and implementations exist in various directory services, network operating systems, and distributed applications complicating network security management. Directory services commonly enhance network security by integrating multiple security standards and technologies, providing the scalable security and access control mechanisms required in an enterprise network. Current directory products also commonly provide support for industry security and encryption standards such as X.509 public key certificates and the Kerberos protocol, in addition to the network-specific security models.

Regardless of the technologies implemented, there is a basic functionality supported by all (in whatever form, to whatever degree). To allow access to the directory, the identity of the user (or process) must first be confirmed and the permissions to access specific directory information must be determined. Directory services provide two fundamental security functions:

- **Authentication**—All administrators face the fundamental issues of controlling which users can connect to the directory. Authentication is the mechanism that verifies the identity of the individual user.
- **Access Control**—A directory must also deal with the question of who can access which data and network resources. In locating information in the directory, the directory service also compares the user's permissions and the access control entries on the requested objects to determine whether to allow access. This *access control* mechanism provides differential levels of access to directory information and services, depending on the user's permissions.

Security in a centralized directory, where each server controls security for its own resources, is both a simple and a complicated task. For example, with an early network directory such as NetWare or NT, users had to be authenticated at every server or domain they accessed. If clients access resources attached to only a single server (perhaps assigned by physical location or workgroup), the security provided by a nondistributed directory may be adequate. If so, it will certainly be much faster to configure such a network for a small group of people than to deploy a full-scale distributed directory.

A large network with this localized style of security management requires significant configuration of interdirectory exchange of security information; however, this is a very complex security model to implement for a large or distributed network. The integration of network security services with directory services can effectively provide controlled access to all network resources and information.

Because security controls can be assigned on an object level, an object can be moved and all its access rights will move with it. When a distributed directory is used as the storage location for users and network objects, the associated access rights can be stored as part of the object, allowing for distributed security control. As a directory is partitioned and distributed among network servers, both security privileges and administration can be logically subdivided within the directory.

The namespace design also affects the approach to implementing directory security:

- A flat namespace uses groups to assign differential security permissions—users are assigned to groups and inherit their permissions from the group.
- A hierarchical namespace uses container objects in the tree for assigning security permissions—users inherit their permissions from cumulative parent objects in the tree. Groups may also be used to provide collective assignment of permissions.

Early NOS Security Models

Early directory implementations used application server or domain-based access rights, requiring a separate user account for each server or domain, complicating network operations for administrators and users alike. Some of these directories, such as that supplied with NT 4, have mechanisms for authentication and access control support across domains. However, this may require a rather complicated configuration of *domain trusts* (the NT method of exchange of security information between domains) to support interdomain operations.

As you can imagine, such centralized security models require substantial administrative overhead when used in large-scale or diverse heterogeneous networks. By comparison, a distributed, hierarchical directory (which encompasses all network resources) provides access to the entire network with a single logon and simplifies security configuration.

Hierarchical Security Model

In contrast to a flat directory, a hierarchical directory can provide structure for the assignment of security information. The structure of the directory tree can be leveraged to implement administrative and security areas, a somewhat different security model from early application and network directories.

Hierarchical directory services define containers (objects that can contain other objects), as well as user and group accounts as objects within the directory namespace, and assign access rights to the objects. Each object in the directory can contain a full set of security descriptors, controlling actions taken on the object, in addition to the security settings for the underlying information or resource represented by the directory object.

A hierarchical directory tree provides a framework for the flow of assigned security permissions downward through the directory (known as *inheritance*). Permissions assigned anywhere in the tree are implicitly assigned to the entire subtree below that point, unless explicitly blocked. *Filters* are (optionally) employed at the container level to block an inheritance of permissions, providing the means to create a security boundary around a specific portion of the directory.

Rather than requiring the assignment of access rights for individual users or groups, permissions assigned to a directory container object apply to all objects in the container. By attaching security assignments to a container object, rather than the individual objects within it, directory management can be streamlined. To assign permissions, which are related to being in a specific location or department (or any logical group represented by a container object), you only have to create an object in that container. All the appropriate security assignments are automatically made. If an object is moved from one container to another the security assigned to the new container will immediately apply.

Taking advantage of this security design can ease managing the control of access to directory information. For example, network administrators can simplify the management of an enterprise network. Permissions that apply to the entire company, such as the capability to browse network resources, can be granted close to the root (top) of the directory tree and thus *implicitly* applied to everyone via inheritance.

More specific rights, such as the capability to write to a file share, can then be assigned to the container holding the objects representing the people or groups who need to write to the share. Departments that need to be isolated, such as Sales or Development, can have the rights inheritance blocked and specific permissions granted only to those users and groups who need to access the information.

Groups can also be used in combination with the hierarchical directory security model, to support assignment of common permissions for users located in different tree locations. In addition, the usual capability to grant access rights to individual users remains. The combination of these methods of assigning permissions provides the framework for robust, yet easy to manage security.

Granularity

Access control can generally be set on a per property basis, providing a high degree of granularity on directory object security settings. This capability to allow access to some objects and attributes, while blocking the viewing or modification of other attributes, provides a great deal of control over what directory contents users can see and change. In many enterprise applications of a directory service, this degree of control is very useful (and sometimes absolutely essential) in managing access to directory information.

This level of granularity also enables a directory administrator to delegate management tasks while ensuring unauthorized administrative actions are blocked and guaranteeing confidentiality of sensitive data.

Multiple Security Technologies and Providers

Although leading directory service and NOS vendors commonly use proprietary algorithms for encryption and authentication, a number of new technologies and standards are being integrated into directory products. The use of Public Key Infrastructure (PKI) security technologies in directory authentication and access control mechanisms is becoming widespread, although there is not always consistency in adherence to PKI standards between vendors.

Many directory services are supporting open standards for security protocols, including Kerberos as well as public key certificate channels such as *Secure Sockets Layer (SSL)* and *Private Communications Technology (PCT).* Implementing PKI and supporting protocols in directory services provides additional support for strong authentication. Because these significant security standards are increasingly being used by directory services, let's take a brief look at each of these mechanisms.

PKI

A Public Key Infrastructure is the implementation of a security technology based on the exchange of authenticated certificates (public keys). Certificates are a form of security token detailed in the X.509 specification.

Communications that are encoded via public key encryption provide the security needed for financial transactions and other sensitive information. Even within a single organization, the need to manage PKI certificates brings with it the need for a straightforward administration method.

Directory services excel at supporting PKI, providing the core repository for storage of the digital certificates as well as supporting applications that use these security credentials.

Kerberos

The Kerberos protocol is a shared secret authentication methodology in which both the user and the security services share a single use session key. Kerberos security utilizes an encrypted form of the user's password, on which a security token called a ticket is based. This ticket is then used to authenticate user access to network resources.

Utilizing the Kerberos authentication protocol provides a directory service with faster server authentication, delegation of user authentication, and transitive security relationships.

SSL/PCT

Directory services may also implement public key certificates to establish secure communications channels via Secure Sockets Layer (SSL) and Private Communications Technology (PCT) that are employed for user authentication and access control.

The SSL and PCT security protocols use X.509 certificates to support strong authentication for directory clients. Directory services support this by storing a user's public key certificates as an attribute of the user object in the directory.

Some directories have a proprietary extensible security framework, and thus multiple providers can be supported by the directory, with the application selecting the preferred provider. Other common extensible security frameworks are those used for LDAP operations:

- *Simple Authentication and Security Layer (SASL)* is a security model defined in RFC 2222 that supports the use of different security providers in LDAP 3. SASL allows connection-oriented protocols such as LDAP to specify an authentication method and optional encryption security layer.
- *Generic Security Service API (GSSAPI)* defines a security framework for interoperable Internet security systems and is a principal SASL provider. GSSAPI, defined in RFC 2743, is a protocol-independent interface to security methods based on public key and secret key technologies.

X.509 Certificate Repositories

Publicly available X.509 certificate repositories are one use of a directory service. One example of this is VeriSign, which has a public repository of the individual (personal) public key certificates it has issued at:

```
https://digitalid.verisign.com/cgi-bin/Xquery.exe
```

General-purpose, meta-directory, and network directory services frequently provide the same sort of PKI support as VeriSign, just with a different focus.

Directory Administration

The administrative capability needed is another aspect that drives the design of directory services. Approaches to directory administration can vary with the type of directory service implemented. In the X.500 design, the original focus was on a global directory in which the need was for distributed administration on a country, regional, and organizational basis. In contrast, with a centralized e-commerce directory or network-focused directory, the support for distributed administration may be less.

Just as with security, the directory namespace design affects the approach to administration:

- Centralized directories with a flat namespace commonly use groups to assign administrative permissions. Delegation of administration is highly limited and usually only done on a per server or domain basis.
- Directories with a hierarchical namespace allow delegation of administration for any subtree at the container level. The flexibility to truly distribute administration of a subportion of the namespace is necessary in functionally distributed applications of the directory service (such as a global directory or the infrastructure of an international enterprise).

Hierarchical namespaces have implications for the approach to administration, and provide capabilities, which we discuss next.

Hierarchical Administration Model

An X.500-based directory service uses the properties of the hierarchical tree structure and inheritance to control access and provide a framework for delegation of administration and management. The directory tree provides a logical structure for assigning administrative and security areas, and facilitates easy delegation of administrative control and administrative tasks. This powerful administration model, focused around the organization of the directory tree, provides the capability to delegate administration for any subtree, as well as defining control over administrative access down to the attribute level.

Because of the flow of security assignments discussed earlier, administrative rights also flow down the tree via inheritance and administration of a portion of the directory can be delegated

Single Point of Administration

While the specific demands of various directory service implementations are unique, the underlying principles of directory management are consistent. The directory provides a single point of administration for a myriad of users, resources, and processes.

easily. The capability to block the flow of rights means that if a portion of the directory contains information that should not be managed by the usual administrators, that subtree can be excluded from the delegated information set.

Distributed directory services can provide a framework for secure delegation of administrative responsibilities within an enterprise by supplying a highly granular resource management and security capability. Delegation can be done for an entire subtree, certain object types (those related to printing, for example), or particular properties (such as passwords or e-mail addresses). This enables administrators to delegate a subset of tasks, such as password management, while protecting other data from unauthorized access.

Delegation of Administration

The overall flexibility of administration when using directory services makes it possible for an individual to administer any aspect of the directory, or to delegate management tasks. Directory management can be divided among (and delegated to) a number of local administrators in areas isolated by security boundaries or geographic regions. Administration can also be delegated based on the type of directory data being managed.

The scope of the delegation can take on several forms:

- An entire subtree can be delegated—typically a geographic or organizational subdivision.

Tree Can Reflect Business and Administrative Structure

The directory service is implemented as a logical tree that can model the structure of your enterprise, providing security and administrative boundaries. When designing a directory tree, you can use the hierarchical properties of directory objects to reflect your organizational structure, network topology, and operational needs. You can use the inherent properties of the object hierarchy and flow of access rights to help structure and streamline the administration of your directory tree. The hierarchical modeling of your organizational structure in the directory facilitates easy delegation of administrative control and tasks.

The actual structure of any given directory tree, however, is dependent on the requirements of each deployment. If you are running an e-commerce application supported by multiple DSAs, the directory tree will reflect the organization of the information used for customer information management and order processing. Yet, if you are using a directory service to manage a geographically distributed enterprise network the directory tree will likely reflect geographic, and perhaps organizational or operational, divisions.

- Control of a particular type of object(s), such as the set of objects used to manage printers and print servers.
- A subset of specific object attributes. This could be used to enable people to manage *only* their own telephone numbers.

Administrative permissions may be assigned at multiple points in the hierarchical directory tree, effectively delegating administration for a specific subtree. The administrative permissions assigned may vary, however, depending upon which permissions are needed for the expected tasks (such as user account management).

Directory services commonly include tools that provide the means to assign control of an object or subtree in a distributed directory, allowing effective delegation of administration for discrete subsections of the directory. Predefined groups, with rights designed for particular subsets of administrative functionality are also commonly provided.

Granular Administration of Access

Due to the underlying security model of a directory service, access rights can be set on individual attributes of a directory object, providing enhanced control of information. The increased granularity of access control available in hierarchical directory services greatly improves the ability to control and assign discrete administrative tasks.

By comparison, in a directory based in a centralized and flat namespace, administration is commonly granted, on an all or nothing basis, to a designated group. For that namespace, all administrators usually have the same permissions and administrative access, and access to directory objects (user and machine accounts) is largely unfiltered.

Hierarchical directory services provide a much finer degree of control of access to information, enabling access filtering on objects and attributes. This granularity provides the administrator with far greater control over the information to which a user has access, as well as providing the means to control the user's ability to change the information.

Delegation May Be Proprietary

Some directory services will define proprietary delegation mechanisms, allowing delegation only at specific points in the tree, and administrative permissions may be limited to the assigned container.

Because many functional aspects of a distributed directory are affected by the information storage methods, the next chapter looks at those aspects in depth.

Self Administration Capabilities

Another important way that a directory supports delegation of directory data management is by providing a way for the source to update information directly. For example, in an enterprise network, the person who cares most about an employee's home address being correct is probably the employee. By allowing employees to update their addresses themselves, two things happen:

- The administration workload decreases because such updates are self-administered.
- The source most likely to have and provide accurate, up-to-date information controls the information.

Directory-Enabled Network Administration

In most large organizations, management of the enterprise networks requires substantial administrative resources. Network administrators use directory services to manage distributed networks and the users, resources, applications, services, and information that they contain.

The integration of network resource data provided by directory services consolidates the tasks involved in administration of the network and minimizes task complexity with regard to managing services, systems, and user accounts.

Storing Directory Information

CHAPTER

3

...the petals are scattered to the wind, yet the flower remains intact...

IN THIS CHAPTER

At its core, a directory is an information repository, and how that information is stored and managed is of critical importance. What is perhaps not quite as obvious is that the methods used for the storage and management of directory information impact many aspects of directory functionality. How effectively information is stored, retrieved, and distributed can directly impact the overall scalability, performance, and reliability of the directory.

This chapter examines how directory data is stored and managed in a distributed directory environment, and it discusses how directory information is subdivided and replicated to multiple directory servers. This chapter also examines the methods of maintaining data consistency among the distributed portions of the directory.

The Directory Database

The unified collection of objects managed by the directory is stored in a database, commonly called the *Directory Information Base (DIB)*. The DIB contains the directory objects representing information and entities such as users, network resources, applications, and so on along with the administrative data (such as security settings) needed to manage and control access to those objects.

The X.500 standards do not specify how the information is stored and retrieved—the database storage mechanisms are not considered part of the scope of the X.500 standards.

The methods used in directory database storage and retrieval mechanisms are implementation specific and can vary widely. Some vendors, such as Novell, write proprietary database engines to meet the specific needs of their directory service. Other vendors have chosen to use a relational database as the repository for directory information.

Because there will always be many more queries than updates performed on a directory, many vendors optimize the search engine and provide highly available catalogs to speed up resolution of client queries.

What Is Stored Depends on Focus

What information is stored depends entirely on what the directory service is being used for. For example, a directory service that is used to manage an enterprise network stores information not only on users, but also the servers, network services and resources, applications, and other information necessary to administer the network. Likewise, a directory that is used to manage an e-commerce site stores information on the users, and user preferences data.

Storing the Directory Database on Disk

Keep in mind that this description is about how the information is written to disk—the actual data storage mechanism—not about partitioning and replication, which is discussed throughout the rest of this chapter. The description that immediately follows assumes a unified (nonpartitioned) directory, or a single partition of a larger, partitioned directory.

Although the DIB is generally spoken of in the singular, it should be noted that this is only true in a logical sense—frequently more than one file makes up the DIB. A directory database may be contained in a range of storage structures, from a single file containing the directory information, to a collection of files containing subsets of directory data with a table of pointers used to link and organize the files.

A directory that has a specialized and small information set is more likely to use a single file than a large general-purpose directory. A quick look at two extremes will help illustrate why.

- **Single file**—At one end of the spectrum is a directory with a relatively simple and small dataset—the Domain Name System (DNS). DNS, in most implementations, stores its information in text files that are very small and consist of a small dataset that can be searched quickly. Of course, DNS has one of these text files for each zone (a zone is analogous to a partition); therefore, the *DNS directory* is made up of a distributed database of *millions* of these little text files.
- **Multiple files**—At the other extreme is Novell's eDirectory, a more general-purpose directory that commonly contains a large amount of information of varied types. To support the flexibility needed by eDirectory, Novell has devised a storage method that uses a series of files, each containing a particular portion of the data that makes up the DIB. One file stores basic information about directory objects; a variable number of others store most of the actual property value information (that is, the data) associated with those objects.

Distributing the Directory Database

Whatever the specifics of a particular DIB implementation, directory service designers must contend with some fundamental data management issues. Obviously, support for the distribution of the DIB must be explicitly defined for a directory to function with a distributed datastore. The support for a distributed datastore is implemented via partitioning and replication of the DIB. Concomitantly, a directory service must define a method of linking the partitions into a complete directory tree, as well as a means to pass queries and other information between partitions.

DIB replication presents other critical issues of data access and information consistency between the distributed replicas. When using multiple copies of the directory datastore (replicas), data integrity between the copies of the information must be maintained. All replicas must (eventually) be updated whenever changes are made to any replica. Additionally, to maintain the consistency of the directory information, some form of data synchronization must be performed.

The next section describes partitioning, and later sections examine replication and data consistency concepts and operations.

Partitioning the Directory

The DIB can be subdivided into smaller sets of data called *partitions* (described as a *naming context* in X.500). A partition is a physical subdivision of the directory database stored on and managed by a specific directory server.

A partition is implemented at the container level and consists of the container object and its associated subtree. The *partition root* is the container object at the root of the directory partition and usually names the partition. The subtree that begins at the partition root is a single partition, unless another container object within it is designated as the root of a new partition.

Note that different directory service implementations have different rules for how and where partitions can be established. Depending on the specific directory service, partitioning may be constrained or limited in fundamental ways.

To help you see how all these things fit together, take a look at Figure 3.1. In this example, the Mythical organization has a directory with two partitions. The first partition is named by its partition root `o=mythical` and managed by the `Phoenix` server. The second partition is `ou=US` and is managed by `Unicorn`. `Phoenix` and `Unicorn` each have information indicating the location of the other partition.

Even when the DIB is partitioned on many servers throughout an enterprise, the directory is still represented as a unified tree when viewed by users of directory information. This means that although the DIB is physically stored on separate directory servers, the information contained in it must be combined somehow before presenting it to the user. The directory is responsible for keeping track of where all the data is actually stored and assembling it into a single tree for presentation. Therefore, even though the DIB itself may be in many pieces spread around multiple locations, the user's view of the directory information is seamless.

Example Companies: Mythical and Netmages

This section uses two example companies: a multinational firm called the Mythical organization; and a small, single location firm called Netmages. These examples highlight directory service factors from the perspective of both small and centralized networks, as well as large and distributed networks.

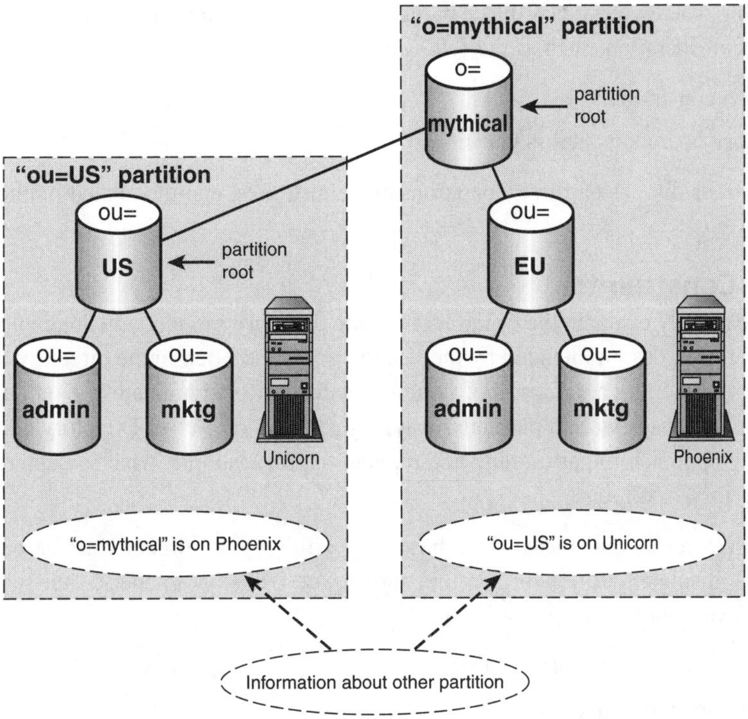

FIGURE 3.1
A directory tree can be divided into partitions, each of which is a contiguous subtree of the DIT.

Managing Partitions

From an administrative perspective, partitions are created for a number of reasons. Use of partitions:

- Provide a key element in scalability by allowing the DIB to be subdivided into many parts.
- Can be used to limit replication traffic across WAN links or to any single server.
- Can divide the server load (from queries) to improve directory performance.

Some partitioning decisions—such as subdividing the DIB when the directory tree spans WAN links—are relatively clear, but others take considerably more thought. If you need to implement additional partitions for scalability, for example, you probably have several possible partition boundaries from which to select. Choosing the best partition design should involve identifying critical operational contingencies of both the directory and the entities that use it.

When deciding where you want to place partition boundaries, you should take some less-obvious aspects into consideration, such as the following:

- Partition constraints
- Directory operations across partitions

The next sections discuss partition operations and constraints, and the related implications for directory design.

Partition Constraints

You should carefully evaluate the capabilities of the directory product you are deploying, and the sort of partition design intended by the vendor, early and often in the directory design process. The partitioning approaches of various vendors differ significantly. Don't assume that partitioning will always work a particular way; it just may not. Active Directory has a rather nontraditional approach to partitioning and replication, for example, which Chapter 10, "Active Directory," explores.

A few of the clearer contingencies about how you partition your directory are based on the capabilities of a single partition or directory server. You will want to check your selected directory software for limitations, such as:

- Number of objects per partition
- Size of partition file(s)
- Numbers of references to subordinate (child) partitions
- Restrictions on placement of partitions
- Number of replicas per server
- Maximum number of replicas per partition

Operations Across Partitions

You should also consider the effect of directory operations that span partitions as crossing partition boundaries slows the search process, even if all the servers holding the partitions are on the same LAN. For every query that is not resolved using a local partition, referrals (redirecting the query to another server) are generated and additional servers must process the query, increasing search time.

The cross-partition delay is usually not significant enough to be problematic for users and applications on LANs. If the servers are separated by WAN links, however, the query has to span these links, which are the slowest connections on a network. What should be a fast request can be delayed or even aborted as the request passes through slow links while attempting to complete the request.

In addition to the obvious example of user queries about objects that reside in a remote partition, directory operations will need to access multiple partitions at other times. Applications, and the directory itself, may perform operations that require access to the entire directory tree. If the directory is partitioned across WAN links, this process may take significant time and bandwidth. You should assess the operations of your directory-enabled applications to be sure that, if they frequently traverse the entire tree, adequate replicas are available to support their operations without excessive network traffic.

The following section, "Partitioning Examples," provides several examples of partitioning for single-location and distributed directory implementations.

Consider Partitioning During Tree Design

When you are designing your directory tree, you should keep partitioning in mind. Because a partition can be implemented only at the container object level, you must design your directory tree to support your partitioning needs. Well, okay... you don't have to design your tree to support your partitioning requirements—you can always redesign your tree to support the partitioning needs of your directory implementation (an undesirable and expensive process). In any case, it will be helpful if you remember that the design of your tree determines where the possible boundaries of partitions fall.

Partitioning Examples

To help clarify how partitioning is used, consider the following examples of how and why a directory is partitioned. To begin with, consider the substantial differences between how partitioning is used with small and large directories.

- Small directories commonly start with a single partition because when the number of directory objects and replicas is small, the best performance and least administration overhead can be achieved with a single partition and minimal number of replicas. As demonstrated in the following examples, when the directory grows to include more users and resources (and perhaps additional physical sites), the DIB can be partitioned to accommodate the changes.
- Large directories must use partitions for scalability. If the directory usage is restricted to a single physical location, partitions may be devised based solely on allowable number of objects per partition or other criteria. In geographically distributed directory installations, the partitions at the top of the directory tree usually reflect WAN topology. If needed, additional partitions may be created within a geographic area for scalability, availability, or administrative reasons.

The following examples discuss some of the factors involved in partitioning decisions.

Limiting Objects in a Partition

A directory might support a million, tens of millions, or more objects in a single directory tree; however, the number of objects that can be stored in an individual partition is often much smaller than that. Accordingly, a common reason for partitioning the DIB is to limit the number of objects per partition.

Even when a directory starts small, it is not necessarily going to stay that way. What starts out as a fairly small directory tree, with few enough objects that a single partition works fine, can outgrow that design and require additional partitions. As the directory grows, existing partitions may need to be adjusted to provide the needed scalability. The focus turns next to what happens when this occurs.

Assume, for example, that the Netmages directory has been operating with a single partition so far. Recently, the network has grown considerably, to the point that the limit on objects per partition is being approached. When this happens, a new partition must be created as a means of subdividing the DIB. Also assume that you know that the `corp` department in particular has been undergoing rapid growth. Because that department already has its own OU in the directory tree, adding another partition, rooted at `ou=corp`, should be simple. (Note the words *should be simple*; not all directory software makes it quite that easy, but it should.)

The directory tree in Figure 3.2 is divided into two partitions, one that starts at the root of the tree and another that begins with the `corp OU`. Each of these partitions is named by the container object at the partition root; therefore, they are `o=netmages` and `ou=corp`.

As the directory continues to grow, the DIB can be broken into more partitions to ensure that partition limits are not exceeded and directory performance does not degrade.

Controlling Replication Traffic

Another reason for partitioning is to control replication traffic (the data sent across the network to replicate directory changes) by restricting the distribution of directory information to locations where that data is needed. This is usually done when the directory spans multiple locations, and thus spans WAN links. It may also be desirable (or necessary) on a LAN when the directory is updated frequently.

After you have determined that replication traffic needs to be controlled, more questions arise:

- Where is the replication traffic being generated?
- Who needs access to the data being updated?

If a specific department generates a considerable amount of replication traffic for information that is relevant only to that department, you may want to implement a partition to reduce network traffic.

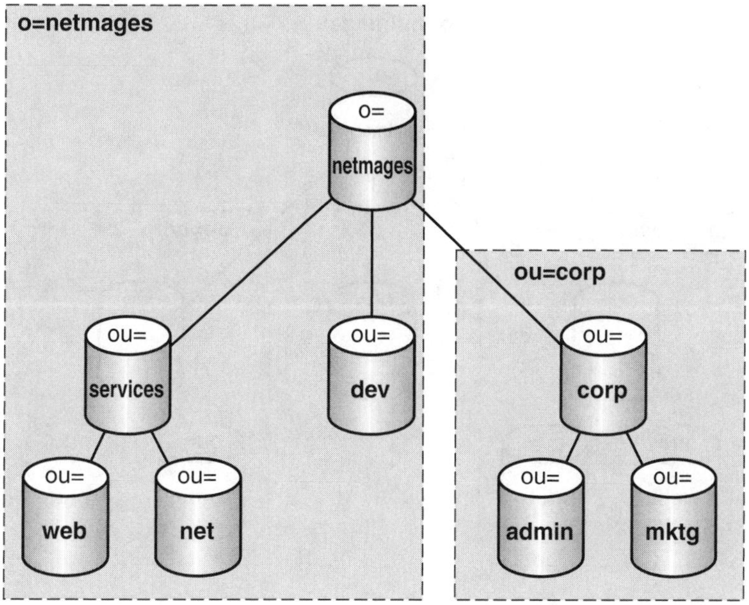

FIGURE 3.2
As the directory grows, partitions can be added to provide scalability.

For example, the services department of the Netmages company has decided to use a directory-enabled version of customer tracking and project management software. Accordingly, each Netmages customer has an entry in the directory that stores customer data, information related to ongoing projects, certificates used for secure communication between the customer and the development team, and so on. This is great for the people who provide services because much of their customer and project management has been moved to the directory.

As there is now a considerable amount of customer information stored in the directory, however, and because that information is updated frequently, there are performance implications for the network. In the case of the customer information stored in the `services ou`, few people outside of that division will be accessing the customer information; therefore, it doesn't make sense to replicate that information to the rest of the company. Accordingly, a partition should be created to segregate replication traffic.

As displayed in Figure 3.3, the tree originally shown in Figure 3.2 has now been divided into three partitions: the two that existed already (starting at the root of the tree and the `corp ou`) and the newly created partition rooted at `ou=services`.

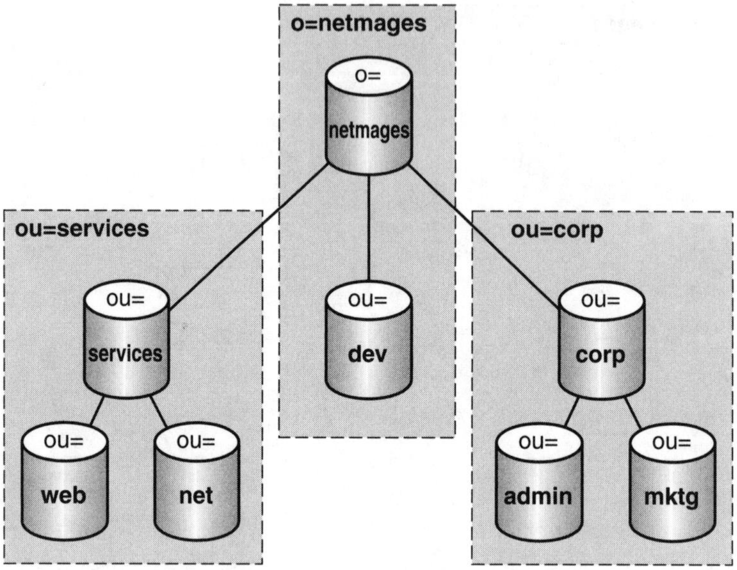

FIGURE 3.3
This directory tree is now divided into three partitions to segregate replication traffic generated within `ou=services`.

Implementation of this partition will improve the performance of the directory and reduce the network bandwidth used. The directory servers holding replicas of the `netmages` partition will not be burdened with unnecessary replication traffic for information seldom accessed by their clients. Because there will be substantially fewer updates without the information used by the services department, the server availability for client requests will also be increased. In addition, the set of data held in the `netmages` partition is now much smaller, so searches will be faster.

The next example looks at what is perhaps the most obvious reason for partitioning—WAN links.

Partitioning for a WAN

One of the most often repeated guidelines concerning partition design is "Don't span the WAN" with a partition. (In other words, don't create partitions that cross your WAN links.) This is generally a useful guideline because most administrators want to control replication traffic across slow WAN links. Because most WAN links are substantially slower than the rest of the network, the potential for replication traffic to bottleneck exists. It is probably true that, as "slow links" get faster, and vendors get more creative about replication methods, this factor will diminish—but not yet.

In many large directory installations, partitions in the upper levels of the directory reflect the WAN topology. In this case, partitions in the lower levels of the directory might reflect company structure, such as departments. This is a common method of dividing a directory when the contents span different geographic regions. Partitions are kept physically proximate to the resources represented within them and the users who will be accessing those resources to minimize WAN traffic in service fulfillment.

To explore how directory partitioning works on a network consisting of LANs connected via WAN links, consider the example of a different company. This example uses the Mythical organization, a large multinational firm with offices on several continents.

As shown in Figure 3.4, the Mythical organization has added more sites and decided to further partition the directory tree along the same lines as the LAN/WAN borders. This will restrict the bulk of the directory traffic for each partition to a single physical site, minimizing WAN traffic for both replication and lookups.

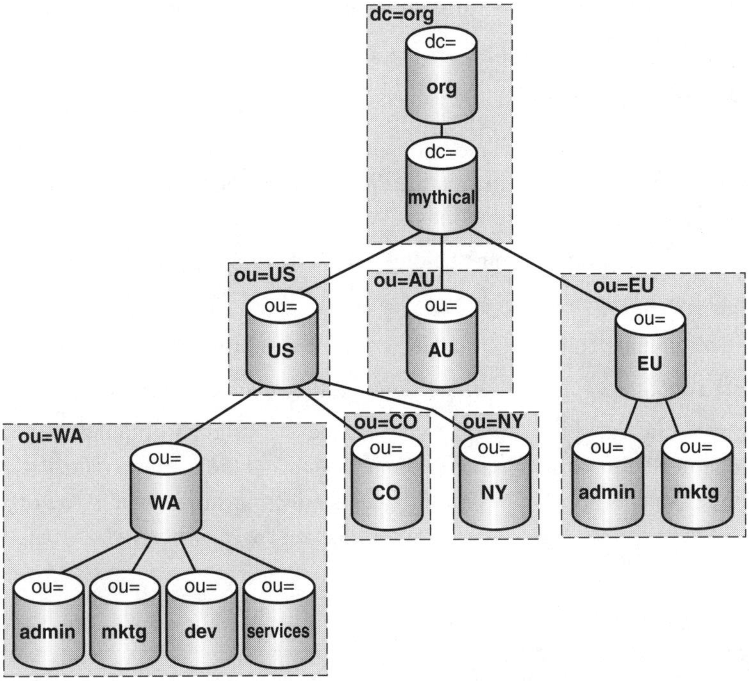

FIGURE 3.4
The Mythical organization has partitioned its directory along geographic boundaries.

As you can tell, a large, geographically distributed company can have an elaborate partitioning scheme for its directory. In addition to the first level of partitions, more partitions could be added within a specific location if needed for scalability or other reasons.

If you choose a partitioning scheme that divides the DIB across WAN boundaries, as described in the preceding scenario, you may want to consider a couple of factors:

- If a WAN link goes down, portions of the DIB may become unavailable. To provide for this, you may want to place a replica of any critical partition in a secondary location such as a dedicated replica server in the IT department.
- The type of replica placed at each location may limit the operations that can be performed locally. If people frequently modify directory information from a particular location, you may want to place a writeable replica of the relevant partition(s) there to minimize referral traffic to a master replica. Of course, this entails additional traffic for updates, but allows for faster query responses.

Invalid Partitioning

Now that you have reviewed what can be done with partitions, take a look for just a moment at what *can't* be done with them. When creating directory partitions, you should remember that partitions have some operational limitations:

- Each object in the directory must belong to exactly one partition.
- Partition boundaries cannot overlap.
- Each partition must contain a complete, connected subtree.
- Two peer containers cannot be in the same partition without their parent.

The directory tree illustrated in Figure 3.5 does not have a valid partitioning scheme for several reasons. To begin with, the partition rooted at `o=netmages` and the partition rooted at `ou=services` have overlapping boundaries. As a result, the `o=netmages` partition contains the object `ou=services`, which also serves as a partition root for another partition (which can't work).

Does Partitioning Impact Directory Operations?

Optimally, users of the directory should be blissfully unaware of all this partition creation and rearranging. Some directory services require that the DIB be locked during partitioning operations so that no other changes can be written to it. This may unavoidably interrupt some directory functionality (most things that require write access to the DIB) briefly, but it won't affect most users because most of the directory use by nonadministrators only requires *read* access.

In addition, `ou=admin` and `ou=mktg` are peer containers and, therefore, cannot be in the same partition without their common parent, `ou=corp`. (It's not even possible to name this partition because it functionally either has two partition roots, or none at all!)

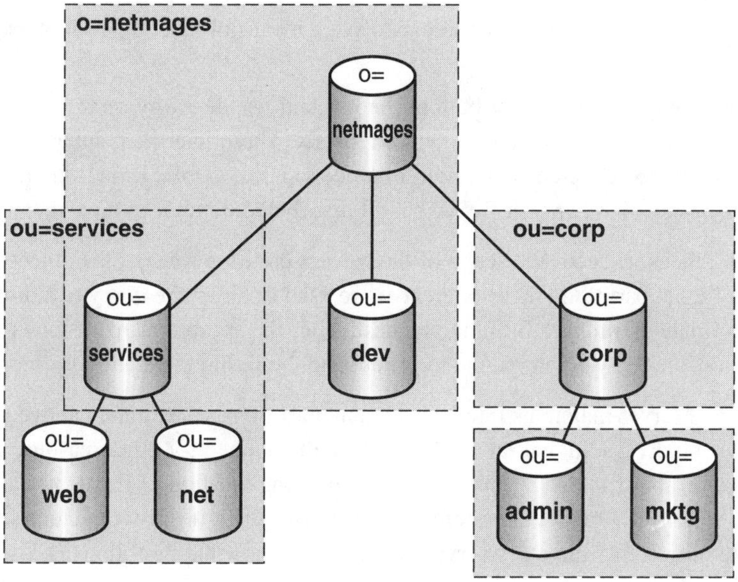

FIGURE 3.5
The examples shown here display two partition designs that cannot *work in directory partitioning: overlapping partitions and peer containers without their parent.*

Now that you have learned how the DIB is broken into smaller pieces and spread around the network, take another look at how it's linked back together. The next section discusses how objects are located when the directory is partitioned.

> **But I Can't Do That, Can I?**
>
> Most directory software is intelligent enough that it won't actually let you create invalid partitions. However, you should determine the functional limitations of the partitioning allowed in your selected directory service, and use this in planning your directory implementation.

Name Resolution Across Partitions

When the directory database has been divided into partitions, two problems present themselves:

- Multiple partitions must be logically linked to form the complete directory tree—a unified logical representation of the contents of all partitions in the directory.
- Servers holding different partitions must have a means of locating each other to communicate.

To provide the linkage necessary for both of these functions, directory servers maintain internal references to partitions whose data is not stored locally. These internal pointers to other DIB subdivisions are named differently in different models (for example, *knowledge references* in X.500, and *name server records* in DNS), but all distributed directories have them.

When a client request exceeds the scope of the current partition (that is, the object sought is not contained in that partition), these references are used to direct the query to a directory server with the appropriate partition to fulfill the request. After the appropriate partition is found, the object is located, the reply is returned to the client and the desired operation is completed.

At a minimum, a server maintains references to any partitions immediately above and below the partitions it holds. Additional references may be maintained for other reasons, such as directing all referral traffic to a specific server or speeding location of frequently accessed partitions by specifically maintaining references to them. Even if every directory server cannot directly locate every other directory server, the assumption is that by following a series of references, any entry in the directory can eventually be located. The process of following a series of references from partition to partition is frequently called *tree-walking*.

User Authentication Across Partitions

When directory queries span partitions, some method must be chosen to handle user authentication to the directory server holding other partitions. In general, this is handled one of two ways:

- The referring directory server passes the user's credentials to the secondary server.
- The directory client resubmits the user's credentials directly to the second server.

If you are going to be dealing with directory operations in a nonsecure environment, you should see how your directory service product handles authentication across partitions. If unencrypted information is passed between directory servers, security information may be inadvertently exposed.

Knowledge Information

Although the types of knowledge information supported are implementation specific, knowledge references fall into some general categories, namely the following:

- **Superior**—The partition immediately above the current one, which is used to walk up the tree.
- **Subordinate**—The partition directly below the current one, which is used to walk down the tree.
- **Root**—The partition at the root of the Directory Information Tree (DIT), which is used to locate the tree root.
- **Other**—This kind of knowledge reference can be anything other than the preceding ones in this list, which might be used to speed lookups to frequently accessed partitions, control directory referral traffic, support replication, and so on.

Figure 3.6 shows the knowledge information used to link the servers holding the partitions in the Netmages tree. In this case, the directory servers maintain only the name of the immediately superior and subordinate partitions. By consulting a series of these references in sequence, any entry in the Netmages tree can be located and accessed.

How the directory obtains the information about servers holding other partitions varies considerably between directory service implementations. Some directory services automate the process entirely and build the appropriate references whenever partitions are created; however, others require manual configuration of the information used in name resolution. Manual configuration of knowledge references can create a substantial administrative load, and present operational issues when directory servers are added or replaced.

A knowledge reference commonly contains the following data:

- **Type of reference**—Superior, subordinate, and so on
- **Identification**—Description of the partition subtree
- **Server**—Name and network address of the server holding the specified partition

A single directory server may store references to multiple replicas of the same partition, each of which is stored on a different server. When servers store multiple references to a single partition, additional information may be added to the knowledge reference to support differentiation between types of partition replicas (such as master or shadow).

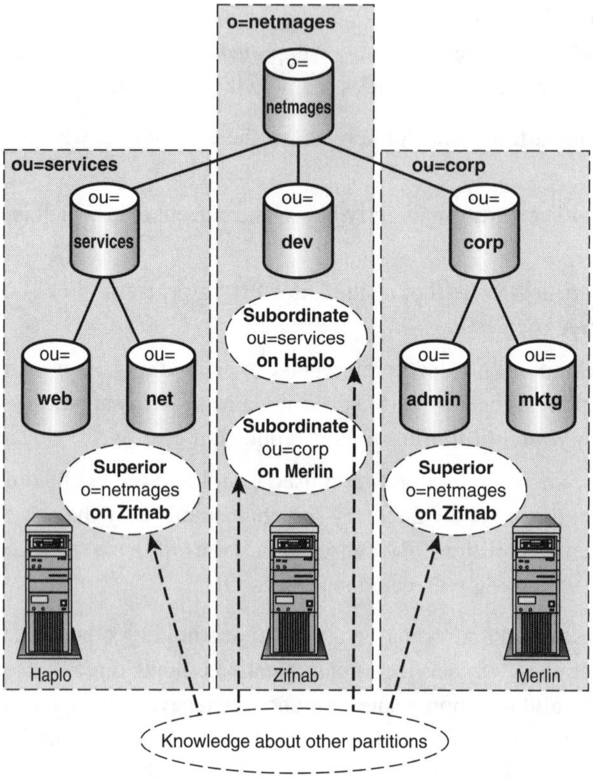

FIGURE 3.6

The directory stores knowledge information, which is used to connect separate partitions into a single DIT.

How Knowledge References Are Used

Now that you know that the directory contains information used to link the various partitions into a single tree, you might be wondering how it actually works. Consider how the name resolution process is handled during a typical client query. Well, *almost* typical, because the example shows a *generic* representation of the name resolution process. An actual directory service operation would likely use a different specific path to resolve the name and provide the results back to the client.

In this example, Natashia (who works in marketing) needs to get the phone number of Kara Stone, a customer (information stored in the `services` partition). Because Natashia is a member of the marketing team, her default directory server is in the `corp` partition. For Natashia to obtain Kara's phone number, the directory first has to find the object representing Kara. Figure 3.7 shows the name resolution process across partitions.

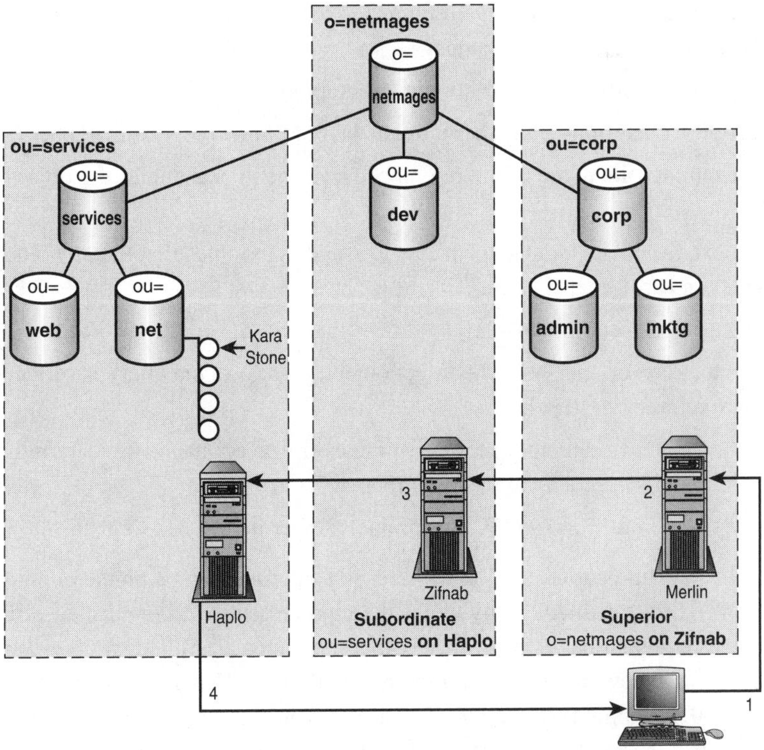

FIGURE 3.7
The name resolution process across partitions.

The following list explains what is going on during the name resolution process shown in Figure 3.7 in a bit more detail:

1. Client submits query to local (default) directory server.

   The directory may be queried for Kara Stone's phone number in a variety of methods, depending on the client; via a form that enables you to specify query parameters and filters, or maybe even a natural language query that enables you to just ask the question.

2. The local directory server determines whether it holds the object, and processes the query accordingly.

   Natashia's default directory server, `Merlin`, examines the name of the referenced object (`cn=Kara Stone`, `ou=net`, `ou=services`, `o=netmages`) and determines the object is not contained within the local partition.

Merlin then checks its knowledge references to determine which partitions it can locate directly. In this case, it's o=netmages.

The query is then passed to Zifnab, the directory server holding o=netmages.

3. The next server determines whether it holds the object and processes the query accordingly.

   Zifnab examines the name of the referenced object and determines the object is not held locally.

   Zifnab next checks its knowledge references and determines that Haplo holds the ou=services partition.

   The query is then sent to Haplo.

4. The directory server *does* hold the target object; therefore, the query is serviced and the results are returned to the client.

   Haplo, the services directory server, examines the object name and determines that it *does* hold the object in a local partition replica.

   The query is then fulfilled and Kara's phone number is returned to Natashia.

Remember, this diagram denotes the logical return of the data (Kara's phone number) to the client (Natashia). The actual methods by which these processes are accomplished vary according to directory service implementation. In X.500, these methods are called *chaining*, *referrals*, and *multicasting*, and they are discussed in more detail in the "X.500 Operations" section of Chapter 4, "X.500: A Model for Directory Services." Now that you understand partitioning in some detail, it's time to switch to a related aspect of distributed storage: replication of directory data between directory servers.

Directory Replication

As described previously, the DIB can be (and commonly is) distributed to multiple directory servers to improve network responsiveness and provide the redundancy necessary for a robust directory service. These copies of the directory database are called *replicas*, and the process of creating and updating these copies is referred to as *directory replication*. Replication is performed on a per-partition basis—that is, each replica is a copy of a single partition.

Replicas provide two substantial benefits:

- **Fault tolerance**—Replication increases fault tolerance by providing secondary (backup) copies of the directory information. This provides the mechanism to prevent the directory from becoming inaccessible if a single directory server goes down. With a directory that is replicated to multiple servers, when one directory server becomes inaccessible, other directory servers holding replicas for that partition can still fulfill any requests.

- **Performance**—For a directory to provide fast service, a sufficient number of directory servers must be deployed to handle the task load and still remain responsive. Replication reduces response latency in directory lookups and authentication services, and it increases directory availability. Replication also supports distribution of the task load for directory data retrieval to multiple directory servers distributed throughout the network.

Managing Replication

You must consider many things when determining replication approaches for your directory, such as the selection of the data to replicate, periodicity of data synchronization, and server roles in the synchronization process. Replication factors such as these can have implications for the performance and manageability of your network. Keep in mind that different directory service implementations support various ranges of replication capabilities.

You should consider a number of replication factors in conjunction with the specific operating contingencies of the directory service software and network environment. These replication factors include the following:

- Types of replicas supported
- The replication strategy
- The specific dataset replicated and amount of data sent with each update
- The synchronization latency period (that is, the length of time it takes for changes to reach all directory servers)
- The data synchronization method employed
- The bandwidth of the network connections used for replication

One Replica of a Partition Per Server

Although many directories allow a server to hold more than one replica and, therefore, more than one partition, a single server can have only one replica of any specific partition.

When managing a directory service, you may have limited options when it comes to fine-tuning replication traffic because much of the replication methodology is predetermined by the design of the directory service. Even if you cannot change a specific replication factor, however, you should be aware of the implications of the directory's replication design on your network operations, as well as your application of the directory service. For example, the amount of data transmitted in each replication matters more when replicating an e-commerce directory across WAN links, than it does when replicating a network directory across local high-speed LAN connections. By having a thorough understanding of a particular vendor's approach, you can discover which factors can be manipulated to optimize replication in your particular environment.

The next section describes the different types of replicas you can use while working with a directory services implementation.

Replica Types

All replicas are *not* created equal; replica types and the operations that they support vary widely. At the most simplistic level, replicas can be divided into two types: those that can be written to, and those that cannot. In the X.500 model for directory services, these two types of replicas are referred to as *masters* and *shadows*, respectively.

Although the differentiation between writeable and non-writeable is stark, in practice there are variations on each of the fundamental replica types. An examination of the different replica types will help you to better understand what functionality each provides.

What Is The "Right Number" of Replicas?

Each directory deployment is different, with individual replica requirements. The directory processes a substantially higher number of queries than changes or updates to the directory database. This means that, in almost all cases, the network traffic generated by queries will be of a much greater magnitude than replication traffic. You need to keep this ratio in mind as you plan your directory and be sure that you are placing adequate numbers of replicas to service requests promptly.

This doesn't mean that you should put a replica of every partition in your directory on every directory server. Especially when no WAN links are involved, however, you should not hesitate to put extra replicas in places where they seem useful. You can always remove them if replication traffic proves to be more of a detriment to network performance than expected.

Replicas are used to provide fault tolerance as well as to improve availability. Yet a minimum number of replicas for each partition need to be implemented to provide fault tolerance in case of server failure—for example, Novell recommends having at least three replicas for each eDirectory partition.

Writeable Replicas

A *writeable replica* supports complete (or almost complete) directory functionality. A server holding a writeable replica can accept directory modifications and is responsible for replicating those changes to other servers holding a replica of that partition. Although the specific capabilities of the replicas supported by any given directory service implementation will vary somewhat, writeable replicas come in two basic flavors.

- **Master replicas** are fully functional, allowing all directory operations. Everything in the directory—objects, tree design, the schema, and so on—is updateable via a master replica. At least one master replica must exist per partition. Whether there are more writeable replicas than that depends on the directory service implementation.
- **Read/write replicas** allow most operations, but they may restrict a few high-level operations such as schema modifications or tree-level changes. Read/write replicas provide additional points of administration for day-to-day directory operations. There are no requirements for read/write replicas—they are totally optional.

Non-Writeable Replicas

A *non-writeable replica* is a read-only copy of the master replica. Although there is generally no requirement for read-only replicas of any kind, their use can greatly enhance directory performance by providing additional replica servers for load balancing purposes.

This type of replica has limitations, some of which may not be as apparent as the inability to update objects directly. If a replica is not writeable, for example, any operation that requires updating the directory cannot be performed on that server. Therefore, a directory server maintaining a non-writeable replica may perform the lookups needed for locating network resources, but not provide logon authentication because properties of the user object may be updated at logon (such as logon time or workstation address).

A few basic types of non-writeable replicas exist:

- **Read-only replicas** contain a complete partition and are generally distributed as needed to support directory lookups. Because, from the user's perspective, a read-only replica is indistinguishable from a writeable one, a server holding a read-only replica commonly has a way of transparently redirecting write requests to an appropriate replica.
- A **catalog** is a read-only copy of a subset of directory objects and attributes; generally those properties commonly used in queries. Catalog servers usually hold a partial set of data from every directory partition, so that they can provide high-speed lookups for the entire directory. Catalogs are not considered authoritative—they are commonly a high-speed index used to locate the directory server with the partition that contains the object sought.

- **Cache replicas** are less well-defined, implementation-specific, read-only collections of directory information. Typically, information obtained during client lookups is stored for a specified period of time and used to satisfy repeated requests for the same data, increasing availability of directory information.

Figure 3.8 shows the various replica types. The replica types are displayed in a continuum of replica capability, ranging from less to more functionality and completeness of the dataset. As shown, the functionality of a replica grows as its dataset grows.

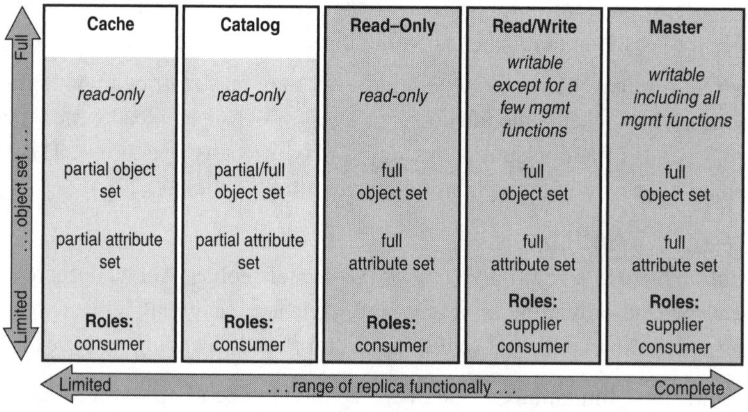

FIGURE 3.8

The various types of replicas have different read/write status and contain different sets of directory data.

Replicas interact in different ways depending on the replication strategy used. The following section examines the different strategies used for replication.

...of Servers and Replicas

Although it's discussed that way for simplicity, the relationship between directory servers and replicas is not necessarily one to one. In fact, it is somewhat more complicated than that. For instance:

- Copies of partition data (called replicas) are almost always held by more than one server for performance and fault-tolerance purposes.
- In many directory implementations, servers can hold more than one replica. This is particularly useful. If you can store replicas of multiple partitions on a single server, you can distribute adequate partitions to service requests without the expense of a separate server for each replica.

• A directory server may well have different roles in relationship to each partition it manages. A single directory server may hold the master replica of one partition, and a read-only copy of one or more others.

Replication Strategies

The number, capabilities, and status of the master replicas for a directory determine how replication operates. In general, a directory supports one of these three variations:

- Single master
- Multimaster
- Floating single master

To explain the sort of functionality each of these replication approaches provides, the following sections focus on the basic styles of replication.

Single Master

Many directory vendors use a single master model when designing their replication strategy. This is primarily because, from a programmatic perspective, it is by far the easiest method. When a directory has a single master, data can be modified on only one directory server—although copies of the information usually reside on other servers. The directory server holding the master replica is also responsible for updating all other replicas whenever there is a change to the directory.

The directory replication process in a single master model, as shown in Figure 3.9, is relatively straightforward. Directory updates are transmitted unidirectionally from the server holding the master replica to the servers holding read-only and catalog replicas. Because those replicas do not accept changes from users (only from the master replica), they do not need to transmit any directory updates.

Single master replication is the easiest style to implement because no real data integrity issues arise—all updates come from a single supplier, so no possibility of conflict exists. This method has its drawbacks, however, primarily that this scheme requires that the master replica be available for all modifications to directory information. If the master replica becomes unavailable, directory operations will be limited until the master is brought back online or another replica is designated as the new master.

A directory service may be able to compensate for loss of the server holding the master replica by allowing selection of a new master from among the existing replicas. This selection may be done automatically by providing for election of a new master upon failure of the current one, or it may require the directory administrator to manually promote a replica to serve as the new master.

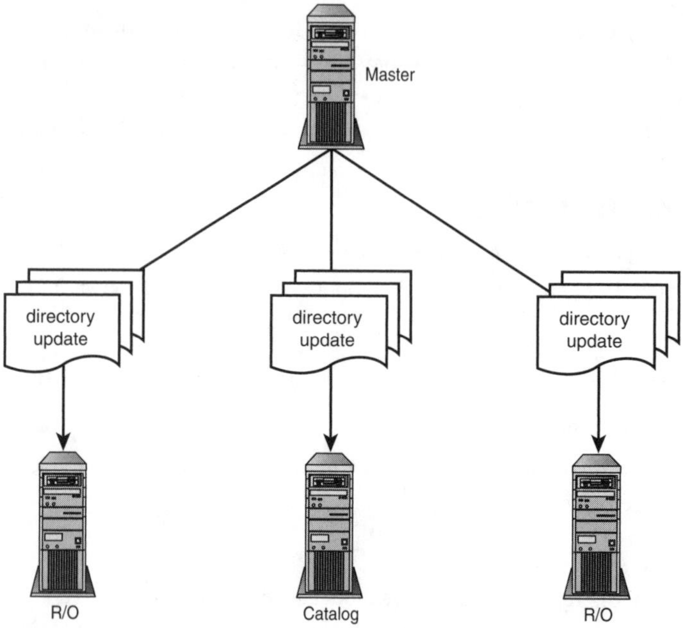

FIGURE 3.9

Single master replication operates in one direction, from the master to all subordinate replicas.

Single master replication offers a simple model for managing replication, such that the X.500 standards still define only a single master replication model. Individual vendors have overcome the obstacles raised by the single master design, however, and have independently developed a number of (highly similar) multimaster replication models, as discussed next.

Multimaster Replication

Replication of directory information can also be implemented in a *multimaster* style, where more than one replica can accept changes. Use of multimaster replication ensures that non-availability of a given replica will not impede the use or administration of the directory.

In multimaster replication, all writeable replicas might be considered equivalent and perform exactly the same functions, or there may be a mix of master and read/write replicas. In this model, most (or all) replicas can perform all directory functionality for that partition. Changes usually can be written to the directory on any available directory server, instead of needing access to the server holding the single master. Any directory server holding a writeable replica is responsible for accepting changes and propagating those changes to the other master replicas as well as any servers containing down-level replicas (such as catalog servers). Figure 3.10 shows a directory using a multimaster replication scheme with three master replicas and a catalog. As you can tell, the paths taken by directory updates have increased.

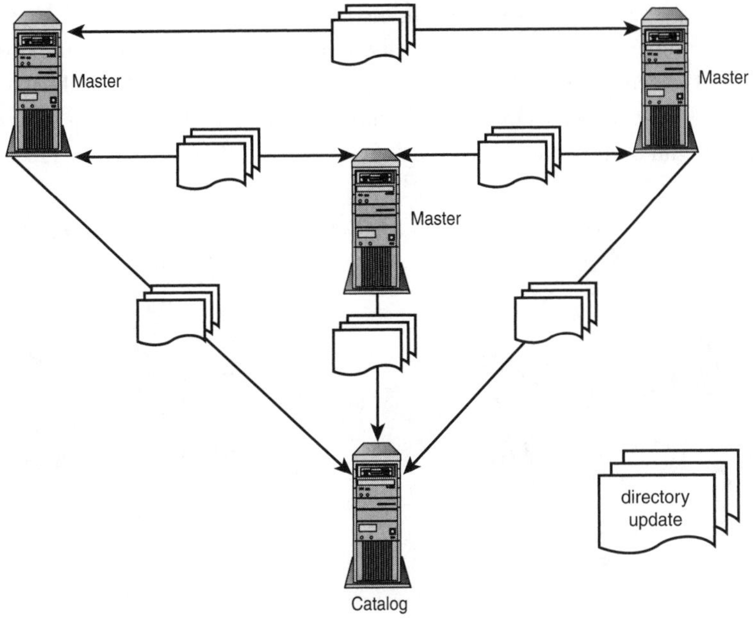

FIGURE 3.10
With multimaster replication, directory update traffic takes many different paths.

Of course, multimaster replication is much more complicated than single master replication. Because multiple writeable copies of the same information exist, some form of data synchronization must be employed to reconcile multiple updates to the same object. Methods of directory data synchronization are discussed later in this chapter.

Floating Master

You might come across less-common variations on the single master model. The designation of the master replica may not be static, for example, but may be assigned to different directory servers as needed. This is considered a *floating master (FM)* or *floating single master (FSM).* A floating master operates exactly like a single master—just a temporary one. A directory may use a floating single master all the time, or only to provide support for a specific operation. Active Directory, for example, employs a number of floating single masters to manage various aspects of directory operations.

Another use of FSMs is by directories that normally use a multimaster model. When more than one replica is writeable, some operations require temporary designation of a single master to guarantee directory integrity. Operations such as schema modifications and partitioning (which change basic directory parameters) must ensure that the replica being operated on is the *only* one currently accepting any changes. Accordingly, a floating single master is often designated for the duration of the operation.

Figure 3.11 demonstrates how this works. On the left side of the figure, a multimaster directory with four master replicas is shown. If an operation that requires selection of an FSM occurs, the directory will effectively switch to the operational mode shown on the right side of the figure. After the FSM determines that the operation is complete, the directory will return to the mode on the left with multiple masters.

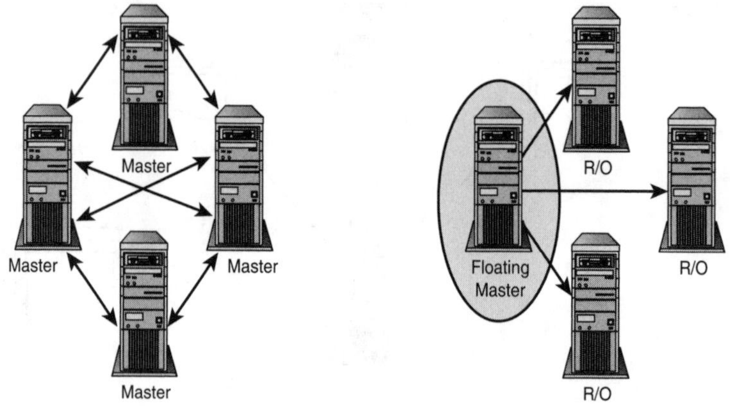

FIGURE 3.11

Some directory operations require election of a temporary floating single master.

An operation that requires the election of a single master is called a *floating single master operation (FSMO).* The FSM functions just like a single master for that period, and it is responsible for replicating changes to all appropriate servers prior to relinquishing its floating master status.

The details of how replicas exchange information are defined in the replication agreement established between the servers holding the two replicas, which is examined in the next section.

Initial Population of the Directory

As the directory database may contain anywhere from tens of thousands to tens of millions of directory objects, the initial entry of the objects in the directory is a significant factor that must be planned for.

The process of initially populating the directory is as significant as the volume of objects to be added to the directory datastore. For example, if the directory entries are loaded off the local hard disk of a directory server it can be a relatively fast process, yet if the same directory entries must be updated across slow network connections (such as WAN links) this process can be excruciatingly slow.

> Many directory service products provide some sort of bulk loading utility to enable the initial loading of directory objects. Most of these bulk loading utilities use the LDAP Data Interchange Format (LDIF) to support the loading of new directory entries. LDIF is a text-based method of storing directory entries in a structured format which facilitates populating a directory via LDAP.
>
> For a geographically distributed enterprise the initial population of the directory datastore presents technical challenges, especially if the directory holds large amounts of data. Attempting to initially populate a directory with many millions of objects across WAN links to multiple locations is problematic at best. It is clearly more effective to distribute the directory contents as compressed LDIF files to the remote locations and having administrative staff load the directory entries locally.
>
> However you approach the initial population of the datastores on directory servers, it is a factor that deserves serious consideration.

Replication Operations

For replicas to exchange information to keep the directory updated, they must first enter into some sort of *replication agreement*. This agreement specifies the parameters that will govern the replication process, including factors such as:

- **Roles**—The roles that each server will take during the replication processes
- **Replication dataset**—The directory information that is to be replicated
- **Replication schedule**—The periodicity of replication transmissions

The following sections explore these aspects of replication agreements, starting with roles.

Replication Roles

As mentioned during the discussion of replica types, a directory server can take one of two roles during a replication process:

- **Supplier**—The directory server sending the update
- **Consumer**—The directory server receiving the update

A single replica can be a supplier, a consumer, or both (yet only one at a time). Although a directory server is designated as either a supplier or consumer for a particular replication agreement, servers can have reciprocal agreements.

In a multimaster environment, every directory server holding a writeable replica of a particular partition is likely to have a pair of replication agreements with every other server holding a writeable replica of that partition—one replication agreement for each role (supplier and consumer). The servers may transfer data in both directions during a single replication session, or require a separate process for each update.

The following section explains how the dataset that will be sent during a replica update is determined.

Replication Dataset

One of the things that directory servers must agree on prior to replication is the set of information that will be transferred during replication. This is sometimes described as the *unit of replication*—that is, the dataset sent with each directory update (also referred to as the *replication dataset*).

The primary delineation of the replication dataset is the contents of a partition. Many agreements between directory servers will specify this as the unit of replication because most replicas need to be fully updated with all the changes to the objects in the partition. Not all replicas need the entire partition contents, however.

Consequently, although the *initial* scope of replicated data is tied to the partition boundary, some directory services provide methods of fine-tuning the dataset to be sent during replication. Filters can be established to selectively transmit updated directory information, usually based on object or attribute type. This enables an additional level of control over replication—you can exclude directory information from being replicated, even if it has changed.

Filtering replication information can be useful in several ways:

- Catalogs of directory information can be maintained for high-speed lookups.
- Replication traffic is reduced because directory information is not unnecessarily updated.
- Filtering the information available to replicas in less-secure environments can strengthen security (such as replicating only username and e-mail address, and not salary or other sensitive data).

The use of replication filters means that the amount of data a directory server sends can vary from one replica of a partition to another. This variance is part of what is specified in the replication agreements. For example, if an update is being sent to another master replica, every piece of updated information is likely to be sent. If the same server were sending the "same" update to a catalog server, however, the dataset sent would be greatly reduced via the use of filters.

Modifying Filters

Many directories allow modification of default filters, like the one used for replication to catalog servers. However, filtering is a capability that should be used carefully. Be sure that you thoroughly understand the ways that any specific directory data is used before you exclude it from being updated during replication.

> You may also want to *add* properties to the set that is replicated to the catalog. For example, an application might need frequent access to objects not normally included in catalog replicas. Without catalog entries, every lookup of one of these objects would require referrals to another directory server just for name resolution (and, thus, increase server and bandwidth consumption). By adding these objects to the catalog, queries may be fulfilled more quickly and without unnecessary referrals to other directory servers.

Catalogs, which are supported by many directories, are probably the primary use of this filtering capability. By providing an index of objects, along with a few commonly searched for attributes, catalog servers can service the name resolution needs of many lookup requests. However, this limited focus (as an index to directory objects) means that catalog replicas typically need to contain only a small subset of the possible attributes of any object type.Of course, the catalog server could just accept a normal replica update and ignore, or discard, the extra information, yet this would occupy network bandwidth unnecessarily. By filtering data prior to replication, however, network traffic and directory update time is reduced, and the target datastore remains as small as possible, speeding responses to directory searches.

After the replication dataset has been defined, some kind of replication schedule must be arranged between the directory servers. The following sections examine the scheduling of replication.

Scheduling Replication

Most directory updates are scheduled for replication in relationship to when the change took place—five minutes after the modification occurs, for example. The vendor predetermines the default schedule for most replication processes, however, you may be able to customize replication scheduling somewhat.

> **Replication Granularity**
>
> Replication granularity is a continuum—a directory server can send anything from a complete copy of the DIB to only a single attribute-value pair (that is, an attribute and the data paired with it, such as `Username=Steve`) when transmitting updates to another directory server. The amount of data sent with each directory update can significantly impact the performance of both the directory and the network.

Directory services that support differential scheduling priorities for discrete types of directory changes can provide greater flexibility in directory management, improve security, and help minimize the traffic caused by directory updates. A specific directory service may schedule replication based on the following:

- **The property being updated**—Different properties can be replicated according to different schedules, based on the importance of the information related to that property. A directory may replicate a password change immediately, for example, to ensure integrity of critical security information. In the same directory, and for the same user a change to a home phone number may not be propagated to other replicas quite as quickly as the password change. This type of prioritization provides a means of allowing rapid updates for the truly important information while not incurring too much unnecessary traffic in the DIB update process. For example, attributes in eDirectory can be designated for either *fast synchronization* (10 seconds) or *slow synchonization* (5 minutes), to control the delay in synchronization.
- **Destination of the update**—Replication across WAN links may be scheduled on a slower schedule than updates to other directory servers on the local network. This may be done to allow more time for aggregation of directory changes, minimizing the number of individual updates. Replication across WAN links may also leverage store-and-forward protocols usually used for e-mail, such as the *Simple Mail Transfer Protocol (SMTP),* to handle replication traffic between physical sites.

After scheduling of the replication is established, another aspect to consider is the variation in the set of information transmitted during replication. The actual set of data sent will depend on whether the directory service uses complete or incremental replication, as discussed next.

Complete Versus Incremental Replication

Another factor in replication is whether the directory server sends the entire contents of the unit of replication even if it has not been changed. Two basic methods are used:

- **Complete replication** sends a copy of the entire datastore, sometimes including schema information and other overhead as well as all objects, to each server with every directory update. To cut down on network traffic, updates may be scheduled infrequently, perhaps only once a day, preferably at a time when network traffic is light. Because of this, the data contained in the various replicas will generally be somewhat more "out of sync" than in a directory using more frequent replication.
- **Incremental replication** sends only a subset of the DIB, containing the data that has been changed. The update information sent may be only the data that has actually changed, or a superset of the changed objects and attributes. Obviously, incremental replication is a much more efficient method of synchronization than complete replication.

As you can imagine, complete replication is a bandwidth-intensive method of transmitting directory changes. If you just add a user, for example, sending the entire DIB to every directory server will consume unnecessary network bandwidth and take longer to synchronize the DIB contents across the enterprise.

Most current directory products use incremental replication for normal operational updates and reserve the use of complete replication for special cases such as initial population of a new replica or repair of a damaged replica.

Replication Processes

As mentioned earlier, directory servers perform replication using supplier/consumer roles. It's largely the same process for most directory services with a few variations in specific behavior. In general, the replication process follows these steps:

1. The directory servers connect and authenticate. Either the supplier or the consumer may trigger this.
2. The supplier assesses what directory information needs to be updated (by an implementation-specific method).
3. The supplier then transmits data to the consumer, which updates its replica.
4. The information used in Step 2 is updated with the values that will be used in the next replication process.

The information used in Step 2 is used to ensure data consistency, and is based on the data synchronization method used. Data consistency is discussed in the following section.

Data Consistency

When more than one copy of a piece of information exists (as happens with a replicated partition), it is critical to ensure that the information contained in those multiple copies is the same and that they contain the correct dataset. Therefore, when multiple replicas of a directory partition exist, changes made in one replica must also be made in all other replicas.

When all replicas of a partition contain the same data, the replicas are considered *synchronized*. Synchronization of the replicas ensures data consistency throughout the directory.

When a directory uses a single master design, ensuring consistency when multiple users are making changes to one directory object is comparatively easy. Simply put, the server holding the master copy of the information accepts all the writes and is the sole supplier for all the update operations.

When using multiple *writeable* copies of a directory partition, however, data consistency among the different replicas on the network becomes a key issue. Clearly a method of providing updated information to all directory servers has to be addressed, while also guaranteeing the integrity of the data contained in the DIB.

Approaches to Data Consistency

Data consistency can be thought of as the degree of correlation between the directory data contained within the replicas. *Convergence* is the state achieved when the contents of the replicas are identical. Approaches to replication can be viewed by the required degree of consistency between directory servers and how quickly changed data is replicated. For a fuller understanding, consider replication from the "consistency-of-the-data" perspective, ranging from *tightly consistent* to *loosely consistent*.

Approaches that require all replicas to always have the same data are defined as tightly consistent—that is, all replicas of the partition are quickly updated when changes are made to any master replica. Tightly consistent replication may work in a transactional fashion, requiring that all replicas of a partition be updated before a directory modification is successfully completed. This guarantees that all the data in every replica of a partition is always exactly the same. If a single replica becomes unavailable, however, no directory updates can take place until it is once again available, or removed from the replication group.

With loosely consistent replication, the data on all directory servers does not have to be exactly the same at any given time. Changes to the DIB are replicated more slowly and network servers gradually "catch up" to the changes made on other directory servers. Loosely consistent replication does not immediately replicate changes to other servers. Instead of sending each individual directory update, numerous small changes to the directory can be aggregated and replicated as a group. Directory services that use a loosely consistent process for most DIB updates may nonetheless use an immediate update method for certain types of information (such as data used in authentication and access control).

Most current directory service implementations, including Active Directory and NDS eDirectory, are considered to be loosely consistent.

Synchronization Methods

In a distributed directory that allows writes to multiple replicas of a partition, the potential for conflicting updates of the same directory information always exists. The directory server must

Failed Replication Processes

Some replication processes are designed in such a way as to require the completion of replication to every directory server holding a replica of that partition before replication is considered a success. If a particular replica is not available, it could stall the replication process (for directory servers sharing that partition), possibly requiring administrative intervention to remedy the situation.

have some way of resolving these update conflicts. Where multiple changes to the same directory objects occur, the directory server must then evaluate the submitted changes and select the correct change to commit to the DIB.

A directory synchronization method is commonly based on one (or more) of these three approaches:

- Time of change
- Sequence number of change
- Changelog file

Defining Propagation and Synchronization

Although propagation and synchronization are often used as synonymous terms when describing directory operations, they actually refer to two distinctly different processes used to update directory replicas:

- **Propagation** is an unconfirmed process where a server unilaterally sends directory updates to other servers containing partition replicas. The servers may or may not receive the data and update their copy of the DIB; in any case, propagation does not provide a means of knowing whether the directory update completed successfully.
- In contrast, **synchronization** is a transaction-like process in which a master replica updates a subordinate replica, where a successful update must be confirmed by the other replica before the update replication is considered completed.

Interdirectory Data Synchronization

Data synchronization factors must be given serious consideration in directory implementations that support operations on multiple directory services at the same time. For example, the question of synchronization between a directory service that uses sequence numbers for synchronization and a directory service that uses time stamps can become complex and should be considered carefully before deploying an enterprisewide solution. Meta-directory technologies are commonly employed for synchronizing disparate directory service implementations.

Time Stamps

One common method of resolving multiple updates to the same object is comparison of the time of the change to ensure that the latest change is the one written to the DIB. When a change is made to the directory, the information is marked with the time of the modification. When directory replication occurs, the time stamp of the change is checked against the time stamps of other changes to the same object or property to ensure that the latest change is written to the DIB.

In a directory service using time-based synchronization, all directory servers must share the same time, requiring that time services be provided. Time servers may provide time to directory servers, client systems, or both. The time may be based on either an arbitrary network time or external clocks representing the "actual" time.

For example, Novell's NDS eDirectory uses a time-based synchronization method, which is discussed in more depth in Chapter 9, "eDirectory."

Sequence Numbers

A directory implementation may use another kind of event stamp, such as an *Update Sequence Number (USN),* to indicate the order of the directory changes. Each directory server maintains internal counters on each entry, and generates the next number in sequence when a change occurs. During the replication process, the consumer replica is provided all changes with any USN later than the last USN received from that supplier.

Using sequence numbers to mark updates and synchronize directory data can be substantially more complex than using time stamps because each change must be tracked, and reconciled, on a per-server basis. Microsoft's Active Directory uses a USN-based synchronization method, and is discussed in more detail in Chapter 10.

Changelog File

Another method of updating directory information is done using a changelog file. A *changelog* is essentially a file containing a log (listing) of all the changes that have been made to the directory. When a replication process is initiated, the supplier just "replays" the changelog to the consumer, effectively processing every directory update just as it was received by the supplier server.

Although this is a straightforward approach, and doesn't require the sort of extensive behind-the-scenes work of the preceding two methods, it also has the disadvantage of sending a raw list of updates. This means that if a single object has been updated multiple times, the same property may be updated several times during a single directory update.

DIB Management—Flexibility Matters!

<rant>

If serious thought has been given to the overall robustness of a directory service, flexible partitioning and replication will be seen as essential. Directories intended to meet the requirements of modern businesses must allow customization of partitioning and replication schemes. By doing so, vendors will provide the means to optimize DIB management for a particular organization.

Some directory services provide a default replication and partitioning configuration that works surprisingly well for many businesses. This is a great start; we can always hope for intelligent defaults. However, it is seldom that simple—networks change, business reorganizations happen, and the directory service needs to change right along with everything else. This may mean rearranging partitioning because of changing security concerns, changing where replica servers are placed, or rearranging where specific replicas reside.

This does not mean that the actual management of the DIB must be complicated; in fact, it needs to be easy to configure the desired replication and partitioning scheme because errors can be costly (in terms of recovery time if nothing else). What is most critical is that a directory service design enables you to use a customized partitioning and replication scheme and that you be able to do so without an inordinate amount of hassle.

</rant>

X.500: A Model for Directory Services

CHAPTER

4

...study closely the ancient runes...

IN THIS CHAPTER

The X.500 standards are the basis for much of the current development in directory services—they are the archetype of most directory service designs—so it's important to take a look at the major aspects of a directory service and its operations from the perspective of X.500. This chapter describes the X.500 standards for distributed directory services, explores the X.500 models, and examines the underlying structures and operations of an X.500 directory.

As you look at X.500, it will become clear that, from a theoretical standpoint, some parts of the X.500 specifications are more significant than others. Because of this, some portions of the X.500 design (such as protocols) are discussed only briefly, while other areas (models, for example) are covered in substantially more detail.

Introduction to X.500

The X.500 standards collectively specify the design of a distributed directory service for managing information. These standards define a global directory service that contains and manages a set of information that is distributed within an array of supporting servers. X.500 directories were initially proposed for an international "white pages" to support messaging applications. X.500 was designed to provide a distributed, network-independent directory service for the messaging systems described in the X.400 specification.

X.500 is actually a set of standards, although people generally use the singular "X.500" as a reference to the entire collection. The collected specifications in the X.500 standards define the information structure of the directory service and the protocols required for accessing and managing the information contained in the directory. Table 4.1 lists the documents comprising the X.500 standards.

TABLE 4.1 The X.500 Standards

Document Number	*Title*	*Year Introduced*
X.500	The Directory: Overview of Concepts, Models, and Services	1988
X.501	Models	1988
X.509	Authentication Framework	1988
X.511	Abstract Service Definition	1988
X.518	Procedures for Distributed Operation	1988
X.519	Protocol Specifications	1988
X.520	Selected Attribute Types	1988
X.521	Selected Object Classes	1988
X.525	Replication	1993
X.530	Use of Systems Management for Administration of the Directory	1997

The X.500 standards are the common industry reference for the design fundamentals of directory services; most directory implementations derive their base taxonomy and architecture from these standards. Although the X.500 standards are the common starting point for many directory service designs and models, they are only baseline definitions—allowing for different design interpretations and divergent implementations.

X.500 describes a rich set of directory models and functionality, but a comprehensive explanation of every detail is well beyond the scope of this chapter. An in-depth exploration of the X.500 specifications could fill multiple books, yet this material will instead focus on describing the core components of the X.500 design for directory services. If you are interested in a more comprehensive look at X.500 directory services, excellent references are available (some of which are listed in Appendix A, "References").

X.500: An Evolving Set of Standards

The X.500 standards should be considered an evolving set of specifications. The International Standards Organization (ISO) and the International Telecommunications Union (ITU) initially developed them in 1988, and revised in 1993 and 1997; 2001 documents are currently in the draft stage. Therefore, you will sometimes hear X.500 (or an X.500 component) referred to as 1988 X.500, 1993 X.500, 1997 X.500 and so on—this just indicates compliance with, or reliance on, a particular revision.

Since the origins of X.500 in 1988, new models have been introduced that describe many additional aspects of directory information and operations. Revisions have also addressed key areas of management and control of the DIB, security mechanisms for effective access control, interactions between Directory System Agents (DSAs), use of collective attributes, and internationalization.

X.500 Terminology

The X.500 standards define a set of specific terms to describe directory services. Table 4.2 lists by functionality key terminology used in X.500 to describe the different components or operations.

TABLE 4.2 Vocabulary Correlations

Functionality	*X.500 Term*
Directory entries	Objects
Object subentries	Attributes
Definition of directory contents	Schema
Logical representation of directory	Directory Information Tree (DIT)

TABLE 4.2 Continued

Functionality	*X.500 Term*
Data storage	Directory Information Base (DIB)
Subdivision of directory	Naming context (partition)
Data updates	Replication
Server agent	Directory Service Agent (DSA)
Client agent	Directory User Agent (DUA)
Query resolution	Chaining and Referral

Defining a Distributed Directory Service

The X.500 models define a hierarchical directory that operates within a unified namespace and store information in a distributed datastore. X.500 uses a structured method of naming objects in the directory that allows an object to be unambiguously identified and accessed.

The X.500 directory stores objects, which represent the components of the information system the directory is designed for (such as a general-purpose directory, or a network-focused directory, and so on). Because X.500 was initially designed to contain a distributed "white pages," the base object set included only the relatively few objects (such as users) and attributes (such as name and telephone number) needed to provide the "white pages" lookup functionality. In contrast, current general-purpose directory service products provide a customizable object set, which can be focused on a wide range of information systems management.

The directory is represented as a number of objects arranged in a hierarchical *Directory Information Tree (DIT)*. Container objects are used to form the structure of the DIT, with objects representing information entities (in the case of a network-focused directory, network users or resources) placed in the containers, providing access to these resources within an intuitive structure. The directory tree structure is also utilized as a framework for assignment of access rights, security permissions, and other administrative controls.

The X.500 standards specify storing the directory data in a distributed datastore called the *Directory Information Base (DIB)*. This database structure allows for partitioning the directory into multiple naming contexts (subdivisions of directory information). The DIB is distributed across multiple directory servers, to reduce lookup latency and increase fault tolerance. The X.500 standards support a single master replication model, where changes are only written to the master replica of a naming context, which updates all other replicas of that partition.

X.500 directory services operate using a client/server exchange between a server agent, which accesses the DIB, and an agent providing services to the network client. The server agent also provides a means for communication between server components to allow multiple physical servers to act as one logical directory. In the X.500 design, directory services operate as an OSI application layer process with directory servers and clients communicating via OSI-defined protocols.

This interaction between the directory client and server agents, providing location services and controlled access to the directory, is employed by users and applications alike—to gain access to directory service functionality and directory information.

X.500 Client/Server Agents

The directory services specified in X.500 use a client/server approach in which a client agent interacts with a server agent to perform directory operations.

- The server component of the X.500 client/server model is called the *Directory System Agent* which manages all the directory operations.
- The *Directory User Agent* is the client application used to access the directory.

This architecture provides for information exchange between a directory client and the directory server managing a specific portion of the directory. It also affords a method for directory servers to communicate with each other to collectively provide access to the entire directory.

Directory Integration into Network Platforms

Networking vendors have, to varying degrees, integrated some of the functionality described in the X.500 standards, extending the scope of objects managed by the directory to include the information needed to manage a distributed network.

In this context, the directory contains additional objects representing network resources including computers, groups, or individual users, and the corresponding network and security properties for each object. The management of network resources can then be performed via operations on the associated directory objects.

There are significant differences in how each vendor of networking directories has implemented directory service operations. Comparing these directories to the standards in X.500 can provide useful contrast.

Directory System Agents

In X.500, a *Directory System Agent (DSA)* is an OSI application layer process that accesses one or more naming contexts, responding to requests from directory clients and other DSAs to perform directory searches, modifications, and other directory operations. DSAs interoperate as a *system*, where multiple DSAs are logically linked to transparently provide client access to the distributed directory.

The term DSA does not refer to a single protocol or software component, but is rather a system of services and protocols working with the portion of the DIB they manage. The DSA is the application running on the directory server, which is performing all the server-side directory operations.

Each vendor creating an X.500 DSA for a commercial directory service product will have implementation-specific design factors, yet will adhere (to varying degrees) to the standards described in the X.500 specifications. Most DSAs in common use support the 1993 X.500 extensions, providing enhanced management functionality compared to 1988 DSAs.

Directory User Agents

A *Directory User Agent (DUA)* is the network client application that constructs and verifies queries (requests to the directory for information), communicates with the required DSAs, and provides query results to the user or application. The directory is seen by the DUA as a single unit that is accessible through a local DSA, which will generally be used by the DUA as a starting point for directory operations. Directory clients are frequently designed to mask the intricacies of the directory, most commonly by simplifying complex X.500 names and providing simple browsing and search methods.

Some DUAs are more powerful than others and participate more actively in directory operations such as searches, allowing the DSA to return referrals back to the client for completion. The DUA then contacts additional DSAs to pursue the resolution of the query. A DUA can take many forms, because the term refers not to the design or user interface of the agents but to conformance with the *Directory Access Protocol (DAP)*. DAP, along with the rest of the X.500 protocols, is discussed next.

X.500 Protocols

The X.500 standards specify a set of network protocols for operating the server and client aspects of the directory service. All X.500 protocols operate at the application layer of the OSI stack. DAP is the only protocol that provides client access to the directory; the three others support operations between DSAs.

To understand what functionality each one provides, take a brief look at each of the X.500 protocols:

- **Directory Access Protocol (DAP)**—DAP functions as the communication channel between the client DUA and the server DSA. DAP supports a number of operations, allowing the contents of the directory to be read, searched, and modified. DAP is also responsible for managing the association between the DUA and the DSA (establishing the connection between client and server agents).

- **Directory System Protocol (DSP)**—DSP supports the interaction between DSAs necessary for supporting the distributed directory operations. To simplify, DSP is essentially DAP with chaining operations and is (not surprisingly) used by DSAs to chain operations to other DSAs (chaining, where multiple DSAs share in resolving a query, is explained in detail later in this chapter). DSP may be configured to allow the caching of query requests and responses by the DSA, speeding lookup response time for frequently accessed directory objects.
- **Directory Operational Binding Management Protocol (DOP)**—A pair of DSAs use DOP to establish a binding agreement for use in distributed operations. These binding agreements (establishing an association between the DSAs) define knowledge references and replication agreements. Each DOP entry is comprised of data including the identity of each DSA, the nature of the agreement, and additional parameters such as information governing replication (frequency, role definition, and so on). The two DSAs involved in the binding agreement have reciprocal DOP entries.
- **Directory Information Shadowing Protocol (DISP)**—DISP is used by a DSA to replicate a naming context (partition) to another DSA. DISP is also used to transmit information during replica update operations. DSAs that are establishing an agreement to shadow the DIB must enter into a DOP agreement prior to DISP being used for actual data exchange.

Figure 4.1 illustrates how these protocols interoperate to provide directory services. The client and DSA uses DAP to communicate. The DSAs use DSP for servicing directory requests, DOP is used to form agreed upon relationships between DSAs, and DSAs use DISP for replication.

Additional Protocols Used by X.500

X.500 relies on the following three additional OSI-defined standards:

- **Access Control Service Element (ACSE)**—X.500 uses ACSE to create and tear down associations between directory agents, essentially managing the *bind* (connect to a DSA) and *unbind* (disconnect) processes.
- **Remote Operation Service Element (ROSE)**—ROSE provides support for the request/reply style of interaction between X.500 protocols.
- **Abstract Syntax Notation One (ASN.1)**—ASN.1 defines the syntax used for storing information that will be exchanged between different systems. ASN.1 stores data in a series of type-value pairs.

FIGURE 4.1
X.500 directory services use different protocols depending on which agents are communicating and why.

Application Programming Interfaces in X.500

X.500 defines *Application Programming Interface (API)* support, enabling application developers to use the directory information and functionality. Two methods of access to programmatic interfaces for X.500 directory application development are

- **XDS** (Open Directory Service) was initially developed by X/Open (now the Open Software Foundation) and the XAPI Association as a programmatic interface to X.500 DSAs. XDS provides the same set of functions, arguments, and results as the X.500 DAP. The XDS API has also been used as the basis for other proprietary directory APIs such as those used by Novell Directory Services.
- The **LDAP C API** (specified in RFC 1823) is a low-level programming interface used in the development of directory applications written for the C language. The LDAP C API supports all DAP operations, albeit sometimes with slightly different names (such as `modify` versus `modifyEntry`).

X.500 Models

The X.500 standards use a number of models to describe various aspects of the directory structure and operations. Each model takes a snapshot of one dimension of the directory service, abstracting a particular layer of directory functionality to provide a distinct view of the directory's contents and operations.

Lightweight DAP (LDAP)

To provide a simplified access to X.500 directory services, an alternative access protocol called Lightweight DAP (LDAP), was implemented as an open standard. LDAP was originally designed to support all DAP-compliant directory services operating over TCP/IP (instead of OSI-based protocols).

LDAP is gaining widespread acceptance, not only as an additional access method, but also as the native access method. Recently, directory servers based on LDAP, such as iPlanet, have been coming on the market. Chapter 5, "LDAP: Lightweight Directory Access Protocol," examines LDAP in detail.

The combined X.500 models describe the data structures, operations, administration, and security framework of the directory service. By examining these models one at a time, individual aspects of an X.500 directory service can be understood and then related to each other to gain a clearer picture of the overall directory functionality.

The original 1988 X.500 specification defined only the *Directory Information Model*, which deals with the most basic view of directory—that which a typical directory user sees. Since then, notably in the 1993 X.501 standard ("The Directory: Models"), a number of additional models have been defined. Some of the significant X.500 models are as follows:

- **Directory Functional Model**—Provides the "big picture" of how the directory works.
- **User Information Model**—Looks at the directory from the perspective of a user.
- **Operational and Administrative Information Model**—Shows what the directory looks like to an administrator.
- **DSA Information Model**—Describes how DSAs interoperate to provide directory access.
- **Directory Distribution Model**—Defines the rules for distributing information among DSAs.
- **Directory Administrative Authority Model**—Defines how the directory is administered and how administration is delegated.
- **Security Model**—Defines the authentication/access control framework.

The following sections discuss these models. Keep in mind that only the most significant models are examined here—X.500 contains a number of other models, some of which explain only a single small subset of administrative detail. To gain information on all the X.500 models, you will need to read the actual X.500 specification documents.

The Directory Functional Model

The *Directory Functional Model* states that the directory is one or more DSAs that collectively provide DUAs with access to directory information (via *access points*). When multiple DSAs support the directory, it is considered a *distributed* directory. This model assumes that some form of pairs of application processes (such as DUA-to-DSA, or DSA-to-DSA) will interact forming the directory service operations. Yet, how the DSAs interact with each other is transparent to this model—it is not concerned with the fine points of how this is accomplished, just the big picture.

> <visualization> Think of the different layers of models as different colored transparencies—each layer adding its particular filter or "hue" to the perception of the directory. <visualization>

Figure 4.2 shows the directory from the perspective of the Directory Functional Model. This is clearly an oversimplified view of the directory, but that is the approach of the X.500 models—subdividing the directory information, administration, and operations into simplified, abstracted layers as a means of explaining them.

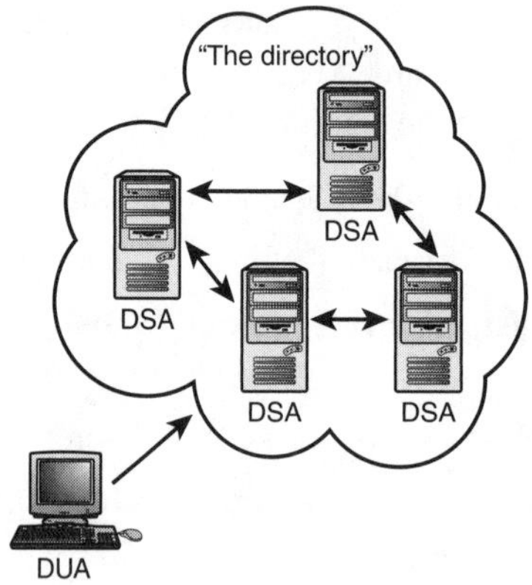

FIGURE 4.2
The Directory Functional Model sees the directory as a collection of servers responding to clients.

The User Information Model

The *User Information Model* describes the directory as a typical user would see it. The entire directory tree seems to exist just as the logical representation describes it—one large tree with no boundaries. All objects in the directory can be seen and manipulated (subject to appropriate access rights), without consideration as to where the information about those objects is stored. The User Information Model does the following:

- Determines the relationship of objects, attributes, and syntax as described by the schema.
- Defines how individual directory objects are named and how X.500 names are constructed.

The information visible by this model is referred to as *user attributes*. User attributes store the information about a directory object that is accessed and manipulated by most people using the directory. As shown in Figure 4.3, the user attributes make up only a portion of the total attribute set of any given object. This means that although a directory user can see some object information, the user is blocked from viewing administrative and operational data.

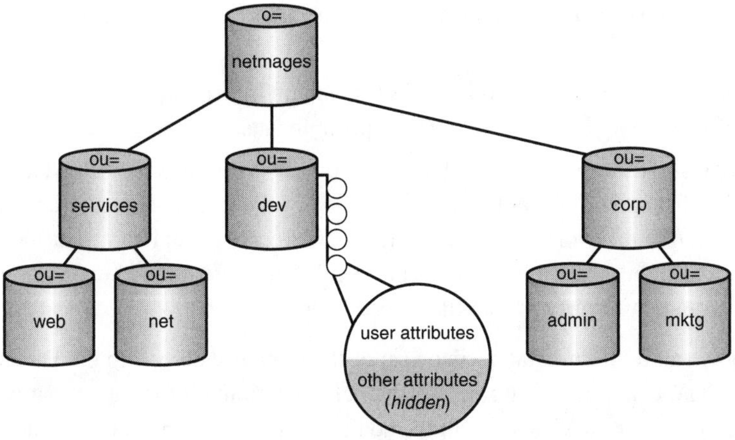

FIGURE 4.3
Only user attributes are visible according to the User Information Model.

The current User Information Model has replaced the Directory Information Model defined in the 1988 X.500 specifications. The User Information Model is one of the two models that make up the Extended Information Model, the other is the Directory Administrative and Operational Information Model, discussed next.

The Directory Administrative and Operational Information Model

The *Directory Administrative and Operational Information Model*, as you might guess from the name, is essentially the directory as the administrator sees it. As in the User Information Model, the entire directory is seen as a single large DIT with no regard for actual DIB distribution. In fact, only one substantial difference exists between these two models—operational attributes and subentries are visible in the Directory Administrative and Operational Information Model.

Take a look at what information the two additional categories of attributes provide:

- **Operational attributes**—These contain information used internally by the directory to keep track of directory modifications and subtree properties. Typical operational attributes would include such things as schema information, access control data, and information used in directory replication. Operational attributes are unlike user attributes in that they are not returned as part of a normal directory query, but must be specifically requested. There are three types of operational attributes:
    - **Directory operational attributes** are used for operational parameters that apply to every DSA, such as access control.

- **DSA-shared operational attributes** store information used between DSAs to perform replication.
- **DSA-specific operational attributes** contain information that applies to a single DSA, such as the time of the last replica update.

- **Subentries**—These are used to select a subportion of the directory and define specific properties that should be applied to that portion of the DIT. A subentry contains the description of a directory subtree and the security controls, collective attributes or sub-schema that should be applied to the subtree. Subtrees are defined under the Directory Administrative Authority Model (described later).

Figure 4.4 shows more of the total attribute set of the directory object. In the Directory Administrative and Operational Information Model, operational information that was hidden in the preceding model is now visible. With the additional properties available to the directory user, management operations can now be performed.

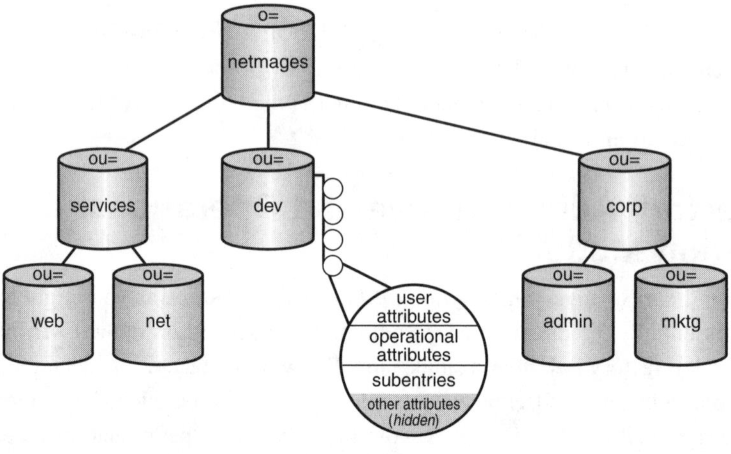

FIGURE 4.4

The Directory Administrative and Operational Information Model provides access to the additional directory information required for administration.

The DSA Information Model

The *DSA Information Model*, which is based on the X.518 Distribution Model, states that the directory entries should be structured into a directory information tree (DIT). The model also acknowledges that the contents of the DIT are held in a database that is divided into multiple naming contexts and shared among DSAs. The information contained in this model describes the DSA's location in relationship to other DSAs and how they interact to control the directory information.

The information seen by this model includes DSA *operational attributes* in addition to all the attributes viewable by the two previous information models. DSA operational attributes identify where a particular naming context fits in the directory tree. They also control interaction between DSAs during the replication process.

Knowledge Information

A DSA uses *knowledge information* to identify and describe the relationship of one DSA to another. *Knowledge references* hold references to portions of the DIB that are not contained within a local naming context. X.500 defines both mandatory and optional knowledge references. There are four mandatory knowledge references which are used for basic directory functionality, specifically the superior-subordinate and supplier-consumer pairs.

The mandatory knowledge references are used as follows:

- **Immediate Superior**—Contains a single pointer to a DSA holding the naming context that is the parent of the naming context held by the current DSA. Obviously, first-level DSAs will not contain an Immediate Superior reference because there is no actual root object to reference. First-level DSAs contain Subordinate references to all other first-level DSAs as a means of immediately locating all the naming contexts subordinate to the DIT root.
- **Subordinate**—Specifies naming contexts that are children of the naming context held by the current DSA. A Subordinate knowledge reference contains the *Relative Distinguished Name (RDN)* of the child naming context as well as the access point for the DSA holding it.
- **Supplier**—Contains information used in replication to identify the DSA that will be providing the update, specified in the replication agreement that has been made with the supplier DSA.
- **Consumer**—Holds information on the replication consumer. This information is the reciprocal of that in the Supplier reference.

It should be noted that the Immediate Superior/Subordinate and Supplier/Consumer references occur in pairs. Figure 4.5 illustrates the relationship between the different types of knowledge references. `Merlin` has a Supplier reference to `Zifnab`; therefore `Zifnab` has a Consumer reference for `Merlin`. Likewise, `Zifnab` contains a Superior reference to `Haplo`, and `Haplo` has a Subordinate reference to `Zifnab`.

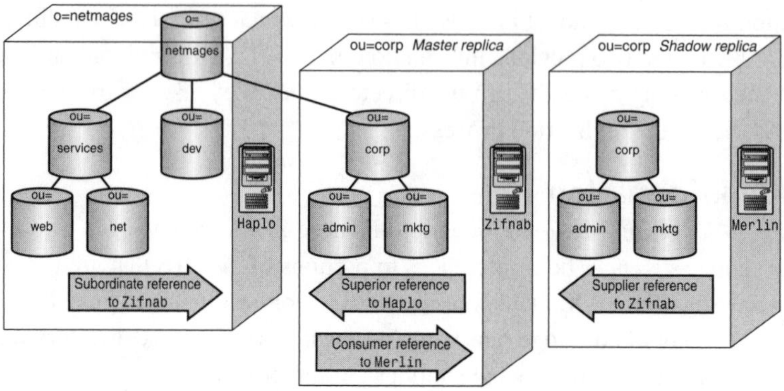

FIGURE 4.5

Each DSA uses knowledge references to locate DSAs holding other naming contexts for object location and replication.

Two additional (optional) knowledge references are defined by X.500:

- **Cross-references**—These are used to point to another naming context that is neither superior nor subordinate to the current naming context. Cross-references can be used to speed referrals to frequently accessed DSAs.
- **Non-Specific Subordinate references (NSSRs)**—A special type of subordinate reference containing the name of a DSA holding a child naming context, but not the RDN of that context. NSSRs were designed as a method of protecting the data in a subordinate naming context that is handled by another administrative authority.

DSA-Specific Entry

Each entry (object) in the directory tree is likely to be referenced by multiple DSAs. The information stored with the object in each of these DSAs will probably be at least somewhat different. To reflect this difference, the term *DSA-specific entry (DSE)* is used. Essentially, a DSE is an entry in the DIT as held by a specific DSA.

An object with its complete set of attributes, for example, will be stored by the DSA holding the naming context containing the object. Any shadow replicas will also have a copy of that object, with most of the same attribute values, except for a few DSA-specific attributes. In addition, a reference to that object with a partial set of its properties may exist in other DSAs as part of a catalog, cache replica, and so on. The DSA Information Model describes a *DSA Information Tree*. A DSA Information Tree is comprised of the complete set of object names (and associated DSEs) known by a specific DSA.

The Directory Distribution Model

The *Directory Distribution Model* makes the rules controlling how directory information is shared by multiple DSAs. According to the Directory Distribution Model, a single DSA shall hold the master copy of each directory entry—the copy of the object considered authoritative. That DSA is called the *master DSA* for that entry. Correspondingly, a DSA holding a shadow copy of an object is considered a *shadow DSA* for that object.

Each DSA manages one or more naming contexts, which are collectively referred to as a *DIB fragment*—that is, the portion of the DIB that is held by a single DSA.

As shown in Figure 4.6, `Haplo` has a single replica, the master of `o=netmages`, making `Haplo` the master DSA for the entries in that naming context. Likewise, `Zifnab` is the master DSA for the `ou=corp` naming context. `Merlin` has two replicas, `ou=corp` and `o=netmages`, both shadows, making it the shadow DSA for both naming contexts. Each of the DIT fragments contained by `Zifnab` and `Haplo` consists of a single naming context, while `Merlin` has two naming contexts in its DIT fragment.

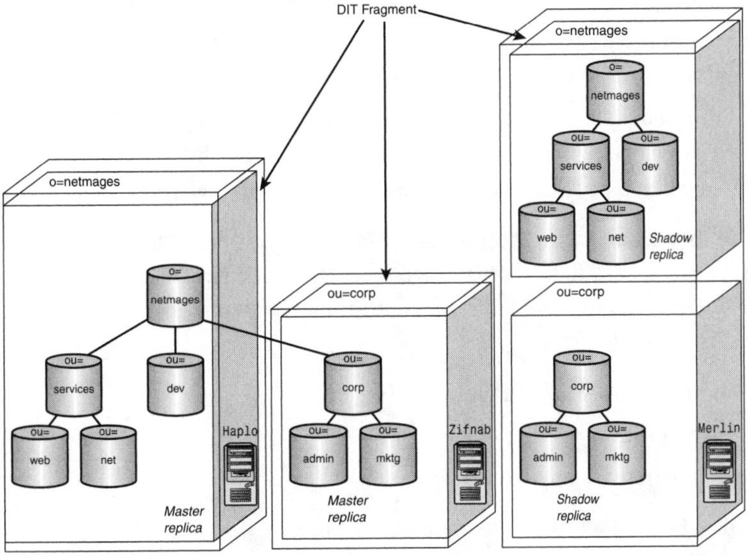

FIGURE 4.6
The Directory Distribution Model defines how DSAs interact to share management of directory information.

The Directory Distribution Model defines a *naming context* as a subtree of the DIT that is held on a single DSA and managed by a common Administrative Authority, which is part of the next model discussed.

The Directory Administrative Authority Model

The *Directory Administrative Authority Model* acknowledges that different people or organizations will administer different parts of the directory tree. This model provides a way for the DIT to be divided into *subtrees*, management of which can then be delegated as needed.

A directory subtree starts at a container object and extends downward until another subtree definition is encountered. The subtree description can also be filtered by object type so that, for example, a subtree could consist of only the User objects within a directory subtree.

Each of these subtrees is designated as a particular kind of administrative area. These administrative subtrees define areas with different types of administrative controls placed on them. The subtrees defined within this model include:

- **Autonomous Administrative Areas (AAA)**—These are managed by independent organizations, each of which is completely responsible for its portion of the directory tree.
- **Specific Administrative Areas (SAA)**—Subtrees of autonomous administrative areas in which entries are viewed from a specific administrative perspective.
- **Inner Administrative Areas (IAA)**—Defined within an organization to designate an area with delegated administrative tasks or collective attributes. A collective attribute is one that is defined once and attached to every object in that IAA.

Each administrative area has a corresponding *administrative point*, which is the node (container object) at the root of the administrative area. By attaching subentries to the administrative point, different types of administrative control may be defined. The name denotes the type of administrative area it begins:

- Autonomous Administrative Point (AAP)
- Specific Administrative Point (SAP)
- Inner Administrative Point (IAP)

Figure 4.7 shows how a DIT is divided into administrative areas. In this figure, a single AAA encompasses the entire `netmages` tree. The entire tree is also defined as one SAA. Because the AAA and the SAA are congruent, the same node (`o=netmages`) is used as their respective administrative points, the AAP and SAP.

The tree also has two IAAs defined, one at `ou=services` and one at `ou=web`. The IAP for the two IAAs are at `ou=services` and `ou=web`, respectively. Unlike the SAA, IAAs can be nested inside each other, because the IAA boundary is somewhat permeable (allowing settings to cross IAA boundaries).

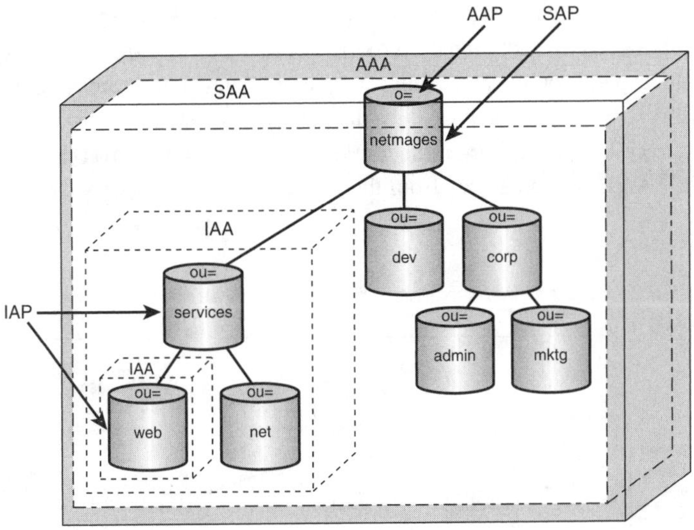

FIGURE 4.7

The Directory Administrative Authority Model divides the DIT into delegable zones of authority.

When an AAA is created, three SAAs are also implicitly created, mirroring the AAA boundary. Each type of SAA controls a single aspect of administration. A Specific Administrative Area is defined in one of three forms:

- **Access control**—An *Access Control Specific Area (ACSA)* manages some portion of the security policy for this portion of the DIT.
- **Collective attributes**—A *Collective Attribute Specific Area (CASA)* administers those attributes applied to an entire subtree.
- **Subschema**—A *Subschema Specific Area (SSA)* defines the schema that applies to this portion of the DIT.

Administrative Areas Are Not Naming Contexts

The boundaries of administrative areas and naming contexts do not necessarily coincide, although they may. Administrative areas describe logical zones of administrative control, but naming contexts are physical subdivisions of the DIB. Administrative areas may span naming context boundaries, and therefore DSAs.

Within an AAA, thereare always three SAAs—one each of the three types just listed. The AAA may be further subdivided into additional SAAs. The boundaries of a specific type of SAA cannot overlap. Figure 4.8 expands on the preceding example of administrative areas by showing the individual SAAs. Where the borders of the three different SAAs were first shown as congruent, this is not necessarily the case. Although it is true that SAA borders cannot overlap, it is only true for the same type of SAA. As you can see from the figure, each type of SAA can have its own set of boundaries.

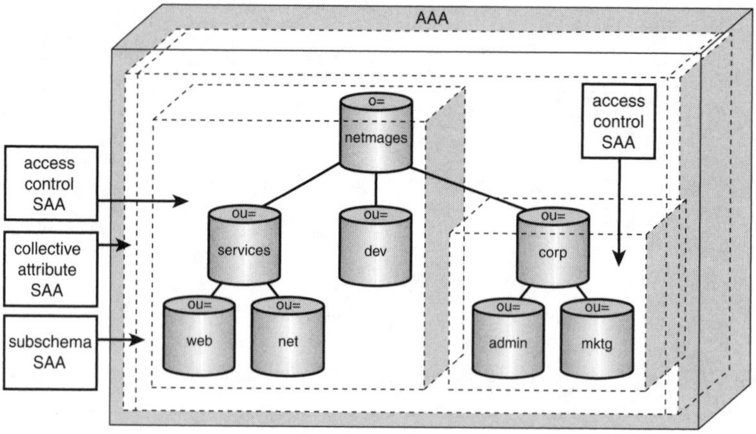

FIGURE 4.8

Each AAA contains three types of SAAs, which may or may not have the same boundaries.

The 1993 extensions to X.500 provided the following distinctions to support policy-based management:

- **DIT Domain**—The section of the global DIT managed by a specific administrative authority, referred to as the *Domain Management Organization (DMO).* A DIT Domain consists of one or more AAAs, which may be unconnected. Policies applied to the DIT Domain apply to information, such as those that govern subschema.
- **Directory Management Domain (DMD)**—A set of DSAs and DUAs administered by a specific organization. DMD policies apply to DSA operations and can be used to limit the operations and services provided by one or more DSAs.

There is a one-to-one correspondence between DMDs and DIT Domains—they are the same things looked at from two perspectives. As shown in Figure 4.9, a DMD is a management area concerned with the directory operations, while a DIT Domain is a management area over directory *information*. Policies can be applied to each of these management areas.

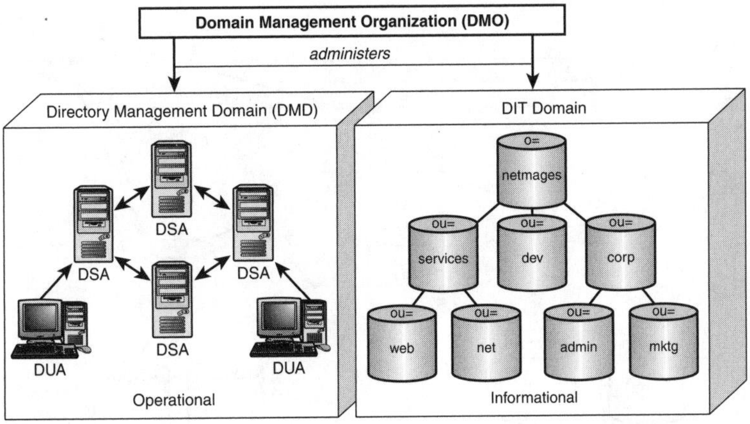

FIGURE 4.9
A DMO manages both the informational and operational aspects of the directory.

The Security Model

Security within the X.500 framework is defined by application of the Directory Administrative Authority Model to security provisioning within the directory, supporting delegation of security administration. The security divisions within the directory *exactly* parallel the administrative divisions.

When viewing an administrative area from a security management perspective, the relationships shown in Table 4.3 apply.

TABLE 4.3 Correlations Between the Security Model and the Administrative Authority Model

Administrative Model	*Security Model*
Specific Administrative Area (SAA)	Access Control Specific Area (ACSA)
Inner Administrative Area (IAA)	Access Control Inner Administrative Area (ACIA)
Specific Administrative Point (SAP)	Access Control Specific Point (ACSP)
Inner Administrative Point (IAP)	Access Control Inner Point (ACIP)
Administrative Authority (AA)	Security Authority (SA)

As shown in Figure 4.10, an AAA contains one or more ACSAs that have non-overlapping borders. An ACSA is an autonomous area of security, such that access control information will not be recognized across ACSA boundaries. Each ACSA can contain one or more ACIAs, which may be nested. An ACIA provides for *partial* delegation of access control administration.

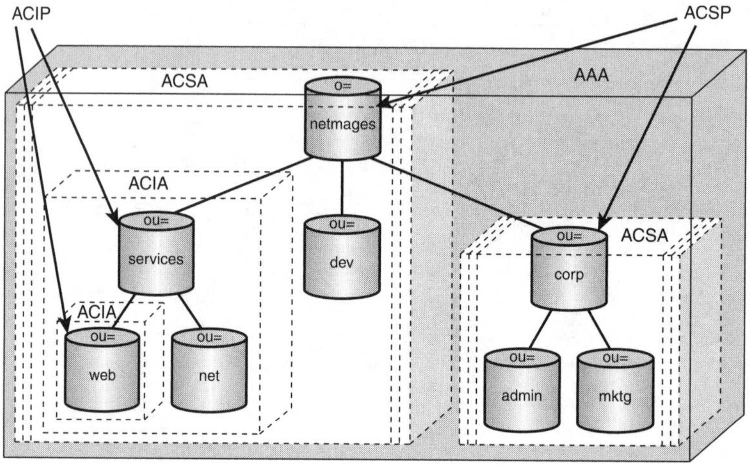

FIGURE 4.10

The AAA is subdivided into ACSAs, and can be subdivided into further ACIAs.

Authentication and access control mechanisms are applied within the access control area by adding a subentry to the administrative point (either ACSP or ACIP). The subentry has *access control lists (ACLs)* containing the access control policies. When determining access control for an object, the directory assesses the collection of permissions from all ACIPs above the object location up to and *including the first ACSP or AAP encountered.*

Take another look at Figure 4.10 and the two examples that follow to see how this works:

- If an object exists in `ou=web`, its inherited security permissions will be the combination of the access control information (ACI) attached to `ou=web`, `ou=services`, and `o=netmages`. The first two administrative points are ACIPs, which are both used in the evaluation of security information. `o=netmages` is the first ACSP encountered, so the collection of ACI stops at that point.
- An object in `ou=admin` will inherit access control information from the ACSP `ou=corp` only. Because the first administrative point (`ou=corp`) is an ACSP, the administrative point at `o=netmages` will not be included in the evaluation of security information.

An access control area can also be subdivided into sets of directory entries, in a form called a *Directory Access Control Domain (DACD)*. This enables the administrator to apply security policies to a diverse set of directory objects within a subtree, by collecting them into this logical access control domain.

X.500 Directory Objects

Directory objects are commonly thought of as being limited to those objects used to represent tree structure and visible directory entries. However, a directory service also uses many "invisible" objects for internal operations.

X.500 defines three major types of object *classes*, based on their purpose in the directory. Each object is constructed from one or more *class definitions*. The three major class categories in X.500 are as follows:

- **Abstract**—The use of abstract classes is very limited, although they are critical to the directory. There is currently one abstract class defined by the X.500 standards: top. The top class provides a basic set of properties used by every object in the directory.
- **Auxiliary**—Auxiliary classes are sometimes called *noneffective objects* because they are not used in the formation of directory trees. Auxiliary classes are used internally by the directory service to create the actual objects used in the formation of the tree. An auxiliary class contains a set of attributes defined to support a specific derivation of an existing object. As an example, an application vendor might add an auxiliary class defining the additional properties needed by various entities using their application and then add that class to an existing object. The auxiliary classes can be thought of as the building blocks for structural class objects.
- **Structural**—The structural (or effective) classes are those objects that form the directory tree and are commonly viewed and manipulated by network users and administrators. When a structural object is created, certain properties are required and must contain valid information. New objects cannot be created unless all mandatory attributes have valid entries. The structural classes that are generally used by all X.500 directory services can be subdivided into three types based on their intended functionality:
    - **Container objects**—Provide structure and organization for the directory objects contained within.
    - **Leaf objects**—Represent an actual entity available in or using the directory.
    - **Alias objects**—Secondary representations of existing objects, which merely function as pointers to the original object.

The base set of structural directory objects (and attributes) is actually rather small, a couple of dozen types of *structural* objects in all. The X.521 specification contains the object definitions of the fundamental classes, or types, of directory objects. Clearly the class definitions published in the standards consist of a rather minimal set of objects.

The X.521 object set is considered to be a base set of internationally standardized objects. The standards state that national administrative authorities and other entities are expected to implement additional object sets. Therefore, the object classes described in the base X.500 schema are not the entire set of objects allowed for a particular directory service. Vendors of X.500-based directory products commonly extend the X.521 object set to include all the classes needed to support the basic scope of directory operations for their implementation. Objects may also be added, or modified, by directory-enabled software, directory administrators, and so on. All this is also true of the attribute set described in X.520.

Container Objects

The *container objects* are classes of objects that may contain other objects. In a directory, container objects are used to create and structure the hierarchical tree within the directory namespace.

The container objects were designed with fairly specific purposes in mind. Accordingly, they have different limitations on where they can reside and what kinds of objects they can contain. The container objects fall into the following classes:

- **Country (C)**—A Country object is used to organize a DIT into international subdivisions, and can be contained only within the root. Country objects are optional and are most frequently used when placing an organization in a global X.500 directory. Country designations are two-letter character codes ("us" for United States, "de" for Germany, and so on) and are defined in ISO 3166.
- **Locality (L)**—The Locality object is used to organize directory trees into geographic subdivisions, and can be contained within the Country, Locality, and Organization classes.
- **Organization (O)**—An Organization object is used to specify the top-level organizational node in the DIT, and can only be contained within the root or a Country object. The Organization object is the top-level object in a DIT that can contain leaf objects (users, servers, and so on). An Organization object is subdivided by creating Organizational Units within it.
- **Organizational Unit (OU)**—An Organizational Unit is used to subdivide a DIT into logical administrative units, and can be contained within an Organization, Organizational Unit, or Locality object. The OU is the most commonly used container object in the directory, and is used for most logical subdivisions of the DIT.

Leaf Objects

The *leaf objects* in an X.500 directory service represent users, resources, and information stored within the directory. As previously mentioned, the defined X.500 object set is small—leaf objects correspond primarily to variations on people, groups, and objects used for directory operations. But remember, in a commercial directory service product, the schema will commonly be extended so that leaf objects correspond to a wide range of individual directory elements (such as users, security entities, groups, and so on), as well as logical groupings of resources, properties, and processes.

The following list shows the set of leaf objects defined by X.521:

- Application Entity
- Application Process
- Certification Authority
- Certification Authority-V2
- CRL Distribution Point
- Device
- DMD
- DSA
- Group of Names
- Group of Unique Names
- Organizational Person
- Organizational Role
- Person
- Residential Person
- Strong Authentication User
- User Security Information

The Root

The root is a fictitious object; although it is referred to and treated as though it were a normal directory object, it is actually made up of entries in each of the DSAs that hold naming contexts immediately subordinate to the root. The root object is a DSA-Specific Entry in that it may be different in each of the DSAs that reference it.

Aliases

An *alias* is an object that functions solely as a pointer, or reference, to another object within the directory (roughly analogous to a shortcut in Windows). An alias is placed in the directory as a reference to an existing object instead of creating a new object to represent the same resource. Aliases are particularly useful for providing multiple references to a single object.

Suppose that an enterprise wanted to make a single person from the development unit easily available to the entire corporation. As the directory administrator, you might create an alias for a development contact and place it in the directory tree at an easily found location. By assigning the alias to point to a particular developer, you would ensure that everyone could use a single point of contact for development and changes to the actual contact would be transparent to end users.

Figure 4.11 shows a possible implementation of this idea. Brynna exists as a user in the `dev` OU and is also referred to by the alias `devcontact` in the `net` OU. In this example, the actual user object for Brynna is considered the *target object*. By using an alias, when Brynna is promoted, and someone else replaces her as the development contact, only the internal reference on the alias must be updated to point to the person taking on those responsibilities and the `devcontact` name remains unchanged.

Aliases can be created when moving an object to serve as a redirector to the new location. Some directory services do this automatically while others require that the administrator manually create the alias object.

If a Leaf Can't Contain an Object, How Can You Have a Group of Users?

Leaf objects may not contain other objects, although some, such as groups, appear to contain other objects (in this case, users). However, the users contained in that group are actually values of an attribute that holds a members list. These types of objects use an attribute called a *multi-valued* attribute.

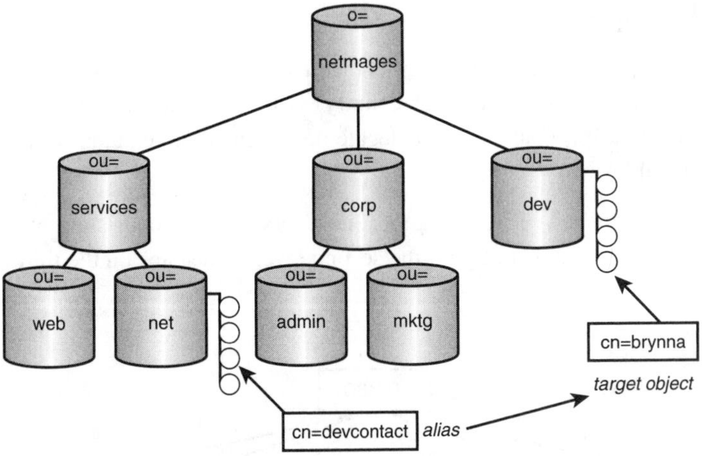

FIGURE 4.11

The `devcontact` *alias object just contains a reference to* `o=netmages, ou=dev, cn=brynna.`

Directory Information Tree

In the X.500 specifications, the objects in the directory are organized into a Directory Information Tree—the complete collection of directory objects logically represented in a hierarchical tree. A set of container objects is used to create the tree structure.

A DIT logically organizes the directory content for display in both management and user applications. The DIT structure can simplify the location of directory resources, especially for people trying to locate information in large and complex directories.

The directory access control methods use the DIT to delimit differential areas of directory security. In addition to access control, the DIT is also used for other administrative subdivisions (such as subschema or collective attribute), as well as for administrative delegation.

In a general-purpose directory, the DIT is often structured to represent divisions in the organization and information. The DIT may reflect the structure of an e-commerce application, for example, or a range of other communications or information systems.

In a network environment, a DIT is generally structured to represent the underlying network infrastructure and/or corporate structure, as a means of organizing directory management and simplifying object location.

The Global Tree

An assumption of the original X.500 design was that a single tree would define a global namespace subdivided by nation and region. Each country would have the administrative authority for its section of the namespace, and could delegate the administrative authority on a regional, state, or organizational level.

The DIT was originally conceived from a "global directory" model, consisting of a root entity at the top of the DIT, with each country on the second level, and states on the third, as shown in Figure 4.12.

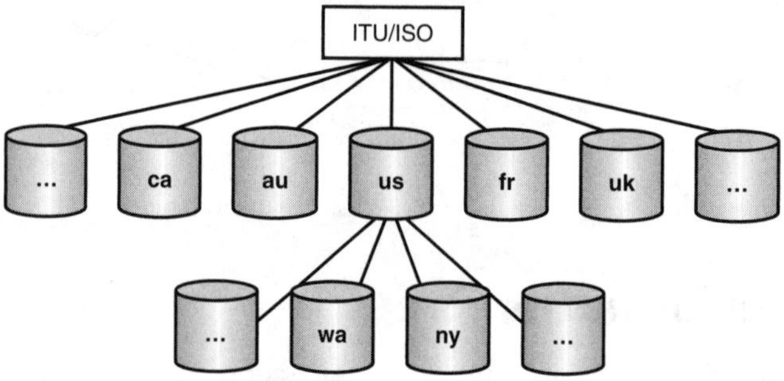

FIGURE 4.12
The X.500 tree was originally designed to support a global namespace.

Dante NameFlow at `www.gateway.nameflow.net` provides a public access point to the root of this global X.500 tree.

The national representatives to the ITU/ISO manage their subportions of the global DIT. These administrative authorities delegate administration of a portion of the DIT to each organization as they request a name for their enterprise.

> **DIT Functionality May Vary**
>
> The specific process and limitations of DIT organization are highly dependent on the vendor implementation. The functionality of DIT operations varies among vendors and may vary among different implementations by the same vendor.

Structuring the DIT

The directory tree is built according to the structure defined in its schema. The *structure rules* determine the relationship between objects in the directory, and how an object can be named.

Structure rules can be broken down into two major components:

- **Superior rules**—Define a set of container objects where each object can possibly reside
- **Name form**—Determines how the object is named

The superior rules proscribe where in the directory an object can exist, defining the possible arrangement of objects in the directory tree. The name form controls the attribute used to name each object, and whether the RDN is single or multi-valued. Objects are arranged according to the superior rules, and are named in accordance with the name form.

DIT Roles in X.500 Models

The DIT is a logical structure that provides the basis for the representation of directory information for multiple X.500 models. When you look at the DIT as viewed in each of the models, its role in the directory service operations becomes clearer:

- The DSA Information Model defines structuring directory entries into a distributed DIT with multiple naming contexts shared between DSAs.
- In the User Information Model, the DIT is used to organize and display usable objects such as users, servers, and so on.
- In the Directory Administrative and Organizational and Information Model, the DIT display includes both the usable objects as well as the management functionality on those (and other) objects.
- In the Directory Administrative Authority Model, the DIT provides the structure used in administrative subdivisions of the directory objects.
- The Security Model describes using the DIT structure for access control subdivisions of the directory.

DIT Permissions Flow

The directory tree also provides the structure for the flow of security settings. Particular types of properties may be assigned to a container, and via *inheritance*, to all objects within it. When a directory object is created within a container object, it inherits the security attributes of its parent container objects.

Most directory implementations also allow for the blocking of rights inheritance at the container object level. This is usually done through an *Inherited Rights Filter (IRF),* which enables the directory administrator to select which rights should not be inherited by objects in a particular container. IRFs are described in more detail in Chapter 9, "eDirectory."

This inheritance of security control is enabled by the assignment of access control areas. Access control areas may be defined as a permeable (ACIA) or non-permeable (ACSA) portion of the DIT, which has associated access control information. This is discussed in more detail in the "Security in X.500" section later in this chapter.

X.500 Naming

The X.500 standards define a structured approach to the naming of directory objects. One of the more familiar directory naming models is the one defined in the X.500 specification and its derivatives. Many directory implementations provide support for X.500, LDAP, or other naming formats derived from these specifications (for example, NDS eDirectory uses an unattributed form of X.500 naming).

X.500 naming starts with a simple premise, that each directory object has both a name assigned to it and a specific location in the DIT. By concatenating the series of object names between the specified directory object and the root of the tree, the object's *Distinguished Name (DN)* uniquely identifies each object in the DIT.

Each directory object has a name assigned by the directory administrator or application at the time the object is created. The object name is the contents of one or more attributes designated by the class definition as its naming attribute.

Every *naming attribute* uses its own abbreviation in typed naming of directory objects:

- **C** = Country
- **L** = Locality
- **O** = Organization
- **OU** = Organizational Unit
- **CN** = Common Name (any leaf object)

The X.500 standards describe a naming convention in which each object in the directory has a *Relative Distinguished Name (RDN)*. The RDN is just the name of the object combined with the appropriate naming attribute abbreviation with no additional information identifying its place in the tree (for example, `cn=angela`). In general, a directory may contain objects with duplicate RDNs as long as the RDN is unique within a specific container object.

Each entry in a directory tree also has a fully qualified name, the DN, which uniquely identifies and places the object within the directory tree. A DN is the comma-delimited string of RDNs starting with the object name closest to the root and continuing down the directory tree to the object. Each component of a directory object's DN is the RDN of the object to which it is referring.

In the tree represented in Figure 4.13, the DN of the Public Relations Manager named Angela is `o=netmages,ou=corp,ou=mktg,cn=angela`. As you can see from this example, DNs in a large tree could easily become long and confusing. For this reason, you may want to consider using short names or abbreviations as container names when feasible.

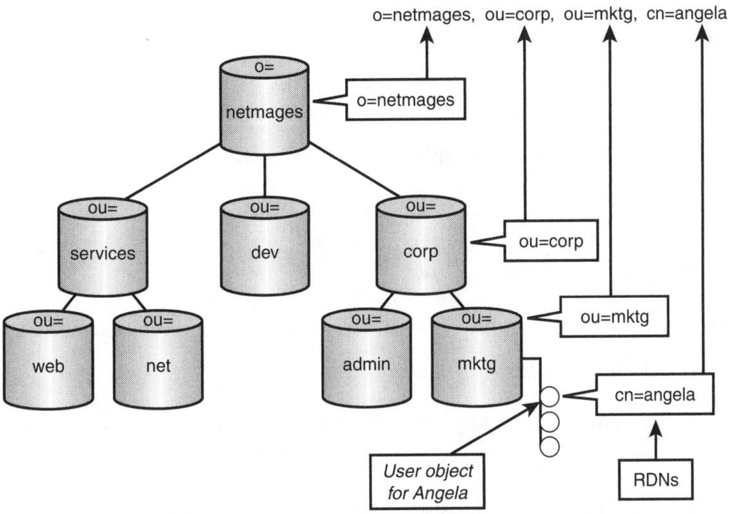

FIGURE 4.13

The Distinguished Name uniquely identifies both the object and its location in the tree.

A multivalued RDN occurs when an object has more than one designated naming attribute. Multivalued RDNs could be used for various reasons; to add additional information needed for object location or directory management, or to distinguish between multiple objects that would otherwise have the same name.

Multivalued RDNs are concatenated with a + symbol as in this example which assumes that Angela (from the previous example) works out of the Seattle office:

```
o=netmages,ou=corp,ou=mktg,cn=angela+l=seattle
```

When Is a CN Not a CN?

In X.500, a common name (CN) is used to refer to leaf objects, not container objects. Each container object has it own unique naming attribute (such as C, L, O, OU). It is worth noting, however, that some directory implementations differ from the X.500 usage of these naming attributes. For example, Active Directory also uses CN as the name type attribute for a default set of container objects.

X.500 Directory Schema

The objects contained within an X.500 directory are specified in a set of data structures and rules called the *schema*, which defines the directory objects and their properties. The schema defines the contents and structure of the directory service, as well as possible relationships between objects. These definitions specify all the properties of the objects, attributes, and syntax that comprise the directory.

The X.500 schema definition is distributed throughout the documents comprising the X.500 standards. There are system schema component definitions in X.501 describing operational attributes and other schema information in the documents defining the related portion of the directory.

An internationally standardized base schema for a core set of structural objects is defined in two documents:

- **X.520: Selected Attribute Types**—Defines attributes and matching rules.
- **X.521: Selected Object Classes**—Defines object classes.

The schema in the standards documents is meant to be supplemented by additional schemata devised by various national administrative authorities, vendors, and so on.

Most current X.500 directory products store the schema as objects in the directory. This allows the directory to dynamically accommodate schema changes, easily replicate those changes to other DSAs, as well as provide support for differing schemata in discrete directory subtrees. This is a significant improvement over earlier X.500-based directory implementations that stored the schema in a text file that was loaded when the DSA was initialized. In this configuration, the schema was generally static until the DSA was shut down and restarted.

Typeless Naming

If the name type abbreviation is used when forming an X.500 name, it is considered typed, or attributed naming; whereas X.500-style names without abbreviations are considered typeless. The X.500 specifications do not support typeless naming, although some X.500-based derivations, such as eDirectory, support both typed and typeless naming. From the user's perspective, the obvious advantages of typeless names are their simplicity and "friendliness."

The X.500 directory schema has three major components that combine to form the internal structure of the objects in a directory tree. The three components of the directory schema are as follows:

- The *classes* are the set of objects allowed within the directory.
- The *attributes* of each object class are the set of properties allowed by that class of object.
- The *attribute syntax* determines syntactical constraints of the attribute and matching rules.

These components follow rules, which are used to constrain the contents of the directory objects and allow their appropriate placement in the directory tree:

- *Content rules* define the contents of the objects—specifying the attributes that each object class contains. These rules are governed by the contents of the `Must Contain` and `May Contain` fields of the object class definition.
- *Structure rules* define the tree—specifying the logical structure of the directory by determining where objects can reside and how they are named. These rules are governed by the contents of the `Superior Rules` and `Name Form` fields.

In many directory implementations, only one directory schema is allowed to exist per tree. As noted in the section on X.500 models, however, the 1993 extensions to X.500 define subtrees as a method to attach differing schemata to some portions of the DIT. (Note that LDAP also supports this method of attaching a subschema to a specific subtree.) This subschema control is particularly useful (at least theoretically) as a means of facilitating data exchange between directories with different schemata, by allowing multiple schema definitions within a single DIT.

Object Class Definitions

Object class definitions specify which objects can appear in the directory tree, what information is required to create the object, and how those objects work in relationship to other objects in the directory. Every object in the directory belongs to one class, and each class has *superclasses*. Superclasses serve as a means of adding template-like sets of properties to objects within the directory.

An object is defined via a set of subdefinitions, which are linked to provide the complete object description. The components used to define an object class are as follows:

- **Object class**—Defines the attributes the object must or may contain, as well as *kind* and *subclass* information.
- **Name form**—Designates which attributes are used for naming.
- **Structure rules**—Determines the name form and superior rules.

This information works to define each object, its possible placement in the directory tree, and its purpose in the directory. In the following, a complete object class definition is examined in more depth to clarify how the subdefinitions work together to form the directory objects and constrain how the objects can be integrated into a tree. The contents of an object class definition includes:

- **Object identifier**—Each object type has an *object identifier* (OID) that uniquely identifies the object class.
- **Kind of object**—The 1993 standards added a designation of the *kind* of object the class is defining: structural, auxiliary, or abstract.
- **Name form**—The name form defines the allowable RDN values for a specific structural object class. Name form definitions contain at least one attribute whose value is used to form the RDN of a directory entry. A name form may also contain the names of additional attributes whose values may optionally be used to form a multivalued RDN.
- **Superior rules**—The superior rules define the possible structure of the directory tree, by delimiting which container objects can hold a specific object class. The superior rules list for a specific object is the list of containers the object may be created within.
- **Mandatory attributes**—As you can imagine, the mandatory attributes of an object are those that must have values assigned to them at the time of object creation. Mandatory attributes, listed in the `Must Contain` field, must be maintained for the life of the object for the object to be recognized by the directory. If an object loses a mandatory attribute, it becomes an unknown object and must be re-created. Most objects have only a few mandatory properties that are used for critical functionality (such as the attributes used for naming or identification).
- **Optional attributes**—Optional attributes are those properties for which values may be assigned, but which are not required for object creation. The `May Contain` field of the object class definition lists the optional attributes. Many directory objects have a large number of optional attributes that are used to track information about the object that, although useful, are not required for the object to function correctly.
- **Superclasses**—Superclasses act as building blocks for directory objects by providing logical sets of attributes to add to an object definition. An object is comprised of the information contained in the definition of the object class, and the definitions of its superclasses (and their superclasses, and so on). For example, all objects have `top` as a superclass, either directly or via inheritance from another superclass. Superclasses are denoted in the schema as entries in the `Subclass Of` attribute.

Directory objects have a hierarchy, in that they go from more general to more specific (an *object-hierarchy*, distinct from a directory tree hierarchy). To illustrate, consider the `organizationalPerson` object.

As shown in Figure 4.14, the `organizationalPerson` object is constructed from the combined definitions of the `top`, `person`, and `organizationalPerson` objects. The `person` object contains attributes common to all persons (`surname`, for example); `organizationalPerson` contains additional attributes with information specific to a person within a business context (such as `title`).

You may notice that rather than solely specifying individual attributes, the `organizationalPerson` definition lists several attribute sets (`LocaleAttributeSet`, `PostalAttributeSet`, and so on). These sets provide a convenient way to add a collection of attributes to an object class, and are discussed in more detail in the following section.

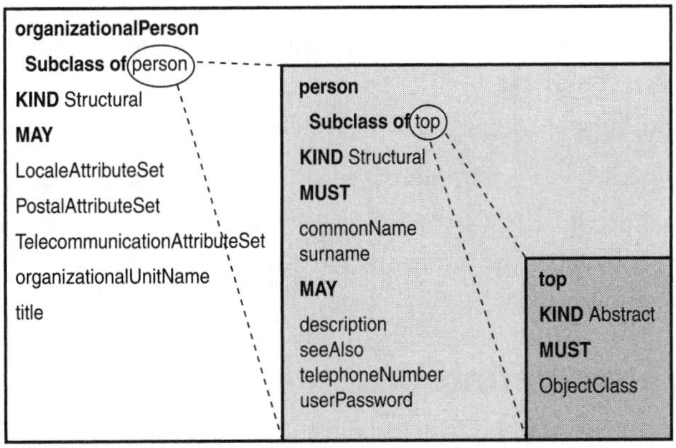

FIGURE 4.14
A directory object is built from the collected definitions of the object class and all the object's superclasses.

The `person` object is also used as a superclass of the `residentialPerson` object, as well as providing a base for custom objects representing persons.

Attribute Definitions

An *attribute definition* in the directory schema specifies the structure (as opposed to the content) of an attribute. Each attribute (also referred to as a *property*) that can be assigned to an object in the directory must first be defined in the schema. The attribute definition includes the attribute syntax and any constraints placed on the attribute, such as whether it is limited to a single value.

Each attribute has a particular syntax that constrains the data type of values entered into it and defines how the attribute value is processed. The matching rules used when comparing values are defined by the attribute definition.

Attributes have a `Subtype Of` field, which operates a lot like the object `Subclass Of` field. An attribute's super type provides portions of the attribute definition, usually the acceptable syntax and matching rules.

Useful Attribute Sets

X.500 designates several collections of attributes as *useful attribute sets*. These sets are designed to provide a way to quickly add a logical collection of attributes, providing support for a particular functionality, to an object. As you saw in the illustration of how the `organizationalPerson` object class is built (Figure 4.14), the attribute sets make it easier to define a new structural object class.

The X.500 standards describe four such sets of attributes, including:

- **Telecommunication attribute set**—Defines a set of attributes containing information used for business communications.
- **Postal attribute set**—Provides a set of attributes related to the physical delivery of mail.
- **Locale attribute set**—This attribute set identifies a location geographically.
- **Organizational attribute set**—Contains attributes an organization typically possesses. This attribute set includes properties such as passwords as well as the three previously defined attribute sets.

Attribute Syntax Definitions

The *attribute syntax* defines how the attribute value is constrained by data type and syntax limits set within the schema. Attributes of the same syntax type can be compared for ordering, equality, and substring matches. The attribute syntax is defined in two parts—*ASN.1 syntax* and *matching rules*.

Although a directory schema is usually extensible, the syntax list is often fixed when the base schema is developed. This means that although you can add new object types and extend existing objects by adding new attribute types to them, you may not be able to define a new type of syntax for the values contained within that attribute. If a wide variety of attribute syntaxes are already defined, however, this constraint may not be problematic.

Extending the Schema

X.500 directory schemata are easily extensible, allowing the integration of new objects and attributes into the directory as needed. The method used to extend the directory schema varies with the specific directory service implementation, yet most commercial directory implementations provide some sort of tools and APIs for schema extension.

Many directory-enabled applications will modify the schema as part of the installation process. This provides a method for implementation of specific objects to support extended application functionality.

Directory administrators who need to customize existing objects, or create new ones, can also perform schema modifications. This is a powerful capability because it provides a way to directly customize the directory contents to support new directory functionality.

Directory Information Base

X.500 specifies that the directory data is stored in a distributed Directory Information Base (DIB), which provides for replication of the directory datastore to reduce lookup latency and increase fault tolerance.

X.500 doesn't specify back-end storage methods, however, so vendors use many different approaches. In its simplest form, the DIB can be stored as sequential ASN.1 entries in a text file. On the other end of the spectrum, however, using a relational database (such as Oracle) for directory storage is not uncommon.

Naming Context

A *naming context* (*partition*) is a portion of the DIB that is stored and managed by a specific DSA. A naming context is a subtree of the directory with the metadata used by the DSA to place the naming context within the DIT. Multiple naming contexts are linked to form a large directory tree, collectively managed by multiple DSAs.

Removing Objects from the Schema

It is important to remember that removal of a class definition from the directory schema can have substantial consequences. Removing the class definition of an object that has been added to the schema, for example, will turn any objects of that class currently in the directory into unknown objects. This would have substantial ramifications for the performance of applications that rely on those objects, a factor that should be considered prior to removing schema extensions or restoring the original schema.

Note that certain directory repair operations can return the schema to its default configuration. In such a case, objects that belong to classes added via extensions to the basic schema will appear as unknown objects.

The complete contents of a naming context are as follows:

- The *subtree* of the directory containing the entries managed by this DSA (the set of objects and information contained within this partition of the DIB).
- The *context prefix* identifying the placement of this naming context in the tree.
- The *superior reference* identifying the DSA holding the parent naming context.
- The *subordinate reference(s)* pointing to any naming contexts that are children of this one.
- *Cross-references* are optional for any naming context.
- *Supplier/consumer references*, which are used for replication.

Replication in X.500

As discussed in previous chapters, *replication* is the copying of a partition, or subsection of the DIB, to another DSA; *synchronization*, on the other hand, is the process of keeping the contents of the DIB consistent.

This section briefly examines how X.500 approaches directory replication and synchronization, and is discussed from the organizing perspective of replication used in Chapter 3, "Storing Directory Information." This chapter also summarizes each key point of how X.500 defines replication. To review general information on directory replication and synchronization, refer to Chapter 3.

Root Context

There is no actual directory object representing the root of an X.500 directory tree—the root is a fictional node. Still, the directory must store information concerning the root of the directory tree to support name resolution and communication between DSAs at the top of the tree.

This information is held in the root context, which is not an actual directory object but rather a logical construct referring to the entries immediately subordinate to the root of the directory tree. These entries, which refer to one or more naming contexts, may be held by a single DSA or, frequently, distributed across multiple DSAs.

DSAs that hold naming contexts immediately subordinate to the root of the tree store cross-references to peer-level DSAs rather than a superior reference to the nonexistent tree root. By using these cross-references during the referral process, DSAs can locate entries held by other naming contexts. DSAs are not required to have a cross-reference entry for every peer-level naming context; however, all naming contexts must be reachable via a series of cross-references within the root context.

Replica Types

Replication for X.500-based directory services is explained in X.525, which describes the types of replicas and replication operations (referred to as *shadowing*):

- **Master**—The master replica in X.500 is referred to as the *master DSA*, which contains the writeable master copy of the data held within the naming context.
- **Shadow**—A shadow is a read-only copy of the naming context held by the master DSA. Only `Read`, `List`, `Search`, and `Compare` operations can be performed on a shadow DSA.
- **Cache**—Although X.525 describes caching, the details of caching are considered beyond the scope of X.525, and it does not attempt to define specific caching processes.

Each replica contains the naming context of a specific DSA.

Replication Strategy

X.500 defines a replication mechanism called *shadowing*, which operates on a single master model. Shadowing in X.500 uses a single master DSA that has administrative authority for the naming context and replicates changes to shadow DSAs. A shadow DSA is a read-only replica of the naming context held by the master DSA.

Replication Operations

The two forms of shadowing are called *primary* and *secondary* shadowing. As shown in Figure 4.15, *primary shadowing* is where the shadow consumer gets data directly from the master DSA. In *secondary shadowing*, a shadow consumer becomes a shadow supplier for other shadow consumers. In secondary shadowing, instead of receiving updates via the master DSA, the update comes from another shadow.

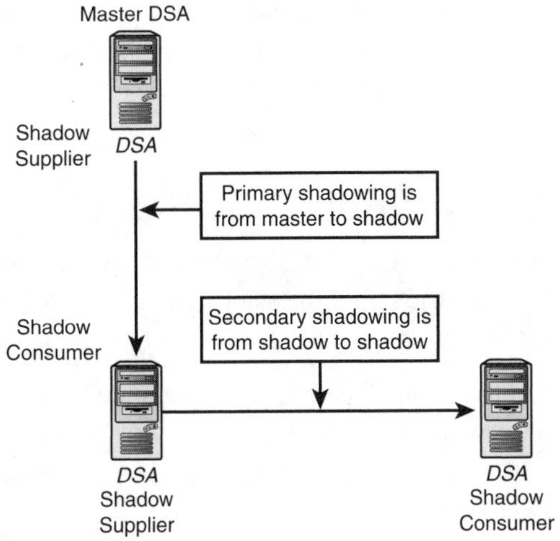

FIGURE 4.15

The difference between primary and secondary shadowing is the source of the data.

The key aspects of how X.525 defines replication can be viewed in the following summary:

- **Replication agreement**—Before shadowing can occur, a shadowing agreement must be established between DSAs. The shadow operational binding defines the DSA roles, and a shadowing agreement defines the update mode and unit of replication.
- **Roles**—Shadowing always operates between two specific DSAs that are assuming reciprocal shadowing roles, where a DSA is either a *shadow supplier* or a *shadow consumer*.
- **Replication dataset**—The replication dataset is derived by factoring the specified scope of the DIT to replicate, and the attributes selected for replication.
- **Scheduling replication**—The update mode specified in the shadowing agreement defines the update scheduling which sets the periodicity of the update refresh.
- **Total versus incremental**—Two methods of supplying shadow updates are defined. *Total refresh* is where all the contents of the naming context are copied from the shadow supplier to the shadow consumer. *Incremental refresh* is where only the contents of the naming context that have changed are copied.
- **Replication processes**—The X.525 specification describes both "push" and "pull" replication operations. Push replication is where the shadow supplier initiates the update to the shadow consumer. Pull replication is where the shadow consumer initiates the update.
- **Data consistency**—Time stamps are used to mark all directory changes, to maintain data integrity during synchronization of directory updates, providing consistency of information across all the directory servers.

X.500 Operations

X.500 operations revolve around DSAs that handle client queries and perform search operations on behalf of clients (and other DSAs). Core operations include authentication, object location, object manipulation, and searching the directory. In addition to the basic set of operations, directory operations can be enhanced to allow for further directory functionality using service controls and extensions.

Binding and Authentication Operations

For communication between a DUA and a DSA, they first have to agree to talk. A `DirectoryBind` operation (commonly called a `Bind`) is used to establish an *association* between a DUA and a DSA.

The `DirectoryBind` establishes an application-layer association between a DUA and a DSA, and is also used to perform authentication. Authentication can be done using simple or strong authentication (as per X.509), or via an external mechanism. To end the association, the DUA sends a `DirectoryUnbind` message to the DSA.

In addition to `DirectoryBind`, the `Compare` operation may also be used in authentication, by comparing the stored value of a particular attribute to a client-provided value. The intended use of `Compare` is as a mechanism for verifying passwords without retrieving the data.

Object Name Resolution

Every directory operation must start by locating the object or objects that are the focus of the operation. In a distributed directory, DSAs work together to determine the location of any object in the directory. This object location process is referred to as name resolution.

X.500 defines the methods used by a DSA to provide name resolution, specified as *chaining, referral, and multicasting*. The primary difference between these methods is which software agent is responsible for performing most of the work and verifying completion of the task. Both DUAs and DSAs should support all three modes of agent interaction, with the default being the referral style. DUAs may request a particular mode of operation, which can be accepted by the DSA or rejected in favor of the DSAs selected mode.

Chaining

When a DUA submits a query to the local DSA, it can request that the query be processed using chaining. A chaining request tells the DSA to provide the DUA with a complete response to the query (via all necessary DSAs) rather than only providing referrals for the DUA to pursue. If the server does not support chaining, it will override the client request and handle the request using the referral process.

In the chaining process, after a query has been submitted to a DSA, the DSA attempts to satisfy the query locally and, if necessary, passes the query to other DSAs. This process will be repeated by each receiving DSA until the entire scope of the directory operation has been explored and a definitive result for the originating query is obtained. The query may pass through many servers, collecting data at each one, before being able to access the entire scope of the directory query. At that point, the last DSA in the chain returns the query results back through the chain of DSAs to the originating DSA, which forwards them on to the DUA.

Chaining includes a mechanism to allow compilation of data from multiple sources, deletion of duplicate data, and transparent delivery of the results to the client. The results from multiple DSAs are compiled and returned to the DUA as if one DSA had provided all the returned data.

As shown in Figure 4.16, the chaining process is commonly conducted by a DSA on behalf of the DUA, and occurs in a sequence of directory operations.

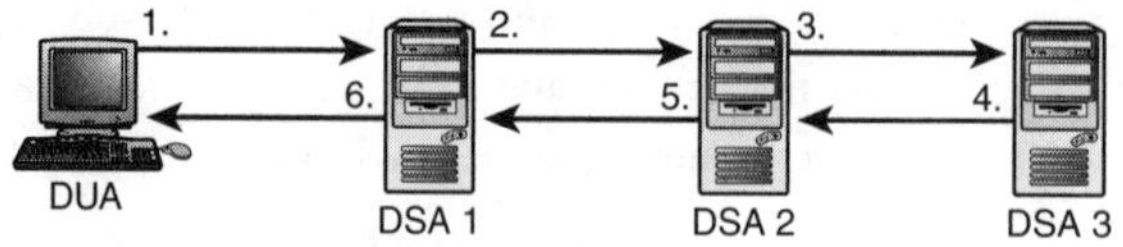

FIGURE 4.16

During the chaining process in query resolution, the DUA requests the DSA to return definitive results from all available DSAs.

The process is as follows:

1. The DUA sends a query to DSA 1.
2. DSA 1 doesn't have the object or the entire scope of the query, and sends the query to DSA 2.
3. DSA 2 also does not have the object or the entire scope, and sends the query to DSA 3.
4. DSA 3 completes the scope of the query, results are compiled, and returned to DSA 2.
5. DSA 2 compiles cumulative DSA results, and returns the results to DSA 1.
6. DSA 1 compiles cumulative DSA results, and returns the results to DUA.

Referrals

Referrals are a mechanism that requires the client to perform most of the work involved in a search and free up the DSA to service other client requests.

When a DSA cannot fulfill a query, it can provide referrals to other DSAs. When using referrals, after a DSA has attempted to fulfill a request from its portion of the DIB, it will return any results to the client. If the DSA cannot complete the request locally, it will also provide locations (or "hints" about possible locations) of other DSAs that may be able to fulfill the request. The client is then responsible for contacting other DSAs to satisfy the directory request, as the DSA will not try to contact the other DSAs for the DUA (see Figure 4.17).

As shown in Figure 4.17, the referral process occurs in the following sequence:

1. A DUA submits a query to DSA 1.
2. DSA 1 first tries to resolve the query within the local naming context. If the query can be resolved via the naming context held on DSA 1, the server returns the requested data. This example assumes that the query cannot be resolved locally, and that DSA 1 returns data (partial answers) as well as a reference to the closest relevant DSA (that is, DSA 2). The DUA will then use these DSAs to pursue the query.
3. The DUA sends the query to the DSA 2.
4. DSA 2 tries to resolve the query locally (and will return results if available). Again, this example assumes that the query is not resolved locally, and again DSA 2 may return data and references to other DSAs (that is, DSA 3).

5. The DUA sends the query to DSA 3.
6. DSA 3 successfully resolves the query and returns the query results to the DUA.

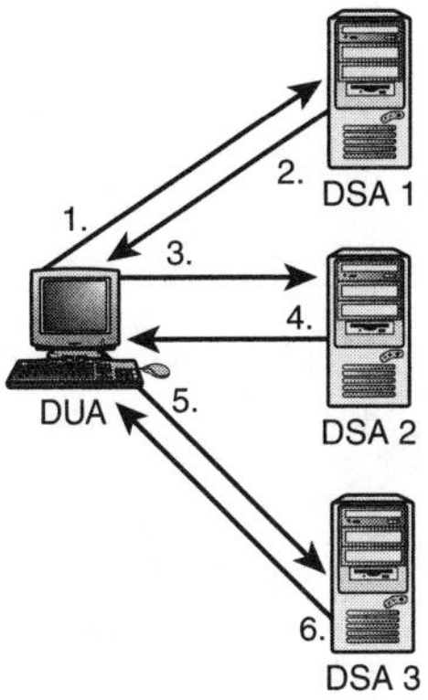

FIGURE 4.17

The referral process requests data that the DSA has available, yet does not request the DSA to pursue query resolution beyond the scope of the naming contexts held locally.

Multicasting

Multicasting occurs when a directory client simultaneously sends information to multiple DSAs. For example, the client DUAs using multicasting submit a single query to multiple DSAs at the same time. DSAs that can provide results do so; all others discard the query. Most current directory service products do not commonly employ multicasting.

Dereferencing Aliases

One aspect of X.500 operations is the capability to specify special handling options for aliases as part of the query process. An alias object is a pointer to another object located elsewhere in the directory. An alias is *not* the object it represents, and does not contain attributes of the referenced object (only attributes of the alias itself).

Sometimes, however, a directory query must locate the *aliased object* itself (not the alias). *Dereferencing* an alias is a process whereby the directory goes to the underlying object to which the alias is referring and continues the operation from there. The indication of whether to dereference aliases is specified as part of the query (if the operation supports it). Dereferencing is used by the following operations:

- **Read**—Aliases are always dereferenced.
- **List**—Aliases are not dereferenced by default, but can be on user request.
- **Search**—Aliases are not dereferenced by default, but can be on user request.

No other DAP operations support dereferencing, and as a result, you can perform actions such as `Add` and `Remove` on the alias itself.

An example alias, and how it might be processed during a search, should make this a bit clearer. This example uses the `devcontact` alias described earlier to demonstrate how the dereferencing process works. If a search that includes the `devcontact` object within its scope is requested, the DSA will handle the search operation differently depending on whether dereferencing is requested by the client.

In Figure 4.18, a DUA has requested a search of the entire DIT for all objects with a name starting with the letter *b*. The `devcontact` alias does not meet the search criteria, but `brynna`, the underlying object referenced by it, does.

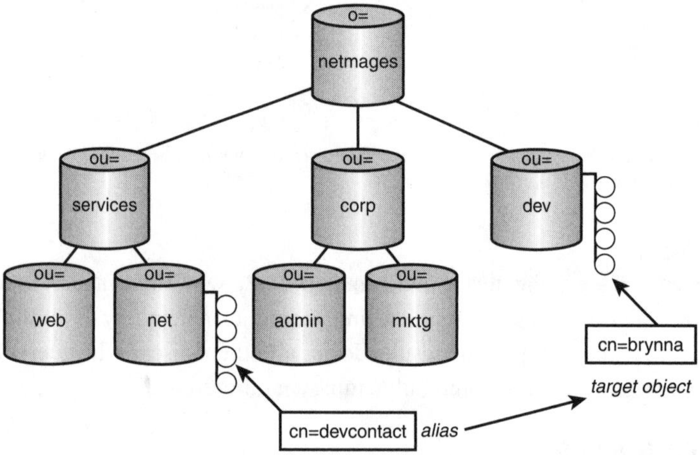

FIGURE 4.18

The actual information returned in response to a directory query varies depending on how aliases are handled.

Depending on whether the client requests alias dereferencing, one of two things will happen:

- If the object is *not* dereferenced during the search, the alias object `cn=devcontact` will be examined during the search. Because the alias name starts with *d*, it will not be returned as part of the search results.
- If the object *is* dereferenced during the search, the alias will be examined, and the referenced object name retrieved. The referenced object is then examined, and the information returned will refer to the aliased object `cn=brynna`. In this case, the object does match the search criteria and will be included in the query results.

Directory Access Operations

A set of operations can be performed on directory objects, including searching, adding, deleting, modifying, as well as other operations. The Directory Access Protocol (DAP) provides most of the commonly used directory operations. Table 4.4 displays the DAP operations for accessing directory objects.

TABLE 4.4 Directory Access Operations

Operation	*What This Operation Does*
`Read`	Reads information from a single directory entry, and enables you to specify a range of attributes to be returned.
`List`	Lists the contents of a single container (all subordinate entries). `List` is roughly analogous to a `dir` command in MS-DOS or `ls` in UNIX.
`AddEntry`	Creates a new directory object in the selected container. The object must meet schema restrictions to be created.
`ModifyEntry`	Changes the value of one or more attributes of a single directory entry. Attribute values may be added, deleted, or replaced by this function. The `ModifyEntry` operation is atomic, in that if all changes are not successfully completed, none of the changes are applied.
`RemoveEntry`	Deletes a single directory object, either a leaf or an *empty* container. Subtrees cannot be deleted using this operation.
`ModifyRDN`	Changes the RDN of an object.
`Search`	Searches can be performed on a single directory entry, a single container and its contents, or an entire subtree. Additional information contained in the search query defines the treatment of aliases and filters.
`Abandon`	Used in conjunction with other object operations to signal query termination. `Abandon` is sent by a client to tell the DSA to stop servicing an outstanding request, and can only be sent for operations that may involve multiple DSAs—`Read`, `List`, and `Search`. A DSA receiving an `Abandon` request ensures that no results are returned to the DUA. `Abandon` terminates a single operation only and does not close the association between the DSA and DUA.

Mechanisms in X.500 provide support for per-query constraints on operations called *service controls*, as well as *extensions* to the base set of operations. This capability may be used for directory enhancements ranging from special handling of query results to security measures. Service controls and extensions are invoked with parameters attached to the original DAP request.

A *service control* is a method of specifying constraining information for a single query. Service controls can be used to specify preferred modes of functionality or restrictions on how the DSA handles a particular request. Some of the things service controls can indicate include

- Selection of chaining or referrals
- Alias-handling preference
- Limits on time allowed for query completion
- Limitations on amount of data to be returned

Extensions allow the use of arguments to support new operations, and may be defined by either vendor or specification. Extensions rely on a prearranged agreement between the communicating directory components on the set of new operations, along with the methods used to invoke the functionality. Extensions can be designated as critical or noncritical by using the *criticality subcomponent.* If a request contains a critical extension unknown to the server, the query is not processed and an error code is returned to the client.

Security in X.500

Specifications for X.500 security models and operations are defined in multiple documents, most notably the X.500 and X.509 specifications.

In the X.500 security design, the directory is both a security provider as well as a user of the security services. As a security provider, the directory provides authentication and access control services to applications and other network services. As a consumer of security services, the directory uses authentication and access control over its objects.

Security permissions to access directory objects can be assigned on a very granular basis. Security descriptors can be assigned to an object and will remain with the object even if it is moved or renamed, which allows a high degree of flexibility in security administration.

As discussed earlier, in X.500 the Directory Administrative Authority Model is applied to security provisioning within the directory, where the DIT is divided into security divisions that directly parallel the administrative divisions. When viewed from a security management perspective:

- Each security subdivision, an Access Control Specific Area (ACSA), is an autonomous area of security, where access control data doesn't cross ACSA boundaries. An ACSA can be subdivided into multiple discrete ACSAs. The root of an ACSA is an Access Control Specific Point (ACSP).
- An Access Control Inner Administrative Area (ACIA) can be nested inside of an ACSA, providing for delegation of access control administration; each ACIA can contain nested ACIAs.

- The *security authority* is the specific administrative authority for the area.
- A Directory Access Control Domain (DACD) is an access control area subdivided by sets of directory entries.

Authentication and access control mechanisms are applied within the ASCA or ACIA. The access control policies that will be applied are contained in access control lists, which are subentries attached to the administrative point. The access by a DUA to any specific directory object is controlled by the entire set of permissions specified in the chain of superior Access Control Inner Points (ACIP), up to and including the first ACSP or Autonomous Administrative Point (AAP).

Authentication

Before a directory can allow a user to access or manipulate an object, it needs to validate the user's identity. The directory uses the *authentication* process, which is the set of operations that verify the user identification.

The X.509 specification documents a framework for authentication in a directory service and defines three security services: *simple authentication*, *strong authentication*, and *digital signatures*.

Both simple and strong methods of user authentication provide the basic functionality of authenticating the user to the directory. The following sections discuss these in more detail. First, however, it's important to review the basic differences between the cryptographic approaches used in the authentication methods.

Approaches to Cryptography

X.509 describes the two cryptographic methods used in the authentication process—either symmetric or asymmetric cryptography. Although simple authentication provides basic user identification, the symmetric cryptographic methods used in this authentication process are not considered secure. The X.509 specification is clearly focused on the use of asymmetric public key cryptographic methods and certificates for strong authentication. Approaches are

- **Symmetric cryptography**—With *symmetric* (also called *shared-secret* or *private-key*) cryptography, the sender and receiver share the same key. In symmetric cryptography, the user provides the secret key that is stored and used to authenticate that user in subsequent processes. A common example of this cryptographic approach is the password that users supply to authenticate to the directory.
- **Asymmetric cryptography**—*Asymmetric* (or *public-key*) cryptography uses pairs of keys (public/private) to encrypt information. These keys may also be *permutable*—in some asymmetric encryption methods, either key in the pair can be used to encrypt the message contents, and the other key can be used to decrypt the contents.

Simple Authentication

In the simple authentication process, the directory uses clear text names and passwords to verify the identity of its users. Simple authentication may use `Bind` or `Compare` operations, in which the submitted name and password are checked against the directory contents, but the name and password are not encrypted. Simple authentication processes are characterized by DSAs that store DN/password pairs, and DUAs that transfer username and password in clear text. There are two derivations of simple authentication:

- **Protected password**—Protected password authentication transfers the name in clear text, but the password is encrypted via a one-way hash function.
- **Mutual authentication**—Both the simple and protected password methods involve a one-way authentication process where the DUA authenticates to the DSA. In mutual authentication, the DSA returns its credentials with the results of the DUA's authentication request, and is also authenticated by the client. This ensures that the client can trust the DSA.

Strong Authentication

Strong authentication uses *public key (PK)* cryptography to produce security credentials, providing controlled access to the directory. Because it uses PK encryption, strong authentication is considered far more secure for transmission of sensitive data.

Public keys are stored in the directory so as to be accessible to applications, users, and directory operations. For users to access other public keys, the DUA must trust the DSA providing the public key.

Strong authentication uses a point-to-point scheme with a chain of trust between DSAs. An example of a chain of trust is where a DUA trusts a specific DSA (DSA 1), and that DSA trusts another DSA (DSA 2), and as a result the DUA will trust DSA 2.

Authentication takes place when an association between DSA and DUA is established. In strong authentication, the user credentials are established via the user's public key, by one of three different methods:

- **One-way exchange**—The sender provides explicit validation, but only implicitly validates the receiver.
- **Two-way exchange**—This is the same as a one-way exchange, but the receiver sends back a reply token explicitly confirming the identity of the receiver.
- **Three-way exchange**—In addition to the two-way communication, a third exchange is used for synchronization between the DUA and DSA.

Although X.509 does not specify an encryption algorithm, it does require permutable public-key encryption algorithms be used. An example is the RSA algorithm (named after Rivest, Shamir, and Adleman, 1978).

Access Control

Besides verifying the identity of the directory user, you also need to be able to control access to directory elements based on that identification. *Access control* mechanisms are used to provide differential levels of access to directory objects and operations, and directory data is available only when a DUA has access permissions.

The initial X.500 specifications described two models for providing this differential access control:

- **Basic Access Control**—X.500 specifies a basic access control model that defines entry access and attribute access permissions, and the use of these permissions to control categories of directory operations (such as `Add`, `Read`, and so on). Application of permissions is segregated via access control administrative areas.
- **Simplified Access Control**—Simplified access control is functionally a subset of the basic access control scheme. Simplified access control does not support ACIAs.

Basic Access Control Model

The *basic access control* (BAC) model describes mechanisms for controlling access to the contents of the directory. The BAC model defines a set of access control components and categories of access types.

The initial X.500 specifications defined *access control schemes* for managing access to directory information. An access control scheme is set as an operational attribute, and defines the procedures to specify the access control information and to manage access control operations. The BAC model specifies access control information controlling user access to protected items in the directory via assigned object permissions, including

- **Objects to be protected**—A *protected item* is any directory element that can be individually controlled (that is, names, entries, attributes, and values).
- **Access control information**—The *access control information* (ACI) is the data stored with each protected item in the directory that is used to determine which users are granted access, and what kind of access is granted. *ACI items* are the operational attributes that collectively control access to protected items in the directory. All ACI items have a range of priority called *precedence*, where higher-precedent ACIs overrule lower-precedent ACIs. Each ACI item also has an *authentication level* value indicating the type of DUA authentication required. A group of ACI items implemented as a set is known as a *security policy*.
- **Distinct classes of users**—*User classes* distinguish different categories of directory users, and the DUA initiating the operation is described as the *requestor.*

- **Permissions to access objects**—*Permissions* can be thought of as the right to complete an operation, and are stored with directory objects as ACI items. Permissions are divided into categories by type of access (*entry* or *attribute*) and are applied to directory elements to control access. An *Access Control List* (ACL) contains sets of ACI items used to specify the user classes and types of access assigned to a directory object. Because directory operations need to make programmatic access control decisions regarding protected items, the *Access Control Decision Function* (ACDF) is the algorithm used to determine access. The access control decisions are processed by the ACDF algorithm, which determines whether to *grant* or *deny* access based on the content of the ACI items of both the object and client.

Access Control Permissions

In this model, access control types are subdivided into *entry access* and *attribute access* categories:

- **Entry access**—Entry access is when the access to the directory entry is as a named object.
- **Attribute access**—Attribute access is when the access is to the attributes, or to the attribute values (containing operational and/or user data).

The two categories of permissions correspond to their related forms of access control, *entry access permissions* and *attribute access permissions.* In the BAC model, access to the directory information is regulated by the DSA granting or denying permissions to the requested object. Access to data in the directory is effectively controlled by the permissions assigned to the directory entry or attribute, and the permissions of the requestor attempting to access it.

Entry Access Permissions

The following entry access permissions apply to objects (entries) within the directory, as shown in Table 4.5.

TABLE 4.5 Entry Access Permissions

Permissions	*These Permissions Allow*
`Read`	Read access to specifically named objects
`Browse`	Access to operations using non-explicit names
`Add`	Creation of a new directory object
`Remove`	Removal of a directory object
`Modify`	The contents of an object to be changed
`Rename`	The renaming of a directory object
`Disclose on Error`	The object name to be disclosed upon error
`Export`	An object to be moved out of the present location to a new location in the directory

TABLE 4.5 Continued

Permissions	*These Permissions Allow*
`Import`	An object (and subordinates) in another location to be moved into the present location
`ReturnDN`	The DN to be returned as the result of a directory operation

Attribute and Value Access Permissions

Table 4.6 shows the attribute access permissions that apply to attributes and values within the directory.

TABLE 4.6 Attribute and Value Access Permissions

Permissions	*These Permissions Allow*
`Compare`	Operations to be compared to the values or attributes the permissions are applied to
`Read` tions	Values or attributes to be provided in search or read opera-
`FilterMatch`	Filter processing with applied search parameters
`Add`	Creation of a new attribute (or attributes), or allows the creation of a new value (or values)
`Remove`	Removal of an attribute or value
`Disclose on Error`	Attribute or value to be disclosed upon error

Access Control Precedence

ACI items are evaluated based on precedence, where higher-precedence ACI items override lower-precedence ACI items. This effectively allows a "weighted value" to be assigned to each ACI item, providing a method to implement an access rights hierarchy.

> **Access Control Constraints Vary**
>
> Not all directory operations share the same access control constraints. For example, some directory operations require that all access control decisions succeed for the operation to succeed. In contrast, other directory operations do not require that all access control decisions be successful for the operation to be completed.

The precedence of ACI items is a value between 0 and 255 that is applied to all ACI items. This allows ACI items to be evaluated along an axis of precedence. In brief, the rules of precedence are as follows:

- High-precedence ACI items override lower-precedence ACI items.
- If multiple ACI items have the same precedence, but dissonant access permissions (granted and denied), denied access overrides granted access.

Rule-Based Access Control

Besides Basic Access Control and Simplified Access Control, later revisions (1993) of the X.500 specifications include a *rule-based* access control model. The rule-based model focuses on access control decisions and regulates directory access via user *clearances* and *security labels* on directory objects. Rule-based access control applies rules of the security policy, denying or granting access based on congruency between security labels and clearance. The rule-based model determines access control by comparing the security labels and clearance values in the access control decisions of each operation.

A security label is access control information that is linked to an attribute value (via a security label context). Security labels are properties of attribute values, and are bound to the values of attributes via a digital signature or other security mechanism. A security label is a single-valued context, allowing only one security label to be associated with the attribute value.

In rule-based access control, the clearance of a user (rather than the identity of the user) is what determines whether access to attribute values is denied or granted. A clearance is access control information linked with the user requesting a directory operation. A clearance is bound to a user's DN via a certificate extension field or attribute certificate, and is compared against a security label of an attribute to determine access. A named entity (such as a DUA) is linked with a clearance via a *clearance attribute*. A clearance attribute has the following components:

- **`policyId`**—Identifies the security policy that the `securityCategories` and `classList` relate to.
- **`classList`**—List classifications (`unmarked`, `unclassified`, `restricted`, `confidential`, `secret`, `topSecret`).
- **`securityCategories`**—Defines other restrictions in the `classList` context.

A *security policy* (applied to the ACSA) describes how security labels enforce the policy. The security policy defines the security rules to be used in making access control decisions. The performing of directory operations requires making access control decisions for each attribute value accessed. The access control decision function uses the security policy rules to determine authorization for access based on the clearance of the requestor and the security label applied to the attribute value. With rule-based access control, access denial crosses operations—when access is denied by rule-based access control to all attribute values of a directory entry or attribute, access is denied for all operations to that entry or attribute.

Both rule-based access control and basic access control may be used in combination, and may be applied in any order. Yet if access is denied via either access control mechanism to an entry, attribute, or attribute value, it cannot be granted via the other mechanism.

Digital Signatures

Digital signatures are a means to verify that transmitted information was validly received, and to confirm the identity of the sender. A digital signature is essentially a summary of the data produced by a one-way hash function encrypted with the sender's public key.

Digital signatures provide the following functionality:

- **Message integrity**—Ensures that the data didn't change in transmission (via comparison of hash values).
- **Message authentication**—Verifies the source of the data (via the public key).

A quick review of the basics of how digital signatures are created might help you to better understand them. The phrases "signing the data" and the data is "signed" refer to the process of creating an encrypted summation of the specific set of data (the message) and appending the encrypted value to the data. The data is signed in the following three-step process:

1. Data is hashed (mathematically represented).
2. Hash value is encrypted with the sender's public key.
3. Encrypted hash is appended to the data.

The encrypted hash value is referred to as the *digital signature*. The sender and receiver agree on the specific hash algorithm prior to transmission.

Next, it's important to briefly examine how a digital signature is used to verify message contents and authentication. Digital signatures are used to validate the integrity of the transmission of the data across the network. Note that this ensures data integrity only (that is, proving that the data is unchanged); it does not encrypt or protect the data during transmission.

The following process describes the common steps of how a digital signature is used:

1. The data (unencrypted) and the digital signature are transmitted.
2. The data and signature are received and separated.
3. The digital signature is unencrypted using the sender's public key, and the hash algorithm is determined.
4. The receiver rehashes the (unencrypted) data.
5. The receiver compares its generated hash value to the hash value transmitted by the sender.
6. If hash values are the same, the message is considered authenticated; otherwise, the data is rejected.

X.509 Certificates

The X.509 standards define certificates based on public key (PK) technology, also referred to as *asymmetric cryptography*. To encrypt and decrypt data, PK cryptography uses a key pair comprised of a published *public key* and a secret *private key*. Key pairs are implemented in such a way that any messages encoded with either key may be decoded only by the other key (referred to as *permutability*).

The certified public keys are contained in certificates. A *certificate* is essentially a collection of data that associates the public key of a directory user with their DN in the directory, and is stored within the directory as an attribute of their user object. A certificate serves as validated identification to the directory.

Directory services use certificates to provide client authentication, where the identity of the network client is established by examining the certificate provided. This provides bilateral authentication—the directory provides validation while receiving the client validation. When authentication is performed, DAP is used to access the directory to obtain the public key certificates, and DSP is used to access certificate data when communicating with another DSA to complete the authentication.

In a public key encryption methodology, the user works with a *Certificate Authority* (CA) to create a certificate that validates the user's private and public keys. The CA is used to generate and validate CA certificates, user certificates, as well as server certificates. For more information on certificates or CAs, check out the VeriSign site at `www.verisign.com`.

X.500 defines a generic model for the design of a distributed directory services. While the standards were written based on assumptions of the underlying OSI networking model and protocols, the current directory implementations are commonly built around TCP/IP networks. For example, the Lightweight Directory Access Protocol is based on TCP/IP, and has become the industry standard protocol for directory access and interoperability. The next chapter describes LDAP in detail, highlighting its design and functionality in directory operations.

LDAP: Lightweight Directory Access Protocol

CHAPTER

5

...leveraging is the sincerest form of flattery...

IN THIS CHAPTER

Although X.500 provided the most widely adopted directory service model, the access protocol defined by the X.500 standards has not been widely implemented in readily available clients. In recent years, Directory Access Protocol (DAP) has been supplemented, and in some cases replaced, by the *Lightweight Directory Access Protocol (LDAP)*. LDAP has become the access protocol of choice for many directory vendors and has helped accelerate directory development efforts.

This chapter examines LDAP in some detail. This chapter relies on information contained in Chapter 4, "X.500: A Model for Directory Services," and assumes an understanding of the general structure and operations of X.500. If you're not familiar with X.500, you may want to read Chapter 4 before reading this chapter.

Introduction to LDAP

LDAP is a dedicated client access protocol for communicating with a directory and viewing or manipulating the objects contained within the directory. LDAP was designed as a simplified subset of the X.500 DAP to provide basic access to X.500-based directories. LDAP was originally targeted at management and browser applications that provide interactive access to directories. LDAP can be implemented as a protocol to access X.500 (or proprietary) directories or as the foundation for a standalone server.

A key goal of the initial LDAP design was to minimize the complexity of the access protocol to encourage widespread implementation of directory-enabled applications. As such, it succeeded admirably. LDAP is now considered the de facto standard directory access protocol and has been adopted as an open standard for directory services. Most vendors offering directory services have released, or announced plans for, directory products that support LDAP v.3, including Microsoft, Novell, and the Netscape|Sun Alliance.

Request for Comments

You should keep in mind that the LDAP specification is contained within a series of *Request for Comments* (RFC) documents. RFCs are the end result of the process by which open standards to be used on the Internet are defined. Proposed standards are first written as *drafts*, and then enter an open review process during which different people advocate for divergent versions of the proposed RFC.

Some RFCs, including the LDAP ones, define a minimal level of expected functionality as well as suggestions for an enhancements—labeled as mandatory and optional. Accordingly, some portions of the LDAP specifications are mandatory for implementation; others are recommended or totally optional.

Many vendors of directory services and related product are represented in the *Internet Engineering Task Force* (IETF) working groups that are continuing to develop LDAP. As you can imagine, this means that although quite a bit of agreement occurs among vendors as to core aspects of LDAP, it is still a little less "standardized" than some standards. Novell is working on one set of LDAP replication methods, for example, and Microsoft is working on another; they may both be accepted as standards in the future. If this happens, although both vendors would comply with "LDAP standards," the standards they comply with would still differ.

LDAP Standardization Efforts

There are organizations, both official and informal, working on LDAP standardization and compliance issues. These groups are focused on consolidating information resources for administrators, facilitating application development efforts, and encouraging corporate adoption of LDAP. The Open Group, for example, has created the "LDAP Works 2000" branding campaign to identify directory servers and applications that are fully LDAP v.3 compliant, enabling the selection of LDAP products with confidence they will work together. The LDAP section of Appendix A "References" has the URLs of several groups that are devoted to furthering the development and adoption of LDAP.

Features of LDAP

Although the X.500 specifications defined a powerful data model and protocols to support a robust directory, the original DAP described in the X.500 specifications has had somewhat limited acceptance. LDAP has been designed to compensate for the perceived disadvantages of DAP while leveraging the strengths of the overall X.500 directory design.

LDAP offers a number of features that have contributed to its widespread adoption including:

- Lower Overhead
- TCP/IP Based
- Can Use DNS for Global Namespace
- Widely Accepted APIs

Taken as a set, and placed in the context of the Internet, these aspects of LDAP combine to offer a powerful yet easily accessible interface to directories.

Lower Overhead

The X.500 specified DAP operates at the application layer level of the *Open System Interconnect* (OSI) stack, mandating a considerable amount of processing for each interaction between the directory client and server. By comparison, LDAP maps its messages directly onto the TCP byte stream, bypassing much of the handling required by DAP (newer versions of DAP also map directly to TCP). In addition, *Connectionless LDAP* (CLDAP) has been defined to provide some of the functionality of LDAP over a connectionless protocol, in this case User Datagram Protocol (UDP).

TCP/IP Based

The X.500 design focused on the directory service being comprised of many Directory System Agents (DSAs), connected via OSI-defined networking protocols. With the explosion of Internet usage and the concurrent demand for TCP/IP support in almost every networking environment, the TCP/IP protocol has emerged as the clear enterprise networking protocol of choice, while the OSI protocols have fallen out of favor.

Accordingly, the decision to design LDAP predicated on using TCP/IP has proven to be a wise one. Most networks run the TCP/IP protocol stack, if not because it is required by the network operating system, then at least for Internet connectivity purposes. Because of LDAP's dependency on TCP/IP, LDAP operates only on networks employing TCP/IP as a protocol.

What Is an LDAP DSA?

Many different types of directory servers, such as X.500, eDirectory, and Active Directory, as well as LDAP-only servers, can be accessed by LDAP clients. In this chapter, "LDAP DSA" means any directory server that is being accessed by an LDAP client. See Chapter 8, "LDAP-Only Directory Services," for a more in-depth discussion of LDAP-only servers.

Can Use DNS for Global Namespace

Another assumption of X.500 was the establishment of a widely accepted and utilized global namespace. This worldwide X.500 directory tree requires an assigned authority to manage the top level of the tree, both within each country and internationally. Although some companies currently using X.500-based directories choose to have a corporate presence registered in the worldwide X.500 tree, not all have chosen to do so.

Yet, there is currently a worldwide namespace in widespread use and supported on virtually every platform: the *Domain Name System* (DNS). Again, the designers of LDAP have made a wise decision to employ widely implemented Internet technologies and have begun to define methods by which LDAP can use DNS. This allows LDAP to leverage the worldwide use of DNS as the top layer of its directories, obviating the need for an additional set of registrars and namespaces.

Two primary methods of LDAP and DNS integration have been proposed:

- A DNS service (SRV) record entry provides a way of locating LDAP servers. This allows clients to query their local DNS server as a means of locating an LDAP directory server.
- LDAP is also incorporating DNS name components as part of LDAP names. This means that the DNS domain "`mythical.org`" could be given an LDAP name of "`dc=mythical, dc=org`" providing congruence between an organization's directory tree and its DNS domain tree.

Because the RFCs that define these integration methods are not a part of the core LDAP v.3 specifications, it is important to note that all vendors will not necessarily support all the DNS/LDAP integration proposals. The integration of DNS and LDAP is discussed in more depth in the "LDAP Naming" section of this chapter.

Using DNS as a Locater for LDAP Directories

One benefit of creating a directory tree with a root that is congruent with a DNS domain is the ability to use standard DNS queries to locate directory servers. The exact means of implementing this functionality is, of course, dependent on the vendor. eDirectory, for example, can locate external eDirectory trees that are rooted at a DNS domain using regular DNS lookups and seamlessly switch back to eDirectory protocols once a directory server for the secondary tree has been contacted. Active Directory, by comparison, requires that all trees be rooted at a DNS domain but uses DNS service (SRV) records to locate Active Directory servers.

Widely Accepted APIs

LDAP provides APIs that are easy for programmers to write to and are widely supported by vendors. The need for a widely accepted API was initially addressed with the adoption of the LDAP C API (RFC 1823). RFC 1823 defines a simple method of interacting with an LDAP directory using the C programming language. Since then, several more APIs have been proposed either as an open standard, or via proprietary methods. The "LDAP Programming" section of this chapter discusses the current state of LDAP APIs.

The Evolution of LDAP

The *International Standards Organization Development Environment* (ISODE) Consortium at the University of Michigan designed LDAP v.2 as a lightweight protocol replacement for DAP as specified in X.500. The LDAP v.2 protocol was published in March 1995 as RFC 1777, making RFC 1487 (LDAP v.1) obsolete. LDAP v.2 defined a small set of simple, yet powerful, operations and provided a common starting point for the much broader design of LDAP v.3. Common programming language API support was provided when the LDAP C API was specified in August 1995 in RFC 1823.

The Internet Engineering Task Force accepted the core set of LDAP v.3 protocols in December 1997. Although these RFCs serve as the basis for LDAP v.3-compliant implementations, they do not address all areas of directory functionality. The portions of LDAP that have been agreed on and published as RFCs include the basic protocol structure and operations, a minimal schema, and definitions of LDAP names and search filters. Table 5.1 lists the RFCs that form the base of LDAP v.3.

TABLE 5.1 The Core LDAP v.3 RFCs

RFC Number	*Name*
2251	Lightweight Directory Access Protocol (v.3)
2252	Lightweight Directory Access Protocol (v.3): Attribute Syntax Definitions
2253	Lightweight Directory Access Protocol (v.3):UTF-8 String Representation of Distinguished Names
2254	The String Representation of LDAP Search Filters
2255	The LDAP URL Format
2256	A Summary of the X.500 (96) User Schema for use with LDAP v.3
2829	Authentication Methods for LDAP
2830	Lightweight Directory Access Protocol (v3): Extension for Transport Layer Security
2831	Using Digest Authentication as a SASL Mechanism

Much like the 1993 extensions to X.500 broadened the scope of the defined directory design and operations, LDAP v.3 expands on the very simple LDAP v.2 base. In fact, the expansion of LDAP in many ways mirrors the 1993 X.500 extensions:

- LDAP v.3 fully supports all LDAP v.2 protocol elements.
- A data model that encompasses many aspects of the multiple X.500 information models has been introduced.
- Support has also been added for referrals, schema and security enhancements, and operational attributes.

All Versions of LDAP v.3 Are Not the Same

By design, each time LDAP is modified by any means other than extension, the newly modified version will be assigned a new version number. This version information will be sent to a client when a `Bind` operation is performed.

Some of the more important aspects of LDAP v.3 are

- **Referrals**—LDAP v.3 is enhanced to provide support for referrals as a mechanism of resolving directory queries for data not contained in the local copy of the DIB.
- **Schema publishing**—The schema for an LDAP v.3-compliant directory is contained in the directory as a series of objects, providing easy access to the schema entries for modification or extension.
- **Subschema**—Another significant improvement to LDAP v.3 is the capability to use subschemas to support different schemas for subtrees within a directory tree and facilitate the exchange of information with other directories.
- **Extensible operations**—LDAP v.3 provides a mechanism for extending many aspects of the directory, including directory operations.
- **Improved security**—LDAP v.3 supports the *Simple Authentication and Security Layer (SASL)*, *Secure Sockets Layer (SSL)*, and *Transport Layer Security (TLS)*. These changes address a major deficiency of LDAP v.2: security mechanisms that were limited to plain text and Kerberos 4 authentication.
- **Internationalization**—Another enhancement to LDAP v.3 is Unicode support, which allows text to be represented in virtually any language. Distinguished names and attribute values use the ISO 10646 character set.

The published RFCs are the basis for LDAP v.3 implementations, but they do not address some key areas of directory functionality. Because of this, work is ongoing on a variety of LDAP extensions, from schema extensions to replication strategies.

In addition, vendors are releasing directory servers based on LDAP, with a lot of proprietary features and functionality on the back end, inevitably limiting interoperability. In more than a few instances these vendors are then offering their proprietary LDAP enhancements as proposed RFCs to be added to the core LDAP specifications, something which may eventually help ease the interoperability issues.

IETF LDAP Working Groups

The IETF has three working groups that are continuing to develop LDAP:

- LDAP (v3) Revision (ladpbis) works on keeping the core LDAP v.3 RFCs up-to-date.
- LDAP Extension (ldapext) defines extensions to LDAP such as security, server location, and APIs.
- LDAP Duplication/Replication/Update Protocols (ldup) is working on defining a framework and methods for managing replication.

How far the expansion of the LDAP standards will go is still up in the air, yet it is clear that LDAP is being asked to be much more than just an access protocol. The ongoing work on standards seems destined to cover much of the same territory as X.500, perhaps eventually specifying much of the functionality required of a full-fledged distributed directory service. This has led some members of the LDAP community to comment that perhaps Lightweight DAP should be renamed *Heavyweight* DAP.

Some of the more important directions for the future of LDAP are discussed in the "Proposed LDAP Extensions" section at the end of this chapter.

LDAP v.2 Is Still Being Enhanced

Interestingly enough, even though LDAP v.3 has been an accepted standard for some time now (the core LDAP RFCs were accepted in 1997), LDAP v.2 is still being improved. Two proposed standards to support public key security have been released as the following RFCs:

- RFC 2559 "Internet X.509 Public Key Infrastructure Operational Protocols — LDAP v.2"
- RFC 2587 "Internet X.509 Public Key Infrastructure LDAP v.2 Schema" (June 1999)

LDAP Models

Like X.500, LDAP includes models that describe individual aspects of LDAP structure and operations. Because LDAP was designed to support DAP (and thus X.500-compliant) operations, as you might expect, these models cover areas somewhat similar to the X.500 models. The models describing the two basic LDAP perspectives are

- The Data Model
- The Protocol Model

The following sections examine each of these models.

Data Model

The LDAP Data Model essentially combines most of the significant elements of the X.500 information models to describe the structure and contents of the LDAP directory. The Data Model defines the object set used by the directory as well as how those objects will be organized. The LDAP Data Model includes the entire directory schema, including both user and operational attributes and other information.

The structure of object class definitions is basically the same as in X.500. Directory objects are comprised of attributes that are either required or optional for the object class. Attributes can contain one or more data values, each of which is of a designated syntax type. The syntax type definition constrains the data type of the attribute value.

The Data Model also defines how information contained in the directory is named and organized. The LDAP naming structure roughly corresponds to the X.500 naming model, with each object having a *Relative Distinguished Name* (RDN) and the RDNs being concatenated into a *Distinguished Name* (DN) to uniquely identify each object in the tree.

An LDAP DN is constructed in *reverse* order from an X.500 DN, however, with the leafmost object first. This means that if the X.500 name of an object is `cn=jo, ou=corp, o=netmages`, the LDAP DN for the same object is `o=netmages, ou=corp, cn=jo`. The method of translating an X.500 name string to an LDAP DN is defined in RFC 2253.

As in X.500, *entries* are organized into a *Directory Information Tree* (DIT), which may be subdivided into multiple naming contexts and distributed to multiple directory servers. Each of these naming contexts (partitions) is written into a portion of the DIB called a *replica*. More than one server may hold a replica of a particular naming context, and the replicas may be of the master, shadow, or cache type.

Protocol Model

The Protocol Model defines LDAP query and update operations. LDAP assumes a client/server model, where directory clients perform protocol operations (queries and so on) against directory servers. In this model, the LDAP client transmits a request for a directory operation to a server which performs the necessary operation on the specified directory objects and returns a response to the client. Client/server communications in LDAP are *asynchronous*, meaning that multiple client requests can be sent while the results from earlier requests are still pending.

A directory server that supports LDAP operations will normally listen on port 389, the designated standard port for LDAP communications—LDAP over SSL uses port 636. Specific implementations may use additional ports for communication, allowing the network administrator to designate the ports selected for use. This allows the use of nonstandard ports with proxy servers, for security or other purposes.

The LDAP Protocol Model specifies operations to perform basic directory functions, including create, delete, modify, rename, or query a directory entry.

The Protocol Model also defines the methods by which DSAs handle requests for directory objects that are outside the scope of their naming context. LDAP v.2 only provided support for chaining as a means for a directory server to resolve requests for directory operations on objects it does not hold. LDAP v.2 does not actually *perform* chaining operations; because it was designed to front-end X.500 directories, it relies on the underlying X.500 directory's chaining functionality. Referrals, which require more processing on the part of the client, were added to LDAP in v.3.

The "LDAP Operations" section of this chapter takes a look at LDAP protocol operations in more detail.

The LDAP Directory Objects and Schema

As you might expect, the LDAP schema is highly similar to the X.500 schema. Two RFCs combine to provide the basic schema for LDAP directories:

- **A Summary of the X.500 (96) User Schema for use with LDAPv3** (RFC 2256) lists the minimum set of X.500 objects an LDAP v.3 server should support. It draws on the X.500 standards X.501, X.509, X.520, and X.521 as the basis for its definitions.
- **Lightweight Directory Access Protocol (v3): Attribute Syntax Definitions** (RFC 2252) defines additional *LDAP-specific* objects, attributes, syntax, and matching rules that should also be supported.

As with X.500, the schema designed for LDAP clearly indicates vendors are expected to expand the base schema as needed to support their specific directory implementations. Further IETF draft documents can be written to define additions to the schema. Since the adoption of LDAP v.3, a number of draft proposals for LDAP schema additions have been written, and it is expected that many of these will be adopted over time.

The schema for an LDAP v.3 directory is published in the directory instead of being stored in a text file as in earlier directory implementations. Each schema entry (object, attribute, and so on) has a corresponding directory object in a special container object within the root *DSA Specific Entry* (DSE). Schema publishing allows easy access to all schema entries for modification or extension. Changes to the schema can be sent to other DSAs using the directory's usual methods for updating replicas.

LDAP Directory Objects

Because LDAP was initially designed to operate as a replacement for DAP in an X.500 directory service, the X.500 schema forms the base for the LDAP object set. The actual requirements for LDAP schema contents are rather minimal, however. LDAP servers are *required* to support only two objects: `top` and `subschema`. Neither of these objects is structural; they are used internally by the directory.

It is recommended (although not mandated) that LDAP servers support 21 additional X.500 structural objects, essentially the base X.500 schema. The structural objects defined in X.521, along with the `alias` object, form the suggested LDAP schema. The recommended LDAP schema consists of the same entries as those listed in the "Objects" section of Chapter 4.

LDAP v.3 defines two additional object classes for use by servers: `subschema` and `extensibleObject`. As mentioned earlier, support for the `subschema` object is mandatory, while the `extensibleObject` is optional. The following sections take a brief look at each of these objects to show how they fit in the LDAP schema.

The `subschema` Object

One of the major improvements in LDAP v.3 is the incorporation of mechanisms that allow directories with different schemas to communicate more effectively. While X.500 uses operational attributes to support subschemas, LDAP uses the `subschema` object to accomplish the same thing. Each directory subtree has a single `subschema` entry containing the schema definition for that portion of the directory tree.

By using `subschema` entries, the directory can define schema information for a subtree and exchange this schema information with other directories. This exchange of schema information takes place before any information about objects in the directory is exchanged. If a server holds a writeable replica, it is required to provide access to `subschema` entries. Clients use these entries when querying the directory for the list of supported objects, attributes, and syntax.

The `subschema` object is an auxiliary object and has seven attributes:

- `objectClasses`
- `attributeTypes`
- `dITStructureRules`
- `nameForms`
- `dITContentRules`
- `matchingRules`
- `matchingRuleUse`

Each of these attributes is multivalued, listing all the classes, attributes, and so on supported by a DSA. The objectClasses and attributeTypes attributes are mandatory because they define critical aspects of the schema contents. The other attributes are optional and can be used to provide additional information regarding the schema description, tree structure, and directory operations.

The extensibleObject Class

The extensibleObject class is an auxiliary class that adds *every* attribute in the schema to the mayContain list (that is, the list of the attributes an object may contain) of the object it is added to. Because there are likely to be hundreds of attributes defined in a directory schema, the extensibleObject does not actually have every attribute in the schema listed in the mayContain list of its class definition. The additional attributes are *implicitly* added as a function of assigning this auxiliary class to an existing object.

Adding this class to a class definition has no effect on attributes already defined as mandatory for the object class. Any attribute that is mandatory for the object class prior to the extensibleObject being added will still be mandatory after the extensibleObject definition is added to it.

It is important to note that not all LDAP servers support this object class. Any LDAP server that does not support the extensibleObject class will refuse to add entries that contain it as an auxiliary class.

In addition to the classes defined in the relevant RFCs, vendors and developers may decide that they need additional objects. LDAP allows for schema extensions, whether by vendors of commercial products or by developers and administrators in an enterprise.

Additional objects may be supported as long as the following conditions are met:

- Class definitions must not conflict with existing LDAP RFCs.
- Class definitions must be published in the subschema entry.

The Root "Object"

As mentioned during the discussion of X.500, the root of the DIT is not an actual object, but rather a DSE held by each server holding a naming context immediately subordinate to the root of the tree. In LDAP this entry is called the *root DSE*. Information contained in the root DSE identifies critical operational factors that apply to a specific LDAP server.

LDAP defines LDAP operational attributes, which are only found in the root DSE. An LDAP server is required to recognize these attributes, although there is no requirement that the attributes exist or have values. The attributes found in a root DSE are

- altServer—Lists other servers to contact in the event that this server becomes unavailable. Clients can cache this information in case it is needed.
- namingContexts—Contains a list of naming contexts held by the DSA.

- `supportedControl`—Contains a list of the *Object Identifiers* (OID) of controls the DSA supports. An OID is a globally unique identifier for objects and attributes assigned by various international standards organizations including American National Standards Institute (ANSI) and the Internet Assigned Numbers Authority (IANA).
- `supportedExtension`—Contains a list of the OIDs of the extensions the DSA supports.
- `supportedLDAPVersion`—Lists LDAP version(s) supported by an LDAP server.
- `supportedSASLMechanisms`—Names SASL mechanisms supported by a DSA. The SASL framework is discussed in the "LDAP Security" section of this chapter.

Besides these attributes, a root DSE entry is likely to contain vendor-specific information used to identify the capabilities of the directory and to manage it. A root DSE in Active Directory, for example, contains entries for a `dnsHostName` and an `ldapServiceName`.

The root DSE is likely to differ in each DSA that holds a reference to it. As this may seem odd—that multiple references to the same root DSE could differ—take a quick look at how this works.

The root DSE entry holds some information that will be common to all the LDAP servers holding a naming context immediately subordinate to the root. Generally, operational information, such as supported LDAP versions, controls, and so on will be the same across multiple directory servers. However, some of the information contained in the root DSE is specific to a particular directory server. For example, the list of naming contexts held by a server is likely to vary from one LDAP server to another.

The root DSE is named with a zero-length DN and can be queried by performing a search on the base object of the root DSE with an `objectClass` of `*`. An LDAP URL that performs this query on the `unicorn.mythical.org` server would look like:

```
ldap://unicorn.mythical.org/?*
```

Dynamic Directory Objects

An extension that provides a mechanism to implement dynamic directory objects is defined in RFC 2589. *Dynamic directory entries* are nonpersistent directory objects that, if not periodically refreshed, disappear from the directory after a designated length of time. These objects are essentially standard directory objects that have been modified by the addition of a *Time-To-Live* (TTL) value.

Three schema additions are defined to support this functionality including

- The `dynamicObject` is an auxiliary object that adds the `entryTtl` attribute to an object.
- The `entryTtl` property is an operational attribute that contains the TTL of the object measured in seconds. If no value is supplied for this property, the server will assign one.
- `dynamicSubtrees` is an attribute that defines the portion of the DIT that can contain dynamic entries. If this entry is contained in the root DSE, dynamic entries are permissible anywhere in the DIT.

Dynamic objects can be used to represent transitory resources that both require a directory entry and have a finite life span. The intent is that dynamic objects will be used for entries that are useful for only a limited period of time. Some examples of this might be a person who has an entry only when logged on to the network, or a meeting whose directory entry disappears when it is over.

As an administrator, the advantages of having such objects automatically delete themselves when they are no longer needed is obvious. When such objects are used within a directory, however, administrative concerns also arise. What happens if the TTL of a dynamic object expires while it still contains a child object with an unexpired TTL, for example? Concerns of this type can confound the process of performing a simple modification (adding a TTL) to an existing directory object.

LDAP Attributes

Not surprisingly, like in X.500, LDAP attributes can also be divided into user and operational categories. These attributes are defined in the same way for LDAP as for X.500. Let's quickly review the two categories of attributes:

- **User attributes**—Those that appear in the directory when viewed through common administrative tools. User attributes contain information used by the network administrator, applications, services, and clients in day-to-day directory operations. A wide range of information is contained in user attributes—everything from names (such as a `CN`) to security information (such as a `userCertificate`) to custom information (such as employee photos) may be found in an LDAP directory.
- **Operational attributes**—Those used internally by directory management processes. These attributes identify the operational capabilities of a DSA and track directory changes. Generally, operational attributes are maintained invisibly by the directory and are not directly modifiable by an administrator, although they may be viewable by someone with appropriate security permissions.

Because the base LDAP schema contains about 70 attributes, it's impractical to go into detail on each attribute in this chapter. If you would like to review the complete list of LDAP attributes, refer to RFC 2252, "Lightweight Directory Access Protocol (v.3): Attribute Syntax Definitions," which also contains information about attribute syntax and matching rules.

LDAP Attribute Syntax

Most LDAP attribute values are encoded as alphanumeric strings. Even so, each attribute is assigned a specific syntax type as part of its definition. The syntax definition constrains the value of the data that may be entered for a given attribute, ensuring that a value is entered and interpreted correctly.

The LDAP v.3 schema specifies 33 syntaxes for use in an LDAP directory. The syntax definitions for LDAP include a variety of methods for interpreting numbers (such as phone numbers, OIDs, and so on), text (Boolean, country codes, and so on), as well as binary definitions.

As with attributes, the number of syntax definitions in the base LDAP schema makes it impractical to go into detail about each one here.

Matching Rules

Besides the syntax type, an attribute definition may include *matching rules* instructing the directory on how to handle filters used in directory queries. Matching rules contain information concerning how to handle the value of a property when a filtered directory operation is presented.

There are matching rules defined for both different filter types and some specific attribute types. The core LDAP schema contains matching rules for `Equality`, `Inequality`, and `Substring` filters, as well as rules used for subschema attributes.

The Directory Information Tree

In keeping with its initial goal of accessing X.500 directories, LDAP describes essentially the same DIT structure as X.500. Container objects are arranged to form the tree structure, and leaf objects representing network resources and entities are distributed into the appropriate containers. DNs are derived by concatenating the RDNs of the referenced object and its parents.

However, critical differences exist between both the structure and naming methods used by X.500 and LDAP. The differences are essentially the following:

- **Structure**—The possible arrangement of objects within the tree is much looser than that implemented by X.500, where an object class may only exist within specified container objects (such as `OU`s within `O`s, but not vice versa).

  In the LDAP schema, an object class has *no* constraints regarding the container objects classes in which it can reside. This doesn't mean that an LDAP server cannot place additional constraints on DIT structure, just that the LDAP standards do not. If an LDAP directory is a front end to an X.500 directory, however, the more restrictive X.500 containment rules will apply.

- **Naming**—LDAP DNs are written starting at the leafmost object and proceeding to an entry immediately subordinate to the root. This is the *opposite* of X.500 naming, which starts at the root of the DIT and proceeds to the referenced object.

Unlike X.500, LDAP does not make assumptions about the existence of a global directory tree structured to facilitate the location of X.500 servers. Instead of creating an LDAP-specific global namespace as a means of locating LDAP servers, LDAP vendors have chosen to approach the issue from a different angle, such as using the *Service Location Protocol* (SLP) or DNS. The exact resolution to the problem of locating distributed LDAP directory servers in an environment such as the Internet is still under consideration. However, there is some ongoing discussion in the IETF working groups concerning methods of locating LDAP servers.

One method currently being used relies on the existing DNS namespace as a form of top-level locator service. DNS has been extended to support service (SRV) records, which supply a means of locating a server providing a specific service, such as LDAP, via DNS lookups. Of course, this requires that the top of an organization's DIT mirror the organization's registered DNS domain name. Concomitantly, LDAP supports a method of using DNS name components as part of an LDAP DIT. (Microsoft has chosen this approach for Active Directory.) The "DNS Domain Names in LDAP" section later in this chapter discusses in more detail how DNS names work with LDAP.

LDAP Naming

The primary method for LDAP naming is defined in RFC 2253 and is modeled on type X.500 naming. Additional RFCs describe an LDAP URL format used by clients such as Web browsers and a mechanism to use DNS domain names in LDAP directories.

The following sections explain what each RFC specifies in the way of naming support.

LDAP Naming RFCs

The RFCs that define LDAP names are

- RFC 2253 "Lightweight Directory Access Protocol (v.3): UTF-8 String Representation of Distinguished Names"
- RFC 2255 "The LDAP URL Format"
- RFC 2247 "Using Domains in LDAP/X.500 Distinguished Names"

LDAP Names

Because LDAP was designed to support X.500 directories, the ability to map an X.500 DN to an LDAP DN accurately is of critical importance. RFC 2253 describes a way to convert X.500-distinguished names from the X.500 format to a UTF-8 string for use by LDAP.

At first glance, an LDAP DN may look like an X.500 DN—it is constructed of a series of X.500-style RDNs separated by commas. On closer examination, however, you'll notice that an LDAP DN lists the string of RDNs in *reverse order* when compared to an X.500 DN.

To illustrate how this works, take a look at an example directory entry from the perspective of both X.500 and LDAP. Figure 5.1 shows the directory object for a user named Michael.

The LDAP DN for this directory object is as follows:

```
cn=michael, ou=mktg, ou=corp, o=netmages
```

However, the X.500 DN for the same object is as follows:

```
o=netmages, ou=corp, ou=mktg, cn=michael
```

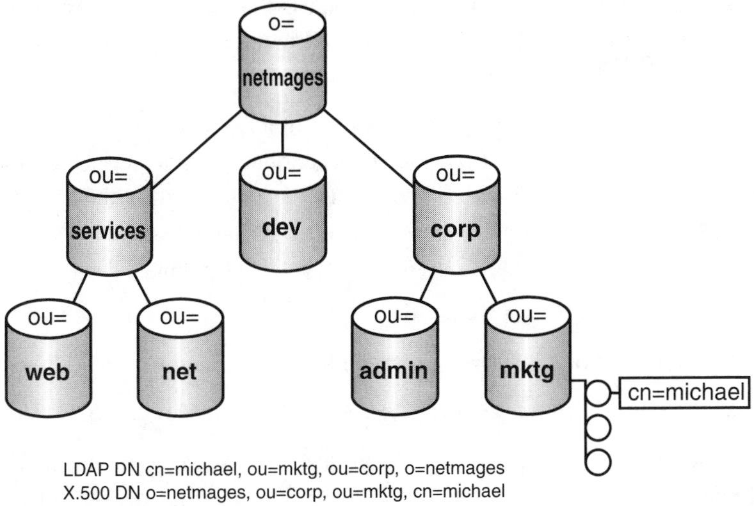

FIGURE 5.1
The order of the RDNs in an LDAP DN is the reverse of that in an X.500 DN.

RFC 2253 also specifies the actions to take in special cases such as when encountering a multivalued RDN, when RDNs contain special characters, or when the RDN attribute type is not recognized by LDAP. This can be rather complex in practice, and you may want to read RFC 2253 if you will be working with many directory implementations that use special cases in naming. The following sections briefly look at a few examples to show how this works in general.

Multivalued RDNs

Sometimes an object has more than one naming attribute designated. This might be done to distinguish between objects that would otherwise have the same name, or as a means of adding additional information for location or management purposes.

Multivalued RDNs are concatenated with a + symbol as in the following example:

```
cn=michael+l=seattle, ou=dev, o=netmages
```

Unrecognized Attribute Type

As mentioned earlier in this chapter, a typed RDN is created by combining the abbreviation for the naming attribute with the object name, resulting in an RDN such as `ou=dev` or `cn=michael`. However, sometimes a directory object uses an attribute type that is unknown to a particular directory server for its name. In such a case, it is not possible for the directory server to create an RDN using the name type abbreviation.

Every attribute in the schema has an OID that can be used to identify the attribute type. When an LDAP server encounters an unknown name type attribute, it uses the OID to form the RDN rather than the unknown attribute type abbreviation.

The next example assumes that an object uses a portion of a DNS domain name as an RDN component. The OID for the *Domain Component* (`dc`) attribute, which names this type of object, is `0.9.2342.19200300.100.1.25`. Because this is not a mandatory part of the LDAP schema, however, all LDAP servers might not recognize it. If a server did not contain the `dc` attribute in its schema, it would use the following RDN to refer to the object named by the `dc` name type:

```
0.9.2342.19200300.100.1.25=mythical
```

And if that RDN were part of a DN string, it might look something like the following:

```
ou=us,0.9.2342.19200300.100.1.25=mythical,0.9.2342.19200300.100.1.25=org
```

As you can see, OIDs are not very friendly and are not easy to use or remember. Therefore, using an OID when naming directory objects is undesirable; but this mechanism does at least allow LDAP servers to cope with unknown attributes.

Special Characters

Some characters require special handling when they are used in an object name. If the CN structure chosen for user objects is "lastname, firstname," for example, a problem presents itself. As LDAP uses commas to separate the components of a DN, the comma might be part of the CN attribute or it might be the separator between RDN components. The directory must have some way to distinguish between the two uses of the comma.

To facilitate this distinction, LDAP uses a process called *escaping* to identify such characters when they occur as part of an RDN rather than as part of the DN structure. The following characters occurring within an RDN require escaping—that is they must be preceded by a backslash (\):

- A space at either the beginning or end of an RDN string
- A # at the beginning of an RDN string
- A comma (,), semicolon (;), plus sign (+), double-quotation mark ("), backslash (\), less than (<), or greater than (>) occurring anywhere within the string

Some organizations may choose to use these special characters within the attributes used to name an object. Consider the example of a username in the format "lastname, firstname"—that is, `cn=smith, michael`. If you wanted to reference this object in an LDAP name, you would need to escape the `,` character in the RDN, like this:

```
cn=smith\, michael, ou=mktg, ou=corp, o=netmages
```

This example points out the need to carefully consider the ramifications of your naming models when constructing your directory. If you expect that your clients will be performing lots of queries using LDAP URLs, you may want to avoid the use of special characters to minimize confusion.

Compatibility Factors in LDAP Names

Naming compatibility issues exist between LDAP v.2 and LDAP v.3. RFC 1777, which defines LDAP v.2, is considerably more lenient than RFC 2253 when it comes to naming objects. Naming compatibility issues between LDAP v.2 and LDAP v.3 are addressed, however, such that an LDAP v.3 DSA will accept any name that is compliant with LDAP v.2, yet not generate LDAP v.2 names.

LDAP v.2 naming constraints differ from LDAP v.3 in the following ways:

- Semicolons as well as commas are acceptable as RDN separators.
- Whitespace characters are allowed on either side of the separator characters, equal signs (=), and plus signs (+)used in multivalued RDNs.
- Quoted RDN strings are allowed by LDAP v.2.
- Some normally escaped characters within quoted strings do not require the leading backslash.
- OIDs used in place of attribute name in RDNs were prefixed with the text `OID`.

LDAP v.3 implementations must accept any of this syntax. When an LDAP v.2 style name is encountered, semicolons are replaced by commas, whitespace is ignored, and other processing is done as needed to create an LDAP v.3—compliant DN.

LDAP URLs

Accessing directories via a Web browser is becoming more common, whether it is done on a corporate LAN to find employee information or across the Internet to a publicly accessible database of names and phone numbers. An *LDAP Uniform Resource Locator* (URL) format has been defined to provide access to LDAP directories using a client such as a Web browser.

LDAP URLs were originally defined at the University of Michigan under a National Science Foundation grant and were first released as RFC 1959. The original standard has been superseded by RFC 2255, which updates LDAP URLs for LDAP v.3 and also defines an extension mechanism for use as a means to enhance the LDAP URL format.

Format of an LDAP URL

An LDAP URL begins with the protocol designator `ldap` and may designate a hostname as well as the DN of the directory object being referenced. The URL can also specify search parameters, authentication data, and other information needed to complete the query.

The most basic form of an LDAP URL follows:

```
ldap://[hostport]/[dn]
ldap://netmages.org/cn=felisha,ou=dev,o=netmages
```

The complete LDAP URL syntax is as follows:

```
ldap://[hostport][/dn[?[attributes][?[scope][?[filter][?extensions]]]]]
```

The components of an LDAP URL contain the following information:

- **`ldap`**—The URL begins with a *scheme* prefix denoting the protocol to be used when handling this URL. The `ldap` designation indicates that the URL references one or more entries in the directory held by the specified LDAP server.
- **`hostport`**—The `hostport` specifies the LDAP server that should be contacted and, optionally, the TCP port that should be used. If no `hostport` is specified, the client must have information telling it which LDAP server to contact. The default LDAP port of 389 is assumed unless otherwise noted. If a TCP port is specified, it is separated from the host name by a semicolon, as in `zifnab.netmages.org:389`. The `hostport` specification is defined by RFC 1738, section 5.
- **`dn`**—The `dn` is an LDAP DN identifying the base object to be used in the search. The DN should be constructed as a `distinguishedName` defined by RFC 2253, section 3, as discussed in the previous section.
- **`attributes`**—This part of the URL indicates which attributes should be returned as a response to the directory search. This is formatted as an attribute description, as defined by RFC 2251, section 4.1.5.
- **`scope`**—This indicates the range of the directory entries to be searched. The options for scope are as follows:
  - `base`—Only the specified object should be searched.
  - `one`—Indicating a search of single level of the directory tree.
  - `sub`—The entire subtree, starting at the specified object should be searched.

- `filter`—This portion of the URL indicates the filter to be applied in this search. It is constructed as defined in RFC 2254, section 4. If no filter is specified, the default value of `*` is assumed and all user attributes should be returned by the directory server.
- `extensions`—This construct allows URL extensions to be specified as part of a query. Extensions are written as a `type=value` string, with the `value` being optional unless required by the specific extension. Multiple extensions can be written on a single query by separating them with a comma. Extensions are discussed in the "LDAP Operations" section of this chapter.

The structure of the attributes, filter, and extensions is discussed a bit more in depth in the section on LDAP searches later in this chapter.

As you can see, the LDAP URL provides a powerful mechanism for performing queries using a Web browser. This enables you to examine the directory from any computer with an LDAP-enabled Web browser. Internet Explorer and Netscape Communicator (v.4 and later of either) provide some degree of LDAP support, although the method by which information is handled may vary.

Examples of LDAP URL

The following URL queries the DSA at `netmages.org` and returns the entire set of user attributes for the specified user:

```
ldap://netmages.org/cn=felisha,ou=dev,o=netmages
```

The next query only returns the surname (`sn`) attribute of the same user.

```
ldap://netmages.org/cn=felisha,ou=dev,o=netmages?sn
```

This query returns the `objectClass` attributes for all objects in the subtree under `ou=dev, o=netmages`.

```
ldap://netmages.org/ou=dev,o=netmages?objectClass?sub
```

These are just a few examples of how LDAP URLs can be used to query a directory. If you are going to be using LDAP queries extensively, you should refer to the appropriate RFCs for more detailed information. Appendix A includes information regarding the location of the RFCs.

Processing an LDAP URL

An LDAP URL should be processed in the following manner:

1. The client must obtain a connection to the LDAP server specified in the `hostport` of the URL or, if no server is specified, an LDAP server selected by the client. If a session already exists with an appropriate LDAP server, it may be reused.
2. If required, the client is then authenticated to the LDAP server. This step is optional unless a critical bind name extension is specified within the URL.

3. The search operation specified in the URL is performed and the results returned to the client.
4. After receiving the results of the search, the client may maintain the connection to the LDAP server or disconnect.

LDAP URLs commonly use DNS names to identify the DSA to which the query should be sent. LDAP also uses DNS domain names in other ways, however, as discussed in the following section.

DNS Domain Names in LDAP

Mechanisms have been adopted to allow the use of DNS domain names within an LDAP directory. RFC 2247 specifies a means of using DNS domains as part of LDAP DNs. This was designed to provide a simple method of translating DNS domain names for use within an LDAP DN.

The algorithm for converting DNS names to LDAP DNs is straightforward. Start with an empty DN and add an RDN for each component of the DNS name, in the same order as the DNS name. These RDNs are named with a `dc` naming type attribute and have a value of one component of the DNS name.

Using this method, the DNS domain `netmages.org` can be translated to the following LDAP DN:

```
dc=netmages,dc=org
```

A DN that consists solely of `dc` components, or that subportion of a longer DN, can be mapped directly back to a DNS domain name. This is done by concatenating the value of each RDN that corresponds to a portion of the DNS name, using a period (`.`) to separate them. Therefore, the LDAP distinguished name `dc=netmages,dc=org` can be easily translated back to the DNS domain `netmages.org`. The `dc` name type makes it easy to determine which portion of the LDAP DN corresponds to the DNS domain.

To support this functionality, two new object classes have been created: `dcObject` and `domain`. There is one critical difference between a `dcObject` and a `domain`—the `domain` class is *structural* and can appear in the directory, but the `dcObject` is *auxiliary*. This means that the `dcObject` is used to extend the functionality of objects that correspond to an existing directory object, and the `domain` object is designed for objects that exist primarily as a placeholder for the DNS name component. A `dc` attribute has also been created, which is used to name the `domain` object. The following sections explain these new objects and attributes.

dcObject

The `dcObject` is an auxiliary class that has been defined to allow the addition of the `dc` attribute to a standard container object, such as an Organization or an Organizational Unit.

There is a single user attribute, `dc`, which is mandatory for the class `dcObject`. The `dc` attribute has as its value a single component of a DNS name and is used to name an object that has the `dcObject` added as an auxiliary class. In fact, the addition of the `dc` attribute to the definition of an existing container object is the only function of the `dcObject`. Although this may not seem like a lot of functionality for an entire object class, this simple change provides a mechanism for congruence of the LDAP directory and DNS domain names.

`domain` Object

On the other hand, the `domain` class is a structural object that, although its basic function is the same as the `dcObject` (providing a way to use DNS names in a directory), also provides a more complete object definition. As with the `dcObject`, the `domain` object requires the `dc` attribute only; it does have a number of optional attributes, however, that provide additional information about the object represented.

The optional attributes of the `domain` object include telecommunications, postal, and other attributes. This information is useful when performing directory administration and queries.

`dc` Attribute

The `dc` attribute type has as its value a single component of a DNS domain name. The value of the `dc` attribute is used as the name of the `domain` object or the container object to which the `dcObject` auxiliary object has been added. In keeping with the DNS standard, the value of the `dc` attribute is not case sensitive.

Notes on DNS Names in LDAP Names

As previously mentioned, DNS domain names are also used when constructing an LDAP URL. This can lead to portions of a DNS name being referenced multiple times when constructing an LDAP name, which may get a bit confusing. If you are using an LDAP URL to access a directory that uses `dc` components you could run into a URL like this:

```
ldap://netmages.org/ou=dev,dc=netmages,dc=org
```

The first time the domain name is used (`netmages.org`), it is as the host portion of the URL, and is resolved by a DNS server to locate the appropriate LDAP server. The second time the domain name is used, (`dc=netmages,dc=org`), it is as part of the LDAP path and is resolved by the LDAP server as part of the path to the directory object.

Also note that some directory implementations use DNS domain names in a variation of the method described in RFC 2247. For example, Active Directory masks portions of the domain name in some instances. No *top-level domain* (tld) name is presented via Active Directory clients; therefore, `netmages.org` appears as `dc=netmages` or just `netmages` when viewed via some Active Directory tools.

Given these factors, it is important to remember that the path to the same directory object may differ, depending on how that object is accessed—that is, which tools are used.

The Directory Information Base

As LDAP is an access protocol that was designed to support X.500 directories, it relies on the underlying directory to define its own methods for storage and handling of DIB functionality. Therefore, LDAP doesn't address most aspects of the DIB that are dealt with by the X.500 model. Synchronization, replication, partitioning, and actual DIB structure are not currently addressed by any of the RFCs that define the core LDAP protocol.

Although this approach has simplified the protocol design, it is not without its drawbacks. The existing LDAP specifications don't define a replication method, leaving it up to vendors to decide how, or even *if*, replication should be performed. Because there is no standardized method for replication, severe limitations are placed on the type of interoperation between LDAP-only directories. This is likely to change in the future as vendors recognize the need to allow directories to work together.

The LDAP protocol design does, however, acknowledge that there will be multiple copies of the DIB and that the access protocol must address security constraints. Most importantly, servers that hold shadow or cache replicas are required to place the same constraints on data access as the server holding the master replica.

Much work is ongoing on the subject of LDAP replication and the section "Proposed LDAP Extensions" at the end of this chapter looks at some of those developments.

LDAP Operations

LDAP supports operations to perform the directory functions previously performed by DAP. Because of this, most LDAP operations are essentially the same as DAP, although the names may differ.

Table 5.2 lists the LDAP operations defined in the core LDAP RFCs.

TABLE 5.2 LDAP Operations

Operation	*What It Does*
`Bind`	Functions like a DAP `directoryBind`. Bind operations were required by the LDAP v.2 specification but are optional under LDAP v.3.
`Unbind`	Functions like a DAP `directoryUnbind`.
`Search`	Functions like a DAP search request. Searches are discussed in more detail later in this chapter.

TABLE 5.2 Continued

Operation	*What It Does*
`Modify`	Functions like a DAP `modifyEntry`. This operation will not remove any portion of an object's Distinguished Name; that must be done with a `ModifyDN` operation.
`Add`	Functionally the same as a DAP `addEntry` operation.
`Delete`	Equivalent to a DAP `removeEntry`.
`Compare`	An LDAP `Compare` operation is the same as a DAP `Compare`.
`Abandon`	Functionally the same as a DAP `Abandon` request.
`ModifyDN`	The `modifyDN` operation can be used to do two things: change the RDN of an object, or move an object or subtree to another location in the directory tree. This operation changes one or more components of an object's DN. The LDAP v.3 `modifyDN` request is essentially the same operation as an LDAP v.2 `modifyRDN` with the addition of one parameter, `newSuperior`. The `newSuperior` value is used to designate the DN of the object that will become the new parent of the entry being modified.
`Unsolicited notification`	An unsolicited notification is sent by the server to signal a condition of which the client should be aware. The only unsolicited notification defined in the core LDAP v.3 specification is a notice of disconnection, which is sent to notify the client that the server is closing a session. This would be used in the case of the server receiving an LDAP message it cannot parse, underlying security failures, or the server becoming unavailable for some reason.
`Extended operation`	The extended operation provides a mechanism for adding new operations to the LDAP protocol. These extensions may be created for a specific implementation or defined via RFC. The extended operations are discussed in more detail later in this chapter.

Name Resolution

Remember that LDAP was initially an access protocol, not a server protocol—LDAP was designed to rely on the underlying directory service for name resolution. This generally meant that an X.500 DSA would use its chaining capability to locate secondary DSAs when needed.

Because referrals require more intelligence on the part of the client, and LDAP was specifically designed to be simple to implement, LDAP v.2 only supports chaining, and then only when the

DSA does. The first LDAP-only servers, which were based on LDAP v.2, were implemented as single server directories, without the inherent ability to deal with queries outside the scope of the naming contexts held by that server. LDAP v.3 added the ability to send referrals back to the client using an error field in the LDAP reply.

LDAP v.3 queries are processed in much the same way as X.500 queries. The server receives a request, evaluates the DN, and fulfills the request or hands it off if it cannot be fulfilled locally.

Both chaining and referral were discussed in detail in the "Name Resolution" section of Chapter 4. Briefly, the two processes work as follows:

- Using referrals, a DSA resolves its portion of a directory query, and then passes the results back to the client, as well as pointers to other DSAs with which to continue the search. LDAP v.3 supports referrals as a mechanism of resolving directory queries for data not contained in the local copy of the DIB.
- Chaining requires that directory servers pass a query down a line of servers and back via the same path to resolve queries. Using chaining results in more work for the directory server and can be used with less intelligent client software. You should remember that LDAP v.2 clients do not support referrals and must rely on the DSA's chaining capability.

LDAP Searches

Because most of the use of LDAP will be for queries, a powerful, yet simple search mechanism has been defined as part of the LDAP v.3 specification.

LDAP searches can be performed on a single directory entry, the contents of a single container, or an entire subtree. Each LDAP search request contains a `baseObject` that is the LDAP DN designating the starting point of the search. Additional information contained in the search query defines the scope of the search, treatment of aliases, filters, and so on. Although many of the following parameters are similar to those used in LDAP URLs, there are some differences.

The syntax for a search request is as follows:

```
[baseObject], [scope], [derefAliases], [sizeLimit], [timeLimit], [typesOnly],
[filter], [attributes]
```

The definitions of the search parameters are as follows:

- `baseObject` —The LDAP DN of the object at which to start the search.
- `scope` —Specifies the scope of the search request.
    - `baseObject`—Search only the `baseObject` for matching attribute values.
    - `singleLevel` —Search only the immediate subordinates of the `baseObject`, *not including* the `baseObject`.
    - `wholeSubtree`—Perform the search on the entire subtree, *including* the `baseObject`.

- `derefAliases`—Specifies alias-handling preferences. The process of dereferencing aliases is discussed in the "Name Resolution" section of Chapter 4.
  - `neverDerefAliases`—Do not dereference aliases for purposes of either locating the `baseObject` of the search or performing the search.
  - `derefInSearching`—Dereference aliases when performing the search, but not for locating the `baseObject`.
  - `derefFindingBaseObj`—Dereference aliases when locating the `baseObject`, but not when performing the search.
  - `derefAlways`— Dereference aliases for both `baseObject` location and searches.
- `sizeLimit`—This parameter restricts the number of entries that may be returned by search results. A `sizeLimit` of `0` means that no limitations are requested by the client, although servers may restrict the number of entries returned. Valid values for `sizeLimit` are any positive integer.
- `timeLimit`—This value indicates the number of seconds allowed for completion of a search. The value can be any positive integer. An unlimited search time is indicated by a value of `0`.
- `typesOnly`—This parameter accepts a Boolean value. Setting the `typesOnly` value to `TRUE` tells the server to return only attribute types and no values. A setting of `FALSE` indicates the server should return both attribute types and values on the search.
- `filter`—Possible filter entries are: `equalityMatch`, `substrings`, `greaterOrEqual`, `lessOrEqual`, `present`, `approxMatch`, and `extensibleMatch`. Additional filter operators of `and`, `or`, and `not` may be used to form queries using combinations of the preceding filters. These filters are evaluated in exactly the same way as in the 1993 X.511 standard (section 7.8.1) and return a value of either `TRUE`, `FALSE`, or `UNDEFINED`. If the evaluation of the filter results in a `TRUE` response, the appropriate attributes are returned in the search results. Otherwise the entry is ignored during the search operation. For more detailed information on the use of filters in LDAP queries, refer to section 4.5.1 of RFC 2251.
- `attributes`—A search request can identify a subset of attributes to be returned by specifying the names of those attributes as part of the query. Two special values are also used: a null value, and the asterisk (`*`), both of which return all *user* attributes. Although a client can request that all attributes be returned, normal access control and other directory restrictions will limit actual search results. An attribute description of `1.1` is used to specify that the client does not want any attributes returned in the search results. Due to the large number of values for some operational attributes, they are never returned in search results unless they are requested by name. The `*` is used when requesting all user attributes in addition to specific operational attributes.

Extended Operations

Extended operations allow new directory functionality to be defined and existing operations to be extended. Mechanisms have been added to LDAP v.3 to provide support for extensions to the base set of LDAP operations and query handling. The extended operations can be defined either as a lasting extension to the directory or dynamically (as part of a directory query, for example).

These extensions can be used for enhancements ranging from special handling of query results to security measures. One area in which a great deal of operation extension work has taken place is on various mechanisms to customize the delivery of directory query results to the client. Methods to allow a directory server to incrementally deliver subsets of a large query have been devised as a way to allow the client agent more control over the directory search process.

Not surprisingly, the methods used for the extension of LDAP operations are essentially the same as those used by X.500 extensions and controls, but the names of these mechanisms aren't quite the same between the two specifications:

- **Operational extensions**, which correspond to X.500 *extensions*, provide a method of defining new LDAP operations, either privately or by RFC.
- **Controls**, which are analogous to X.500 *service controls*, are a means by which extended handling information can be specified for a single query.

Extensions

The extension mechanism provides a way to dynamically add functionality to query strings. Operational extensions allow the use of predefined syntaxes and methods to support operations not included in the basic LDAP specifications. A likely use of an operational extension would be for additional security measures, such as digitally signed operations. Operational extensions may be defined via RFC or by an individual vendor or developer.

Operational extensions can be designated as critical or noncritical (that is, whether the extension is *required* for the operation). Extended operations are marked as critical by prepending an exclamation mark (`!`) to the extension syntax portion of the request. It is important to remember that extensions may or may not be supported by the system processing the request. LDAP servers should follow these rules when processing LDAP extensions:

- Supported critical extensions *must* be processed.
- Requests with unsupported critical extensions *must not* be processed.
- Supported noncritical extensions should be processed.
- Unsupported noncritical extensions may be ignored during processing.

The operational extensions supported by a given LDAP server are listed in the `supportedExtension` attribute of the root DSE entry.

Controls

A *control* is a method of specifying extension information for a single LDAP request. Controls can be used to support added functionality such as sorting, paging, or other special handling of search results. A list of supported controls is located in the `supportedControl` attribute of the root DSE entry.

Controls can be designated as critical or not, either by the developer or at the user's discretion. Unlike operational extensions, however, controls are marked as critical (or not) by a Boolean value in a criticality field within the control syntax. Controls are evaluated and handled according to the same rules as operational extensions.

LDAP Data Interchange Format

The *LDAP Data Interchange Format* (LDIF) has been defined as a means of describing directory entries in a standardized text format. LDIF (RFC 2849) facilitates the exchange of directory data by implementing a simple text listing of a directory entry. LDIF can be used to import and export directory data, as a means of exchanging information between LDAP-compliant directories, or to delineate a set of changes to the directory information. An LDIF file can contain either a set of directory entries, or a set of changes to existing directory entries, but it cannot contain both in the same file.

Common LDAP operations, such as "add," "delete," and "modify" can be performed using LDIF. Many LDAP utilities read and write LDIF, as do most development tools designed for use with LDAP directories. Most directory vendors include an LDIF utility, primarily to support bulk loading and the export of directory information.

The following is an example of an LDIF file with two entries:

```
version: 1
dn: cn=David Allan, ou=Research, dc=netmages, dc=com
objectclass: top
objectclass: person
objectclass: organizationalPerson
cn: David Allan
sn: Allan
uid: dallan
telephonenumber: +1 213 555 1212

dn: cn=Debra Karren, ou=IT, dc=netmages, dc=com
objectclass: top
objectclass: person
objectclass: organizationalPerson
cn: Debra Karren
sn: Karren
telephonenumber:  +1 202 555 1212
```

LDAP Security

One of the most important considerations for any network service is security. LDAP defines some of the methods by which secure access to data and network resources is provided.

Both LDAP v.2 and v.3 provide a mechanism for simple authentication and support for Kerberos. LDAP v.2 supports Kerberos v.4.1 or a simple authentication method using clear-text passwords.

LDAP v.3 also adds support for SASL, which is a powerful means of providing secure communications using a variety of methods, including Kerberos.

Many drafts related to security are circulating in the LDAP Extensions (LDAPExt) working group of the IETF. To review the current status of the work on security, you should visit the LDAPExt page at:

`http://ietf.org/html.charters/ldapext-charter.html`

LDAP Security RFCs

Several RFCs relating to authentication and security were published by the LDAP Extensions working group after the original LDAP v.3 RFCs were released in 1997. These RFCs, which are considered part of the core LDAP v.3 specifications, are

- RFC 2829 "Authentication Methods for LDAP" delineates a minimum set of security methods that an LDAP v.3 server or client should implement to ensure interoperability.
- RFC 2830 "Lightweight Directory Access Protocol (v3): Extension for Transport Layer Security" defines the LDAP extension for TLS, the form of the request and response, and result codes.
- RFC 2831 "Using Digest Authentication as a SASL Mechanism" describes using HTTP Digest Authentication [Digest] as a SASL mechanism for LDAP, mail, Web, and other protocols.

The following sections briefly look at each of the LDAP security mechanisms. Because the security mechanisms used by LDAP are varied and complex, however, you may want to refer to the relevant RFCs for more complete information.

Access Control

There has not been agreement on an access control model for LDAP, leaving individual vendors to implement proprietary methods to manage this aspect of security. This is clearly a significant gap in the current state of LDAP. Drafts defining access control requirements and models are currently under discussion, and it can be hoped that some agreement will be reached soon, allowing work in this area to move forward.

Authentication

Unlike the access control factors, LDAP has defined authentication mechanisms. LDAP supports non-authenticated access (access by anonymous entities), as well as the following three authentication methods:

- Simple Authentication
- Simple Authentication via SSL/TLS
- SASL-based authentication

Anonymous Access

LDAP allows *anonymous* (non-authenticated) access to the directory, providing a means for anyone to access the information managed by an LDAP server if so desired for the specific LDAP application. This is very useful if the LDAP service is being used to provide information for something like an Internet directory of email addresses. Non-authenticated access does not require an entry in the directory.

Simple Authentication

LDAP supports a *simple authentication* method that allows connecting to the directory and authenticating with a clear text password (where the password is transmitted unencrypted across the network). Although this method does provide a modicum of security, it is not recommended in most environments unless some other security mechanism is in place to prevent inadvertent disclosure of passwords and other security information.

The simple authentication method is also used for non-authenticated connections. In this case the password is set to a zero-length entry, as is the distinguished name portion of the authentication string. LDAP v.2 clients often use this method for non-authenticated access to the directory.

Simple Authentication via SSL/TLS

By combining the convenience of the simple password authentication method with the added security of an encrypted connection, the authentication process can be made more secure. This can be accomplished by using the *Secure Sockets Layer* (SSL) or *Transport Layer Security* (TLS), the successor to SSL. Of course, this approach requires that both the client and server obtain public key certificates for use in the SSL/TLS process. Because public key certificates require management, this method is not quite as simple for the administrator, but it does add some security to the process.

Simple Authentication and Security Layer

LDAP v.3 implements an extensible security model using SASL, which allows for the use of different security providers. SASL provides a way for connection-oriented protocols to specify an authentication method and optional security layer (encryption) for protocol interactions.

When using SASL, the client specifies the desired authentication mechanism (or method). If the contacted server supports the specified SASL mechanism, it will initiate the authentication process. Authentication then takes place in accordance with the specified authentication mechanism. If the client also requests that the optional security layer be implemented, this encryption takes place immediately on completion of the authentication process.

As defined in RFC 2222, mechanisms used with SASL must be registered with the *Internet Assigned Numbers Authority* (IANA). SASL currently supports the following mechanisms:

- Kerberos v.4
- GSSAPI
- S/Key
- External

The next sections briefly examine each of these SASL mechanisms.

Kerberos via SASL

Kerberos technology was developed by MIT in response to the need for secure communication across what is essentially an insecure environment, the Internet. Kerberos operates by authenticating clients and then issuing tickets to be used for authentication of the client to the service. The ticket consists of the client identity and a temporary *session key*, which is then sent to the service by the client. This session key contains a unique shared encryption key that is used by both the client and service during that one session. The client and service can then encrypt all communications using the session key, thus providing a means to operate securely over a public medium such as the Internet.

Kerberos uses both an *Authentication Server* (AS) and a *Ticket Granting Server* (TGS), collectively referred to as a *Key Distribution Center* (KDC). Network clients and services each have a secret key (password) that is registered with the AS. When the client is authenticated by the AS, a *Ticket Granting Ticket* (TGT) is granted to the client by the AS. The TGT, which is essentially a session key for use between the client and the TGS, is presented to the TGS, which then issues the actual ticket and session key for use between the client and service.

This method of ticket management ensures that user passwords are used only once, at the beginning of a session, and need not be reentered or cached, removing a possible weakness in the security implementation. As an additional layer of security, Kerberos tickets are valid for a short period of time only, further limiting the ability of a third party to intercept the ticket and use it to impersonate someone with access rights that the third party does not have.

Generic Security Service API

Generic Security Service API (GSSAPI) defines an interoperable security system for use on the Internet and is another one of SASL's principal providers. GSSAPI provides a protocol-independent and mechanism-independent interface to underlying security methods based on public key and secret key technologies. GSSAPI was initially defined in RFC 1508, then RFC 2078, and now RFC 2743, the current version of GSSAPI.

S/KEY One-Time Password System

The *S/KEY One-Time Password system*, described in RFC 1760, was designed to prevent intruders from obtaining user passwords via packet sniffers and so on. The S/KEY system is designed to counter a replay attack, where an intruder captures and then replays a username and password to gain entry to the network.

The S/KEY One-Time Password system uses a secret pass phrase factored with a server-provided seed value, and then applies a secure hash function multiple times to produce a sequence of one-time passwords which are used to implement secure communications. The S/KEY hash function is based on the MD4 Message Digest algorithm.

Using the S/KEY system, only a single-use password is ever transmitted across the network. The user's originating secret pass-phrase is never transmitted and is, therefore, not exposed to compromise.

External SASL Mechanisms

The use of an external SASL mechanism enables you to plug in a security protocol or method that is otherwise unsupported by SASL. This can be used to provide support for a variety of security approaches such as TLS, SSL, or IP Security (IPsec).

LDAP Programming

One of the critical factors for widespread support of the LDAP protocol is the availability of APIs. In August 1995, RFC 1823 was published, defining the LDAP API. RFC 1823 defines a C language programming interface to perform queries and modifications on an LDAP directory (commonly referred to as the *LDAP C API*).

The original LDAP API was written for LDAP v.2. Since then, there have been several proposed additions and extensions to the original LDAP API issued as Internet drafts. This includes, most importantly, `draft-ietf-ldapext-ldap-c-api-05.txt`, an update of the LDAP C API to support features new to LDAP v.3 such as extended operations.

Synchronous and asynchronous modes of operation are both supported. Synchronous operations return the actual results of the operation to the client. Asynchronous routines return the message ID of the operation; this message ID can be used by the client when querying later for results.

Interfaces that support the functions listed in Table 5.3 are provided.

TABLE 5.3 LDAP API Functions

API Name	*Function*
`ldap_init()`	Opens a connection to the LDAP server
`ldap_simple_bind()`	Authenticates the client to the directory using simple authentication
`ldap_sasl_bind()`	Authenticates the client via SASL mechanisms
`ldap_unbind()`	Unbinds and closes the connection
`ldap_search()`	Searches the LDAP directory
`ldap_modify()`	Modifies an existing LDAP entry
`ldap_modrdn()`	Modifies the name of an existing LDAP entry
`ldap_add()`	Adds a new entry to the directory
`ldap_delete()`	Removes an entry from the directory
`ldap_abandon()`	Abandons an operation in progress
`ldap_result()`	Obtains results of a previous asynchronous operation

There are also provisions for routines to parse the results returned by these operations. Entry names and attribute values can be retrieved and the viewing of results can be managed by these routines.

In addition to the LDAP C API, a number of other APIs to access LDAP directories have been developed:

- There are several IETF draft proposals for a Java API for LDAP, implemented as a set of Java classes.
- Netscape has a freely available Java SDK that fully supports LDAP v.3.
- Perl-LDAP provides support for Perl scripting as an interface to LDAP directories.
- Java Naming and Directory Interface (JNDI) is Sun's proprietary API that provides access to LDAP, eDirectory, and other directory services.

Proposed LDAP Extensions

It is important to remember that *X.500 is a set of standards* that define directory service structures and services, and *LDAP is a protocol* that is designed around X.500 information models and supports X.500 DAP operations. The initial intent of LDAP was purely as an access protocol for X.500 directories. Because of this focus, many aspects of directory design and operations were not specifically addressed in the LDAP standards but just assumed to be X.500 compliant.

The scope of LDAP is broadening, however, to the point that some directory products (such as iPlanet) are being built around LDAP, with no underlying X.500 directory. This means that much more than client access methods need to be defined. DSA-to-DSA interaction does happen with LDAP; it just requires that one of the DSAs be seen as a client by the other DSA. As LDAP develops, it is likely to expand to provide more direct support for a broader range of interactions between disparate DSAs.

The RFCs that define the LDAP v.3 protocol are just a starting point for what are sure to be highly variant LDAP implementations. Literally dozens of IETF drafts have been proposed as additions to LDAP. Many of these drafts address simple topics such as the definition of a single new object or a simple operation extension; others address considerably larger issues such as replication. You can check on the status of any IETF working group by visiting its Web site at `www.ietf.org`.

It is worth taking a brief look at a few areas of the LDAP protocol that (although they have not been finalized yet) have been circulating in draft form for an extended period of time. These drafts address some of the key issues that still face the developers of directories, especially as they relate to directory interoperability.

Replication

Replication has proven to be one of the more difficult aspects of LDAP. Although a number of other facets of LDAP v.3 have been resolved, no consensus has been reached on methods of directory replication. There has, however, been significant work taking place in this area.

The *LDAP Duplication/Replication/Update Protocols* (ldup) working group is working on both single master and multimaster replication methods. This working group has created a number of Internet drafts defining replication requirements and architecture as well as the controls, extensions, and schema additions needed to use LDAP as a replication protocol. This includes those for replication agreements and topologies, consistency models, replica management and administration, as well as conflict detection and resolution. The ldup working group charter and status can be found at `ietf.org/html.charters/ldup-charter.html`.

In the meantime, vendors have proceeded with implementation of proprietary replication approaches, limiting interoperability. Some of these proprietary designs have been proposed as solutions to the LDAP replication question. Microsoft has proposed a multimaster replication scheme to the IETF, and although it has not been accepted as part of the standard, it does form the basis for Active Directory's replication design.

Broader Schema

The LDAP v.3 schema, as described by the core LDAP RFCs, does not go much beyond the basic X.500 schema. In fact, the LDAP object set contains only two classes in addition to those defined by X.500; and both these classes define objects used internally by the directory. This limited schema provides the basic directory objects and properties that all directories require as a starting point.

Numerous IETF drafts describing additions to the LDAP schema have been published by a wide variety of organizations and businesses involved in directory development. Some of these drafts propose extensions to existing objects; others define new object classes and associated property sets. As you might expect, support for extensions to the LDAP schema will be vendor specific.

LDAP also makes it possible for programmers and administrators to independently extend the directory schema; therefore, if a needed class or property is not defined within the vendor's product, it can be added. This is not without complications, however, and should be carefully considered in the context of the corporate network before implementation. If two DSAs have different schemas and try to replicate data, for example, some objects may be unrecognized and unusable.

DNS: The Domain Name System

CHAPTER

6

...simplicity belies the breadth...

IN THIS CHAPTER

Domain Name System (DNS) provides network clients the capability to find network servers and services via their logical name instead of having to know and use the server's IP address. The location services provided by DNS are now integral to the operations of most enterprise networks, and are increasingly integrated with directory service implementations.

This chapter describes the DNS from a directory service perspective, covering DNS from domain namespace design and name resolution to zone files and resource records. This review of DNS is based on RFCs, and vendor-specific approaches are not discussed. For details on specific DNS implementations, take a look at the DNS references listed in Appendix A, "References."

Introduction to DNS

The Domain Name System is a service used to locate network servers on the Internet and many corporate networks. DNS is a network name service that enables you to find a server's network address by supplying the server's host and domain name. This process of locating a server's IP address via its host and domain name is referred to as *name resolution.*

DNS is a client/server implementation that uses two fundamental components:

- A network server providing DNS services (the *name server*)
- The client running the DNS *resolver* (which may be either a workstation or another DNS name server)

Similarities and Differences

Like X.500 directory services:

- DNS describes client agents that submit queries to server agents to locate information in a distributed datastore.
- DNS queries are either client-intensive (iterative) or server-intensive (recursive) queries.
- The DNS data storage and administrative models are based upon a distributed architecture.

Yet, a key difference between DNS and an X.500 directory service, is that DNS does not perform user authentication or provide access control over directory information. This is fine for DNS's purpose, as DNS clients are always anonymous. From the X.500 perspective, however, this is a major shortcoming; user management and security are integral parts of the X.500 design.

To understand the functionality and underlying architecture of DNS it can be useful to view it from a directory service perspective.

In a nutshell, DNS servers provide lookup services for DNS clients. They perform name resolution for requested DNS domain names and supply IP addresses for the servers within the specified domains.

DNS is a service designed to operate on TCP/IP-based networks, allowing network clients to use the names of network servers (as opposed to having to use IP addresses). A DNS server translates the "friendly name" (hostname) of a network server (for example, `dragon.mythical.org`) into its corresponding IP address (for example, `192.168.111.90`).

DNS implements a hierarchical naming strategy to associate a logical DNS hostname to a corresponding IP address. The DNS namespace is organized in a logical tree structure, arranging network servers within a hierarchical tree of domain nodes. DNS supports the delegation of management, a clear necessity in such a large implementation as the Internet.

DNS operates by storing (and providing) domain name information in a distributed database contained on DNS *name servers* located within the TCP/IP network. The name servers store their portion of this distributed database in DNS *zone files*. Each DNS zone file stores the domain name information for the pertinent DNS region (*zone*) in DNS *resource records* (RRs).

From a general networking perspective, the DNS service corresponds to the application layer of the OSI model, and it can be implemented over either TCP or UDP on port 53.

Prior to DNS, the association of IP addresses and the Internet server's hostname was done by storing the server (host) names and corresponding IP addresses in a HOSTS.TXT file (as per RFC 952). The name-to-IP address mapping was initially centralized, with Internet servers periodically downloading the updated HOSTS.TXT file. When the number of servers exceeded the design capacity of this strategy, DNS was adopted.

One of the core goals in the design of DNS was to replace the centrally administered HOSTS.TXT file strategy with a distributed database that provided a hierarchical namespace, extensible data types, distribution of administration, and no operational limits on database size. The central specifications for DNS (RFCs 1034 and 1035) were accepted as standards in 1987.

Hosts Files in Enterprise Networks

On intranets, there was a corresponding host/address file called *hosts* on Unix servers, and `hosts.txt` on Windows servers. A DNS implementation may also support these files for backward compatibility with the host/address mapping.

DNS Terminology

Although DNS is not a general-purpose directory, it does share many of the basic characteristics of a directory service—that is, a defined namespace, distributed data storage, client/server agents, and delegated directory servers that process client queries. From this perspective, DNS looks very much like a directory service. Even though much of the high-level design and functionality of DNS is similar to an X.500-style directory service, the specific mechanisms that DNS uses differ somewhat.

An important distinction between DNS and the directory services discussed to this point is the language used to describe their components and operations. Unlike many directory service implementations, which may use a term or two a bit differently from each other, DNS uses a vocabulary almost entirely different from X.500, but it still has some functions, which parallel those in X.500. Being able to connect the two sets of terminology may help you to more fully understand how DNS is both similar to and different from most directory service products on the market today.

To highlight the difference in vocabulary, this discussion reviews DNS, examining the parallels between DNS and X.500, and draws connections between the terminologies employed. To start, Table 6.1 shows the correlation between terminology used in DNS and X.500.

TABLE 6.1 Vocabulary Correlations

Functionality	*DNS Term*	*Analogous X.500 Term*
Directory entries	Resource records	Objects
Object subentries	Fields	Attributes
Definition of directory contents	Resource record definitions	Schema directory contents
Logical representation of directory	DNS domain namespace	Directory Information Tree (DIT)
Data storage	Zone files	Directory Information Base (DIB)
Subdivision of directory	Zone	Naming context (partition)
Data updates	Zone transfers	Replication
Server agent	Name server	Directory Service Agent (DSA)

TABLE 6.1 Continued

Functionality	*DNS Term*	*Analogous X.500 Term*
Client agent	Resolver	Directory User Agent (DUA)
Query resolution	Recursive and Iterative	Chaining and Referral

Although these analogies may be only somewhat helpful, a summary of the basics of DNS may prove instructive.

DNS as a Specific-Use Directory

DNS is a highly specific, limited-use directory, primarily used to locate servers on the Internet and other TCP/IP networks. DNS operates as a network service that performs name-to-IP address resolution for domain and hostnames. DNS contains records used to locate various hosts (servers), frequently those performing specific roles (mail servers, name servers, and so on) or using a generic name to advertise a service (for example, WWW, FTP).

A *resource record (RR)* is a single entry in the DNS database that is analogous to a directory object. A resource record consists of a series of *fields* (analogous to attributes), including information that identifies the type of resource record and the identification of the network host represented by the record. Each type of resource record is designed to represent a particular resource or service and contains the fields required for that type of record.

The *DNS schema* is comprised of the entire set of all possible resource records. These resource records are defined through the RFC process and may or may not be eventually implemented by industry vendors. Compared to general-purpose directories, the traditional DNS schema has historically been very simple with a limited scope of content—a small set of resource records describing hosts on the network. Multiple RFCs and drafts propose ways to enhance the functionality of DNS, from storing security data to locating network services. These new RFCs are discussed in the "Defining the DNS Schema" and "Proposed DNS Extensions" sections later in this chapter.

The *DNS domain namespace* describes a hierarchical tree of domains. Each domain component (similar to an X.500 RDN), is a single, separate portion of the DNS name. Domain components are separated by a single period (.) between the host, subdomain, and domain names. The highest level of the domain namespace tree structure is called the *root*, the nodes on the next level are referred to as *top-level domains* (tld), and the next level nodes are called *second-level domains*.

DNS uses *name servers* to provide DSA-like functionality—that is, name servers process client queries and return results and referrals to other name servers (but with a much more limited capability than X.500 DSAs).

The information base for DNS is distributed as sets of resource records divided into zones, which are generally stored in text-based *zone files*. Each zone file contains a set of resource records and is limited in size to 64KB. A zone is a functional subdivision of the DNS database and, like a partition, each DNS zone contains a contiguous subtree of the DNS namespace.

Similar to X.500 replicas, DNS makes copies of the data it maintains in the zone files, using a single-master style replication model. There is a single *primary name server* for a given zone, which holds the master copy of the DNS data, and generally functions much like a directory server holding a master replica. There are also additional *secondary name servers,* which act much like read-only replicas and provide redundancy for load balancing and fault tolerance for DNS services.

Replication of DNS data (called *zone transfers*) commonly transmits the entire zone, but support for incremental transfer of just the zone data that changed is also supported. Although zone transfers traditionally required the secondary name servers to request updates at predetermined intervals, a notification mechanism (defined in RFC 1996) allows a primary name server to initiate the process.

Analogous to an X.500 DUA, the client-side software component in DNS is referred to as a *DNS resolver*. Although many general-purpose directories do have an application or interface to view the DIT as a hierarchical tree, DNS implementations do not commonly provide this.

Although the specifics of the name resolution and query resolution process differ, the basic approach is similar to that of X.500 in that DNS provides both a client-intensive (iterative) and a server-intensive (recursive) process. These processes are described in the "DNS Name Resolution" section later in this chapter.

DNS Client/Server Agents

Like other directories, DNS is based on a client/server network model and employs specific software agents to conduct client and server operations. The following two software components are used by DNS:

- **Name servers**—Provide the server-side functionality of DNS.
- **Resolvers**—Act as the client component of DNS.

DNS is implemented such that a DNS client requests services of a name server by submitting a query, requesting information about a specified node within the DNS namespace. Each DNS name server manages a specified portion (that is, a zone) of the DNS domain namespace and related resource records. When a DNS server cannot provide a resolution to a query, it will commonly use a list of referrals to other DNS servers in order to locate a name server that can provide an authoritative response to the submitted name query.

The following sections review each of these components in a bit more detail.

DNS Name Servers

The DNS component that operates as a network service and handles information about a specific portion of the DNS domain namespace is called a *name server*. A name server is designed to store, manage, and provide DNS information to network clients. Each name server is responsible for one or more DNS zones (analogous to partitions) for which it is required to respond to name queries.

To specify a name server in the related zone file, the Name Server (NS) resource record is used to designate the DNS server that is performing authoritative name resolution services for the assigned zone. Name server records should always point to an authoritative name server for the designated zone. The use of the term *authoritative* in DNS has a specific meaning—for a name server to be authoritative, it must contain current resource records for the designated zone.

The DNS server component is provided as a network service and can be implemented in a variety of server roles. The following terms are used to describe the roles a name server can take:

- **Primary**, **secondary**, and **master** apply to replication roles.
- **Authoritative** and **caching-only** refer to (operational roles) in the name resolution process.

Each of these roles is discussed later in the appropriate section of this chapter.

Correctly configured primary and current secondary name servers are authoritative for the designated DNS zone by default. From a lookup perspective, there is no operational distinction between primary and secondary name servers because the algorithm used in DNS name resolution uses the NS resource records for the referenced domain in the submitted order. The distinction between primary and secondary is important to the replication process, however, and these roles are discussed in more detail in the “Replication of DNS” section of this chapter.

DNS Resolvers

There is a client side to the DNS server operations, the component (called a *resolver*) which formulates the URL lookup into a DNS query and communicates with DNS name servers. To understand what the resolver does, consider how a Web browser uses DNS to look up a Web site.

When the URL of a Web site is provided to a browser, the browser passes the domain portion of the URL to the resolver, which processes and forwards it as a DNS name query to the locally assigned DNS name server. The name query refers to a host (or alias such as `www`), which exists within a designated DNS domain (such as, `mythical.org`), and is specified (with the protocol) in URL format as `http://www.mythical.org`.

The name query is referred to an authoritative DNS name server for the specified DNS zone, which responds to the name query by returning the corresponding IP address of the host to the resolver (which then passes it back to the client application, the browser). The browser then uses the host IP address to initiate direct communication with the host server.

A resolver interacts with the name servers to obtain DNS domain, host, or service information; it is commonly built in to the operating system's TCP/IP protocol stack. Both DNS clients and name servers provide resolver functionality, managing DNS communications between clients and servers as well as server to server.

DNS resolvers format data submitted by the client into DNS query packets to be sent to name servers, and they handle and interpret DNS reply packets from those name servers, passing the results back to the requesting client. Results from name queries can be cached for use in subsequent query resolution.

A DNS resolver commonly requests the following three types of operations for DNS clients:

- **Name-to-address translation**—A process of deriving the corresponding IP address from a submitted DNS domain name. The name-to-address translation is sent to the DNS name server as a request for a host address resource record.
- **Address-to-name translation**—The reverse process of deriving the DNS host and domain information from a submitted IP address. To resolve an address-to-name translation request, the octet values of the IP address are reversed and concatenated with the reserved domain name suffix, `in.addr.arpa`, by the resolver. The address-to-name translation is then sent to the DNS name server as a request for a type PTR resource record (referred to as a *pointer record*).
- **General lookup function**—An operation involving searching the DNS zone files for records of a particular name, class, or type. General lookup functions are not commonly used, but they are employed by DNS utilities (such as NSLOOKUP) for troubleshooting DNS configuration problems.

Models/Views in DNS

Unlike X.500, the DNS RFCs do not specifically define informational or functional models. Yet, similar to the way that X.500 describes models from the perspective of users, administrators, DSAs, and so on, DNS describes both components and views employed by DNS (RFC 1034).

The components defined by DNS include the domain namespace, resource records, name servers, and resolvers. In addition, three *views* of DNS are described:

- DNS defines the *user view*, which is analogous to X.500's User Information Model because it views the DNS directory from the user's perspective where the DNS namespace is comprised of a single unified tree. Users can query any portion of the DNS tree without having to understand the structure of the underlying distributed database.

- DNS also defines a *resolver view*, which doesn't correlate directly to an X.500 model, although it does provide some of the functionality described in the X.500 DSA Information and Distribution Models. The resolver views the DNS namespace as an unknown number of name servers, each of which contains a static portion of the DNS database.
- DNS also defines a *name server view*, which roughly corresponds to the X.500 DSA Information Model. The name server sees individual zones and recognizes that the information contained in those zones is somewhat dynamic, requiring refreshing to remain current. A name server maintains internal references to child and parent domains and provides query resolution services by using those references for referrals.

DNS Objects: Resource Records

All the information in a DNS database is stored as entries called *resource records*, which contain information about network hosts and services. These resource records are defined by the RFC process and, as a result, are an evolving set of entries providing ever-increasing functionality.

A dozen or so resource records are in common use, although many more are defined in the collected RFCs. Table 6.2 shows the resource records most often found in DNS.

TABLE 6.2 The Set of Commonly Used Resource Records

Resource Record Type	*Content*	*RFC Number*
`A`	Address	1035
`CNAME`	Canonical name	1035
`HINFO`	Host information	1035
`MINFO`	Mailbox or mail list information	1035
`MX`	Mail exchange	1035
`NS`	Name server	1035
`PTR`	Pointer	1035
`SOA`	Start of authority	1035
`TXT`	Text	1035
`WKS`	Well-known service	1035

TABLE 6.2 Continued

Resource Record Type	*Content*	*RFC Number*
`ISDN`	ISDN	1183
`NOTIFY`	Notify	1996
`SRV`	Service	2782
`UPDATE`	Dynamic update	2136

The section "Defining the DNS Schema" later in this chapter takes a closer look at resource records.

The DNS Tree

DNS is a system comprised of a distributed database of names logically structured as a hierarchical tree called the *domain namespace*. The DNS namespace is represented as a structure of domain nodes organized in an inverse tree. Each node in the DNS tree represents a domain that can contain one or more child nodes representing subdomains.

Each node in the DNS domain tree database (with all its child nodes) is defined as a *domain*. A domain may contain multiple subdomains or servers (hosts). Every DNS subdomain is 'owned by' its parent domain. Every host, service, or subdomain that is owned by a specific domain is considered to be contained within that domain's namespace.

Organizations that register domain names are assigned (delegated) authority for that portion of the DNS domain namespace, and they manage the subdivision, naming, and administration of that subtree of the domain tree structure.

DNS domain references consist of logical components of the DNS name separated by a dot (.) delimiter. The five possible components of a DNS domain name are shown in Table 6.3.

TABLE 6.3 The Components of a DNS Name

Component	*Example*
The root of the domain tree	`.`
The top-level domain	`org`
The second-level domain	`mythical`
A subdomain name	`sales`
A hostname	`dragon`

The Root Domain

The root of the DNS tree is a reserved value that is unnamed (null) and, as mentioned earlier, is referenced in DNS resource records via a trailing period (`.`), designating the highest level of the domain tree hierarchy.

At the heart of DNS operations (and the top of the DNS tree), the root name servers contain the zone information for all top-level domains. The root name servers are the authoritative servers for most top-level domains and can identify authoritative servers for the remaining top-level domains.

The root DNS servers control the core of the DNS database for the Internet. The root DNS servers and the IP addresses they refer to are under the authority of the Internet Corporation for Assigned Names and Numbers (ICANN) which assumed these responsibilities from the Internet Assigned Numbers Authority (IANA) in 1998.

The root name servers play a key role in DNS name resolution, as DNS servers on the Internet are usually configured to refer name resolution requests to the root name servers whenever local name resolution is not possible.

When a DNS name server cannot resolve a name query, it performs the DNS referral process from right to left, beginning at the root. The name server forwards the query to a root name server, which replies with the address information for the authoritative server of the appropriate top-level domain. The name server then queries the top-level domain name server, requesting information on the second-level domain name provided in the query. This process continues until the query has been completed.

Top-Level Domains

Top-level domains are divided into the following three primary subdivisions of domain types:

- **Organization types**—Associated with a corresponding abbreviation (commonly, a three-letter abbreviation such as .com). These top-level DNS domains are primarily used for U.S. organizations and are subdivided by type of organization.
- **Country-code Top Level Domains (ccTLDs)**—Implemented by using the two-character country codes established in the ISO 3166 specification maintained by the ISO 3166 Maintenance Agency (ISO 3166/MA). These ccTLDs are administered by agencies in each country. For example, the `.us` domain is managed by the U.S. Domain Registry at the Information Sciences Institute of the University of Southern California.
- **`in.addr.arpa`**—A special domain reserved for use in reverse name lookups, where the normal lookup process (DNS domain name to IP address) is inverted, and an IP address is resolved to a DNS domain name.

Figure 6.1 shows some of the currently available top-level domains. This figure does not, however, show any representation of the `in.addr.arpa` domain in the DNS tree.

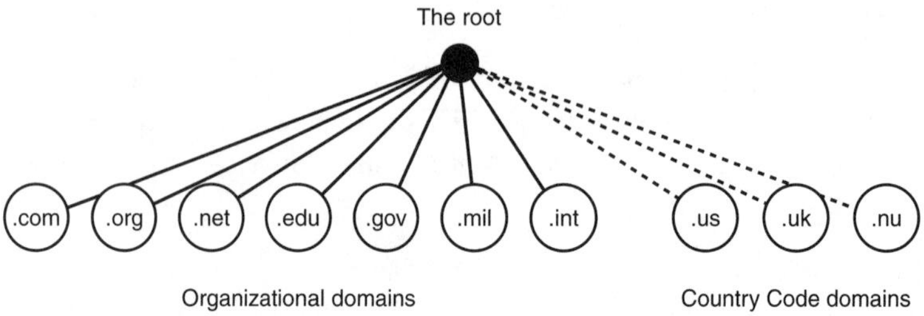

FIGURE 6.1
The top-level of the DNS domain namespace.

The most familiar (and coveted) top-level domains are those used by businesses and other organizations (such as .com). The following domain names comprise the most commonly used top-level domains, including

`.com`—For *commercial* entities (though not restricted to commercial entities).

`.org`—Used for *noncommercial* organizations (but use is not restricted to solely those organizations).

`.net`—For *networking* organizations (although use is also not actually restricted).

`.edu`—Reserved for qualified *educational* institutions.

`.gov`—Reserved for *governmental* organizations.

`.mil`—Reserved for solely *military* organizations.

`.int`—Reserved for organizations established by *international* treaties.

Various organizations manage the top-level domains:

- Network Solutions (NSI) currently manages the most common organizational top-level domains (`.com`, `.org`, `.net`, `.edu`). Until 1999, NSI enjoyed a monopoly on the domains they manage. However, NSI now shares the responsibility for these domains with other registrars.

Accredited Registrars

For a list of accredited registrars, go to: `www.internic.net/alpha.html`.

- The Department of Defense (US DOD Network Information Center) manages the `.mil` domain.
- The General Services Administration manages the `.gov` and `.fed.us` domains.
- The IANA manages the `.int` domain, which is used only for registering organizations established by international treaties between governments.
- Other top-level domain registries (based on country code) provide registration and name resolution services to the general public, such as registries using the `.nu` (Niue) and `.tm` (Turkmenistan) top-level domains.

Proposed Additional Top-Level Domains

At its November 2000 meeting, the Internet Corporation for Assigned Names and Numbers selected seven new top-level domain names. The new top-level domains provide new subdivisions of the DNS namespace. The introduction of these (and other) new top-level domains will ease the existing namespace constraints on domain names (especially in the `.com` domain). These new proposed top-level domains include the following:

`.biz`—Restricted to businesses.

`.info`—Unrestricted and may be used by anyone.

`.aero`—For commercial air transport industry.

`.pro`—Used by providers of accounting, legal, and medical professional services

`.coop`—Used for commercial cooperatives.

`.museum`—Reserved for museums.

`.name`—Used for individual name registration.

Second-Level Domains

Second-level DNS domains are domains created by, and assigned to, specific organizations or people. The second-level domain name is a single DNS name component, like an X.500 RDN. However, a second-level domain is usually referenced by combining the selected second-level domain name (such as `mythical`) and the top-level domain (`.org`), into a single domain name expression, as in `mythical.org`. When the term *domain name* is used in common parlance (as in seeking a Web site), it is commonly the combined domain names being referred to.

Figure 6.2 shows two second-level domains as they are delegated to the organization(s) that created and registered them.

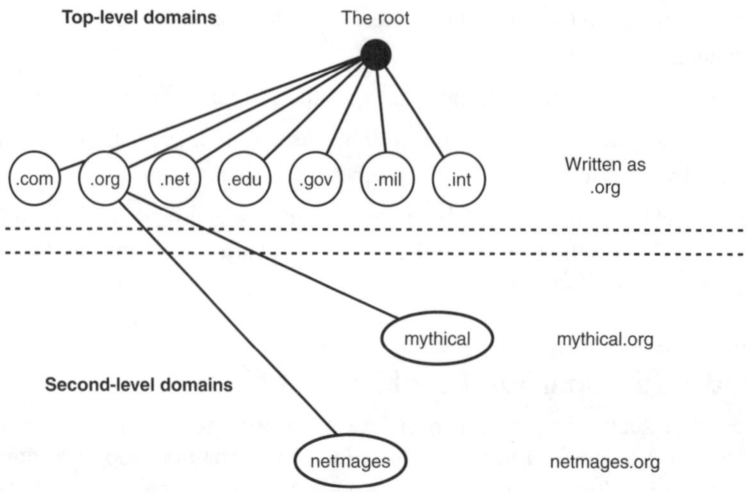

FIGURE 6.2

The second level of the DNS domain namespace is where various registrars register and delegate DNS domains to organizations and individuals.

When an organization registers a second-level domain name with a registrar, the responsibility for managing the DNS namespace from that second-level domain downward through the DNS tree is delegated to that organization or its assigned technical contact. Organizations can then define DNS subdomains and hosts to match their actual network configuration and usage requirements.

After the domain is divided into subdomains, local administrators can further delegate the management of those subdomains. This structure of namespace management, where a registrar delegates DNS namespace control to organizations, and the organization delegates to subdivisions within the organization, provides for decentralized administration of DNS domain names.

Control of Domain Names

Control of DNS domain names is a significant issue for many businesses. Many businesses initially registered a `.com` domain name (such as `netmages.com`), and subsequently have sought to register the `.net` (`netmages.net`), `.org` (`netmages.org`), or other versions of the domain name as a means of protecting the intellectual property asset value of the name.

Yet with the range of possible domain names, it is not feasible, nor economically useful, to try to register a second-level domain name under all the available top-level domains. To register and administer a domain name in all top-level domains would be costly, time consuming, and ultimately not very productive. As a result, most businesses are selectively choosing the domain names to register and support, yet many businesses are still ending up with many domain names to manage and to protect.

A variety of factors must be considered in selecting, registering, and implementing domain names:

- Which domains are relevant to the business operations and interests?
- How many domain names and under which top-level domains (such as `.com`, `.org`, `.net`, and so on) does the business need to control?
- What trademarks, copyrights, and business operations are you attempting to protect in the registration of these domain names?

Protecting a Domain Name

Protecting a domain name requires a business to monitor for (what is perceived as) infringing domain name registrations or usages, and then to send "cease and desist" letters, file legal actions, or initiate domain dispute resolution processes.

This process of monitoring for infringements and addressing domain disputes requires substantial investment of business resources. Many businesses are implementing cross-functional teams of personnel with legal, technical, marketing, and operations expertise.

What constitutes an infringement of domain name registration or usage remains unclear. ICANN has established the Uniform Domain-Name Dispute-Resolution Policy (UDRP), a process followed by all `.com`, `.net`, and `.org` registrars, to address disputes in the registration of domain names.

In general, the UDRP will not support a claim to a domain name if:

- The domain name is identical to a service mark or trademark belonging to another entity.
- The domain name has been registered in bad faith, such as registering it merely to sell it to the owner of the trademark.

For details on the UDRP process, see `www.icann.org/udrp/udrp.htm`.

Subdomains

The use of *subdomain names* is optional within the DNS namespace. Subdomains are specified to the left of the second-level domain name and are commonly used to specify organizational subdivisions (for instance, `sales.mythical.org`), as shown in Figure 6.3 (next page).

Subdomains can be multiple levels deep, allowing for detailed subdivisions within the DNS namespace controlled by an organization (for example, `oem.sales.mythical.org`). Subdomain names are not managed by registrars and are entirely controlled by the organization that has registered the second-level domain name.

Although technically any domain is a subdomain—even the top-level domains are subdomains of the root—the term *subdomain* is generally used to describe domains *below* the second level—that is, the section of the DNS tree created and managed by the organization delegated responsibility for a second-level domain.

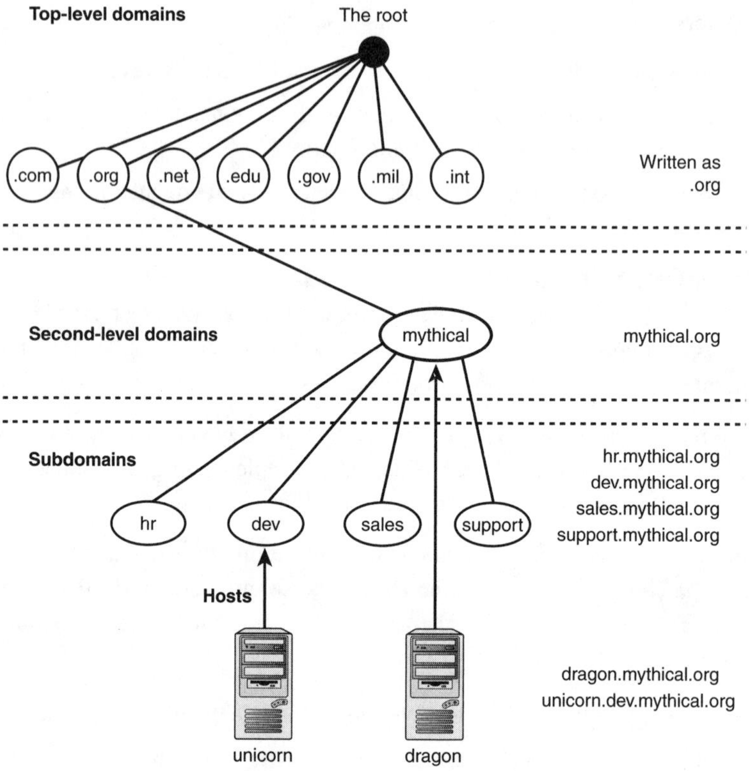

FIGURE 6.3

All domains under the second level of the DNS domain namespace are subdomains assigned and administered by the organization registering the second-level domain name.

DNS Hosts

In DNS, a *host* is a computer—generally a server supplying some sort of network service for the specified domain. Each host has at least one name and may also have aliases to allow location via multiple names. This is particularly useful because some of the common network services have universally accepted names associated with the server providing the service (such as `www` for Web servers).

In DNS naming, the hostname appears on the leftmost side of the DNS name, separated from subdomain and domain names by the dot (.) delimiter. If a server named `dragon` were providing DNS services for the `mythical.org` domain, for example, the DNS name would be constructed as `dragon.mythical.org`. Similarly, if the `unicorn` server were providing DNS services for the `dev` subdomain of `mythical.org`, the DNS name would be constructed as `unicorn.dev.mythical.org`.

DNS Naming

The names of each of the domain components are used in the DNS name string, except the root, which is represented by a period. These components are combined to form a DNS name in the following manner:

```
<host>.<subdomain>.<second-level domain>.<top-level domain>
```

Such as in the previous example of:

```
unicorn.dev.mythical.org
```

The DNS naming convention specifies a dot (`.`) delimiter to separate name components. The number of dot delimiters in the construction of a DNS domain name indicates the relative domain position within the DNS hierarchy.

DNS has a few basic rules governing the construction of names:

- The minimum information required to resolve a DNS name is shown here:

  ```
  <host>.<second-level domain>.<top-level domain>
  ```

  For example:

  ```
  dragon.mythical.org
  ```

- Subdomain components of a DNS name must be unique within the containing parent domain.
- The character set allowed is only A–Z (uppercase and lowercase), 0–9, and the hyphen character (`-`). DNS is not case sensitive, meaning that a *Z* and a *z* are considered equivalent.
- Components of a DNS name can be as many as 63 characters in length (with the exception of the root domain).

DNS names are evaluated as either a fully qualified domain name, or a relative domain name. The key distinction between these is the use of the terminating dot (`.`) to signify the complete name to the root. The difference is

- **Fully qualified domain names**—A *fully qualified domain name* (FQDN) is specified with the complete set of required values and has the terminating root delimiter (`.`) as the rightmost value (for example, `host.domain.tld.`). FQDNs are typically constructed by starting with the hostname and specifying the domain components from the host up to the root of the DNS tree, and concatenating the host (or alias) and domain components with the dot delimiter, as follows:

  ```
  host.subdomain.domain.tld.
  ```

  For example:

  ```
  www.dev.mythical.org.
  ```

- **Relative domain names**—All DNS domain names that do not end with a trailing (`.`) delimiter are not FQDNs, but rather are referred to as *relative DNS names*. Relative DNS domain names are more commonly used and are constructed by starting with the hostname and specifying all domain components up to the top-level domain (rather than to the root of the DNS tree as an FQDN does). Relative DNS domain names are structured as `host.domain.tld`, as in `www.mythical.org` (which does not have the trailing period). A hostname may be omitted if a null host address record is written to the zone file for the local host.

Defining the DNS Schema

Like other directories, DNS has to define a schema of some sort (the underlying definitions of objects, attributes, and syntax). While the DNS RFCs do not explicitly define the set of resource records as a *schema* (the use of schema here is borrowed from X.500), the total set of resource records defined in DNS RFCs constitute the effective DNS schema.

The schema (the combined set of all DNS resource records) has been incrementally defined via RFC processes. The number of resource record types supported by all DNS servers is relatively low (a much smaller set of object types than in a directory service). Compared to general-purpose directories, the DNS schema has historically been very simple with a limited scope of content—a limited set of resource records describing hosts on the network. Unlike many other directory services, DNS does not publish its schema as part of the available DNS information.

Although there have been a number of RFCs proposing additional DNS resource record types over the years, few have been widely adopted by industry vendors until recently. Now a number of proposed standards for new resource records will effectively extend the DNS schema. For example, RFCs have been written proposing ways to enhance the capability of DNS to manage security, both for the DNS service and the network in general. Several of these RFCs define ways to allow DNS to hold security tokens (such as X.509 certificates, Diffie-Hellman keys, and so on). These RFCs are listed in the "Proposed DNS Extensions" section later in this chapter.

Only certain ASCII characters are considered valid within DNS resource records, specifically the characters A–Z, a–z, 0–9, and the hyphen (`-`). In addition to this base character set, special characters are used within a zone file's resource records, characters that are used to denote defaults (default domain), wildcards, or other special properties within a zone file. These characters are as follows:

- The (`@`) symbol is used within DNS zone records as a shortcut reference to the current default domain.
- Parentheses `()` are used to encompass arguments that span multiple lines.
- The asterisk (`*`) is used for wildcard expressions.
- The semicolon (`;`) is used to begin a comment line, where everything after the semicolon is ignored.

DNS Resource Records

DNS resource records are entries in DNS zone files containing specific information about the domain or host, and can be categorized by resource record *class* or *type*.

A resource record *class* indicates the class of network. The most commonly used resource record class specified in a zone file is the Internet class specified by the `IN` class record entry. Although RFC 1035 also defines the following three additional classes, they are rarely used:

- `CS`—`CSNET` class (obsolete)
- `CH`—`CHAOS` class
- `HS`—`Hesiod` class

A resource record *type* indicates the nature of the resource record, type of data contained within each record, and specifies the data format employed for that resource record type. For example, the host address resource record type accepts a hostname and IP address parameters.

This section describes the most common resource record types employed in conventional DNS zone files including the *start of authority* (SOA), *name server* (NS), *mail exchange* (MX), *host address* (A), and the *canonical name* (CNAME) records. In addition, the DNS *service* (SRV) resource record is employed to indicate TCP/IP services locatable via DNS queries.

The Start of Authority Record

A *start of authority* (SOA) record is the first entry within a DNS zone file, and refers to the primary DNS server that is authoritative for the specified DNS domain.

An SOA resource record entry in the DNS zone file is structured as shown here:

```
<domain> IN SOA <source> <contact> <serial#> <refresh> <retry><expire> <TTL>
```

- `<domain>`—The fully qualified DNS domain name. A common shortcut used in DNS zone files is the `@` symbol referring to the default domain.
- `<source>`—The `source` field specifies the host where the zone file is stored.
- `<contact>`—The `contact` field specifies to the e-mail address for the zone file administrator. This e-mail name format requires replacing the customary `@` symbol with a period.
- `<serial#>`—The `serial#` field specifies the version number for this zone database file, which is a number that should be incremented every time zone records are updated (either by administrator or programmatically). This field is used to tell the secondary name servers when an update is needed.
- `<refresh>`—The `refresh` field specifies the amount of time (in seconds) that a secondary DNS server delays before checking with the primary DNS server to see whether a zone transfer is needed.

- <retry>—The `retry` field specifies the amount of time (in seconds) that a secondary DNS server delays before retrying a zone transfer that did not complete.
- <expire>—The `expire` field specifies the amount of time (in seconds) that a secondary DNS server will continue attempting to perform a zone transfer. If the time limit expires without a successful zone transfer, existing zone information for this specific zone is discarded.
- <TTL>—The `TTL` field specifies the amount of time (in seconds) that a DNS server is permitted to store resource records from this specific zone file in its cache.

The following is an example of an SOA resource record entry:

```
@          IN    SOA    dragon.mythical.org. info.dragon.mythical.org. (
 8
 10800
 3600
 604800
 86400 )
```

Specifying Name Server Records

A *name server* (NS) resource record is used to specify a name server for a designated zone and is always specified within a zone file, as well as in the reverse lookup zones defined in the `in-addr.arpa` DNS domain.

The NS resource record specifies the DNS server responsible for authoritative name resolution for the designated zone. NS records should always point to authoritative name servers.

The NS resource record entry in the zone file is structured as shown here:

```
<domain> IN NS <host>
```

For example:

```
@ IN NS dragon.mythical.org
```

> **Order of DNS Records**
>
> The order of entry of the resource records in a zone file is not preserved in the operation of DNS.

Supplying Host Address Records

A *host address* (A) resource record is used within a zone file to specify the linkage between a hostname and its corresponding IP address. The host address resource record is one of the most common resource records used in DNS forward lookup zone files.

Every zone file must contain at least one host address resource record for every host within the DNS zone and for every IP address assigned to that host. The host address records may comprise a substantial number of the entries contained within the zone file.

The host address entry in the DNS zone file is structured as shown here:

```
<host> IN A <IP address>
```

For example:

```
dragon IN A 192.168.111.90
```

A reserved host record address is defined that refers to the local host—which is implemented in the same format as host address resource records—and is created in most zone files by default. This address record for the local host provides a means to perform lookups on the local computer by associating the local hostname with a standardized IP address (`127.0.0.1`) commonly used to perform loopback testing on host network adapters. *Loopback testing* is used to verify that the TCP/IP protocol is installed and functioning on the local machine. The format for the local host resource record entry is structured as follows:

```
localhost IN A 127.0.0.1
```

Aliases: The Canonical Name Records

A *canonical name* (CNAME) resource record is used within a zone file to specify an alias for a hostname. CNAME records specify only the host and alias names; therefore, CNAME records depend on existing host address `A` resource records already defined within the zone file for the designated host. Using aliases via CNAME resource records provides a mechanism to isolate client access to resources from the details of network server implementation.

The CNAME resource record provides a way to associate multiple logical names with a single host, allowing a single server to host multiple services. A common use of the CNAME record, for example, is to specify the server providing FTP services for a domain (for example, `ftp.mythical.org`). The CNAME resource record entry in the DNS zone file is structured as follows:

```
<alias> IN CNAME <host>
```

For example:

```
ftp IN CNAME dragon
```

Should the FTP services for the designated domains be required to move to a new host server, the new server's host address resource record could be added, and the CNAME alias updated to reference the new server. The change of host servers would be transparent to the FTP clients.

> **Glue Records**
>
> In DNS deployment, a condition arises in which references to the name server for a domain exist only within the domain for which it is the name server. For example, when the only reference to a name server for a subdomain is within the zone file of the subdomain, name resolution cannot be completed (as no reference to the child subdomain is contained within its parent domain).
>
> To accomplish effective address resolution, a *glue record* must be used to append the host address to the name server reference in the parent domain. The glue record is employed only in the name server delegating the domain, and it is not employed in the target domain.
>
> Assume you are referencing a name server for `dev.mythical.org` from the parent `mythical.org` name server, for example, and that the name server for `dev.mythical.org` is `unicorn.dev.mythical.org`. In such a case, the NS record and glued A record would be specified as follows:
>
> ```
> dev.mythical.org.     NS unicorn.dev.mythical.org.
> unicorn.dev.mythical.org.    A 192.168.111.83
> ```

Using Service Resource Records

The *service* (SRV) resource record is a new DNS record type introduced in RFC 2052 (replaced by RFC 2782) and is used to specify the location of named TCP/IP-based network services. SRV records enhance the capability of DNS to locate network resources by identifying the specific *services* provided by a particular server. The SRV record maps the name of a network service to the IP address of the server providing the service.

From the perspective of directory services, the SRV record is one of the more important new resource records because it supports the identification of service hosts such as LDAP servers. This is one of the ways DNS and LDAP are being integrated to provide directory service functionality—DNS acts as the location service to find the directory server, and LDAP provides the structured query support for accessing the information stored within the directory.

The DNS service resource record entry in the DNS zone file is structured as shown here:

```
<service>.<protocol>.<name> SRV <TTL><priority><weight><port><target>
```

- **<service>**—The `service` field accepts the symbolic name of the service provided, which is specified in accordance with the standardized abbreviated code specified in RFC 1700 (such as `http`).
- **<protocol>**—The `protocol` field specifies the transmission protocol to be employed for network communications. The protocol types most commonly specified in this parameter are the Transmission Control Protocol (`tcp`) and the User Datagram Protocol (`udp`).
- **<name>**—The `name` field is optional and is commonly employed to indicate additional domain name data to be prefixed to the domain name of the current DNS zone.
- **<TTL>**—The `TTL` field sets the time in seconds that a DNS server is permitted to cache SRV records from the zone.
- **<priority>**—The `priority` field is used to establish a priority scale (0-65,535) for each host of a named domain target.
- **<weight>**—The `weight` field is designed to effect load balancing between target domain hosts for the specified service.
- **<port>**—The `port` field is used to specify the TCP/IP service port number for the specific type of service. Standard assigned service port numbers are specified along with their abbreviations in RFC 1700.
- **<target>**—The `target` field of the service resource record specifies the host domain name supporting the server lookup requests. A corresponding host address `A` record must exist in the appropriate zone file for every host listed in the target parameter of an SRV record.

The Distributed DNS Database

The logical DNS tree of domains and subdomains is stored in a distributed database contained on servers spread throughout the network. In its Internet implementation, the network spans the entire world. The DNS database is subdivided via domain delegation and is partitioned using DNS zones.

Partitioning the DNS Database

To store the DNS data, the resource records of the domains and subdomains are grouped into zones. A *zone* is a set of resource records representing a single contiguous subdivision of the DNS namespace. A zone is comprised of DNS resource records managed in a specific file, referred to as a DNS *zone file*.

DNS domains and DNS zones are not the same thing. The key distinction between a DNS domain and a DNS zone is that a DNS domain represents the logical structure of the DNS namespace, whereas a DNS zone represents the physical distribution of DNS information to specific name servers.

Every zone is anchored to a specific domain node referred to as the zone's *root domain*. DNS servers can manage one or more domains contained in one or more zone files, as shown in Figure 6.4. A zone must be a contiguous subdivision of the DNS namespace (a subtree) because a zone may not contain records from discontiguous domains.

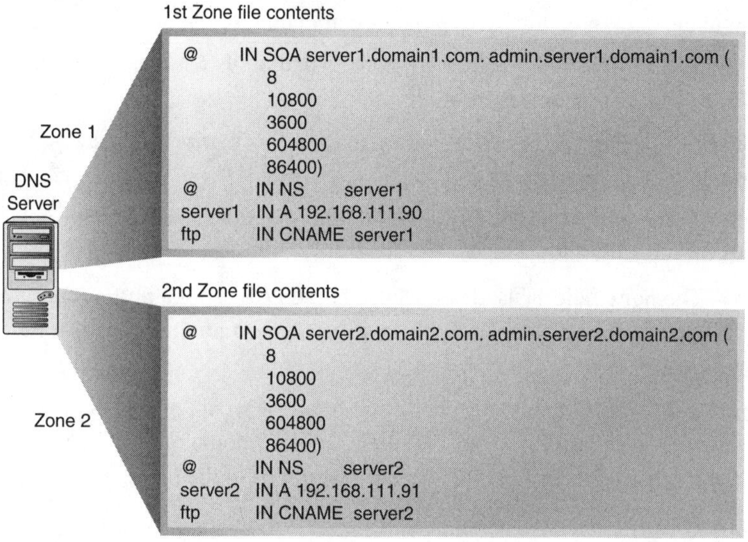

1st Zone file contents
@ IN SOA server1.domain1.com. admin.server1.domain1.com (
8
10800
3600
604800
86400)
@ IN NS server1
server1 IN A 192.168.111.90
ftp IN CNAME server1
Zone 1
DNS
Server
Zone 2
2nd Zone file contents
@ IN SOA server2.domain2.com. admin.server2.domain2.com (
8
10800
3600
604800
86400)
@ IN NS server2
server2 IN A 192.168.111.91
ftp IN CNAME server2

FIGURE 6.4

DNS servers support one or more DNS zones (a collection of resource records representing a contiguous subtree).

Subdividing the logical DNS domain namespace and defining corresponding zones can facilitate management of distributed DNS services. Resource records contained within each zone can be replicated from primary to secondary name servers via a *zone transfer*. Secondary name servers are employed to provide backup DNS name servers for the zone. Distributing secondary name servers throughout the network can provide load balancing for heavily utilized DNS services.

Zone Delegation

Zone delegation is the process by which a name server is delegated responsibility for handling a specific zone. This is specified in the zone file by the use of the delimiting name server (NS) and address (A) resource records following the SOA record.

DNS Zone Files

DNS is commonly configured via text-based zone files that contain the necessary resource records defining host, domain, and DNS services. A zone file describes a specific portion of the DNS database and contains the specific set of resource records defining that zone. Other standard DNS files include the cache and reverse lookup files. These distributed zone, cache, and reverse lookup files are collectively referred to as the DNS database.

DNS Boot File

A *DNS boot file* is not specified in the RFCs for DNS, or required for RFC-compliant DNS operations. Implementations of DNS either support the use of a boot file to specify startup parameters or provide other support for the DNS startup command functionality. For example, the Berkeley Internet Name Domain (BIND) is a UNIX implementation of a DNS name server that specifies the use of a boot file for startup functionality. A BIND-compliant DNS boot file is a text file called `named.boot` (BIND 4.x) or `named.conf` (BIND 8.x) that allows startup commands controlling DNS behavior, including the `directory`, `cache`, `primary`, `secondary`, `forwarders`, and `slave` commands. The following sections briefly look at each of these command entries in the boot file.

`directory`

The `directory` entry is used to specify the location of external files referred to within the boot file. A `directory` entry is structured as follows:

```
directory <directory path>
```

For example:

```
directory /usr/dns
```

> **Lame Delegation**
>
> When a DNS name server is delegated as authoritative for a specific DNS zone and yet does not respond to name queries with authoritative results, this is referred to as lame delegation. The condition of lame delegation usually results from incorrect configuration of the DNS name server, where the name server is not configured to respond authoritatively for the specified zone but is supposed to be (such as where a parent domain has a name server record pointing to that name server, but the name server does not have the needed Start of Authority record).

cache

The cache entry identifies the DNS cache zone file specifying the root name servers. A cache entry is structured as shown here:

```
cache . <DNS cache filename>
```

For example:

```
cache . cache.dns
```

primary

The primary entry specifies both the DNS domain for which the name server is authoritative and the zone file containing the resource records for the designated domain. A DNS boot file may contain multiple primary entries, one for each configured primary zone. A primary entry is structured as shown here:

```
primary <domain> <zone filename>
```

For example:

```
primary mythical.org mythical.dns
```

secondary

The secondary entry is used to specify the DNS domain for which the server is authoritative, the master server IP addresses from which to download zone information, and the name of the local file used for caching transferred zone information. A DNS boot file may also contain multiple such secondary entries, with every entry describing a secondary zone. A secondary entry can contain more than one host IP address. The structure of a secondary entry is as follows:

```
secondary <domain> <IPaddressesOfHosts> <local cache filename>
```

For example:

```
secondary mythical.org 192.168.111.90 mythcache.dns
```

forwarders

The forwarders entry is used to specify the IP addresses of name servers that will perform name resolution on forwarded name queries. A forwarders entry is structured as shown here:

```
forwarders <IPaddressesOfHosts>
```

For example:

```
forwarders 192.168.111.98  192.168.111.99
```

slave

The `slave` entry is used to specify that using the forwarders is the only method of name resolution. Versions of BIND after 4.9 will support the use of the `options forward-only` entry as equivalent to `slave`. A `slave` entry can be used only subsequent to a `forwarders` entry and is a single-word entry, as shown here:

```
slave
```

or

```
options forward-only
```

DNS Cache File

The *DNS cache file* contains host address resource records for the root DNS name servers. The DNS cache file is required to resolve name queries for DNS names for which the local name server is not authoritative (that is, domains not contained in the server's zone files). The Internet root name servers are the most common entries contained within a DNS cache file; for networks not connected to the Internet, however, the DNS cache file should contain host address resource records for the root servers of the local network.

Reverse Lookup Files

The *DNS reverse lookup files* are zone files referenced when a DNS name server is searching the `in-addr.arpa` domain to perform a reverse lookup (finding a hostname based on an IP address). One reverse lookup file per subnet exists, containing the information necessary to resolve an IP address to its corresponding hostname. Similar to forward lookup zone files, a reverse lookup zone file also contains NS and SOA records. However, reverse lookup files differ in their use of pointer (PTR) records instead of address (A) records. Pointer records are employed in two ways in reverse lookup operations: to either identify a specific host, or to identify a specific network.

PTR Records to Identify a Host

A PTR resource record is used within a reverse lookup zone file to associate an IP address to a hostname in a reverse lookup zone within the `in-addr.arpa` domain. The PTR resource record is a counterpart to the host address (A) resource record specified in a forward lookup zone.

To create a PTR resource record, the IP address values are written in reverse order with the `in-addr.arpa` domain concatenated to the end of the reverse IP address. The PTR record is structured as shown here:

```
<reverseIPaddress>.in-addr.arpa IN PTR <host>
```

For example, the PTR record for `dragon.mythical.org` at `192.168.111.90` is as follows:

```
90.111.168.192.in-addr.arpa IN PTR dragon.mythical.org
```

Gateway PTR Records

Gateways for a specified network can be located using the `in-addr.arpa` domain. Although gateways are specified with PTR resource records in the same manner that hosts are specified, they also have additional pointer records used to find them solely by network number.

These additional PTR records will use one, two, or three octets of the IP address in the construction of the `in-addr.arpa` domain name, depending on whether they are Class A, B, or C networks. Therefore, a gateway PTR record would look like the following:

- `10.in-addr.arpa` for a Class A network
- `18.128.in-addr.arpa` for a Class B network
- `111.168.192.in-addr.arpa` for a Class C network

Replication of DNS Data

The replication of DNS data follows the single-master replication model discussed in Chapter 3, "Storing Directory Information." This section describes the replication roles used by name servers and the replication operations they use to propagate the changes to the DNS data.

Replication Roles of DNS Name Servers

DNS name servers can be implemented in a range of roles and functionality:

- Primary
- Secondary
- Master

Although DNS name servers are commonly referred to by their role (as a primary name server, or just primary), the server component remains the same (only the tasks performed by the server differ).

Primary Name Servers

A *primary name server* is the server containing a master copy of all DNS information files used in supporting the services for the specified zone. All changes to zone information, including adding hosts, services, or domains, are performed at the primary name server. The primary name server commonly is also the master name server—that is, the source of the resource records transmitted during a zone transfer.

A primary name server acquires its zone information by accessing local DNS information files (zone files), as shown in Figure 6.5. The primary name server for a specified zone is an authoritative name server for that zone.

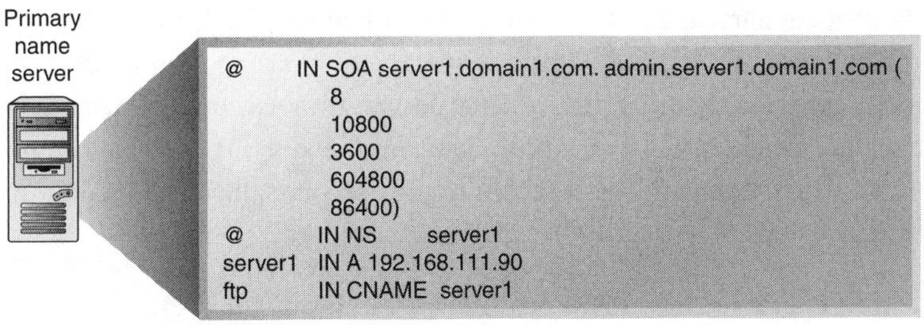
Primary
name
server
@ IN SOA server1.domain1.com. admin.server1.domain1.com (
8
10800
3600
604800
86400)
@ IN NS server1
server1 IN A 192.168.111.90
ftp IN CNAME server1

FIGURE 6.5

The primary name server obtains zone information direct from local zone files.

Secondary Name Servers

A *secondary name server* is essentially a backup name server for a DNS zone that receives its zone information from an authoritative name server (typically the primary name server for the zone). Secondary name servers commonly are used as backup servers to heavily utilized DNS servers, providing name resolution support on a distributed basis.

Secondary name servers obtain their zone information via periodic replications (that is, zone transfers). During a zone transfer, the secondary name server receives the zone's resource records, typically from the primary name server for that zone (which sends current zone data to the secondary zone server), as shown in Figure 6.6.

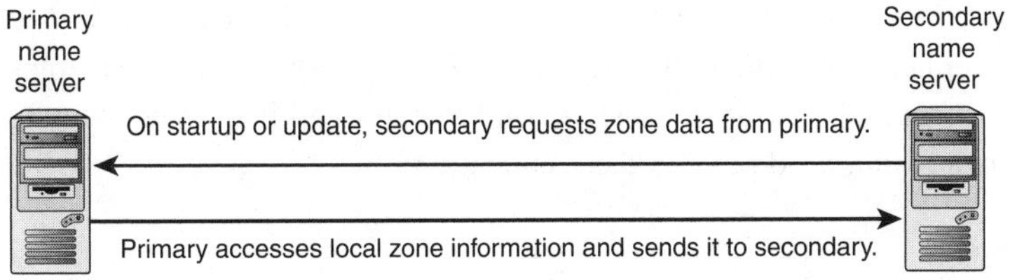
Primary
name
server
Secondary
name
server
On startup or update, secondary requests zone data from primary.
Primary accesses local zone information and sends it to secondary.

FIGURE 6.6

The secondary name server obtains zone information from the primary name server during period updates (zone transfers).

A secondary name server initially requests the zone information from the primary name server upon startup and, from then on, periodically checks for updates by comparing its serial number in the SOA record to the serial number in the primary's SOA record. When the primary's serial number differs from the secondary's, the secondary initiates a zone transfer request.

The frequency of secondary updates is controlled by three key fields in the SOA record, specifically the `refresh`, `retry`, and `expire` fields. Every `refresh` number of seconds, the secondary name server checks the primary name server. If the secondary name server fails to complete the update check, it will retry the update check every `retry` seconds until it succeeds. If it does not complete the update check within `expire` seconds, the zone records are discarded, and the server returns errors to queries in that zone.

Master Name Servers

The designation of a name server as a *master name server* merely specifies that it is the *source* of the DNS zone resource records during a zone transfer. For a secondary name server to acquire its zone information, a name server from which to obtain the zone records must be specified. Although this can be either a primary or secondary name server, in either case it is referred to as the master name server.

> **Name Servers Can Be Both Primary and Secondary**
>
> From the description of the roles performed by name servers, you may have gotten the impression that these are exclusive roles, but that is not the case. Because a name server can support more than one zone, it can be a primary name server for one zone and a secondary name server for another.

Replication Processes

Replication in DNS takes place using some kind of zone transfer. Originally, DNS supported only complete replication—where the entire zone file is sent with each zone transfer. With newer DNS implementations, zone transfers can be performed in an incremental fashion to minimize the bandwidth used in DNS data replication.

Zone Transfers

A *zone transfer* is the process whereby a secondary server receives a complete copy of the zone information from an authoritative name server. A zone transfer essentially transmits a copy of all resource records of a specific zone to the receiving (secondary) server.

Figure 6.7 shows the zone transfer process, which is as follows:

1. By default, the secondary name server periodically checks with the master name server to determine whether zone records have been changed. The secondary requests the SOA record to evaluate the serial number (the version number) of the zone records.
2. The master name server sends the SOA record to the secondary.

3. The secondary server compares version numbers and requests zone transfer if the version number has changed.
4. The master name server begins the zone transfer, transmitting zone file contents to the secondary name server.

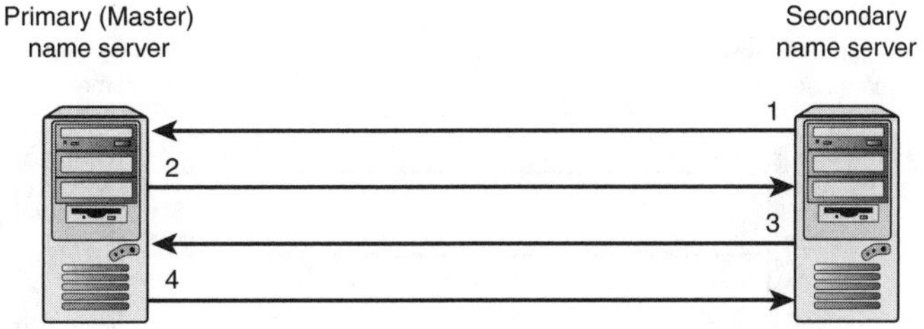

FIGURE 6.7
DNS zone transfer from primary to secondary server.

To accomplish a zone transfer, the secondary name server must specify the name server from which to obtain the zone information. Although the source of the zone transfer can be either a primary or secondary name server, it is always referred to as the master name server.

Incremental Zone Transfers

Initially all zone transfers required transferring the entire set of resource records for the zone during every zone transfer, yet this took more bandwidth than necessary when small changes were made. To enable more effective replication, RFC 1995 described an incremental method for propagation of zone file update information. Incremental zone transfers allows the master name server to send only the resource record information that has changed since the last zone transfer with that secondary server. Because substantially less information must be transmitted, incremental zone transfers are a far more efficient method of DNS zone replication.

Incremental zone transfers require the master name server to maintain not only the updated master zone file, but also a recent history, logging changes to resource records that occurred with each update of the zone file (and its corresponding version number). When the master name server receives an incremental zone transfer request, it compares the version numbers; if they differ, the master name server sends the resource record changes that have occurred between versions.

Zone Transfers with DNS Notify

Instead of waiting for a secondary name server to request an update, a push mechanism for a master name server to notify selected secondary name servers of changes to zone files was defined in RFC 1996 called DNS Notify. DNS Notify allows name servers to push the zone changes to secondary name servers as they occur. The DNS Notify operation requires the specification of the name servers to push updates to, and limits the pushed zone transfers to those designated name servers. Although secondary name servers commonly "pull" (`refresh`) zone updates from master name servers, the DNS Notify "push" implementation provides more timely updates and ensures consistency of DNS zone information (see Figure 6.8).

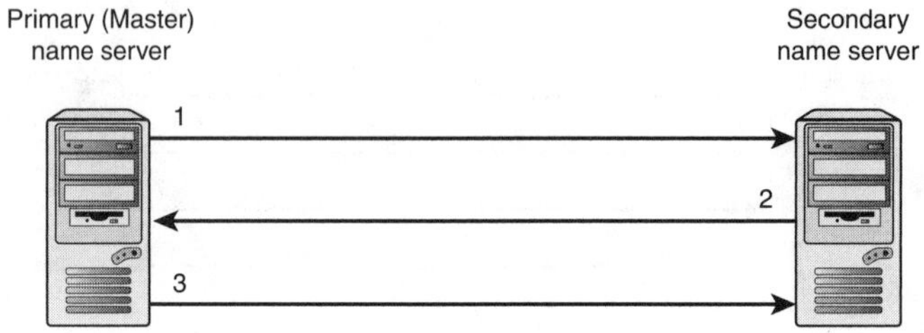

FIGURE 6.8
DNS zone transfer from primary to secondary server using DNS Notify.

1. A DNS Notify process occurs when zone records on the master name server change, and the serial number field in the SOA record is incremented. The master name server sends a DNS Notify message to servers contained within the notify set, and those servers respond with an SOA type query to check the zone file version.
2. The secondary name server compares version numbers; and if the master name server's zone file version exceeds the secondary's zone version number, the secondary name server requests a zone transfer.
3. The master name server copies all resource records for that zone to the secondary name server. When complete, the secondary name server is again authoritative for the designated zone.

For DNS Notify to operate, the IP address of every secondary name server must be contained within the master name server's notify set. After the secondary name server IP addresses are listed in the master name server's notify set, the zone information will be pushed to that set of secondary name servers only.

DNS Operations

DNS provides the operations necessary to support resolution of domain names to IP addresses, as well as to identify hosts of network services. DNS name servers can be assigned different (operational roles) and can be configured to perform different degrees of query processing (such as when configured with `forwarders` or `slave` entries).

Similar to X.500, DNS provides two forms of query resolution:

- One that requires the client to perform most of the lookup processing (an iterative query)
- Another that offloads the query process management to the server (a recursive query)

This section discusses the fundamentals of name resolution, and describes how each of the query types is handled.

DNS Name Resolution

DNS name resolution is the process by which a DNS name server resolves a DNS name to its corresponding IP address. Typical DNS approaches to resolving a name query are referred to as *recursive name resolution* and *iterative name resolution*, prompted by the corresponding type of query. In addition, a special kind of name query allows for reverse name resolution process (from IP address to name), commonly referred to as a *reverse lookup*.

A naming system strategy that uses a distributed database (such as DNS), is commonly presented with a condition in which a name server receives a client query that can be resolved only by another name server. A DNS name server that receives a name query but cannot perform the name resolution itself will refer (or provide) the name query to another name server.

The following section discusses the different roles in which a name server operates, and then describes how DNS name queries work. The section also reviews the specific recursive and iterative name resolution processes.

Operational Roles of Name Servers

Fundamentally, DNS name servers operate in one of two operational roles:

- Authoritative
- Caching-only

Authoritative Name Servers

A DNS name server may control one or more zones containing one or more domains. A name server has *authority* for each zone that it controls and is referred to as an *authoritative* name server. For a name server to respond positively to a name query, it must be an authoritative server for the zone containing the queried name.

The primary name server for a specified zone is an authoritative name server for that zone. If the secondary name server's zone data is current, the secondary name server is also authoritative for the specified zone.

The authority for a DNS name server to provide name information within a specified zone is defined using an SOA record. When a name server contains the SOA record in its zone file for a particular DNS domain or subdomain, that name server is referred to as *authoritative* or as an *authoritative server* for that zone.

Caching-Only Name Servers

A *caching-only name server* is not linked to any specific zone and does not contain its zone files. When a caching-only name server initializes, it has no information on zones or domains and relies exclusively on other primary or secondary name servers for its information. A caching-only name server builds its DNS information from queries passed to primary or secondary name servers and stores the information in its local name cache.

The caching-only name server (see Figure 6.9) directly processes additional queries referencing the DNS information stored in its local cache. The sole function of caching-only name servers is to perform name queries, store the responses in their local cache, and return the query responses to the client submitting the query. The cached DNS data remains in the cache until the Time-To-Live (TTL) expires or the next reboot of the server.

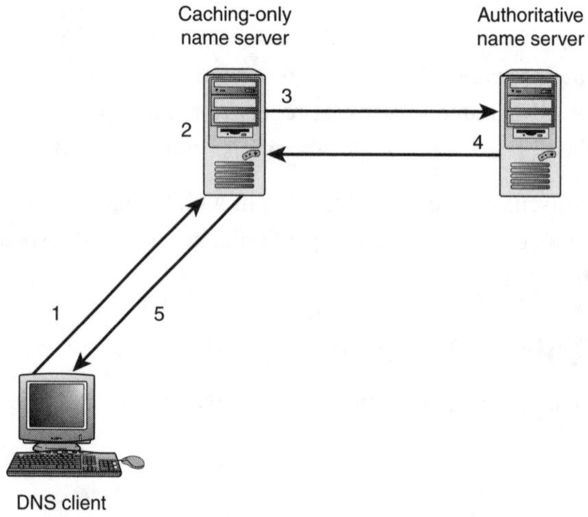

FIGURE 6.9

A caching-only name server does not have local zone files and builds its cache from name query requests it handles.

Figure 6.9 shows how a caching-only server performs, which is as follows:

1. A DNS client submits a recursive query.
2. The caching-only DNS server is not linked to any zone (and does not contain local zone files) and, therefore, looks in cache for resource records matching query.
3. If a match is not found in cache, the name server queries other name servers.
4. The authoritative name server for the zone returns query results to the caching-only name server.

5. The caching-only name server stores the query results in its local cache for future access and returns the results to the client.

DNS Name Queries

A typical DNS name query (forward lookup) is initiated by a client resolver requesting name resolution for a specific host or domain name. The DNS client resolver (or a name server) may submit either iterative or recursive name queries to the name server.

The key difference between an iterative name query and a recursive name query is:

- When a client passes a *recursive query* to the name server, it requests the name server to complete the name resolution process on its behalf (by querying other name servers).
- With an *iterative query*, the client requests the server to provide only whatever local information it has (and not to query other name servers).

A DNS name query is resolved starting from the left side of the submitted DNS name (containing the most specific portion), proceeding through the domain components to the right side of the submitted DNS name (containing the most general portion of the domain name). The name resolution process uses each component of the domain name in an effort to locate an authoritative name server for the submitted name query.

When a name server receives a resolver query for a specific domain name, it first checks the zone files for which it has authority. If it finds the name, it provides the authoritative result to the client. If it does not have the name in its zone records, it checks its local cache to see whether it has resolved the query before—if it has, it provides the authoritative result to the client.

A name server will commonly pass DNS requests it cannot resolve to a higher-level server in the DNS tree (using the NS records of the parent domain to locate the right servers to query for the requested domain). If the DNS server is presented with a query for an unknown domain name, the resolver may query other name servers higher in the DNS tree or may redirect the query to the root name servers. The resolver typically continues to query other name servers until it receives an authoritative response to the query.

Caching DNS Query Results

DNS name servers temporarily store name query information results in a local cache, allowing the name server to retrieve commonly requested DNS information rapidly, without having to access other name servers. DNS information that is stored in the local cache has a TTL value applied to the cached resource records. Although all DNS name servers will cache the results of name queries that have been submitted to them, *caching-only* name servers will not be authoritative for any domain and will merely contain DNS query results for name queries that they process.

Iterative Name Resolution

Iterative name resolution is like the X.500 referral process because the name server receiving the name query either answers the query authoritatively or refers the client to another name server. When the information requested in an iterative name query is not found in local zone files or cache, the name server does not query other name servers on behalf of the client.

An iterative name resolution request instructs the name server to attempt to complete name resolution from within its own DNS dataset (see Figure 6.10). If the contacted name server contains the requested information, it will provide it to the client; otherwise, it may return pointers to other name servers that may contain the queried data (but will make no attempt to contact the other name servers on behalf of the requesting client).

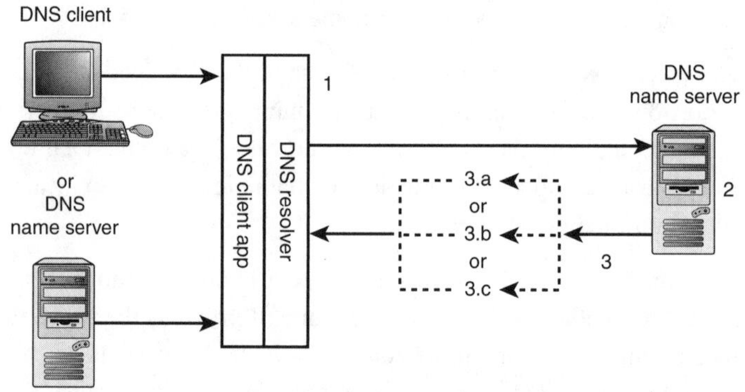

FIGURE 6.10

An iterative query to a name server essentially asks for the best information the name server has available but does not request the name server to pursue the query for the requesting client.

Figure 6.10 shows how an iterative name query to a name server occurs, which is as follows:

1. DNS client resolver (can be a DNS client or another name server) submits an *iterative* query to a name server.
2. The receiving name server first tries to resolve the name query within local zone records.
3. The name server provides one of the following three responses to client:
   - 3.a—If the query can be resolved via local zone records or cache, the name server returns the zone data (zone resource records with corresponding hostnames and IP addresses) in query results to the client.
   - 3.b—If the query cannot be resolved locally, the name server returns a referral (best guess at closest relevant domain name server) to the client, for the client resolver to use in further name queries.

- 3.c—When an authoritative name server for the zone cannot resolve the query from its zone records or cache, it will return an error to the requesting client specifying that the requested data is not found.

Iterative name resolution is also referred to as a *nonrecursive name resolution* because the name server responds to the query based on its own DNS information and does not recursively send the query to other name servers.

Recursive Name Resolution

Recursive DNS queries are similar to the X.500 chaining process, in which query resolution is pursued on the server side and only complete results are returned to the client. Recursive name resolution is where the server receiving the query pursues name resolution with other name servers on behalf of the client submitting the query. DNS name servers must be specifically configured to allow recursive forwarding of name queries.

Submission of the recursive query tells the name server to provide the client with a complete response to the query—not just a reference or a pointer to an alternative DNS name server. The name server queries other name servers until a definitive result for the originating query is obtained:

- A definitive positive response to the name query occurs when an authoritative name server verifies that the target of the query exists and provides the requested results in the query response.
- A definitive negative response to the name query occurs when an authoritative server verifies that the target of the name query does not exist.

Recursive DNS server operations are commonly employed by *stub resolvers* (a resolver component that provides a minimum functionality) and rely on recursive operations for name resolution and address translation. Stub resolvers are frequently configured to query a specific set of servers, and they expect to receive an authoritative response to queries (as opposed to referrals).

Figure 6.11 shows a specific example of recursive name resolution, in which the client submits a recursive name query on the domain name `www.mythical.org` to a local DNS name server that queries the DNS root name servers to resolve the domain name. This process is as follows:

1. The DNS client resolver submits a recursive query for `www.mythical.org`.
2. The local name server fails to resolve the name query within its zone records.
3. Because the query cannot be resolved locally, the name server submits an iterative query to the DNS root name servers.
4. The root DNS name server is not authoritative for zone, so a referral to the `.org` domain name server is returned.

5. The local name server queries the `.org` name server.
6. The `.org` name server is also nonauthoritative, but it does contain reference to the authoritative name server for `mythical.org` and, therefore, returns a referral to the `mythical.org` name server.
7. The local name server queries the `mythical.org` name server.
8. The `mythical.org` name server is the authoritative name server for the zone that includes `www.mythical.org` and, therefore, returns the requested host IP address, `192.168.111.90`, to the local name server.
9. The name server then returns definitive query results (the IP address of `www.mythical.org`) to the requesting client.

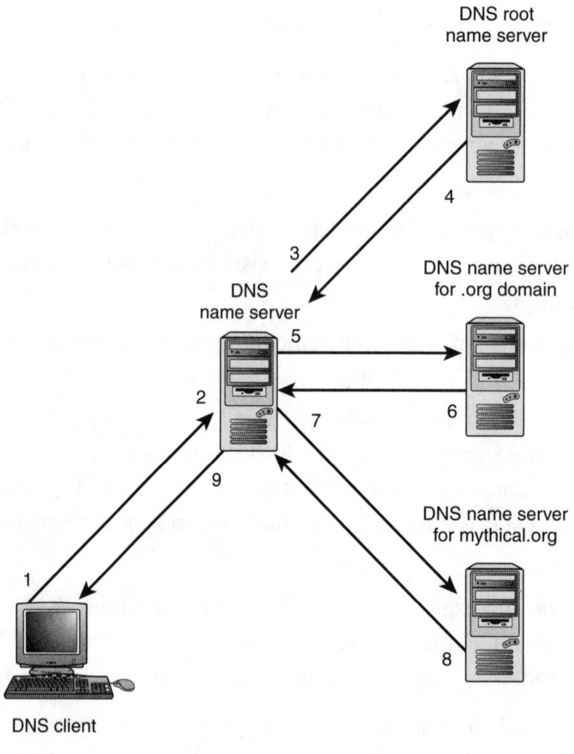

FIGURE 6.11
In recursive name resolution, the local name server pursues a query on behalf of a client until it is resolved.

Reverse Lookups

In most DNS queries, the client submits a DNS host and domain name, requesting the corresponding IP address (a forward lookup). Yet sometimes a resolver will submit an IP address to receive the assigned DNS hostname from a name server. A DNS query that requests this address-to-name resolution is referred to as a *reverse name query*, or *reverse lookup*.

There is no structural correlation in the assignment of DNS domain names and IP addresses, a factor which by default would require a search of all domains within the namespace to provide a resolution to a reverse lookup. To provide the capability to effectively perform reverse lookup operations, a special domain called `in-addr.arpa` was created within the DNS namespace. The `in-addr.arpa` domain functions by naming its nodes with the numbers used in IP addresses.

DNS domain names become less specific from left to right, with the most specific (hostname) information on the left side, to the least specific (top-level domain name) on the right side. In contrast, IP addresses become more specific from left to right, with the network number represented in the first octet(s) and the host identifier represented in the remaining octet(s). This differential direction of specificity in the ordering of DNS names versus IP addresses requires the reversal of the IP address octets in the delineation of the `in-addr.arpa` tree. In other words, because DNS and IP go from less-specific to more-specific in opposite directions, the `in-addr.arpa` structure reverses the IP address.

Like address records used in forward lookups, in the `in-addr.arpa` domain PTR records are used to correlate IP addresses to hostnames in reverse lookups.

As an example of the reverse lookup process, consider this: To locate a hostname for the IP address `192.168.111.90`, a client resolver would submit a query to a DNS name server for a pointer record indicating `90.111.168.192.in-addr.arpa`. If the submitted IP address is not contained within the local DNS domain, the name server will begin at the DNS root and perform sequential domain node name resolution. When the sequential name resolution reaches `111.168.192.in-addr.arpa`, the zone records would be searched for a pointer type resource record for host `90`, which would resolve to the domain host `dragon.mythical.org`. At this point, the reverse lookup process would be completed and the results returned to the client.

Name Resolution with `forwarders`

DNS servers can be configured with `forwarders` entries to control DNS lookups to name servers. `forwarders` entries enable you to specify the order and the scope of a DNS lookup process and provides a means to control the flow of DNS query traffic for security or other operational reasons. Generally, in an enterprise network with connectivity to the Internet, direct DNS lookups to external servers would be restricted to specific internal name servers.

If a name server has `forwarders` specified, it can also specify that it should only use `forwarders` as a `slave` (queries are not sent beyond the name servers specified in the `forwarders` entry). `forwarders` and `slave` entries are optional entries in the DNS boot file.

DNS Servers Configured with the `forwarders` Entry

In DNS, `forwarders` are essentially a list of name servers to query first. The `forwarders` entries are added to the beginning of the list of name servers to query if the requested domain information is not available in local files. If the `forwarders` entry is present, other name servers (such as the root name servers) will only be queried if the `forwarders` provide no response within a short period of time.

These `forwarders` are commonly used in enterprise networks to provide a means to have all DNS lookups search the internal DNS namespace first, and to access external name servers (such as the root name servers) only after internal resources have been exceeded. In common configuration, only specified internal name servers would be allowed to forward name queries to external DNS servers. Depending on results received, the name server will respond in one of two ways:

- If a name server receives a name query that it cannot resolve, it first forwards (sends) the query to the other name servers specified in the `forwarders` entry. The specified name server then processes the forwarded name query and returns the query results to the requesting name server.
- If the forwarder does not answer the query within a specified period of time, the originating resolver will transmit the query to other name servers.

DNS Servers Configured with the `slave` Entry

A name server configured with the `slave` entry in the boot file requires an existing `forwarders` entry (in other words, the `slave` entry is dependent on a `forwarders` entry being present). A name server configured with the `slave` entry must either use only the name servers specified in the `forwarders` entry or return a failure message if they cannot resolve the name query request. A DNS server configured with the `slave` entry does not attempt to contact alternative name servers if the name servers on the `forwarders` list cannot resolve the name query.

The DNS `slave` entry works in combination with the `forwarders` entry, specifying that the list of name server records will *replace* (instead of being added to the beginning of) the list of name server records to query when queries cannot be resolved locally. The `slave` entry effectively prevents referral of DNS name queries to the name servers other than those specified in the `forwarders` entry. Using the `slave` entry, if the query cannot be resolved by the specified list of `forwarders`, the query will not be resolved at all.

Slave Operations in BIND

Some DNS implementations, notably later versions of BIND, use the syntax options `forward-only` to indicate that the name server should function as a slave.

Name Resolution Processes with `forwarders`

In Figure 6.12 (see next page), two forms of name resolution are displayed with the lookup processes using `forwarders` and `slave` entries specified in the DNS boot file. The diagram begins with a DNS client submitting a name query for a DNS hostname, as follows:

1. A DNS client submits a name query.
2. The name server attempts to resolve the query within local zone records. When a name server fails to resolve a name query, it performs different name resolution processes (depending on whether it has `forwarders` or `slave` entries specified). These variations on name resolution are demonstrated in A and B:

   A. If configured with a `forwarders` entry—A DNS name server is required to first use a designated list of forwarders to resolve all queries outside the local zone, *before* attempting to contact other name servers (including the DNS root name servers). DNS name servers to query first are specified in the `forwarders` entry in the DNS boot file and are operationally prefixed to the NS lookup records.

   3. The name server first queries the name server(s) specified in the `forwarders` entry.
   4. The name server receives a response indicating query failure.
   5. The name server then queries the DNS root name servers.

   B. If configured with a `slave` entry—A name server configured with the `slave` entry (in the DNS boot file) forwards DNS queries to designated forwarders *only* and does not attempt to contact DNS name servers outside of the designated forwarders list. A `slave` name server depends entirely on the specified list of forwarders to provide query resolution, whereas name servers without a `slave` entry are allowed to relay DNS queries to name servers in the DNS cache file (usually the DNS root name servers on the Internet) after a designated period of time.

   3. The name server first queries the name server specified in the `forwarders` entry.
   4. Upon receiving a response, the name server makes no further attempt to contact other name servers.

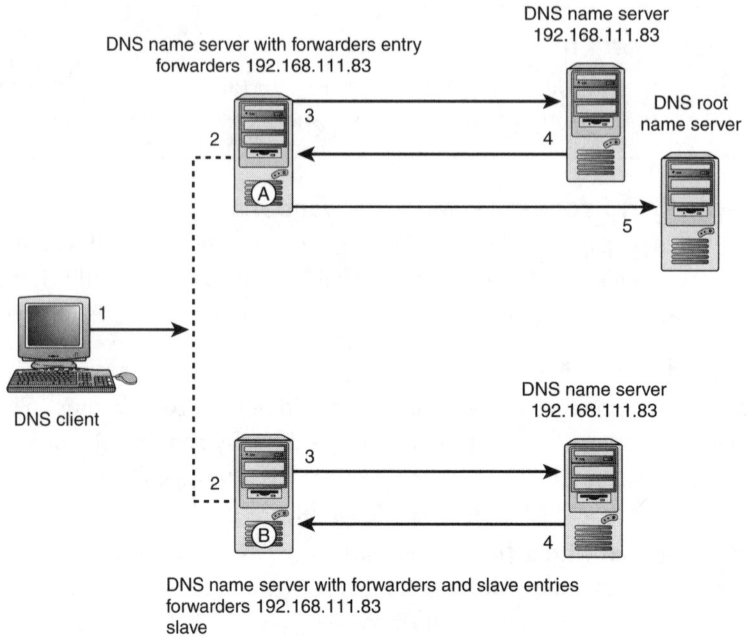

FIGURE 6.12

DNS name resolution with `forwarders` *or* `slave` *entries.*

Proposed DNS Extensions

DNS is an evolving technology with new functionality and operations being continuously proposed. Besides the base DNS operations, proposals for dynamic updates, IPv6 support, network service location, and security mechanisms are being considered. DNS is also being integrated into directory service implementations such as Active Directory and NDS eDirectory.

Support for dynamic updates of DNS data (Dynamic DNS) is described in RFC 2136, "Dynamic Updates in the Domain Name System (DNS UPDATE)."

Integration of network service location is described in RFC 2782 (replacing RFC 2052), "A DNS RR for Specifying the Location of Services (DNS SRV)."

Additionally, extensions to DNS to provide IPv6 support are proposed in the following RFCs:

- RFC 1886, "DNS Extensions to Support IP Version 6"
- RFC 2373 (obsoleted RFC 1884), "IP Version 6 Addressing Architecture"
- RFC 2874, "DNS Extensions to Support IPv6 Address Aggregation and Renumbering"

DNS Security

The security considerations in DNS differ from directory services, in that it does not perform user authentication or access control over the information stored in its directory. DNS does not have user objects, does not track users as a discreet information entity—clients accessing DNS services are always doing so anonymously.

This lack of user and security management makes DNS's role as a specific-use directory more apparent. It is not designed to track or control user access to DNS information —it is simply supposed to provide it upon request, irrespective of the origin of the query.

While there are several RFCs which are describing security mechanisms for DNS, they are not intended to authenticate the user nor provide user access control.

Although accepted DNS standards do not specify security mechanisms for DNS operations and are not commonly implemented, the following RFCs suggest support for public key (PK) technology and DNS security operations. Given the widespread support for use of X.509 certificates in network security operations, implementation of PK technology in DNS seems likely. Security related DNS RFCs include

- RFC 2065, "Domain Name System Security Extensions"
- RFC 2137, "Secure Domain Name System Dynamic Update"
- RFC 2230, "Key Exchange Delegation Record for the DNS"
- RFC 2535, "Domain Name System Security Extensions"
- RFC 2536, "DSA KEYs and SIGs in the Domain Name System"
- RFC 2537, "RSA/MD5 KEYs and SIGs in the Domain Name System"
- RFC 2538, "Storing Certificates in the Domain Name System"
- RFC 2539, "Storage of Diffie-Hellman Keys in the Domain Name System"
- RFC 2540, "Detached Domain Name System Information"
- RFC 2541, "DNS Security Operational Considerations"
- RFC 2931, "DNS Request and Transaction Signatures"

DNS in Directory Services

DNS is being integrated as the location service (and more) into many networking directory service products such as Active Directory. Because LDAP is the most widely accepted directory service access protocol, the integration of DNS and LDAP is significant in that DNS provides the location services and LDAP provides the query functionality. Use of DNS domains in LDAP and X.500 is proposed in RFC 2247, "Using Domains in LDAP/X.500 Distinguished

Names." The integration of DNS and LDAP was described in detail previously in Chapter 5 in the "Features of LDAP" and "DNS Domain Names in LDAP" sections. With this integration, directories will be containing, managing, and distributing DNS information, reducing the need for standalone DNS servers, and cutting the cost of DNS network administration.

Dynamic DNS (DDNS)

Dynamic DNS allows DNS resource records to be dynamically updated to reflect changing server availability and IP addresses. The addition of DDNS is a significant improvement because it provides the functionality to resolve hostnames to dynamically assigned IP addresses. Traditional DNS resource records are static records written in the DNS zone file. All changes made to DNS zone records had to be individually and manually modified.

DNS Is Providing More and More Functionality

DNS lacks a number of things one would expect of a full-featured directory service: user management; schema flexibility; adequate security; and most critically, DNS has an extremely limited set of possible objects (or in DNS terms, resource records). In any case, whatever you call it, DNS doesn't have very many different things it could manage.

This isn't really a problem. DNS isn't supposed to manage many different things; it is just supposed to provide the most highly accessible, massively scalable, distributed directory ever. And it succeeds amazingly well.

`<consider>`

Take just a second and consider what DNS actually does, as a global directory of domain names, and how well it works, and how seldom it breaks. Then consider that it is managed by a collection of hundreds of thousands of people (of widely varying skill levels and experience) who almost never communicate with each other. And the data is stored in text files, not a fancy database, but text files....

Pretty impressive, huh?

`</consider>`

Even though DNS has these initial limitations in scope, new functionality is being added to DNS to address needed capabilities in security, integration with LDAP, and location of network services (as described previously). Further, to enable the support for dynamic changes in the networking environment, Dynamic DNS is being implemented on a variety of platforms, and for a variety of purposes. While DNS has performed its original tasks admirably well, it is being extended to address the emerging needs of network and directory technologies.

However, *Internet Service Providers* (ISP) and enterprise networks commonly rely on the *Dynamic Host Configuration Protocol* (DHCP) to supply IP addresses to network clients. Unfortunately, there has not been a way to include the dynamically assigned TCP/IP addresses within the static DNS files. DDNS provides this critical mechanism, enabling administrators to dynamically include DHCP clients in the DNS database.

As proposed in RFC 2136, DDNS specifies a new resource record type called `UPDATE`, which provides a means of performing dynamic updates of resource records on a zone's primary name server.

Using a network with DDNS implemented provides certain key advantages, most notably that changes to DNS zone data can be automatically performed by the DNS name servers (thus minimizing DNS administration). Another advantage to using DDNS is that it can work with DHCP and other dynamic registration services (such as WINS) to synchronize all name-to-address mapping throughout the network.

The updating method used in DDNS is consistent with earlier static DNS in allowing zone updates to be performed on a zone's primary name server only. Using dynamic updates, a primary name server can be provided a list of authorized name servers that are allowed to initiate the zone updates. These authorized dynamic update servers can include secondary name servers as well as DHCP servers.

There are controls over how updates take place in DDNS. In its application, DDNS allows the specification of a set of conditions that must be met for the dynamic update to be performed. DDNS is effectively atomic in nature. Therefore, only if all conditions are met will a DNS update be allowed. For a DNS update to occur, the following conditions must be met:

- The request must confirm that the required resource record (or resource record set) exists or is in use.
- The request must confirm the requesting server is allowed to update the specified resource record.
- The request must confirm the requesting server is allowed to initiate dynamic update of the specified zone.

After all conditions are satisfied, the primary name server proceeds with updating the specified resource records.

X.500 Directory Services

CHAPTER

7

...forms summoned forth from ancient runes...

IN THIS CHAPTER

Although X.500 defines the general architecture for most directory services, only some directory products on the market are *truly* X.500 compliant. These X.500 directory services are general-purpose products; the information, management, security models, and distributed operations can be applied to a wide range of requirements.

This chapter looks at several X.500 directory services, noting in particular their level of adherence to X.500 and how they differ from X.500. Although many aspects of X.500 directories are highly similar, differences in the focus of individual vendors are played out in the final products.

Introduction to X.500 Directory Services

The X.500 standards thoroughly define a distributed directory service. Information, administration, and security models, as well as distributed operation methods, client and server protocols, and APIs are described in detail.

Some aspects of the directory service specified in the X.500 standards leave little room for variance; they must be implemented in a particular way to ensure interoperability. The X.500 information model, for example, determines the directory contents, organization, and naming, while the protocols are also standardized so that any X.500 client can communicate with any X.500 server.

Because of these similarities, some design and operational dimensions can be assumed to be true for all X.500 directory services. During the discussion of these products, the following aspects of a directory service should be considered essentially the same:

- **Objects and Schema**—The base schema described in the X.500 standards is implemented by each of these directory servers, along with their own selected enhancements. Many

> ### A Design Guide, Not a How-To
>
> Although this book is clearly not an administrative "how-to" guide, it aims to help you understand why different directory services work the way they do—from an architectural perspective. By understanding the underlying directory structures and operations, you can more clearly see how the design decisions made by a particular vendor influence the resultant directory service offering.
>
> Accordingly, this book examines a number of directory service products, starting with X.500 in this chapter, followed in later chapters by LDAP-only directories, eDirectory, and Active Directory. During each product's discussion, you'll see how it implements different aspects of a directory service to help you understand how the underlying architectural assumptions influence its ultimate capabilities.

additional schema are available from vendors and organizations, among others, any of which can be used to extend the default directory schema.

- **Directory Tree**—The directory tree defined by X.500 is also used by all these directories, with trees that are geographically modeled and/or based on the enterprise organization being common.
- **Naming**—Naming is another facet of the directory that the X.500 standards mandate. Every X.500 directory service supports the same naming style, although they might also implement additional naming forms due to LDAP support or for other reasons.

Any significant deviations from, or additions to, the standards are noted in the introduction to each product.

Rather than reiterating what is essentially the same data about each directory (things common to X.500 directories), this chapter focuses on those things that are different from one product to the next. Some of the things that differ from one X.500 directory to the next include

- **Intended use**—Is the directory service meant for general-purpose user management or is it part of a messaging platform? This influences the specific features available in the product; a directory for military use has extremely stringent security demands, for example.
- **Related products**—What sorts of bundled and/or related products are provided? How do they enhance or extend directory functionality?
- **Data storage mechanism**—Most X.500 directories use a commercial database to store the directory information; however, no two vendors use the same one. The selection of database technology has a significant impact on the ultimate directory performance.
- **Style of LDAP support**—Most X.500 directory services support LDAP access to the directory, although the exact methods of supporting LDAP vary quite a bit. Some directories provide native LDAP and integrate external LDAP directories into the X.500 directory, while others offer a simple DAP-LDAP gateway.
- **Distributed operations**—One area where optimization of the directory is possible is in the implementation of distributed operations. eTrust, for example, separates its routing and chaining functionality into a router module that is optimized for managing distributed directory operations.
- **Technical aspects of security**—Although it's true that the X.500 security model requires that the products are largely the same in the high-level design, the specific security mechanisms used can vary.
- **Administration approach and tools**—The administration model supplied by X.500 controls some of the overarching administrative structures, however, the specific capabilities provided and the administrative tools supplied will differ.

Each of the vendors focuses on a different portion of the directory market and molds its directory offerings in that image. Nexor, for example, has demonstrated a dedication to the government and military messaging market, and accordingly, its directory is part of a high-security messaging platform.

Computer Associates' eTrust Directory

eTrust Directory is positioned as an e-business enabler; a globally scalable directory service that can integrate information regarding employees, clients, partners, and vendors to enable new ways of doing business. Computer Associates describes eTrust deployments by large corporations, banks, ISPs and government agencies in applications including white pages, PKI, and other Internet security, e-mail, user authentication, voice integration, and catalogs.

Introduction to eTrust

eTrust is a fully X.500-compliant directory service designed to deliver extremely high performance in a large-scale, globally distributed environment. Scalability is linear, based on processor and storage capabilities; increasing processor throughput allows an eTrust DSA to service more requests, while increasing available disk space allows for more data to be stored.

eTrust uses patented indexing algorithms, and comprehensive knowledge references that are used to carry out shortest path routing between DSAs, speeding directory lookups. Directory performance is further enhanced with features such as query streaming and load balancing. This has helped eTrust demonstrate subsecond search performance in a directory holding tens of millions of entries.

eTrust Directory is fully LDAP v.3 compliant, and also supports a number of extensions, including server-side sorting, virtual list views, and persistent searches. External LDAP servers, such as iPlanet or eDirectory, can be integrated into the eTrust backbone, allowing any LDAP server to transparently act as part of a unified directory tree. The DSA manages queries directed to the LDAP directories along with the eTrust DAP (X.500) traffic.

eDirectory as an X.500-Style General-Purpose Directory

eDirectory provides another interesting perspective on general-purpose directory development. X.500 is the architectural base for eDirectory, providing it with the same highly scalable, general-purpose information management framework as the X.500 directories discussed in this chapter (although without support for X.500 protocols such as DAP). Moreover, Novell has ported eDirectory to most major platforms, freeing it from its earlier dependencies on NetWare, and is positioning it as a general-purpose directory that *also* can manage networks.

The eTrust Directory is part of the eTrust security product line from Computer Associates. The eTrust security products have been bundled into three general solution sets, addressing different critical business needs. Each solution bundles a number of components that combine to supply the needed functionality. The eTrust solution sets are:

- **eTrust Internet Access Solution Set**—Web client authentication and access control supporting single sign-on for Web sites and services, X.509 certificate management, dynamic personalization for portals, and virtual private networks (VPN).
- **eTrust Management Solution Set**—Centralized enterprise and security management.
- **eTrust Defense Solution Set**—Internet security and monitoring; antivirus; firewall; and guards against hacking, denial-of-service attacks, and intrusion.

eTrust Directory was previously called OpenDirectory.

Client/Server Agents

DXserver employs a pair of DSA agents; a *router DSA* and a *data DSA*. As you might guess from their names, they manage the routing and distributed searches and the directory information, respectively. The use of separate modules allows the optimization of each module for the specific processes it carries out. The router DSA can be deployed without the data DSA to serve as a DSP switch or relay for directories, firewalls, and proxy servers.

DXserver has two integrated subcomponents:

- **DXlink**—Integrates external LDAP servers into an eTrust tree, allowing any LDAP server to function as part of the eTrust enterprise directory.
- **DXtools**——Data management utilities that import, export, and synchronize information from external data systems.

The DSA

DXserver, the eTrust DSA, is a fully X.500 and LDAP v.3 compliant DSA that doubles as a directory router. It is designed to run in a small memory footprint regardless of the amount of data or number of clients being managed, and performance is unrelated to the size of the directory database.

Patented Technologies

Computer Associates holds 30 patents on technologies developed for eTrust Directory. These include the design of the metadata table and SQL interface used to connect to the Relational Database Management System (RDBMS), and its method of indexing every attribute of every object in the directory.

A one-to-one relationship doesn't necessarily exist between servers, DSAs, and databases. The relationship between DSAs and databases might be one of the following:

- Multiple instances of the eTrust DSA can be run on a single server to increase the maximum possible concurrent clients handled. Each DSA instance can manage a different database, or multiple DSAs can share a single datastore.
- A single datastore (replica) can be managed by multiple DSAs (running on one or more servers) to improve performance and provide failover capabilities for the DSA. Additional replicas can be created for data redundancy or to distribute replicas proximate to clients that need the data.
- A single instance of DXserver can manage more than one database as well, transparently switching between multiple datastores as needed.

eTrust is available for these platforms:

- Windows 2000
- Windows NT Server 4
- Solaris (SunSparc) v.2.6, 7, and 8

eTrust Clients

eTrust communicates with any client that uses DAP, LDAP, or LDAP over Secure Sockets Layer (SSL). This means that DAP and LDAP clients from other directory products, such as Active Directory or iPlanet, can interoperate with DXserver.

Two client applications are provided with eTrust:

- **JXplorer**—A graphical user interface (GUI) LDAP browser written in Java.
- **DXplorer**—Lightweight 16-bit Windows client using DAP.

Programming eTrust

XDS, the common means of accessing X.500 directories, is supported; XDS is essentially a programmatic version of DAP supporting all DAP functions and arguments. To support eTrust's LDAP functionality, the LDAP C API is supported.

Scripting tools are also provided to allow for the automation of directory management tasks.

> ### The eTrust Schema
> A number of standard schema, in addition to that defined by X.500, are included with eTrust. These schema include those used for DEN, ISP, CTI/IVR, postal, security, government, financial services, document management, and catalog services, among others.

The eTrust Directory Information Base

Computer Associates used its *Ingres* relational database as the storage subsystem for eTrust. Ingres brings with it a strong set of capabilities and tools. Performance is enhanced with caching and query optimization, and tools are provided to optimize, tune, and monitor the database.

Single master replication is performed in accordance with the X.500 standards, employing both primary and secondary shadowing mechanisms.

In addition to the standards-based replication method, a second synchronization method, the *DXreplicator Option*, is provided. DXReplicator uses a two-stage transactional process that employs checkpoints and has rollback capabilities.

All the DSAs holding a particular naming context can be updated simultaneously using eTrust's *multiwrite* capability. Multiwrite allows a group of peer-level DXservers to be kept in sync without interruption to service. DSAs being updated via multiwrite can continue real-time directory operations while the updates are being processed. If one server in the peer group fails, the router module redirects queries sent to the inaccessible DSA to another DSA in the group.

Replicated information can be filtered at the attribute level, providing a control over which data is replicated to any other system. This can offer a measure of security by blocking the replication of sensitive data, or provide replicas with smaller datasets for catalogs or address books.

eTrust Operations

DXserver can perform both chaining and referral in its distributed operations. The DXserver router module is responsible for much of the directory's distributed operations, including routing, knowledge information management, and load balancing. The router module also manages chained operations, performing tasks such as compiling search results and routing queries to alternate DSAs as needed.

Storing eTrust's Data

eTrust doesn't store the active copy of the DIB in RAM, as some directories do, using the data stored on the disk instead. This lessens the chance of data loss in the event of server failure. DSA startup time is also drastically reduced—to as little as *five seconds* according to Computer Associates—because there is no need to load a large datastore into RAM.

Directory traffic is prioritized and routed based on the type of action being requested, ensuring that queries, which require fast responses, are not held up by modification requests, which take more time. Routing is based on the current state of the network, dynamically changing to provide optimal performance.

With DXserver's routing capabilities, a number of DSAs can work together to provide a highly responsive directory backbone that can manage a high volume of traffic. Queries can be distributed to multiple DSAs, often the entire directory backbone, so that *all* the DSAs can collectively perform more simultaneous operations and provide faster results.

Comprehensive knowledge references are stored, allowing shortest-path routing to other DSAs. This can greatly speed name resolution and server location, especially in large, widely distributed directories. Parallel multicasting speeds distributed operations to subsecond—eTrust has been tested at 1,500 searches per second.

Patented algorithms are used to fully index the directory database to enable extremely high performance when servicing directory queries. By indexing the entire directory, eTrust provides performance that is unrelated to the amount of information the directory holds. Any single piece of data can be retrieved with only two hits to the hard disk. The combination of shortest-path routing and the fully indexed database ensures that distributed operations and directory lookups are performed quickly, using a minimum number of tasks.

DXserver can be deployed without a datastore to serve as a *dedicated* router for directories, firewalls, and proxy servers. The dedicated router can be designated to manage the directory traffic for other eTrust DSAs, both those managing a specific database and load-balancing DSAs.

The router module is also responsible for distributed operations, load balancing, routing, and knowledge information management for connected LDAP directories.

eTrust Security

DXserver complies with (1993) X.500 authentication and access control mechanisms. Clients can be authenticated to eTrust via the usual X.500 methods of simple or strong authentication. As an LDAP v.3 server, DXserver also supports Kerberos, SSL, and SASL for LDAP operations.

Strong authentication is provided using X.509 certificates and tokens, such as smart cards. PKI certificates from a number of vendors, including Entrust, Verisign, and Baltimore Technologies, are supported. Mutual authentication between DSAs affords an extra degree of security during chained operations and replication.

eTrust uses the X.500 access control model, including basic and simple access control, as well as rules-based access. Permissions can be assigned for a filtered or unfiltered subtree, individual objects, sets of objects, or individual attributes. Access control rules are applied universally across a management domain.

Routing performed by DXserver can be subject to access controls, providing an additional layer of security for distributed operations. Credit-based controls can be used to stop denial-of-service attacks.

eTrust Administration

DXserver management is eased by the capability to share a common configuration among a network of DXservers. Knowledge information between servers is managed automatically as well. Database management, including swapping out and adding databases, can be done while the DSA is operational, without interrupting the handling of client queries.

Two management tools are provided with eTrust:

- **DXplorer**—This tool provides database management functionality, including data loading, dumping, archiving, and replication. The schema can be imported or exported as well.
- **JXplorer**—A Java-based management console that supports configuration and fault management, index and database table tools, LDIF (Lightweight Directory Interchange Format) data import and export, as well as schema management.

Audit, fault, and performance logging is available. Comprehensive audit logs can be created for statistical and accounting purposes. X.700 and SNMP (Simple Network Management Protocol) are supported for alarms, logging, and tracing directory operations.

Scripting tools also are provided to facilitate the automation and customization of directory information management.

Real-Time Validation of PKI Certificates

eTrust OCSPro is a companion product to eTrust that performs real-time validation of X.509 certificates. OCSPro uses the *Online Certificate Status Protocol* (OCSP) to obtain the current status of certificates from the appropriate certificate authority. OCSPro also offers alarms and tracing, and can create audit trails to maintain a record of all status transactions for certificates. OCSPro is available for Sun Sparc Solaris (versions 2.6, 7, and 8), Windows NT, and Windows 2000.

Training on eTrust

Computer Associates offers several classes on eTrust Directory for network administrators, focusing on security aspects of the directory. These classes cover topics such as introduction to eTrust, directory administration, intrusion detection, access control, and single sign-on.

Information on these classes is available at `ca.com/education/descriptions/etrust.htm`.

Siemens DirX

As a general-purpose, fully LDAP-compliant directory solidly rooted in the X.500 architecture, *DirX* supplies the scalability and flexibility needed for application as an enterprise directory service. DirX is designed to handle information on users and distribution lists, as well as network devices, applications, and services.

The range of applications for which DirX is suitable encompasses the entire range of enterprise and distributed applications/operations: from a "white pages" lookup service for employees, partners, suppliers, and customers, to an enterprise-wide security solution supporting PKI, and single sign-on capabilities to provide cross-platform authentication and access control.

Its foundation in the X.500 architecture provides DirX with the underlying framework for truly distributed directory service operations and functionality. This enables DirX to operate across a geographically and operationally diverse enterprise while maintaining reliability and availability to directory clients in every location.

Introduction to DirX

The directory service supplied by DirX is fully compliant with the X.500 (1993) specifications as well as the related ISO-9594 standards. The DirX DSA implements the X.500 user and DSA information model, administrative model, as well as schema and access control. It provides (among others) support for collective attributes, subtree-specific schema definitions, subtree-specific access control rules, operational attributes, and attribute subtyping.

DirX is a robust distributed and replicated X.500 directory service, using a proprietary database built on top of a commercial ISAM kernel for its data storage backend. Directory data integrity and recovery is ensured via the database's secure, transaction-based data management and rollback capabilities.

LDAP v3 has been comprehensively integrated into the DirX directory product, providing full support for LDAP applications. LDAP support in DirX is provided by an LDAP server component that integrates with the X.500 DSA. Full support for LDAP v.3 is provided including RFCs 2247, 2251–2256, 2559, 2605, and 2696. Further integration with LDAP-enabled applications and services is provided via DirX's support for the LDIF data import and export.

DirX is a high-performance system, providing high availability and responsiveness. Performance is enhanced by the use of indexes in the database and holding critical information in memory. There are three levels of memory caching in the system: at the database, at the DSA, and at the LDAP server level. The responsiveness of the DSA and of the LDAP server are optimized through their multithreaded structure and via the various caching mechanisms that enable high rates of throughput on parallel queries.

Client/Server Agents

The DirX product consists of a number of servers and tools, which collectively provide an enhanced LDAP and X.500 directory to standard clients. DirX also includes several user agents, mostly for administration. Extra functionality and access methods, such as HTTP access or integration with other directories are provided by additional products of the suite, which are tightly integrated with DirX. The server-side components of DirX are:

- **DirX DSA Server**—A fully X.500 compliant directory providing services via DAP over either the OSI stack or TCP/IP.
- **DirX LDAP Server**—A fully compliant LDAP v.3 server to any LDAP client as well as to the DirXweb server. The LDAP server runs as a separate process from the DSA, on the same server or a different one, and is managed with standard DirX tools.

The additional server products include:

- **DirXweb**—A Java-based servlet implementing an HTTP to LDAP gateway that allows Web browsers access to DirX information via HTTP.
- **DirXmetahub**—The metadirectory product in the DirX suite, DirXmetahub provides integration and bidirectional synchronization between a variety of directories and data sources. For a more complete discussion of DirXmetahub, see Chapter 11, "Metadirectory Services."

The various server components can be deployed as needed by a given business. Each server product can have a dedicated server or, if the client load is light enough, multiple products can be installed on a single server. For load-balancing purposes multiple instances of the LDAP server or DirXweb can be deployed.

DirX's server architecture is shown in Figure 7.1. DirX is accessed by external applications over LDAP, or over DAP in the case of some legacy tools and applications. Other X.500 DSAs, including other DirX DSAs, employ the usual X.500 protocols DSP and DISP to provide for distribution and replication. The LDAP server(s) and the DSA are tightly integrated over an internal, non-public protocol. Both the LDAP server and the DSA support non public RPC access available only to the DirX management tools.

The DirX administration components and the overall relationship to other clients and servers is shown in Figure 7-2. DirXweb is just a normal LDAP application which can be used with any LDAP v3 compliant directory.

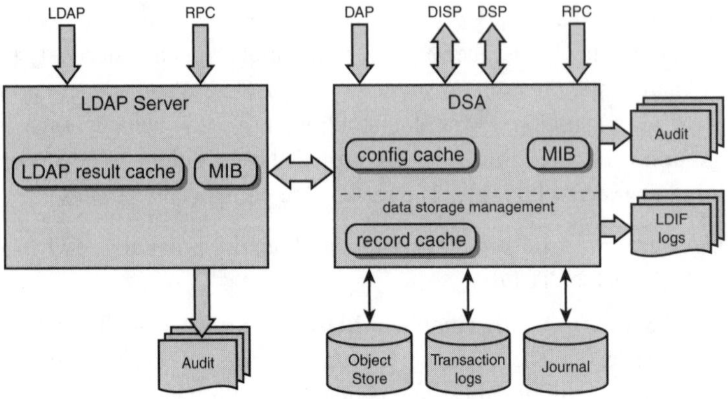

FIGURE 7.1

DirX is comprised of two servers that act together to provide access to directory data across LDAP and X.500 protocols.

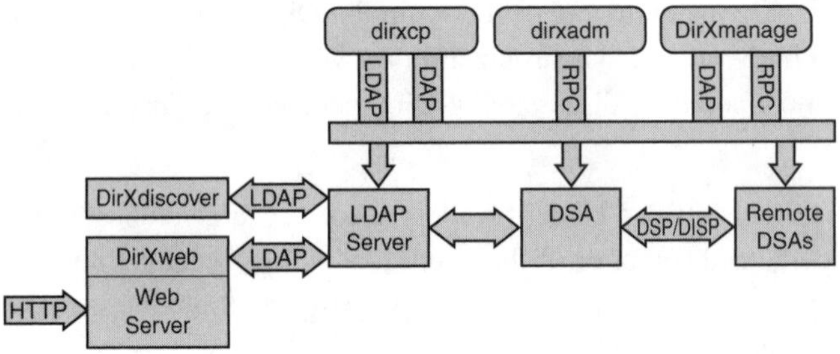

FIGURE 7.2

DirX administration tools use both standard and internal protocols to remotely manage the system, while all other applications access the server over LDAP or DAP.

As shown in Figure 7.2, DirX supplies access to a variety of client applications, which can access DirX using several methods:

- **HTTP**—Web browsers can obtain directory information over HTTP from the DirXweb server.
- **LDAP**—Any LDAP v3 client can perform directory operations. *DirXdiscover* is an LDAP client for corporate resource location and address book; `dirxcp` is a command-driven LDAP DUA.

- **DAP**—The *DirXmanage* and `dirxcp` tools as well as any X.500 DUA can perform directory operations over DAP
- **RPC**—Two of DirX's management tools, `dirxadm` and DirXmanage, use RPC, which allows things not possible over LDAP or DAP, such as starting and stopping the DSA. This is not a public protocol open to other applications.

The DSA

The DirX DSA is fully X.500 (1993) compliant, although not all options of the standards are implemented; a few minor functions are lacking (a seldom-used knowledge reference isn't supported), but nothing you are likely to notice. On the other hand, DirX supports parts of the 1997 X.509 standards so its certificate handling is substantially improved over 1993, storing the latest version of certificates and revocation lists.

The DirX DSA is a robust directory server that uses threads to facilitate the multitasking needs of a directory service supporting a high number of concurrent clients.

The DirX DSA is available on these Unix and Windows platforms:

- AIX
- HP-UX
- Solaris
- Reliant Unix
- Linux
- Windows NT
- Windows 2000

> **Not Limited, Technically...**
>
> In a number of areas, the DirX DSA is described as having no hard limitations. Some of the things described as "unlimited" are:
>
> - Number of objects in directory
> - Number of naming contexts (partitions)
> - Number of simultaneous users

The LDAP Server

DirX includes an integrated LDAP server which implements the full LDAP v3 standard, and supports LDAP v.2 for legacy clients. LDAP provides the standard way for applications to access the directory information and database. The LDAP server can be collocated with the DSA or remote from it, and gets its configuration from the DSA. More than one LDAP server can front-end the DSA providing load balancing and/or for supporting different LDAP configurations.

The LDAP server in DirX is implemented as a high-performance, multithreaded server with a powerful result cache mechanism. It has similar auditing, logging, and monitoring capabilities as the DSA and is available on the same platforms as the DSA. It also implements SSL/TLS for secure LDAP access, with both server and client authentication supported.

DirX Clients

Client access to DirX is provided via LDAP and HTTP (and DAP for some legacy purposes), while management applications also can use the RPC interface. One client for end users, *DirXdiscover*, is provided as a separate product, while several management agents are part of DirX.

DirXdiscover is an LDAP client designed for corporate end users, offering the ability to easily access network resources. This Windows application has a customizable multiple-document interface, allowing the configuration of several views of directory information. A private address book and an offline address book designed for laptops are available.

Users can search the directory, modify their own information (subject to access control), and even export directory data directly to Windows Office applications. Clients can exchange data between DirXdiscover and Windows applications using a number of methods; Microsoft API (MAPI), Telephony API (TAPI), Dynamic Data Exchange (DDE), Object Linking and Embedding Custom Controls (OLE OCX), and OLE Automation.

Clients also can access the directory using DirXmobile, which provides LDAP directory access via the Wireless Application Protocol (WAP) for WAP-enabled telephones.

The most common client platform used to access the directory is Web browsers. DirXweb, which supplies an HTTP to LDAP gateway, enables development of Web pages with dynamic access to DirX data. Both read-only (client) and data management (administrative) scenarios are supported.

Programming DirX

Programmatic access to the DirX directory is supported over LDAP. Application developers can choose among a number of third party LDAP SDKs available for free for most of the relevant platforms and languages.

DirX provides a TCL LDAP (and DAP) client called `dircp`, that can be used to develop scripted applications. DirXmetahub has a sophisticated environment to develop TCL scripted LDAP applications and embed them into synchronization workflows.

A number of APIs are available via DirXdiscover including Microsoft Telephony API (TAPI), Messaging API (MAPI), OLE Custom Controls (OCX), OLE Automation, and Dynamic Data Exchange (DDE).

The DirX Directory Information Base

The DirX DIB is stored in a proprietary ISAM-based database optimized for search and read operations, making extensive use of indexing and caching algorithms. The database ensures data integrity by providing transaction and rollback capabilities at the granularity supported by the wire protocols. An off-line database checking, repairing and reorganization tool called `dirxreorg` is supplied with DirX.

Replication in DirX is based on the 1993 X.500 standards providing for only single master replication. Secondary shadowing, also known as *cascaded replication*, is supported in the DirX directory. This enables a specific replica server to operate as a hub that redistributes the shadowed (replicated) directory information to other DSAs.

When performing replication, the DirX DSA provides a wide selection of shadowing capabilities. Replication in DirX supports both supplier-initiated and consumer-initiated replication operations. Complete replication and incremental replication are both implemented by the DirX directory service, and replication based on data change events, as well as periodic updates, are supported. DirX replicas can be either full copies, or a filtered subset of objects and/or attributes.

DirX Uses Server-Internal Identifiers

Each directory object has a 4-byte identifier, which is used internally by the DSA instead of the distinguished name. This allows a small amount of data to be stored for each object when compared to a distinguished name string. Object names can be compared by comparing the reference number.

The use of a reference number also means that if an object is renamed or moved, resulting in a DN change, most of the behind-the-scenes management work is taken care of automatically. The object name change is made in every place that object is referenced, keeping access privileges, group memberships, and so on, intact.

Everything is not totally automated; PKI certificates for example, have the actual DN embedded within it, thus if the DN for the user changes, the certificate is invalid and a new certificate must be issued. This is because certificates are sealed (signed) and should not be changed dynamically.

Updates can take the form of a *total refresh* or an *incremental refresh*, to use X.500 terminology. Obviously, the incremental refresh method is used most of the time; total refresh is reserved for operations such as populating a new replica or repairing a damaged one.

Both push and pull styles of replication are supported—synchronization can be initiated by either the supplier (master) or consumer (shadow). This allows the master to push important changes to shadow replicas, and shadows to request updates when needed. Synchronization can be triggered by changes to the master or scheduled to occur at a selected interval.

In addition to the X.500 protocol-based replication, DirX supports a public file interface for replication events based on the LDIF format. The whole database, or specific subtrees, can be exported directly from the DSA backend into LDIF content format. Similarly, changes to the database content can be exported in LDIF change format periodically or upon change event. Triggers can be associated with these events to start further processing. This functionality is essential for integrating DirX with other applications and for support of meta-directories.

All the information regarding a DSA's binding agreements is held in the `Cooperating-DSA` operational attribute, providing a single location for all operational binding information.

DirX Operations

DirX can, depending on the need, use either chaining or referral, including LDAP referrals, for distributed operations. More interestingly, DirX can try to resolve any referral or continuation reference it receives during chained operations and, if that does not succeed, pass along the referral to the client so that it can pursue the query on its own. This offers the advantages of chaining with the guarantee that a DSA will not spend an inordinate amount of time chasing down the result for any given query.

DirX Schema

The default schema includes the complete 1993 X.500 schema and portions of the 1997 X.509 specification. Also all LDAP object classes and attribute types defined in RFCs 2251 and 2252 are supported. Additional operational attributes are defined for use in managing the DirX DSA. Schema definitions from the X.402 "Information technology—Message Handling Systems (MHS): Overall Architecture" specification are also included. Additional schema elements can be easily defined using the management tools.

The common knowledge references (subordinate, superior, and so on) are supported, although the nonspecific subordinate reference (NSSR) is not. DirX uses cross-references to speed name resolution; to ensure that access control information is passed correctly between DSAs, and that the DSAs mutually authenticate, the cross-references must be explicitly created, not acquired via DSP.

Information caching is used to improve directory performance. Frequently used information is organized into data structures that the DSA holds in RAM to speed access. This is commonly used for access control information to provide for extremely fast security decisions.

DirX Security

As an X.500 directory service, DirX supports the X.500 security standards for authentication and access control. Support for security technologies, such as SSL/TLS, is provided for LDAP servers and clients for authentication and secure, encrypted communications across nonsecure networks (such as the Internet). Authentication is used in both client-server (LDAP clients to LDAP server or DUA-to-DSA communications), as well as in DSA-to-DSA operations.

The authentication of LDAP clients to DirX include

- Name and password in clear
- Name and password via an encrypted connection (server-side SSL)
- PK user certificate (client-side SSL) also called strong LDAP authentication.

X.500 methods of authentication used by DirX in DAP, DSP and DISP include:

- **Simple-unprotected**—A plain text password is used, stored as an encrypted attribute of the user object.
- **Simple-protected**—An encrypted password is used rather than a plain text one.

DSA associations can require authentication, improving security during replication by ensuring that data is not intercepted or tampered with. The passwords used during DSA-to-DSA authentication are not usually stored in the directory as normal attributes. DSA passwords are usually supplied during the process that establishes the operational binding agreements and stored (encrypted) by the appropriate DSAs.

X.509v3 (1997) certificates are supported in DirX, as well as standardized extensions, and the functionality the PK infrastructure has been tested with certificates from industry-leading certificate vendors. Both certificates and *certificate revocation lists* (CRL) can be stored by the DirX DSA.

Strong authentication via PK certificates in DirX is supported over LDAP and can either be server-based (in which the authentication is via a server-side SSL connection using a server certificate) or client-based (in which the client certificates are used to authenticate the user).

Trust relationships can be created between DSAs (policy operational attributes); trusted DSAs, and users authenticated by them, are not treated the same as untrusted DSAs. This might mean being given different access privileges or having authentication considered valid in circumstances in which the same user chained from an untrusted DSA would not be considered valid.

In a distributed directory, user authentication must be managed between multiple DSAs. When using simple authentication, the client is authenticated by the first DSA encountered and that client identity is passed from one DSA to the next during chained operations. Each DSA maintains a list of the DSAs it trusts, and users authenticated by a trusted DSA are granted appropriate access rights by the trusting directory. Users whose original authentication was done by an untrusted DSA are treated as if they were anonymous clients. This offers a means to easily discriminate between two different security classes.

Granularity of control over objects and attributes is provided in DirX, as X.500 basic access control and simplified access control is supported for objects and attributes. DirX does not provide access control for specific *values* of attributes—which means that you can not provide different access rights to the various values of a recurring attribute.

Access control information is consistently retrieved by all directory operations, and thus quick access to this information is essential. To speed access control decisions, all access control policy information is held in local cache memory by the DirX DSA. Each directory object also has relevant access control information at the beginning of the data comprising its DSE value.

Access control decisions can take into account the quality of authentication as well as the identity of the user. Factors that can be considered include

- The identity of the entity requesting access
- The original authentication methods if known (simple, strong, and so on)
- Whether the DSAs that forwarded the request are trusted

DirX Administration

The administration of DirX is like most X.500 directories, in that both GUI and command-line tools are available to manipulate the directory tree, objects, attributes, schema, partitioning, replication, and other directory operations. To facilitate a reliable and robust directory implementation, DirX administration additionally supports these data management features:

- Database management, including backup and recovery.
- Auditing and logging of directory transactions both for the DSA and the LDAP server.
- Customized indexes of selected attributes can be created to improve search performance.

The DirX administration tools include:

- **DirXManage**—A Windows-based directory browser with an administrative interface that allows management of directory information and directory servers. Directory object and attribute creation, deletion, and assignment of values is supported, as well as directory-management operations. Its strengths lie in the management of schema and policy, access control, LDAP server configuration, auditing and logging, shadowing and distribution as well as the monitoring of servers.
- **`dirxcp`**—A command-line administration tool that uses LDAP or DAP to access and manage directory information.
- **`dirxadm`**—Another command-line directory management tool; `dirxadm` uses RPC, and is thus able to do management tasks not possible over LDAP or DAP (such as starting or stopping the DSA).

The two command-line tools act together to provide complete directory-management functionality. They are based on TCL, a powerful scripting language that can be used in conjunction with the DirX tools to significantly streamline directory administration. Both `dirxadm` and `dirxcp` operate in *interactive* mode, for administrators managing the directory, and *command* mode, convenient for use with TCL scripting.

Integration with Windows NT simplifies directory management; DirX events can be viewed with Windows Event Viewer, for example, and an administrator authenticated for Windows NT also is authenticated for DirX.

Securing the Directory Tools

The administration tools, DirXmanage and `dirxadm`, provide access to information and functions normally hidden not only from users, but sometimes from administrators as well. To guarantee that only authorized people use these two tools, DirX identifies specific administrators via an operational attribute called `DirX administrators`. The distinguished names listed in this attribute identify the administrators able to bind with either `dirxadm` or DirXmanage.

Nexor Directory

Nexor has focused its product line on military and intelligence environments with its rigorous security demands, although it does have some commercial business customers. Nexor describes its directory as a "third-generation" directory service. Nexor makes the distinction based on the data-storage method; directories using b-tree file packages and relational databases are considered first and second generation, respectively.

Introduction to Nexor

Nexor Directory implements an X.500 (1997) compliant directory service, enhanced with an eye toward use in secure environments. The directory serves as the user-management backbone for large-scale messaging systems and is scalable to those needs.

In an approach somewhat different from most X.500 directories (which generally use relational databases), Nexor uses Versant's *object database management system* (ODBMS) to store the directory data. An ODBMS allows directory information to be stored as a number of objects that have defined relationships between them. Performance is improved because the directory tree can be traversed rapidly. Nexor has written a white paper (*"Object-Oriented Databases and Mission-Critical Directories"* June 1998) describing some of the differences between RDBMS and ODBMS and why it selected an ODBMS for its directory. You can download it at

`www.nexor.com/papers/OODB White Paper.pdf`

The Nexor DSA provides native LDAP access, supporting RFCs 2251, 2252, and 2253. Bulk loading of directory data can be performed using LDIF; Nexor reports bulk-loading performance of over 250,000+ entries per hour.

DirX's Management Information Base

A management information base (MIB) is used for monitoring DSA and LDAP server activities. Statistics about DirX and its application layer operations can be provided by these MIBs. DirX supports three MIBs:

- **The Network Services Monitoring MIB (RFC 1565)**—Describes elements that are common to OSI network services.
- **The X.500 Directory Monitoring MIB (RFC 1567)**—Describes elements specific to a DSA, including process and network related aspects.
- **The Directory Server Monitoring MIB (RFC 2605)**— Describes elements that are specific to an LDAP directory.

Nexor has established a significant presence within the government and military marketplace, providing a secure messaging and directory infrastructure. Nexor has made a commitment to delivering products for organizations that have stringent security demands, something its product line demonstrates.

Nexor Defender relies on the Nexor DSA to deliver a high assurance (that is, secure) messaging platform meeting international standards for military class security. Nexor Defender provides an integrated secure e-mail solution with a mail server, directory server, and security extensions for off-the-shelf e-mail clients. In addition to the X.500 DSA, Nexor Defender components are:

- **Nexor Mailer**—A high-performance X.400/SMTP message switch with advanced management features and military-level security (available for Solaris and Windows NT).
- **Directory Guardian**—This directory firewall, built for the high-security market, can completely mask directories from public view while providing access to those with the appropriate authentication (available for Windows NT and Solaris). Users can be granted the right to perform specific tasks, subsets of directory information can be exposed (to provide a public employee directory, for example), works on DAP, LDAP, DSP, and DISP.
- **Defender Client Agents**—Defender also provides agents that extend commercial e-mail clients to provide high assurance messaging for X.400 and Microsoft Exchange. The two agents, *Nexor Defender for Motif* and *Nexor Defender for Outlook*, share a modular security architecture allowing new security libraries to be added as needed. Clients using different security mechanisms can nonetheless communicate with each other securely. Both clients include an LDAP address book.

Client/Server Agents

The Nexor directory provides a single server agent and no clients. The server operates independently to provide an X.500 directory that can be applied to just about any purpose. In conjunction with other components of the Nexor Defender suite, the DSA can provide the sort of secure messaging platform needed by the military or intelligence.

Standards Conformance Testing

Nexor is active in compliance testing with groups including the World Electronic Messaging Association Directory Challenge, NameFLOW-Paradise, and the COS Pilot. Many X.500 directory services being tested for compliance must *first* prove their compatibility with Nexor Directory; it is the reference platform for a number of major conformance-testing bodies, including the U.S. Department of Defense's Joint Interoperability Test Command (JITC) and the U.K. National Computing Centre.

The DSA

Nexor's DSA is fully compliant with the 1997 X.500 standards and offers a native LDAP implementation. The Nexor DSA can hold 20 million objects and manage an unlimited number of concurrent users.

Nexor Directory is available for the following platforms:

- Windows NT
- Solaris
- HP-UX

Nexor Clients

Client access to the Nexor DSA is provided natively via DAP and LDAP. One common use for Nexor Directory is as part of a security infrastructure layer used in conjunction with off-the-shelf mail clients, such as Outlook, to provide a secure messaging platform. Accordingly, one of the common clients to Nexor Directory is an e-mail client, frequently enhanced with one of the Defender secure client extensions.

In addition to the Defender user agents, Nexor provides the Messageware Address Book Service Provider, a MAPI/LDAP address book as a no-charge download from its Web site.

Programming Nexor

Nexor Directory provides support for programming clients to communicate with the directory using DAP. A complete line of SDKs to support the Defender product line, including the Nexor Directory, is available. SDKs are available for Windows NT and Solaris.

APIs supported by the collection of Nexor SDKs include

- **XDS**—Provides access to X.500 directory services.
- **XMS**—Provides access to X.400 message stores.
- **XMT**—Provides access to X.400 mailer functionality.
- **XOM**—Provides object-management functionality underlying the previously listed items.

The purchase of an SDK from Nexor comes with a couple of extremely useful "extras." A two-day training class is included, offering a complete overview of the product and covering each of the supported APIs. Training includes slide presentations, demonstrations, Q & A, and example coding. Full support is also provided.

The Nexor Directory Information Base

The Versant Object Oriented Database provides the data-storage mechanism used by Nexor Directory. Nexor describes the advantages of an object database as including

- Support for all relational database functionality.
- The capability to directly map directory objects without the decomposition required to use a relational database.
- Improved performance due to the direct relationships between directory objects and database objects.

Replication is performed in accordance with the X.500 standards, meaning single-master replication with master and shadow replicas. A shadow server easily can take over for the master if a network or system fails.

Information packaged for replication can be digitally signed to ensure the integrity of synchronized data. Nexor's (or another vendor's) firewall also can filter DISP, the protocol used for replication, guaranteeing that sensitive data is not replicated outside the internal secure environment.

Nexor Operations

Nexor Directory performs distributed operations in accordance with X.500's model for managing distributed directory information. Both chaining and referrals can be performed by a Nexor DSA.

ODBMS are particularly suited for the navigational style of queries used in a directory service. Parent-child relationships between directory objects are directly maintained in the database, speeding the process of walking the directory tree to retrieve information.

Directory operations, both between client and server and between DSAs, can be digitally signed for additional security.

Nexor Security

Authentication and access control are implemented in accordance with the X.500 standards. Authentication is provided using three methods:

- **None**—Anonymous user access is allowed, which is acceptable for read-only public information, but not very useful in most other environments.
- **Simple**—A username and password are needed to log in to the directory; this offers a bit more security, but because the password can be encrypted or plain text, it's clearly not sufficient for Nexor's target market.
- **Strong**—Authentication using strong cryptographic technologies—such as X.509 certificates—is needed for the government and military environment. Nexor also uses digitally signed data to guarantee data is not tampered with during transmission.

Nexor's strong authentication is based on *Secure Data Network System* (SDN) 705, an implementation guide describing exactly how digital signatures can be used over X.500 protocols to provide a secure distributed directory. The National Security Agency (NSA) developed SDN 705 for implementation in U.S. military and intelligence environments.

Both simple and basic access control methods, as defined by the X.500 standards, are implemented. Access permissions can be assigned down to the individual attribute level. Access control templates can be created to make it easier to assign permissions. An access control template contains a set of permissions and can be assigned to a number of users who need the same access rights.

Nexor Administration

Nexor supports standardized administration, per the X.500 (1997) standards, allowing the secure delegation of directory management. Nexor Directory supplies a Web-based management interface that allows multiple directories to be managed simultaneously.

Database recover and restore operations can be performed while the DSA is online, avoiding interruption in service to clients. Database bulk loading also can be done using the Web management tool.

LDAP-Only Directory Services

CHAPTER

8

...a different path through the same forest...

IN THIS CHAPTER

This chapter looks at several directory products that are based on the Lightweight Directory Access Protocol (LDAP) standards. Because LDAP defines only a client access protocol, each vendor has had to decide upon proprietary approaches to provide much of the directory functionality. Because of this, the directory servers discussed in this chapter only share their support for LDAP and have many variations in how they supply directory functionality from one implementation to the next.

Introduction to LDAP-Only Directory Services

Because LDAP came on the scene in the early 1990s, every directory vendor has added support for it to its product lines, with more than a few vendors providing native LDAP, and others offering gateway-style LDAP access. This has helped spur development of LDAP clients and led to broader adoption of directory services in general. Recently, some products have come on the market that are not proprietary or X.500 directory services with native LDAP; rather, they are standalone LDAP-only servers.

Although LDAP is arguably the most widely used method of client access to directory services, it isn't a directory service in and of itself. Remember that LDAP was designed as a lightweight alternative to DAP for accessing X.500 directories. Accordingly, what is described by the LDAP standards only pertains to the directory access protocol, a relatively small portion of overall directory functionality.

Yet, a directory service is a lot more than just an access protocol; it's a system of servers that collectively manages a distributed database while providing security services to clients, applications, and network services. LDAP, by design, doesn't provide any of the server functionality. In its original incarnation as a client to an X.500 directory, the underlying directory takes care of all those complicated details.

A Protocol, Not an Architecture

Two critical points bear repeating here:

- LDAP is a directory access *protocol*, not a directory architecture.
- X.500 provides the *architecture* upon which LDAP is built.

This is a common area of confusion, particularly because LDAP servers have become a viable product category. Admittedly, work continues on enhancing the LDAP standards by defining complex functionality such as replication; at times, this process seems to be reinventing the X.500 wheel. Remember, however, that whatever directory functionality is not defined by LDAP is implemented via proprietary means, potentially hindering interoperability.

Because LDAP doesn't need to deal with the specifics of directory operations, it doesn't. This isn't an oversight on the part of the developers of the LDAP standards; the protocol is supposed to be lightweight, after all. If it had to carry all X.500 definitions on its shoulders, it wouldn't be so light.

The flip side to this is that—given all the directory functionality defined in the X.500 standards, but not in LDAP—if you were planning to design standalone LDAP *servers*, a lot of functionality would have to be added proprietarily. Without a common standard for much of the server functionality, each LDAP directory implementation probably would be somewhat different from the others. However, this wasn't initially a problem because LDAP wasn't designed to be a server; LDAP is, after all, only an *access protocol*.

Well, that was then, and this is now…and, of course, *now* there are standalone LDAP directory servers. Not surprisingly, every standalone LDAP (or LDAP-only) directory server is somewhat different from the rest.

SLAPD (Standalone LDAP Daemon)

Every directory product has its architectural touchstone, and for LDAP servers, it's the *Standalone LDAP Daemon* (SLAPD). The University of Michigan team that first defined LDAP as a means of accessing X.500 directory servers developed SLAPD. The first implementation of an LDAP server was as a gateway to X.500 directory servers. An LDAP server sat between LDAP clients and X.500 servers translating LDAP requests into DAP requests and chasing

Rooted in LDAP

Because each of the directory servers described in this chapter is based on LDAP, they have far more in common than they have differences. All the LDAP-only directory servers support the LDAP data model, naming model, use the same base schema definitions and construct the same DIT. Thus, in the discussion of each directory server, the focus is on each vendor's approach to implementing an LDAP directory to avoid unnecessary reiterations of the basics of LDAP.

A Sampling of LDAP-Only Directory Services

The chapter does not attempt to review every LDAP-only directory service; many fine products are available that are not described here. Rather, the products described here show the range of implementation styles—from classic open-source SLAPD to iPlanet's more ambitious offering.

referrals for clients. This server, commonly called theUMich or U-M implementation, was first released in 1992. This freely available version of LDAP led to the development of a number of LDAP clients.

The team at UMich soon noticed that almost all (99%) the access to its X.500 servers was taking place via LDAP. This meant that the LDAP gateway was translating virtually every client request for the X.500 servers, adding an extra layer of processing to 99% of directory requests. The point of LDAP was, after all, to simplify the directory access process and this was not necessarily *simpler*.

Accordingly, the team decided to create a standalone LDAP server. This server, dubbed SLAPD, was created in 1995. The initial release of SLAPD supported LDAP v.2. For a lightweight implementation of a directory server, the first SLAPD server had some advanced features:

- Choice of data storage mechanism and a database API (Application Programming Interface) allowing the creation of custom data-storage mechanisms
- Multiple databases (linked to naming contexts) per DSA
- Authentication and access control
- Basic replication capabilities using SLURPD (Standalone LDAP Update/Replication Daemon)

There were also some downsides to the initial release of SLAPD, such as the lack of support for X.500 aliases and the default LDBM database had some performance issues with certain types of queries. Overall, however, it was an excellent start at implementing a lightweight directory server.

In addition to the ongoing open source work, a number of commercial LDAP servers have been developed based on SLAPD. These directory products usually have significant proprietary enhancements to add areas of functionality not addressed by SLAPD. The team that created SLAPD and SLURPD went on to spearhead the Netscape Directory Server (now iPlanet) project.

More Information on SLADPD

You can access historical reference information on the UMichSLAPD SLAPD implementation at `www.umich.edu/~dirsvcs/ldap/#servers`. For current information on open-source LDAP software, the UMich site refers visitors to OpenLDAPat `www.openldap.org`. For a discussion of the current state of the open source SLAPD server, please read the "OpenLDAP" section later in this chapter.

SLURPD (Standalone LDAP Update/Replication Daemon)

After a standalone LDAP server was created, it became obvious that replication of directory information was a necessary function. Accordingly a method of providing updates to other LDAP servers was needed. SLURPD records the changes to the information held by a SLAPD server, and provides those updates to other SLAPD servers.

SLURPD uses a *change log* file to record the changes made to the directory. Each change is recorded in the order it is made, and those changes are played back in sequence to the consumer server. LDAP is used for server-server communications during replication.

Change log files are not necessarily the most efficient method of synchronizing data. If multiple changes are made to a single object, each of those changes are propagated, rather than just updating the consumer with the cumulative results. It does, however, provide a relatively simple method of performing synchronization.

Many commercial LDAP-only directory products use a type of change log file to record directory changes that need to be replicated to other servers. This has proven to be a good thing for interoperability efforts; if the LDIF (Lightweight Directory InterchangeFormat) file can be read, and translated to another directory's format, replication can (at least theoretically) take place between them.

LDAP 2000 Certification

The Open Group, in cooperation with the Directory Interoperability Forum (DIF), has developed the LDAP Open Brand initiative to identify LDAP products that fully comply with the standards. These certifications are intended to help promote the adoption of LDAP directory products by providing a neutral certification standard guaranteeing that LDAP products meet interoperability standards.

Open Brand initiative has two certifications:

- Open Brand for LDAP 2000
- Works with LDAP 2000

> **`slapd.conf`**
>
> SLAPD configuration is done via a single text file, `slapd.conf`, which is read in by the DSA when it's started. The entries are read in the order they appear in the file, and many processes stop searching the file when they encounter the *first* entry that fits their needs. This means that you must pay close attention to the construction of `slapd.conf` to ensure the proper operation of a SLAPD DSA.

Open Brand for LDAP 2000

The Open Brand for LDAP 2000 certification is awarded to server products that meet standards for LDAP compliance. This includes conformance with the mandatory requirements for an LDAP server as defined in RFCs 2251, 2252, and 2253. LDAP 2000 branded servers must support the Secure Sockets Layer protocol (SSL) v.3 and supply X.509 v.3 certificates that conform to RFC 2459 for authentication. Referrals and continuation references must be provided in compliance with RFC 2251, and the mandatory requirements of RFC 2254 and 2255 must be met when returning LDAP URLs in referrals and continuation references. These servers have received the LDAP 2000 certification:

- *Injoin Directory Server* v.3.x (Critical Path)
- *iPlanet Directory Server* v.4.11 (Netscape|Sun Alliance)
- *NDS eDirectory* v.8.x (Novell)
- *Oracle InternetDirectory* v.2.x (Oracle)

Works with LDAP 2000

The Works with LDAP 2000 certification is awarded to applications that are certified to work with any server that carries the LDAP 2000 brand. To date, 24 products have been awarded the Works with LDAP 2000 certification including

- *eProvision Day One* (Business Layers)
- *DirXML* (Novell)
- *PeopleSoft Directory Interface for Human Resources* v.1 (PeopleSoft)
- *SAP Directory Interface for User Management* v.6.10 (SAP)
- Distributed Computing Services (DCE) v.3.2 (IBM)

The complete list of products that have been certified for the Works with LDAP 2000 program is available at the Works with LDAP site at `www.wwldap.org`.

OpenLDAP

OpenLDAP comes from an open-source project to develop a high-quality suite of LDAP applications and developer tools, an effort facilitated by the OpenLDAP Foundation, a not-for-profit organization chartered to advance the development of open-source LDAP software and related information.

The OpenLDAP Foundation is continuing the work on SLAPD started at UMich. As OpenLDAP is arguably the "purest" SLAPD-based directory available, many aspects of its architecture and operations apply to the other LDAP-only directories. Much of what is described in this section also pertains to the other LDAP-only directory offerings, although some specifics (such as the included administration tools) vary.

Introduction to OpenLDAP

OpenLDAP is an open-source implementation of a SLAPD server being developed under the auspices of the OpenLDAP Foundation. OpenLDAP is currently on version 2.0.12, which fully supports LDAP v.3, with work ongoing on future versions and enhancements.

As open-source software, OpenLDAP has a strong user community involved in developing additional functionality. In addition to the core directory service code, user-donated components are available, both as part of the distribution package and as additional downloads.

OpenLDAP supports all the core LDAP v.3 standards (RFCs 2251-2256 and 2829-2831) as well as a few other LDAP RFCs. These additional RFCs include

- RFC 2596 "Use of Language Codes in LDAP"
- RFC 2829 "Authentication Methods for LDAP"
- RFC 2830 "Lightweight Directory Access Protocol (v3): Extension for Transport Layer Security"
- RFC 2849 "Lightweight Directory Interchange Format (LDIF) v.1"
- RFC 3062 "LDAP Password Modify Extended Operation"

OpenLDAP directory trees can use domain component (`dc`) objects, as defined in RFC 2247, allowing congruence of DNS and LDAP namespaces. This is particularly useful for the increasingly common Internet directory deployments.

OpenLDAP also supports DNS-based service location via SRV resource records. RFC 3088 "OpenLDAP Root Service: An experimental LDAP referral service" describes an OpenLDAP project that is providing referrals to LDAP servers using DNS (Domain Name System) SRV records.

Client/Server Agents

Interestingly enough, the OpenLDAP server is available in two flavors; *demonstrated stability* or *latest features*. You can decide whether you need a production-quality LDAP server or you can afford slightly less stability in exchange for newer features.

OpenLDAP Server components include

- **SLAPD server**—The core DSA component, an LDAP v.3 compliant server based on the UMich SLAPD server.
- **SLURPD server**—A simple replication server providing synchronization via LDAP.
- **LDAP Gateways**—Several gateways are bundled with the OpenLDAP 2.x distribution including finger, gopher, and e-mail.

OpenLDAP depends on additional software to provide some core functionality. These software packages are available as open source from a variety of organizations. The following software is also required:

- Transport LayerSecurity(TLS) libraries from OpenSSL are required for implementation of SSL/TLS. Without SSL support, OpenLDAP is *not* fully LDAP v.3 compliant.
- Simple Authentication and SecurityLayer Layer (SASL) is provided by a package from Cyrus. As with SSL, SASL is required for full LDAP v.3 compliance.
- Kerberos is supported via SASL or GSSAPI using either the MIT or Heimdal Kerberos package.
- Additional database support is needed to use LDBM, OpenLDAP's primary datastore. You can choose between Sleepycat Software's BerkeleyDB or the Free Software Foundation's GNU Database Manager (GDBM).
- Threads are supported using POSIX pthreads, Mach CThreads, or other thread subsystem.
- TCP Wrappers (IP-level access filters) are recommended and are used automatically if present when OpenLDAP is installed.

The DSA Component

The OpenLDAP DSA is a direct port of the SLAPD server, updated to support LDAP v.3.

OpenLDAP can be configured in four ways including

- **Local Directory Service**—Manages only local directory and has no interaction with other directory servers.
- **Local Directory Service with Referrals**—Manages local directory information and provides referrals to a DSA that manages a superior naming context. This configuration is used when participation in a global directory is desired.
- **Replicated Directory Service**—Replication can be used in combination with either of the previous two listed configurations to provide redundancy of directory data and increase server availability.
- **Distributed Local Directory Service**—A local directory service can be partitioned and distributed to multiple DSAs. Both superior and subordinate references are used to glue the partitions together.

OpenLDAP has arguably the broadest range of supported platforms. It is available for most platforms as source code that must be compiled before running.

OpenLDAP Source code is available for

- Be BeOS
- Compaq (Digital) UNIX (OSF/1)
- Data General DGUX
- FreeBSD
- Hewlett Packard HP-UX
- IBM AIX
- Linux
- Microsoft Windows (NT/98/95)
- OpenBSD
- Silicon Graphics IRIX
- Sun Microsystems Solaris
- Sun Microsystems SunOS

Packaged versions of OpenLDAP are available for

- Debian GNU/Linux
- FreeBSD
- NetBSD
- Red Hat Linux

The Directory Client

Any of the available LDAP clients can access OpenLDAP directories. The only clients included with OpenLDAP are management utilities, a set of command-line tools that rely on the `slapd.conf` file for configuration information.

Programming OpenLDAP

A number of languages and APIs are supported for developing applications to leverage the OpenLDAP directory server. OpenLDAP, of course, supports the LDAP C API, with an LDAP C++ API slated for late 2001. A SDK (software developer's kit) for the LDAP C API is available for download at the OpenLDAP site. A TCL (Tool Command Language) LDAP SDK from Neosoft is included in the distribution.

One of the advantages to the open source approach to LDAP is the availability of user contributed APIs. The current release of OpenLDAP includes user contributed interfaces including TCL, PHP Hypertext Preprocessor, and GIMP ToolKit (GTK).

External data sources can be integrated using languages including Perl, TCL, Shell, and SQL.

OpenLDAP Directory Objects and Schema

Like other directory servers, OpenLDAP's schema defines the set of objects, attributes, and syntax rules governing the content of the directory. OpenLDAP's object set includes the LDAP v.3 default objects. Dynamic objects, per RFC 2589, are also supported. The `InetOrgPerson` object is available in a default installation as well.

The OpenLDAP schema is stored in a series of text files in the `/usr/local/etc/openldap/schema` directory. The individual schema files are referenced in the `slapd.conf` file. To extend the schema, create a new schema file and specify it in the `slapd.conf` file.

As with most directory services, modifying the default schema is not recommended because it is likely to create problems. Schema changes require restarting the OpenLDAP DSA.

Schema specifications included with OpenLDAP are

- **`core.schema`**—Standard schema defined by the core LDAP RFCs 2252, 2256 (required).
- **`corba.schema`**—CORBA object as defined by RFC 2714.
- **`cosine.schema`**—Cosine and Internet X.500 (recommended).
- **`inetorgperson.schema`**—`InetOrgPerson` as defined in RFC 2798 (recommended).
- **`java.schema`**—Java objects as defined by RFC 2713.
- **`krb5-kdc.schema`**—Kerberos v.5 key distribution center.
- **`misc.schema`**—Assorted definitions.
- **`openldap.schema`**—OpenLDAP Project.
- **`nadf.schema`**—North American Directory Forum.
- **`nis.schema`**—Network Information Services.

Only the first of these is required, although as listed here, others are recommended. Other schema definitions are totally optional.

The OpenLDAP Directory Information Tree

An OpenLDAP directory tree takes one of two forms:

- **Traditional style**—This is generally the geographic style directory tree with the top levels representing geographic locale and lower levels modeling the organization's structure or administrative boundaries.
- **Internet naming**—This style uses domain component (`dc`) naming to provide congruence between an organization's DNS domain and its LDAP tree. Using Internet naming also allows the use of DNS as a location service for LDAP servers, which is necessary for e-commerce and other Internet presences.

The trees that an OpenLDAP DSA manages are specified in the `slapd.conf` file by denoting a suffix and a corresponding database. A suffix is the DN string of the partition root, such as `dc=mythical,dc=org` and corresponds to a single naming context.

A single OpenLDAP DSA can have multiple designated suffixes, each representing its own distinct naming context. This is convenient for organizations, such as ISPs, that must manage users for a number of DNS domains, each with its own tree. By creating suffixes and associating databases with them, a directory tree can be arranged, and rearranged, as needed to support directory operations.

OpenLDAP Naming

OpenLDAP conforms with the LDAP v.3 standards for naming, using attributed naming of objects, and concatenating relative distinguished names (RDNs) into distinguished names (DNs) denoting the object location in the directory tree.

Implementing the standard LDAP naming model, the DNs in OpenLDAP are constructed from the RDNs of the object and its parents, beginning with the leafmost object name, up to the container object immediately below the root.

OpenLDAP also supports LDAP URLs, integrating DNS with LDAP naming, allowing DNS domain components to be referenced (such as `dc=mythical,dc=org`) in the LDAP namespace.

The OpenLDAP Directory Information Base

The directory data can be stored in one of several backend databases. Options include LDBM, the default database; SHELL, a database interface to shell scripts; or PASSWD, a password file database.

The initial population of a replica can be done in two ways:

- Although the DSA is online, an LDAP client, such as the included `ldapadd`, can be used to specify an LDIF file, the contents of which should be added to the database.
- If the DSA can be taken offline, several utilities allow the population of a database as well as the creation of indexes and exporting the directory data to an LDIF file.

As with most SLAPD implementations, OpenLDAP uses master and slave replicas in a single master replication configuration. The unit of replication is a partition; there is no capability to filter replicated data.

Replication is done via the included SLURPD server, which runs on the server holding the master replica. The SLURPD server writes a replication log file in a variant of LDIF. The replication log records the changes along with the name of the entity that made the modification and a time stamp. The changes in the change log file are then replayed to the consumer using LDAP during synchronization.

OpenLDAP Operations

OpenLDAP supports referrals for searches exceeding the scope of the data managed by the local DSA. Superior and subordinate knowledge references can be used to link multiple databases together to create a distributed directory tree. These knowledge references are used as follows:

- **Subordinate knowledge references**—These references take the form of a *referral* object with the same DN as the subtree being referenced. The referral object contains an LDAP URL that points to the DSA holding the subordinate naming context.
- **Superior knowledge references**—These references also use a referral object to specify a DSA holding the superior naming context. Superior knowledge references can point to a DSA with a naming context that is actually above the current one, or a DSA with global knowledge for naming contexts at the root of the tree.

OpenLDAP Security

OpenLDAP provides support for three security mechanisms, including

- SASL for strong authentication
- Kerberos v.4 can be used for authentication
- TLS/SSL for secure session communications

TLS/SSL can be implemented by recompiling OpenLDAP and specifying SSL support. This must be done for the OpenLDAP installation to be LDAP v.3 compliant. Red Hat and Turbo Linux packages are available with support for SSL, SASL, and Kerberos.

Access control levels are identified in a hierarchy, and granting a particular level of access implicitly grants all the lesser levels of access. Access rights, in ascending order, are

- **None**—Denies all access.
- **Auth**—Needed to bind.
- **Compare**—Allows comparison of entries.
- **Search**—Allows application of search filters.
- **Read**—Allows reading of search results.
- **Write**—Needed to modify or rename an entry.

An individual's access rights are determined by searching the local access directives, and then the global access directives. The search stops upon encountering the first directive that applies to the entry to which access is being requested. That directive is examined and the first specified entity that matches the requestor is used to determine the level of access granted. As both parts of the assessment process use the *first* relevant entry that is encountered, the order of the data in the configuration files is critical.

OpenLDAP Administration

Administration of OpenLDAP is done via configuration files and command-line tools.

Configuration of the OpenLDAP DSA is performed via entries in the `slapd.conf` file. This file is read when the DSA starts so the OpenLDAP server must be restarted for changes to take effect. The `slapd.conf` has three major sections including

- **Global**—This information pertains to the OpenLDAP server as a whole.
- **Backend**—This is data controlling a specific type of backend management, LDBM, for example. The backend information applies to every instance of a backend type. Every backend can support all the configuration options, although each one must have its own set of configuration information.
- **Database**—This configuration data is associated with a specific *instance* of the directory database. Again, every database can support all the possible configuration options, however, a single set of database configuration settings can apply to any single database instance.

The three sections of the `slapd.conf` file occur in the order listed here, and configuration settings in one section can override the settings in earlier sections. Therefore, more specific settings take precedence over more generic ones.

A number of command-line tools are included to allow the manipulation of the directory database:

- `ldapadd` is used to add the contents of an LDIF file via LDAP.
- `slapadd` creates a database and indexes for it.
- `slapindex` performs index-management tasks.
- `slapcat` dumps the contents of the database to an LDIF file for backup or offline manipulation.

No GUI (Graphic User Interface) tools are provided with OpenLDAP, although you can use any of the publicly available LDAP management tools and browsers to manipulate the data.

IBM SecureWay

SecureWay is a SLAPD-based directory intended for user management and e-commerce on the Internet. SecureWay is a part of many IBM offerings, such as Tivoli Policy Director and WebSphere, as well as operating systems including AIX, OS/390, and OS/400.

The SecureWay directory server is fully LDAP v.3 compliant and is available as a free download. It also supports directory browsing via HTTP (Hypertext Transfer Protocol).

SecureWay acts as the authentication and access control point for much of IBM's product line including its Web application development platform, WebSphere Application Server, and security offerings such as Tivoli Policy Director.

SecureWay implements the original set of core LDAP v.3 RFCs, 2251–2256. All LDAP v.2 and v.3 operations are supported. IBM, along with its business units Lotus and Tivoli, is involved in the ongoing work of the IETF (Internet Engineering Task Force) on the LDAP standards, including access control, base schema, and replication. Because SecureWay directory is compliant with LDAP v3 standards, many LDAP v3 compliant directory applications can operate on the SecureWay platform—common Public Key Infrastructure products, provisioning tools, ERP products, and meta-directory products.

SecureWay Focus

All directories have an area of focus, and for the SecureWay directory, the priorities are scalability, reliability, and cross-platform support. IBM claims (and can demonstrate) that because of the scalability of the DB2 backend, SecureWay directory can store tens of millions of entries in the directory tree with very little affect on the observed performance.

In addition, SecureWay uses DNS to support its directory operations, using domain components in LDAP naming, and handling LDAP URLs and SRV records for server location. SecureWay supports the following DNS related RFCs:

- RFC 2052 "A DNS RR for specifying the location of services (DNS SRV)"
- RFC 2219 "Use of DNS Aliases for Network Services"

Client/Server Agents

The SecureWay server consists of several components that combine to provide the directory service. The SecureWay package includes

- **SecureWay Directory**—Core DSA components.
- **DB2**—Database used for directory data storage.
- **IBM HTTP Server**—A compatible Web server is required, although not necessarily IBM's.
- **Global Security Kit**—GSkit is an optional component, required for SSL support. GSkit comes in two versions; *U.S.*, which includes 128-bit and 3DES encryption, and *Export*, which has only 56-bitDES support.

A Web server is also required for the Web-based administration of SecureWay. If a compatible server is not detected during setup, IBM HTTP Server is installed automatically. IBM lists these Web servers as compatible:

- Apache Server
- Lotus Domino Go Webserver

- Lotus Domino Enterprise Webserver
- IBM HTTP Server
- Microsoft Internet Information Server (IIS)
- Netscape Enterprise Server
- NetscapeFastTrack Server

The DSA Component

SecureWay's DSA is a SLAPD implementation leveraging IBM's DB2 relational database as the backend storage management system.

SecureWay is available for a number of platforms, including

- AIX
- Security Server for OS/390
- OS/400
- Solaris
- Windows 2000 Server
- Windows NT 4 Server
- Linux (in beta)

SecureWay Clients

Clients can access SecureWay via either LDAP or HTTP. The directory client included with SecureWay runs on the Windows platform. Like the server component, the client requires that GSkit be installed if SSL support is needed. The SecureWay SDK includes an LDAP v.3 client for Java with Java Naming and Directory Interface (JNDI) support.

Programming SecureWay

Available SDKs include C and JNDI for AIX, HP-UX, Solaris, and Windows NT. Developer kits for plug-ins to extend the directory in areas such as auditing, LDAP operations, and database-related functionality are also available. The SecureWay SDK includes

- LDAP shared libraries
- C header files
- LDAP v.3 client for Java with JNDI support
- Sample programs

Supported APIs for developing applications to leverage the SecureWay directory include C, Java, JNDI, SQL, and ODBC.

SecureWay Directory Objects and Schema

SecureWay supports the core LDAP v.3 schema. In addition, dynamic objects and the Directory Enabled Networking (DEN) schema are part of the default SecureWay installation.

The SecureWay schema is published in the directory (instead of being stored in a text file), providing easy access to all schema entries for update or extension. Changes to the schema are sent to other DSAs during the replication cycle.

The SecureWay Directory Information Tree

As SecureWay is an LDAP-based directory server, it supports the organization of the directory objects into an LDAP-compliant directory tree. In the SecureWay directory tree:

- Container objects form the tree structure and hold leaf objects representing resources, entities, or information.
- Any object class can reside in any type of container object, providing directory design flexibility.

Like other LDAP v.3 directories, a SecureWay directory tree can be based on either of the following:

- **X.500**—Country/locale base of the directory tree, and O and OUs modeling the organization's IT or administrative structure.
- **DNS**—With domain components at the top of the tree reflecting the domain hierarchy, and OUs below that reflecting organizational subdivisions. Using the DNS model allows you to leverage DNS as the location services for your directory.

SecureWay Naming

As an LDAP directory using the LDAP naming model, SecureWay's DNs are built from the RDNs of the object and its parents, starting at the leafmost object and proceeding to an entry immediately subordinate to the root.

The SecureWay directory server supports the LDAP v.3 naming model, and includes support for the use of domain components to reference DNS domains in the context of the directory tree. The LDAP URL format, supported by SecureWay, uses DNS domain names for directory server location, integrating the DNS naming model with the LDAP naming model.

The SecureWay Directory Information Base

SecureWay uses DB2 as the data-storage mechanism, leveraging IBM's existing highly scalable database to manage the directory data. SecureWay allows database backup, and restore operations can be done while the database is online.

Each SecureWay database is available on one network node. A SecureWay server can manage the contents of one or more DB2 databases without paying attention to the actual details of data management.

Replication in SecureWay is either single-master or peer- master. Neither configuration supports cascaded replication. Replication uses change logs, and must be manually configured. In SecureWay's implementation, the unit of replication is a partition, and does not support the filtering of objects and attributes for replication.

SecureWay documentation describes the directory server or servers holding a read/write directory datastore as *masters*, and all other (shadow) directory servers as *replicas*. The master directory server performs all replication operations, propagating updated directory information to all the replicas.

In a peer-master configuration, two or more masters are used. Each of the masters holds a writeable copy of the entire directory tree, and propagates all changes to each of the other masters and replicas. The peer-master configuration can be used in combination with load balancing products, such as the IBM WebSphere Edge Server, to provide high availability deployments. Another option for high availability is the deployment of the directory on an AIX *High Availability Clustered MultiProcessor* (HACMP) cluster.

A limitation of the peer-master configuration is that if replication conflicts occur because a given entry is simultaneously changed on several masters, there is no conflict reconciliation. Such conflicts are very rare, but require administrative intervention to correct.

SecureWay Operations

A connection is established with the SecureWay directory server via an LDAP `bind` operation, passing the user's DN (if an authenticated connection is sought) and the requested directory operations to the directory server. A user can open multiple connections with the directory server at the same time, sending multiple requests for directory operations.

The SecureWay directory server can provide referrals to directory clients whose queries cannot be satisfied locally. In SecureWay's implementation, these directory referrals require manual configuration by the administrator.

SecureWay Security

SecureWay supports the SSL, SASL, Kerberos, GSSAPI, and CRAM-MD5 security mechanisms. Authentication can use passwords, certificates, or administration-defined methods. Password authentication can use SHA, crypt, or imask. The SecureWay DSA can be configured to run with or without SSL support.

Two different forms of user-authorization are employed in SecureWay, namely, role-based authorization (a role has implicit permissions) as well as group-based authorization.

SecureWay has two kinds of groups:

- **normal groups** (of object class `GroupOfNames` or `GroupOfUniqueNames`)—the default X.500/LDAP groups.
- **access groups** (of object class `AccessGroup`)—for collective access control.

Access control lists (ACLs) are used by SecureWay to control user access to objects in the directory. ACLs can be applied to limit access to an object, and to determine whether the ACLs should be propagated to child objects. During access control assessments, ACLs are evaluated by comparing the user's access control information (ACI) linked to the `access Id`, `Group`, and `Role` and the information in the object's ACL.

Valid access control permissions in SecureWay are defined as *Read*, *Write*, *Add*, *Delete*, *Search*, and *Compare*.

Object attributes are grouped in *attribute access classes*; essentially defining the sensitivity of those attributes. There are five classes; three are designated for user attributes; *normal*, *sensitive*, and *critical*. An additional two classes deal with special cases; *restricted attributes* are for ACL information, while *system attributes* are used for operational attributes.

Membership in these classes is defined in the schema. Individuals are granted access to one or more attribute access classes. The use of attribute access classes reduces the number of individual ACLs that must be created.

SecureWay Administration

The management of SecureWay is flexible and detailed. Administration of directory information can be delegated to the attribute level. SecureWay includes tools for installing, configuring, and managing directory operations and users.

The administration tools in SecureWay allow you to

- Install and configure the SecureWay directory.
- Manage directory server operations including creation, backup, and restoration of directory databases, as well as server startup and shutdown.

SecureWay Groups and Access Control

In SecureWay version 3.1, only access groups could be used in access control, yet this was changed in version 3.2 so that all groups can be used for access control purposes.

- Manage security; access control lists, encryption, certificate management, and group membership.
- Manage server settings, database settings, performance tuning, directory activity, and configure directory replication.

A number of tools are used to administer SecureWay:

- **Server Administration**—A Web-based tool used for DSA configuration and management, requiring a frames-capable browser. This tool supports database operations, including back-up and restore, and replication management. Security settings for encryption, certificates, and Kerberos, as well as auditing are also managed via Server Administrator.
- **Directory Management Tool**—A Java-based tool that allows manipulation of directory data, schema customization, and access control management.
- **LDIF tools**—Provide the means to bulkload directory information, move data to and from relational databases, and create LDIF files from standard input.

Sun|Netscape iPlanet

The Sun|Netscape Alliance produces iPlanet, a native LDAP directory server designed for use on the Internet and intranets.

iPlanet was first released by the Netscape Corporation as Netscape Directory Server in 1996. Following the merger of Netscape and America Online (AOL), the Sun|Netscape Alliance was formed to further develop the Netscape server line. Renamed as iPlanet, the product is now in version 5 and has sold 500 million licenses worldwide.

Introduction to iPlanet

The iPlanet Unified User Management Services platform is a suite of server products centered on iPlanet Directory Server. The iPlanet Unified User Management Services platform provides a management and provisioning solution built on open standards including LDAP and XML (eXtensible Markup Language).

These products make up the Unified User Management Services:

- **iPlanet Directory Server**—The core of the user management services, iPlanet Directory Server is an LDAP v.3 compliant directory that provides authentication services and manages access control for the entire line of iPlanet servers.

> **Multiple Language Support**
>
> SecureWay can store information in multiple languages in a single directory.

- **iPlanet Directory Server Integration Edition**—This product enhances the basic directory server to allow consolidation of user identity from multiple sources within the enterprise, including HR and messaging applications and network operating systems. Bidirectional synchronization can be performed across the disparate directories to simplify administration.
- **iPlanet Certificate Management System**—This is an X.509 compliant certificate server allowing issuance and management of PKI (public-key infrastructure) certificates. These certificates can be used by iPlanet to provide stronger security for user authentication.
- **iPlanet Web Proxy Server**—The Web Proxy Server caches and filters Web content, and controls access to network resources.
- **iPlanet Delegated Administrator**—The iPlanet Delegated Administrator provides a means of distributing administrative tasks across the enterprise. You can manage your own directory information using the Delegated Administrator, offloading many administrative tasks. The included Java Servlet templates allow the simple creation of custom sets of administrative tasks.
- **iPlanet Policy Server**—The Policy Server provides centralized policy management to simplify management of large numbers of users. Single Sign-On (SSO) for Web and application servers is also supplied by the policy module.

There are two enhanced versions of iPlanet, each of which integrates additional services with the iPlanet Directory Server. These products offer different levels of directory-centric user management.

iPlanet Directory Server Access Management Edition

The *iPlanet Directory Server Access Management Edition* provides an integrated policy-based identity-management solution. By establishing a central point of authentication using shared credentials, the management of access to applications can be facilitated.

The iPlanet Directory Server Access Management Edition combines a number of components with iPlanet Directory Server:

- Policy Module
- User Management Module
- Certificate Authority Module
- Web Proxy Module

iPlanet Directory Server Integration Edition

The *iPlanet Directory Server Integration Edition* consolidates user identity within the enterprise. User account information from human resources applications, messaging systems, network operating systems, and other enterprise applications can be combined.

iPlanet Directory Server Integration Edition performs bidirectional synchronization with linked applications to streamline user administration across disparate directories. Dynamic schema mapping speeds and simplifies inter-application communication. An included LDAP proxy server acts as a firewall by filtering directory access and rerouting LDAP requests to provide failover support.

Client/Server Agents

The iPlanet server side components include

- **iPlanet Directory Server**—The core iPlanet LDAP Server (`ns-slapd`) that manages user information as well as server and application configuration data.
- **iPlanet Administration Server**—Manages directory authentication and handles operations that are not done via LDAP (starting and stopping the DSA, for example).
- **Directory Server Gateway(DSGW)**—An LDAP-to-HTTP gateway that runs on a Web server to provide HTTP access to directory information. DSGW provides read-only access via *Directory Express* (an address-book style application) and *Default Gateway*, a set of forms that allow customized lookups and modification of directory information.

Enhancements in iPlanet v.5

A number of significant enhancements were made in version 5 of iPlanet, bringing it closer to an X.500 style directory service. Some of the new features are

- Multi-master replication
- Distribution and chaining
- Partitioning
- Improved management tools
- Roles

Along with the introduction of new and improved features, other capabilities have been removed. Support for Windows NT Synchronization, for example, has been moved to the iPlanet Directory Server Integration Edition product.

iPlanet Components

A *component* is any discrete iPlanet server operation or plug-in. The function that verifies certificates, for example, is a component. Certain configuration options can be applied to individual iPlanet components. This means that specific functions can be restricted to the local directory server for security reasons, for instance.

The DSA Component

The iPlanet Directory Server DSA is based on the SLAPD agent and runs as a service on the Windows platform or a daemon on Unix. Multiple instances of the iPlanet DSA can run on a single server. The different instances can hold the same partition or manage different sets of directory information.

iPlanet uses plug-ins to provide enhanced server functionality. Plug-ins can do things such as support chaining operations, provide referential integrity checking, or distribute a single naming context into multiple database files.

iPlanet Directory Server 5 runs on these platforms:

- Sun Solaris 8 (UltraSPARC, 32-bit and 64-bit)
- Sun Solaris 2.6 (UltraSPARC)
- Microsoft Windows 2000 Server and Advanced Server
- Microsoft Windows NT 4.0 Server (x86 only)
- Hewlett Packard HP-UX 11.0 (PA-RISC 1.1 or 2.0)
- IBM AIX 4.3.3 (32-bit, PowerPC)
- CompaqTRU64 support (available via Compaq)

Solaris Extensions for iPlanet Directory Server

The Solaris extensions for iPlanet provide native support of *Network Information Service* (NIS) and *Remote Authentication Dial-In User Service* (RADIUS) to ease management of users and network resources. The Solaris extensions act as a gateway translating NIS calls to LDAP; the translated requests are then handled as regular LDAP queries. Solaris extension components include a RADIUS server, NIS synchronization utilities, *Pluggable Authentication Module* (PAM) modules, and associated administration tools.

NIS Extensions

The NIS Extensions allow storage of NIS maps in iPlanet and bidirectional synchronization of that information with NIS. An NIS emulator services NIS queries. The NIS extensions can replace the entire NIS infrastructure or act as a slave server in an existing NIS configuration.

iPlanet Clients

Client agents for iPlanet include a management console, a GUI client, and the e-mail address book in Netscape Communicator. As an LDAP v.3 compliant directory, any LDAP client can access iPlanet information.

Sun|Netscape has an iPlanet SDK that supports the development of clients using a variety of interfaces and languages.

Programming iPlanet

Like other LDAP-based directory products, iPlanet supports the LDAP C API. Programmatic access to iPlanet is also available via Java, JavaScript, Perl, and HTML (via an HTML Gateway). Custom connectors to external data sources can be created with PerlLDAP. iPlanet SDKs are available for C and Java, as well as PerlLDAP for Windows NT and Solaris.

iPlanet Directory Objects and Schema

The iPlanet schema is based on the LDAP v.3 schema, with the addition of objects used for server operations and management. The entire set of structural objects available in the default configuration is

- `user` (based on inetOrgPerson)
- `group`
- `OU`
- `role`
- `Class of service` (represent shared attributes)

It is a rather lightweight object set; yet it does seem consistent with the intended use of iPlanet as a user management and authentication server in Internet and intranet environments.

Like most directory servers, iPlanet stores its schema as objects in the directory; in this case, in the `cn=schema` container. This allows discovery of the schema and provides easy access for schema modifications.

Netscape refers to *templates*, essentially another reference to a class definition of structural directory objects.

The iPlanet Directory Information Tree

iPlanet's directory tree follows the LDAP conventions for tree structure. The containers in the upper levels of the tree are comprised of `dc` objects, with lower containers being either a `dc` or `OU`. A single iPlanet directory can contain more than one discrete directory tree.

In most iPlanet installations, the user information and the information related to applications and servers are held in different subtrees. iPlanet designates two containers in the directory tree to hold this information and refers to them as:

- **Configuration directory**—Multiple iPlanet servers (Administration server, DSGW, and so on) are configured to use a particular configuration directory to obtain their configuration data. By default, `o=NetscapeRoot` holds configuration information used by iPlanet servers.
- **User directory**—The user directory contains the data used for user management, authentication, and access control. An enterprise can have more than one user directory, the administration server is configured to authenticate against multiple servers. By default, `o=userRoot` contains the user database.

In iPlanet, container objects are referred to as *nodes*. A node that has a database associated with it is called a *suffix*, which is functionally equivalent to an X.500 partition root (the container that is the start of a new partition/naming context). The use of the term suffix in the iPlanet documentation corresponds to a naming context in X.500.

You create a suffix at the point in the tree where you want the new database (partition). An existing database can be *associated* with the suffix, or a new (empty) database can be created. If the suffix has no association, it is disabled until a database is assigned to it. In creating the suffixes and linking a database to each, the DIT can be structured to support needed directory operations.

The root node of an iPlanet tree is called the *root suffix*, and subordinate suffixes are called *sub suffixes*. Each sub suffix has one *parent suffix*, the root suffix at the top of its tree, whereas root suffixes can have many *child suffixes*.

A root suffix must be named by a string of domain component (`dc`) objects. A sub suffix can be named with either `dc` or `ou` objects. The parent suffix is automatically added to a sub suffix's name when it is created. Thus, if you have a root suffix of `dc=netmages,dc=org` and create a sub suffix of `ou=users`, the complete name of the new sub suffix is `ou=users,dc=netmages,dc=org`.

A directory can contain more than one root suffix, allowing the creation of numerous trees, each representing its own discrete naming context. This can be used by organizations that manage users in a number of DNS domains, each domain with its own tree.

Suffixes can be disabled to stop clients from accessing the contents of that naming context. Disabling a suffix is a temporary action; the directory data remains intact and easily can be made available to clients again.

Deleting a suffix, by contrast, actually deletes the contents of the database associated with that naming context. Replication information associated with that database is also removed from the directory when a suffix is deleted.

The default iPlanet tree has three containers:

- `cn=config` has internal configuration information used by the iPlanet Directory Server.
- `o=NetscapeRoot` is the configuration directory.
- `o=userRoot` is the default user directory..

Additional containers can be created and designated as suffixes as needed to support the desired directory tree design.

iPlanet Naming

iPlanet uses standard LDAP naming conventions, with LDAP URLs being the more common method of addressing directory information.

iPlanet supports the LDAP v.3 standards for naming (which specify the attributed naming of objects). Directory objects are named by concatenating RDNs into DNs. As described in the LDAP naming model, iPlanet DNs are constructed starting at the leafmost object, up though the parent objects to the container object just below the root.

The iPlanet directory integrates DNS with LDAP by providing support for domain components via LDAP URLs. This allows DNS domain name resolution to be used for iPlanet directory operations.

The iPlanet Directory Information Base

The directory information is stored in an LDBM database, which is implemented as a plug-in. A commercial relational database, such as Oracle, can be used instead of the standard iPlanet data-storage mechanism.

iPlanet has been tested to 50 million entries on a single server, importing 1 million entries an hour, and handling 5,000 queries per second on a single server.

An iPlanet replica is often called a *database,* with both read/write and read-only replicas that are used to support directory reliability and availability. An iPlanet server can hold as many replicas of either type as is needed. Individual replicas can be placed in read-only mode if needed; this is usually done when the database is being repaired. A server can be placed in read-only mode, making *all* databases on that server read-only.

iPlanet supports single master and multi(dual)-master modes of replication, and relies on master and consumer roles to perform the replication processes.

iPlanet's replication scheme is based on the standards being developed by the IETF's LDAP Duplication/Replication/Update Protocols (LDUP) working group. iPlanet replication can be implemented in three configurations:

- **Single master replication**—The usual single master configuration using one master replica and as many read-only replicas as desired. When a master replica receives an update, it propagates those changes to all the read-only replicas.
- **Multi-master replication**—In iPlanet, this might more correctly be called dual master because it uses only two master replicas with additional read-only replicas for redundancy and performance. In a dual-master configuration, changes made to one master are sent to the other master as well as the consumer replicas.
- **Cascaded replication**—Has a read/write supplier that replicates its database to a *supplier hub*. The supplier hub has a read-only database and in turn acts as the supplier to other consumers.

The unit of replication is a database (that is, a partition); no additional filtering capability is available.

Replication agreements must be manually created, one for each pair of supplier and consumer. This means that if a server is supplying updates to three consumers, three replication agreements must be formed. Likewise, in a dual-master configuration, a pair of replication agreements must be made between the two masters, one with each server as the supplier and the other as the consumer.

The replication agreement can be set to keep directory data in sync at all times by immediately propagating changes to all consumers. Alternatively, replication can be scheduled to take place on specific days of the week and/or at certain times of day.

Either the supplier or consumer can initiate replication, but only one initiator can be designated for each replication agreement. Supplier initiated updates are more common and work well in most circumstances. Consumer initiated replication is useful when the consumer is located at a different location from the supplier, perhaps across a dial-up connection.

The process of creating and configuring a pair of replicas and the corresponding replication agreement is as follows:

1. Create a read-only consumer database.
2. Configure a consumer-replication agreement.
3. Create a read/write supplier database.
4. Configure a read/write replication agreement.
5. Initialize a consumer replica (replicate contents of supplier database).

iPlanet uses a change log file to track changes to the directory. Each change to the supplier directory is given a unique *change number*. The management console displays the number of the last change made on a server as well as the last change replicated to the consumers. This makes it simple to check the status of synchronization between two given servers.

As with any multi-master replication scenario, data conflicts can occur. If a consumer receives conflicting changes, a time stamp on the change is used as a tie-breaker.

The connection used for directory replication is authenticated for security. Replication also can take place over SSL encrypted connections to provide a higher degree of security when transmitting directory updates over public data channels such asthe Internet.

Initial Population of a Replica

When the replication agreement is created, multiple methods of initializing the consumer replica are offered. This can be done as a normal synchronization over LDAP, or the information in the master can be exported as an LDIF file and then imported to the consumer. A manually created LDIF file also can be used. The initial population of the consumer is likely to be time consuming, so the use of one of the LDIF import methods is recommended.

Custom Distribution Plug-In

A *custom distribution plug-in* is available that allows the distribution of the contents of a single naming context across multiple databases. For example, if `ou=clients, dc=mythical, dc=org` has so many users that it is desirable to partition the contents, the database can be *physically* divided without creating another container and moving some of the contents of the `client's` OU.

The objects can be subdivided based on arbitrary criteria. Two physical replicas could be created, each representing a subset of the contents of the clients container.

These two replicas might be

- Users with last names starting with A–L in `ou=clients, dc=mythical, dc=org`
- Users with last names starting with M–Z in `ou=clients, dc=mythical, dc=org`

Note that the objects in the `clients` container all still resolve to the same DN they always have, even though they are in two different physical storage locations. The names of the objects do not change because the objects don't appear to move. This enhancement to replication functionality could be of significant value to organizations with a large (and growing) customer base.

> Keep in mind that databases using the custom distribution plug-in cannot be replicated. To be replicated, a one-to-one correspondence must exist between suffixes and databases. This means that any naming context that has been divided using the custom distribution plug-in cannot be replicated. This is a critical consideration to keep in mind when deciding how to manage the contents of a large directory.

iPlanet Operations

Unlike the other LDAP-only directory products that have been discussed, iPlanet can provide both referrals and chaining.

Referrals can be configured by specifying the LDAP URL of one or more servers to contact in the suffix settings. A directory server can provide referrals in response to all client requests, or only when receiving update requests. The latter allows for the use of read-only databases for lookups, while referring the relatively few write requests to the master copy of the data on another server.

Chaining is provided via a plug-in that is installed by default. Directory entries called *database links* are pointers to data that is stored remotely. These entries must be created manually. Database links are used to chain requests to another server. When a query exceeds the scope of the locally held data, the database links retrieve the data from the remote server and return it to the requesting client. Chained operations can be configured to use SSL for communication between servers.

The *chaining policy* can allow or deny chaining privileges to individual components of the iPlanet DSA. Operations that cannot be performed via chaining are referred to the appropriate iPlanet server. By default, internal DSA operations are not allowed to be chained, and some extended LDAP operations cannot be chained; for example, server-side sorting and virtual list views do not function across database links.

iPlanet Security

iPlanet was designed to provide user authentication services for access to the directory using passwords, SSL/TLS, and X.509 certificates. iPlanet servers also can mutually authenticate to provide a higher level of security for inter-server communications.

Users can authenticate to iPlanet in a variety of ways:

- Passwords
- Passwords over SSL
- X.509 certificates

- Based on IP address
- Based on DNS domain name

Encryption is provided via SSL with ciphers as strong as 128-bit. iPlanet has a certificate wizard that simplifies the process of obtaining and installing the X.509 certificates needed for SSL. These certificates can be used for digital signatures and message integrity checks, as well as for user authentication. Hardware-accelerated SSL is also supported via the PKCS#11 interface.

Directories that use repeating subtree structures can benefit from using macros to apply consistent sets of ACIs to these repeated subtrees. iPlanet's access control mechanism can use macros to minimize the number of individual access control statements, which improves the speed of access control decisions.

iPlanet Administration

Most directory operations can be performed in one of two ways: from the Directory Console or from a command-line utility.

The *iPlanet Console* is the primary administration tool for the entire iPlanet Server suite, providing an integrated point of managing a number of related products and services. When the console is loaded, it connects to the Administration Server via HTTP.

The iPlanet administration tools include

- iPlanet Administration Server
- iPlanet Console (the server management application)
- Directory Server Gateway (DSGW) (an HTTP server that provides access to user information)
- SNMP Monitor

iPlanet also includes command-line tools that perform the following:

- Database operations (importing and exporting data, and indexing)
- Account inactivation and deactivation
- LDIF operations
- Kernel tuning

The following tools are included in iPlanet:

- **admconfig**—Used to manage an iPlanet server, allowing configuration of access, directory, encryption, and network settings.
- **administration ip.pl**—A Perl script that updates the IP address of the server in the local server configuration file (`local.conf`) and the configuration directory (the contents of the `o=NetscapeRoot` subtree).

- **ldapsearch**, **ldapmodify**, and **ldapdelete**—Perform search, modify, and delete LDAP operations.
- **sec-activate**—Starts and stops SSL for a given instance of iPlanet.
- **sec-migrate**—Moves PK certificates and keys from a version of Netscape lower than 4 to an iPlanet server.
- **modutil**—Manages PKCS#11 and hardware token configuration.

Groups have traditionally been used to manage iPlanet users. iPlanet groups come in two forms, *static* and *dynamic*. Static groups have members added individually, whereas dynamic groups determine membership based on an LDAP query. To determine the membership of a dynamic group, the group object is queried and the query representing the filter is returned to the client. The client then runs the filter to determine the actual membership in a group.

Roles, introduced with v.5, are more efficient for directory clients to use. Roles can be read from the user object assigned to that role, whereas group membership must be enumerated from each group object. This reduces the time it takes to determine a user's security settings or configuration.

iPlanet defines three kinds of roles:

- **Managed roles**—Membership is explicitly defined.
- **Filtered roles**—Membership is based on an LDAP filter.
- **Nested roles**—Membership consists of other roles.

Class of Service (COS) is iPlanet's term for what X.500 calls collective attributes. Using CoS allows dynamic retrieval of data used by many different objects from a single directory entry. This dramatically lessens the administrative burden while improving data quality. CoS templates are used to define the set of attributes to be assigned.

Roles are also used in connection with CoS settings. When combined, roles and CoS provide *role-based attributes*. These are collective attributes that are attached to objects based on their membership in a particular role.

eDirectory

CHAPTER

9

...power derived from classic forms...

IN THIS CHAPTER

This chapter provides a concise theoretical overview of Novell's eDirectory (previously known as *Novell Directory Service* or NDS). eDirectory Because eDirectory is rooted in the X.500 standards, you will find many similarities in architecture and approach. Accordingly, only the differences are highlighted here, avoiding a re-explanation of X.500 concepts and terms.

Introduction to eDirectory

eDirectory has been around a long time, at least from the perspective of a directory service. Introduced in 1993 as a method of managing NetWare networks, eDirectory has evolved significantly over the years and now manages much more than NetWare. eDirectory has also expanded its reach beyond just the NetWare platform, and now runs natively on most major network operating systems.

eDirectory is a mature product with a broad scope of network-management capabilities and cross-platform support—something Novell is promoting by positioning eDirectory as a standalone product. Novell is supporting this focus on eDirectory with a number of eDirectory-related offerings, along with active participation in industry directory-service partnerships and initiatives. However, before examining eDirectory in detail, let's look at where eDirectory came from.

Prior to the introduction of NDS with NetWare 4 in 1993, NetWare used a bindery rather than a directory service. To describe a bindery by the information organization and management aspects discussed earlier, a NetWare bindery is a flat namespace, using a physical naming model and a centralized database. A bindery manages a limited set of objects (such as users, groups, print servers, and print queues) for a single server, requiring a separate user account on each server. In the early days of NetWare, this was a reasonable approach.

As networks grew, and the number of users and resources grew, the bindery was no longer the best method; in this context, the bindery was becoming an inadequate approach to network management. Recognizing this, Novell released *NetWare Name Services (NNS)* in 1990 as an add-on to NetWare 3. NNS was designed to aggregate and synchronize the binderies on a group of NetWare servers; this group of servers was called (perhaps not surprisingly) a domain.

It wasn't a perfect approach—synchronization had to be performed manually and was only functional with a small number of servers in the domain. Even with those limitations, NNS *did* provide access to any server in the domain with a single login. Still, NNS was only designed as a stopgap measure until NDS was ready. Accordingly, only one version of NNS ever shipped and Novell discontinued support for NNS in 1994.

With the introduction of NDS in 1993, Novell shifted its network-management focus from a server-centric view to a network-directory focus. NDS was initially released with NetWare 4.0 as a network-focused directory service designed to manage distributed NetWare networks. The Novell engineers who were designing NDS decided to start with a clean slate, architecturally speaking. They drew heavily upon the X.500 standard, adapting it as needed to operate well on local area networks (LANs), and ultimately, in the NetWare environment.

Although NDS initially managed a basic set of network resources and processes, it has been extended greatly over the years. eDirectory now supports management of not only basic network resources, but also a broad range of applications, services, and other network information.

NDS was ported from NetWare to other platforms as a means of managing network users and resources. Novell introduced an "NDS for…" product line, first with *NDS for NT*, followed by *NDS for Solaris*. These early offerings were not without their limitations; the initial release of NDS for NT, for example, required a NetWare server to store the directory information. NDS for NT 2.x eliminated this storage requirement.

Novell continued to enhance NDS, and fostered the development of directory-enabled applications. Novell, along with thousands of ISVs (independent software vendors), has developed powerful solutions for directory-enabled business, taking on tasks such as automating provisioning and supply-chain operations. As a result, eDirectory now provides a central point for administering not only the network, but many aspects of the business operations as well.

In the meantime, a fundamental technological shift was taking place—the Internet, and more importantly, the World Wide Web, was everywhere; and everyone was on it (or so it seemed). Suddenly, there was a crying need to securely manage huge numbers of clients to support Web-based applications such as e-commerce, customized content provision, and business-to-business (B2B) operations. LDAP (Lightweight Directory Access Protocol) was gathering steam, heterogeneous networks were the order of the day, and there was a lot more to manage than what was going on inside the corporate firewall.

What Version Is That Anyway?

As various aspects of eDirectory are discussed, the focus will be primarily on eDirectory v.8.x. Many businesses, however, are still using earlier versions. For this reason, multiple versions of eDirectory are mentioned in this chapter when significant differences between them exist. If a version number is not otherwise specified, assume eDirectory 8.5.

The product name has been through a few changes along the way. It was first *Netware Directory Service* (NDS) and then *Novell Directory Service*; although few people could tell you *exactly* when the change occurred, it was *NDS* in either case. With version 8, the name was changed to *NDS eDirectory*, and finally, the NDS was dropped at the end of 2001, leaving simply *eDirectory*.

Accordingly, eDirectory (starting with v.8) represents a substantial shift in Novell's approach to directory services. With eDirectory, Novell completely separated the directory from NetWare, creating a standalone, cross-platform directory service to support e-commerce, B2B relationships, and Internet-based applications.

The architecture of eDirectory was overhauled, resulting in a directory that scales to billions of objects. Novell states it has tested with one billion objects in the directory on several platforms, including a Solaris deployment with a billion objects on a single server! With eDirectory, many functional limitations on the directory contents have seemingly disappeared—there are no limits on partition size, a directory can hold billions of objects per tree and millions of objects per container. Other enhancements include the ability to create custom indexes, filter replicas, and improved search speed.

Enterprise-management functionality, such as user and group management, as well as file and print services, which had been closely tied to earlier versions of NDS, were delinked from the core directory service. With the release of eDirectory v.8.0, user- and group-management services for Unix and Windows NT, which had been integrated with the "NDS for…" line, became available as NDS Corporate Edition. When eDirectory v.8.5 was released, NDS Corporate Edition was renamed to Novell Account Management.

eDirectory has broad market support; it is currently running on 4.5 million servers with 163 million licensed clients worldwide. According to Novell, over 80% of the Fortune 500 companies have deployed eDirectory. Similarly, over 40,000 ISVs are developing to eDirectory and 1,800 eDirectory-enabled applications have already been released. With Novell's focus on the directory as a core product, eDirectory has staked out its spot in the rapidly expanding directory service market.

The "Full Service Directory"

Novell has defined what it calls the Full Service Directory (FSD) —essentially the criteria for what Novell sees as a fully capable directory service. Novell says that the FSD is "… a general-purpose database that manages discovery, security, storage, and relationships." The FSD taxonomy presents an interesting perspective on Novell's approach to a directory service. It is available at `www.novell.com/products/nds/fsd/fsd_taxonomy.html`.

NDS Design Overview

When Novell set out to design a directory service in the late '80s, the first X.500 specifications were being developed. Novell chose to use these standards, adapted for the PC environment, as the basis for its directory service. eDirectory leverages the X.500 models, directory operations, namespace, and naming model, as well as DIB (Directory Information Base) management.

NDS Terminology

Again, it is useful to make the correlations between terminology clear. Table 9.1 compares eDirectory terms to X.500 terms. As you can see, there aren't many significant differences between the two.

TABLE 9.1 eDirectory/X.500 Terminology Comparison

Functionality	*eDirectory Term*	*Analogous X.500 Term*
Directory entries	Objects	Objects
Entry attributes	Attributes	Attributes
Definition of directory contents	Schema	Schema
Logical representation of directory contents	Directory tree	Directory Information Tree (DIT)
Data storage	DIB DIB Set	Directory Information Base (DIB)
Subdivision of directory	Partition	Naming context
Data updates	Synchronization	Replication
Server agent	Replica server NDS server	Directory Service Agent (DSA)
Client agent	Client	Directory User Agent (DUA)
Query resolution	Tree-walking and referral	Chaining and referral

eDirectory Design

As you examine the design of eDirectory, you can see the influence of X.500 in a number of ways.

The eDirectory namespace defines a single hierarchical directory tree, although multiple trees can be federated for management purposes. eDirectory naming is also highly similar to X.500 naming. The eDirectory schema specifies a wide range of class, attribute, and syntax definitions and is easily extensible.

The eDirectory DIB can be partitioned as needed, and partitions are stored on DSAs as required. Servers can hold multiple replicas, although only one of any specific partition. eDirectory generally uses multi-master replication with a static single master for some operations, such as partitioning and schema modifications.

eDirectory servers provide the expected DSA functionality—manage client login, fulfill queries, and provide referrals to other eDirectory servers. eDirectory network client software is available for Windows, Macintosh, and DOS.

eDirectory operations are much like those in X.500, using proprietary protocols, of course. eDirectory performs distributed operations using both referrals and chaining. Client queries, for example, are satisfied by a combination of the two. Object location is done by a form of chaining that Novell calls *tree-walking*. A referral to the server holding the object is then generated to route clients to the appropriate server.

eDirectory is implemented as a set of components that provides a cross-platform directory service:

- **Replica server**—The eDirectory DSA component. Replica server is feature equivalent and fully interoperable across all supported platforms.
- **Administration Utilities**—User libraries, replica monitoring and administration tools, cryptographic libraries, and LDAP components.
- **ConsoleOne**—Provides an extensible Java Console for managing the directory along with the core set of snap-ins.

eDirectory Models

Although Novell does not directly discuss directory models when describing eDirectory, it's clear when you examine the design and operations of eDirectory that the X.500 models apply.

LDAP and eDirectory

As with just about every other directory service, eDirectory supports LDAP v.3. Novell calls its implementation of LDAP support *Novell LDAP* (NLDAP), sometimes called *LDAP Services for NDS*. eDirectory v.8.5 supports LDAP natively, as it has since NetWare v.5. Earlier versions required an add-on package to support LDAP services.

The LDAP implementation provided with eDirectory v.8 has been optimized for searches and (according to Novell) performance doesn't degrade with large directory trees. This is particularly important when the directory service is to be deployed as part of a large e-commerce or Web site management solution.

LDAP services and servers are represented in the directory as objects, and administration is done with ConsoleOne, the standard eDirectory management console. As part of installation, an *LDAP group* object is created and mappings between eDirectory and LDAP classes and attributes are configured. The LDAP group contains a list of eDirectory servers that are governed by a common configuration controlling LDAP operations. The LDAP group is also used to configure security, distributed operation mode (referral, chaining, or both), and the proxy user for anonymous LDAP access. Each server running LDAP Services has an *LDAP Server* object that controls server-specific operational parameters such as search handling, SSL (Secure Socket Layer) configuration, port settings, and filtered replicas.

The LDAP data interchange format (LDIF) is supported and a utility is provided to allow LDIF import and export, as well as the exchange of information directly between LDAP directories. eDirectory uses an extended version of LDIF that can handle access control and index management, as well as schema definitions and mapping.

DNS and eDirectory

With the shift to native TCP/IP in NetWare 5, Novell had to address the need for IP services such as DNS and DHCP. eDirectory v.8's native LDAP also brings with it requirements for DNS to provide support for resolving LDAP URLs. Not surprisingly, Novell decided to thoroughly integrate both its DNS and DHCP implementations into eDirectory.

All DNS and DHCP information is stored as directory objects and configuration is performed via those objects. Each DNS zone is stored as a directory object, for example, and replicated via the usual eDirectory methods. Even with this storage mechanism, NetWare DNS servers interoperate fully with other DNS implementations and are compatible with BIND 4.9.5.

DNS in NetWare supports a proprietary form of Dynamic DNS, registering DHCP clients with eDirectory. Each DHCP-assigned DNS entry consists of several directory objects representing hostnames, IP addresses, and additional resource records.

Novell's DNS uses the Service (SRV) resource record for a range of services, such as FTP However, LDAP is not listed in the selection for type of SRV records when one is created. eDirectory doesn't use DNS to locate directory servers (as Active Directory does), but rather uses the *Service Location Protocol* (SLP) as specified in RFC 2165. SLP is used for advertising and locating services for distributed IP networks.

eDirectory uses a process called *DNS federation* to allow communication between eDirectory trees. eDirectory trees that are rooted at a DNS domain can be located by eDirectory servers using DNS queries. After the external tree is located, standard eDirectory protocols are used to carry out directory operations. DNS federation is a powerful method of accessing directory trees belonging to partners, vendors, or other businesses. DNS federation is covered in more detail later in this chapter in the "eDirectory Operations" section.

Client/Server Agents

Like other directory services, eDirectory is implemented via a client/server model, in which a DSA services client queries and interacts with other directory servers to manage directory information. Although eDirectory is very X.500-like in design and operations, the protocols used are primarily proprietary.

Even there, however, eDirectory doesn't stray far from its X.500 design roots. Novell's version of the directory access protocol (DAP) is called Novell DAP (NDAP), for instance, and supports all the functionality provided by DAP. Likewise, eDirectory does not use X.500 replication mechanisms, but rather employs a proprietary replication method.

DSA Component

The core DSA component in eDirectory is called the *replica server* (prior to eDirectory v.8, it was called NDS server). A replica server can manage one or more partitions of directory information, providing client access and supplying updates to other eDirectory servers. Replica servers perform all DSA operations, including user authentication, directory information management, partitioning, and replication. The replica server also manages the physical storage of directory replicas.

> **eDirectory Is Certified as LDAP 2000 Compliant**
>
> eDirectory v.8.x has been awarded the "Open Brand for LDAP 2000" by the *Directory Interoperability Forum* (DIF). DIF gives the Open Brand for LDAP 2000 to server products that meet standards for full LDAP v.3 compliance.

eDirectory is notable as a directory product because it operates on multiple networking platforms. Client libraries and LDAP tools are available for all platforms. eDirectory is available for these operating systems:

- **NetWare**—eDirectory v.8 requires NetWare 5, although earlier versions of NDS run on NetWare 4.
- **Windows**—eDirectory v.8 runs on Windows NT and 2000. Prior to the release of eDirectory, there was a separate product for Windows, *NDS for NT*, which ran on Windows NT 4.
- **Sun Solaris**—eDirectory v.8 supports Solaris v.2.6 (SPARC version) and Solaris v.7 and 8. NDS 8 supports Unix applications that use the Unix PAM framework APIs (Application Programming Interfaces) for login services. eDirectory 8.5 is the first, and so far only, directory service to achieve SunTone certification by proving its performance, scalability, and security on Solaris.
- **Linux**—eDirectory requires Linux 2.2 and glibe 2.1.3.
- **Compaq TRU64**—eDirectory runs on TRU64 4.0 and 5.0. Tru64 has a directory-aware security structure, allowing eDirectory to manage TRU64 user accounts without add-on products. A pure 64-bit version of eDirectory for TRU64 is under development.
- **IBM AIX**—Novell says it is currently working on a version of eDirectory for IBM AIX.

eDirectory Clients

eDirectory clients take a number of commonly used forms: network user authentication, e-mail, and Web browser, for example. Don't forget, however, that directory-enabled applications, whether commercial or homegrown, make up another important group of clients. With 1,800 applications written for eDirectory, many people use it daily without realizing it. In addition, any of the growing number of LDAP applications can act as eDirectory clients.

However, in discussing eDirectory clients, you should first look at the clients designed for use on the corporate network. These include the following:

- **Novell Client for Windows**—This is Novell's recommended client for computers running Windows. It is designed to be high performance; the core component is a *virtual device driver (VXD)*, and it employs 32-bit versions of the IPX (Internetwork Packet Exchange) and TCP/IP protocols. The full range of NetWare services and management utilities are supported, and the client is fully integrated into Windows Explorer. (The functional equivalent of this client was previously called Client32.)
- **Microsoft Client for NetWare Networks**—Windows ships with an eDirectory-aware client. Even though the client is eDirectory-aware, it is still limited, primarily providing access to NetWare file and print services. Some earlier NDS management tools are not operational when using this client. Microsoft's client also requires the use of NWLink (Microsoft's version of IPX) and does not work with NetWare 5's native TCP/IP.

- **NetWare for Mac**—As of NetWare 5, Novell no longer provides a Macintosh client. Prosoft Engineering, Inc. now provides all Macintosh client support for NetWare. Prosoft's first NetWare client, NetWare for Mac, is a fully eDirectory-aware IPX client for NetWare 4 and later. You can reach Prosoft at `www.prosofteng.com`.
- **Bindery clients**—eDirectory supports bindery clients by providing a bindery-style view of a portion of the eDirectory tree. When clients access eDirectory via bindery services, they can only see the object classes that existed in the NetWare bindery. This means that only the user, group, print queue, print server, and profile objects are visible. Bindery services do *not* support a single client login to the network—connections to additional servers must still be made manually.

Although these clients provide access to the range of eDirectory functionality needed by a network user, a lot more than network management is being done with eDirectory. One significant area of eDirectory-enabled application development is enterprise management: human resources, automated provisioning, and supply-chain management.

Every eDirectory-enabled product functions, often transparently, as a directory client. To facilitate the distribution of applications using eDirectory, Novell repackaged the redistributable core client agent as a single unit (`NDSBase`). Only two files—`NDSBase` and a platform-dependent support file—are required for applications to access eDirectory.

Clients for NetWare 6

With the release of NetWare v.6, Novell is taking an interesting approach to eDirectory clients. A range of client options is available including using standard eDirectory clients and the native clients from other NOSs (Windows 2000, Macintosh, and so on). More interesting, however, is the new direction in eDirectory clients, the use of a standard Web browser. This provides a universal means of accessing eDirectory.

Macintosh and OS/2 Clients

Prior to NetWare 5, Novell supplied clients for Macintosh and OS/2 as well as Windows. Although these clients are no longer available from Novell, they will probably remain in use for some time yet. The Novell versions of these clients are

- **NetWare Client for Mac OS**—A fully eDirectory-aware client supporting both client and administrative functionality.
- **NetWare Client for OS/2**—Provides eDirectory client functionality to OS/2 workstations.

eDirectory APIs

eDirectory supplies numerous APIs for accessing the directory, providing a robust search capability with comprehensive object-management interfaces. Available programmatic interfaces include:

- **DSAPI**—This is the traditional method of programming eDirectory; it is functionally a port of the XDS APIs from X.500.
- **LDAP C API**—eDirectory uses its integrated LDAP services to provide native LDAP programmatic access to directory contents.
- **ADSI (Active Directory Services Interface)**—Programmers also can access eDirectory via ADSI, which is Microsoft's API for Active Directory.
- **JNDI (Java Naming and Directory Interface)**—Part of Sun's Java API set that provides easy network-resource discovery for Java clients.

Support for scripting is available with:

- JavaBeans
- JavaScript
- Perl
- REXX
- Open Database Connectivity (ODBC)
- Novell script (was NetBasic 7)
- ActiveX
- NetBasic 6/7

eDirectory Is Free for Developers

As part of its drive to encourage the development of directory-enabled applications, Novell is giving eDirectory away to developers. ISVs can get eDirectory server software and *250,000* client licenses free, providing a powerful incentive to use eDirectory as the directory on which to build their applications. Details of the offer are available at `http://developer.novell.com/edirectory/`.

Support for Industry Initiatives

A number of organizations are working on directory-related initiatives. Some of these efforts are aimed at developing open standards for interoperability or promoting directory-centric development. Industry initiatives supported by Novell include the following:

- **Directory Interoperability Forum (DIF)**—Novell is one of the leaders in the DIF, a group of vendors supporting the development of directory-enabled application development and open directory standards.
- **Directory Enabled Networking (DEN)**—A collaboration between network infrastructure-device vendors and directory-service vendors seeking to enable directory-based control over infrastructure devices (such as routers and switches). Novell has forged partnerships with a number of leading network-hardware vendors to provide directory-based management of their network devices, including Lucent, Cisco, and Nortel.
- **Directory Services Markup Language (DSML)**—A number of vendors are working on directory markup languages based on the Extensible Markup Language (XML), which is emerging as an open standard for content exchange. The *Organization for the Advancement of Structured Information Standards (OASIS)* is serving as the primary body working on a vendor-independent method of XML access to directories, which it is calling the Directory Service Markup Language (DSML). DSML v.1 has been released, and DSML v.2 is under discussion.
- **Active Digital Profile (ADPr)**—ADPr is an XML-based method of automating directory-enabled provisioning processes. ADPr provides support for user management across a broad range of enterprise resources. Business Layers, a leading vendor of eProvisioning software, developed ADPr, which has been submitted to OASIS for adoption as a proposed standard. Novell is one of a growing number of vendors endorsing ADPr, joining security providers such as Checkpoint Software in the growth in this important area of directory-related development.

Ubiquitous Administration

Although earlier versions of NDS had some limitations on non-Windows clients, primarily in the availability of administrative tools, eDirectory introduced a new administrative console that eliminated most of those limitations. *ConsoleOne* is a Java-based, platform-independent console that provides access to eDirectory administrative functionality from any platform. Another new tool, *iMonitor*, allows monitoring and administration of directory servers from anywhere on the network via its browser-based interface. These tools, which add substantial platform independence to eDirectory, are discussed later in the "eDirectory Administration" section of this chapter.

eDirectory Objects and Schema

eDirectory clearly reflects the models that X.500 applies to the schema and objects. eDirectory objects are comprised of attributes, each of which has a designated syntax. Objects have constraints on where they can be created and how they are named.

The schema is stored as objects in the directory, allowing dynamic schema changes, and replication of those changes. The base schema reflects its origin as a network-centric directory service. All the objects used to manage an enterprise network are present.

Because a high degree of structural similarity exists between the objects and schema used by eDirectory and X.500, only some aspects of this topic are described here (and briefly).

Directory Objects

eDirectory directly incorporates the X.500 object model, supporting the base X.521 container and leaf objects. In addition, many other directory objects are created for informational and network-management purposes.

Container Objects

The eDirectory container objects all have analogs in X.500 objects, although the class definitions might not be exactly the same. Container objects serve the same basic function as in X.500, providing organization to facilitate information distribution, administration, and security. The following container objects are available in the default schema:

- **`[root]`**—eDirectory has a visible (and often mentioned) `[root]` object, which is functionally the root of the tree. The `[root]` is automatically created when the eDirectory tree is created and is not explicitly named. Rather, it is referred to as either the `[root]` or (less often) by the tree name. The `[root]` object is essentially the top class instantiated as an effective object. The `[root]` can contain Alias, Organization, or Country objects.
- **Country**—The Country (C) object can be created under `[root]` only. The country class can contain a range of objects representing services and applications. However, it cannot hold OUs (Organizational Units) or many common network entities (such as computers and users). An object of the country class must be named with a two-letter code that complies with ISO 3166.
- **Locality** and **State**—Use of the Locality (L) and State (S) objects is optional. To create either object, you select a Locality as the class of object to instance, and then select Locality or State/Province. The Locality/State object can hold more classes than a Country, yet not as many as an O or OU. Instances of the class can be placed beneath Organization, Country, or other Locality/State objects.

- **Organization**—eDirectory requires the creation of one Organization (O) object during installation. There can be additional Organization objects directly beneath either the `[root]` or Country objects.
- **Organizational Unit**—An *Organizational Unit (OU)* is used in eDirectory for organizing directory information to facilitate administration and use. The OU is by far the most common container in most eDirectory trees. An OU can be contained by an Organization, Locality, or far more often, another OU.

Leaf Objects

The leaf objects contained in the eDirectory base schema are highly similar to the X.500 objects, although there are quite a few more classes. Classes in the base schema can be divided into some general categories based on what they are intended to manage:

- **User Management**—The most common objects in most directories are probably users; groups and profiles are some of the objects used to manage users.
- **Network Resources**—This group includes those used for basic network management such as computers and printers.
- **Services**—Objects are created as needed to manage services, such as DNS, DHCP, and LDAP.
- **File System**—A number of objects are used to manage file resources, including the NCP Server, and AFP Server, Volume, and directory map classes.

Object ID

When an object is created, each server that holds a replica with the object assigns it a unique object ID. This object ID is a 4-byte value that is used by most eDirectory operations as a unique identifier for the object. Each object also has the object ID of its parent object.

`Tree Root` Class

The `tree root` class defines an effective (one that can be used in a tree) container object, although it isn't exposed by every administrative tool. However, the `tree` object is visible in `ConsoleOne`. A tree name (T) attribute is used to name an instance of the `tree root` class. The class definition for `tree root` is visible in the Schema Manager tool.

Some objects are presented in subsets depending on the context or tool; DNS objects, for example, are manipulated in the DNS/DHCP Management Console, schema objects are visible in Schema Manager, and so on. DNS objects appear in the tree, but their contents are hidden from within the usual tree administration tools, and they function primarily as pointers to the DNS management tool.

Interestingly enough, the tool that you use to manage the eDirectory tree affects the object classes that you can select from when creating a new object. After an installation of NetWare v.5, eDirectory v.8, and DNS, you can create about 23 base classes via the legacy NWAdmin administrative tool. The current eDirectory administrative tool, ConsoleOne, exposes dozens of additional classes!

eDirectory Schema

Like early versions of X.500, early versions of NDS used a static schema, which was read when the server initially loaded and remained the same until the server was restarted. However, also like X.500 (as of 1993), current versions of eDirectory publish the schema in the directory as objects. Storing the schema in the directory facilitates schema replication and discovery, and allows developers and administrators to easily access the schema to modify it.

From a structural perspective, the eDirectory schema is similar to the X.500 schema. Obviously, the specifics of the class definitions vary; however, because you are now familiar with the basics of how the X.500 schema works, the eDirectory NDS Manager schema should make a lot more sense.

What Is an Unknown Object and Why Do I Have One?

An unknown object represents an object that eDirectory does not recognize, usually because one of its mandatory attributes no longer exists. An object might become unknown as a transitional effect during synchronization, or the change can be permanent. A permanently unknown object is created, for example, when a server is deleted prior to its volumes. The volumes become unknown because the object for the server they belong to (which is the value of a mandatory attribute) no longer exists.

Browsing the eDirectory Schema

You can browse the eDirectory schema with the Schema Manager, which is available from the ConsoleOne or eDirectory Manager Tools menu.

Object Class Definition

eDirectory class definitions look a lot like X.500 class definitions. The same rules for building classes apply: Classes inherit part of their definition from super classes; containment and naming rules are largely the same. eDirectory class definitions are comprised of the following set of fields:

- **Class Flags**—Class flags define the type of class (effective, non-effective, or auxiliary) and the designation as a leaf or container. Ambiguous naming or containment also can be set. (In this case, ambiguous means a class without a specified value for the `named by` or `containment class` attribute.)
- **ASN1 ID**—The ASN.1 (Abstract Syntax Notation One) ID, like the X.500 OID, is a globally unique number assigned by Novell when schema extensions are registered. If schema extensions are being used for an application that is to be Novell certified, an ASN.1 ID is required.
- **Super Classes**—Identifies the additional classes that also should be included in this class definition. As in X.500, all eDirectory classes have `top` as a super class and are likely to have others as well.
- **Containment Class**—Lists the types of objects this object class can be created within, such as OU or O.
- **Named By**—Identifies one or more attributes that will be used to name instances of this object class.
- **Mandatory Attributes**—Contains a list of properties for which the object class must have values. Mandatory attributes can be assigned to a class definition during creation only.
- **Optional Attributes**—Additional properties for which an instance of the object class might or might not have values.
- **Default ACL Template**—Each class has a default set of ACL (Access Control List) settings as well as an ACL that it inherits from top. This determines the initial ACLs for an instance of that class.

Classes can be added to the schema, and classes created via extension can be removed from the schema. To maintain base compatibility, however, classes that are part of the standard eDirectory schema cannot be removed from the schema.

Attribute Type Definition

eDirectory has quite a few attributes defined—eDirectory 8 without any extensions has well over 500! Just in case that isn't enough, or an attribute doesn't exactly meet your needs, you can add more. However, existing attributes (including those added by extension) cannot be modified.

Attributes that have been made part of the schema via extension can be removed as long as they are not currently being used in any object-class definition. Attributes that are part of the standard eDirectory schema cannot be removed.

The attribute class definition consists of these fields:

- **Attribute Syntax ID**—Identifies the syntax to be used for a particular attribute.
- **ASN1 ID**—The ASN.1 ID serves the same purpose as in the class definition, uniquely identifying the attribute definition.
- **Used In**—Contains a list of the classes that use this attribute.
- **Constraint Flags**—Quite a few constraints can be placed on an attribute, including whether it is multivalued, hidden, read-only, or has range or size limitations. Synchronization settings for the attribute also can be assigned, determining whether the attribute synchronizes immediately, on a normal schedule, or not at all.

Attribute Syntax Definition

As described in Chapter 4, "X.500: A Model for Directory Services," the syntax definition specifies the data format acceptable for the value of an attribute. The syntax defines how a value is constrained by data type and syntax limits. The eDirectory syntax definition contains the following:

- **Syntax Name**—Descriptive name of the syntax.
- **Syntax ID**—A 32-bit integer that uniquely identifies the syntax type. This is the value designated in the Attribute Syntax ID field of the attribute definition.
- **API data structure**—Specifies a C structure supported by the XDS API.
- **Syntax Flags**—Contains matching rules to be used when comparing values using this syntax, such as ordering, equality, and sub string matches.
- **Used In**—Contains a list of the attributes that use this syntax.

Schema Extensions

eDirectory provides support for extending the schema, enabling administrators and developers to create needed objects and attributes. The schema is extensible via a number of methods:

- **Schema Manager**—The eDirectory Schema Manager is a ConsoleOne snap-in that provides a graphical interface to browse and manipulate the schema. Schema Manager allows full schema administration and includes wizards that walk through extending the schema in half a dozen steps.
- **Novell Import Conversion Export (ICE)**—ICE is the eDirectory LDIF tool that allows for schema modifications using LDIF files.

- **NDSSH**—A DOS command-line tool that ships with eDirectory 8 and is used to import schema modifications from a text file. Novell provides many of the schema extensions for add-on NetWare services in the form of text (SCH) files.
- **MAPUTIL**—Used to manage the eDirectory LDAP class and attribute mapping. It imports and exports mappings from an LDAP group object, allowing backup, restoration, and customization of eDirectory/LDAP relationships. MAPUTIL is available on Novell's Developer Web site.
- **SCHMAP**—Reads in an LDIF file, performs the schema extensions, and then configures the LDAP-NDS mapping in a single step. This DOS command-line tool is available from the Novell Developer site.
- **SCHMIG**—A DOS command-line utility that converts a Netscape directory server schema file into an LDIF file for import into eDirectory.

It is worth noting that changes to the schema always imply compatibility issues with other eDirectory servers. To deal with this, schema information for the directory is held in a schema partition, a replica of which is held by each replica server. Schema changes are synchronized to all other replica servers to maintain schematic integrity throughout the tree.

You can find additional information on the eDirectory schema at `developer.novell.com/nds/schema.htm`.

Schema Registry

Novell has a registry for developers who are extending the eDirectory schema. The registry contains the base eDirectory schema, along with additional schemas from independent developers. By maintaining the schema registry, Novell aims to promote the development of standard schemas and to reduce problems due to schema incompatibilities.

Developers can be assigned an OID (like an X.500 OID) and a name prefix, which is used at the start of the new class or attribute name (for example, `MyCompany:MyClass`) to uniquely identify the schema addition. Novell-assigned name prefixes are designed to map to OIDs in much the same way that DNS hostnames map to IP addresses.

Novell's Developer Web Site

Novell has a number of excellent resources concerning the eDirectory schema and schema extensions available at `http://developer.novell.com`.

The eDirectory Tree

Novell recommends that most eDirectory deployments implement a single directory tree, although in some instances, such as multinational corporations that span widely differing geopolitical boundaries, multiple trees might be required. Beyond that, Novell has a flexible vision of how eDirectory trees should be designed.

One result of designing eDirectory around the X.500 standards has been directory trees that often look and function a lot like X.500 trees. Because partition design and management is generally the final determinant in upper-level tree design, geographic or business divisions are often represented at the top of the tree. Directory administration is often the more important factor lower in the tree, building a framework to streamline directory management and facilitate security.

Because eDirectory removes most limitations on tree and partition capabilities, eDirectory trees need only support the requirements of the business deploying them without regard for product limitations. This means that the trees of a directory used to manage a corporate network might have a lot of structure, reflecting the business organization. By contrast, the tree of an e-commerce directory might have only a few OUs, even though it has many more users than the corporate tree.

Novell's approach to network administration includes a design that builds the business logic into the tree, streamlining network management. Any object (container or leaf) acts as a security principal, and can have permissions granted to it. In the case of container objects, those permissions are also automatically granted to all objects within it via inheritance.

Inheritance supplies a powerful mechanism for managing NDS security because much of the access control information can be attached to the tree structure and applied based on an object's location. In this way, container objects function as a sort of "structural group"—a group built into the tree structure. When an object is created, it is a "member" of its parent container and gets "membership rights." eDirectory uses container objects for much of the functionality that would otherwise be provided by groups.

Inheritance is an iterative process; an object can inherit rights from each node between it and the root of the tree. By designing your tree to take advantage of inheritance and carefully considering your business requirements, you can substantially reduce the time spent on directory administration.

Naming in eDirectory

Although eDirectory uses the general X.500 model for names, some differences exist in exactly how naming is implemented. By using an X.500-style naming convention, Novell made it easy for eDirectory to exchange information with other X.500 and LDAP directories, which has proved useful.

Individual objects are named as in X.500 attributed naming, using a designated naming attribute and its associated value (for instance, `cn=tabitha`). Novell refers to attributed naming as *typed* (or *typeful*) naming. Unlike X.500, however, unattributed, or *typeless*, naming is also supported, allowing the use of names such as `tabitha` without the naming attribute. In a few circumstances, eDirectory tools require the use of typed names, although typeless names are more commonly used due to their relative simplicity.

As far as eDirectory is concerned, the following names are equivalent:

```
cn=tabitha
tabitha
```

DIB Capabilities and Tree Design

eDirectory's partitioning requirements have historically had a lot of influence on tree design. Because each partition requires its own node in the tree to function as the partition root, large enterprises have necessarily had some OU structure that was only there for partition management.

Suppose, for example, that there are 10,000 users with largely the same permissions and configuration; from a management perspective, these users could all reside in the same OU. With NDS v.7 or earlier, however, a single partition would normally hold only a few thousand objects. Accordingly, those users would have to be divided between multiple OUs strictly for scalability.

With the introduction of eDirectory v.8, the capacity of a single partition has increased dramatically. With little need to partition the directory for scalability, eDirectory trees no longer require much of the OU structure formerly used to support partitioning.

LDAP Naming

eDirectory provides a native, fully compliant implementation of LDAP v.3 and thus supports standard LDAP naming conventions. The usual style of LDAP name is essentially the same as a typed eDirectory name, and LDAP URLs are also fully supported.

eDirectory Names

Like X.500, eDirectory naming uses a concatenated series of object names to form distinguished names that are unique across the tree. However, individual object names are combined to form a distinguished name (DN) starting at the leafmost object, like LDAP. Object names are combined using the period (.) as a separator between name components.

In accordance with its X.500 foundations, eDirectory has several distinct types of names that refer to different styles of referencing objects:

- **Distinguished name (DN)**—Just as with X.500, an eDirectory DN is the name of the object combined with all objects in the path to the tree root—starting at the leafmost object. For example:

  `ian.dev.netmages`

- **Fully distinguished name (FDN)**—A FDN (also called fully qualified distinguished name) is a DN preceded by a period (.) to indicate to eDirectory that the name should be treated as complete and resolved from the root. For example:

  `.ian.dev.netmages`

- **Relative distinguished name (RDN)**—Although they use the same name, an eDirectory RDN is not like an X.500 RDN. An X.500 RDN, you'll remember, is the attributed name of a single object, such as `cn=ian`. An eDirectory RDN, by comparison, is a partial DN, described *relative to the location of the object referencing it*. This could be as simple as the standard X.500 RDN if it is referencing an object in the local context (same container), such as `cn=ian`. Alternatively, it can provide a partial path to the object if it exists in another context (different container). Instead of giving the DN, the object name is given in relative reference to the user's current location in the tree structure (or context). For example, if a user in the `netmages` OU is referencing the `ian` user object, the RDN is `ian.dev`—a relative reference. This is complicated, so it is explained in more detail in the "Periods in eDirectory Names" section later in this chapter. Throughout the rest of this section, you'll learn the variety of ways eDirectory uses RDNs to identify and locate directory objects.

Typeless Naming Is Cool

Typeless names require typing far fewer characters, they are visually analogous to DNS, and are cognitively easier to remember and use. However, typeless names can lead to ambiguity. For example, `.anna.dev.netmages.us` could be `.cn=anna.ou=dev.ou=netmages.o=us` or `.cn=anna.ou=dev.o=netmages.c=us`.

A number of constraints apply to eDirectory names:

- Duplicate object names are allowed within the directory tree, but not within a single container.
- The length of any individual object name cannot exceed 64 characters, and a DN string cannot exceed 255 characters.
- NDS names are not case sensitive (that is, `dev` is processed the same as `DEV`).
- The following characters should be avoided because they require special handling or might conflict with internal directory uses of the same character:

  `, . ; : + = \ / ? *`

- Spaces and underscores (_) are considered interchangeable by eDirectory, but are handled differently. Underscores can be used as normal text in name strings; however, names containing spaces require quotation marks, making them more awkward to use.

All RDNs Are Not the Same

In some references, the usual X.500 definition of RDN is applied to eDirectory. According to these sources, the RDN is just the object name, represented in either typed or typeless format as shown:

`cn=ian` (typed)

`ian` (typeless)

However, Novell currently defines an RDN as a value relative to the location of the object referencing it (as previously described).

SAP Naming Constraints

When eDirectory uses IPX as its communication protocol, it uses the Service Advertising Protocol (SAP) to advertise the network services it is providing, bringing some additional name constraints into play. File servers and printers that connect directly to the network (such as the HP JetDirect series) must follow the SAP guidelines. SAP requires the following:

- Name must be unique across the entire network.
- Names cannot be longer than 47 characters.
- Spaces are not allowed in names.

Directory Context

eDirectory defines an object's place in the directory tree as its *context*. An object's context is referenced by the string of object names between it and the tree root. Another way to look at it—a DOS analogy would be the current directory as denoted by the path.

Each network client is assigned a default name context, which is the DN of the OU containing the user object. In the case of `chloe.dev.netmages`, Chloe's context is `dev.netmages`. This information is stored in a local configuration file on the network client. At login, the username is concatenated with the name context and resolved to the specific user object for authentication. Because of the eDirectory tree design, a person's name context generally represents a logical group sharing resources or security settings.

You change your current context in one of two ways:

- As you navigate in any of the eDirectory client or administration tools, your context changes.
- By using the `CX` (change context) command (executed at a command line). The `CX` command is similar to the DOS `CD` (change directory) command, except that it applies to the directory service tree rather than the file system tree. You can use `CX` to change your context in several ways:
  - You can change your context to another container by specifying that container's FDN. As an example, "`CX .corp.netmages`" would change your context to the `corp.netmages` container, regardless of your current context.
  - If you specify the RDN rather than the FDN or DN, your context changes relative to your current position in the tree. If your current context is `netmages`, for example, you can move to the `corp` context by typing "`CX corp`". This moves you down a level of the tree into the corp container, much like typing "`CD dos`" from the root of `C:` moves you into the `dos` directory.
  - You can move up the DIT by using periods (`.`) to indicate the desired number of levels up the tree. If your context is `corp.netmages` and you need to change it to `netmages`, for example, you can just type "`CX .`" to move up one level in the tree. Similarly, "`CX [root]`" will change your context to the tree `[root]`.

eDirectory objects also can be easily located relative to your current context. When accessing an object in your current context, for example, you are only required to use the object's RDN. When you request an object using its RDN, eDirectory uses your current context to locate it in the tree.

Periods in eDirectory Names

In addition to using the period (.) as a separator, eDirectory uses periods in names to identify how a particular name should be treated:

- A leading period indicates that the replica server should consider the name to be an FDN and assume the name string ends immediately below `[root]`. This is similar to the use in a DNS Fully Qualified Domain Name (FQDN), except that DNS uses the period at the end of the FQDN (a trailing period), whereas NDS uses a leading period to signify the FDN.
- The lack of a leading period designates the object name as an RDN, telling the replica server to resolve it from the current context.
- Trailing periods are used to identify an *object relative to the user's current context*. This can be used either in the CX command (as described earlier) or in an object name. This can be a bit complicated, so let's look at how it actually works.

Figure 9.1 shows two user objects, `Ian` and `Jody`. If Ian needs to locate Jody's user object, he has two choices: He can use the FDN of `.jody.net.services.netmages`, or he can shortcut it by using periods to indicate the object location relative to his name context. In this case, the RDN would be

```
jody.net.
```

The single trailing period indicates to eDirectory that it should first move up one level in the tree (to the `services` OU) and then move down the tree to resolve the name. If Ian wanted to access the `dev` OU, he could enter the following:

```
dev..
```

eDirectory reads the two trailing periods, moves up two levels to the `netmages` OU, and then resolves the name to the `dev` OU immediately beneath `netmages`.

Contextless Logins

NetWare 5 introduced contextless logins, which enable a user to log in to the network without needing to know their context. A user just enters their first name and selects the appropriate user object from the presented list, which is created from the eDirectory catalog. This is especially useful with roaming users who might not always be at an appropriately configured computer.

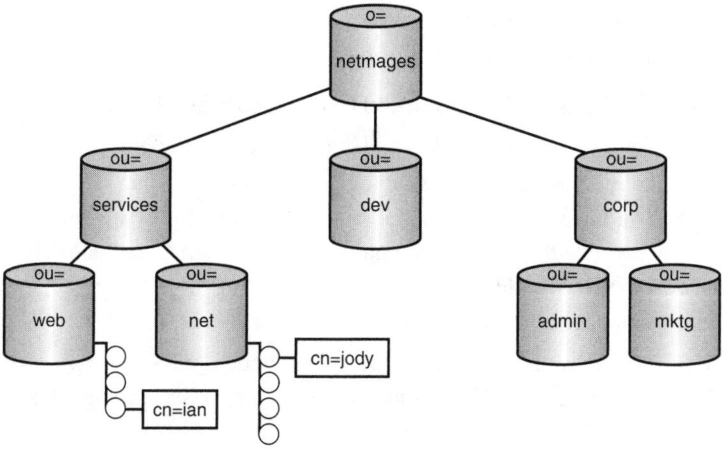

FIGURE 9.1
Using periods in NDS names can simplify object locations.

eDirectory Directory Information Base

The eDirectory database is commonly called the *DIB Set*. In keeping with the X.500 design, the DIB Set can be partitioned and distributed to multiple servers. eDirectory is said to be a loosely consistent directory service, meaning that although mostly all replicas contain the same information, they will not necessarily match exactly in every detail at any specific point in time.

Unlike X.500, the replication model used by eDirectory is multi-master in most aspects, although a single-master replica is designated and used for a few operations. Replica placement is flexible—servers can hold more than one replica and might also have varying types (master versus read/write) of replicas of different partitions. The collection of servers holding replicas of a single partition is called a *replica ring*.

Storage Method

The method that a directory service uses to store directory information to disk can vary between versions as well as between vendors. Although NDS has historically used a multiple file structure for storing directory information, the specifics of the file structure have changed with eDirectory v.8. These changes have brought about a significant increase in the storage capabilities of a single partition.

eDirectory v.8 File Structure

NDS 8 uses these files to store directory information:

- **DS.DB**—This is the control file for the eDirectory DIB Set. It also contains a *rollback log*, which is used to undo transactions that have not completed.
- **DS.01**—All the records and indexes on a given replica server are contained in the NDS.01 file. The NDS.01 file has a 2GB limit. Additional files are automatically created as the limit is exceeded; these files are named NDS.02 and so on. Attribute indexes contained in the NDS.0x file include the `Object Class`, `dc`, `Unique ID`, and `CN` fields, as well as strings beginning with `Given Name` and `Surname`.
- **DS*.LOG**—The NDS*.LOG file is used for DIB update transaction tracking. Incomplete transactions are logged in this file, which is used as a *roll-forward* log, allowing completion of interrupted transactions.
- **Stream files**—Streamfiles hold attribute information that is of variable length, such as login scripts and print-job configurations. Stream files have an `.nds` extension and are named with hexadecimal characters (0–9, A–F).

NDS File Structure (v.7 and earlier)

In NDS 7 and prior versions, the RECMAN database was used to store directory information. It consisted of the following:

- **PARTITIO.NDS**—PARTITIO.NDS holds a list of all the partitions on the NDS server, including system, schema, external reference, and bindery.
- **ENTRY.NDS**—The ENTRY.NDS file contains an entry for each object in any replica on the server.
- **VALUE.NDS**—The VALUE.NDS file contains the values for each object in the ENTRY.NDS file.
- **BLOCK.NDS**—This file is used for overflow data from the VALUE.NDS file.
- **Stream files**—Stream files are much like those in eDirectory, holding the same data and using the same names.

Interesting Heritage

The current eDirectory storage method is known as the *FLexible and Adaptable Information Manager (FLAIM)* database. FLAIM was originally developed as a means of managing very large amounts of genealogical data.

Versions of eDirectory prior to 8 used Novell's *Transaction Tracking System* (TTS) to guarantee integrity of the DIB by providing a means to roll back changes in the event of incomplete transactions. eDirectory v.8 uses a rollback log contained in NDS.DB instead of TTS.

Partitioning the DIB

eDirectory provides flexible partition design—any container object can function as a partition root (and names the partition). This flexibility is perhaps far more significant than it might appear at first. The ability to partition at *any* OU enables an administrator to subdivide the directory as needed for performance or operational reasons—and not all directory services allow that.

The number of partition-level operations that eDirectory is capable of indicates its overall flexibility:

- **Create a new partition**—This is probably the most common partition-level operation. To create a new partition, you select the container that you want to be the new partition root. eDirectory places replicas of the new partition in a configuration that mirrors the replica placement of the parent partition—by default, the server holding the master replica of the parent is given the master replica of the child, and so on.
- **Merging partitions**—This operation merges a child partition into its parent. First, each eDirectory server with a replica of the parent is sent a replica of the child, and vice versa, and then the partitions are joined. This is likely to generate a substantial quantity of network traffic while copying replicas, so manually placing replicas on all the appropriate servers before starting might be a good idea.
- **Move container**—Moving a container (such as an OU), requires that two conditions be met: the container must be a partition root, and it must not have any child partitions. When you move an object, you are offered the option to create an alias to replace it. This is particularly a good idea for a container because any process looking for the old object will be transparently redirected to the new location.
- **Changing replica types**—eDirectory enables you to change the type of a replica between master, read/write, and read-only. Because any partition must always have a master replica, you cannot directly change the master replica to a read/write or read-only. To change the status of the master replica, you promote another replica to master status, which automatically makes the old master a read/write replica. Other replicas can just be changed between read/write and read-only types.
- **Removing a replica**—Removing a replica is simple; unless it's a master, you just delete it. If you want to remove the master replica, you must first designate a new master, and then remove the original master replica afterward.

In addition to being flexible, eDirectory partitioning is independent of directory functionality that is not directly related to DIB management. Partitioning the DIB has no inherent impact on security or administration of the directory information.

Prior to version 8, NDS trees required partitioning for scalability. Partitions could only contain a few thousand objects, whereas an NDS tree was likely to hold many more. eDirectory v.8 increases the capabilities of an individual partition dramatically—theoretically to millions of objects. This is a substantial improvement in the scalability of eDirectory. Although partitioning is still required for managing replication traffic and might be desired for administrative reasons, it won't be required for scalability quite as often.

Replication of the DIB

eDirectory uses a multi-master method of directory replication, even though it uses one master replica (with multiple read/write replicas) to do so. Most operations can take place on any writable replica, although a few are restricted to the single replica designated as the master.

eDirectory uses five replica types:

- **Master**—There is only one master of any partition. The master replica is required for partition and replica creation and deletion operations.
- **Read/write**—Read/write replicas can perform most of the functions of the master replica. Read/write replicas are used for redundancy, information distribution, and load balancing.
- **Read-only**—Used for lookups only, read-only replicas cannot support updates, user authentication, or bindery services.
- **Filtered Read/write**—These replicas contain a filtered view of a directory partition. That is, a custom-configured partial set of objects and attributes created when a replication filter is employed. The replica is functionally equivalent to a standard read/write replica. Filtered read/write replicas might be used to support catalogs or applications that need to accept updates.
- **Filtered Read-only**—This replica also contains a filtered view of a directory partition, and is, as you might guess, functionally equivalent to a standard read-only replica. Filtered read/write replicas are appropriate when only lookups need to be performed.

How Big Is a Million?

According to Novell, the DIB for an eDirectory v.8 tree with one million objects occupies about 1GB of hard drive space.

The last two replica types are new to eDirectory v.8.5, and were implemented to support filtered replication.

Given the differential level of functionality provided by the various replicas, careful consideration should be taken when determining type and placement of replicas. Read-only replicas are used less often due to their limited functionality.

By default, eDirectory creates three replicas of a partition, one master and two read/write replicas. The first server installed into an eDirectory tree (that is, the server that creates the tree) receives a master replica of the entire tree, and the next two servers installed into the tree each receive a read/write replica by default. If the DIB is partitioned, this distribution is applied on a per-partition basis.

An eDirectory server is capable of holding 250 replicas, although only one of any specific partition. This is particularly useful if you want to, for example, have one or more dedicated replica servers.

As previously mentioned, the collection of servers holding replicas of a particular partition is considered a *replica ring*. Replica rings can contain up to 50 servers, meaning there can be 50 replicas of a specific partition—a lot more than is needed for most partitions. Synchronization is generally performed directly within the replica ring. eDirectory keeps track of the members of a replica ring with a replica pointer table.

Filtered Replication

eDirectory provides *filtered replication* as a means of replicating a selected subset of a partition, something that is useful for creating custom partitions of specific data. Filters can easily be created by administrators or developers, specifying the object classes and attributes to be replicated. One or more partitions are then selected for the filter to be applied to, creating a new filtered replica. The filtered replica can be designated as read/write or read-only.

Filtered replicas might be used for an application that only needs a few attributes of an object, or to create publicly available directories of employees with limited contact info while shielding most of the staff information. By including only a few attributes per object, extremely small replicas can be created, even when many objects are in the replica. This allows for many copies of a partition without incurring undue overhead for synchronization.

The *replica pointer table* contains a list of all the servers holding a replica of a given partition, the replica type held by each server, and the current status of the replica. Every server in a replica ring must have a matching copy of the replica pointer table for synchronization operations to work properly.

Replica pointer tables contain the following:

- **Server name**—The DN of the server holding the replica.
- **Replica type**—Master, read/write, or other designation.
- **Replica state**—This indicates the operational status of the replica, and is usually on. Other states include new, join, and split—each of which indicates that a particular partition operation is underway.
- **Replica number**—A unique number is assigned to each replica upon creation.
- **Partition root object ID**—The object ID of the object that serves as the partition root is unique to each server holding a replica.
- **Address**—Network addresses for the server are listed in this field. Multiple addresses can be listed if the server supports multiple protocols.

Figure 9.2 shows the partitioning scheme for the `netmages` tree. The four servers that participate in the `services` replica ring are shown. The partitions held by each server are listed immediately below the server. Three of the servers have only replicas of the `services` partition, but `Merlin` has two others as well.

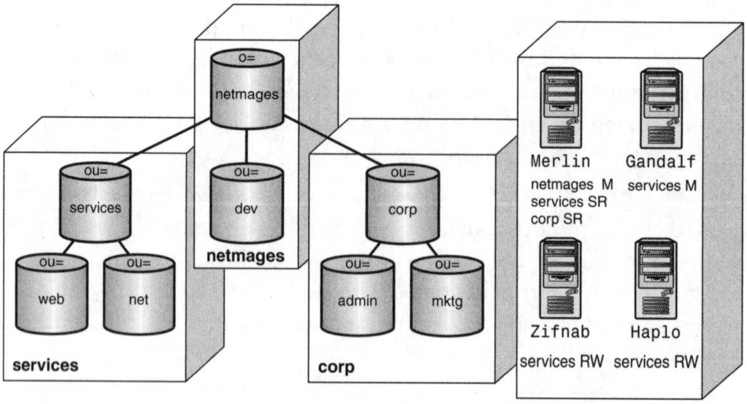

FIGURE 9.2

The netmages tree and eDirectory servers holding replicas of the services partition.

Table 9.2 shows the replica pointer table for the `services` partition. There are four replicas of the partition: one master, two read/write, and one subordinate reference (SR) (as discussed in the following section).

TABLE 9.2 The Replica Pointer Table for the Services Partition

Server	*Replica Type*	*Replica State*	*Replica Number*	*Partition Root Object ID*	*Address Name*
Gandalf	Master (M)	On	1	02972405	192.168.200.42
Zifnab	Read/write (RW)	On	3	93755822	192.168.200.75
Haplo	Read/write (RW)	On	2	03947289	192.168.200.18
Merlin	Subordinate reference (SR)	On	4	15005920	192.168.200.145

Subordinate Reference

eDirectory creates subordinate reference replicas to glue together portions of the directory contained in multiple partitions. Subordinate references function like X.500 knowledge references in providing linkage between distributed portions of the DIT. A subordinate reference is placed on a server that contains a partition that has a child, but does not hold a replica of the child partition. In the previous Figure 9.2, `Merlin` has a replica of the `netmages` partition, but not `services`; therefore, a subordinate reference is placed on `Merlin` to provide linkage to the `services` partition. Note that `Merlin` is also referenced in Table 9.2, shown previously.

A subordinate reference is a small replica containing a single object—the partition root of the child partition. The object that serves as the partition root contains information identifying all the servers in the partition's replica ring. By using this information, eDirectory can locate a server holding a complete replica of the child when it needs to walk down the tree.

However, this also means that all subordinate references are members of the replica ring and must participate in synchronization and partition-level operations. The impact of subordinate references on eDirectory operations should be kept in mind when partitioning NDS.

External Reference

The *external reference* partition contains temporary pointers to objects in the tree that are not part of a partition held on that replica server. eDirectory automatically creates external references when it needs to reference information about an object that is not part of a local replica. replica servers create external references for a number of reasons:

- **Complete a DN**—The entire path from any given object to the root of the tree must be represented for every object referenced by any replica server. Accordingly, every object between the partition root of any local replica and the root of the tree must have a local reference—if the object is not local, eDirectory creates an external reference. When an external reference is created, additional external references to complete the tree framework between the initial object and the root of the tree also can be created.

- **Authentication and access control**—External references are created to support user authentication to a server not containing a replica of the user's context.
- **Objects that are also values**—eDirectory must track information about objects referenced as a value of another object. If a group has members who are not referenced in a partition held by its server, an external reference is created to maintain the linkage between them.

External references contain the object name and an object ID, assigned by the replica server creating the external reference. They might contain additional information depending on why they were created. For instance, an external reference to a user used for authentication caches the user's public key to improve performance.

Distributed Reference Links

Every object has an attribute that corresponds to the external reference, called a *distributed reference link* (DRL). A DRL maintains a list of all the external references created for an object. DRLs are periodically verified, and if the associated external reference no longer exists, the DRL is deleted.

This functionality was provided by a *backlink* prior to NetWare 5. Although they are highly similar, there is one significant difference between DRLs and backlinks:

- Backlinks use the server DN to locate servers holding replicas containing the external reference for maintenance. This requires that every eDirectory server be able to communicate directly with every other eDirectory server, something no longer guaranteed with NetWare 5.
- In contrast, DRLs reference the DN of the partition rather than the server, allowing the use of transitive synchronization, which was also added to NetWare 5.

Synchronization Method

Synchronization is the term used in eDirectory to describe the replication of directory updates to other servers. Directory synchronization in eDirectory uses time stamps to ensure that data is correctly synchronized across the network.

Whenever an object is updated, the change is also marked with a time stamp (this is done on a per-attribute basis). That time stamp is used to determine which information should be sent when synchronizing replicas. Time stamps also can be used to resolve data collision issues that occur in a multi-master environment.

Each replica server stores the time of last update performed on every other server in the replica ring in a *SynchUpTo vector*. During the synchronization process, the supplier checks the time stamp indicating the most recent update to that consumer. Only changes that occurred after that time are sent to the server. At the end of the process, the SynchUpTo vector is updated for use in the next replica synchronization process.

Because each attribute has a time stamp indicating when it was last updated, the existing time can be compared to the time stamp on the updated value for an attribute. If the update about to be applied contains information that was written to the DIB prior to the existing data, it can be discarded. This method of synchronization guarantees that the last write to any individual attribute is written to the DIB.

Unlike many other directory services currently on the market, eDirectory propagates changes on a prioritized basis. This means that important changes are promptly sent to all other replica servers, and less-important changes are sent out on a lower priority. eDirectory supports two different synchronization speeds:

- **Fast synchronization**—Most updated directory information is synchronized every 10 seconds.
- **Slow synchronization**—Information associated with user login, such as login time and network address, is synchronized every five minutes.

Transitive Synchronization

With NetWare 5, Novell introduced native TCP/IP and dropped the requirement for IPX. This brought with it some changes in NDS. Communications issues arose—for example, how can a server running only IPX and a server running only TCP/IP synchronize NDS data?

TCP/IP Changed NDS

The change to native TCP/IP with NetWare 5 required several changes in NDS. It is now a protocol-independent network service, running on IPX or pure IP equally well. However, some specific internal methods and supportive services needed adjustments. A few particularly significant changes due to TCP/IP are as follows:

- Backlinks were replaced with distributed reference links due to changed interserver communication processes.
- Transitive synchronization capabilities were added to support mixed-protocol replica rings.
- SLP was introduced as a method of locating IP services.

To support the switch to native TCP/IP with NetWare 5, Novell had to modify the synchronization process somewhat. Prior to NetWare 5, every server in a replica ring had to be able to directly contact every other server in the replica ring.

eDirectory now supports *transitive synchronization*, allowing indirect replication within a replica ring. Transitive synchronization occurs when a replica server using different protocols synchronize replicas through an intermediary eDirectory server that supports both protocols.

Each eDirectory v.8 server uses a *transitive vector*, which stores information pertaining to its replica update status (that is, synchronization). When a synchronization operation is triggered, the source of the update checks the target server's transitive vector to determine whether an update is needed.

In addition to supporting replication within a mixed protocol replica ring, transitive synchronization is, in theory, a more efficient method of replication in large networks. This is because each replica server does not have to contact every other server in its replica ring individually, but can exchange the data aggregated from a number of replica servers with a single server.

Time Services

The directory synchronization scheme used by eDirectory requires time synchronization across the network—all servers must be using the same network time to avoid corruption of the directory information. To accomplish this, replica servers also function as time providers and all client system clocks are synchronized with the network time when the user logs on (which can be disabled if required).

To provide consistent time among the time servers, a polling process occurs periodically. A time server compares its time to the other time servers on the network and adjusts its clock according to a weighted priority. Several types of time servers exist, each of which participates in the time synchronization process differently:

Synchronization in a Mixed IPX and TCP/IP Environment

Prior to NetWare 5, TCP/IP was supported only as an additional service. Beginning in NetWare 5, however, TCP/IP is native. eDirectory servers can now support both IPX and TCP/IP, or only one of the two—a situation that presents replication issues.

For a replica ring with replica servers running "IPX only" and "TCP/IP only" to complete the synchronization process, one member of the replica ring must support both protocols. This server acts as an intermediary during synchronization. Updates that need to pass between servers with different protocols can do so through the replica server supporting both.

- **Single reference**—A single reference time server acts as controller, setting the time for all other computers on the network. This type of time server never adjusts its clock based on the polling process. Secondary time servers are the only other time servers allowed with a single reference server.
- **Reference**—Similar to a single reference, but will exist with additional time servers (that is, primaries). Like the single reference, a reference server never adjusts its clock based on the polling process. Reference servers have a polling weight of 16, meaning that primary servers always adjust their clocks to match that provided by a reference server.
- **Primary**—When a primary time server is used, at least one additional primary must be present. Any additional time servers required, other than a single reference, can be present with the primary server. Primaries have a weight of 1 in the polling process and participate equally in the adjustment process. When a primary polls other time servers, it collects the available times from primaries and averages them—the result is the new time.
- **Secondary**—Secondary time servers are considered consumers of time services in that they rely on other time servers to provide the accurate time. A secondary changes its time to exactly match the time it is given by a provider. Secondary time servers enable less capable, redundant local time servers to provide more robust time services to local clients and servers.

The default configuration for eDirectory is for the first server to be designated as a single reference and all others as secondaries. Although this is a simple configuration, it is generally used only on smaller networks (20–30 servers), due to inherent limitations with a single time source.

Larger networks commonly use a cascaded configuration in which there is one reference server, a few primaries, and a number of secondaries. This configuration provides adequate availability of time services without the overhead involved with a large number of servers participating in the polling process.

External Time Sources

eDirectory servers can be configured to get their time from an external time source, not other eDirectory servers. This is commonly done when an absolute universal time is needed, perhaps to provide a common time source for disconnected networks. The external time source can be an Internet Time Server, a dial-up connection to a government time source, a radio-based time source, and so on.

eDirectory Operations

eDirectory operations, in general, fall into line with X.500 operations. Replica servers handle authentication, object location, and manipulation, as well as searching the directory. Due to the similarities between X.500 and eDirectory, this section briefly explores the server-location process and name-resolution operations, as well as the bindery-emulation services.

Server Location

Initial server location is performed via one of three methods, depending on eDirectory version, the communications protocols in use (IPX or TCP/IP), and the protocol used to access the directory:

- **SLP**—Designed for advertising and location of services for distributed IP networks. SLP is specified in RFC 2165, and provides functionality similar to SAP. SLP performs discovery of servers (eDirectory, DNS, DHCP) and can take advantage of IP multicasting (but doesn't require it). SLP also encapsulates SAP when running in IPX compatibility mode, and allows IPX clients to find IP servers and vice versa.
- **SAP**—When a workstation using IPX boots up, the eDirectory client broadcasts a SAP service request with the desired tree name. Servers holding a replica of a partition in that tree respond to the service request, performing user authentication and providing access to resources.
- **DNS**—Can be used to locate eDirectory trees that are rooted congruent with a DNS domain. Although this is not the usual method of locating eDirectory servers for network clients, it is useful as a means of federating eDirectory trees or accessing eDirectory via LDAP.

Name Resolution

To begin the lookup process, a client passes the DN of the object it wants to locate to its local eDirectory server. The replica server examines the DN to determine whether the object is held within a local replica. The client request specifies the required type of replica (master, read/write), so the replica also must be the right kind.

If the sought object is held locally, the server returns its own network address to the client. The client then reconnects to the server with the complete query (for example, a request to read an object).

If the object is not held locally, eDirectory uses a chaining process Novell calls tree walking to locate it. The server does a partial match on the object DN to determine whether it needs to walk up or down the tree. To do this, each portion of the DN is examined starting at the `[root]`. By comparing the DN of the requested object with the replicas held locally, the server determines whether the object is up or down the tree.

If the object is located down the tree from the current server, the server uses the subordinate reference replica to locate a partition and continues the tree-walking process. Each time that a partition boundary is encountered, eDirectory uses subordinate references (if needed) until the desired object is located.

If the object is located up the tree, the root-most partition on the server is examined. The replica pointer table of this partition contains information concerning a subordinate reference held by another replica server. eDirectory contacts that server and continues walking the tree in the same fashion until it finds the object.

After an appropriate replica containing the object is located, the server returns the network address of the server holding it to the client. The client then connects to the new server to complete the query.

DNS Federation

Each eDirectory tree represents its own discrete namespace, providing administrative and security capabilities that extend only to the contents of that tree. For many years this was fine; until recently when limited interconnection between trees belonging to different organizations and security concerns often outweighed perceived benefits.

With the advent of the Internet, however, this all changed. Businesses now *want* to share the information in their directory. Indeed, there are many advantages to this sort of information exchange—relationships between partners and vendors can be enhanced, supply chains can be automated, and business operations can be streamlined.

eDirectory uses a process called *DNS federation* to allow communication and shared management functionality among eDirectory trees. eDirectory trees that are rooted at a DNS domain are considered to be installed under a pseudo-tree named "DNS." eDirectory trees created under the DNS pseudo-tree can be located by replica servers using DNS queries. After the external tree is located, standard eDirectory protocols are used to carry out directory operations. All eDirectory security still applies in federated trees, allowing secure sharing of information.

Bindery Compatibility

eDirectory provides backward compatibility with NetWare 3.x bindery clients via the bindery service, and supplies eDirectory-based management of NetWare 3.x binderies via NetSync.

Bindery Services

eDirectory provides support for NetWare 3.x clients through *bindery services*. The bindery service designates a container (by default, the container the replica server is in) to serve as the bindery context. When bindery clients access eDirectory, they are presented with a subset of the contents of the bindery context.

Bindery services can logically combine up to 16 separate contexts (that is, the contents of up to 16 container objects) on a single server. This allows a single replica server to present tens of thousands of objects to bindery clients. Down-level clients see the complete contents of the bindery context as a single flat namespace, equivalent to a single server under NetWare 3.x.

When eDirectory is installed on a server, the server's bindery context is automatically set to the container the server is in. This server must hold a writable replica of the partition of which it is a member (that is, the partition containing the server object).

When a client accesses eDirectory via bindery services, the client sees only the objects that existed in earlier versions of NetWare. This means that only the user, group, print queue, print server, and profile objects are visible. (The profile object is not actually a bindery object, rather it is provided for compatibility with NetWare Name Services.)

NetSync

NetSync was designed as a temporary solution for administering a mixed NetWare 3.x–4.x environment during the transition to NDS. Many years later, however, it is still being used on many networks that use both versions of NetWare. The primary advantages to NetSync are that it allows management of bindery objects via the standard eDirectory administration tools and provides a cluster of up to 12 NetWare 3.x servers with a more comprehensive, shared database of users, somewhat like NetWare Name Services.

NetSync operates via a pair of agents:

- **NETSYNC4**—The eDirectory server loads NETSYNC4.NLM.
- **NETSYNC3**—NetWare 3.x servers load NETSYNC3.NLM.

Installing NetSync is a fairly simple process requiring a few actions on each involved server. The eDirectory server requires a list of the 3.x servers that will be in the NetSync cluster. Each of the NetWare 3.x servers must also have an eDirectory server specified. After configuration is complete, the users and groups from the bindery of each NetWare 3.x server in the NetSync group are imported into the directory as standard objects.

The complete contents of the replica server's bindery context are then copied to the NetWare 3.x server. The bindery context contents consist of the binderies of all the servers in the NetSync cluster as well as any bindery-compatible eDirectory objects that exist in that OU (users, printers, and so on).

After NetSync is installed, all management on the down-level servers should be performed via eDirectory tools (ConsoleOne or NWAdmin). This ensures that eDirectory changes the contents of the bindery context rather than the bindery itself. Changes made by down-level administration tools, such as SYSCON, are not made in eDirectory, but rather in the actual bindery. Changes made to the bindery are not transmitted to the eDirectory server, so any changes made in this way remain only on the 3.x single server.

Security in eDirectory

eDirectory provides a substantial degree of administrative flexibility in its security management. eDirectory uses a distributed security architecture, employing the directory to contain and provide the information and the (C-2 level) security services for authentication.

Like X.500, the eDirectory namespace is structured around a hierarchical directory tree, providing a logical mechanism for security subdivisions. In this hierarchy, each container can be assigned inheritable rights. Filters can be used to determine which of those rights are inherited to subcontainers.

Because every object in the directory tree is considered a security principal, eDirectory provides a substantial degree of control over all directory objects and information. As a consequence, eDirectory provides a powerful mechanism to manage the security of your network and your information.

Novell uses a proprietary set of security mechanisms for authentication and access control based on the Public Key Infrastructure (PKI), and it also supports related Internet security protocols.

PKI technologies supply data integrity and confidential communications across nonsecure networks (such as the Internet). PKI employs digital certificates and asymmetric (public-key) cryptography. eDirectory also provides support for X.509-compliant certificates, and certificate authorities.

In addition, eDirectory provides support for SSL 3.0. SSL is used to encrypt LDAP passwords and provide a secure communications channel between an eDirectory replica client and a server.

Authentication Methods

eDirectory leverages both proprietary and standards-based technology in the provision of user authentication services. eDirectory uses shared secret authentication methods as well as PKI certificates for establishing user identity. Both private and public-key technologies are used for authentication. eDirectory uses RSA public-key technology security to provide for a single login and encrypted authentication.

During the login process, eDirectory establishes the user's identity by walking the tree to find a writable partition containing the user object. After the user has been authenticated, the user's private keys are retrieved and eDirectory provides background authentication to other services and servers as needed.

eDirectory provides support for authentication via the following:

- Encrypted passwords over SSL
- X.509 certificates
- SmartCards

Novell Modular Authentication Service (NMAS) provides an extensible framework for authentication to eDirectory using methods such as biometrics and security tokens. Using NMAS, eDirectory supports differential access (varying levels of access) based on the authentication method. Using differential access, a directory service can allow access to some resources (e-mail, for example) based solely on a password, while requiring biometric authentication for access to more sensitive data (such as financial records).

Access Control

As one of its properties, every eDirectory object has an ACL, which is used to determine access permissions. An ACL consists of the security assignments for the object or its properties. eDirectory ACLs support a high degree of granularity because access rights can be established at the property level on individual objects. Other directory services might allow access control decisions to be made for groups of objects, but not for a single one.

Objects are protected by ACLs with the following entries:

- **Trustee**—Contains the object ID for the trustee. (A *trustee* is an object that has been granted rights to another object.)
- **Type of rights**—Designates whether the ACL is for object or property rights.
- **Type of access**—Lists the rights being granted.

The default ACL template determines the rights for a new instance of a class of objects. For example, a user object is created with the right to modify certain properties of itself, such as the password.

eDirectory Rights

eDirectory defines a range of object and property rights that can be set on any directory object.

Object Rights

Object rights apply to an object as a whole rather than to the individual properties of the object. eDirectory object rights are

- **Supervisor**—Grants all object rights.
- **Browse**—Grants the right to see the object.
- **Create**—Grants the right to create a new object.
- **Delete**—Grants the right to delete the object.
- **Rename**—Grants the right to rename the object.
- **Inheritable**—This option is new to NetWare 5 and determines whether permissions granted at the container level flow down the tree. Inheritable is on by default for compatibility with previous versions of eDirectory.

Property Rights

Property rights apply to the individual properties of an eDirectory object. Access rights can be set for all object properties as a group or for one (or more) individual properties:

- **Supervisor**—Grants all property rights.
- **Compare**—Grants the right to compare contents of two properties.
- **Read**—Grants the right to read the property.
- **Write**—Grants the right to write (change) the property.
- **Add self**—Grants the right to write to the object's ACL.
- **Inheritable**—Functionally equivalent to the same setting on an object.

Permissions

eDirectory uses a system of directly assigned and inherited security assignments to determine the access permissions for any object in the tree.

Access rights are determined using a combination of several settings:

- Trustee assignment
- Security equivalence
- Inheritance
- Inherited rights filter (IRF)

The effective rights of a particular object are determined by the combined assessment of these factors.

You need to look at each piece of the eDirectory security picture in a little more depth to understand how it all works together to control access to directory information.

Trustee Assignment

With eDirectory, every object in the directory is a security principal. This means that any object in the directory can be made a trustee of another directory object, or granted rights to that object. For example, a user who has rights to access a server is a trustee of the server and is in the server's trustee list.

After a trustee assignment is made, permissions can be associated with that object. Default permissions are sometimes associated with an object during an initial trustee assignment. eDirectory also grants a number of objects default trustee assignments when they are created. The `admin` object is granted supervisor rights at the `[root]` of the tree, for example, providing full access to all eDirectory objects.

Security Equivalence

One of the important concepts of security in eDirectory is that of *security equivalence*. eDirectory relies heavily on the use of security equivalence as a means of assigning rights within the directory. Security equivalence can be created in a number of ways:

- **public**—Every user is considered the security equivalent of the public object. It is important to note that this security equivalence applies before the user is logged in to the tree, to allow tree browsing before being authenticated. Because unauthenticated users have the same rights as public, you should be careful which rights are assigned to the public object. For this reason, only object rights, and not file system rights, can be assigned to the public trustee.
- **[root]**—Any person who is logged in to eDirectory has security equivalence to the [root] object. You should grant [root] the permissions that apply to everyone on the network.
- **Containers**—This is the primary use of security equivalence in eDirectory. By default, any object is considered to be the security equivalent of every container above it, all the way to the root of the tree. To determine which containers a specific object is considered to be a security equivalent of, look at the object DN. An object is the security equivalent of every container used as a name component in its DN. You should assign those rights that you want all users in a particular container to have to the container they reside in.
- **Groups**—When you create a group in and assign a set of access rights to that group, all people who are added to the group are considered to be a security equivalent of the group object. Any permissions granted to the group are given to the individual objects in its members list. Groups are used to control permissions at a finer level than a container.
- **security equals attribute**—The direct assignment of security equivalence can be done by selecting one or more other directory objects as values for the security equals attribute. This is particularly useful if, for example, you need to temporarily assign someone administrator rights. By adding admin (or another appropriate object) to the security equals property of a user object, that user will be granted the administrator's rights. The object administrator can be removed from the security equals property when this is no longer needed. Although this is a powerful method of quickly assigning rights within NDS, you should also carefully keep track of what rights have been granted via this method. Most eDirectory object class definitions include the security equals attribute.

Rights granted via security equivalence cannot be masked by an IRF on the object that has been granted the security equivalence.

Inheritance

Security permissions flow down an eDirectory tree via *inheritance*. Inheritance is a process that allows the rights granted to an object higher in the tree to flow downward, applying to objects below it. Inheritance is based on the tree hierarchy, allowing the tree structure to control much of the general security for the directory with only exceptions needing to be assigned individually.

If the admin object is given the `[Supervisor]` permission at `[root]`, for example, the admin object has that permission throughout the entire tree structure. Rights granted via this method are known as *inherited rights*. Inherited rights can include object rights and property rights, either for all properties or selected individual properties.

Inherited Rights Filters

In the context of a hierarchical directory tree that allows for inheritance of access rights, it's also important to have a means of stopping the inheritance of rights. eDirectory provides this mechanism via an *Inherited Rights Filter (IRF)*, which blocks the inheritance of access rights from higher in the tree.

An IRF is used at the container level to determine which rights the objects within a container *do not* inherit. IRFs can filter inheritance of rights that were granted to the entire object, for all properties, or for only selected properties. This is particularly useful for directory administrators—blocking the hierarchical flow of access rights to an entire subtree in one configuration setting.

Note that an IRF cannot grant any permissions; it can only block the inheritance of those that were granted higher in the tree.

> **Runtime Inheritance**
>
> In eDirectory, an object's ACL contains only the permissions granted directly on the object. When access to the object is requested, the directory dynamically determines the access rights by gathering ACLs from that object and the other objects that contain relevant security information (such as parents). eDirectory assesses the collection of ACLs to determine the effective permissions on the requested object. Runtime inheritance guarantees that the access control decision will be based on absolutely current data, although there might be a nominal trade-off in access time.

Effective Rights

An object's *effective rights* are the set of access rights that result when all the security factors are combined and assessed. Effective rights denote which operations the object can actually perform. Effective rights are determined using the object's ACL, explicit assignments, and security equivalents.

To calculate effective rights, eDirectory does the following:

- Determines the explicit trustee assignments between the object and the partition root.
- Factors in the applicable IRFs.
- Obtains inherited ACL from partition root.
- Adds in the ACL of any object that this object is security equivalent to.

This process is done for the two objects in question—the object being accessed and the object doing the accessing. The collection of these security settings determines the effective rights for any given object.

eDirectory Administration

This book describes the design and operations of directory services, encompassing architectural and theoretical dimensions. Likewise, it describes eDirectory administration from the architectural perspective, explaining the range of administrative tools and functionality provided, rather than providing an administrative "how-to" manage eDirectory. Several excellent books do just that, however, and they are listed in Appendix A, "References".

Powerful, flexible tools do just about everything you need done out of the box. As stated previously, *ConsoleOne* is a platform-independent administrative console that supplies a centralized administrative interface to eDirectory. This console can be easily extended to provide new management capabilities. The LDAP utility that comes with eDirectory, *Novell Import Conversion Export (ICE)*, adds a wizard to the administrative console that allows LDAP import, export, and bulkloading of data. You also can monitor the eDirectory servers on your network from any Web browser with *iMonitor*.

> **Inherited ACL**
>
> Each partition root has a property called an *inherited ACL*, which contains the effective rights for that partition. The effective rights are the combination of all the trustee assignments made minus all the IRFs applied in higher levels of the tree. If no IRFs are applied at the partition root, the rights contained in the inherited ACL will be inherited by all the objects in the partition. By using the inherited ACL, eDirectory can calculate effective rights without having to actually walk the entire tree.

Administration Tools

eDirectory's administrative tools have changed considerably as the directory service has gone cross-platform. Prior to v.8, NDS shipped with a suite of tools, primarily for Windows, although some utilities were run from the NetWare server console.

With the release of ConsoleOne, management functionality began migrating from the older tools to the new Java console. iMonitor replaced other directory-management utilities, while ICE replaced still others. As this point, Novell refers to these earlier administrative applications as "legacy tools."

Most eDirectory management can be performed with either the new tool set, or the legacy tools, although a few directory components and operations require a specific tool to manage them.

eDirectory Tools

A highly distributed, cross-platform directory service needs highly centralized, platform-independent management tools. ConsoleOne and iMonitor are the core of the eDirectory management applications—most aspects of the directory can be managed with these two tools. Several additional utilities manage data exchange via LDIF and internal eDirectory operations.

The current set of administrative tools used to manage eDirectory is ConsoleOne, iMonitor, Novell ICE, DSMERGE, and Index Manager:

- **ConsoleOne**—An extensible Java console that centralizes a wide variety of directory-management tasks. Directory information, DIB operations, schema modification, and reporting can all be managed from a single interface. Multiple eDirectory trees can be managed simultaneously.

Certified Directory Engineer

Novell's *Certified Directory Engineer* (CDE) program provides specialized training for people who work with directory services. The CDE training covers directory technologies, along with eDirectory design, implementation, and troubleshooting. A hands-on practical exam (done on servers at Novell via the Internet), and a requirement for ongoing education and testing, ensures that CDEs have current, proven skills.

The CDE program has a prerequisite of a technical certification; *Certified Novell Engineer* (CNE), *Microsoft Certified System Engineer* (MCSE), *Cisco Certified Internetworking Expert* (CCIE) or *Cisco Certified Networking Professional* (CCNP), or *IBM Certified Specialist*. CNEs must complete two or three classes, while students with other certifications must take five; all students must pass the practicum.

ConsoleOne, which replaces the Windows-only NWAdmin, is extensible, furnishing a framework for enhanced management capabilities. *Snap-ins* provide extended functionality needed to manage objects and services that aren't a native part of eDirectory. An application that modifies the directory schema to include application-specific objects, for example, must also provide a means to manage those objects. By installing a snap-in, a vendor can provide access to the objects and properties that were added to the schema.

ConsoleOne features include

- Powerful search capabilities enable ConsoleOne to deal with large trees by paging search results and providing virtual list views.
- Multiple objects can be selected and property values for the entire group edited at the same time.
- Capability to manage all partitions and replicas in the directory.
- Individual property pages can be sorted and hidden for any directory object, enabling customized console configurations.
- A centralized point to launch additional management tools for services such as DNS/DHCP and remote console access to the eDirectory server.

ConsoleOne is available for NetWare, Windows, Solaris, Linux, and TRU64. ConsoleOne is available in many languages, including Chinese (Simplified and Traditional), English, French, German, Italian, Japanese, Korean, Portuguese, Russian, and Spanish.

A Brief History of ConsoleOne

ConsoleOne was introduced with NetWare 5 and has had two rather different incarnations as a network-management tool. ConsoleOne 1.1, which shipped with NetWare 5, was a server-based console rather than the client-side ConsoleOne provided with eDirectory v.8. The original ConsoleOne tool was highly limited, rather slow, and not very well accepted.

To its credit, Novell publicly acknowledged this was perhaps not the best approach to dealing with a portable administration tool and thoroughly redesigned ConsoleOne prior to releasing it with eDirectory v.8. ConsoleOne 1.2 provides support for all the functionality in the preceding administration tool, NetWare Administrator; supports enhanced operations; and, because it is a Java-based utility, is platform independent.

- **iMonitor**—Provides a Web-based method of monitoring and working with eDirectory servers from anywhere on the network. Using iMonitor, you can the check the status of your replica servers and perform many server-level operations, such as working with replica rings, logging eDirectory operations, and administering time services.
- **Novell ICE**—The ICE utility provides a method of importing and exporting LDIF formatted data. (As mentioned earlier, LDIF is the LDAP data interchange format, a text representation of directory objects used as an implementation-independent method of exchanging data between directories.) ICE also allows the exchange of information directly between LDAP directories without the need to perform LDIF translations first. ICE, which replaces the LDAP bulkload utility, is available as a ConsoleOne snap-in called the eDirectory Import/Export Wizard, or a command-line client utility. Data being manipulated with ICE can be processed using XML rules (the same rules as DirXML) to provide the following sorts of functionality:
  - Creation rules enforce prerequisites for creating new directory entries, such as requiring that objects match specified property values, supplying default information for mandatory properties whose values are empty, and designating a template to use in object creation.
  - Placement rules use conditions to govern where in the tree new objects are created and which attribute should be used as a naming attribute.
  - Schema mapping rules reconcile the inevitable differences in schema when moving data between directory services, allowing mapping of objects and attributes.
- **DSMERGE**—Used to perform tree operations such as merge, graft, and rename. DSMERGE also allows you to check the status of replica servers, and monitor time synchronization. DSMERGE is available for NetWare, Windows NT, and as NDSMERGE for Linux, Solaris, or Tru64.
- **Index Manager**—Allows for the creation and configuration of custom indexes, used to speed directory searches.

Delegating Administration

You can use the tree in eDirectory to delegate administrative authority for discrete parts of the directory, granting specific administrative rights for designated containers and subtrees. OUs are most commonly used for such delegation to subdivide the administration for business or operational purposes.

Legacy Tools

These tools are considered "legacy tools"—they formed the NDS management tool set prior to eDirectory v.8:

- **NetWare Administrator**—This predecessor to ConsoleOne is a Windows-only directory management tool, and was the primary NDS tool beginning with its inception in 1993.
- **NDS Manager**—NDS Manager supports partitioning and replication of the DIB. NDS Manager also can verify synchronization status, trigger synchronization, and initiate the repair of a remote database. NDS Manager replaced the DOS-based *Partition Manager*, which provided this functionality in earlier versions. ConsoleOne cannot perform a few NDS Manager operations, such as remote replica repairs and partition continuity checks.
- **LDIF Bulkload**—eDirectory provided the LDIF Bulkload utility prior to the introduction of ICE, enabling administrators to easily add, delete, or modify large numbers of directory objects.
- **SCANTREE**—This is a DOS-based, read-only utility that produces a basic inventory of the eDirectory tree. SCANTREE is available from Novell's Web site as `dsscan.exe`.
- **DSTrace**—You can observe eDirectory operations in real-time by using the DSTrace utility. Numerous options enable you to view processes such as synchronization.
- **DSREPAIR**—DSREPAIR is a NetWare server console tool that examines, repairs, and compacts the DIB. Recent versions of DSREPAIR work on a single partition, allowing most operations to be performed without locking the entire DIB.
- **DSMAINT**—DSMAINT is designed to support replacing replica servers. Using DSMAINT, an administrator can back up eDirectory, replace the server hardware, and then restore eDirectory to the new server with all object IDs intact. Recent versions of DSREPAIR have also included this functionality.
- **SBACK**—SBACK is a basic backup utility that provides a method of backing up the DIB to tape and restoring it. Although it does afford a simple backup method for eDirectory, that is about all it does. Because most network backup software also includes a mechanism for backing up NDS, however, it is not widely employed in large network environments.

Login Script Processing

eDirectory provides comprehensive support for multiple levels of login scripts, assessed according to a predetermined hierarchy. Login scripts are processed in the following order:

- **OU login script**—The OU login script is used first.
- **Profile login script**—If a profile is assigned, the profile login script is used next.
- **User login script**—A login script assigned to the specific user is next.
- **Default login script**—The default script is run unless one of the two following conditions occur: Either there is a user login script, or the default script is told not to run using the appropriate variable in one of the other login scripts.

Groups in eDirectory

Groups are used to collect a set of users, generally for assigning common access permissions. Like other eDirectory objects, groups are security principals, so you can assign group permissions and all members will be granted those permissions. A group object does not have login scripts associated with it, although groups can be referenced within a login script.

When group memberships are enumerated, member names are returned one at a time. This means that if the group is not held in a local replica, the process to enumerate members of a group might generate some additional network traffic, and be somewhat slower than if performed locally. Therefore, you might want to keep in mind the relative locations of groups and their members when designing your network.

Integrated Novell Management Technologies

Novell has integrated a number of management technologies with eDirectory. These technologies assist network management in common administrative and infrastructure tasks. The following are just a few examples:

- **iChain**—iChain provides a security and management infrastructure for Web-based applications and content. iChain, which is built on the Volera Excelerator Caching Server, provides Proxy, Authentication, Authorization, Web Single Sign-On, and Community Services.
- **Single Sign-on**—Single Sign-on provides a method for securely storing and retrieving passwords used by applications other than eDirectory. Passwords to multiple systems are stored within eDirectory and used to authenticate the user as needed. Provisions are

> **Profile Objects**
>
> Each user can have only one profile object assigned. The profile object affords an additional method of attaching a login script to a user. No security equivalence is conferred via profile objects.

made so that stored passwords cannot be easily compromised. Single Sign-on can be configured so that if a user's eDirectory password is changed by an administrator, it will request the old password at the next use of the stored application credentials. This helps ensure that someone impersonating an administrator cannot easily access and alter stored secret information. Among the first applications supported are Lotus Notes and PeopleSoft.

- **ZENworks** for Desktops—ZENworks for Desktops is a desktop-management system, allowing desktop management and troubleshooting from a remote location. ZENworks integrates policy-based management of workstations with NDS to deliver network-wide support for roaming users and centralized administration of clients. ZENworks stores desktop, application, printer configurations, and help-desk information. This information is stored in the directory and pulled by clients upon login. Administrators can perform tasks such as remotely gathering computer inventories, installing software on client machines, and securely accessing workstations from remote locations. A recent addition to Novell's product line is *ZENworks for Servers*, which provides a similar style of centralized management of servers.
- **BorderManager**—BorderManager provides security at the network boundaries to provide secure Internet and intranet management. BorderManager lets you define security and service rules for devices and services. You can use BorderManager to manage Virtual Private Networks (VPNs), firewalls, proxy services, and caching.

digitalme™

Novell has developed *digitalme*, a new kind of personal information management system. digitalme extends eDirectory's secure information management capabilities across the Internet and enables individuals to manage their online identity. Novell envisions digitalme using eDirectory as a relationship manager to "integrate the digital world around the person."

digitalme uses an *identity server*, which is run on a Web server, making it accessible on the Internet. The identity server stores digitalme information securely, while making it available according to user-configured policies. Because it is based on standard eDirectory technology, the identity server can offer capabilities such as Single Sign-on.

Each person who registers with digitalme creates one or more profiles. Profiles are specific "views" of a person based on context such as business, family, or a special interest. These profiles are called *mecards*. Each mecard can have its own set of attributes and information, making it possible to have customized personas for various aspects of your Internet identity.

Users can form relationships to the mecards, which grant another entity (such as a Web site or another digitalme user) access to the information in that mecard. After a relationship is established with a Web site, digitalme can perform actions such as automatically log the user in to the site, fill in forms, and otherwise offload repetitive tasks.

For further information regarding digitalme, visit `www.digitalme.com`.

The Future of eDirectory

As mentioned at the beginning of this chapter, eDirectory has been around for a number of years. As a product, it has expanded considerably over the years, both within the core eDirectory product as well as in ancillary offerings. That growth is continuing, extending onto the Internet and integrating an ever-increasing number of new technologies.

Let's take a brief look at just a couple of the things that Novell has up its sleeve for eDirectory in the near future.

DirXML

XML, the emerging open standard for content exchange, is being used in accessing and representing directory-service content. XML, along with *Extensible Stylesheet Language* (XSL) and *XSL Translation* (XSLT) are the core technologies used in *DirXML,* Novell's meta-directory solution. DirXML runs on top of eDirectory v.8, providing data synchronization between multiple directories and a single point of management for the disparate data sources.

DirXML uses drivers to create an application-specific view of the information stored in a directory service. The information contained in that application view can then be replicated via XML and an XSL processor. XSL consists of a language used to transform XML documents and a vocabulary used to describe formatting semantics. The XSL processor in DirXML can customize the data to the needs of any application.

DirXML drivers are currently available forNDS eDirectory, iPlanet, Active Directory, Exchange, and Lotus Notes. Nexor has recently partnered with Novell to develop DirXML connectors to X.500 directories, expected to be available by the end of 2001. Developers can create customized DirXML drivers for applications, databases, or directories in Java or C++ with an SDK (software developer kit) available from Novell.

DirXML is described in more detail in Chapter 12, "Directory Markup Languages."

Interesting NDS Deployments

Some of the most exciting developments around eDirectory aren't coming from Novell. An impressive array of NDS eDirectory-based products and business solutions have been developed in recent years by third-party vendors.

Many governments are deploying eDirectory so that they can manage the affairs of their citizens securely online. Much of this activity is happening at the city level; services being provided in the first stages include booking parks and recreation facilities, involvement in city planning activities, permitting processes, and sometimes e-commerce such as utility and tax payments. Communication between the city and the residents, as well as with elected representatives, can be facilitated with a directory. Future plans for these implementations commonly call for broader e-commerce applications (payments of benefits to citizens, for example), and even voting.

Many of the cities trying e-government are small to medium size (ten to a hundred thousand or so), but not all of them; Toronto, Canada is taking its government online for 2,500,000 residents. And, it's not just *city* governments that are taking their services online with eDirectory. Cap Gemini Ernst & Young announced recently that the French government purchased eDirectory with 35 million client licenses.

Novell has a registry of eDirectory-enabled products available on the Web at the Novell Solutions Site (`developer.novell.com/nss/`).

Active Directory

CHAPTER

10

...all domains shall be as one, and speak in tongues of LDAP...

IN THIS CHAPTER

This chapter examines the architecture and operations of Active Directory, Microsoft's directory services integrated with Windows 2000 and Windows.NET Server. Although the scope of the technical information on Active Directory can fill many books, this material provides a concise summary of key factors describing Microsoft's entry into the networking directory service market.

While reading this chapter, you will use much of the information learned in previous chapters. Active Directory is designed to integrate core Internet technologies with the Windows 2000 and Windows .NET Server networking and security services, leveraging the global DNS namespace and location services, and using LDAP as the core directory protocol.

Introduction to Active Directory

Active Directory is one of the more technologically inventive network directory service implementations in the industry. Active Directory integrates Microsoft's key directory service and network technologies, such as LDAP and DNS, with its Windows 2000 networking platform. Active Directory represents a significant step in the evolution of Windows network management. A brief review of Microsoft's approach to Windows NT network management might help illustrate how the pieces fit together.

First, there were Windows NT domains, which allowed management of a limited set of objects, users, groups, and network devices such as printers and servers. An NT domain is a flat NetBIOS namespace that provides network account management and security services (authentication and access control) to a collection of users, servers, and workstations. The information for each domain is stored in a centralized and replicated *Security Accounts Manager* (SAM) database.

Each NT domain can theoretically contain up to 40,000 objects, although many contain substantially fewer, requiring some businesses to use a number of domains to manage its enterprises. There is no inherent relationship between domains, although interdomain relationships can be created to ease administration. These interdomain trusts *were* useful, but given the number of trust relationships that must be managed in large organizations, the complexity of trust administration and maintenance was problematic.

Then along came the development of Windows 2000 and Active Directory.

Microsoft clearly chose to support the substantial installed base of Windows NT networks in the design of its new directory service, integrating the existing Windows NT domain mechanisms in the core of Active Directory's design and security operations. Adding to this Windows NT 4 base, Microsoft leveraged the X.500 data model for structuring the directory contents, the LDAP protocol for access to the directory information, and DNS as the location services and core namespace. The result of this integration of technologies is Active Directory, as implemented with Windows 2000 and Windows .NET Server.

Active Directory's support for Windows NT network environments includes a Primary Domain Controller (PDC) Emulator to communicate with down-level domain controllers and servers (NT 3.51–NT 4), as well as clients (Windows 98/95 and Windows NT Workstation). This integrated support for the Windows NT 4 networking platform enables IT departments to leverage its existing Windows NT infrastructure, while upgrading to the directory-enabled networking environment of Windows 2000.

In the Active Directory design, Microsoft also enhanced its location services. Windows NT domains used broadcasts to locate a domain controller, and supported TCP/IP location services via *Windows Internet Naming Service* (WINS), which provides NetBIOS name registration and resolution to IP addresses. Windows NT 4 also supported DNS domain name resolution (yet the DNS domains and the NT domains were distinct and separate). Due to the Internet, both TCP/IP and DNS are now ubiquitous—and even LDAP has been extended to integrate with DNS domains with the introduction of domain component objects. Active Directory uses DNS as a location service to find domain controllers, as well as servers that provide Kerberos and LDAP services.

Microsoft decided on a native-LDAP implementation, choosing to go with the de facto industry standard for directory access. LDAP brings with it the information models of X.500, but does not describe distributed operations. For storage of the directory information, Microsoft already had a distributed directory engine (*Jet Server*) for Exchange Server and that technology was leveraged to manage Active Directory's datastore.

The decision to build on the NT domain model led to Active Directory having distinct design and operational differences from many other directory services.

Active Directory blends support for DNS, LDAP, and NetBIOS namespaces; an Active Directory tree is fundamentally a tree of DNS domains, each of which is also an NT-style domain and thus its own NetBIOS namespace. Objects in the directory tree are accessed via LDAP, which is used to locate directory objects within the domain.

The domain in Active Directory is still a security boundary, just as in NT 4—yet trust relationships between domains are created automatically. Security identifiers link objects created in a domain to that domain. There is a one-to-one correlation between Active Directory domains and directory partitions; the domain boundary is also the partition boundary.

In building Active Directory this way, Microsoft provided the necessary compatibility with existing NT networks, as well as support for the industry standard directory access protocol (LDAP) and location service (DNS). This design formed a solid application platform for both Win32 and LDAP application developers and vendors, while supplying advanced directory functionality for administrators to leverage.

In reviewing the architecture of Active Directory, keep in mind that Active Directory was designed to support the existing Windows NT domain and security models. You can see the integration of various components of the Windows NT 4 platform with Active Directory. This includes the NetBIOS networking components, such as the Universal Naming Convention (UNC) NetBIOS, namespace and WINS, as well as the NT domain security boundary and the Security Accounts Manager (SAM) interface.

By designing this support for its previous networking platform, Microsoft enabled down-level applications to run on the Windows 2000 platform, and supported the integration of existing NT networks into Windows 2000.

For IT environments with NT networks, this design supplies the upgrade path to directory-centric administration of distributed networks, as well as the use of directory-enabled applications, facilitating business operations such as provisioning and procurement.

Active Directory Design Overview

The architecture of Active Directory integrates Windows 2000 networking and domain security with a native LDAP directory, framed in the DNS domain namespace and using DNS location services. Because Active Directory natively uses LDAP, it incorporates aspects of the X.500 models and general methodological approach; however, the need to integrate support for NT domains, as well as the linking of partitions to domains, and Microsoft's decision to leverage DNS as the fundamental namespace, have led to some divergences from "classic X.500"—and an interesting finished product.

Active Directory Terminology

Before delving into detailed descriptions of Active Directory architecture, let's take a look at an analogy between terms used in Active Directory and X.500. Table 10.1 shows the correlation between terminologies.

TABLE 10.1 Vocabulary Correlations

Functionality	*Active Directory Term*	*Analogous X.500 Term*
Directory entries	Objects	Objects
Object subentries	Properties	Attributes
Definition of directory contents	Schema	Schema

TABLE 10.1 Continued

Functionality	*Active Directory Term*	*Analogous X.500 Term*
Logical representation of directory	Forest Domain Tree Directory Tree	Directory Information Tree (DIT)
Data storage	Store	Directory Information Base (DIB)
Subdivision of directory	Domain, partition, or naming context	Naming context
Data updates	Site replication	Replication
Server agent	Domain Controller (DC)	Directory System Agent (DSA)
Client agent	Active Directory client	Directory User Agent (DUA)
Query resolution	DNS Recursive & Iterative LDAP Referral Global catalog lookups	Chaining & Referral
Security boundary	Domain	ACSA

Active Directory as an NOS-Based Directory Service

Active Directory is a networking-focused directory service, designed to manage distributed Windows 2000 networks. Active Directory runs as a discrete service within the Windows 2000 security subsystem, supplying a client/server set of directory services via a structured information model, and providing access to network resources in a logically unified namespace.

Active Directory uses *domain controllers* (DCs) to provide DSA functionality, that is, handle client logon, queries, return results, and referrals to other DCs. The client-side software for Active Directory is built in to Windows 2000 Professional and available as an extension for Windows 95/98 clients.

Active Directory leverages the X.500/LDAP data model with directory *objects* comprised of a series of *properties*. The Active Directory *schema*, however, goes well beyond the base X.521 object set with its wide range of classes, attributes, and syntax.

The *Active Directory namespace* uses DNS to define one or more *Domain Trees*, which is a tree of domains that comprise a contiguous DNS namespace. Active Directory uses a *forest* to contain multiple disjoint (noncontiguous) domain trees.A *domain* in Active Directory is also a functional subdivision of the Active Directory database; each *partition* is stored on the DCs in that domain. Active Directory abstracts replication management to *sites*, which automatically perform local replication and allow configurable replication for local and remote DCs. Active Directory uses multimaster replication with flexible single-master operations for schema (and other) updates.

LDAP and Active Directory

Microsoft implements LDAP (version 3) as Active Directory's core directory protocol. Active Directory is constructed as a native LDAP directory, handling LDAP queries directly and without translation. LDAP provides a rich query capability for directory information access, supplying access to all directory functionality, including managing the schema and query scoping.

In its strategy white paper, "Comparing Microsoft Active Directory to Novell's NDS," Microsoft describes Active Directory as an inherently scalable LDAP server product that can contain over a million objects in a single partition. (In other documentation, Microsoft describes testing the Active Directory storage subsystem with 40 million objects.)

DNS and Active Directory

Active Directory integrates DNS at its core, using DNS for naming and location services. The use of the DNS structure for domain names is a significant change from the NetBIOS name structure used in previous versions of its Windows server platform (Windows NT).

Domains in Active Directory are structured as DNS domains (and use DNS names) while retaining its NT domain security properties. The top of the domain tree can be (and commonly is) the internal or external organization name in the DNS namespace (for instance, `mythical.org`). Alternatively, for businesses without an assigned DNS name and who are not connected to the Internet, an arbitrary DNS name can be selected.

An Active Directory Forest

The *forest* is a concept unique to Active Directory. A forest represents the ultimate root of an Active Directory namespace, existing *above* the root of any given Active Directory tree. The forest can contain one or more Active Directory trees, and Active Directory trees always exist within a single forest. Forests share a common schema and configuration information, and trees within a forest have implicit trusts automatically established between them.

Active Directory is dependent on an RFC 2136–compliant version of *Dynamic DNS (DDNS)* to provide dynamic updating of DNS zone entries. Active Directory does not require that you run Windows 2000 DNS, although it is highly recommended. Using DDNS, Active Directory servers can do the following:

- Dynamically publish SRV records containing information about its services, ports, and IP addresses.
- Periodically check its DNS registrations to ensure correct IP address assignment.
- Update the DNS records as servers and services become available or unavailable.

Active Directory adds multiple SRV records to the base DNS configuration, denoting various servers, services, protocols, and ports used in Active Directory operations. Active Directory clients use the SRV records to locate the Global Catalog and DCs for network logon and authentication.

DNS provides the core location services, and therefore, correct DNS configuration is essential to effective Active Directory network operations. DNS has the critical role of locating domain controllers and key services in the Active Directory namespace. Clients use DNS as the location service that connects them to the DC containing the directory information needed for logon and query resolution.

Client/Server Agents

Active Directory uses a client/server implementation, where its DSA (a Windows 2000 Domain Controller) receives directory requests from clients, and interacts with the storage engine layer to access the requested object data. The operations of the DSA effectively isolate Active Directory clients from physical storage management issues for directory objects.

Core Information Source

The information in this chapter is primarily based on the Windows 2000 product and other information provided by Microsoft. Because this chapter documents the core directory service architecture, technologies, and operations, barring substantial and fundamental directory redesign efforts by Microsoft, changes in future Active Directory releases (such as Windows .NET Server, code-named Whistler) that affect this information should be minor. Changes to Active Directory in Windows .NET Server are noted where appropriate. Technical feedback is invited and can be submitted to `uds@src.nu`.

The DSA Component

A core component in any directory is the DSA, which handles access to the DIB, performing all directory read/write operations and management tasks. The *domain controller (DC)* is the DSA of the Active Directory architecture, providing access to its portion of the DIB (called the *store*), and supplying updates to remote DSAs and the Global Catalog on changes to its DIB partition. A DC contains a single partition of the directory information. The DCs supply the DSA interface to which clients and applications can bind to access the directory information held in that partition. Throughout this chapter, when the term *DSA* is used, it refers to a Domain Controller.

In addition to these base domain controller operations, a DC may be used in a variety of roles including

- **Global Catalog (GC) servers**—A GC server contains an index to all directory objects in the forest, providing an efficient means for applications and users to query the directory for objects based on one or more known attributes. GCs contain a partial replica of every domain in the forest.
- **Operations masters**—Active Directory uses flexible single-master operations in replication processes. Active Directory defines five *operations master* roles: the *Domain Naming Master* and *Schema Master* (required once in each forest), as well as the *Relative ID Master, Infrastructure Master*, and the *PDC Emulator* (required for each domain).

The various roles performed by DCs are discussed in more detail in the "Active Directory Operations" section later in this chapter.

The DUA Component

An Active Directory client accesses directory information by using one of the specified interfaces to connect to the DSA and requests the needed operation for the selected directory objects.

The DUA client's connection methods vary, as follows:

- Active Directory clients use LDAP v.3 to connect to the DC.
- Clients using the Microsoft Messaging API (MAPI) use the MAPI remote procedure call (RPC) interface.
- Down-level clients use the SAM interface.

Active Directory APIs

Active Directory supports a number of Application Programming Interfaces (API) allowing access to the directory contents and directory service operations. Active Directory APIs include a new Microsoft proprietary method for accessing the services and information, an

LDAP-based interface to enable application access, as well as MAPI and the SAM APIs to provide backward-compatible interfaces to support Microsoft's email and Windows NT domain functionality. These Active Directory APIs are

- **ADSI**—The primary API is called the *Active Directory Service Interface* (ADSI). ADSI is an object-oriented interface to Active Directory objects and methods, masking the details of the underlying LDAP communications. The ADSI design abstracts the functionality of multiple types of directory services and integrates directory access and management into a set of unified interfaces. An ADSI *provider* supports a namespace-specific implementation of directory objects. Active Directory includes an ADSI namespace provider for NT 4, NDS, NetWare 3.x, as well as LDAP (versions 2 and 3). Applications written for ADSI have the capability to perform directory operations across disparate namespaces. ADSI interfaces are also accessible to scripts, easing the automation of administrative tasks. ADSI provides application development support for multiple scripting languages, including Visual Basic Script, JavaScript, Perl, as well as the Windows Scripting Host environment.
- **LDAP C API**—The LDAP C API can be used to access Active Directory services and objects.
- **MAPI**—Active Directory supports the *Messaging API* (MAPI) interface for compatibility with applications based on MAPI; however Microsoft does recommend that new applications use ADSI.
- **SAM API**—The *Security Accounts Manager* (SAM) interface is a protected subsystem used by Windows 2000 to administer user and group security account information maintained within the Registry. In NT 4, security principals (either local or domain) are stored in the SAM database; therefore, when Active Directory operates in mixed mode (with both Windows 2000 DCs and NT 4 BDCs on the network), down-level NT clients use the SAM APIs for authentication. The SAM APIs are also used in mixed mode for replicating the SAM database to down-level domain controllers. Security account information for workstations is stored in a registry (of the local computer); however, the DC security account information is stored within Active Directory.

Directory Initiatives

The Directory Enabled Networks (DEN) initiative is advanced by Microsoft and Cisco (among others) and is designed to integrate network hardware management into directory services, including Active Directory. Integrating the network infrastructure devices (such as switches and routers) can supply the capability needed to control the network via policies enforced by the directory.

Additionally, Microsoft and other vendors have allied with Bowstreet Software to develop the Directory Services Markup Language (DSML) for accessing directory services via a common markup language. DSML will support vendor efforts in developing directory-centric applications. Bowstreet has also made substantial advancements in the integration of Web Services and directory operations, developing an application called the "Business Web Factory" to expedite automating the connection of business operations and interbusiness relationships.

Active Directory Models

In its white paper "Active Directory Technical Summary," Microsoft defines the architecture of Active Directory as subdivided into a number of primary components and several models. Although these models do not have the depth or focus of the X.500 models, they can be useful in assessing Microsoft's design intent for Active Directory.

The Active Directory models include

- **Data model**—Microsoft describes the Active Directory data model as deriving its origins from the data model defined in the X.500 specifications. In Active Directory, the directory is an information datastore containing objects that represent network resources and users (and a wide range of information). Each of the objects in the datastore is defined by the schema that specifies each object class, and the optional and mandatory attributes for that object class, its container class, and permissible attribute syntax.
- **Security model**—The Active Directory security model fully participates in the Windows 2000 security infrastructure and uses *access control lists* (ACLs) to protect directory objects, where user permissions to access objects are validated against the object's *access control entries* (ACEs) by the Windows 2000 access validation routines. While the Active Directory security model differs from the X.500 security model, it is backward compatible with, and extends, the Windows NT security model. Active Directory employs multiple security technologies and protocols, using Kerberos for authentication and transitive trusts (automatic trust relationships between domains), SSL/PCT for encryption, and SAM for authentication with down-level systems.
- **Administration model**—The Active Directory administration model differs from the X.500 administrative authority model, yet supports a finely detailed delegation of administrative tasks. Active Directory allows the authorization of selected people to perform specific sets of actions on designated sets of objects or attributes within a specified subtree or organizational unit. The capability to specify ranges of actions that can be performed, and to set the scope of the subtree in which the operation can be performed, provides for delegation of appropriate authority over the specified directory tasks.

- **Replication model**—In its Windows 2000 SDK, Microsoft also defines a replication model—one that is substantially different from X.500's single-master model—using a more robust approach called multimaster replication. Microsoft describes this model as "*multimaster loose consistency with convergence*," where a directory is comprised of a system of replicas, and changes made at any replica are propagated to all others. The directory content is only loosely consistent because the replicas are not necessarily the same at any given point in time. Convergence occurs after all changes are propagated to all replicas, and the directory information is consistent between all replicas.

Active Directory Objects and Schema

This section briefly describes the objects and schema used in Active Directory, primarily noting the distinctions and differences presented. While the directory objects in Active Directory include objects described in the X.500 and LDAP data models, an extensive number of additional objects are defined in the Active Directory schema.

Active Directory Objects

At a basic level, the Active Directory objects and properties are fairly consistent with X.500, but the approach is also somewhat different. Only two types of container objects are available in the primary management tool, for example—a container is either a domain (with all the related contingencies) or an OU.

Active Directory defines a substantial number of objects—more than 125 *structural* objects in the base schema alone. Although the range of objects may seem extensive, you are actually only presented with a handful of context-appropriate classes from which to select when you create an object.

Container Object Classes

As just mentioned, Active Directory supports only two administrator-created classes of container objects in the directory tree: domain and OU. The X.521 base container object classes Country, Locality, and Organization are not supported in the tree by Active Directory, which uses the domain component objects instead. There are many similarities between the domain object and the OU. They both provide containers for directory structure, administrative rights can be delegated at either level, and a group policy can be attached to either object. They differ significantly, however, in its structure and usage:

- **Domain**—The domain object is one of the most critical objects in Active Directory, providing the basic tree structure, as well as security and partitioning boundaries. A domain object is created (from the `domainDNS` class) automatically when `DCPromo` is used to create a new domain. To guarantee the continuity of the DNS namespace, domain objects can only be created immediately subordinate to other domain objects—except at the root of the tree, of course. Attributes for this class primarily consist of SAM information. In fact, the only attribute not from `Top` or one of the SAM classes is the `dc` attribute, which is used as the naming attribute of the class. The definitions of the two auxiliary SAM classes, `SAMDomain` and `SAMDomainBase`, supply the properties necessary to support NT domain functionality.

- **OU**—The Active Directory OU is similar to an X.500 OU in that it provides a container for objects without any inherent security or partitioning boundaries. OUs are used to subdivide the contents of a domain into smaller units for administrative purposes. An OU can be contained by either a domain or another OU. Administrative permissions can be assigned at the OU level, enabling the delegation of administrative tasks within the OUs.

Leaf Object Classes

Active Directory uses a substantial number of object types to represent the resources and entities on the network. Active Directory leaf objects correspond to a wide range of individual network elements (printers, servers, users), as well as to logical subdivisions of resources, properties, and processes.

These objects are presented in subsets depending on the management task being performed (that is, which tool is being used and what the context is). Quite a few Active Directory objects are created automatically by the system as part of an installation or configuration process and cannot be created manually through normal administrative tools.

The list of leaf objects is far too long to include here. It is possible, however, to look at a few general categories as an example of what Active Directory provides:

- **Network management objects**—Objects providing basic network management such as `users`, `computer`, `printers`. These objects are available via the *Active Directory Users and Computers* console.
- **Replication management objects**—Objects such as `sites`, `site links`, and `site link bridges` are used in DIB management. Replication-related objects can be accessed via *Active Directory Sites and Services* console.
- **Service management objects**—A set of objects for managing services is also provided, including DHCP and PKI services. Service objects are also available via the *Active Directory Sites and Services* console, although they are hidden by default. To view service objects, you must select the option to view the Services node in the Sites and Services management tool.

Clearly, many other objects are available in Active Directory. Some of these objects will become apparent when you encounter them in a management tool; however, others you will never see unless you dig into the "hidden" portions of the directory (via the Active Directory Schema snap-in, for example).

Active Directory Schema

From a general perspective, the Active Directory schema is similar to the schema defined in X.500. Although the class and attribute definition details vary, the underlying model is the same.

Active Directory stores its schema as objects in a schema container subordinate to the configuration node. There is one schema, and therefore one schema container, per forest. The configuration partition (and, therefore, the Active Directory schema) is replicated to every domain controller in the forest. Here is an example of the default DN of the schema container:

```
cn=schema,cn=configuration,dc=mythical,dc=org
```

By storing the schema in the directory, Active Directory allows applications and developers to easily access and modify schema information. This access to schema information provides necessary support for directory-enabled applications, and allows applications to verify and extend the schema. Active Directory also supports dynamic schema updates, allowing applications to use its schema extensions immediately.

Class Definitions

Class definitions in Active Directory specify possible directory objects, the information used to create those objects, and valid object relationships. Class definitions define the structure rules, as well as mandatory and optional attributes. Each class is derived from its parent object class (analogous to an X.500 superclass). Every object is created as an instance of its specified class.

Active Directory uses the following fields in the class definitions:

- **Class Type**—The class type defines the type of object (structural, abstract, or auxiliary) and the designation as a container or not.
- **X.500 OID**—This is the object identifier (assigned by industry organizations such as ANSI).
- **GUID**—The globally unique identifier assigned to the class.
- **Category**—This field specifies the LDAP name for the object class. Active Directory LDAP agents and Active Directory clients use the LDAP name to read or write the class.
- **Parent Class**—Identifies the parent class definition from which this class inherits portions of its definition.
- **Auxiliary Class**—Lists additional classes from which this class derives some portion of its definition.
- **Possible Superior**—Lists the types of objects this object class can reside within.
- **Common Name**—Identifies the attributes that will be used to name instances of this object class.

- **Mandatory Attributes**—Contains a list of properties for which the object instance must have values.
- **Optional Attributes**—Additional properties for which an instance of the object class may or may not have values.

It should be noted that the preceding list is what is viewable from the Active Directory Schema snap-in. The system uses other fields, but these are not visible in the schema browser. Other schema options control whether instances of a particular class are displayed for browsing. A default security template (ACL) can also be associated with each class.

Attribute Definitions

Attribute definitions describe the properties of an object including the specific sort of information it can contain and whether it is single-valued or multivalued. Attribute definitions in the schema are not directly linked to a specific object, enabling any attribute to be applied to multiple object classes as needed.

Attributes can be added to the Active Directory schema, but once added, they cannot be modified. Attributes that have been made part of the schema via extension can be removed as long as they are not currently being used in any object class definition. Attributes that are part of the standard Active Directory schema cannot be removed from the schema. The ability to delete *custom* attributes from the schema, however will be supported in the Windows .NET Server version of Active Directory.

The attribute definition in the Active Directory schema consists of these fields:

- **Description**—The descriptive text that explains the purpose of the attribute.
- **Common Name**—The LDAP CN is the name by which the attribute is referenced in the class definition.
- **X.500 OID**—The object identifier assigned to the attribute.
- **GUID**—The globally unique identifier assigned to the attribute.
- **Syntax**—Identifies the syntax to be used for a particular attribute.
- **Range**—Identifies minimum/maximum range values; for integers, this represents actual allowable numeric values, while for strings it identifies the string length.

Within the attribute definition, you can select whether the attribute is multivalued, shown while browsing, indexed, and whether it is replicated to the GC. You can also determine whether to copy the attribute value when duplicating a user.

Syntax Definitions

The syntax definitions specify the format of the data to be used within the attribute and matching rules. The syntax definition consists of

- **Syntax ID**—Uniquely identifies the syntax type, which is the value designated in the attribute syntax field of the attribute definition.
- **Syntax Name**—Descriptive name of the syntax.
- **Syntax Flags**—Contains matching rules to be used when comparing values using this syntax.

Extending the Schema

The schema is managed through Active Directory schema objects. Extending the schema creates new objects representing class or attribute definitions. Extensions to the Active Directory schema can be implemented in a variety of ways:

- The Active Directory Schema MMC snap-in enables administrators to directly alter the schema.
- The schema can be extended programmatically using ADSI interfaces, MAPI, or the LDAP C API.
- Schema extensions can also be performed via LDIF files.

Active Directory doesn't currently allow deletions from the schema, but objects can be disabled (The Windows .NET Server version of Active Directory, however, does support schema deletions.) The following conditions apply when disabling components of the Active Directory schema definitions:

- Classes and attributes with certain access category values cannot be disabled. The access category indicates the type of rights required to access Active Directory information.
- Disabling an attribute definition requires that no class definitions are using the attribute. If a class definition includes the attribute, the class must be disabled or removed before the attribute can be disabled.
- Disabling a class definition prevents new instances of the object from being created, but it has no effect on current instances of the class.

The Active Directory DIT

The *Directory Information Tree (DIT)* in Active Directory differs significantly from the namespace used in Windows NT, and has interesting differences from the DIT defined in X.500. The Active Directory tree contains a unique blend of aspects of DNS, LDAP, and NT domains. This integration of NT domains provides critical backward-compatibility for the Windows NT 4 domain model and existing NT installations and applications.

The Active Directory namespace can be viewed as stratified into three aspects:

- The *forest* is a collection of one or more noncontiguous Active Directory trees.
- A *domain tree* is a tree of contiguous DNS domains representing the higher-level nodes of the Active Directory tree.
- The *directory tree* is a single complete tree of domain components (`dc`) and organizational units (`OU`), from the root of the tree to the leaf objects.

The Forest

Active Directory uses a construct called a *forest* to support multiple Active Directory trees in a common (shared) logical namespace. This is useful for companies that need to accommodate more than one DNS name for multiple business subdivisions, or want to maintain different namespaces on each side of a firewall.

Forests are not used *only* when multiple directory trees are present—rather, a forest is an inherent part of Active Directory. A forest is created when a new domain tree is created, unless the domain tree is installed to an existing forest. Just as partitions and trees have a root node, so do forests. The first domain of the first tree in the forest defines the *forest root*. Note that the forest root cannot be changed without destroying the forest and completely re-creating it. This can cause a substantial amount of IT administrative work and cost, and thus forest, domain, and tree design should be thoroughly planned and carefully designed before implementation.

As shown in Figure 10.1, a forest is a collection of noncontiguous DNS namespaces, each of which is an independent Active Directory tree. In this example, the triangle symbol represents a single domain tree in the forest. This figure shows three Active Directory trees, `mythical.org`, `netmages.org`, and `src.nu`, each comprising its own domain root within the shared forest. The figure also shows the LDAP name that corresponds to the DNS domain name. Domain controllers are located using DNS, and objects within the directory are then accessed using LDAP.

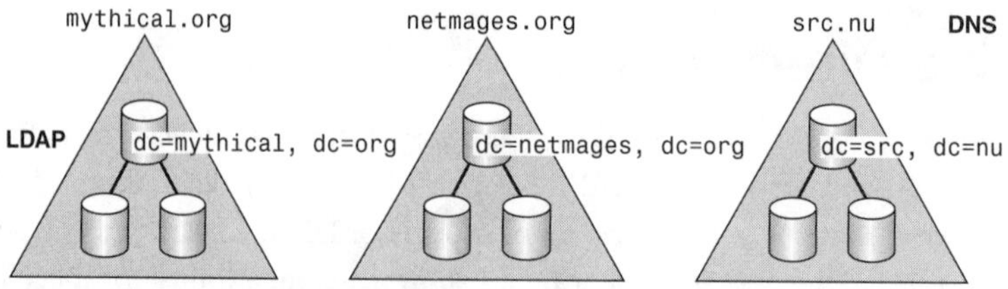

FIGURE 10.1
The Active Directory forest of disjoint/discontiguous Active Directory trees.

Characteristics of a forest include the following:

- Contains one or more Active Directory trees
- Common schema, configuration, and Global Catalog (GC)
- Automatic trusts between trees in forest

From a technical perspective, forests exist as a set of Kerberos trust relationships and cross-references between the member trees. However, there are limitations on forests. LDAP searches do not cross trees in a forest, for example, because LDAP does not natively represent the forest construct. Also, in the Windows 2000 version of Active Directory, there are no trust relationships between forests. The Windows .NET Server version, Active Directory, supports cross-forest trust relationships.

The Domain Tree

One of the more significant Windows 2000 features for NT administrators is the capability to arrange domains into a hierarchical structure with automatic trusts established between domains. When looking at the namespace in this fashion (that is, consisting of a tree of domains), Microsoft defines it as a *domain tree*. A domain tree is a tree of contiguous DNS domains contained within an Active Directory forest.

As shown in Figure 10.2, the domain tree represents only the domain component (`dc`) container objects of the directory tree. The three DNS domains shown are each a single node in the domain tree. Note that the portion of the LDAP directory tree contained *within* each domain is ignored from this angle—only the objects representing domains are relevant.

Active Directory enforces security boundaries at each domain, thus administrative privileges assigned high in the tree do not flow downward across domain boundaries. From a directory perspective, the domain boundary effectively subdivides (partitions) the directory on administrative and security lines, creating discrete administrative and security areas—one for each domain. The automatic two-way transitive trust established between domains provides automatic user authentication across all the domains in the domain tree.

Forest-Level Design Considerations

In creating a forest in Active Directory, consider how you want to use the logical grouping of domain trees. Do you want

- a single DNS namespace and therefore a single Active Directory tree?
- noncontiguous Active Directory trees to provide for different internal and external DNS trees?
- noncontiguous Active Directory trees in a forest with enterprise partners?

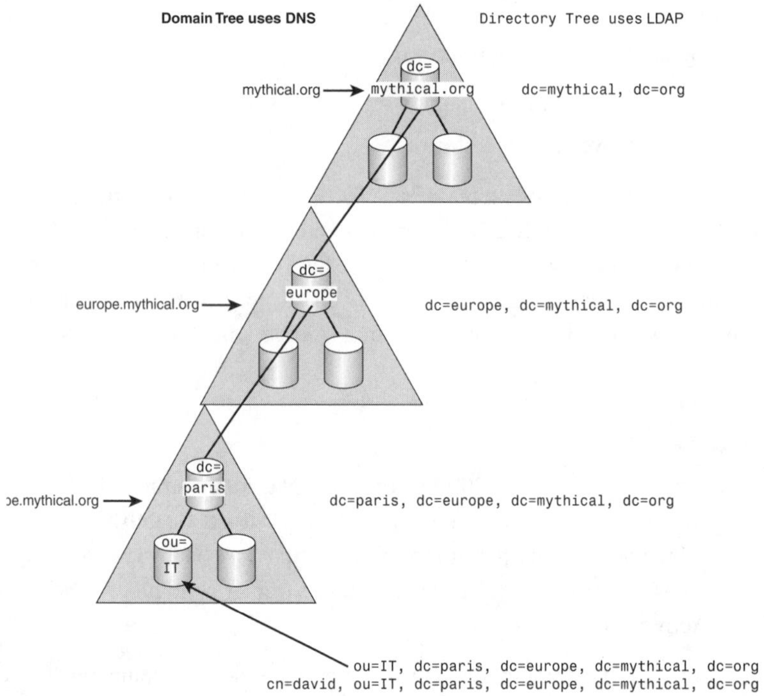

FIGURE 10.2
A domain tree describes the domain structure of the directory.

All the domains in a single domain tree share the following common characteristics:

- A contiguous namespace
- Transitive trusts between domains
- Common schema, configuration, and Global Catalog (common to forest)

Domains in Active Directory

Active Directory domains are a security, administrative, and storage partition of the directory requiring one or more (usually multiple) domain controllers on dedicated servers. A single Active Directory domain can theoretically contain millions of objects, representing network users, resources, services, and so on. For larger enterprises with networks that are more complex and contain a large number of objects, multiple domains can be linked into a single Active Directory domain tree.

Key benefits of Active Directory domains include the following:

- Segregation of domain object information and administration
- Centralization of security management by domain policy

In Windows 2000, Active Directory domains, once established, could not be renamed. The version of Active Directory included with Windows .NET Server, however, allows the renaming of domains. This is a substantial improvement in Windows domain management, providing needed flexibility for today's rapidly changing business environment.

Domain Hierarchy and Transitive Trusts

Nodes in the domain tree are arranged in a hierarchy, establishing logical parent-child relationships between domains. By default, Active Directory parent domains automatically have a two-way trust relationship with all child domains. The creation of a child domain establishes a two-way parent-child trust between the parent domain and the new child domain.

Active Directory supports transitive trusts, allowing all domains within a forest or a domain tree to automatically trust each other. A transitive trust is where a trust relationship with a specific domain is automatically extended to any other domain trusted by the trusted domain. (If C trusts B, and B trusts A, then C trusts A.) Referring back to the `mythical.org` tree, for example: If `paris.europe.mythical.org` trusts `europe.mythical.org`, and `europe.mythical.org` trusts `mythical.org`, then `paris.europe.mythical.org` trusts `mythical.org`, and vice versa. (This example also helps illustrate the issues that arise with long names.)

Four different types of domain trusts exist, including

- **Tree root**—Trust between domains and the tree root
- **Parent Child**—Trust between parent and child domains

Domain Tree–Level Design Considerations

When creating an Active Directory domain tree, think about how you want to use the hierarchical grouping of domains. Consider these aspects of your domain tree design:

- Assess constraints, such as the effects of domain subdivision on security and partition boundaries.
- Carefully examine domain boundaries, considering replication load on your network bandwidth in your domain design.
- Determine the number and placement of DCs that are required in each role to adequately support each domain given your expected usage levels. Be sure to factor in the required operations master roles for each domain.

- **Shortcut**—A cross-link trust to a peer domain
- **External**—A trust to an external domain

A *trust path* is the set of trust links between domains used for passing authentication requests. A trust path is the route between the DC for a server receiving a request and the DC in the domain of the requesting user.

You can also still explicitly create a nontransitive trust where needed. Nontransitive trusts can be used to establish a trust relationship between Active Directory domains in different forests, or between an Active Directory domain and a down-level NT 4 domain. Trusts between NT 4 domains and Active Directory domains are *always* nontransitive.

The Directory Tree

The DIT represents the logical organization of the *entire* directory. Active Directory is an LDAP-based directory, and the Active Directory tree can be looked at like an LDAP directory tree.

It may be helpful to examine how Active Directory structures its LDAP directory tree:

- There are two kinds of container objects: domain and OU.
- A single domain must exist immediately below the root node, and additional domains can be contained only by other domains.
- OUs can only exist under a domain or another OU, not in the root.

Figure 10.3 shows the entire LDAP directory tree for the `mythical.org` Active Directory tree. Notice that both domain objects and other OUs form the structure of the directory tree.

The directory tree can be viewed from two perspectives:

- As a complete LDAP tree comprised of all objects from root to leaf objects
- As a domain subtree consisting of the portion of the LDAP namespace that exists *within* a single domain

A domain subtree (consisting of the hierarchy of OUs and the leaf objects they contain) can be used to model your organizational subdivisions or operational requirements. From an NT 4 perspective, the hierarchy provided in Active Directory is a valuable administrative addition. The hierarchy can be used to group business efforts, systems, and people, while supplying access control and the capability to delegate authority over organizational subdivisions. Instead of being limited to domain or server administrative options, Active Directory administration can be delegated for each OU.

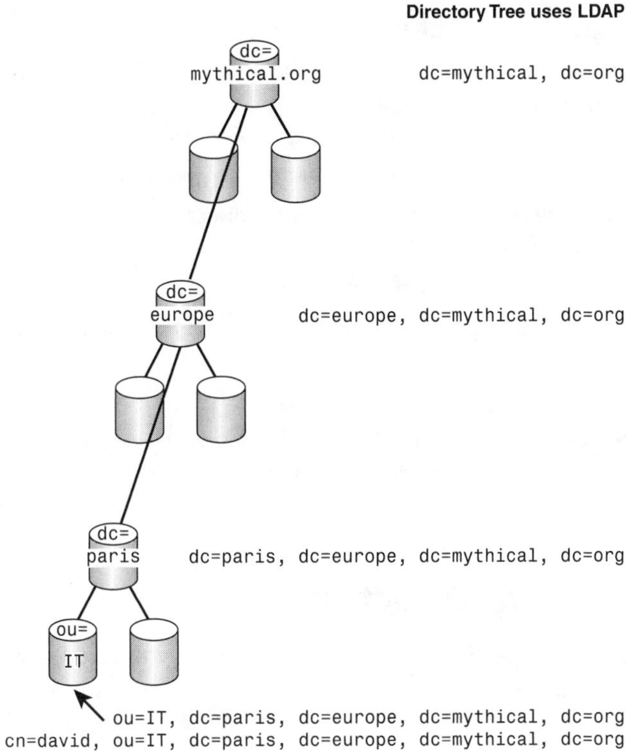

FIGURE 10.3
The LDAP directory tree in Active Directory.

This provides you with the following:

- **Logical organization within a domain**—Domains can be further subdivided into OUs to facilitate delegation of administration tasks.
- **Finer ability to delegate authority**—Administrative rights over object and attribute access in OUs can be delegated.

Within a domain, users can inherit administrative permissions from parent objects. They can also choose to filter those permissions that can be inherited by child user objects. These administrative permissions do not cross the domain boundary, and thus security principals in a child domain cannot inherit administrative permissions assigned in a parent domain.

Directory Tree–Level Design Considerations

When structuring your directory tree, consider how you want to use the hierarchy of OUs. The hierarchy supplies the mechanism to enable you to more effectively structure your network directory to model your business operations.

Directory tree factors to keep in mind include the following:

- Carefully examine the needs and reasons for directory subdivision (usually business, organizational, or operational).
- Use OUs to establish a hierarchy of management and operational subdivisions.
- Use subsequent OUs to delegate administration of business units within a larger division.
- Policies can also be applied at the OU level.
- Keep your tree relatively shallow—don't make unnecessary OUs in the hierarchy because deep hierarchies make long and complicated DNs.

Naming in Active Directory

Naming is a little different in Active Directory from many other directory services. Instead of natively representing a single namespace, Active Directory uses multiple namespaces as shown in Figure 10.4:

- **DNS**—Active Directory uses DNS for naming and location of domains and DCs. Domains, hosts, and some services are represented in the DNS namespace, but only domains are part of the Active Directory domain tree.
- **LDAP**—Active Directory uses LDAP for naming and accessing directory objects. Every directory object has an LDAP name.
- **UNC/NetBIOS**—Active Directory supports the use of NetBIOS names (for users, computers, and domains), and it supports the UNC naming convention for access to network resources.

Windows 2000 security principals must be represented in each of these namespaces. This requires Active Directory to support multiple forms of naming for each computer, user, and domain. These naming forms are compliant with the namespace they support, NetBIOS, DNS, or LDAP.

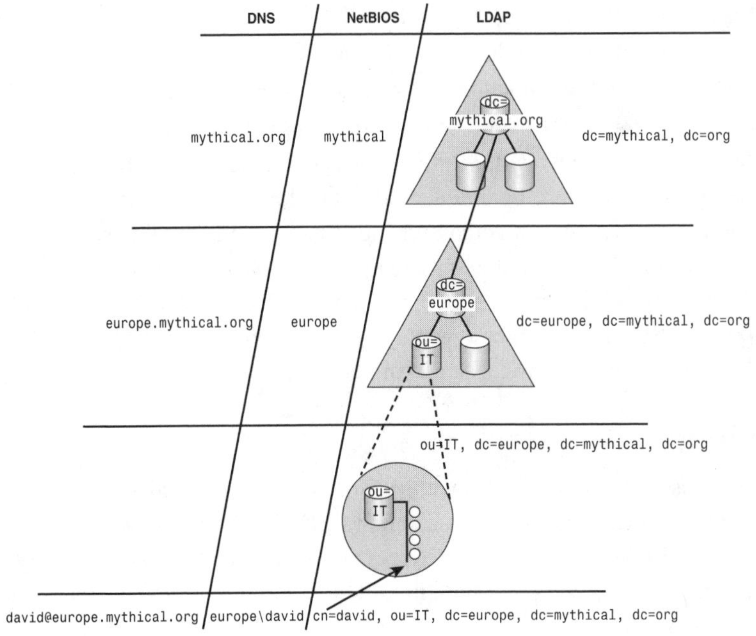

FIGURE 10.4
Active Directory naming uses DNS, NetBIOS, and LDAP.

NetBIOS Naming

Windows 2000 uses NetBIOS names and UNCs for backward-compatibility with NT 4 and the Windows client operating systems. NetBIOS namespace support provides compatibility with NT domains and for communications with down-level clients and applications.

NetBIOS names and UNC naming conventions are familiar to many people from its use in Windows networking. In Active Directory, NetBIOS names are comprised of (up to) the first 15 characters of the name assigned to the user, computer, or domain. NetBIOS user and computer names must be unique within the domain, and are concatenated with domain names to form full computer names or usernames in the form of `domain\user`.

DNS Naming

Active Directory integrates DNS domain naming and resolution, and it follows the DNS naming convention. Active Directory uses DNS names in these ways:

- **DNS domain names**—The DNS domains used in Active Directory are named in accordance with the DNS naming convention, using a dot-delimited domain hierarchy (such as `oem.sales.mythical.org`).

- **DNS hostname**—Windows 2000 uses the DNS hostname to identify the security account for the computer at the local domain controller. The domain name is appended to the hostname, to form a full computer name (such as `dragon.mythical.org`).
- **User principal names (UPNs)**—To ease user access to the directory, Active Directory specifies users and groups with *user principal names* (UPNs). A UPN is an attribute of the user object, and it must be unique within the domain. UPNs are comprised of two parts: the UPN prefix, which is the user logon name; and the UPN suffix, which is the DNS name of the domain containing the user object. The two parts are combined with the "@" symbol to form the familiar email-style name. For example, the UPN for `Shawn` within the `mythical.org` domain would be constructed as `shawn@mythical.org`. UPNs are substantially shorter than DNs, and are easier for people to remember and use.

LDAP Naming

LDAP naming is used to access objects within the directory tree. Active Directory uses LDAP attributed naming with LDAP URLs, and it follows LDAP naming conventions as described in Chapter 5, "LDAP: Lightweight Directory Access Protocol." For the three security principals reviewed here, the user and computer both use `CN` as its naming attribute, and domains use the LDAP standard of `dc`.

Active Directory supports multiple LDAP naming forms:

- **LDAP DN**—The full DN of the object name such as `cn=rvoss,cn=admin,dc=dev,dc=netmages,dc=org`
- **LDAP URL**—The LDAP URL format of the object name such as `ldap://dragon.dev.netmages.org/cn=rvoss,cn=admin,dc=dev,dc=netmages,dc=org`
- **Active Directory Canonical Name**—Windows 2000 uses a derivative form of the LDAP DN by default. The canonical name uses the DNS dot-delimitation for the domain names, is constructed without the naming attributes, and is ordered in reverse of an LDAP name, starting from the root of the domain downward such as `dev.netmages.org/admin/rvoss`.

Unique to the Domain

Active Directory guarantees LDAP DN uniqueness by the usual method of not allowing two objects with the same RDN to exist under the same parent object. Windows 2000 domains have a requirement that each username (UPN) and computer name (DNS hostname) be unique within a domain. This is different from X.500 where user names only have to be unique within the specific container.

The Globally Unique IDentifier

To implement the location of directory objects via a query on object attributes, every object in the directory has a *Globally Unique IDentifier (GUID)*. The GUID is a unique 128-bit number generated for each directory object at the time that it is created.

The GUID is never changed or altered, even when a directory object is moved or renamed, providing a consistent internal identifier unique to every object. The use of the GUID allows directory-aware applications to store an object's unique identifier and reliably retrieve that specific object from the directory irrespective of the object's current DN.

The global catalog utilizes the GUID as its primary index reference to objects within the directory. The algorithm generating the 128-bit value controls the uniqueness of a GUID.

The Active Directory DIB

Directory information storage in Active Directory has been substantially enhanced beyond the capabilities of its NT 4 predecessor. The Active Directory information *store* (Microsoft's term for the DIB) is based on the Exchange directory data structure and storage engine, supplying fast indexed access to directory information.

Storage Method

Active Directory employs a unified storage mechanism for all the directory information. As shown in Figure 10.5, Active Directory abstracts layers of directory information storage, providing database and tree support to the DC with indexed, transaction-based storage. These layers are as follows:

- **Database layer**—The database layer operates as an abstraction layer between the data store and applications, including the Active Directory DSA. Directory clients access the database layer either indirectly (via the DSA layer) or directly via (MAPI). This layer also structures the entries in the DIB into the DIT for the DSA, and forms DNs from RDNs for name resolution. The database layer constructs the directory hierarchy from the parent-child relationships of objects contained within the directory.
- **Extensible Storage Engine**—Active Directory uses a proprietary database engine called the *Extensible Storage Engine* (ESE) as its data storage layer. The ESE is an enhanced version of Jet, an *Indexed Sequential Access Method* (ISAM) table manager, which is used by Exchange and other Microsoft applications. The ESE employs a transaction-based storage system, using log files for transaction verification. The ESE uses the NTFS subsystem for storage to disk.

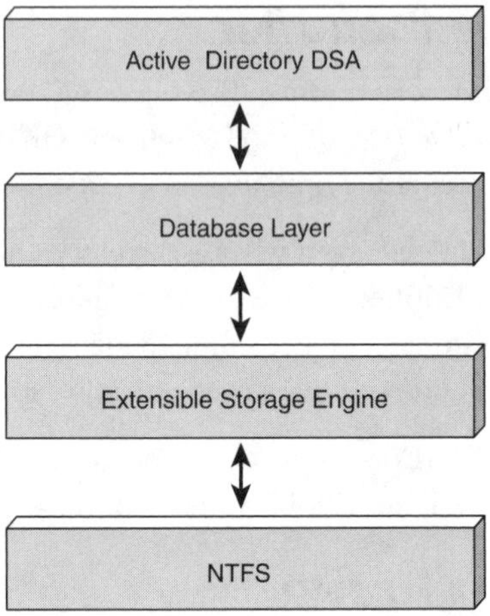

FIGURE 10.5
Storing Active Directory information.

Active Directory information is written to the `%SYSTEMROOT%\NTDS\NTDS.DIT` file, which must be on an NTFS partition on the DC. Microsoft recommends storing the Active Directory DIB on mirrored file system partitions and, for performance, dividing the Windows 2000 operating system files, the Active Directory DIB file, and the Active Directory log file among separate drives on the server.

Theoretically, an Active Directory database can reach 16 terabytes in size and hold millions of objects per domain—the Windows 2000 Resource Kit states that the Active Directory database has been tested with 40 million objects per domain.

Defragmenting the DIB

When objects are deleted from the Active Directory database, they are first tagged with *tombstone* status—marking the object as logically deleted but still partially stored—which also tells replication partners the object is deleted. The *garbage collection* process is a periodic task that deletes tombstones and defragments the database.

Active Directory supports online defragmentation of the Active Directory database (via the ESE), which rearranges content without releasing the allocated file system space. To free allocated space while defragmenting the DIB, the DC must be taken offline, booted into Directory Service Repair mode, and defragmented with a command line tool (NTDSUTIL.EXE), which creates a new defragmented copy of NTDS.DIT in another directory.

Partitioning the DIB

Like most other directory services, linkage between partitions is maintained automatically. Active Directory takes a different approach to partitioning the DIB, however, as partition management is largely done in an indirect fashion:

- Active Directory partitions the DIB at every domain boundary, meaning each domain is *required* to be its own partition of the DIB (as shown in Figure 10.6). Because Microsoft has linked DIB partitioning to domain boundaries, normally unrelated factors (such as security boundaries) come into play whenever a partition is created.
- A DC can hold only one full replica—a single domain directory partition containing the objects for a specific domain. Although every DC also contains the schema and configuration partitions, a DC only contains directory information for one domain.
- Replication traffic routing is handled via sites (that is, areas of high-speed connectivity) and managed by configured connections between the sites.

Although this may mean that administrators will not have to spend as much time manipulating DIB partitioning as they might with other directory implementations, it also means that there is less flexibility in partitioning. Active Directory requires a dedicated directory server for *each* replica of a domain partition—a single directory server cannot contain *full* partition replicas for more than one domain.

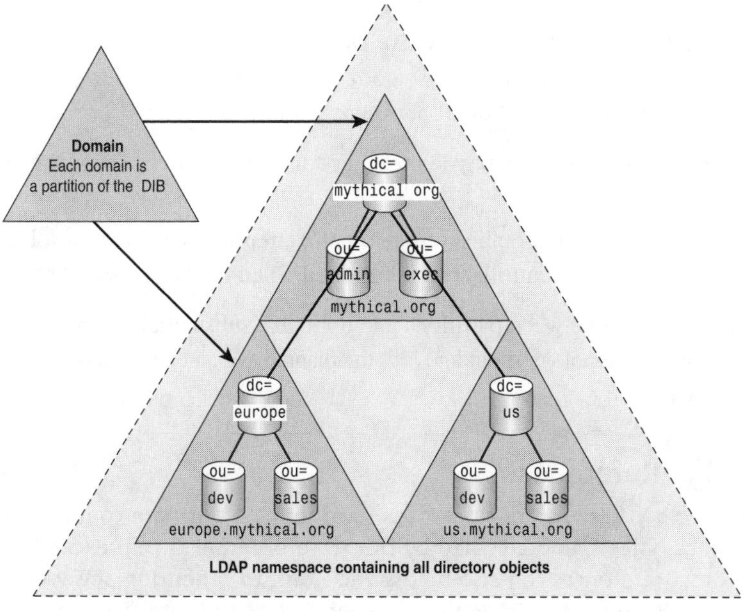

FIGURE 10.6

An Active Directory domain constitutes a partition of the DIB.

Each Active Directory DC holds three partitions:

- The *schema* partition contains the schema data—that is, the set of definitions of all possible objects and attributes in the directory. The schema partition is replicated to every DC in a forest.
- The *configuration* partition contains configuration information for the entire forest. The configuration partition contains the replication topology (sites) information, configuration information on services, and directory metadata—references to domain partitions, trees, and forests, as well as the locations of GCs and DCs. This partition is replicated to every DC in the forest, providing every DC with the logical topology for the entire directory.
- The *domain directory* partition contains all the objects within a given domain, and it is only replicated to DCs for that specific domain. Some information from a domain will be replicated to the Global Catalog. If an attribute that is indexed in the GC is changed in the DC for a specific domain, the GC will be updated with the changed attribute information, yet only that very limited data will be replicated to the GC. In contrast, all the DCs in a domain will share full replicas of all objects and attributes within the specific domain. A domain directory partition can be considered a *domain subtree* because it contains the subtree of objects belonging to a single domain (Microsoft has described this as a *Directory Partition Subtree* in the Windows 2000 Resource Kit documentation).

Throughout this chapter, when partitioning is described, it refers to the domain directory partitions, not the schema or configuration partitions (unless explicitly specified).

Partition handling is mostly automatic as Active Directory is designed to perform most partition and replication management without administrator intervention. There are few partition operations in Active Directory, and administration of partitions is rather indirect:

- Because a partition is a domain, you create and delete partitions as you create and delete domains.
- Because a DC must hold a replica of its domain, a replica is created for a DC when it is promoted (to a domain controller) and destroyed when the DC is demoted.

As a result of this linkage between partitions and domains, substantial review of namespace allocation and replication topology should go into the planning of an enterprisewide implementation of Active Directory.

Knowledge References

In Active Directory, knowledge references to other partitions are contained in cross-reference objects, and are used by DCs to refer requests that exceed the local partition. Cross-references can also be used to point to other domains within a forest or external LDAP directories. Referrals are generated when contacting a nonauthoritative DC, or when searching the domain tree.

Replication of the DIB

Microsoft describes the Active Directory replication model as using a *multimaster loose consistency with convergence* approach with *nondeterministic latency* (an unknown degree of update latency).

Multimaster replication in this context means that each Active Directory server can function as a master (writeable) replica of the partition and can propagate changes to other DCs within the domain. Multiple DCs with replicas of a domain partition can be established to distribute the client-access load and increase fault tolerance of the directory service.

Active Directory uses two forms of replicas:

- *Full replicas* are writeable and contain a complete copy of the data in a given partition. A full replica contains either the schema, configuration, or a domain directory partition. A DC has one of each of these replicas.
- *Partial replicas* are used solely for the Global Catalog, and contain a selected subset of directory attributes from all domain directory partitions. Domain controllers that are also GC servers contain both the full replica for its host domain, as well as the GC partial replicas from all other domains within the forest.

Active Directory uses a store-and-forward mechanism with full replication. After objects are updated, the other DCs in the domain are notified of the changes after a set period. Upon notification, the DCs in the domain contact the source DC and obtain the updated directory information.

Active Directory doesn't use a change log file to track replicated changes to the directory database, but rather uses a state-based replication mechanism in which updates are made to the replica as the changes arrive.

Directory information is updated on a per attribute basis in Active Directory, minimizing the amount of information that must be transmitted across the network to synchronize partition replicas.

Replication via Sites

Microsoft uses the term *site* to designate a set of TCP/IP subnets with good connectivity (such as LAN speeds of 10Mbps or more). A site commonly houses multiple DCs and may contain DCs from multiple domains. DCs for a domain may be distributed across multiple sites—for example, a DC for a remote domain may be placed within the local site topology for administrative purposes.

Active Directory uses the topology information stored in the site objects to determine directory replication. The specific site topology should reflect the physical topology of your connected LANs. Sites can be used to manage replication bandwidth allocation, isolate logon traffic, and locate proximate resources.

Site links represent the connections between networks and tell Active Directory how to use the network connection for replication of the DIB. Replication frequency, cost, and availability can be configured for each site link. Site links that overlap can be combined into *site link bridges*.

Active Directory automatically configures connections within a site, but site links usually are not configured (unless the site is already a site link and has a DC). DCs use site links to communicate with remote DCs and, therefore, cross-domain updates depend on these site links. Active Directory supplies flexible inter-site replication using variable scheduling and multiple protocols to support WAN-linked communications.

Replication Roles

Active Directory uses more than one type of DSA role in replication. Active Directory divides replication roles into intrasite (via DCs) and inter-site (via bridgehead servers) operations management.

- **Domain Controllers (DCs)**—DCs automatically handle replication between all DCs within the local site. A DC replicates all object updates to all other DCs within its domain.
- **Bridgehead server**—A bridgehead server is used to manage replication between sites, and across slower communications links (commonly WAN connections). Intersite updates are managed by designated bridgehead servers, which are responsible for updating the intrasite domain controllers. Each site can have one bridgehead server. Although bridgehead servers are the preferred server for intersite replicating of directory updates, other DCs can be configured to perform replication between sites.

Directory Replication

Inter-DSA communications for replication use many different types of connections and transport protocols. Replication in Active Directory uses three types of connections:

- High speed, uniform (via RPC over IP)
- Low speed, point-to-point, synchronous (via RPC over IP)
- Low speed, store-and-forward, asynchronous (via SMTP)

Active Directory performs replication differently within sites and between sites. Replication operates using one of two methods:

- *Intrasite* replication is always done via *Remote Procedure Calls* (RPC) over IP, is automatic, and doesn't use compression. Intrasite replication is optimized to minimize replication latency, frequently updating all DCs within the site.
- *Intersite* replication notifies DCs of updates using RPCs over IP, or SMTP, and can be compressed and scheduled. Intersite replication is optimized to minimize network bandwidth required to replicate directory updates between sites (as these connections are commonly WAN links).

Updates to the directory replicas may occur rapidly via synchronous point-to-point links (RPC over IP), or on a delayed basis using asynchronous store-and-forward links (SMTP).

A process called the *Knowledge Consistency Checker* (KCC) creates the replication topology. The KCC determines replication routes between DCs in a site based on the quality of available connections.

Active Directory defines the configuration, schema, and domain directory partitions as individual units of replication. These are replicated as follows:

- The schema and configuration partitions are replicated to all DCs in the forest.
- The domain directory partition containing all objects and properties within a given domain are replicated to each DC in that domain.
- All objects (with a small subset of properties) are replicated to the GC. GCs are updated in tandem with the replication cycles, ensuring that catalogs remain current.

Synchronization

Active Directory implements a replication model that allows updates to occur at any of multiple replicas (multimaster replication). Consequentially, replicas must then be synchronized to ensure directory consistency. Although some directory services rely solely on time stamps to control replica synchronization, the method employed in Active Directory relies on unique 64-bit *update sequence numbers* (USN). Active Directory uses USNs to track directory changes, and it uses volatility and time stamps as a tiebreaker in cases of collision of replicated data.

When changes are replicated, only objects with a higher USN are sent to the receiving replica. As an object is written to the receiving DC, it is assigned a new USN and a version number incremented at every change to the object (as well as a digital signature of the supplier DC), and this information is stored with the object. As part of the replication process, each replica requests all changes with any USN later than the last USN received and is provided all relevant changes.

Replication Depends on Mode

Pure Active Directory networks update all DCs using multimaster replication, but mixed NT 4 and Active Directory networks perform replication in compliance with NT 4 methods using the SAM interface.

Defining Your Sites

To determine the subnets that will comprise each site, review your network infrastructure, determining numbers and locations of subnets, bandwidth of each subnet, speed of remote links, amount of replication data crossing remote links, as well as the overall capacity and utilization of your networks.

USNs are organized using a table of USNs maintained at each DC. A DC receives its table entries (USNs) from its replication partners, tracking the highest USN received (called the *high-watermark*) from each replication partner. During replication, a DC requests all directory changes with USNs higher than the USN stored in its table for the replication partner. The incrementing and storage of the USN, as well as the write operation on the designated object or property, succeeds or fails as a unit. The USN tables on DCs simplify recovery on directory failure—to reinitialize a DC, the DC requests changes from all replication partners with USN numbers greater than what is stored in its USN table. An interrupted replication cycle can be restarted without duplication or loss.

A replication collision can occur if multiple changes are made to a property on multiple replicas before the first replica change has been supplied to all other DCs. Active Directory manages collision detection with version numbers on properties, and by tracking the original updates. Active Directory uses propagation dampening to prevent redundant updates.

Active Directory handles replication collisions via the following mechanisms:

- **Property version numbers (PVNs)**—Active Directory's replication model uses PVNs to manage replication collisions. PVNs are property-based replication values (in contrast with the server-based USNs) directly associated with an object property. A PVN is instanced the first time an Active Directory object property is written to.
- **Originating writes**—PVNs are incremented by *originating writes* on the associated property (a successful write updating a property on the DC initiating the change). Updates via replication are not considered originating writes and will not increment the PVN. If a DC receives an update PVN higher than the stored PVN, the update is valid and applied (if lower, the update is rejected).
- **Replication collision**—A *replication collision* happens when a replicated PVN is received that is the same as the stored PVN, and the property's values are not the same. If a replication collision occurs, the update time stamp is evaluated, and the receiving replica will apply the changes with the latest time stamp.

- **Propagation dampening**—Active Directory implements *propagation dampening* to prevent redundant transmission of changes. Active Directory's replication process uses *up-to-date vectors* for propagation dampening (also called *up-to-dateness vectors* in the Windows 2000 Resource Kit). An up-to-date vector is a set of server-USN pairs maintained by every replica server. The up-to-date vector for a replica lists all other replicas for that site, and contains the highest USN received from each replica server. During replication, a server receives an update and sends its up-to-date vector to the initiating server, which uses it to filter propagated changes.

Active Directory Operations

Although there is far more detail to the operations in Active Directory than fits within the scope of this material, this section very briefly discusses the key server roles and operations. For more detailed information, refer to the Windows 2000 online help or Resource Kit books.

DSA Operational Roles

The domain controller (DC) is the Active Directory DSA, managing access to the information stored in its partition and providing updates to other DCs and the Global catalog (GC) server. The following points highlight some aspects of what the DCs contribute to Active Directory operations:

- **DCs play an active role in site management**—From the perspective of the domain controller, a site is a system of domain controllers on a high-connectivity set of IP subnets. The site information for the entire forest is stored in the `Configuration` container on the DC. DCs use site information to compare client IP addresses to known subnets, thus determining the appropriate site and DC for client logon and authentication.
- **DCs help manage DNS records**—The NetLogon service is responsible for creating the initial DNS records during installation of Active Directory. Each DC dynamically manages service (SRV) resource records locating and identifying servers by service type or protocol. SRV records are used to locate LDAP and Kerberos services and to indicate the site in which the DC is located. DNS in Active Directory searches for site-specific records prior to searching the general records.
- **DCs publish its services**—DCs publish its name and address at startup, where each DC server registers its name with DNS and WINS. Each DC dynamically updates DNS with a host address (A) record to register the IP address of the DC for the specified domain. In addition to DNS, a DC advertises its NetBIOS name via broadcast or directly to a specified WINS server, allowing down-level Windows clients to also locate the DC.

In Active Directory, in addition to acting as a domain controller for a specific domain, a DC may perform a variety of other roles such as a being a Global Catalog server or other operations master roles.

Global Catalog Servers

To facilitate faster directory lookups, Active Directory implements a forestwide index called the *Global Catalog (GC)*. A GC server is a DC containing a partial replica of each domain in the forest, and a complete replica of one domain. The first DC installed into a forest is a GC by default.

The GC server must be a domain controller, and it can be located at any point within the directory hierarchy. Although you are required to have one GC in each forest, you should put one GC server at every site.

The GC is used within Active Directory to help network users locate resources and information represented by directory objects. The GC enables network clients to quickly locate directory objects without knowledge of the domain in which the objects are contained, and to find directory objects across noncontiguous namespaces. Each Active Directory object has an entry (with summary object information) within the GC, which allows a fast multiattribute search for directory objects.

Besides a partial read-only replica of every domain directory partition in the forest, the GC contains structural information about Active Directory, including the schema and configuration partitions. All partitions on a GC server are written to one database (NTDS.DIT), which also contains the GC attributes stored as additional data. Object and attribute security is enforced at the GC; therefore, lookup of Active Directory information is constrained by the domain security services.

The replication process implemented by Active Directory automatically builds the GC (as changes are propagated, the GC is updated). Although Microsoft has defined a set of properties that are replicated to the GC by default, Active Directory administrators can specify additional properties as needed by modifying the schema. Attributes to be included in the GC can be selected in the Active Directory Schema administration tool.

Operations Masters

Although Active Directory implements multimaster replication, some directory *operations* require a single master. Microsoft terms this type of operation a *flexible single-master operation* (FSMO). Active Directory defines five operations master roles, each of which is responsible for a core set of operations, such as schema management, used in Windows 2000. Some of these operations master roles are required for each forest; others are required for each domain. Active Directory requires the following operations master roles:

- **Domain Naming Master**—The Domain Naming Master controls the additions and deletions of domains within the forest and ensures the uniqueness of the domain names. These changes, and the creation of cross-references to external directories can only be made on the DC configured as the Domain Naming Master. The Domain Naming Master operates on a forestwide basis, so there must be only one within the forest.
- **Schema Master**—The Schema Master is responsible for controlling all changes to the schema. Only the DC that is configured as the Schema Master can write changes to the schema. You must connect to this DC with the Active Directory Schema snap-in to modify the schema. There can be only one Schema Master because it also must be unique within the forest.
- **Relative IDentifier (RID) Master**—The RID Master supplies the RID sequences to all DCs within the forest. A RID is an identifier used with a domain identifier to construct the SIDs for security principals within the domain. To enforce forestwide uniqueness, RIDs are assigned by a single DC in the forest. This DC provides pools consisting of hundreds of unallocated RIDs to each DC for assignment to new objects as needed. Certain operations, such as moving objects into a new domain (via the Movetree tool), require access to the RID Master to complete the operation.
- **Infrastructure Master**—The Infrastructure Master role enforces object consistency for operations that span domains and is performed by one server per domain. An Infrastructure Master is used to synchronize the group-to-user references in the directory when group memberships are altered or updated.
- **PDC Emulator Master**—The PDC Emulator Master (also referred to as PDC Operations Master) supplies compatibility with down-level clients and NT 4 backup domain controllers (BDCs), handling NT 4 client authentication, password changes, and replication. The PDC Emulator also performs the Domain Master Browser role for NT 4 networks. Only one DC in each domain can be used to perform the PDC Emulator role.

Client Logon

As Active Directory supports down-level clients, there are multiple forms of user logon to an Active Directory domain. When a user logs on to a domain, one of the following name forms is used:

- **DNS**—If the logon uses a DNS domain name (Active Directory client), NetLogon uses DNS to find a domain controller for authentication. Once located, the client uses LDAP to connect to the DC.
- **NetBIOS**—If the logon uses a NetBIOS domain name (down-level client), NetLogon sends a mailslot message to find a DC performing the PDC emulator role for the domain. Once located, the down-level client uses the SAM interface to connect to the DC.

- **MAPI**—E-mail clients, such as Exchange 5.5 connect to Active Directory via an RPC interface using the messaging API.

On client startup, the client Locator initiates a remote procedure call to the local NetLogon service and passes the information (domain name, GUID, site, and flags) needed to select a DC. Again, this process varies depending on logon name:

- A client using DNS names locates a DC by querying a DNS name server. DNS returns the list of IP addresses indicated in the SRV records, and the client sends an LDAP query to each IP address. The first DC that responds to the query is returned to the client for logon.
- A client using NetBIOS names locates a DC via WINS (or other NT 4 transport-specific discovery method). When an NT 4 (NetBIOS) domain name is sought, discovery begins on the NetBIOS name query from the client NetLogon service and uses the DC providing the domain's PDC emulation.

Name Resolution

As Active Directory is designed as an LDAP directory, it uses LDAP queries for access to directory objects. The name resolution process uses DNS to locate the DCs and LDAP to locate objects within the directory. Active Directory object names must be specified in accordance to LDAP RFC 2247, and they are located in the directory by the object's DN.

Active Directory uses DNS name resolution for location of domain controllers and network service providers. DCs operate as the Active Directory name server, performing name resolution for all directory operations. Using its knowledge of the DIB, a DC determines whether the query can be fulfilled locally, or whether it must be referred to another DC.

Because DNS domains and LDAP domains differ, Active Directory also provides a DNS-to-LDAP mapping of domain components, via the standard LDAP method that maps an LDAP domain component for each DNS domain name component. For example:

- **DNS**—`mythical.org`
- **LDAP**—`dc=mythical, dc=org`

With Active Directory's integration of LDAP, when an LDAP string contains domain components, resolution depends on the following:

- If the contacted DC is a member of the sought domain, the DC can process the operation.
- If the contacted DC is not a member of the domain, the DC returns a referral to another DC, or supplies an error message denoting operation failure.

Active Directory resolves a submitted LDAP URL by performing the following steps:

1. Using DNS, Active Directory locates a GC server.
2. Using the server IP, Active Directory submits an LDAP query to the GC server.
3. With the reply IP information supplied by the GC, Active Directory submits an LDAP query to a DC with a replica containing the object(s).

Active Directory also provides backward-compatible support for UNC naming conventions and NetBIOS names. NetBIOS names are provided to DCs for name resolution by WINS or another transport-specific mechanism. Down-level clients use NetBIOS names in logon and authentication.

Native Versus Non-Native Mode

The Active Directory "mode" references aspects of the domain controller's behavior in the Active Directory authentication and replication infrastructure:

- **Mixed mode**—Mixed mode is the default mode, and provides the maximum compatibility with down-level servers and clients, needed when operating in network environments with Windows NT 4. Mixed mode supports NT 4 replication methods as well as Active Directory domain replication and uses either one, depending on whether the client is a down-level BDC or an Active Directory domain controller. With down-level domain controllers, Active Directory replication works like single-master replication, where the DC functions like a PDC (via the PDC Emulator), which does all updates.
- **Native mode**—Native mode uses multimaster replication between DCs and, thus, removes the backward-compatible support for NT 4 BDCs. However, native mode provides other enhancements. New types of groups (Universal, Domain Local) and nested groups are supported. Native mode must be specifically selected and, once implemented, cannot be undone.

A Mixed Environment Is Not Mixed Mode

A mixed environment refers to having Active Directory in native mode (where all DCs are running Windows 2000) but still having servers and clients on the network that are not Active Directory-aware. In contrast, mixed mode applies to the configured status of Active Directory *domain controllers* when operating as a mix of Windows 2000 and NT 4 domain controllers.

Extensibility

Active Directory is a native LDAP directory service, and LDAP operations can be easily extended. Active Directory currently supports LDAP extensions or controls that provide enhanced search capabilities such as server-side sorting and paged results.

Microsoft has also proposed an extension to LDAP called DirSync to serve as a synchronization mechanism between Active Directory and Novell Directory Services (NDS). Synchronization performed via DirSync is either one-way synchronization (Microsoft calls this forward synchronization)—from NDS to Active Directory—or two-way synchronization that includes synchronizing directory information from Active Directory to NDS (which Microsoft calls reverse synchronization). This functionality is embodied in its Microsoft Directory Synchronization Services (MSDSS) application (an advanced implementation of DirSync), which provides bidirectional synchronization between Active Directory and NDS.

Security in Active Directory

Active Directory is designed with a distributed security architecture, which uses the directory to manage the information and enhanced Windows 2000 security services for authentication. A new set of distributed security services is tightly integrated with Active Directory, allowing more flexible management of user accounts and much finer control over network objects and properties than was possible in NT 4.

Moving Beyond Windows NT Security

Security operations in Windows NT are rooted in a domain model that provides domainwide security with user access to domain resources. Security accounts for each domain are maintained in a flat namespace by the Security Accounts Manager (SAM), and the user and group account information is stored in a secure section of the PDC's registry.

For NT domains to allow users from foreign domains to access resources, a trust relationship between domain controllers must be manually established. NT interdomain trusts are connected via an explicit one-way or two-way trust relationship that is specified at each participating domain controller.

Although the NT 4 domain trust and pass-through authentication features provided some degree of flexibility in security account and resource management, the degree of scalability was inadequate for enterprise networks. As the number of domains increase, the domain trust relationships become increasingly complex.

New Security Capabilities

Active Directory runs as a service in the Windows 2000 security subsystem. The *Security Reference Monitor (SRM)* is the enforcing authority in the security subsystem, and the Active Directory DSA is part of the *Local Security Authority (LSA)*.

One significant enhancement to security in Windows 2000 is that Active Directory uses Kerberos to supply an automatic trust relationship for all domains within a domain tree. This vastly reduces the amount of administrative effort required to allow users to access resources between domains. Additional security enhancements supported by Active Directory include the following:

- **Directory stores security data**—Active Directory contains the security policy and account information for the network—all user and group account data, as well as domain, OU, and local access policies. As the policies are stored in a group policy object, Active Directory distributes the security information by replication operations to other domain controllers within the domain.
- **Security and directory interdependence**—In Active Directory, the directory services and security services are interdependent subsystems relying on each other for basic operations. Directory operations obtain authentication and access from the security services, and the objects that the security services act on are accessed via the directory services.
- **A security hierarchy**—Another substantial enhancement is the new security functionality in the hierarchical structure of the Active Directory namespace. This hierarchy provides the structure for security inheritance, administration delegation, and permissions filtering (within domain boundaries).
- **New security policy management**—The new integrated Group Policy Editor allows centralized administration of domainwide security policies, as well as application of policies to specific OUs. The domain policy can even be linked to IP security policies to provide control over the encryption of IP network traffic.

Security Is Based in Domains

An Active Directory domain is part of a directory tree, yet the Windows domain-level security boundaries apply. Security is implemented within the context of the domain—all security principals are defined within a domain and are "owned by" that domain.

> **Other Security Features in Windows 2000**
>
> Other security additions in Windows 2000 include its use of IP Security (IPSec) for encrypted networking, as well as the Encrypted File Systems (EFS) for file system security.

You can envision domains in Active Directory as comprised of the following:

- **Windows 2000 domain**—Controls security, authentication, access control
- **DNS domain**—Provides naming and location service
- **DIB partition**—Stores domain directory information

In Active Directory, user authentication can extend beyond the domain boundary via automatic interdomain trusts. Administration permissions granted within a domain are blocked at the domain boundary, however, as shown in Figure 10.7.

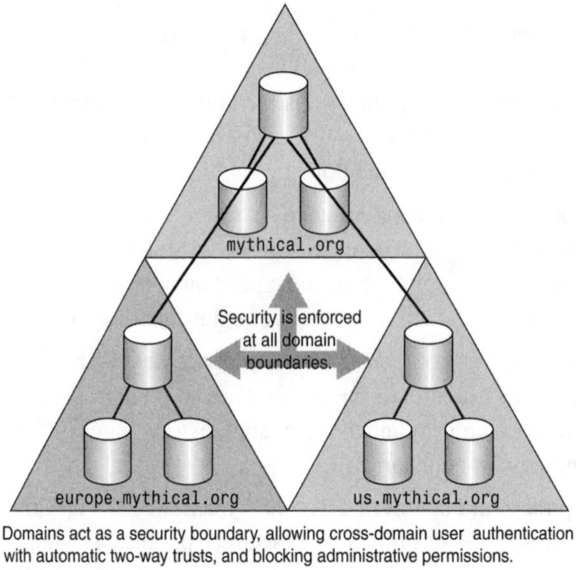
mythical.org
Security is enforced at all domain boundaries.
europe.mythical.org
us.mythical.org
Domains act as a security boundary, allowing cross-domain user authentication with automatic two-way trusts, and blocking administrative permissions.

FIGURE 10.7
Security in Active Directory is based in domains.

Interdomain Trusts

Windows 2000 implements a new security model in which the domains in a tree (and a forest) are automatically interconnected via Kerberos-based *implicit* trust relationships. Domain trust relationships have been built in to the Active Directory tree, allowing treewide transitive trusts, as shown in Figure 10.8. A transitive trust is effectively authentication by referral from an implicitly trusted source—in Active Directory, a domain trusts any other domain that shares a common ancestor (parent, grandparent).

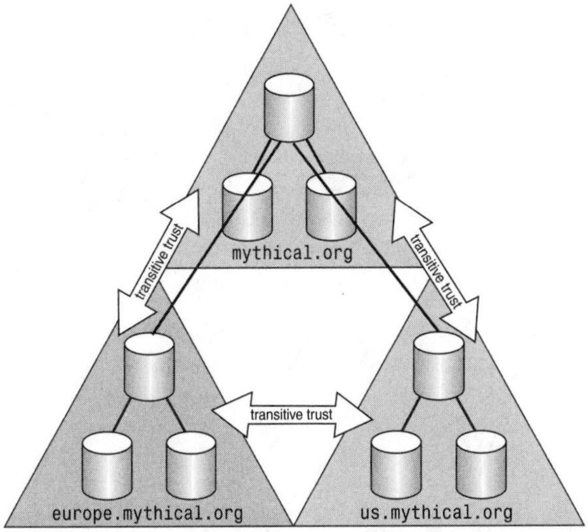
transitive trust
mythical.org
transitive trust
transitive trust
europe.mythical.org
us.mythical.org
NT domain security is enforced at all domain boundaries, yet automatic transitive trusts between domains allow users to be authenticated in all domains within the domain tree.

FIGURE 10.8
Active Directory supports transitive trusts between domains.

Hierarchy Within Domains

Active Directory objects are linked to its domain and controlled by its domain policy, but security policy and administration can also be assigned at the OU level. Within a domain, rights are controlled by the hierarchy of the policies assigned at the domain and OU levels, as well as by the permissions inherited from parent OUs.

By using the hierarchy of the Active Directory tree, administration can be subdivided by OU, delegating administration where needed by network or business subdivisions, as shown in Figure 10.9. Within a domain, Active Directory provides the ability to assign security values at nodes high in the directory tree and to have these values inherited by all child nodes lower in the tree. Users can inherit permissions to entire directory objects or only specific attributes.

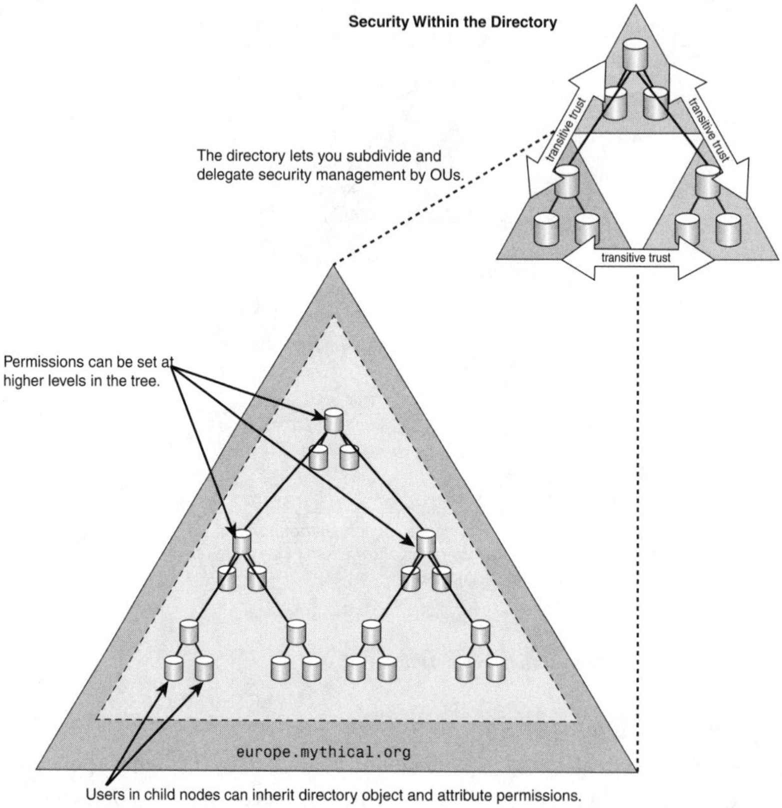
Security Within the Directory
transitive trust
transitive trust
transitive trust
The directory lets you subdivide and delegate security management by OUs.
Permissions can be set at higher levels in the tree.
europe.mythical.org
Users in child nodes can inherit directory object and attribute permissions.

FIGURE 10.9
Active Directory allows hierarchical security delegation within domains.

Security Standards and Protocols

Because corporate networks are connected to the Internet, additional security concerns are being addressed via the development and use of Public Key encryption and Certificate Authorities.

Windows 2000 supplies flexibility in its supported security protocols, which include the integration of Kerberos, support for PK and X.509 certificates, extensions of Kerberos for PK, as well as Secure Sockets Layer (SSL), and Private Communications Technology (PCT) security protocols for authentication. Active Directory integrates the key security protocols via the *Security Support Provider Interface (SSPI).*

Active Directory employs multiple security methods, including:

- **Kerberos**—Active Directory uses Kerberos, an Internet security protocol based on RFC 1510. Kerberos implements a *Key Distribution Center (KDC)*, which is comprised of two components: an *authentication server (AS)*, which provides the user authentication services; and the *ticket-granting server (TGS)*, which supplies the tickets used in subsequent authentication processes. Kerberos is implemented as an Active Directory security provider that utilizes the SSPI.
- **X.509 certificates**—Certificates are used in Active Directory to grant access for Internet users, remote users, and systems not supporting Kerberos version 5. Certificate-based security in Active Directory is integrated with other services such as Internet Information Server (IIS). In Active Directory, X.509 certificates are security tokens derived from the CryptoAPI Version 2 certificate library APIs, but applications that handle public key certificates can use any standard format.
- **SSL/PCT**—Active Directory also provides support for the Secure Sockets Layer (SSL) 3.0 and Private Communications Technology (PCT) channel security protocols.

Authentication

Windows 2000 includes security protocols that provide strong authentication based on Kerberos and NTLM Challenge/Response (the Windows NT 4 authentication mechanism). Active Directory also supplies strong client authentication by mapping public key certificates to user accounts. The authentication protocol used is determined by the client and server capabilities; Windows 2000 clients and servers use Kerberos, and down-level clients and servers use NTLM.

Certificate Services

In Active Directory, a certificate authority (CA) is used to create and validate certificates for network servers and users. The user certificate authenticates the user to all network servers, services, and other users. A network administrator needs to select which certificate authorities are trusted on the network and to control which certificates can be used for authentication and access.

Windows 2000 includes the Microsoft Certificate Server for creation, management, and revocation of X.509-compliant certificates. The Microsoft Certificate Server enables you to establish the CA for your network, and to create a hierarchy of certificate authority. For external networks or Web sites, a commercial CA (such as VeriSign) can be used to provide industry recognized validation and credentials. You can implement MCS as an enterprise CA (or subordinate) and a standalone root CA (or subordinate).

Kerberos is the default authentication protocol for Windows 2000. Kerberos is used when the user is logging on with a Windows 2000 computer, and the computer and user accounts are in a Windows 2000 domain. A Kerberos *ticket-granting server (TGS)* supplies the *ticket-granting tickets (TGTs)* used by clients to obtain session tickets that provide access to the specific servers and applications.

When an Active Directory client authenticates via Kerberos, the client's security identifier (SID), as well as those of any groups the user is a member of, are sent to the KDC. If there is more than one domain in the directory tree, the KDC queries the GC and collects SIDs from universal group memberships. The collection of SIDs is listed in the authorization data field of the TGT.

When the client requests a session ticket, the KDC puts the SIDs listed in the TGT into the authorization data field of the session ticket. If the session ticket is to be used in another domain, the KDC also queries Active Directory for group memberships in that domain and adds those SIDs to the session ticket. When a user connects to a server, the server can directly validate session tickets obtained by the client from the TGS.

One extension of the security in Active Directory is mutual authentication, where the client authenticates to the DC, and the DC also authenticates to the client. To supply this capability, a *Service Principal Name (SPN)* is used to identify and register a specific instance of a service in Active Directory. The SPN is registered in the directory on installation of the service and must be a unique name. When mutual authentication is performed, the client retrieves the service SPN from directory and then uses the SPN in the authentication of the service.

Access Control

Active Directory access control is conducted by validating users access permissions (*authorization*) to determine its access to directory objects and attributes, and the operations that they are allowed to perform. Active Directory leverages the Windows 2000 security infrastructure, using Access Control Lists (ACL) to protect all objects in the directory. An ACL consists of a set of access control entries for the directory object.

Down-Level Authentication

The NTLM Challenge/Response authentication protocol is supported for down-level clients. When a down-level NTLM client connects to a server, that server contacts the domain PDC Emulator DC to provide the authentication service to verify the client.

An *access control entry (ACE)* is a single security-related directory entry linked to a specific object. An ACE can grant or deny a particular user (or group) a specific set of access rights to a directory object. (One key element of an ACE is the SID of the security principal to which the ACE applies.) The set of available access rights directly corresponds to related operations on the directory object.

Active Directory uses the Windows 2000 security subsystem to control access to objects by validating the user permissions against the list of ACEs in the object's ACL. Access requires authentication and validation of the permissions of the security principal. Access control is operationally controlled by the security reference monitor and the security subsystem. The *security context* for access control is comprised of the user account data (including SID, groups, and privileges), and it is implemented when a user attempts to access a protected object.

An ACL is stored in a binary form called a *security descriptor*. A directory object is available only when its security descriptor grants access rights to the requesting security principal.

If an ACL changes, and those changes are to be inherited by subordinate objects, the ACL is marked. When the ACL change is replicated to other DSAs, the inherited changes are propagated locally. This approach uses much less bandwidth than the alternative—applying the inherited change locally and then replicating every object that is changed.

Directory Permissions

In Active Directory, you can grant or deny permissions and determine how the permissions are applied and propagated. Active Directory supports the following types of permissions:

- **General permissions**—Five general object permissions are provided, including `Full Control`, `Read`, `Write`, `Create/Delete All Child Objects`, and `Apply Group Policy`.
- **Advanced permissions**—Advanced permissions include all general permissions, as well as `List Contents`, `Delete`, `Delete Subtree`, `Read` and `Modify Permissions`, `Modify Owner`, `All Validated Writes`, and `All Extended Rights`.
- **Permission to create and delete specific objects**—You can grant or deny permissions to create or delete `User`, `Computer`, `Contact`, `Group`, `Printer`, `Shared Folder`, `Trusted Domain`, and other specific objects.
- **Permission to read or write properties**—Property read/write permissions in Active Directory include the permissions on all properties or a subset of selected properties.
- **Application of permissions**—You can determine how permissions are applied. Permissions may be applied `to this object`, `this object and all child objects`, `child objects only`, or specific classes of objects (by name). You can determine whether these permissions propagate or apply only to objects within the local container.

Inheritance of Administrative Rights

Active Directory enables you to assign administrative permissions at any node of the domain subtree. These permissions are subsequently inherited by objects in child nodes. Inheritance can be combined with administrative delegation to easily grant rights to manage designated directory subtrees.

Inheritance is a property of the container object that allows the values of an ACE to propagate to all child objects. Inheritance is controlled via Security Descriptor Inheritance, where a new object inherits the combined security descriptors of the process creating the object, the parent container, and the class definition.

When inherited permissions are determined varies among directory service vendors. Active Directory uses create-time inheritance rather than the runtime inheritance used by NDS eDirectory. When an object is created or its ACL modified the change is calculated and written to the object's ACL. When the permissions granted to an object need to be determined, the directory just reads the ACL. This provides a fast response in security decisions, but does not guarantee the results are the most current because, depending on synchronization latency, the ACL may be slightly out of date.

Group Policy

A *group policy* is a set of policies enforced on a group of computers or users within the directory. Domain-based security is set by policy and assessed via a hierarchy of policy settings.

Active Directory uses group policies to enable administrators to configure security, desktop, application, and Start menu selections for users and computers within an OU or a domain. Policies only apply to Active Directory computer and user objects. Computers receive an additional *local group policy object (LGPO)* by default. An LGPO only supplies security-specific policies.

Policies can be Registry-based, or can contain a range of policy data from domain security, IP security, scripts, to file or application deployment.

Multiple policy settings are collectively assessed to create the effective policy (except where settings conflict). Policies overwrite previous policies by default when settings differ and are applied in the following order: NT 4 policy file (NTCONFIG.POL), local, site, domain, and OU.

> **Schema Objects**
>
> The schema objects defining object classes and attributes are also controlled via ACLs, allowing only authenticated and authorized users to modify the directory schema.

A *group policy object (GPO)* is a uniquely named set of policies that can be applied to a domain, OU, or site. GPOs are either stored in the group policy container that contains version, status, and other policy information (application objects), or in the group policy template (found in the domain controller's System volume) that contains deployment, software policy, script, and file-based data.

Active Directory Administration

As the range of administration funcionality in Active Directory far exceeds the scope of this material, this section only briefly discusses key management tools, delegation of administration, and groups in Active Directory.

Delegation of Administrative Authority

Active Directory enables you to delegate administrative authority to users, granting specific administrative rights for designated OUs and subtrees. In general, use OUs (rather than domains) for administrative delegation of business or management subdivisions.

OUs are the nodes in the tree commonly used to do the following:

- Delegate total administrative control
- Delegate administrative control over certain object types or properties
- Delegate administrative rights to create and delete objects or certain types of objects

The Delegation of Control Wizard simplifies the assignment of administrative responsibility for specific tasks or for an entire directory subtree. Using the Delegation of Control Wizard, you can delegate one of these tasks or any combination. You can delegate administrative rights to the following:

- **User management**—Read all user information, create, delete, and manage user accounts, and reset passwords on user accounts
- **Printer management**—Create, delete, and manage printers
- **Group management**—Create, delete, or modify the members of a group, and manage group policy links

Alternatively, you can create a custom task to delegate control (at the OU level) of the current folder, existing objects, and/or in creating new objects; or you can delegate control on specified objects only (determined by class membership).

You can selectively delegate general permissions, the permission to create and delete specific object(s) (as described previously under "Directory Permissions"), and property-specific permissions.

You can also delegate the property-specific permissions that provide read and write access control on individual object properties, including `Managed By`, `countryCode`, `street`, `postalAddress`, `postalCode`, and others.

Administrative Tools

Administrative tools for Active Directory are mostly provided through a common interface—the *Microsoft Management Console (MMC)*. Active Directory supports the delegation of administrative tasks via customizable tool sets and flexible directory permissions.

The MMC is a Windows 2000 console interface that integrates the Active Directory administration tools. The MMC is *only* a console in that it provides no management capability but only hosts programs constructed as snap-ins. The MMC provides the mechanism to add, remove, and manipulate snap-ins. The MMC enables you to customize which administration tools will be contained within the console, and to store the configuration into portable files.

The administration tools for Active Directory are provided in the form of MMC snap-ins. Snap-ins are modular software agents that supply a limited functionality, and which are designed to handle a specific set of operations. Snap-ins are constructed in one of two forms:

- *Standalone snap-ins* provide independent management functionality and operate without dependence on any other snap-in.
- *Extension snap-ins* extend (and depend on) another snap-in type. For instance, the Group Policy snap-in is an extension snap-in of the Active Directory Users and Computers snap-in.

The MMC enables you to create custom sets of snap-in tools, and to save them into .msc files. These files are portable, enabling a network administrator to design custom tools for delegated tasks and easily distribute copies. By default, Active Directory administration tools can be invoked from different menu selections; but they can also be organized into a single MMC console. You can use MMC to create a new console and add all snap-ins needed for your directory administration.

Four primary directory tool snap-ins enable you to manage domains, users, computers, sites and services, as well as the directory schema. These tool snap-ins include

- **Active Directory Domains and Trusts**—The Domains and Trusts snap-in enables you to manage domain trusts between domains. This MMC tool supports managing interdomain relationships and allows a multiple domain view of Active Directory (you can see and work with domain trees). The Domains and Trusts snap-in operates on the domain tree, enabling you to view, create, edit, or remove any specific trust relationships established between domains.

- **Active Directory Users and Computers**—This snap-in enables you to manage the users, computers, and related properties within a domain. The Users and Computers snap-in provides management access to domain subtree contents, the OU structure, users, groups, and network resources. Each domain represented in Active Directory Users and Computers includes the `Built-in`, `Computers`, `Domain Controllers`, `ForeignSecurityPrincipals`, `LostAndFound`, `System`, and `Users` nodes that contain corresponding directory objects. Using the Active Directory Users and Computers snap-in, you can create a new computer, contact, group, OU, printer, user, or shared folder, delegate control, assign operations masters, or locate objects within the directory.
- **Active Directory Sites and Services**—The Sites and Services snap-in is used to manage site configuration for replication management, and supports service management functionality. The `Sites` node supplies access to intersite replication parameters, enabling you to create and delete sites, as well as to delegate administrative control. Windows 2000 publishes service information via Active Directory, providing greater availability and easier management of the service. The Services node is not displayed, however, unless you select `Show Services Node` from the View menu. The `Services` node contains information on Public Key, RRAS, and Windows services.
- **Active Directory Schema**—The Active Directory Schema snap-in is used to manage the contents of the directory schema, and it supplies the means to view and modify the objects and attributes within the schema. The Active Directory Schema snap-in lets you set schema permissions, reload the schema, determine which attributes are replicated to the GC, and whether the permissions are inherited.

Besides the four primary Active Directory snap-ins just described, some other tools are used to manage Active Directory. These include the following:

- **DCPromo**—The DCPROMO.EXE program is used to promote a server to an Active Directory domain controller. When a server becomes a domain controller, you can choose to install it into either a new or existing forest, and you can select to create a new domain tree or to create a new child domain within an existing domain tree. To remove DC status from a server, run DCPromo again, and demote the DC to a member server.
- **Group Policy Editor**—Active Directory includes a Group Policy Editor to simplify the creation and editing of security policies. The Group Policy Editor can be launched from the `Group Policy` tab of an OU or domain's property sheet. The Group Policy snap-in enables you to import, review, configure, and apply a group policy object.
- **DNS**—The DNS administration tool is another MMC-based console. The Active Directory DNS snap-in differs substantially from the DNS tool in NT 4, but provides similar functionality. The DNS Wizard is a nice enhancement, simplifying the creation of

DNS domains and zones. The representation of the DNS information in Windows 2000 is rather complex, displaying an unusual arrangement of zone entries arranged in an extended tree. (Some DNS records even use an Active Directory object GUID in place of a host-name, obscuring some DNS configuration details.)

Groups in Active Directory

Active Directory uses groups for security as well as for providing distribution lists. In Active Directory, security groups are the method of implementing security for directory and network resources. In the Active Directory security model (like NT), users are assigned to groups, and groups are assigned permissions to access resources. In general, groups may contain users, groups, and shared resources existing on the local server, in the local domain tree, or in remote domain trees in the forest.

Active Directory contains both the NT-compatible groups called Built-in groups, as well as new Security groups.

The Built-in groups correspond to the default NT 4 built-in local groups, and provide the same functionality. The Built-in groups on an Active Directory server are `Account Operators`, `Administrators`, `Backup Operators`, `Guests`, `Print Operators`, `Replicator`, `Server Operators`, and `Users`.

The Security groups incorporate the NT 4 domain groups and provide additional Security groups specific to Active Directory. The security groups include the following categories:

- **Administration**—`Enterprise Admins`, `Domain Admins`, `DnsAdmins`, `Schema Admins`, `Group Policy Creator Owners`, and `DHCP Administrators`
- **Computers**—`Domain Computers`, `Domain Controllers`, `RAS` and `IAS Servers`, `Cert Publishers`, and `DnsUpdateProxy`
- **Users**—`Domain Guests`, `Domain Users`, `WINS Users`, `DHCP Users`

Security Groups and Distribution Lists

If the Active Directory-integrated version of Exchange (Exchange 2000) is installed on the DC, security groups can also be used for distribution lists. Active Directory security groups have features supporting distribution lists, such as allowing nonsecurity members to exist in a group, and allowing the disabling of security for a group.

Scope of Security Groups

Active Directory security groups have three distinct ranges, or *scopes,* to which they apply. These ranges are defined as being of *Universal*, *Global*, and *Domain Local* scope. The groups with a Universal scope (that is, Universal groups) provide forestwide access, whereas Global groups operate between domains, and Domain Local groups are used within a specific domain.

When operating in native mode, Active Directory also enables you to *nest* groups within other groups, providing a hierarchy of group security membership. This can be especially beneficial for enterprise network administrators who can use this capability to manage large environments. Nesting a group within another group makes it a member of that group. Nested (child) groups and all members within the group can inherit assigned permissions. This nesting capability substantially extends the functionality of groups for use in security organization and control.

Universal Groups

In brief, groups with Universal scope can provide all selected users within any domain tree in the forest the capability to access resources in all other domain trees. Universal groups are most commonly used in large-scale enterprise environments with multiple domains or trees, and can:

- Accept members of all domains, users, Global, or Universal groups in the forest
- Be a member of Domain Local and Universal groups
- Grant permissions on all domains in the forest
- Be used in an ACL on any object in the forest

> **OUs for Administration, Groups for Security**
>
> Active Directory groups should be used differently from OUs:
>
> - Use OUs for administrative hierarchy within a domain.
> - Use groups to control user access to resources throughout the domain tree and forest.
>
> Unlike most directory services, in Active Directory, permissions *cannot* be assigned or granted to objects other than the security principals (user, computer, and groups) and are specific to the domain in which the object exists. This fundamentally affects how you organize and manage people and resources within your directory tree.
>
> As explained in the preceding chapter, with NDS eDirectory if you grant permissions to an OU, all objects within that OU inherit these rights. Active Directory uses groups rather than the OU structure (as NDS does) to provide permissions to users. Each user is added to one or more (usually more) groups and those groups are granted the permissions. Group membership is also restricted to security principals.

When updating Universal groups, the entire membership list is replicated to all GCs in the forest. To avoid undue replication traffic related to Universal groups, keep membership as static as possible, and keep the total number of objects as small as possible. Universal groups require that more than one domain exists within the forest—an Active Directory forest that contains only one domain will not support Universal Groups.

Global Groups

Groups with a Global scope are equivalent to the NT 4 global groups and can be used throughout the forest. Global groups can do the following:

- Accept as members only Global groups and users within the parent domain of the group
- Be a member of all groups in the forest
- Grant permissions on all domains in the forest
- Be used in an ACL on any object in the forest

Domain Local Groups

Groups with a Domain Local scope are new in Active Directory, and they are used to grant access to resources within the domain. Domain Local groups can do the following:

- Accept members from Global and Universal groups and users from all domains in the forest, as well as Domain Local groups within the parent domain of the group
- Be members of only the Domain Local groups within the parent domain of the group
- Grant permissions on only the parent domain of the group
- Be used only in ACLs on objects within the local domain

The Future of Active Directory

Active Directory is approaching its second release, establishing the foundation of what it offers as a directory service product. It is not clear at this point exactly how Active Directory will evolve, what features will be added, and which technologies will be incorporated. However, a quick look at what *is* known about plans for Active Directory development and enhancements provides some hints:

> **GC Required at Logon for Universal Groups**
>
> Universal groups are only stored on GCs; therefore, if Universal groups are used, the GC must be available on logon. If the GC is not available, the logon process uses locally cached data.

- **Cisco Networking Services for Active Directory**—Cisco, in partnership with Microsoft, is developing *Cisco Networking Services for Active Directory (CNS/AD)*, a set of services designed to enable the integration of network device management with information contained in Active Directory. This integration will enable administrators to use Active Directory to manage Cisco network devices. CNS/AD will allow the provisioning of network services according to profiles and Active Directory security information. Cisco also will publish a standard schema, allowing third-party application developers to access the services provided by CNS/AD.
- **Integration of metadirectory technologies**—Microsoft is currently working on version 2.2 of its Microsoft Metadirectory Services (MMS), integrating metadirectory technologies with Active Directory. Incorporating metadirectory functionality allows Active Directory to integrate user identity across disparate namespaces in the enterprise network. These additions to Active Directory will provide user access to resources managed by different directories and applications with a single logon. The integration of these metadirectory capabilities can provide synchronization of the Active Directory information with these external namespaces.
- **Directory-enabled applications**—Products are being released that take advantage of the services offered by Active Directory. Exchange 2000, for example, leverages Active Directory's management rather than relying on its own directory service. Business Layers has released an Active Directory version of its innovative directory-based DayOne eProvisioning application, which automates the provisioning process for enterprise employees and contractors.

The business awareness of the need for—and uses of—directory services is rapidly expanding, and Microsoft seems committed to delivering comprehensive directory solutions for enterprise networks. Active Directory is an ambitious undertaking and Microsoft is hitting the ground running with many available directory-enabled applications, business partnerships, technical support alliances, and plans for enhancements.

As the cornerstone of Microsoft's approach to network management, and with support from application vendors, Active Directory is clearly a serious contender for the enterprise network. Whatever the future holds for Active Directory, it should be an interesting product to watch.

Metadirectory Services

CHAPTER

11

...pay no attention to the DSA behind the curtain...

IN THIS CHAPTER

Metadirectory services are an interesting area of technology. They provide a powerful means of integrating and managing disparate sets of information, which reside in other directories or databases. As a product class, however, metadirectories are a diverse lot—the architecture and mechanisms of each product vary greatly from one to the next.

This chapter provides an overview of the common functionality that all metadirectory services offer, and the general methods that must be implemented to provide them. After that, it takes a look at several products, each of which approaches the concept of a metadirectory from its own particular angle.

Introduction to Metadirectory Services

The concepts and operations of a metadirectory service are a little complex, so before we start talking about what a metadirectory service is, what it provides, and how it works, let's take a look at what is behind the need for metadirectory technologies.

Fundamentally, the underlying business need is that enterprises have multiple unconnected directories that contain overlapping sets of data—most notably, about the users of the various directories, and the information related to the users.

Businesses have invested a significant amount of money and administrative effort in creating and maintaining these multiple directory namespaces. These unconnected directories and data sources for applications take many forms—e-mail directories, network directories, HR databases, and many others.

Each of these directories contains much of the same information about the people in the organization, the groups to which the people are assigned, and their various administrative, operational, and security roles. As a result, each directory contains redundant information about the people, groups, and roles, requiring additional storage space, network bandwidth, and administrative effort to create and manage this information.

Although the underlying information is frequently overlapping, these directory namespaces generally do not interoperate or use a common information storage mechanism, but rather operate within application-specific and network-specific frameworks.

It is costly in terms of time and expense to manage all this duplicated directory information. Every time a person is added to the HR directory, for example, the same user information must be added to multiple other directories such as the network directory, e-mail directory, and so

Just a Sampling of Metadirectory Technologies

The chapter does not attempt to review all metadirectory products, nor does it cover the range of directory synchronization tools available. There are many good metadirectory products, which are not addressed. Products with distinctive characteristics were selected to provide an overview of the scope of metadirectory implementations.

on. Similarly, if information about a user is changed in one database or directory, the same information must be manually changed in all the other directories in the company.

Clearly, integrating the information in all the directories maintained by a company can reduce the administrative burden and facilitate access to information.

The integration of existing directories into a single unified directory simplifies resource location and access, and can reduce administrative overhead. Some of the benefits of a metadirectory include

- Integration of the disconnected information into a single logical namespace provides a consistent access point for the information existing in all the company's directories.
- Management of complex sets of user and resource information in multiple directories is simplified by providing a single point of administration.
- Administration costs are reduced due to elimination of duplicated tasks required to manage redundant directory information.

Information and Implementation Factors

Directory integration is not merely a matter of addressing the technical issues involved with connecting the various directories within an organization. The integration of directory information is often as much a political/organizational issue as it is a technical/connectivity issue. Issues surrounding sharing enterprise information can at times far outweigh the technical ones.

The connectivity is, after all, a relatively straightforward matter of installing software and getting the configuration right—no small trick in and of itself. However, getting *every* department in your company to agree on a new method of managing *its* information is often a much greater challenge. Each directory that is to be integrated belongs to one group or another—few departments are going to easily give up control of *their* data.

Information Issues

The political and organizational issues center on the control and administration of the information itself—issues that must be dealt with in any metadirectory implementation. Central issues related to information include

- **Ownership**—With the distributed ownership and control of enterprise information, you need to be able to select which information is authoritative so that ownership of the information stays where it is needed.
- **Organizational**—Every directory in an organization is managed and maintained by a specific department or business unit that has a vested interest in the integrity and control of the information contained within the directory. For instance, the information stored in a HR database is commonly under the control of the HR department, and must be protected according to both company policies and government regulation. If that database is going to be connected to a metadirectory, there must be the assurance of security.

- **Political**—Given some of the political and legal issues over control of information, an integration solution needs to allow the incorporation of selected subsets of information while excluding others.
- **Administration**—A core administration issue is the necessity to manage redundant information stored in the directories distributed throughout the enterprise. A metadirectory provides the automation needed to handle change management for user related information. Less administrative work is required because the metadirectory can automate actions in multiple connected directories based on an event in any one directory.

Implementation Issues

Besides the organizational and political issues, there are a variety of implementation issues involved in integrating the content of multiple, different directories. These issues are present in directory integration both within the enterprise and in its partnering efforts with other companies.

- **Connectivity Issues**—There are fundamental issues of how to connect the different directories that use different namespaces, naming conventions, and protocols for accessing and managing the information.
- **Directory Design**—In evaluating how to integrate a set of diverse directories, there are core issues around the differences in the design of the directory namespace—how to connect different directories that do not share the same tree structure or schema.

What Is a Metadirectory?

A *metadirectory* integrates information—it is a programmatic approach to integrating distributed information resources. In its simplest form, a metadirectory supplies the programmatic logic needed to integrate distributed information, and to provide consistent access to that information. This information, can reside in a variety of sources and take many forms (see Figure 11.1).

A metadirectory can be thought of as a "meta" approach to managing diverse information assets in directories and databases within the enterprise network. The metadirectory integrates selected sets of information stored in the connected directories into a single logical directory. As a result of connecting and integrating the enterprise information, a metadirectory can provide a core index to the information contained in the various repositories.

What Does a Metadirectory Do?

A metadirectory connects multiple directories and/or databases, and represents the collective information in a single logical directory. It provides the infrastructure used to create and maintain accessibility and data integrity between multiple connected directories. A metadirectory creates a unified namespace, with a common naming model for the naming of directory objects, and a common access point to the directory information for users and applications alike.

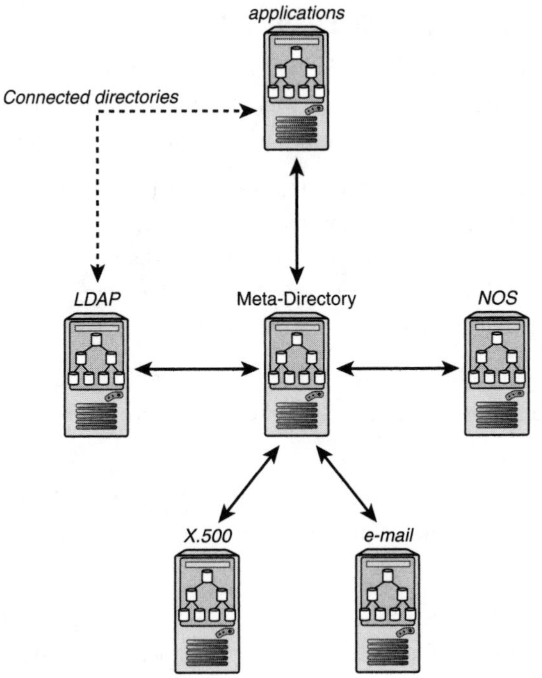

FIGURE 11.1
Metadirectories can integrate a variety of data sources into a single point of management.

The metadirectory provides a way to integrate, locate, access, secure, and synchronize heterogeneous directory resources. Although offering this unified view of the directory, the assignment of ownership and administration of directory information must be maintained by the metadirectory.

The flow of information between the connected directories is managed by the metadirectory, which controls the replication and synchronization of directory additions, deletions, and modifications.

A metadirectory also extends the directory functionality—it is designed to perform directory operations across diverse namespaces. Cross-directory operations can be automated, offloading common and duplicated management tasks such as user account creation and deletion. This capability can also enhance security, for example, by ensuring that employee's network accounts and permissions are inactivated as soon as they leave the company.

How Does a Metadirectory Work?

The key functionality of a metadirectory is the aggregation of subsets of information from an assigned group of directories and databases. Metadirectories create a new logical directory, one that integrates selected subsets of the data from the connected information sources.

Each object in the metadirectory is constructed from selected attributes of objects from each of the external directories. The aggregation of object attributes from multiple external directories to form the composite metadirectory object can be considered a *joining* of the various related objects into a single metadirectory object. An employee, for example, would have a metadirectory object that aggregates network accounts, e-mail, HR info, and so on.

The information in the metadirectory is a subset of the totality of data in the connected directories. The metadirectory transparently makes this information globally available to users and applications.

To integrate directory information, a metadirectory supports one or both of two common methods—*information brokering* (links to directory information) or the *join* (copies directory data to a common datastore).

In either method, *connectors* (also called *namespace connectors*) are used to pass information between the metadirectory and the other directories. Connectors can be filtered to limit the data crossing them, providing the ability to exclude data from the metadirectory set.

Metadirectory Design

A metadirectory is a set of services and functions that is designed to integrate complex and diverse sets of information from disparate sources. The aspects of metadirectory technology examined here include

- **Namespace Integration**—Internal namespace structure, how it manages the integration of multiple namespaces, integrating disparate directories (and possibly databases and other information sources) into a unified directory
- **Scope of Interoperability**—How it provides connectivity and interoperability with multiple directories, supporting the interdirectory operations to exchange information

Source of the Term

The term "metadirectory" is generally attributed to The Burton Group, which defined the concept of a metadirectory in its 1996 publication *Metadirectory Services*. The Burton Group can be credited with much of the conceptual work on metadirectory technology, as well as for increasing awareness of this product category. For more information on The Burton Group, take a look at their Web site at `www.tbg.com`.

- **Methods of Integration**—The integration method of the selected directory information
- **Metadirectory Components**—The namespace connectors and the underlying engine which handles integration and synchronization
- **Information Management**—The object and attribute mapping, filtering, and management of information flow between directories
- **Data Synchronization**—The data synchronization functionality between directories
- **Storing the Data**—The store and retrieve operations for directory information
- **Event Management** —How directory events are managed to dynamically respond to changes
- **Interdirectory Security**—The managing of authentication and access control across multiple directories

In the following sections, each of these aspects is discussed in a bit more detail.

Integrating Multiple Namespaces

Most enterprise environments maintain multiple directories, which hold functionally discrete sets of information. A typical enterprise network includes NOS directories, e-mail directories, application directories such as HR, as well as various other line of business and enterprise directories. The basic functionality that a metadirectory provides is the integration of this range of namespaces into a cohesive whole (see Figure 11.2).

A metadirectory must know how to connect to diverse information resources (directories, databases, and so on), and read from and write to these information resources. Each of these directories is likely to have a different naming convention, proprietary datastore, and set of administrative tools. Every directory implementation has its own schema as well, further complicating directory interoperability.

The integration of dissimilar directory namespaces requires that the metadirectory address a number of technical issues:

- Naming discrepancies between disparate namespaces must be eliminated or, at a minimum, a translation mechanism to allow effective interdirectory communication must be provided.
- To support the integration of multiple directory services with different schema, some method of resolving schema discrepancies between directories must implemented. This usually takes the form of configurable schema mapping.
- As there is not as yet a broadly accepted standard for directory replication and synchronization, there is no easy way for information to be dynamically shared and updated. Therefore, namespace-specific software components (connectors) are used to communicate with each directory in its native protocol.

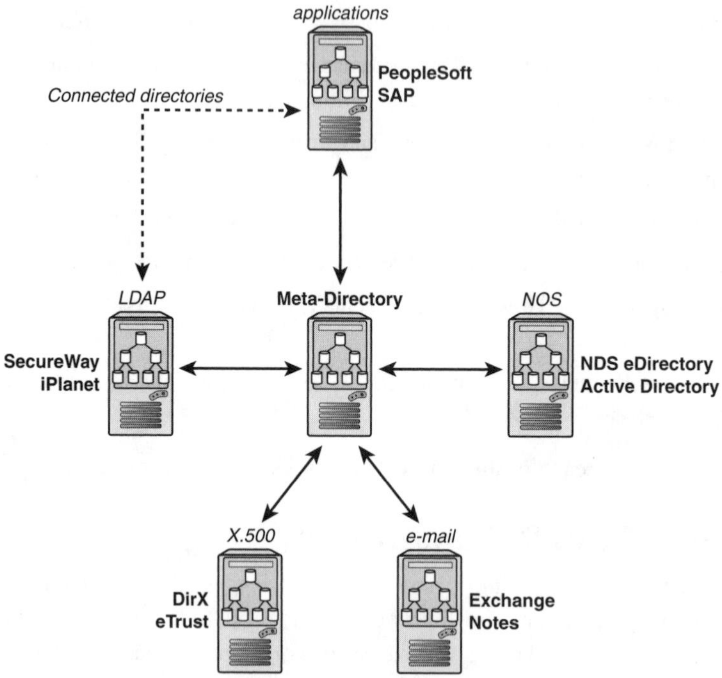

FIGURE 11.2
Most enterprises have a core set of applications, representing critical data, which needs to be integrated.

- If a metadirectory allows updates to information in the underlying directories, complex data synchronization issues can occur. Accordingly, information ownership must be assigned and maintained to ensure that only the assigned entities are allowed to change their information and at the designated repository.
- Security issues are a critical concern. Access control must be correctly maintained when information is accessed via a metadirectory connection.

Metadirectory Namespaces

To provide a single point of access to the information it manages, a metadirectory must have a namespace of its own. Within this namespace, the metadirectory represents the objects as they exist to it, with the aggregate data set from the connected directories. This internal metadirectory namespace generally takes one of two forms:

- It is sometimes integrated into the underlying X.500 or LDAP directories (perhaps as extensions to existing objects).
- It is sometimes integrated into a two-part namespace—one representing the connected directories, and the other representing the metadirectory.

Scope of Interoperability

A metadirectory service can provide a range of interoperability. It might support only a limited set of directories, communicating only with LDAP or X. 500-based directories, or it might also communicate with NOS, e-mail, and application directories, as well as databases and other datastores. Each of these external datastores has important information, much of which it could be integrated into the metadirectory.

As shown in Figure 11.3, the information sources that a particular metadirectory can manage may be limited to a small set of proprietary directories, extend to a number of application directories and databases, or include standard access methods such as LDAP. The vendor may fix the scope of interoperability of a particular metadirectory, or the metadirectory may be flexible providing a means of incorporating additional data.

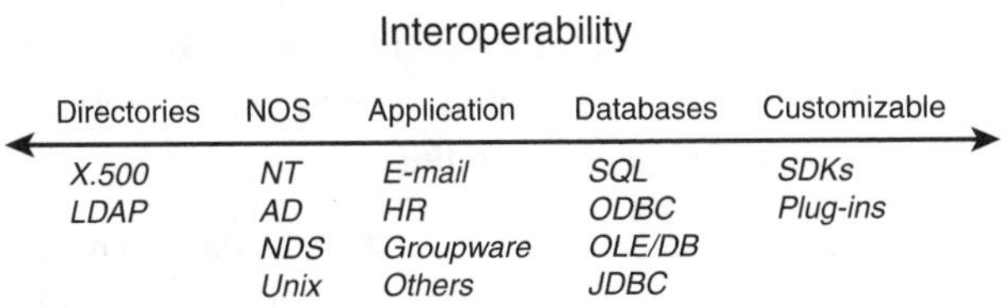

FIGURE 11.3
The range of interoperability for a given metadirectory can vary considerably.

Any enterprise has a considerable investment in its network operating system, which contains user, resource, and security information needed in the metadirectory. A metadirectory may support integration of one or more networking directories, such as Novell Directory Services, Active Directory, Windows NT, and Unix.

Integration of information in enterprise applications such as e-mail, HR, groupware, and other key information repositories is an important part of the metadirectory's interoperability.

A critical information store in most enterprises is the e-mail directory, which contains the e-mail addresses and names of all the people in the enterprise. E-mail is one of the most critical applications used by many businesses; they rely on it as a channel to communicate with their employees, clients, vendors, partners, and others.

Another core information repository for the enterprise is the HR database, which contains the most detailed and sensitive information on employees. This information is also often in high demand, thus integrating some HR information into the metadirectory is likely.

Some metadirectory products can also access databases (such as SQL), providing a means to communicate with backend applications containing critical information. Many SQL databases are the repositories for the line-of-business information, used to facilitate and manage business operations.

Besides interoperating with standardized directories or databases, some metadirectory approaches allow for a customizable interface to external information sources. Interfaces and development tools are supplied as SDKs and/or plug-ins, allowing administrators or developers to specify the structures and methods of the information exchange. This kind of flexibility enables access to needed information regardless of how was stored. Novell's DirXML, for example, allows for directory engineers to use connectors to communicate with external namespaces, and XML-encapsulated data structures to exchange the information.

The more data sources that can be integrated into the metadirectory, the more valuable it will be to an enterprise. This is particularly true when you consider the automation functionality the metadirectory may offer. Each task that can be automated frees up administrators for more productive work, and can reduce administrative costs.

Methods of Integration

Although there are a variety of products offering varying degrees of integration, there isn't exactly a consensus on the functionality required of a metadirectory service, nor even on the terminology used to describe metadirectory capabilities.

Yet thanks to some leading industry research groups (The Burton Group, Gartner Group, and others), some general approaches to implementing metadirectory technologies have been identified. These approaches can be viewed by their method of data integration. They are

- **Join/Full Directory Synchronization**—A metadirectory using the *join* method replicates data into a unified directory, aggregating content from multiple directories. Entries in the tree are *copies*—a selected superset of objects and attributes in remote directories.
- **Information Brokering**—A metadirectory using the *broker* method contains only *links* to data stored in connected directories. Entries in the metadirectory tree are *aliases* to the entries in the remote directories.
- **Directory Synchronization Tools**—Synchronization tools simply update a limited set of attributes of linked objects held in a specific directory. These tools are usually applied in a fairly limited way, such as password synchronization, and no unified view of the directory information is provided.

In assessing the available products supplying interoperability between directories, there is a range of functionality ranging from metadirectory services (which commonly employ both brokering and join methods), virtual directory services (using brokering the method only), and synchronization tools (which just synchronizes two directories).

Although directory synchronization tools have their purposes, they clearly aren't metadirectories. We will discuss the role of synchronization tools later in this section. Because they are a peripheral topic, however, for now we're going to look at the two methods of metadirectory integration.

As shown in Figure 11.4, these two methods primarily differ in whether or not the metadirectory maintains a copy of the information. Most metadirectory products support both the brokering and join methods of integrating directory information.

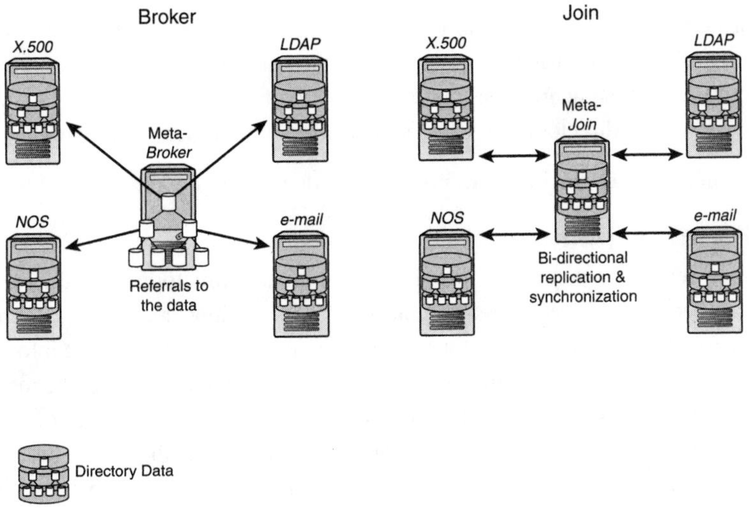

FIGURE 11.4

A virtual directory service uses only the broker method, whereas a metadirectory service supports both join and broker methods.

The joining (combining) of the attributes and objects from multiple directories into one unified directory tree, can be done as either the (solely) logical joining of the information into a single logical DIT (tree), or as the physical joining of the information into a common DIB (database).

In a logical joining, all directory objects and attributes are represented in a unified logical namespace and accessed through a unified interface. All approaches to metadirectory integration must do a logical join to represent the data.

In the physical joining, all globally shared objects and attributes are *also* replicated into a unified datastore. The storing, replicating, and synchronizing of the information is the aspect that differentiates the *join* from brokering.

Some metadirectories use a *virtual directory* design (based on the information brokering method), where the data remains in the directory of origin and is never moved between directories. In this approach, the directory is a logical join, providing a view of directory data that links to data that *only* exists in the original source directory.

Other metadirectory solutions support both the physical and logical joining of the directory information, supporting both the brokering method in linking to the information, as well as the join method of integrating the information.

In assessing the different approaches, you have to look at the granularity of the objects that are involved in the integration process. You also have to evaluate the degree of processing and transformation the objects are subjected to—assess if whole entries, attributes, or even single attribute values are accessible for the join process and the associated transformations.

How the information is stored affects how the information is accessed when queries are sent to the metadirectory for that information. It can also determine how up-to-date the information is. Due to the complexity of synchronization between directories, there may be a bit of latency in data updates with a metadirectory that does a physical join, and thus stores data.

This next section examines the join and broker methods in more detail.

Joining the Information

The Join method replicates the information from the external directories into the metadirectory DIB. The metadirectory acts as an accessible source of the information and supplies information directly to requests. Because a metadirectory using the join method replicates the information, entries (objects) in the directory tree are copies of the information. An object in the metadirectory that is joined from multiple connected directories is a selected set of attributes derived from the corresponding objects in all the remote directories. The selected attributes can be copied directly from the remote directories or can be subjected to considerable transformations to account for semantic and syntactic differences between the different repositories. (See also the discussion on schema mapping later on in this chapter.)

A joined metadirectory:

- Creates meta-objects from the collected set of object attributes in the underlying source directories.
- Aggregates information from the connected directories into the metadirectory storage.
- Optionally distributes parts of this consolidated information to some of the original sources.

The desired directory objects are mapped from the external directory to the metadirectory, providing linkage between objects. The selected attributes are copied to the centralized metadirectory, which constructs its objects from the aggregate attributes for each object from all directories. A metadirectory object, as shown in Figure 11.5, appears to be a single object, and is stored as one, although the data it is constructed from is derived from a number of external sources.

Administrators are faced with a number of decisions in implementing the join process for establishing the join criteria (a unique field across all external directories, successive matching rules of multiple attributes, heuristics, and manual procedures), building the distinguished name of the joined entry, and the mapping of the selected attributes.

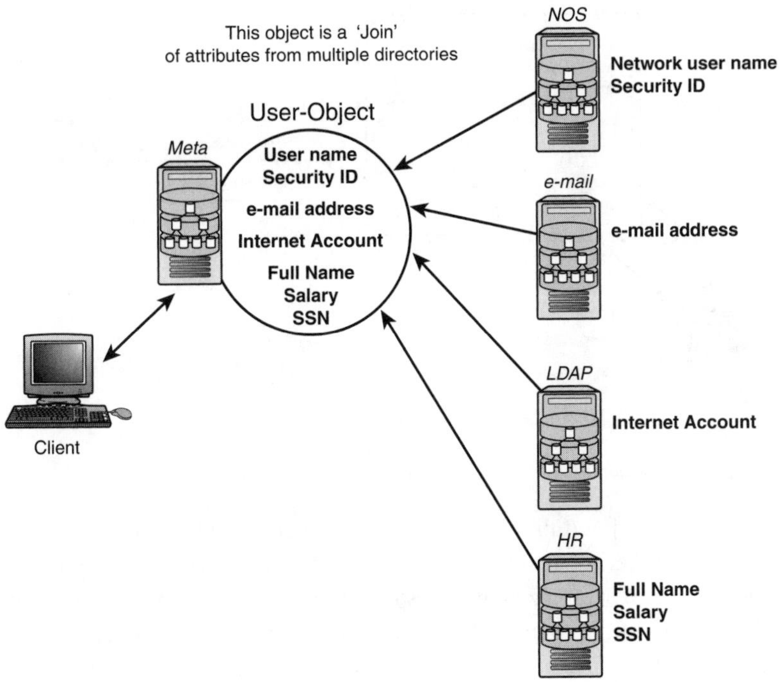

FIGURE 11.5
A metadirectory object consists of data from a number of objects in other directories.

Once configured, a metadirectory using the join method will replicate all the selected information from each connected directory into the metadirectory DIB, thus creating a physical join as well as a logical join of the information sets.

Once replicated, the metadirectory must keep its data current by synchronizing its directory information with the connected directories. To do this, the metadirectory synchronization and security infrastructure mechanisms must be robust—flexible, interoperable, granular, and so on.

When a query is sent for information that a metadirectory has in its joined DIB, the metadirectory acts as the source of that information, supplying the information to the client. If that information is physically held in the metadirectory, the metadirectory server provides the data directly to the requesting client. If the data is *not* held locally, however, the metadirectory will request the source data from the external directory and then supply that data to the client (in the information brokering style). As shown in Figure 11.6, a metadirectory server can use one or both of these methods.

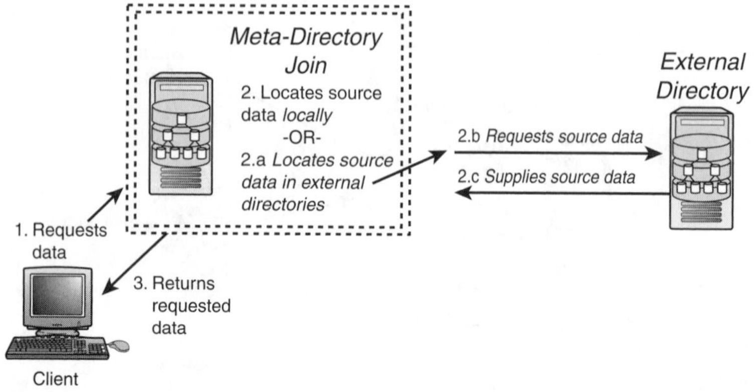

FIGURE 11.6
A metadirectory supplies data that it has, and broker requests for data it does not have.

Metadirectories using the join/full integration approach can provide better performance (than those only using the brokering method), yet they may do this at the expense of data latency. The complexity of data synchronization grows as the numbers and types of data sources increase, and due to the sheer volume of data, synchronization may be scheduled, and thus not occur in real-time. Not all metadirectory products do dynamic updates— some rely on manual data imports.

Information Brokering

Information brokering is another method used by metadirectories to integrate information from the connected directories. When information brokering is used, the integration is in the form of a *logical* join rather than a *physical* join. This means that the metadirectory *solely* maintains links to the information stored in the source directory, as Figure 11.7 shows, and doesn't replicate that data into a common datastore.

Because a DSA using the broker method only contains links to the data, broker entries in the directory tree are aliases to the real entries in the remote directories. For clients requesting the data, the metadirectory essentially acts as a broker for the information stored in the connected directories, handling all access requests for the information.

A metadirectory using the brokering method handles incoming queries for information by contacting the authoritative source directories, retrieving information, and supplying it back to the requesting client.

When a query is sent to a broker-style metadirectory, rather than looking up the actual data (as the joined metadirectory does) the broker uses a link to find the directory to query. The broker requests the information from the external directory, as shown in Figure 11.8, and when it receives a response, provides the data to the client that originally requested the information.

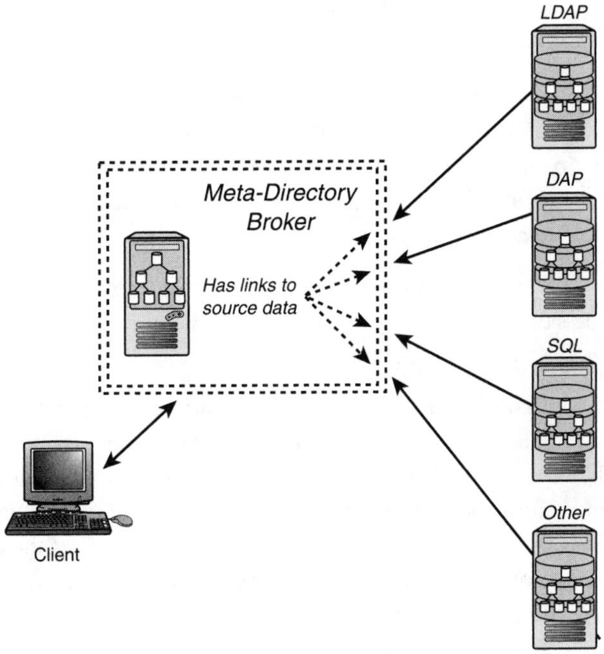

FIGURE 11.7

A metadirectory using the information brokering method does not store any data locally; its objects consist only of links to data in external sources.

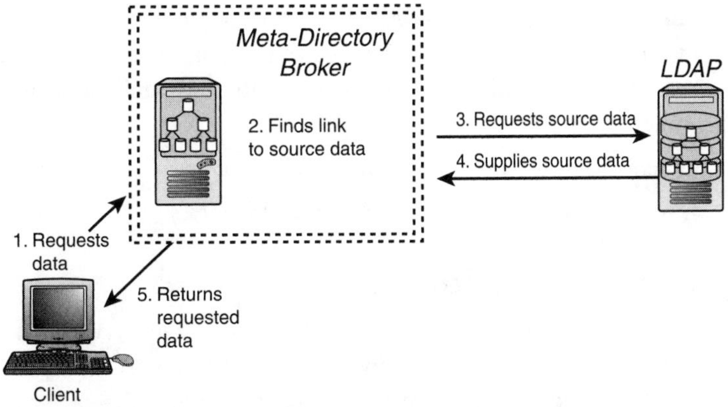

FIGURE 11.8

The broker style of metadirectory queries the external directories on behalf of the clients requesting data.

A metadirectory using only information brokering is commonly referred to as a *virtual directory*, named such because it can create only a solely logical join of the information contained in the connected directories. This creates the tree representing all the directory objects, yet no information from these remote directories is stored on the virtual directory server.

A virtual directory only supports brokering, completely relying on the connected directories for the information. A virtual directory supplies front-end views of data in underlying directory without creating any local objects containing that data. Each entry in the virtual directory is an alias to the source objects in a connected directory. A virtual directory does not commonly attempt to synchronize data between connected directories.

There are two types of virtual directory services, server-based and client-based. Each one provides much of the same functionality, but uses somewhat different methods. Consider the differences between these two approaches:

- **Server-based virtual directory**—A virtual directory can be implemented as a server-based application that acts as an information broker between dissimilar directories or databases. The virtual directory processing a client request for directory information repackages and reformats the information appropriately and then routes the request to the source directory. When the directory sends back the results of the query, the virtual directory server reformats and repackages those results and sends them back to the client. A server-based virtual directory:
  - Looks like an LDAP server
  - Acts as a gateway to the source directory
  - Repackages/reformats and routes to source, and does the same in reverse on the way back
- **Client-based virtual directory**—A virtual directory implementation also can be constructed as a client application, where the application is designed to communicate with a variety of directories integrating information into a logically unified whole. A client-based virtual directory:
  - Uses client application which can access all directories
  - Retrieves information directly from source directories

Directory Synchronization Tools

Directory integration products aren't always a complete metadirectory service, but are sometimes just tools that exchange information between two specified directories. The synchronization tools work by replicating selected data between specified directories, with each directory holding its own data. This synchronization takes one of two forms:

- **One-way synchronization—**A synchronization tool might only provide one-way synchronization of directory information—where a designated directory replicates information out to the connected directory, but does not allow the connected directory to replicate information back. One example of this is how Active Directory talks with the Novell NetWare bindery; Active Directory replicates its directory information updates to the NetWare bindery, but does not allow changes in the bindery to replicate to Active Directory.

- **Two-way synchronization—**Many synchronization tools provide bidirectional synchronization between the connected directories—where each connected directory provides updates to the other directory when directory objects change. The information sent in one direction is not necessarily the same information that is sent in the other; given a pair of directories, an e-mail address could come from one directory and network logon information from the other.

This type of directory synchronization method is generally deployed with rather modest goals; keeping passwords and other basic information synchronized. Although these tools do synchronize some of the contents in each of the connected directories, however, what sets them apart from metadirectories is what they *lack* in directory integration functionality. One essential distinction between these synchronization tools and metadirectory products is that synchronization tools have no intermediate logical structure supporting the aggregate directory content. This sort of synchronization tool has no unified namespace, nor is there a centralized unified administration interface for managing the aggregate directory information.

To clarify the differences between synchronization tools and metadirectories, Figure 11.9 displays some delineations between the various approaches to directory integration.

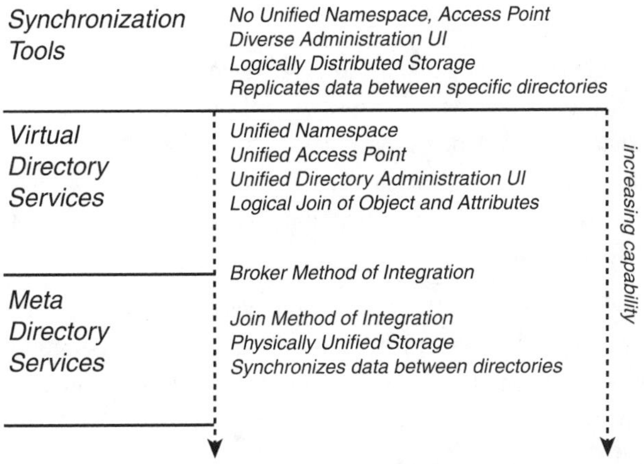

FIGURE 11.9

The distinctions between synchronization tools, virtual (brokering-only) directories, and metadirectories (full join).

Metadirectory Components

Although metadirectory architecture depends on the vendor designing and implementing it, because of the baseline functionality that the metadirectory service must provide, a common set of components are usually employed. These components can be grouped by functionality:

- A *meta engine* carries out the integration and synchronization processes
- *Namespace connectors* communicate with the different directory namespaces

The exact methods these components use varies between implementations, yet the functionality that they provide will be similar. In addition, a metadirectory that does a physical join requires some sort of data storage mechanism, often provided by an underlying directory service.

Meta Engine

The operations of the meta engine (like other components) vary between implementations. The meta engine commonly manages the process of exchanging information between directories by controlling and filtering the information flow, implementing schema mapping, and handling interdirectory security mechanisms.

Sometimes a standalone application is used to carry out the meta engine operations, whereas other solutions rely on the underlying directory service to conduct metadirectory functions. The Siemens metadirectory product, DirXmetahub, for example, uses a standalone executable to manage the metadirectory activities; in contrast, Novell's DirXML metadirectory technology leverages the underlying NDS eDirectory service for its meta engine capability.

Namespace Connectors

Each metadirectory implementation has some kinds of agents, often called *namespace connectors*, which communicate with each of the different types of directory and database namespaces (and other types of data stores). A namespace connector is usually responsible for the details of communicating with a *single* connected directory. The connector commonly controls directory-specific items such as object and attribute mapping, data filtering rules, and translation of information content formats.

Most metadirectories have a number of specific connectors; one to communicate with NDS eDirectory, another to communicate with Windows NT, another to communicate with LDAP directories, and so on. In addition, the capability to create custom connectors may also be supplied.

Information Management

An important aspect of the metadirectory is the flexibility it offers when managing directory information. A metadirectory enables mapping the objects and attributes within the metadirectory and connected directories, and controlling the information flow between directories. Filtering the objects and attributes allows the selective integration of data from connected directories, and can minimize the replication of directory updates.

The logical and/or physical joining of the directory information can vary in the scope of attributes and objects that are integrated from the connected directories. For example, in some cases only a few selected attributes and objects may be integrated from other directories, or in other cases most of the objects and many of the attributes from the other directories may be integrated into the metadirectory.

When the information is integrated, the data must be either periodically or dynamically synchronized.

There are multiple aspects to consider, including

- **Schema mapping**—The mapping of related objects and attributes between directories is fundamental to the exchange of information. If that information can be manipulated and transformed during this exchange, it can help streamline complex business processes.
- **Information filtering**—If the selection of which information is used can be controlled at a highly granular level, you can gather exactly the information you need, and none that you don't need.
- **Authoritative data source**—It is also necessary to identify which directory owns that information, and maintain that relationship, and at a highly granular level.

Each of these factors affects the overall information management flexibility, and ultimate usefulness, of a given metadirectory product.

Schema Mapping

There will, of course, be a different set of objects and attributes contained in each of the directories; even the objects and attributes that represent basically the same thing in each of the directories are likely to be named differently. The differing directory schemas must be taken into account and administrators must have a mechanism for mapping objects in one directory to objects in another directory. Likewise, administrators have to be able to map the attributes in one directory to attributes in the other directory.

Anything Worth Doing...

The integration of disparate directory data is never without administrative costs, in terms of directory service management and tool implementation. Substantial administrative work is required for the smooth integration of complex sets of discrete directory information. The detailed configuration of object and attribute mapping alone, for example, entails substantial administrative efforts.

Careful consideration must be given to the possible outcome of a poorly implemented metadirectory, which could simply add an additional layer of directory management requirements without adequately compensating long-term gains.

Although the specifics of how the object and attribute mapping is done can vary widely between metadirectory implementations, every metadirectory solution provides some method of mapping objects and attributes between directories. Rules are commonly used to control the mapping of objects and attributes. These rules range from a fixed one-to-one mapping (object-to-object and attribute-attribute) to a flexible mapping of any object to any other object, any attribute to any other attribute, even a single object (or attribute) to multiple objects (or attributes).

In addition to mapping, the systems may have to perform transformations on the various objects and attributes to account for semantical and syntactical mismatches between the various directories and databases. One example of this is when two or more attributes (or fields) in one system have to be combined into a single attribute on another system, such as when the first datastore knows name, given name, and middle initial as separate fields, and the second one only needs a common name attribute. Syntactic differences (sensitivity to capitalization or lack of it, different character sets) may also require processing the values before (and sometimes even after) the mapping.

Information Filtering

It is usually desirable to integrate only selected objects and attributes from the connected directories into the metadirectory. To control the information that is integrated via the metadirectory, mechanisms must be provided to allow the selection of the specific objects and attributes that are to be used (or blocked).

A metadirectory commonly enables some sort of filtering of objects and attributes from the external directories, though different metadirectory implementations may vary in the degree of filtering supported. This capability can range from the limited filtering of objects and attributes, to (optimally) the ability to selectively filter at the attribute level from all the other directories.

Authoritative Data Source

In an enterprise environment where many directories fulfill highly specific functions, control of the information contained within those directories commonly resides with the business units chartered with maintaining this information.

> **Commonalities in Schema Mapping**
>
> The whole schema and attribute mapping and the associated processing bears a close similarity to metadata management and the ETML (extract, transform, move, load) paradigm of data warehousing.

The human resources department, for example, always controls information stored in HR database. Employee information, such as job title or manager's name, is clearly its responsibility. Much of the information stored about employees is sensitive and confidential information, and control over this data is of significant importance to HR management. Therefore, the HR database must remain the authoritative source of that information.

Likewise, the network operating system controls a user logon name and password needed to provide access to directory and network resources (and is managed by the IT department). Because the network operating system is the access control infrastructure for network resources, the NOS should remain the authoritative source for the user logon information.

Yet, even with the ability to control ownership, not all information from remote directories and databases should even be integrated, but should rather remain in the source datastore. Information such as the employee salary should not be made commonly available via the metadirectory.

Data Synchronization

Data synchronization is another issue between disparate directory services. For businesses attempting to track user and resource information across a distributed network with different directory databases and different storage and update mechanisms, the synchronization of directory content is a key issue for integrated directory operations.

If information about a user is changed in one directory, this change must be propagated to other directories (that commonly use different synchronization methods). These differences are handled by the individual namespace connectors, which communicate data changes in the method needed by a particular directory.

Both push and pull methods of replication are commonly supported, therefore a directory can either request information, or it can be sent (unsolicited) when a directory information change event occurs. Some connectors periodically read change logs or poll the connected directory for changes.

Metadirectory implementations vary in their support for replication or synchronization between the various connected directories.

Storing the Data

How the metadirectory information is stored is related to its method of integration. As shown in Figure 11.10, storage takes two basic forms:

- If a metadirectory relies solely on the brokering method of integration of the connected directories, it will store only the links to the actual information.
- If the metadirectory relies solely on the join method of integrating multiple directories, all selected objects, attributes, and values will be replicated from the connected directories into the metadirectory's DIB.

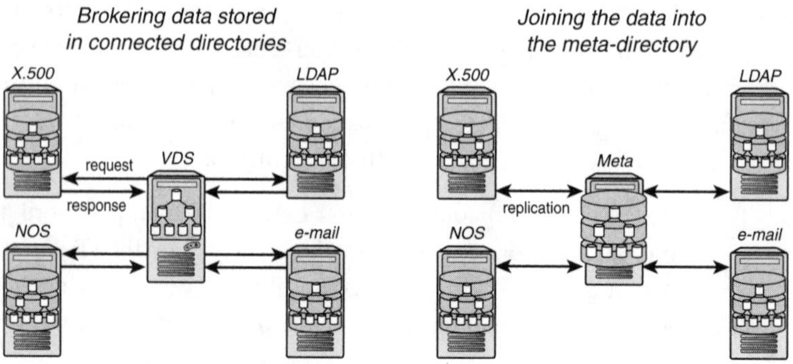

FIGURE 11.10

The different forms of storage depend on the integration method.

If a metadirectory uses both of these methods, the metadirectory will still have a centralized DIB, yet will contain only some of the information locally. It will contain links to the information it brokers that is stored in the connected directories.

Event Management

Metadirectories may support some form of event management, in which changes to directory objects can trigger related events in other directories. For example when a new user is added to a metadirectory, it must signal the connected directories to create a new user object. Likewise, when a new user is added to a connected directory (such as the HR database) the metadirectory must also add a corresponding new user object and then relay those changes to other directories as needed.

A metadirectory can provide only limited event handling, where only the creation or deletion of objects and attributes triggers a corresponding creation or deletion in connected directories. Conversely, a metadirectory might provide very flexible event handling mechanisms, where a simple change in a single value can trigger an entire set of event-related directory actions.

Day One eProvisioning (by Business Layers) is a directory-based application that monitors changes to employee status (such as hiring and firing), and then handles the entire provisioning (or deprovisioning) process. Provisioned resources typically include a broad range of IT resources, PBX systems, and security for facilities access, among other things. This provides the means for a relatively small change (perhaps a transfer to another state) in the HR database to result in the updating all necessary IT directories and databases for that employee.

Interdirectory Security

Because information is accessed across multiple directories (frequently on multiple platforms), interdirectory and interplatform security mechanisms must communicate to implement consistent authentication and access control policies. Some metadirectories rely on the security mechanisms employed in the source (connected) directories while others provide their own.

A metadirectory can provide support for pass-through authentication, where the security credentials for a user are translated into the specific security protocols needed by each connected directory, giving the user a single sign-on access to all directory information.

In an enterprise network, each different directory has its own security mechanisms and protocols for handling and authentication and access control processes. Yet, to provide an integrated access to the information stored in each of these different directories, a metadirectory has to supply security mechanisms that will work across directory and security architectures. For example, the security mechanisms used within a network directory such as Windows NT (SAM/NTLM) or Active Directory (Kerberos) differs substantially from the security mechanisms used in LDAP directories (SASL, SSL). Yet to integrate these directories, a metadirectory solution must provide a way for security mechanisms to interoperate, such that access is controlled consistent with the users permissions across all directories.

Siemens DirXmetahub

Integration of enterprise directories with the help of the *DirXmetahub* metadirectory provides enterprisewide integrity and consistency of directory information, and a centralized point of administration via any LDAP client.

DirXmetahub Version 6.0 operates on the foundation of the Siemens *DirX* DSA, a massively scalable X.500 and LDAP-compliant directory service, or of some other commercial LDAP directory. The X.500 base of DirX supplies a robust platform to support the integration of many directories from across the enterprise into the metadirectory.

Platforms and Dependencies

Platforms:

DirXmetahub runs on Windows NT, Windows 2000, and Sun Solaris. Other Unix platforms will be supported in the future. Some DirXmetahub agents are available only on Windows NT and Windows 2000.

Dependencies:

The DirXmetahub requires an LDAP v3 directory server as its underlying data store and configuration store. In addition to Siemens' own DirX server, the iPlanet directory and the Oracle Internet Directory are also supported, with more to follow. IBM's MQSeries messaging product is also required, and is bundled together with DirXmetahub.

Namespace Integration

DirXmetahub integrates information from distributed directories, networks, and databases into the namespace of its underlying LDAP directory product. The metadirectory objects are contained within the LDAP directory tree.

DirXmetahub integrates a wide range of common industry namespaces including those used by X.500, LDAP, NOS, and e-mail directories, as well as common HR, PBX, and relational databases. Namespaces implicitly contained in XML files or other types of structured files can also be easily integrated.

Methods of Integration—The DirXmetahub metadirectory supports the full join method of integrating multiple directories, allowing the replication of objects and attributes from the connected directories into the metadirectory datastore. Administrators can also choose not to copy all objects or all attributes from selected directories (filtering) into a common datastore. The capability to synchronize directory information in both directions is supported.

Scope of Interoperability

DirXmetahub provides bidirectional synchronization with many common industry directories and databases. DirXmetahub can synchronize with X.500 and LDAP directories such as Netscape/iPlanet, Oracle OID, IBM SecureWay (and of course Siemens' own DirX server). Enterprise networking directories, including NDS eDirectory, Windows NT, and Active Directory are accessible via DirXmetahub, providing integration of the core data about the enterprise network.

Application directories include e-mail directories, such as Lotus Notes and Microsoft Exchange, common human resources databases, such as those provided by SAP and PeopleSoft, as well as PBX directories (such as Hicom DMS) and CTI applications.

Additionally, ODBC compliant databases can also be tied into the DirXmetahub system.

Metadirectory Components

Siemens DirXmetahub is built as a distributed system, which uses server processes and executable programs, such as meta agents and the meta controllers, to manage the synchronization of all connected directories. The configuration and meta information is stored in an LDAP directory, which can be the same as or different from the metadirectory datastore, and is administered over a Java-based graphical interface, the DirXmetahub Manager. At runtime all the configuration files and TCL scripts that supply the meta information used during the synchronization processes to the various agents and controllers are created automatically from the LDAP repository. The various components use the LDAP protocol to access the repository and communicate with each other over a JMS-(Java Message Service) compliant bus (DirXmetahub uses IBM's MQSeries as a messaging infrastructure). DirXmetahub's overall architecture is shown in Figure 11.11.

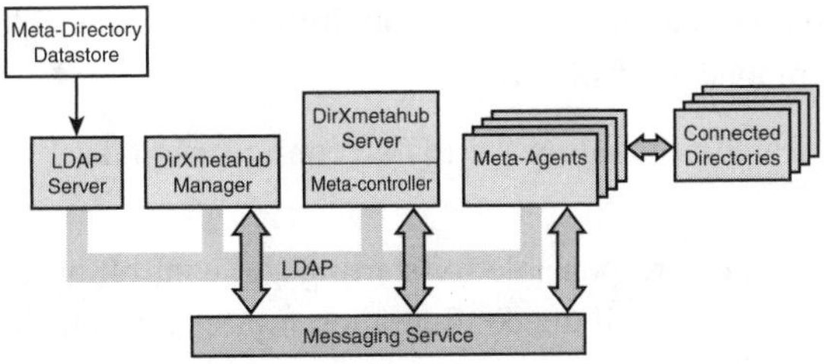

FIGURE 11.11
DirXmetahub is a distributed system where server, agents, and management components communicate over message queues and use a common LDAP repository.

Meta Engine

The DirXmetahub's underlying meta engine consists of three components: the manager, the server and the *meta controller*. Each of these components are discussed in more detail in the next sections.

The DirXmetahub Manager

The manager provides the system administrators with a graphical user interface to do the following:

- Set up the configuration data for all the DirXmetahub components
- Set up the meta information needed for the synchronization processes
- Define, start, and monitor synchronization workflows

The configuration and monitoring information is stored in the LDAP server. To start workflows, the manager interacts over the message queue with the server. Four different views are available for different tasks or skill levels:

- The global view is a high-level, wizard-based tool for dealing with the configuration data.
- The expert view uses a tree and property sheets approach for the same task (Windows Explorer-style).
- The data view is an LDAP access to the metadirectory datastore and helps you follow the results of the synchronizations.
- The monitor view displays the status of running or completed synchronization workflows.
- The manager is an LDAP and message queue-enabled Java application, which can reside on any machine and be present as often as needed in the system.

The DirXmetahub Server

The server is a background process responsible for scheduling, starting, controlling, and monitoring the synchronization workflows performed by the meta controller and the meta agents. It includes exception handling and recovery, and can be present more than once in the system providing for distributed workflows, for example, workflows started by one agent on one machine and continued by another agent on a different machine. It is LDAP and message queue-enabled. The server is implemented as a multithreaded, extensible component container, with the following components available:

- The scheduler, which is based on the LDAP configuration data, starts an instance of the workflow engine.
- The workflow engine is responsible for starting and controlling a workflow. This includes the generation of all the configuration files and eventually the TCL scripts that supply the meta information used by the meta controllers and agents.
- The agent controller is responsible for starting the various executable programs, such as the agents and the meta controllers.
- The status tracker, which monitors and records the status of each running workflow.

The Meta Controller

The meta controller works together with the meta agents, scripts, and configuration files to perform the interdirectory synchronization. It is started by the server, which also automatically generates all the configuration files and TCL scripts out of the LDAP repository, where they have been configured using the graphical interface.

The meta controller is responsible for the core synchronization operations of the metadirectory, including

- Filtering directory objects and attributes
- Mapping attributes between the metadirectory and the connected directory
- Control of authority/ownership policies regarding objects and attributes
- Import and export of information between the metadirectory and the structured files containing the directory information
- Conversion of the structured information files from one format to another
- Manipulation of strings containing attribute values

The meta controller is both the join engine of DirXmetahub as well as an execution environment for synchronization applications. It provides this by incorporating into one executable an LDAP and a DAP client, file parsers and formatters for XML, LDIF, CSV and various other structured files, a TCL interpreter, and making all this functionality available from the command line. Complex TCL applications can be developed using the built-in primitives for:

- Processing meta information
- Processing structured file I/O, including XML and LDIF
- Supporting the directory joins, where the meta controller maps related directory objects from each of the connected directories into a single metadirectory object, then replicates just the pertinent attributes and integrates them into the metadirectory
- Performing LDAP and DAP operations on one or multiple directories in parallel

Namespace Connectors

The namespace connectors—the components that handle connecting to and communicating with each external directory—are described as *meta agents*. A meta agent provides the programmatic interface to a specific type of directory or database. Meta agents are started by the agent controller component in the DirXmetahub server, which dynamically generates all the configuration and meta data necessary for the agent execution out of the LDAP repository. Third-party and customer-built agents can also be integrated into DirXmetahub, because the agent controller can easily start any executable. The necessary configuration information and/or scripts can either be integrated into the repository or provided explicitly in the appropriate form with the new agents.

Some meta agents are designed to connect to a particular type of directory such as those that connect to Windows NT Domain, or Lotus Notes AddressBook. Other meta agents are designed to connect to specific sets of directory or database types, such as ODBC databases or ADSI-compliant directories.

The DirXmetahub metadirectory implementation provides a set of meta agents to communicate with the following directories and databases:

Directory Services

- DirX
- LDAP

Network Directories

- Windows NT Domains
- Active Directory
- Novell NDS

E-mail Directories

- Lotus Notes/Domino
- Microsoft Exchange

Database Directories

- Open database connectivity (ODBC)
- SAP R/3 HR

PBX Directories

- Siemens Hicom domain management system (HDMS)
- Siemens DS-Win

Additional connectors can easily be added to DirXmetahub at various levels of integration and control from the manager:

- At the command line level
- At the configuration files level (which get stored into the LDAP repository and generated at runtime)
- Extensibility of the DirXmetahub user interface (which is XML driven) to reflect the special switches and attributes to control the agents
- Ability to define own wizards through XML configurations, enabling easy set up of workflows for the new agents

Information Management

The DirXmetahub implements its directory information management capabilities at a high abstraction level via a sophisticated object model for configuration and meta information stored in an LDAP repository, and at a lower level of executable meta controllers and meta agents via synchronization profiles (written as TCL scripts) and attribute configuration files. The meta controller synchronizes the connected data sources using the parameters in these scripts and configuration files.

The information flow is controlled by the configuration instructions and parameters contained in the script files and attribute configuration files used by the meta agents during the synchronization process.

Both levels of information management have their justification and advantages:

- The repository-based modeling is the basis for simplifying the management process using wizards, graphical interfaces, parameterized templates, automatic schema import, predefined attribute mappings, and so on. The DirXmetahub server automatically generates fully instantiated lower-level profiles and configuration files needed by the agents and controller.
- The possibility to work directly with the TCL scripts and attribute files, and to provide custom files directly is useful—this provides extra flexibility beyond the object model of DirXmetahub, to quickly customize existing files, to develop opaque synchronization scenarios, or to integrate third-party agents quickly.

The higher-level management is supported by the graphical interface, DirX Manager and its multiple views. Once the object model of the repository is understood, both the global and the expert view are intuitive and self-explanatory. In the rest of this section we will concentrate mainly on the lower-level of information management, which still provides a powerful way to integrate external agents and additional applications.

Schema Mapping

The way the schema in connected directories is mapped, filtered, and the directory information is structured to be exchanged, is controlled in DirXmetahub via the synchronization profiles, attribute configuration files, and the meta agents configuration files.

Synchronization Profiles

A *synchronization profile* specifies how the meta controller implements the designated synchronization activities. The synchronization profile is constructed as a TCL script (or set of TCL scripts) using TCL statements and meta controller commands to delineate the synchronization operations.

This synchronization profile script is subdivided into the *variable*, *mapping*, and *control logic* sections whose contents are dependent on the specific synchronization scenario.

The *variable* section supplies configuration data for the synchronization profile, by employing designated TCL variables (each referred to as a *profile switch*), which set synchronization process parameters. These parameters include

- Name of the source attribute configuration file
- Name of the target attribute configuration file
- Meta controller trace filename
- Trace level for the synchronization process
- Bind and Search parameters for the metadirectory

In the synchronization profile, the *mapping* section provides specifications of the rules for the

- Mapping of objects
- Inclusion and exclusion of objects
- Ownership of objects
- Mapping of attributes
- Inclusion and exclusion of attributes
- Manipulation of attribute values
- Ownership of attributes

The *control logic* section of the synchronization profile contains the specific script code and meta controller operations that are used to perform the directory synchronization process.

At the higher, graphical level of management, the variables are taken care of by the graphical interface, and the mapping by a powerful graphical mapping editor. Even so, direct editing of TCL scripts is supported by a built-in TCL-aware editor, and external scripts can easily be imported into the LDAP configuration store over the GUI.

Attribute Configuration Files

For the meta controller to synchronize the information in a connected directory, a valid *attribute configuration file* for that directory must be available. Attribute configuration files define the set of attributes that exist in a specific connected directory namespace.

Each meta agent has a corresponding attribute configuration file. In this file, one record is written for every attribute that exists within the connected directory, providing a configuration list of all valid attributes within that namespace. An attribute configuration file provides necessary formatting information, which the meta controller uses to process the import and export data files for that connected directory.

To synchronize the connected directory with the metadirectory, the meta controller reads the attribute configuration files for both the metadirectory and the connected directory. The meta controller uses the information in these files to determine the attributes and data file formats to be used in the synchronization process.

At the higher level of management, the information in attribute configuration files is created automatically by importing the schema of connected LDAP directories, or by importing existing configuration files into the LDAP repository. From there it is used to drive the graphical mapping editor and to generate the runtime files.

The Meta Agent Configuration Files

The meta agent, likewise, has configuration files that delineate the meta agent's import and export parameters for the synchronization process.

The name of the configuration files for a meta agent is usually provided on the command line invoking the import or export process. These configuration files set parameters for the synchronization process with the connected directory, including

- The server for the connected directory that is the subject of the import or export operation.
- The category of the directory objects to be imported or exported.
- The specific set of attributes to be imported or exported.
- The degree (full or delta) of the object import or export.
- How integration of imported objects and attributes should be handled—such as deciding the action to take in the case of data conflicts. If imported objects match existing objects, for example, the existing object can either be overwritten completely or updated with the imported data.

Which synchronization parameters are available for a specific connected directory depends on the corresponding meta agent. As with the other configuration files, the meta agent configuration files can also be fully managed through the graphical interface.

Import and Export Data Files

Although the meta controller can do a direct protocol-based synchronization with the LDAP-enabled directories, other directories and databases must use import and export data files for synchronization. These files are used by the meta agents to exchange information with the meta controller. Both the meta controller and meta agents use these files for interim storage of directory information during the synchronization operation.

An import data file employs a specific data format to provide information to the connected directory in a format that it understands. Similarly, each meta agent employs a specific data file format when exporting information from the connected directory.

These data file formats include XML and other tagged file formats such as LDIF, and untagged file formats such as fixed-width tables and character-separated formats. All the supported data file formats used by any of the metametadirectory agents are supported by the meta controller.

Information Filtering

The DirXmetahub filters directory objects (entries) and attributes, allowing administrators to determine which objects and attributes in the connected directories should not be replicated to the metadirectory. Filtering parameters are specified in the mapping section of the synchronization profile, where objects and attributes can be included or excluded from the replication set, or in the DirXmetahub manager graphical mapping editor.

Authoritative Data Source

An essential facet of metadirectory information management is the capability to determine and assign the directory or database that is the owner of any specific piece of information. The data source that maintains the master copy of a piece of data is said to be the *authoritative source* for that data.

Three general approaches to managing authoritative information are defined in the DirXmetahub documentation. These approaches are then mapped to *deployment models*. The three deployment models define the relationship of directory entry (object) ownership between DirXmetahub and the connected directories. These deployment models are

- **The centralized model**—The metadirectory is the central point of administration for the directory objects, and is the owner of the objects. In this model, the metadirectory is the designated owner of all the directory objects, and objects are created or deleted by the DirXmetahub server and then replicated to the connected directories. Either the connected directory or the metadirectory may control attributes.
- **The decentralized model**—The metadirectory is not the owner, and the connected directories are both the owner and administration point for the entry. In this model, the connected directories are responsible for object creation and deletion within their own directory, and the objects are joined and consolidated in the metadirectory datastore. This

constrains the administration of directory entries to the local directory, preserving information ownership and administrative autonomy.

- **The hire-and-fire model**—Both the metadirectory and a connected directory share ownership and administration responsibilities in the management of the directory entry. In this model, a HR database is responsible for the creation and deletion of the object (typically a user object), and after the object is replicated to the DirX metadirectory, the metadirectory is considered the owner of the objects attributes.

Data Synchronization

The DirXmetahub supports both *complete* and *delta* (*differential*) import and export of data for synchronization between the metadirectory and connected directories. The DirXmetahub can directly import from, and export to, any directory that supports either the LDAP, or the DAP, protocol using the meta controller. For all directories that are integrated over meta agents, DirXmetahub supports the import and export of directory information via structured files and file operations.

There are three possible scenarios of interdirectory synchronization supported by DirXmetahub, including

- Exporting directory information from the metadirectory datastore into a connected directory
- Importing information from a connected directory to the metadirectory datastore
- Direct synchronization between connected directories (called *cross synchronization*)

DirXmetahub comes with over twenty preconfigured and easily adaptable default synchronization workflows involving most of the available agent types and structured files, as well as the previously mentioned scenarios. A few typical examples of default workflows are as follows:

- ODBC to metadirectory datastore, full import
- Metadirectory datastore to Active Directory, full export
- Metadirectory datastore to Hicom DMS, full-bidirectional (import, export)
- NDS to metadirectory datastore, delta import

In order to customize one of the default applications for particular requirements, you need to do the following:

> ### Logging and Reporting
> During directory synchronization operations, the DirXmetahub performs detailed logging of all synchronization activities and can provide synchronization reports. All the information is available in the graphical user interface over the monitoring view.

- Copy one or more of the default workflows in the global view of the DirXmetahub Manager and adapt it with the connected directory and workflow wizards to your specific needs. You can, for example, specify configuration information for the servers and use the mapping editor for the mapping of attributes in a specific synchronization.
- If you want to change specific behavior of a workflow, you can access 100% of the functionality of the meta controller and agent features in DirXmetahub's expert view. All parameters and scripts can be accessed, configured, or changed there.
- The expert view can also be used to integrate proprietary agents or to migrate existing scenarios into the system.
- From the global view or the expert view, an administrator can start synchronizations either directly or via schedule. The results are stored automatically as status entries in the configuration database, together with links to a configurable status area in the file system where all generated files are stored (configuration files, data files, trace and report files). This feature is also configurable; for example, you can control which information to save or when these status entries are deleted.

Exporting Directory Information

When exporting directory information from the metadirectory into one of the connected directories, the following steps must occur:

1. The directory administrator creates the synchronization profile (if the DirXmetahub default templates don't match the specific export task). This profile specifies the procedure variables for the export, as well as the attribute mapping rules and format conversion procedures. This profile also supplies the necessary control logic for the export operation.
2. The directory administrator must develop the attribute configuration files for the connected directory and the metadirectory. If the default templates provided with DirXmetahub meet the export requirements, this step is skipped.
3. The export data file that will be imported into the connected directory must be created. To do this, the directory administrator first performs an LDIF export operation on the metadirectory server and then executes the synchronization profile activating the meta controller.
4. Next, the meta controller loads attribute configuration files for both the metadirectory and the connected directory, and parses the LDIF content from the export data file. The meta controller uses the mapping rules and control logic contained in the synchronization profile to convert the export data file content into the format needed by the meta agent that will import it into the connected directory.
5. The directory administrator must provide the meta agent's import configuration file to delineate the import operation parameters used to import the data into the connected directory. Again, templates are provided with DirXmetahub and can be customized as needed.

6. At this point, the directory administrator must execute the meta agent import operation, which parses the export data file and imports the information into the connected directory in the manner specified in the configuration file.

Importing Directory Information

The process of importing directory information into the metadirectory from one of the connected directories, occurs in the following sequence:

1. The directory administrator creates (or selects) the synchronization profile. This profile specifies the procedure variables for the import, the attribute mapping rules, and format conversion procedures to convert the connected directory object and attribute formats into LDAP. This profile also supplies the control logic needed to import the information into the metadirectory.
2. The attribute configuration files for the metadirectory and the connected directory must be selected from the templates (or developed) by the directory administrator.
3. The directory administrator makes (or provides) an import configuration file for the connected directory's meta agent, defining the import operation parameters.
4. At this point, the directory administrator must execute the meta agent export operation on the connected directory that creates the export data file (which will be imported into the metadirectory). This operation also creates a *delta* base file, which can be used in future export operations.
5. The directory administrator now executes the synchronization profile activating the meta controller, which loads the attribute configuration files (for both the connected directory and the metadirectory). The meta controller next binds to the metadirectory, reads the contents of the import data file, and then uses LDAP to import the directory information into the metadirectory server (in compliance with the mapping rules and control logic specified in the synchronization profile.

Note: These import and export steps, which technically are correct, are not so relevant with DirXmetahub V6.0, where the accent is on using the default applications/workflows and the graphical manager to customize them.

Cross Synchronization

The meta controller can facilitate the synchronization of information between two different connected directories without going through the metadirectory at all in a process called *cross synchronization*. The same supporting files—synchronization profile, attribute configuration, meta agent configuration, and export and import data files—are used to implement this process, yet this approach bypasses the metadirectory altogether.

Storing the Data

The DirXmetahub server leverages the underlying LDAP server in the join model as the central metadirectory datastore—the data for all the other connected directories is replicated into the LDAP server. This data integrated through the DirXmetahub into the metadirectory datastore is kept synchronized with the connected directories. When DirX is used as the metadirectory server its database is an ISAM-based threaded implementation—to optimize responsiveness for directory operations, the DIB is mapped to ISAM indexes and records, and commonly accessed data (like access control information) is cached. Both transaction-security and rollback are support by the ISAM database, protecting directory data integrity.

Event Management

All the LDAP directories used by DirXmetahub as its metadirectory datastore provide access to their replication events, either through an LDIF file interface, as DirX does, or over the change log mechanism. This allows the synchronization of the changes in the objects and attributes in the datastore to the connected directory on an event basis. At this time, DirXmetahub is polling the LDAP directories in order to process the events, but trigger mechanisms and event-driven workflows are slated to be supported in the future.

Interdirectory Security

As DirXmetahub leverages the underlying LDAP directory to house the metadirectory data, it also leverages its security capabilities. The standard LDAP security mechanism including SSL/TLS is used for authentication and protocol encrypting, as is the proprietary access control of the various servers. In the case of DirX, the standard X.500 basic access control and simplified access control models are available. Also, various security features of the underlying operating system and messaging middleware are leveraged to protect the information in transit or when stored on disk.

Sun|Netscape iPlanet Meta-Directory

The iPlanet Meta-Directory is designed to integrate information from LDAP-based directories, SQL accessible relational databases, and applications (primarily e-mail). The iPlanet Meta-Directory leverages the iPlanet Directory Server to provide the underlying directory and storage functionality.

iPlanet Meta-Directory is designed to consolidate user identity within the enterprise. User account information from human resources applications, messaging systems, network operating systems, and other enterprise applications can be combined in a unified namespace. It can also provide a single point of sign on so that user access control information can be passed though to connected directories.

Namespace Integration

The iPlanet Meta-Directory structures the information it works with into two distinct namespaces—one of them connects to the external repositories, while the other represents the unified metadirectory namespace. The representation of the connected directories and databases is called the *ConnectorView*. The representation of the integrated objects in the metadirectory is the *MetaView*.

Methods of Integration—The iPlanet Meta-Directory integrates the information stored in directories and databases using the join method, replicating the remote objects and attributes to one or more databases on the iPlanet server.

The MetaView

The MetaView is comprised of the entire set of linked objects. It is the integrated, unified end result of joining the multiple directories or databases represented by their related connector views.

Each object is linked to its corresponding ConnectorView. This link, created in the join process, is the connection between an object in the MetaView and an object in the ConnectorViews, which enables the synchronization of information between the objects represented in each view. This allows for changes made to directory objects in the MetaView to be propagated back to the directory or databases represented in their respective ConnectorViews.

How the information as replicated between the MetaView and the ConnectorViews is based on configuration parameters used by the JoinEngine during the join process. The join process attempts to link objects that exist within the ConnectorViews with an object that exists in the MetaView. By using administrator configured rules, an object will either be added to the MetaView or left unlinked for manual intervention.

Platforms and Dependencies

Platforms:

Windows NT

Dependencies:

iPlanet Directory Server, Perl 5.004-02

Packaging Changes

The iPlanet Meta-Directory is being assimilated with the iPlanet Directory Server and the iPlanet Directory Access Router into a combined package the Sun|Netscape alliance calls the *iPlanet Directory Server Integration Edition*.

ConnectorViews

A ConnectorView is essentially a copy of a set of directory objects that exist in the connected directory. Each entry in the ConnectorView is comprised of a directory object and a subset of its attributes.

The iPlanet Meta-Directory only uses two protocols (LDAP or SQL) to access directory objects from the external directories. Because of this, data sources using another protocols require an extra layer of processing. Accordingly, there are two types of ConnectorViews, based on the protocols used by the connected directory:

- **Direct ConnectorViews** contain objects held in an LDAP-compliant directory (such as Secure Way) or an SQL-compliant relational database (such as Oracle or SQL Server). Because LDAP and SQL are the protocols used by the JoinEngine, the contents of these directories and databases can be directly accessed in the ConnectorView. If the information can be accessed in a Direct ConnectorView, a directory connector is not needed to retrieve the information.
- **Indirect ConnectorViews** describe objects replicated from databases or directories which the metadirectory JoinEngine is not able to access directly via LDAP or SQL, such as Lotus Notes. The information in these repositories is translated to LDAP in the process of being replicated to an Indirect ConnectorView by the directory connector. An Indirect ConnectorView allows the JoinEngine to work with information stored in directories or databases to which the JoinEngine is not able to directly connect.

Scope of Interoperability

The iPlanet Meta-Directory integrates any source that can be accessed via LDAP or SQL. Using the provided directory connectors, the metadirectory can synchronize data with Microsoft Exchange and Lotus Notes. The *Universal Connector* provides a Perl interface to iPlanet Metadirectory, affording a means of connecting any data source that can be accessed via Perl scripts.

Metadirectory Components

In iPlanet, the metadirectory components are described as two types of services that are responsible for integrating information into the metadirectory from the different data stores. These components are

- The *JoinEngine*, which links the entries in the combined namespace. Both the MetaView and the ConnectorViews use the LDAP protocol to communicate with the JoinEngine.
- *Directory connectors*, which are the components responsible for exchanging directory objects and attributes with the external data stores.

The JoinEngine and the directory connectors operate together on the data that is stored in the various repositories to create the ConnectorViews, and then the integrated MetaView.

Meta Engine

The iPlanet meta engine component, the JoinEngine, controls and manages the flow of object and attribute information into and out of the MetaView. The JoinEngine locates the directory objects contained in a ConnectorViews and links each of them into the MetaView.

To join the contents of the ConnectorViews with the related objects in the MetaView, the JoinEngine uses *join rules sets*. These join rules sets are configurable searches performed in sequence, which seek to match objects in the ConnectorViews with objects in the MetaView. The join rules are processed until a match is made; failing that, a specified action can create a new object or leave the ConnectorView object unattached until an administrator can manually link it to a MetaView object.

The essential task of the JoinEngine is to synchronize the information in the MetaView with the corresponding information stored in the connected databases or directories. This synchronization engine monitors for changes that occur in the ConnectorViews, and integrates those changes into the contents held in the MetaView. Similarly, changes that occur in the MetaView are relayed to the ConnectorViews.

Data modification supported by the JoinEngine includes

- **Incremental updates**—Objects in the source databases or directories are updated as they are changed.
- **Object creation and deletion**—An object can be created or deleted in either the MetaView or the ConnectorViews, and the change is reflected in the other view.
- **Object modification**—An object can be changed in the MetaView and the changes are reflected in the related object(s) in any or all the ConnectorViews (and thus the source databases).

Configuring the JoinEngine

JoinEngine components can be configured within the Management Center administrative application to control the flow of information, including filters, join rules, DN mapping rules, attribute flow, and constructed attributes.

How objects are linked between the ConnectorViews and the MetaView relies on the join roles specified in the JoinEngine configuration. During the join process, objects in the MetaView and ConnectorViews are either linked or not, based on whether or not they matched the join rules criteria.

Types of Rules

There are two types of rules that can be used in configuring join rules, distinguished name mapping rules, and constructed attributes:

- **Grammar-based rules**—The JoinEngine has a custom grammar language that can be used to create rules. Join, DN mapping, or constructed attribute rules can be created in compliance with the JoinEngine grammar language.

- **Script-based rules**—The script-based rules are written in a Perl script, which can supply any functionality needed in the conversion or construction of information.

Namespace Connectors

The namespace connectors used by iPlanet are called *directory connectors*. Directory connectors are software agents responsible for replicating data between external data sources and the related Indirect ConnectorView. A directory connector consists of components that manage the configuration of its operation.

These components include

- **Tasks**—Tasks specify how the directory connector should synchronize the connected directory or database with its related connector view.
- **Attribute flow**—Configuration information that specifies how attributes should be contained in the ConnectorView.
- **Default attributes**—Default values used when a source attribute is empty (contains no value), or the attribute is missing.
- **Filters**—Used to specify objects, containers, and or domains that should be excluded from replication.

Each directory connector uses configuration data that specifies which objects should be replicated into the Indirect ConnectorView.

A directory connector can control the flow of objects in both directions between an external datastore and its Indirect ConnectorView.

A directory connector can also filter the objects that are accepted for replication between a connected database or directory and the ConnectorView.

Directory connectors provided with iPlanet's Meta-Directory, include specific connectors for Lotus Notes and Microsoft exchange, as well as a Universal Connector using Perl.

Application-Specific Connectors

Although there are two separate connectors Lotus Notes and Microsoft Exchange, each connector functions in the same way. Both directory connectors support bidirectional replication of data between the application (Lotus Notes or Microsoft Exchange) and the related Indirect ConnectorView.

The connector replicates the changes made to objects in the application (Lotus Notes or Microsoft Exchange) to the corresponding objects maintained in the Indirect ConnectorView. These changes are then replicated to the corresponding objects in the MetaView.

Similarly, every change made to an object in the MetaView is reflected in the ConnectorView for the application, and then replicated back to the application source directory or database.

Universal Connector

Besides the application-specific directory connectors, there is a *Universal Connector* supporting a programming interface based on the Perl language. This Universal Connector can be used to custom configure connections to databases or directories not currently supported by the iPlanet Meta-Directory product.

The Universal Connector supports the bidirectional flow of information between directories and databases and the related Indirect ConnectorViews.

Information Management

The information managed by the iPlanet Meta-Directory can be monitored and managed using iPlanet's Management Center administration tool. In the iPlanet Meta-Directory, the join rules specify how the objects in the MetaView and ConnectorViews are joined, and the distinguished name mapping rules define where in the MetaView namespace that objects are created. Configuration settings that specify the objects and attributes to filter are used by the JoinEngine to filter the information flow.

Schema Mapping

The rules for schema mapping are configured in the JoinEngine, including join rules, distinguished name mapping, and control over attribute flow and information filtering. The critical rules used to map schemas between directories are

- **Join Rules**—Join rules specify the rules for joining MetaView and ConnectorView objects, and can be built via the Join Rule Editor. A join searches the MetaView objects attempting to find a match for an object in a ConnectorView, identifying the specific object in the MetaView to link to the source object. Join rules can be combined into *join rules sets*—ordered sets of joined rules sequentially tested until a join rule succeeds or all fail. Adding objects in a ConnectorView, uses the JoinEngine to search for a match in the MetaView based on existing join rules.
- **Distinguished Name (DN) Mapping Rules**—These rules allow you to control how distinguished names are handled. The DN mapping rules allow you to specify where in the MetaView namespace to create new objects, based on each source object. The JoinEngine concatenates the DN of the source object with the DN of the view location to construct an object's fully qualified DN in the MetaView. *DN Mapping Rule Sets* can be used to group multiple DN mapping rules, to perform multiple rules in sequence. DN mapping rules are unique to each ConnectorView—they can be specified differently for each ConnectorView.

Information Filtering

Object and attribute filtering is controlled by the configuration data, which tells the JoinEngine (if using LDAP or SQL), or the directory connector (in using an Indirect ConnectorView), which objects and attributes to replicate. The filter configuration enables object filtering by specifying the subtree or objects that can be excluded from the MetaView or a ConnectorView. This component allows you to control the replication of information, by specifying the exclusion of objects or entire subtrees, in either the MetaView or the ConnectorView.

Authoritative Data Source

The attribute flow configuration maps attributes between the MetaView and the ConnectorView objects. Specification of an authoritative data source is controlled by the attribute flow rules defined in the configuration parameters of the JoinEngine or directory connectors.

The attributes exchanged between a ConnectorView object and a MetaView object are specified by the *attribute flow rules*. Each attribute flow rule defines the specific attributes exchanged between the linked objects by supplying pairs of attribute names (source and destination) that are to be linked.

Attribute flow rules sets are used to group multiple attribute flow rules for collective and sequential processing.

Two different classes of attributes are

- **Context attributes**—The context of the JoinEngine operation has *context attributes* that are used to specify object ownership, membership, type of operation, and direction of information flow.
- **Entry attributes**—*Entry attributes* refer to the attributes of the source and destination objects, the actual directory data.

Constructed attribute rules enable the creation of new attributes that are built by modifying and combining object information. A constructed attribute is any new attribute not directly specified in the source object, but rather is derived from information in the source object, and written as an attribute in the destination object.

Data Synchronization

iPlanet Meta-Directory performs bidirectional synchronization with linked applications to streamline user administration across disparate directories. Dynamic schema mapping speeds and simplifies interapplication communication. In the iPlanet Directory Server Integration Edition, an included LDAP proxy server acts as a firewall in filtering directory access and reroute LDAP requests to provide fail-over support.

Storing the Data

The iPlanet Meta-Directory software runs on top of iPlanet's LDAP directory server, which stores the metadirectory information. The information contained in the connector views is physically joined and stored in the metadirectory. The directory data is stored in an LDBM database that (initially) contains the entire directory. The iPlanet database can be subdivided and replicated to multiple servers.

Event Management

iPlanet supports system events (for example, data change events)—and employs scripts that can be used by the system events. These scripts are referred to as *event scripts*. The scripts are created in Perl, and must be custom written for the actions required. These scripts provide the events hooks at key information processing points, allowing the scripts to monitor or intervene in the process.

Interdirectory Security

Security is provided in the setup of the user/process accounts on each side of the connection by using existing NOS or directory-specific security assigned to each account by its local security.

Microsoft Metadirectory Services

Microsoft gained an entry into the metadirectory marketplace by leveraging its purchase of ZOOMIT VIA, a metadirectory product developed by the ZOOMIT Corporation. Microsoft renamed ZOOMIT VIA to *Microsoft Metadirectory Services* (MMS) and released its initial version of the metadirectory (MMS 2.1) in December 1999.

Since that initial release, Microsoft has released version 2.2 of MMS, as well as a service pack for the MMS 2.2 product. This latest release of MMS included a specialized management agent optimized for synchronization with Active Directory; this agent takes advantage of Active Directory's advanced replication capability to enhance the integration with MMS.

Platforms and Dependencies

Platforms:

Windows 2000 Advanced Server or Datacenter Server

Dependencies:

Although Active Directory is not required, Microsoft encourages its use as the primary administrative point for objects in the MMS metaverse.

Not a Retail Meta...

Microsoft's metadirectory product is not available as a retail product. Instead, it is only available "to customers who are willing to engage Microsoft Consulting Services, or a trained partner, to assist with their MMS evaluation, solution development, and deployment" (quoted from their Metadirectory Services Roadmap document).

`www.microsoft.com/WINDOWS2000/advancedserver/evaluation/news/bulletins/mmsroadmap.asp`

Namespace Integration

MMS integrates information from the connected directories into two linked logical namespaces called the *connector namespace* (sometimes referred to as the *connector space*) and the *metaverse namespace* (also called the *metaverse*).

Methods of Integration—MMS supports the full join method of integration, replicating objects and attributes from connected directories, and constructing an aggregate object in the metadirectory from this replicated information.

The Connector Namespace

Management agents use the connector namespace as a storage area in which to initially house data imported from connected directories. It is, in essence, a staging area that management agents use for moving information into the metadirectory.

Each external directory is assigned its own area in the connector namespace. Objects from the connected directory are initially imported into its connector namespace area, a process that is controlled by the management agent for that connected directory.

Each connector namespace contains objects referred to as *connectors* and *disconnectors:*

- A **connector object** creates a link between objects in the metaverse and objects in the connected directory, supporting the synchronization process between the connected directory and the metadirectory. Connector objects contain an attribute that has the distinguished name of the corresponding object in the metaverse to which it is connected.
- A **disconnector object** is used to *block* the synchronization between the connected directory and the metadirectory. Disconnector objects do not contain an attribute with the distinguished name of a corresponding object in the metaverse. A disconnector object essentially functions as a placeholder representing an object contained in the connected directory.

The Metaverse Namespace

The portion of the namespace representing the integrated view of the complete set of objects joined from all the connected directories is called the *metaverse*. The metaverse is effectively the operational "metadirectory" as users and applications see and access it.

A single object in the metaverse holds the aggregate of the attributes from the related objects in connected directories. This is a one-to-many relationship—one object in the metaverse maps to many objects in connected directories. Information from source objects in all the connected directories is integrated into a single object in the metaverse.

Although most of the contents contained in the metaverse is imported from the connected directories, you can also have an object in the metaverse which has no corresponding object within any connected directory, or within the connector space itself.

The MMS Directory Tree

Like many other metadirectory services, MMS constructs the information it manages into a hierarchical directory tree. In MMS, the root of the tree is referred to as *The Known Universe*. Directly under the root is the context prefix, which the installing administrator will have to provide, representing the logical beginning of the named objects within the metadirectory.

MMS can be implemented around the X.500 naming standards, or around the Domain Name System standards, as each of them defines a hierarchical directory tree structure to contain entries.

Scope of Interoperability

Microsoft Metadirectory Services can integrate a range of directory services, applications, and databases. Supported directories include Netscape Directory Service, Novell NDS, NetWare Bindery, Windows NT, Active Directory, Banyan VINES, as well as LDAP directories.

MMS also integrates with e-mail applications, such as Novell GroupWise, Microsoft Exchange, Microsoft Mail, Lotus Notes, and cc:Mail. Enterprise applications such as PeopleSoft and SAP, and database servers, including Oracle, SQL Server, and ODBC-compliant databases can also be managed.

Metadirectory Components

The architecture of Microsoft Metadirectory services is logically organized around the following set of components, which work together to form a metadirectory system:

- The *metadirectory* itself, which integrates the information from all the connected directories. It is divided into two related logical namespaces called the *connector namespace* and the *metaverse namespace*.
- MMS uses namespace connectors called *management agents* to manage the metadirectory information import and export process.
- The management agents exchange information with the *connected directories*, which can be one of a range of information repositories (directory, database, and so on).

MMS is based on a client/server model, providing access to the metadirectory, via LDAP-based or HTTP-based clients. The clients include

- The *administrative client* application, which provides management of the metadirectory.
- The *user client* application, which provides access to the directory information stored in the metadirectory—the contents of the metaverse.

Meta Engine

The meta engine is responsible for employing the management agents to control synchronization between each of the connected directories and the metadirectory. The management agents actually perform most of the integration and synchronization operations required to join the information in the metadirectory.

The management agents provide the meta-engine with the instruction it needs to manage object creation and deletion, as well as maintain the integrity of the attribute information. The management agents are also responsible for controlling the relationships between objects in the metadirectory and the connected directory.

Namespace Connectors

Management agents are the MMS namespace connectors, and are primarily responsible for data synchronization between the metadirectory and a specific connected directory.

In a nutshell, the management agents are responsible for moving data into, and moving data out of, the connected directory and the metadirectory. Each management agent is responsible for importing the information from a connected directory into the connector namespace. It is also responsible for synthesizing and merging the information imported from the connected directory with the existing objects in the metaverse namespace.

The management agents in MMS are special objects that reside on the metadirectory server; they contain information that describes how each specific connected directory is to be integrated with the metadirectory. A management agent defines the method in which the metadirectory and connected directory communicate, including the flow rules, transformation rules, control scripts, attribute ownership, and configuration parameters.

These management agents are namespace specific—supporting a single directory. Consequently, the configuration of the management agent differs for each specific connected directory. The management agent's configuration information includes the specifications of how to process information exported by the designated connected directory, as well as how the attributes are mapped between the connected directory and the metadirectory.

Default Management Agents

The following management agents are included with MMS 2.2:

- **Directories**—LDAP, Novell NDS, NetWare Bindery, Netscape Directory Service, as well as Windows NT, Active Directory, and Banyan VINES
- **E-mail applications**—Novell GroupWise, Microsoft Exchange, Microsoft Mail, Lotus Notes, Domino and cc:Mail
- **Enterprise Applications**—PeopleSoft, SAP, ERP
- **Databases**—Oracle, SQL Server, ODBC-based databases, and databases accessed through OLE/DB
- **Data formats**—XML, DSML, LDIF, CSV and other character delimited file formats

Microsoft provides a wizard in Service Pack 1 for MMS 2.2 to enable customizing access to XML, DSML, LDIF, CSV and other types of file formats. New types of management agents can be developed to communicate with sources of directory information beyond those supported by default in MMS.

Operating Modes

MMS management agents have three different operating modes, which effectively specify where a metadirectory object can be created or deleted. These three modes are

- **Reflector**—Creation or deletion of an object in a connected directory is reflected in the connector namespace as well as the metaverse namespace.
- **Creator**—Creation or deletion of an object in the metaverse namespace is automatically extended to the connected directory, where the same operation is conducted.
- **Association**—Creation or deletion of an object in a connected directory causes it to be added to the connector namespace, yet is *not* integrated with the metaverse namespace.

Depending on which mode is used, the administration point from which the objects can be managed differs. This object management determination is divided into two approaches:

- **Localized**—If the object can be managed only at the connected directory it is referred to as a *local management* (or *distributed management*). This approach allows local administrators of directory or database resources to retain control and ownership of the information. Both association mode and reflector mode are locally managed.
- **Centralized**—If the object can be managed only at the metadirectory, is referred to as *central management*. This approach allows centralized directory administrators to control the creation and deletion of directory information.

Although the operating mode of the management agents specifies in which directory object creation or deletion can occur, the attributes of the objects can be changed in *either* directory, irrespective of the operating mode of the management agent. Thus in either mode, the specific information that needs to be controlled by the different departments or divisions of an enterprise can be managed by specifying the control over the attribute's authoritative source in the attribute flow rules.

MMS Clients

MMS supports LDAP and HTTP clients for metadirectory access and administration.

Administrative Client—*Compass* is the MMS administrative client, which uses LDAP to communicate with the metadirectory. This administration tool provides access to the data used to configure and manage MMS, as well as the managed information. Because MMS supports LDAP, any LDAP application can access the information stored in the metadirectory. In addition, MMS can be managed over the HyperText Transfer Protocol (HTTP). Through its support for HTTP, MMS enables access to (and management of) the directory information using a Web browser.

Directory Client Applications—Besides support for all LDAP-based client applications, MMS supports using HTTP, allowing the use of Web browsers for end-users to access the metadirectory.

Information Management

The MMS information flow begins with each management agent creating objects (extending the schema if necessary) in its portion of the connector namespace for each of the objects which exists in the connected directory. This occurs for each connected directory that is to be integrated into the metadirectory.

Schema Mapping

Each connected directory has its objects and attributes mapped to its own designated area of the connector namespace. The management agents for each of the other connected directories, then attempt to map the objects and attributes from the connector namespace to the objects and attributes existing in the metaverse namespace.

The management agents use a template language that can:

- Specify which metadirectory objects should be excluded or included during an update
- Do direct, simple attribute modifications
- Employ built-in functions to do attribute transformations.
- Use conditional control structures to direct the template execution
- Gain additional data from other metadirectory objects

This part of the process is what Microsoft refers to as the *join*—as each of the objects in the connector namespace is joined with (integrated with) a specific object in the metaverse namespace. This joining, or integrating of objects is based around a common unique identifier of some sort contained in an attribute the objects share.

When a link has been established between an object in the connector namespace and the corresponding object in the metaverse namespace, the object is joined. This join is not only between the two metadirectory namespaces, but also indirectly with the connected directory. *Join criteria* can be specified to allow directory objects to be joined automatically, or the administrator can directly initiate the join. The administrator determines the order in which connected directories have their schema mapped from the connector namespace to the metaverse namespace.

Managing the Join

The Compass administration tool enables the specification of a *batch join* option that automatically joins objects using specified criteria. An automated batch join process, for example, can integrate a connecting directory for the first time (commonly in association mode). To enable automatic joins, the join criteria (the rules for how they join, which attributes have to match, and so on) must first be defined.

A *Configure the Join* interface is supplied by both the *Join Action* option in the MMS Compass administration tool, as well as within the management agents. This interface allows you to configure the rules that will be used to join an object in the connector namespace with an object in the metaverse namespace. The batch join can be executed via the *join action* in the Compass administration tool.

The join action uses the search attributes specified in the interface to examine every disconnector in the connector namespace to search for object matches in the metaverse namespace, and uses a set of inclusion rules to assess acceptable join options. If an appropriate match is found, a link is established automatically between the objects.

The process of joining of the objects in the connector namespace with the metaverse namespace may result in a failed join (no match with objects in the metaverse) and the resultant disconnector objects.

During batch join operations, exceptions to the specified join criteria are inevitable, causing objects to be left unjoined (remaining as disconnectors). MMS includes an *Account Joiner* program to handle these objects that are not compliant with the join criteria, and are left unjoined.

The Account Joiner program searches the metaverse for an object which matches, or makes a new object in the metaverse namespace to match the object. You can define rules dynamically with the Account Joiner, and try different search criteria until a matching metaverse object is found.

Schema Extension

Administrators may discover that they need to extend the MMS schema when a connected directory contains attributes for which no match exists in the metadirectory. The schema can be extended by creating new object classes or attributes in the same way that you would create other new entries in the metadirectory, using one of the two following methods:

- Administrators can modify the schema by directly creating or deleting an object class or an attribute. These new schema entries can either be created by using the MMS Compass administrative tool, or by the creation of external files with the new object or attribute definitions, and importing them with a schema utility.
- Management agents can automatically extend the MMS schema by creating new attributes in the metadirectory whenever they discover attributes in a connected directory that do not exist in the metadirectory.

Information Filtering

Directory information is filtered by the management agents that specify the metadirectory objects to be excluded or included during an update. While configuring the join, objects can be selected or excluded from the join process.

The Compass administration tool is used to configure the filtering. It allows join rules to be specified, join actions to be defined, and enables flexibility in filtering of directory information.

Authoritative Data Source

The *attribute flow rules* determine which directory is authoritative for each attribute. When the value in an attribute from a connected directory differs from the value contained in the metadirectory, the attribute flow rules determine which value to use.

When the value of an authoritative attribute in the metaverse namespace is changed, the management agents for each connected directory update the attributes in the connector namespace, and then synchronize each connected directory with the new information.

After the join of the objects is complete, the administrator can specify which connected directory will be authoritative for the values that the attributes hold. Attribute flow rules are effective only for directory objects when the object containing the attribute has been joined in the metaverse namespace.

MMS provides a graphical interface for configuring the attribute flow between the metadirectory and the connected directories. This point-and-click interface simplifies the assignment of authoritative sources on the metadirectory for attributes shared between connected directories.

The ability to simply assign the authoritative source for each of the attributes in the directory is a significant advantage for directory administrators chartered with addressing the organizational, political, and ownership issues regarding control of the directory information.

The attribute flow rules are stored as properties of the management agent object. When you have more than one management agent that updates a specific object in the metaverse, the attribute flow rules must specify which directory is authoritative for each attribute.

Data Synchronization

A management agent is a service that establishes synchronization of the metadirectory with the connected directories. The management agent specifies how the synchronization is supposed to be carried out, as well as actually performing the synchronization processes between their specific connected directories and the metadirectory.

The Synchronization Process

The Microsoft Metadirectory Services uses a multiple phase synchronization methodology. The synchronization process is structured in three distinct phases:

- **Discovery**—During the discovery phase of the synchronization cycle, directory information is imported from the source connected directory.
- **Synchronization**—Import templates and attribute flow rules are used to assess the scope of changes that must be synchronized, and the directory information is processed and stored in the connector namespace.
- **Update** —Information resulting from this integration into the metaverse, which then must be *updated* into the connected directory, is then processed through the *export template*.

The synchronization phase uses import templates and attribute flow rules to assess the scope of changes that must be synchronized with both the metadirectory and connected directory. During the synchronization phase, the directory information is processed through a *parsing template* and a *connector namespace construction template* and stored in the connector namespace area for that specific connector directory.

These entries are processed through a *metaverse construction template,* which compares the entries in a connector namespace to the corresponding entries in a metaverse namespace. The rules specified in the templates are used to resolve and integrate the information into the metaverse namespace.

MMS management agents are designed to handle many of the default attributes specified in the corresponding directory's schema. The scripts and templates used during the synchronization cycle can be edited and modified to fit your specific application requirements for the directory integration.

Transforming Data During Synchronization

A basic function of a management agent is to import directory information updates from its connected directory, and export updates from the metadirectory back to the connected directory. Although occasionally the direct transfer of attribute values is all that is required to update the directory information, more commonly the data must be transformed to comply with the receiving directory's requirements.

Data synchronization factors that should be considered include

- Either the metadirectory or the connected directory may have objects that should not be imported.
- There may not be an exact match for a given attribute.
- For the object to be unique within the metadirectory namespace, additional metadirectory information might be required for the attribute.
- The format of the existing data in the connected directory can be different than the format required by the metadirectory.
- There might not be a one-to-one relationship between the attribute data—more than one connected directory attribute may be required to complete the metadirectory attribute.

The rules for how management agents export and import attribute values are specified in templates written in a scripting language. In MMS, the `IMPORTT` program is used to interpret the template's instructions for the export or import of the metadirectory data.

Storing the Data

The MMS database stores the information contained in the MMS directory tree. This database can be distributed between multiple MMS servers. Future releases of MMS are expected to further leverage Active Directory's data storage mechanism.

Event Management

MMS handles change management via a polling mechanism—MMS periodically compares the contents of the metadirectory and a connected directory. Polling is performed according to a set schedule.

There are two fundamental ways in which the contents of the metadirectory and a connected directory can differ:

- Objects can exist in one directory, but not in the other.
- Objects that exist in both the directories may contain different values for an attribute.

If MMS encounters either of these states, it performs the appropriate data updates.

Novell DirXML

DirXML provides what are essentially metadirectory services, although Novell doesn't call it a metadirectory. They refer to it as a "data sharing and synchronization service." Whatever you call it, DirXML offers an interesting way to perform cross directory integration.

DirXML sits at the center of an information exchange system in which a variety of data repositories are connected to NDS eDirectory. By going through DirXML, the connected directories can communicate with any other connected namespace.

DirXML lets one directory communicate its changes to any of a number of other directories, and trigger actions in those directories if appropriate.

DirXML is built around XML, allowing a considerable amount of flexibility in data transformations and thus enhancing the overall capabilities of the metadirectory. XML provides a highly customizable framework within which to manage multiple data sources while automating repetitive IT tasks.

The connected data sources can be dynamically queried to create address books, differential directories for internal and external use, and so on.

Platforms and Dependencies

Platforms:

DirXML can run on any platform on which NDS eDirectory runs, including NetWare 5 (or later), Linux, Solaris, Tru64 Unix, Windows 2000, Windows NT, AIX (late 2001).

Dependencies:

eDirectory must be running on the server that is running DirXML.

Namespace Integration

DirXML uses eDirectory to supply data synchronization between multiple directories and disparate data sources. The selected objects and attributes from the connected datasources are contained in the eDirectory namespace, and are represented as objects and attributes in the eDirectory DIT.

Methods of Integration—DirXML fully supports the join method of integrating information from multiple connected directories or other information repositories. Objects containing the aggregate of the attributes from the related objects in the connected directories are stored in the eDirectory DIB, and are replicated and synchronized with all the relevant connected directories and other data sources.

Scope of Interoperability

DirXML uses namespace connectors called *drivers*, or *driver shims,* to connect to, and synchronize with, the various directories, databases, and other data sources.

These drivers ship with DirXML 1.0:

- Active Directory
- Exchange
- eDirectory
- Lotus Notes
- LDAP (iPlanet Directory Server, IBM SecureWay Directory, Innosoft Directory, Critical Path InJoin Directory)
- NT Domain
- Delimited Text

Drivers available for separate purchase from Novell include

- PeopleSoft
- JDBC (Supports: Oracle, Microsoft SQL Server, IBM DB2 Universal Database)

Novell has partnered with Nexor to develop DirXML connectors to X.500 directories and expects to have these connectors available by the end of 2001. Customized DirXML drivers for applications, databases, or directories can also be developed in Java or C++ with an SDK available from Novell.

The Role of XML

The *eXtensible Markup Language (*XML), and its related components, the *eXtensible Stylesheet Language* (XSL) and *XSL Transformations* (XSLT), are at the core of the information management system used in DirXML.

XML is used to represent the directory objects in each directory in a universal translation language for manipulation by DirXML. The DirXML technology creates an application-specific view of the information stored in a connected directory by the use of specific directory namespace drivers.

DirXML uses XML rules and style sheets to manage the translation of data between the connected directories. DirXML rules are a series of XML tags representing operations that can be taken by the DirXML engine to transform the data. These operations are schema mapping, object creation, object placement, and object matching.

XSLT is used to describe the transformation of XML documents (which are represented internally as a tree modeled on the document XML hierarchy). The events and data transformations are represented in XSLT. Customized routines can also be described in XSLT and can replace the basic operations.

XML is used to store the business rules that are used to transform data and trigger events in connected directories. Data change events are also described in XML documents. XML rules that determine the processing of these change events are stored in the directory as XML documents as well. The commands used to perform data transformations for synchronization are also represented in these documents.

Configuration information regarding the DirXML driver shim is stored in XML documents in the directory. This information includes names and locations of the server holding the connected directory, authentication information, and so on.

Replication of the information stored in an application view is performed via an XML processor. XSL, a vocabulary used to describe formatting semantics, is used in this process to transform XML documents. Through this XML/XSL processor, DirXML customizes the data it handles to fit the needs of the application.

DirXML uses an industry standard programmatic representation of XML that provides faster processing of XML data than when using serialized XML (standard XML text files).

Metadirectory Components

Like other metadirectory solutions, DirXML uses a meta engine to perform integration operations and namespace connectors to communicate with foreign namespaces.

The three major components to DirXML are

- **eDirectory**—eDirectory holds data shared by the connected directories and supplies security, event management, and synchronization services.
- **DirXML Engine**—The DirXML engine provides the framework for running driver shims and controls the data synchronization process.
- **DirXML Driver Shim**—The driver shim acts as the *connector* and communicates data changes between the connected directory and DirXML. The driver shim can be written to use standards, such as LDAP, or proprietary APIs.

eDirectory

DirXML uses eDirectory as its data repository. The data that is integrated from the connected directories is held in eDirectory where it can easily be shared with those same directories. This allows the leveraging of the eDirectory event system to notify DirXML changes to its objects in real-time.

eDirectory sits at the center of hub-and-spoke style replication, allowing connected directories to synchronize data with each other via DirXML.

Access to objects in the connected directories is controlled by eDirectory's security mechanisms. Data flow in and out of the directory via driver shims is restricted without the appropriate access rights.

Meta Engine

The DirXML Engine is the underlying meta engine that handles interdirectory communication and synchronization. DirXML is capable of using complex business logic during the XML transformation process, triggering a customized set of actions in a number of connected directories based on a single change in one.

As information passes into DirXML it is translated into XML. XML rules and style sheets convert the data into the appropriate data format for the target directory. During this conversion process XML rules are applied to transform objects and events as needed. The DirXML Engine then replicates those changes (now repackaged as commands) to the connected directories.

Namespace Connectors

DirXML namespace connectors are called *driver shims* or *drivers*. The driver shim sits between the DirXML engine and the connected directory and provides application-specific methods, which the DirXML engine can then call. The interface methods used between the DirXML engine and the driver shim mostly take XML documents as parameters and return XML documents.

The driver shim reports object events changes from its directory to DirXML. When a shim is made aware of a change, it constructs an XML document describing that change. The document is sent to the DirXML engine, which processes it and sends the resulting commands to other driver shims.

The driver shim uses an application-specific method of discerning changes in the directory. Connected applications and directories may have an event system; if not, the driver shim can poll the application or read a change log file to check for changes.

Each driver object has an *event cache* in which object change events are stored. This allows changes that should be processed by DirXML to be saved even when the DirXML engine or needed driver shim is not running. An object change event identifies the object, the type of change, and the new values of the changed information.

DirXML includes an SDK to allow the creation of custom connectors, for applications not included from Novell. DirXML drivers can be created in Java and C++.

eDirectory Objects Used for DirXML

A series of directory objects are created to manage DirXML:

- `DirXML-driver-Set`—This is a container object holding the complete set of application drivers on the server. Contains DirXML-driver objects.
- `DirXML-driver`—This container object is used to hold the configuration for one driver shim. Contains a DirXML-publisher and DirXML-subscriber object, as well as DirXML-rule and DirXML-stylesheet objects. The configuration attributes identify the DirXML rules to be used in data transformation and identify and configure the drivers shim itself.
- `DirXML-subscriber`—A container object for the configuration information regarding the subscriber (outbound) synchronization channel. The DirXML-subscriber container has DirXML-rule and DirXML-stylesheet objects, along with filter and rule information.
- `DirXML-publisher`—This container holds the same information set as the DirXML-subscriber container, just pertaining to the publisher (outbound) synchronization channel.
- `DirXML-rule`—This object contains a single DirXML rule in the form of an XML document. This rule is either the create, placement, matching, or schema mapping rule.
- `DirXML-stylesheet`—This object contains a DirXML rule implemented as an XSLT script.

Information Management

The flow of information between DirXML and the connected directory is managed by a combination of filters and DirXML rules. Each DirXML rule performs a single transformation on an XML document.

There are two types of DirXML rules:

- The rules describing well-defined tasks such as object creation and placement, as well as schema mapping and object matching. use an XML vocabulary developed by Novell for DirXML.
- Arbitrary transformations, such as changing the event type or data format, are described via XSLT transformation instructions. XSLT transforms can be swapped in to replace the standard method of doing well-defined tasks.

A series of applied rules transforms the events on a publisher channel into a command on a subscriber channel. When a data change event is processed by a sequence of DirXML rules, an XML document containing a set of commands is produced.

The XML document describing the change to be made is sent to the target directory or application, which makes those changes in its datastore. If any of those changes affect information for which the connected directory server is the authoritative data source, the target directory will send the information back to DirXML. The DirXML engine again transforms that data as needed to trigger changes in other connected applications and directories.

By using XML transformations, the format of data can be changed as needed between applications. One type of event can be changed to another (or several others) using the XML data transformation process. This means that when employee leaves the company a status change in the HR application can trigger the removal of some accounts, the revoking of privileges in other accounts, and the disabling of others.

A given rule is linked to a `DirXML-Subscriber` or `DirXML-Publisher` object if it is only used on one channel for a particular driver shim. If a rule is used on both the subscriber and publisher channels for a particular shim, it will be referenced by the `DirXML-Driver` object instead.

Schema Mapping

There are effectively two parts to DirXML's schema mapping process. Associations on eDirectory objects are used to relate objects in separate directories with each other, and the actual schema mapping must be performed.

Schema Mapping Rules

Schema mapping between eDirectory and the connected directory is done via *schema mapping rules* associated with driver shims. These rules, like much of DirXML's configuration files, are XML or XSLT documents.

On installation of a new driver, schema mappings must be done so that the directories will know how to associate the objects. First, the eDirectory schema is imported into DirXML. Then the driver shim supplies its directory's schema and a simple mapping is done. This mapping can be customized. There is a schema mapping wizard to facilitate the setup process.

DirXML Associations

A DirXML *association* is a list of pointers to information in connected directories. When DirXML is installed, a DirXML association is attached to every eDirectory object, allowing one or more objects in other directories to be associated with it.

A single directory object can be associated with an object in any of the connected name spaces, allowing one-to-one and one-to-many mappings. There are no arbitrary limits on the types of objects between which associations may be formed.

The `DirXML-association` attribute is multivalued and has the following components:

- **Driver object DN—**The name of the driver shim to be used.
- **Application key value—**A value that uniquely identifies an object within the connected application's object set.
- **State—**The current state of the association, such as associated, disabled, and pending. The state is represented as an integer value.

The connected directory supplies the value for the association, which is unique to that directory. This allows any entry in the connected application to serve as the connection point for one or more objects in the metadirectory.

DirXML Information Filtering

The filtering of objects and attributes is done on the publisher and subscriber channels, which are used to exchange information. Each channel has a filter that specifies the types of information that should be passed through it. A filter is expressed as a query and is easily customized to define the exact data to be synchronized.

Authoritative Data Source

A critical concern when combining multiple data sources is maintaining data ownership. DirXML allows information ownership to be maintained by the underlying namespace ensuring that information is only changed by the source with the authority for that information. The selection of the authoritative data source for any given piece of data can be made at the attribute level.

Flexibility and granularity of source authority is established in DirXML by the selection of publisher or subscriber channel:

- If the *publisher* channel is used, then the repository that is publishing it to DirXML is the authoritative source.
- If the *subscriber* channel is used, then DirXML is relating the information from a source authority to another directory.

This means that DirXML objects can be comprised of attributes from many objects in a number of different directories. The objects, with all the common data, are held in eDirectory, which updates all the connected directories except for the authoritative source. The authoritative source in turn is the only one allowed to change in the information managed by DirXML.

Data Synchronization

DirXML Engine controls the data synchronization process. During synchronization, the DirXML engine provides the framework for the XML rules to run in, while the driver shims are responsible for reporting changes to DirXML.

Note that one DirXML driver shim can make a change that triggers an event in one or more other DirXML driver shims. This means that a single administrator initiated event can cause any number of additional events to take place in connected directories, and ultimately perhaps in the initiating directory as well.

The flow of information in DirXML is processed via assigned channels, and DirXML uses two types of channels including

- **Publisher—**Moves information from a connected directory into eDirectory
- **Subscriber—**Carries information from eDirectory to the connected namespace

Each connected directory can use either the publisher or subscriber channel, or both, if bidirectional information flow is desired. Bidirectional synchronization is usually used with DirXML, although unidirectional synchronization can be performed if desired.

Subscriber Channel

The subscriber channel moves data from the eDirectory server to a connected directory/application. The information flow on a subscriber channel is

1. An object change event occurs on the object on eDirectory server. This can be any type of change, made by any method (administrator change, replication, other DirXML shim).
2. The XML engine looks at each driver's subscription filter. If the object complies with this filter, then the event is cached.
3. Each event is read from the event cache in sequence, with the DirXML engine building XML documents that describes the event for each driver shim.
4. XML rules are sequentially applied to the XML documents. If, during processing, the document becomes empty (that is, all data has been removed by the previously applied rules) processing stops on that data change.
5. Each XML document has been transformed to a series of commands, to be passed to the driver shim.
6. The XML document is interpreted by the driver shim, which then invokes its native API for its application.

Publisher Channel

Publisher channel data flow is

1. Information is changed in the connected directory.
2. The driver shim detects that a change has occurred.
3. The event is compared to the publisher filter—if the event matches the filter, an XML document is constructed to describe the event and handed to the DirXML engine.
4. The DirXML engine applies the XML rules in sequence, transforming it to a series of commands—if all data is processed out by the rules, creating an empty document, the event is discarded.
5. The DirXML engine in examines the XML document and makes the corresponding changes in eDirectory.

Storing the Data

DirXML stores the integrated data that it manages in NDS eDirectory so that it can take advantage of NDS's data management mechanisms. Although DirXML can also use the storage of the underlying directories if desired, this is not the usual approach.

Event Management

DirXML can take advantage of eDirectory's robust event engine to provide provisioning capabilities within the connected systems. DirXML rules and stylesheets can perform complex data transformations and trigger events in many linked systems based on a single event.

Consider that, by writing business rules that describe hire-and-fire processes and linking those rules with actions taken on accounts in the human resources database, many related account management tasks can take place automatically. When an employee is hired, DirXML stylesheets can describe how to create standard account names in connected directories, as well as assign security groups and configuration settings, grant network permissions, and so on.

When an employee is fired, the single act of changing employment status in the HR directory can again trigger a chain of events that will result in all accounts and permissions being revoked immediately. This greatly reduces security risks, as well as automating repetitive management tasks.

Throughout this process data ownership is maintained. Although eDirectory instructs all the connected directories on how to construct the user accounts, it does not consider its data authoritative. Rather, once the connected directory takes its actions, creating an e-mail account, for example, it returns its data to DirXML, which considers the (e-mail account) information authoritative. eDirectory stores this information, and also takes any actions triggered by the creation of an e-mail account.

Interdirectory Security

Security for information handled by DirXML and stored in eDirectory is implemented by eDirectory's native security mechanisms. For authentication and access control, NDS eDirectory implements a proprietary set of security mechanisms based on the Public Key Infrastructure (PKI), supporting X.509-compliant certificates and certificate authorities. eDirectory also supports Internet security protocols such as SSL/TLS, using them to provide a secure communications channel between an eDirectory server and client.

Radiant Logic RadiantOne VDS

RadiantOne Virtual Directory Server (VDS) offers an innovative approach to data access, by integrating data from relational databases and directory sources into a virtual LDAP directory namespace. As an LDAP server, VDS Server can, of course, connect to and integrate other LDAP-compliant directory services. That's not really the primary purpose of RadiantOne VDS, however; what RadiantOne VDS is *really* about is databases.

Where RadiantOne's approach is unique in its focus on mapping information contained in relational databases to an LDAP tree. The Virtual Directory Server provides LDAP applications with transparent access to near real-time enterprise data stored in their many existing relational databases. None of the current data storage strategies needs to change—the server simply provides an LDAP interface to all the enterprise data stored in back-end relational databases. To perform the needed mapping, VDS Server employs a unique addressing scheme (called *Information Resource Locators*) to access the information stored in relational databases across the network.

The VDS Server accesses and aggregates the information stored in the databases and directories, but avoids transforming, converting, or replicating the data. Because the information is stored in its original source databases, the relationship information between objects in the datastores remains intact, unchanged by RadiantOne's integrating it into an LDAP directory namespace.

Namespace Integration

RadiantOne VDS integrates information from the connected databases and directories via brokering—creating a virtual directory. This means that VDS Server doesn't maintain any data store of its own, and instead stores a link to the information's location in the source directory or database. This link serves as an effective address for the location of the data referenced by the link.

Because much of the data referenced by VDS Server is in relational databases, a method of addressing discrete data fields had to be implemented. Radiant Logic came up with an addressing scheme where each data record is individually referenced by an *Information Resource Locator (IRL).*

VDS Server tracks information in the databases by constructing a form of address for each part of the data as an IRL. The IRL essentially maps a database record into an LDAP URL, such that a data record can be accessed via common Internet protocols.

These locators are used to retrieve the information that they reference from the relational database. When the virtual directory server is responding to a LDAP query for information in its LDAP directory namespace, these addresses are used to retrieve the set of information from the back-end relational databases to fulfill the requirements of the query.

Platforms and Dependencies

Radiant Logic has different platform requirements and dependencies depending on the kind of deployment for the RadiantOne VDS.

Platforms:

LDAP or Web Deployment—Windows NT, Windows 2000 Server

Developer Deployment—Windows 98, Windows NT, Windows 2000

Dependencies:

LDAP Deployment—An LDAP directory (iPlanet or SecureWay), RadiantOne Plug-In and Microsoft Data Access Components 2.5

Web Deployment—Microsoft Internet Information Server 4, and Microsoft Data Access Components 2.5

Developer Deployment—Microsoft Internet Information Server 4 or Personal Web Server, and Microsoft Data Access Components 2.5

At installation, RadiantOne VDS Server allows the administrator to integrate the selected relational databases and/or LDAP directories. This virtual directory server builds a directory tree using a logical join of the information stored in all the external datastores, merging the selected information into a single, logically unified LDAP DIT.

Methods of Integration—The VDS Server operates solely as an information broker—it does not create or maintain local copies of data, nor does it replicate the information into a common datastore. The RadiantOne server maintains links to the directory information located in all connected databases or LDAP directories. VDS Server intercepts all LDAP queries for data within its virtual directory structure transparently, and routes the LDAP requests for a directory information to the connected directories. VDS Server then compiles all the directory responses, and provides the results back to the requesting LDAP client.

One of the advantages of this brokering based, virtual directory approach is that it leverages the real-time data, which is contained within the relational databases existing on enterprise networks (and supporting enterprise operations). Each LDAP query submitted to the RadiantOne virtual directory server accesses the current information, as it is stored in the relational database (or LDAP-compliant directory).

A Virtual Directory...

It is worth noting that Radiant Logic says in its product information that RadiantOne VDS is not a classic directory solution, noting that it is not intended to supplant either the enterprise or metadirectory. It is rather meant to access data that resides in relational databases via LDAP, and in the context of an LDAP tree. (Source: "The Virtual Directory Server: A pragmatic approach to directory deployment," January 2000.)

Scope of Interoperability

RadiantOne is designed to have a specific scope of interoperability. It doesn't attempt to replace the enterprise directory or the metadirectory, but rather augments the namespace integration with a LDAP directory server that integrates all the relational databases on enterprise network into its LDAP directory tree. It then allows multiple different directory views of that information to be constructed dynamically, enabling the modeling and testing of different LDAP directory tree structures.

RadiantOne VDS Server can communicate with external data sources and services using:

- **Relational databases**—SQL, OLE/DB, ODBC, and JDBC.
- **LDAP v3**—Directory plug-ins are provided for Sun|Netscape iPlanet or IBM Secure Way. VDS Server provides LDAP v.3 compliant referrals to connected directories.

- **Active Directory Services Interfaces** (ADSI)
- **Java Naming and Directory Interface** (JNDI)
- **Wireless**—WAP and the PALM PQA can access RadiantOne VDS directory information.
- **Application platforms**—Lotus Notes, Microsoft Exchange, SAP, PeopleSoft.

RadiantOne VDS supports the eXtensible Markup Language (XML) for import and export of information, encapsulating information into XML objects to ease data transformation and eventual integration.

Metadirectory Components

Compared to metadirectories, RadiantOne VDS uses a different set of core components to supply its virtual LDAP directory service. The primary functionality of the VDS Server is provided by

- The *Virtual Directory Server* (or *VDS Server*) provides brokering of queries to content in the source databases.
- *Intelligent Object Mapping and Cache (IOMC)* speeds location and access to the data by rapidly responding to queries in the RadiantOne cache, or referring queries to the location in the source directory if needed.

Meta Engine

The RadiantOne VDS server acts as the meta-engine, processes the LDAP queries for access to content in its LDAP namespace, translates the LDAP request into SQL query, and directs (brokers) those queries to the content in the source relational databases.

RadiantOne's handling of queries can provide query results in multiple formats (LDAP, ADO, or XML), and can also return the SQL syntax required for a query when using a database interface. Applications accessing the RadiantOne VDS can select the query result format needed for the application's operations. Query results can also be supplied in Directory Services Markup Language (DSML) format, to facilitate communication with DSML-enabled applications.

The VDS Server supports the mapping of object relationships, mirroring their relationships in the database, and automatically translates database schemas to the LDAP schema used by the virtual directory server. This ability to map object (and information) relationships, enables the modeling of business logic in the directory structure. RadiantOne supplies a customizable directory view of the information stored in the relational databases (and other LDAP-compliant directories).

Intelligent Mapping and Cache

VDS server is optimized for accessing information stored in relational databases, and providing it to LDAP-enabled clients. Even so, the fact that VDS Server has to query the remote server holding the underlying database to satisfy every query has performance implications for the data retrieval process. RadiantOne VDS offsets this, however, with the use of its Intelligent Object Mapping and Cache (IOMC) caching mechanism, speeding retrieval of commonly accessed information.

RadiantOne's Intelligent Object Mapping and Cache technology speeds location and access to the data by rapidly responding to queries in the RadiantOne cache, or referring queries to the location in the source directory if needed. The first-time a query is sent to the RadiantOne server and redirects the query (via its database interface) to the source directory. Each time a query is sent for that information, the RadiantOne server supplies the information from its local cache. The updating of this cache can be scheduled as needed. The IOMC distinguishes between three levels of caching—metadata, user access rights, and directory entries.

IOMC 1.5 supports user updates of information represented in the directory, updating the relational database, which is the authoritative source of the information. RadiantOne VDS supports a fully read/write capable LDAP directory interface, allowing changes to be made on objects within its directory namespace to be passed through to the source database. When changes are made, RadiantOne supports related operations including recoverability, replication, transaction, and event triggers. By supporting update capabilities—to be able to write to the relational database that is the authoritative source of information—synchronization is minimized, as the data is being changed at its source, being changed once, and thus replication and synchronization are nominalized.

Namespace Connectors

The RadiantOne VDS communicates with the data sources using three different types of connectors. Each type of connector supports a category of data source, with individual connectors within that category communicating with specific namespaces. The three types of connectors are those for relational databases, directories, and applications.

The Database Connectors

RadiantOne supplies connectors to synchronize with OLE/DB, ODBC, JDBC databases, and can communicate with a relational database that supports any of these database interfaces.

RadiantOne also supports SQL—SQL commands (compliant with the SQL92 standard) are issued by the RadiantOne server when communicating with relational databases. SQL commands are used to access the information stored in the connected databases.

The Directory Connectors

The RadiantOne VDS is fully LDAP 3 compliant, operating as an LDAP-only directory service. In RadiantOne 1.5, the LDAP query filter has been enhanced to support the more robust SQL filter, which has more precise and granular commands, providing a refined set of results.

RadiantOne is also compatible with all ADSI applications, supporting ADSI directly, and integrates seamlessly with common ADSI applications such as Windows Explorer, and ADSI-compliant directories such as the Windows 2000 Active Directory.

Directories supporting the Java Naming and Directory Interface can also be accessed by RadiantOne.

The Application Connectors

A RadiantOne query can provide results in multiple different formats. Applications using RadiantOne can select the format in which to receive the results, such as LDAP, ADO, or XML. RadiantOne can also return the SQL syntax required for the query when going through OLE/DB or ODBC.

Application platforms that are supported by RadiantOne include

- Lotus Notes
- Microsoft Exchange
- PeopleSoft
- SAP

Information Management

RadiantOne synthesizes heterogeneous database data structures into a single logical namespace. To integrate the relational databases with the LDAP directory supported by the RadiantOne VDS, the Schema Manager extracts the schema from the databases, and maps objects and relationships to the LDAP directory namespace.

To facilitate the design of the logical LDAP namespace, RadiantOne provides the DirectoryView Designer. This tool supplies a point and click interface for the modeling of multiple, different LDAP directory trees. This ability to model complex directory structures can facilitate large-scale directory projects by enabling the prototyping of various directory tree designs that can be assessed for usability and efficacy in both IT and business operations.

Schema Mapping

The RadiantOne Schema Manager is used to extract the schema from the relational databases, and supports the mapping of database content to the directory objects in the LDAP namespace. To do this, the schema manager connects to the selected database using the configured connector (OLE/DB, ODBC, JDBC, ADO).

Information Filtering

The filtering of objects and attributes is handled during the initial schema manager importation of the database contents. During this initial load, the schema manager maps objects from the connected directory to the LDAP directory objects in the RadiantOne VDS. The standard method of filtering data in VDS Server is via LDAP filters, which offer a reasonable set of search criteria, for a *directory*.

A database is not a directory, however, and a more robust filtering mechanism was needed. Starting in v.1.5, in addition to the LDAP query filter, the RadiantOne VDS can use standard SQL queries as filters, supplying more precise and granular database querying commands, producing more refined results. The capability to select data via tightly defined SQL queries allows the use of information in the VDS virtual directory for complex real-time applications like e-commerce.

> **RadiantOne VDS Tools**
>
> **Schema Manager**—Extracts the schema from relational databases, mapping it to the LDAP directory.
>
> **DirectoryView Designer**—Enables the designing of the LDAP directory tree via a point and click interface.
>
> **SmartBrowser**—Provides the Web-based client for accessing the VDS Server.

Authoritative Data Source

Storing the addresses to the data, rather than the data itself, allows the information referenced in the virtual directory tree to remain in the relational database of origin. This maintains the database as the authoritative source, bypassing the need to map authoritative data source relationships. This approach also minimizes the ownership and political issues surrounding the information contained in the databases.

> **Another Way to Look at Data Ownership**
>
> Interestingly enough, RadiantOne's documentation talks of the "owner of the data" not as the authoritative data source that literally has *write* control over the data. Rather, it is the administrator of the relational database who has the authority to map database information to the VDS server.

Data Synchronization

Because RadiantOne doesn't store the information represented in the logical structure of LDAP directory tree (but rather only stores links to the information), synchronization issues are minimized. By leaving the data in its source databases, no additional replication and synchronization is required. The lack of replication and synchronization allows the virtual directory server to minimize the network traffic required to provide up-to-date results to the requesting client.

The Intelligent Object Mapping and Cache subsystem maintains query results in its local cache, which need to be updated when the information changes in the source database. The cache can be configured for updating at any specified period.

Interdirectory Security

The RadiantOne VDS provides support for use of its LDAP internal security mechanisms, or any other LDAP directory can be used for authentication and authorization. Full X.500-style access over information in the directory tree is provided in the RadiantOne VDS, using inheritance and inheritance filtering.

RadiantOne VDS implements a roles-based security model, which focuses on linking the authorization and the authority that users have over the information to the specific tasks the users need to perform. Control of access over information in the directory is determined by user authorization and group membership. The access control information can be administered on a granular basis, and the inheritance of security properties by directory objects is supported in the RadiantOne VDS directory tree.

Support is also provided for a number of security mechanisms used by industry vendors including Microsoft, IBM, Oracle, and Netscape.

Directory Markup Languages

CHAPTER

12

...incantations for transformations...

IN THIS CHAPTER

Why create markup languages for directories? As it turns out, the information stored in directories is needed by a range of enterprise applications, and the ability to integrate information stored in a range of diverse directories is essential to streamlining administration tasks.

Directory markup languages can do the following:

- Improve the scope and functionality of the directory service, by allowing it to import from, and export to, any XML-enabled datastore.
- Integrate enterprise directories and datastores
- Provide the data-handling infrastructure that enables leveraging external data
- Integrate B2B efforts, building tighter business relationships
- Automate administrative tasks across directories

Directory markup languages are based in XML, the *eXtensible Markup Language*, which provides them with the flexible underpinnings of XML's customizable vocabulary, as well as provides the common ground to interconnect and exchange information with other directories and datastores. Directory markup languages produce and consume XML documents containing directory entries and/or schema information structured in XML.

So, why base a directory markup language on XML? As it turns out, XML is ideally suited for this. XML can process and transform information stored in hierarchical information structures. XML supplies needed data handling flexibility via customizable elements and attributes, which enable the custom markup of information structures. XML also translates data between different formats, changing data from one format to another via application of XML rules and stylesheets.

So, how is XML integrated with a directory service? It seems that there is already an industry consensus on directory access protocols, namely LDAP—the most common protocol used for accessing directories. Directory markup languages are designed to reflect directory data structures and operations, and to use XML to map directory data and/or processes. XML is a logical addition to LDAP to provide extensible information exchange mechanisms and enable directory services to become more interoperable and Web accessible.

Directory-Focused Markup Languages

Directory markup languages are kind of like HTML—they are specific implementations, specific XML vocabularies—but rather than marking up text like HTML, they are designed to markup directory information; the schema, objects, attributes, and values contained in a directory.

Each directory markup language is a specific XML vocabulary. Directory markup languages are commonly constructed as XML documents, and are largely written using XML to express LDAP directory data structures, operations, and query results. Combining XML with LDAP provides a means to seamlessly perform schema mapping, data transformations, and event management on the directory information being processed, enabling the exchange and integration of directory information.

XML-based directory markup languages represent directory objects, attributes, and schema information within an XML document as a hierarchy of XML elements. Each directory markup language has elements that describe or operate on directory objects, attributes, and values. Similarly, each directory markup language also has distinct elements that describe the directory schema information stored in the XML document.

Introduction to Directory Markup Languages

There are different aspects of representing directory data and operations in XML documents, each addressing different parts of directory information management.

Initially, the objective for Directory Server Markup Language (DSML) was to represent static directory data (structural characteristics and entries). This was the approach used in DSML v.1, where directory entries are represented as XML elements sequentially stored in an XML document.

An important next step (and the focus of DSML v.2) was to represent the directory operations in XML, storing not only directory queries but also the results of the queries in XML documents. The ability to perform directory operations via XML enables the applications to dynamically interact with the directories as an information repository. In DSML v.2, XML documents can contain the information to represent directory service processes as well as directory objects, attributes, and values.

Another key aspect in a directory markup language is the ability to transform directory data between a wide range of formats. The interoperability offered by directory markup languages is largely dependent on XML's underlying ability to handle data transformations flexibly. The data transformations performed via XML can change the format of directory data into the format required by any specific datastore. Data transformations are a key element of exchanging information between dissimilar directory name spaces.

XML Reduces Client Complexity

The use of XML-based directory markup languages results in server-centric operations and reduced complexity on the client-side. No special-purpose client applications are required, as XML-compliant Web-enabled browsers are already widely available.

With information being stored in a variety of directories and databases, there is a pressing need to be able to access and exchange the information. Increasingly, enterprise applications require access to multiple data stores—having a standard means of exchanging directory information facilitates integration across IT platforms and business operations.

Leveraging XML

A directory markup language leverages the capabilities of XML. As a markup language, XML is designed to manipulate information, to transform data from one format to another, and to represent information in a generic form accessible by a wide range of applications and services.

XML is well suited to create directory markup languages, as it stores information in hierarchical structures, allowing relationships between information to be maintained. Needed flexibility in data handling is provided by XML, which enables the transformation of data between different formats via XML rules and stylesheets. XML supports the custom markup of directory information structures via flexible definitions of elements and attributes.

Using XML Structures and Capabilities

XML is characterized by enabling the creation of a custom XML vocabulary—a set of elements and attributes needed to meet the structural requirements of whatever directory, application, or datastore from which the developer is accessing the information.

XML uses namespaces to define the set of XML elements and attributes with which to map the contents of the datastore. XML documents use the namespace to ensure the uniqueness of the element names and the attribute names within a specific XML vocabulary.

The documents used in the directory markup languages are fundamentally structured as XML documents, each specifying a namespace identifier, and containing elements that hierarchically identify the contents within the document. The namespace is specified via the `xmlns` attribute, which establishes the namespace for either an entire document or a specific element, via a *uniform resource identifier* (URI).

> **Standards and Reference Web Sites**
>
> The Organization for the Advancement of Structural Information Standards (OASIS) is the standards organization driving the open development of directory service markup languages.
>
> Useful reference sites include
>
> `www.oasis-open.org`
>
> `www.dsml.org`
>
> `www.xml.org`

Leveraging XML-Enabled Applications

As vendors have striven to increase the interoperability of their applications, they have looked to XML as a standard method of exchanging information. Increasing numbers of applications are XML-enabled, as many vendors are adding XML import and export capabilities to their applications. Leading industry vendors are all using XML in one form or another. (Some vendors are creating their own specific versions of XML to support the functionality they need.)

XML is designed to facilitate the custom markup of information structures, and enables the control of information and the transformation of information between dissimilar formats. If an application (or service) is XML-enabled, it can interconnect and share data with all other XML-enabled applications and services. The ability to exchange information between applications, databases, and directories via XML enables the increased integration of information repositories within the enterprise network.

Current Directory Markup Languages

There are a number of different markup languages focused on representing directory information, yet the scope and focus of each of these approaches differs somewhat. For example, version 1 (v.1) of the Directory Service Markup Language (DSML) represented only the structural characteristics of the directory. Yet the scope of DSML has been extended—DSML v.2 also represents directory operations (such as queries) and the results of these operations.

This chapter discusses two directory markup languages in more detail—the *Directory Service Markup Language* (DSML), and Novell's *DirXML*. Both of these markup languages are described in detail later in the chapter, and are thus only briefly described here:

- **Directory Service Markup Language (DSML)**—As an XML-based method of describing directory structural information, the Directory Service Markup Language (DSML) is an effort initially led by Bowstreet to define in XML the structural characteristics of directory. Since Bowstreet's initial development, DSML has been adopted by many leading industry directory vendors, and is now being extended to represent directory operations in XML.
- **DirXML**—DirXML is Novell's directory markup language, designed to facilitate the exchange of information between dissimilar data sources via XML, using the underlying directory to provide the information management engine. As a markup language that allows considerable flexibility in data transformations, DirXML provides advanced capabilities to exchange and process information between directories. The underlying XML-base enables automation of IT tasks via customizable methods that manage information exchange between many distinct data sources.

While the focus in this chapter will be on DSML and DirXML, there are other markup languages designed to represent directory information and operations. While these additional markup languages are beyond the scope of this material, we will briefly discuss them in sidebars throughout the chapter (a URL for more information is provided in each sidebar). The additional markup languages include

- **XMLDAP**—iPlanet's XMLDAP Directory Gateway XML schema
- **XDAP**—VeriSign's eXtensible Directory Access Protocol
- **DAML**—Access360's Directory Access Markup Language

XMLDAP

The iPlanet XMLDAP Directory Gateway's XML schema defines the XMLDAP markup language. XMLDAP is different from DAML and DirXML in that it does not define an XML Document Type Definition (DTD), but rather defines a template used by the gateway to perform XML data transformations. XMLDAP defines the eXtensible Template Language (XTL), which represents LDAP via defined sets of tags (elements). iPlanet is a product of the Sun|Netscape alliance.

For more information on XMLDAP, visit this URL:

`www.iplanet.com/downloads/developer/2040.html`

Directory Service Markup Language

The Directory Service Markup Language (DSML) is an XML-based method of representing the content of a directory service as XML documents. DSML provides the means to integrate XML-accessible resources with directory services and to communicate with other XML-enabled datastores.

Without DSML, application developers who need directory information must write directory-specific access routines. Such proprietary solutions hinder the exchange of information between companies, and are time-consuming, costly efforts.

DSML provides developers with a common interface to leverage the information stored in directories. Structuring directory information as XML documents enables the use of this directory information over common Internet protocols such as HTTP, for integration in Web, e-commerce, and other XML-enabled applications.

There are currently two versions of DSML: v.1, which defined publishing LDAP directory information as XML documents, and v.2, which extends that into defining LDAP operations.

DSML v.1

Bowstreet, who was quickly joined by leading industry vendors, initiated the development of DSML. The initial draft of the DSML v.1 specification was defined in the XML documents, `dsml.dtd`, `dsml.xdr`, and `dsml.xsd`.

DSML v.1 specifies a simple XML schema that allows a directory to publish its structural information as XML documents that can be exchanged with a variety of services and applications. Yet, while the directory structural information is represented in DSML v.1, directory operations, such as queries, updates, and query results are not represented until DSML v.2.

DSML Documents

The XML vocabulary for DSML is contained in its DTD namespace document. The DSML namespace is referenced in XML documents by using the prefix `dsml` on the XML elements. The use of this `dsml` prefix associated with the DSML Namespace URI signifies that the elements belong to the DSML Namespace.

The DSML Namespace (v.1) is identified by the following URI:

```
http://www.dsml.org/DSML
```

The URI identifies the namespace for the document. The prefix associated with it (such as `dsml`) is arbitrary, and another prefix could be used—or you could use no prefix at all if the DSML Namespace is declared as the default namespace.

The DSML document structure begins with the document element (of type `dsml`).

For example, the DSML v.1 Namespace URI is specified as:

```
<dsml:dsml xmlns:dsml="http://www.dsml.org/DSML">
```

The `dsml` element may contain the XML attribute `complete`—this attribute's value is either `true` (default) or `false`:

- When true, it denotes that the `directory-schema` section contains all `class` and `attribute-type` elements referred to in the document, and no external references occur in the `entries` specified within the `directory-entries` section.
- When `false`, it denotes that there is a reference to another DSML document that contains the schema.

Specifying Directory Entries in DSML

Consider what DSML is designed to do, that is, convert directory information to or from XML. Every DSML document contains XML-encoded references to the directory entries—essentially describing a directory's schema, objects, or both. Every entry in a directory is identified by its distinguished name—a unique reference that specifies both the object's location in the directory, and the type of entry.

Directory entries in a DSML document are declared in the directory-entries section, and may contain one or more child elements of type entry. The directory entries specified in a DSML document are enclosed by elements (such as entry, objectclass, and oc-value, as well as attr and value), which define directory objects and attributes.

In brief, directory entries in a DSML document are structured using the following DSML elements:

- The directory-entries element is a child element of the dsml element, and may contain one or more child elements of type entry.
- Each entry has an objectclass element that can have multiple oc-value elements defining the set of object class definition that make up the object (directly assigned classes and superclasses).
- The attributes for an object entry are specified with the attr child element (each entry has multiple attr elements). The attr element uses the XML attribute name to specify the names of the directory attributes associated with this object, and the value element to contain the associated value.

The dsml element contains the directory-entries element, which contains one or more entry elements defining the directory objects, and one or more attr elements defining directory attributes:

```
<dsml:dsml xmlns:dsml="namespace identifier">
   <dsml:directory-entries>
        <dsml:entry> </dsml:entry>
        <dsml:attr> </dsml:attr>
   </dsml:directory-entries>
</dsml:dsml>
```

Entry Elements

Directory entries described in a DSML document are represented in the directory-entries element. DSML represents individual entries using the entry element type, each of which contains elements that describe its object classes and attributes. The entry's distinguished name is stored as an XML attribute of the entry element—an XML attribute called dn. The dn is used to identify the entry and therefore is stored as an attribute instead of as a child element.

Objects are specified in the DSML document using the objectclass and oc-value elements. Every directory entry consists of multiple object classes that are referenced within the objectclass element. Within the objectclass element, an entry's object classes are specified via oc-value elements:

- **objectclass**—Defines the object classes that the entry belongs to by using oc-value elements.
- **oc-value**—Specifies an entry's object classes—every oc-value specifies a single object class that the entry belongs to.

An optional XML attribute for the objectclass element, ref is a URI to the attribute-type definition for an objectclass directory attribute (enabling extension of the objectclass directory attribute).

An oc-value has a ref attribute that specifies the URI to the class element definition of the object class as specified in the directory-schema section of the XML document.

A DSML entry specifying an object class is written as

```
<dsml:entry dn="Distinguished Name">
     <dsml:objectclass>
          <dsml:oc-value></dsml:oc-value>
     </dsml:objectclass>
</dsml:entry>
```

For example:

```
<dsml:entry dn="cn=margaret sara,ou=dev,o=netmages">
     <dsml:objectclass>
           <dsml:oc-value>top</dsml:oc-value>
           <dsml:oc-value>person</dsml:oc-value>
           <dsml:oc-value>organizationalPerson</dsml:oc-value>
     </dsml:objectclass>
</dsml:entry>
```

Representing Directory Attributes

Directory attributes are described using the attr and value elements, and are specified in the context of an entry element. For each attribute in the directory, an attr element is used to represent each directory attribute in the DSML document. The attr element has a mandatory XML attribute called name and an optional attribute called ref. These attributes work as follows:

- **name**—Specifies the directory attribute's name.
- **ref**—This optional attribute contains a URI referencing an attribute-type definition specified within the directory-schema section of a DSML document.

The value associated with the directory attribute is described in value child elements; multiple value elements are used for multivalued attributes.

An attribute is written as

```
<dsml:attr name="Attribute Name">
     <dsml:value>Attribute Value</dsml:value>
</dsml:attr>
```

For example:

```
<dsml:attr name="email">
     <dsml:value>margarets@mythical.org</dsml:value>
</dsml:attr>
```

Specifying Multivalued Attributes

To handle attributes with multiple values in DSML, a `value` element is specified for each of the multiple values. The `attr` element representing the directory attribute uses multiple child `value` elements, one to describe each specific value.

For example, Margaret has multiple e-mail addresses, all of which need to be represented. Accordingly, the e-mail attribute has multiple values assigned to it to display multiple e-mail addresses:

```
<dsml:attr name="email">
     <dsml:value>margarets@mythical.org</dsml:value>
     <dsml:value>msara@netmages.org</dsml:value>
     <dsml:value>margaret.sara@src.nu</dsml:value>
</dsml:attr>
```

Specifying Binary Data

Some directory attributes contain binary data, such as public key certificates or graphics, instead of text-based information. DSML handles binary data by encoding it—the encoding scheme to be used is specified in the `value` element's `encoding` attribute.

In its first release, DSML only supports base64 encoding (defined in RFC 1521), so the only valid value for the `encoding` attribute is `base64`.

For example:

```
<dsml:attr name="certificate">
     <dsml:value encoding="base64">
     XZi2Gpl0n1Z1Y+9WqLdf8u34jhDF-2klJf9u2Rp8eDlfM3MCOf9q2z3...
     </dsml:value>
</dsml:attr>
```

An Example DSML Entry with Attributes

Combining the preceding descriptions of the DSML entry and attribute elements, the DSML method of structuring directory objects and their attributes into a DSML file becomes clearer.

A directory entry is written as:

```
<dsml:dsml xmlns:dsml="URI">
   <dsml:directory-entries>
     <dsml:entry dn="Distinguished Name">

          <dsml:objectclass>
                <dsml:oc-value>Class Name</dsml:oc-value>
          </dsml:objectclass>

          <dsml:attr name="Attribute Name">
                <dsml:value>Attribute Value</dsml:value>
          </dsml:attr>
     </dsml:entry>
   </dsml:directory-entries>
</dsml:dsml>
```

Thus, a portion of the `organizationalPerson` object for Margaret Sara would be specified as

```
<dsml:dsml xmlns:dsml="http://www.dsml.org/DSML">
   <dsml:directory-entries>
     <dsml:entry dn="cn=margaret sara,ou=dev,o=netmages">

          <dsml:objectclass>
                <dsml:oc-value>top</dsml:oc-value>
                <dsml:oc-value>person</dsml:oc-value>
                <dsml:oc-value>organizationalPerson</dsml:oc-value>
          </dsml:objectclass>
          <dsml:attr name="email">
                <dsml:value>margarets@mythical.org</dsml:value>
                <dsml:value>msara@netmages.org</dsml:value>
                <dsml:value>margaret.sara@src.nu</dsml:value>
          </dsml:attr>

     </dsml:entry>
   </dsml:directory-entries>
</dsml:dsml>
```

Referencing the Directory Schema

Every directory object is a member of one or more classes and has multiple attributes containing values associated with the object. The classes to which an object belongs determine which attributes it must, and may, contain. All the object classes, attributes, syntax, and containment rules for the directory defined within the schema can be represented in DSML.

Like directory entries, directory schema information is also stored in DSML documents. The ability to map the schema in DSML facilitates exchanging data between the directory and any XML-enabled application. The directory schema may be supplied in a standalone DSML document, or provided in the same DSML document as the directory entries.

The `dsml` element may contain an entry of `directory-schema`, denoting that the directory schema is also stored in the document. The `directory-schema` element has `class` and `attribute-type` child elements. These elements are used as follows:

- Every object class is specified in the `directory-schema` section using a `class` element, which has an XML attribute `id` used to identify the object class.
- Every attribute is specified in the `directory-schema` section using an `attribute-type` element.

From the most general view, the schema is specified as multiple occurrences of `class` and `attribute-type` elements:

```
<dsml:directory-schema>
   <dsml:class id="Class Name"> </dsml:class>
   <dsml:attribute-type id="Attribute Name"> </dsml:attribute-type>
</dsml:directory-schema>
```

Defining Object Classes

Every directory object class specified in a DSML document is described by XML attributes and child elements of `class`. Each `class` element has the following XML attributes:

- **`id`**—Contains a locally unique identifier for the specified object class (may be the same value as the `name` element value). The `id` is used to reference the object class from other `superior` or `ref` XML attributes.
- **`superior`**—Contains the URI reference to the object class from which the current object is derived.
- **`type`**—Specifies whether the object class is `structural`, `abstract`, or `auxiliary`.
- **`obsolete`**—Can either be `true` or `false`, and defaults to `false`.

The child elements of the `class` element include

- **`name`**—Contains the designated name of the object class.
- **`description`**—The optional `description` element contains a description of the object class.
- **`object-identifier`**—Contains the assigned OID of the object class.

- **`attribute`**—Contains mandatory and optional attributes of the object class. The `attribute` element has attributes of its own; the `ref` attribute contains the URI for the directory `attribute-type` specification, while the `required` attribute is either `true` or `false`, specifying whether this directory attribute is required for entries of this object class.

A `class` specification is written in DSML as:

```
<dsml:dsml xmlns:dsml="">
   <dsml:directory-schema>
     <dsml:class id="" superior="" type="">
          <dsml:name> </dsml:name>
          <dsml:description> </dsml:description>
          <dsml:object-identifier> </dsml:object-identifier>
          <dsml:attribute ref="" required=""></dsml:attribute>
     </dsml:class>
   </dsml:directory-schema>
</dsml:dsml>
```

For example:

```
<dsml:dsml xmlns:dsml="http://www.dsml.org/DSML">
   <dsml:directory-schema>
     <dsml:class id="organizationalPerson" superior="#person"
➥ type="structural">
        <dsml:name>organizationalPerson</dsml:name>
        <dsml:description>Organizational Person</dsml:description>
        <dsml:object-identifier>2.5.6.7</dsml:object-identifier>
        <dsml:attribute ref="title" required="false"></dsml:attribute>
        <dsml:attribute ref="organizationalUnitName"
➥ required="false"></dsml:attribute>
     </dsml:class>
   </dsml:directory-schema>
</dsml:dsml>
```

Specifying Attribute Type Definitions

Directory attributes are defined in the same way as the object classes, using XML elements to denote the specific directory attributes. A child element of `directory-schema`, the `attribute-type` element, is used to define directory attributes in the DSML document.

The XML attributes of `attribute-type` element identify the directory attribute type and specify the allowable syntax. The XML attributes of the `attribute-type` element are

- **`id`**—Uniquely identifies the specific attribute type.
- **`superior`**—Contains the URI reference to the `attribute-type` from which the attribute is derived.
- **`obsolete`**—Can either be `true` or `false` (defaults to false).

- **single-value**—This `true/false` attribute is used to signify whether the directory attribute is single or multivalued (defaults to false).
- **user-modification**—Also a true/false XML attribute (defaults to `true`).

The child elements of `attribute-type` consist of:

- **name**—Contains the name of the attribute type.
- **description**—Optional, used to hold a description of the attribute type.
- **object-identifier**—Contains the OID of the object class.
- **syntax**—The allowable syntax for this attribute type is referenced in the `syntax` element. The `syntax` element contains the OID identifying the allowable syntax for values. The `syntax` element has an XML attribute `bound` that is used to configure the minimum upper bound.
- **equality**—Contains the OID referencing the LDAP EQUALITY matching rule.
- **ordering**—Holds the LDAP ORDERING matching rule OID.
- **substring**—Contains the OID referencing the LDAP SUBSTR matching rule.

An attribute specified in DSML is constructed as:

```
<dsml:dsml xmlns:dsml="">
   <dsml:directory-schema>
     <dsml:attribute-type id="" superior="">
          <dsml:name> </dsml:name>
          <dsml:description> </dsml:description>
          <dsml:object-identifier> </dsml:object-identifier>
     </dsml: attribute-type>
   </dsml:directory-schema>
</dsml:dsml>
```

For example:

```
<dsml:dsml xmlns:dsml="http://www.dsml.org/DSML">
   <dsml:directory-schema>
     <dsml:attribute-type id="sn" superior="#name">
          <dsml:name>sn</dsml:name>
          <dsml:description>surname</dsml:description>
          <dsml:object-identifier>2.5.4.4 </dsml:object-identifier>
     </dsml: attribute-type>
   </dsml:directory-schema>
</dsml:dsml>
```

DSML Document Types

From the perspective of conforming to the DSML specification, DSML documents can be viewed as four different types of documents based on contents; the primary delineation is based on whether the schema is included. There are four types of DSML documents:

- `Type 1`—Does not contain a directory schema, or reference to external document with directory schema.
- `Type 2`—Does not contain a directory schema, yet has a reference to external document with a directory schema.
- `Type 3`—Contains only a directory schema.
- `Type 4`—Contains a directory schema and directory entries.

The DSML v.1 specification describes the provisioning and processing of DSML documents as *producers* and *consumers* of DSML.

According to the specification, a producer of DSML *must* be able to create type 1 documents, and *may* be able to create DSML documents previously described as types 2, 3, and 4. A DSML producer that can only create type 1 documents is described as a *level one producer*. A producer that can create all types of DSML documents is described as a *level two producer*.

DSML consumers are looked at a little bit differently. A DSML consumer has to be able to process all four document types. If the DSML consumer can utilize the directory schema information, it is described as a *level two consumer*, whereas if it cannot, it is described as a *level one consumer*.

DSML v.2

The DSML v.2 effort sought to go beyond DSML v.1, which, as we've discussed, was limited to representing directory structural information. In DSML v.1 the design intent was to accurately represent an LDAP directory in an XML document. This represented the current state of a directory—a static map of the directory schema and objects—yet it is not designed to describe the operations the directory performs.

Source of Key DSML v.1 Documents

The documents describing DSML v.1 are available at `www.dsml.org`:

- **DSML DTD**—The DTD for DSML is specified in the file `dsml.dtd`.
- **XML schema**—The XML schema for DSML is defined in `dsml.xsd`.
- **Biztalk schema**—The Biztalk schema for DSML is defined in `dsml.xdr`.

DSML v.2 clearly builds on the foundation of DSML v.1 and extends its functionality, going beyond representing only directory structural information into representing LDAP operations and results. DSML v.2 implements these new capabilities by supplying request/response envelopes for handling LDAP operations, as well as handling the results provided by those operations.

The goal of DSML v.2 is to directly map LDAP to XML. DSML v.2 is largely a direct translation of LDAP ASN.1 into XML-Schema—thus the meanings would be consistent between named identifiers in LDAP and elements in DSML v.2 with the same name.

In their proposal for the DSML v.2 specification, Microsoft describes that DSML v.2 "…is not required to be a strict superset of DSMLv1" yet it should follow the DSML v.1 design wherever possible. This proposal is available at:

`http://lists.oasis-open.org/archives/dsml/200106/msg00000.html`

Mapping LDAP Operations

The core focus of the design for DSML v.2 is to represent an LDAP operation (an LDAP request or response) as an XML document. This requires defining methods of representing LDAP queries and updates in XML documents, as well as representing the results of these LDAP queries and updates in XML.

DSML v.2 defines the request and response elements and types that directly correspond to the related LDAP operations. These elements are shown in Table 12.1.

Considered for DSML v.2

Each of the directory markup languages discussed here was provided to the Organization for the Advancement of Structured Information Standards (OASIS) to be considered for use in the DSML v.2 specification. The willingness of the major directory vendors to supply their specifications, as well as the diversity of the approaches considered, demonstrates the directory industry's commitment to open standards.

- Microsoft submitted the proposal that was eventually accepted as DSML v.2.
- Access360 submitted the specifications for DAML.
- Novell as NDS-DTD submitted the XML specification for DirXML.
- The XML schema from the iPlanet XMLDAP Directory Gateway was submitted by the SunlNetscape alliance.
- VeriSign submitted the XDAP specification.

TABLE 12.1 The LDAP Operations Elements in DSML v.2

Request Element	*Request Type*	*Response Element*	*Response Type*
searchRequest	SearchRequest	searchResponse	SearchResponse
modifyRequest	ModifyRequest	modifyResponse	LDAPResult
addRequest	AddRequest	addResponse	LDAPResult
delRequest	DelRequest	delResponse	LDAPResult
modDNRequest	ModifyDNRequest	modDNResponse	LDAPResult
compareRequest	CompareRequest	compareResponse	LDAPResult
extendedReq	ExtendedRequest	extendedResp	Extended Response
		errorResponse	xsd:string

While DSML v.2 leverages LDAP data structures for accessing and manipulating the directory information, DSML v.2 and LDAP differ in significant ways:

- LDAP uses a bind request to authenticate a security principal for an LDAP connection. In contrast, a DSML v.2 document doesn't have a bind request, as it does not need to authenticate the requester of the documents.
- DSML v.2 operates in a request-response method.
- DSML v.2 can specify multiple LDAP operations in a single request document, and wrap multiple responses generated from an LDAP request into a single `searchResponse` element.
- DSML exchanges data between directories by producing and consuming XML documents, whereas LDAP produces queries and consumes results.
- DSML can also be communicated over HTTP using HTTP request/responses.

Types of DSML v.2 Documents

Each DSML v.2 document starts with the namespace reference URI specified within the envelope request or response in a DSML v.2 document:

```
<dsmlEnvelopeRequest xmlns="http://www.dsml.org/DSML/v2">
```

There are two types of documents in DSML v.2—a pair of linked documents described as the *request* and *response* documents. These correspond to the client/server interaction in DSML, between the client requesting information, and the server providing responses.

DSML v.2 defines the request and response envelopes, via the `dsmlEnvelopeRequest` and `dsmlEnvelopeResponse` top-level elements, to enclose the request or response elements.

For every request document received from a client, there is a response document returned by the server. Each request document may contain any number of request elements—the response document likewise may contain any number of response elements.

There is a positional correspondence between the location of requests and responses within the related request/response documents. The relative location of each response in the response document is the same as the location of the related request in the request document.

For example, if a specific request was ninth in the request document, the related response would be ninth in the response document. Even in the case of query processing errors, this correspondence is maintained—every n^{th} request element specified in the request document directly corresponds to the nth response element within the response document.

Request Document

A request document specifies the operation, which the client is requesting of the directory server, and may include processing instructions. The request document contains the envelope header, and a range of possible request operations. A request document has the `dsmlEnvelopeRequest` element as the top-level element of the document, and may contain a *search*, *modify*, *add*, *delete*, *modDN*, *compare*, or an *extended* request.

A simple request document could look something like this:

```
<dsmlEnvelopeRequest xmlns="http://www.dsml.org/DSML/v2">
     <searchRequest></searchRequest>
     <addRequest></addRequest>
     <modifyRequest></modifyRequest>
</dsmlEnvelopeRequest>
```

A `dsmlEnvelopeRequest` element may also contain a `processing` XML-attribute. This attribute is responsible for instructing the directory server how to process the requests—either sequentially or in parallel. The valid `processing` attribute values are specified as either:

- **`sequential`**—Processing of the request elements is performed in the order in which they appear in the dsmlEnvelopeRequest.
- **`parallel`**—The directory server may perform the requests in any order, without regard to the order in the DSML document.

Null Envelopes to Verify Compliance

It is valid for both a request and a response envelope to be sent without request or response elements being contained within the envelope. A null request-response pair (each containing no elements) can be used to verify that a directory can process documents written in compliance with DSML v.2.

Response Document

A response document is sent to the client in response to a request document. A response document has the dsmlEnvelopeResponse element as the top-level element of the document, and may contain a search, modify, add, delete, modDN, compare, extended, or an error response.

A simple response document corresponding to the preceding request document would look like:

```
<dsmlEnvelopeResponse xmlns="http://www.dsml.org/DSML/v2">
     <searchRequest></searchRequest>
     <addRequest></addRequest>
     <modifyRequest></modifyRequest>
</dsmlEnvelopeResponse>
```


Handling Syntax Errors

To address the processing problems around documents with syntax errors, DSML v.2 provides some error handling capability. Documents that have syntactical problems are processed with each request being handled atomically—therefore if a request fails due to a syntax error, the other requests contained in the same document are still processed.

If a request document is not compliant with the XML Schema defined for dsmlEnvelopeRequest—that is, it does not meet the DSML v.2 syntax requirements—the directory server will supply a response document containing information relating to the syntax errors. The errorResponse element denotes the specific line and column number of the syntax error and the offending text is quoted.

Directory Access Markup Language

The Directory Access Markup Language (DAML) was created by Access360, Inc. Like DSML v.2, it extends the scope of DSML v.1 by mapping LDAP operations in addition to directory content. DAML defines how to represent LDAP queries in an XML document. DAML syntax is structured to closely match the syntax of LDAP; DAML, however, is stored as XML rather than stored in the ASN.1 Basic Encoding Rules (BER) encoding of LDAP. In a design that leverages the foundation of the DSML v.1 specification, DAML integrates the DSML v.1 DTD.

DAML is specified in the DAML DTD (stored as daml.dtd). The DAML DTD imports the DSML v.1 DTD (dsml.dtd) and also defines common entities for use throughout the document (including LDAPString, LDAPOID, and relative-distinguished-name).

DAML, like other directory markup languages, uses defined elements to map the LDAP operations to XML. In DAML, LDAP operations are specified via the LDAPOperation element and its request/response pairs of child elements (such as SearchRequest and SearchResponse), which directly correspond to the LDAP protocol operations.

The LDAP operations to connect to a directory service, and to search for or modify directory information, are supported in DAML in the following ways:

- **Bind**—The DAML Bind connects to the directory server, requiring the DN of the requestor, and supporting both simple authentication and the use of SASL credentials for authentication.
- **Search**—A DAML search request structure is defined in the `SearchRequest` element, with attributes that identify the directory objects and scope, determine how to handle dereferencing aliases, as well as accepting filters and attribute name parameters.
- **Modify**—DAML modify requests are specified in the `ModifyRequest` element, which uses the `Modification` element to specify which operation to perform. The `Modification` element has an `Operation` attribute, which can specify `add`, `delete`, and `replace` values denoting the operation to perform. The `ModifyRequest` element has a corresponding `ModifyResponse` element.
- **ModifyDN**—The ModifyDNRequest element requires the distinguished name (DN) and the new relative distinguished name (NewRDN) attributes, yet specifying the DN of the new superior object is implied. The ModifyDNRequest element has a corresponding ModifyDNResponse element.

Further information on DAML (`DAML.DTD`) is available at the following URL:

`lists.oasis-open.org/archives/dsml/200103/bin00000.bin`

Novell's DirXML

DirXML is a directory markup language (and part of a connectivity solution) developed by Novell, and works in concert with eDirectory to provide full data transformation and inter-datastore exchange capability. DirXML was submitted to the OASIS as a possible specification for DSML v.2.

Details on the DirXML elements are available at the following URL:

`lists.oasis-open.org/archives/dsml/200103/zip00000.zip`

Because DirXML is explained in detail in Chapter 11, "Meta-Directory Services," the coverage of DirXML here is centered on its use as an XML-based directory markup language. In brief, DirXML operates with the DirXML engine using namespace connectors, XML data structures, and rules.

The *connectors* (also called *driver shims*) communicate with external namespaces. The driver shim is a software component that creates an application-specific view of the information in a connected datastore. DirXML uses the driver shim to exchange data, translating XML content into native API calls.

DirXML rules structure the flow and transformation of the data between namespaces. During the process of exchanging information between directories, databases, or other repositories by DirXML, the information is stored in XML-encapsulated data structures.

The DirXML engine, which operates via eDirectory, is the underlying component that processes the DirXML documents. eDirectory also stores core DirXML information, such as connector configuration data, which is stored as XML documents in the directory.

DirXML provides a customizable framework that can link diverse data sources while automating IT administration. DirXML provides security for interdirectory access to information, and the connected data sources can be dynamically queried, providing realtime information from distributed datastores. By using DirXML's interoperability, administration costs can be reduced by automating management tasks.

Foundations in XML

The foundations of DirXML are in XML, XSL, and XSLT—Novell's DirXML is built on the *eXtensible Markup Language (XML),* the *eXtensible Stylesheet Language (XSL),* and *XSL Transformations (XSLT).*

DirXML uses XML to represent directory information, handle namespace configuration data, and manage data change events and synchronization. In each of these specific aspects, you can see DirXML's reliance on XML:

Interconnecting the Namespaces in DirXML

Connectors (driver shims) are used in DirXML to communicate with a foreign namespace such as Lotus Notes or Microsoft Exchange. The interface methods of the connectors accept input in the form of XML documents and return XML documents as output.

Novell supplies a default set of DirXML connectors and is developing more. In addition to eDirectory, the default set of connectors includes support for LDAP v3 directories, Lotus Notes, Microsoft Exchange, and Active Directory (with support for Windows NT and Delimited text connectors under development). Novell also supports the development of DirXML connectors by other vendors—as a case in point, Novell is currently working with Nexor on a connector for the X.500 directory access protocol (DAP).

- **Representing directory information**—DirXML uses XML to represent and exchange directory information. Directory information is represented in XML for manipulation by DirXML, which uses XML rules and stylesheets to translate data between connected directories.
- **Handling namespace-specific configuration information**—Directory objects and XML are combined in the DirXML's handling of namespace configuration. DirXML stores its namespace configuration data as XML data structures. Configuration information for the DirXML driver's shims are stored as XML documents in designated eDirectory objects.
- **Data change and synchronization**—DirXML uses XML in managing data change events and synchronization of directory data. Data change events and synchronization commands are represented in XML documents. Data change events, for instance, are described in XML documents with the DirXML rules that determine the processing of these change events. Commands used to transform data for synchronization are also represented in XML, and are stored in the directory as an XML document.

Transforming Data Via XML

DirXML leverages XML for transformations of data—DirXML is designed around XML, XSL, and XSLT, enabling enhanced data transformation capabilities. DirXML uses these technologies as follows:

- **XML**—XML transformations allow data to be changed into the format needed by a specific application, directory, or datastore. Similarly, XML transformations can be used to change the event into other event types. Information is translated into XML as it is passed into DirXML, where data is converted to the needed format according to specified XML rules and stylesheets. When converting the data, XML rules are applied to transform objects and events as needed.
- **XSL**—DirXML uses XSL for formatting data, providing flexible control over the presentation of the data.

Interdirectory Data Exchange

The DirXML Engine, the underlying engine that translates XML documents between dissimilar datastores, performs DirXML's interdirectory communication and synchronization. The DirXML Engine is responsible for replicating changes between all connected directories.

- **XSLT**—DirXML uses XSLT for transforming data, managing the transformation of data from the format it receives to the format it needs provide. XSLT describes the transformation of the XML documents, where each of the events and data transformations is represented. XSLT can be used to define customized routines that can replace basic operations.

DirXML replicates information stored in an application view via an XML processor that uses XSL to transform data in XML documents. Through this data transformation by the XML/XSL processor, DirXML customizes the data to fit the application's requirements.

This transformation of data between formats is a key aspect of how DirXML exchanges information between dissimilar directories (or other forms of information storage).

Rules Manage the Processing

DirXML employs rules to control the processing and transformation of data. DirXML rules operate on an XML document, and are used to transform data and/or trigger events. A single DirXML rule performs a single, specific transformation on an XML document.

Rules control the processing of data change events in DirXML, and are structured as a series of XML tags representing data transformation operations such as schema mapping and object matching, creation, or placement. DirXML rules are defined in XML documents—DirXML rules may be stored as an external text file or stored in the directory as an XML document.

DirXML supports the handling of dynamic events via XML. When a DirXML rule processes a change event, an XML document containing a corresponding set of change event commands is produced and sent to the target datastore.

A combination of filters and DirXML rules manage the flow of information between DirXML and an external datasource. Complex business logic can be supported during the XML transformation process, such as initiating an automated set of operations across a number of connected directories.

Speeds XML Processing

A standard XML document (a text file) supplies serialized XML, yet DirXML uses a programmatic representation of XML, which speeds the processing of XML data.

Rules in DirXML are typically configured in the publisher and subscriber channels, and can be either:

- Rules describing well-defined tasks like schema mapping or object creation, which are written in Novell's DirXML dialect of XML.
- Rules defining arbitrary transformations (such as changing the data format), which are specified in XSLT transformation instructions.

DirXML uses a specific eDirectory object to store a rule—the DirXML rule object contains a single DirXML rule as an XML document. This rule is one of four types:

- **Create**—The *create rule* determines if an object is created depending on the completion of all mandatory attributes. To process an add object event, the create rule is applied to the DirXML document. Default values may also be set for empty attributes by the create rule.
- **Matching**—If an object is unassociated, a *matching rule* (using the specified criteria) will be used to try to locate an object matching the source object. The matching rule can also be constructed as an XSLT stylesheet.
- **Placement**—The placement of a new object in the hierarchical namespace is determined by the *placement rule*. The placement rule identifies the object placement with regard to the location (or designated attribute values) of the source object.
- **Schema Mapping**—The mapping of schemas between eDirectory and an external data-source is performed by *schema mapping rules*. These rules are XML or XSLT documents associated with driver shims.

DirXML Document Structure

A DirXML document is fundamentally an XML document using Novell's DirXML as specified in the DirXML DTD file (`nds.dtd`). Novell's DirXML, like other XML-based directory markup languages, uses a hierarchy of XML elements to represent directory information (objects, attributes, and schema) within an XML document.

Elements that describe or operate on directory objects, attributes, and values, are distinct from elements used to describe the directory schema information, which may also be stored in the XML document.

Top Level Elements

A DirXML document begins with top level elements that are used to structure the input and output flow of information, and to specify the configuration parameters for the specific namespace connector (driver shim).

A DirXML document starts with its top-level elements, notably:

```
<nds>
<driver-config>
```

The nds element specifies the NDS and DTD versions, identifies the document source, and contains all the input and output elements of the DirXML document. The nds element has two attributes, ndsversion (8.5) and dtdversion (1.0), as well as the source, input, and output child elements.

The source element specifies the origin of the DirXML document, and has product and contact child elements for specifying the source product details.

The input element specifies the operation to perform and may contain one or more of the following commands:

add

modify

delete

rename

move

query

query-schema

add-association

modify-association

remove-association

init-params

status

Each of these commands, such as add or modify, can also be used as an element operating as an input event, rather than as an input command.

DirXML sends an output element in response to a received input element. The output element may provide one or more of the following commands:

status

add-association

modify-association

remove-association

instance

schema-def

init-params

The `status` command is mandatory and must be sent in every `output` element.

Configuration data for the namespace driver is specified in the `driver-config` element. The `driver-config` element has a `name` attribute that specifies the DirXML driver name, and has child elements of `driver-options`, `subscriber-options`, and `publisher-options` that describe driver configuration settings, as well as configuring publisher and subscriber roles.

While the top-level elements and the input and output elements have been briefly described, the command and event elements, as well as the other elements are too numerous to address here. For further information on the DirXML elements see:

`lists.oasis-open.org/archives/dsml/200103/msg00004.html`

Schema definition (for either the application or the directory) is specified via the `schema-def` element, using `class-def` and `attr-def` elements to define the object classes and attributes.

The schema definition is written as:

```
<schema-def>
   <class-def class-name="" container="">
   <attr-def attr-name="" case-sensitive="" multi-valued="" naming="
   " read-only="" required="" type=""/>
   </class-def>
</schema-def>
```

Schema Mapping in DirXML

The *schema mapping rules* and related elements (`attr-name-map`) describe the relationship between the objects and attributes in the connected directories. These schema mapping rules, along with the matching rule elements (`matching-rules`), create rule elements (`create-rules`), and placement rule elements (`placement-rules`) collectively define the rules of the data manipulation.

The schema mapping is specified in a DirXML document in the `attr-name-map` top-level element. The `attr-name-map` element contains the rules for mapping the schema—associating the objects and attributes of the connected directory/datasource to the NDS schema.

Object classnames and attribute names both use mapping rules to link to related objects or attributes in foreign directories. The DirXML engine to map all class and attribute entries contained in the DirXML document uses schema mapping rules.

Mapping an object class is done via the `class-name` element, and two other `attr-name-map` child elements called `nds-name` and `app-name`, linking the name of the class in NDS and the class name in the external namespace.

Consider a schema mapping rule, for example, linking the `organizationalPerson` class to the NDS `User` class:

```
<attr-name-map>
     <class-name>
          <nds-name>User</nds-name>
          <app-name>organizationalPerson</app-name>
     </class-name>
</attr-name-map>
```

Mapping an attribute is done via the `attr-name` element, specifying the name of the attribute in NDS in the `nds-name` element and specifying the attribute name in the external namespace in the `app-name` element.

To specify linking the NDS `Common Name` attribute to the `cn` attribute for the external directory, for example, a schema mapping rule would look like:

```
<attr-name-map>
     <attr-name>
          <nds-name>Common Name</nds-name>
          <app-name>cn</app-name>
     </attr-name>
</attr-name-map>
```

eXtensible Directory Access Protocol

The *eXtensible Directory Access Protocol* (XDAP) is an Internet-Draft (`draft-newton-xdap-00`) developed by VeriSign/Network Solutions. XDAP is designed as a transport neutral framework to support search and retrieval operations on directories. Like other directory markup languages, XDAP leverages XML namespaces and XML schemas to structure directory information.

In an XDAP document, the root element must be `<xdap>`, which has `xmlns` as the attribute specifying the namespace identifier. XDAP handles operations via request/response elements (which may both be contained in the same XDAP document).

The request element contains child elements, which request operations from the directory, such as:

- `authenticate`—Authenticates the client, via `authenticationId` and `authenticationPassword` elements.
- `sessionInquiry`—Provides a mechanism to request information about the session.
- `serviceInquiry`—Requests a list of directory namespace identifiers.
- `directorySearch`—Queries the namespace of a directory service, using the `lookupEntity` and `query` elements.
- `quit`—Indicates the client wants to close the session.

For example, a request could be written as:

```
<request>
  <authenticate>
    <simpleAuthentication directoryNamespace="namespace identifier">
      <authenticationId></authenticationId>
      <authenticationPassword></authenticationPassword>
    </simpleAuthentication>
  </authenticate>
</request>
```

The `response` element contains child elements, which the directory uses to provide query results, service results, and status information. These child elements include:

- `sessionStatus`—Status information on the session
- `serviceResult`—Results of a `serviceInquiry`
- `directoryResult`—Results of a `directorySearch`

For example, a response could be written as:

```
<response>
  <sessionStatus>
    <currentlyAuthenticated directoryNamespace="namespace identifier" />
  </sessionStatus>
</response>
```

This is only a brief glimpse at the XDAP directory markup language. For more information, see the XDAP specification and other information at the following URLs:

lists.oasis-open.org/archives/dsml/200106/msg00001.html

www.cto.netsol.com/home.php?inc=projects.inc&content=projects/xdap/draft-newton-xdap-00.html

www.cto.netsol.com/home.php?inc=projects.inc&content=projects/xdap/draft-newton-xdap-domdir-00.html

www.cto.netsol.com/home.php?inc=projects.inc&content=projects/xdap/draft-newton-xdap-ipdir-00.html

Evaluating Directory Services

CHAPTER

13

...investigate in detail, contemplate at length, act with caution...

IN THIS CHAPTER

This chapter switches the focus from directory theory, technologies, and implementations to look at how to assess your directory service needs. The discussion begins by examining key factors to assess in your existing enterprise environment and then explains how to determine what you need a directory service to do. This chapter also presents ideas about how to evaluate the various directory service products in the context of your network.

There are no fixed “right answers” to directory implementation questions. Each section of this chapter does, however, try to highlight key questions that you should ask about your business, directory needs, network platform, and the directory service that you are considering.

Examining Directory Services

The deployment of a directory service represents a significant investment of time, money, and other resources. Such a project requires a substantial amount of corporate effort to research, plan, and deploy. When deployed, the directory service needs to work well for an extended period of time—businesses often rely on the directory service for core operations and don’t change them lightly. Given this, you should evaluate and plan carefully before committing to a particular solution.

Directory service products vary significantly in the scope of services provided and the industry standards supported; the underlying mechanisms of each directory service implementation also differ.

It can be difficult to sort out the competing claims of directory vendors and derive a clear understanding of the technologies and functionality supported by each directory product. It can be particularly difficult to assess the “unseen implications” of the vendor’s architectural decisions on the resultant directory service product.

You must evaluate directory service products in the context of the requirements of your business operations and networking environment. (How does it work with *your* existing directories, key applications, networking infrastructure, and so on?)

To do this, you need to look at three major areas:

- **Assess your directory service needs**—Analyze your business requirements and goals.
- **Assess your environment**—Determine the current state of your enterprise IT environment in detail.
- **Evaluate key directory service factors**—Determine which products provide the directory service features your network requires.

> **Consider the Questions in Context**
>
> A lot of questions are asked while examining assessment and evaluation criteria in this chapter. These questions can be answered only in the context of *your specific* network and business environment.

Assess Your Directory Service Needs

Directory services provide a general-purpose approach to information management, but the operational needs of each business are individual. Chapter 2, "Evolution of Directory Services," discussed how the operational needs drive the design of different sorts of directory services. With this perspective in mind, you want to think about how your business needs impact the design of a directory service for your environment.

As with any significant change in the operation of your business, it is imperative to have clearly defined goals—in this case, the goals for what your enterprise is trying to achieve by implementing a directory service. Some of these goals will be operational (network management, for example), others may be political (such as control of information).

You need to carefully identify, in the context of your specific environment, the business, operational, and network needs you are trying to address. As Melinda (see sidebar) would ask, "*What functionality are you lacking…?*"

The Melinda Question

One day, a customer was complaining that the software from Melinda's company was crashing. Unclear as to the exact nature of the problem, Melinda asked about the process that led to the software failure:

Melinda: Hmmm, when does the application crash?

Customer: When I am opening and closing it.

Melinda: Both opening and closing? Every time?

Customer: Well, I lined up my icons so that I can click to open your program and then click to close it without moving my mouse—real fast, you know? That's when it crashes, when I open and close it a bunch of times in a row real fast—that's when it crashes!

Melinda: (after a long pause) Sir, *what functionality do you feel our program is lacking that you are attempting to add by doing this?*

You can view the implementation of every technology from this kind of perspective (that is, what functionality are you attempting to add?)—when you apply this perspective to directory services, the question becomes:

What functionality is your business lacking that you are attempting to add by implementing a directory service?

Define Your Goals Carefully

To accomplish your goals, you must first know what they are. This is especially true when deploying something as complex as a directory service. Before beginning to design your directory service, look carefully at what you are trying to achieve.

"Simplify network access and management" is a common goal for a directory service. Although this is a useful goal, more specific objectives are required for a successful transition to a directory service, even relatively focused ones intended to manage a network.

You have to examine closely the information management and networking functionality that your existing infrastructure lacks that your business needs and the degree to which a given directory service product can supply that functionality. You should first consider "big picture" issues such as the following:

- What is the purpose of the directory service? E-commerce? Enterprise Directory? Network Management? Line-of-Business application?
- What is the scope of information that you need the directory service to manage?
- What administrative capabilities do you need? Are you planning on centralized or delegated administration?
- How will the directory information be used in network and business operations? By applications?
- What are your baseline operational requirements for the directory service? Does it need to be available for 9-to-5 operations or for 24/7 e-commerce?
- Which groups need to access what ranges of directory information? Employees? Business partners? Customers?

Different entities will have significantly different (as well as overlapping) goals and requirements. It is critical that the needs of all involved be considered when determining what the directory service should do. For the directory implementation to be successful, the common requirements and goals need to be met, and any unique requirements addressed as needed.

The goals and requirements of the following entities should be carefully considered when deciding what the directory service should do:

- Business management
- Network administrators
- Users
- Applications

Business Goals and Requirements

The overall business organization goals are likely to revolve around how the directory service can enhance business operations—reduce cost, generate income, optimize use of network, and improve productivity. These goals are common to most businesses, but it is difficult to quantify an approach to accomplishing them, and even more difficult to measure them. More tangible business goals can take a variety of forms, depending on what your business does:

- **E-commerce**—Your business may need to support e-commerce operations with services such as customer account, security, and certificate management.
- **Web site management**—Managing visitors to Web sites, including providing customized content, is another common need for many businesses.
- **Customer management**—You may also need your customer management information to be available to, and/or integrated with, your core business applications.
- **Partnerships**—An increasing number of businesses require a secure method of sharing business information with partners, clients, and vendors.

Who Should Participate in Planning?

An important part of a directory service deployment is putting together the planning and deployment team. As part of a distributed IT management team, most administrators are directly responsible for only a portion of their network. Because directory services are generally deployed on an enterprisewide basis, however, administrators from across your organization will need to collectively assess the needs of the enterprise as it pertains to the directory service.

As directory services are ultimately about information, expect that nontechnical staff will also need to be involved in the planning and deployment process. You should be sure the Human Resources department is represented, for example, because so much of the directory information is about the people who work in your enterprise. Depending on your implementation and business, you might want to consider legal reviews of policies regarding directory contents, disclosure, and usage.

By inviting people from outside the IT department to participate in the project, you will ultimately improve the quality of your directory service design and implementation. Getting input from people in other departments will also help ensure that you don't plan a technically brilliant solution, only to have it run into an unseen business-related barrier.

Networking Goals and Requirements

Networking requirements are usually concerned with resource management, network security, and monitoring, as well as the ease of management tasks and the capability to delegate administration. You will want to evaluate the required directory service functionality in these aspects of your network:

- **Network management**—Consider the administrative aspects of your network environment. Are there tasks that are needlessly difficult, duplicated management, or other situations you would like to address via the directory service?
- **Security**—For what resources do you need to provide access control? Do you need strong authentication, encryption, data control, privacy, PKI services, and/or digital certificates?
- **Network services**—Is support for location services, dynamic addressing (such as DHCP), routing, and/or QoS services required?
- **Desktop management**—Do you require robust distributed client desktop management capabilities, such as those provided in Novell ZENworks or Microsoft IntelliMirror?

User Goals and Requirements

People want the directory service to make their jobs easier—for most people using the directory this translates to easing access to information and network resources and simplifying management of their directory-related data. The people who use the directory service will expect some of the following capabilities:

- **Resource location**—A directory is frequently used to locate network resources, such as file shares and printers.
- **Address book**—One of the most common uses of a directory service is as an address book with e-mail, phone numbers, and other information about the people within your enterprise.

Customer Management as a Business

Consider an ISP as one example of a business that can significantly reduce the cost of managing clients with a fully integrated, and thoughtfully designed, directory service. A directory service could allow a new user account to be created and configured in a minimum of time—something especially needed in the high client turnover environment of an ISP. Additional fee-based services can also be supported via QoS and other network management technologies that are being increasingly directory-enabled.

- **Application management**—Directory-enabled applications leverage the directory to store related client data (such as security and configuration information). This frees users from having to keep track of application information stored in multiple locations and provides support for roaming users.
- **Multinetwork sign-on capabilities**—Even though most enterprise networks are using multiple operating platforms, user logon to the various networks is seldom integrated. From the user's perspective, this is less than desirable and calls for some form of integration, although from the administrator's perspective it is a security nightmare. Addressing this can take the form of simple password synchronization or more integrated solutions such as a Single Sign-On product.
- **Groupware operations**—The directory can also play a central role in the operations of groupware products (such as scheduling), which rely on access to information about network clients.

Application-Related Goals and Requirements

The core applications that you use in your business operations provide another aspect of the goals and requirements for a directory service. Application-related factors you need to determine include

- **Criticality**—Which applications *must* be integrated into the new directory service? Although it is nice to plan on eventually integrating everything into the directory, it's seldom a fast process. You should prioritize applications relative to the need to integrate them with the directory and assess the time involved to do so.
- **Information**—Determine what information your applications need to store and whether there is overlap between the information required by various applications. You should also determine the size of the data that an application will store. Data storage size can have multiple implications, including increases in the size of the directory and replication traffic.
- **Services**—Which services (such as security or logon) do your applications need the directory service to provide?
- **Application Programming Interfaces**—Which APIs do existing applications require to operate correctly? Are certain programming interfaces needed for in-house programming or future application deployment?

Prepare for Compromises

One of the things that will become obvious in the process of assessment and evaluation is that you are unlikely to locate the "perfect" directory service. In the directory service implementation process, it is likely that everyone will have to make some compromises along the way. Some goals may not be attainable, some business operations too difficult, time-consuming, or expensive to "directory-enable."

Assessing Performance Requirements

Determining requirements for directory performance is another important aspect of the needs assessment. By combining information about the demands that will be placed on the directory (how many clients, queries, and so on) and the performance expected of it, you can gain a clearer vision of the level of service it must provide. This is central in determining the overall quantity and distribution of directory servers required for your environment.

You should consider these issues:

- **Availability**—What level of availability does the directory need to deliver? Is it going to be accessed by the public via the Internet at any time, or will it be used for a 50-hour-a-week business environment, and at what client request loads? Can you afford *any* decrease in level of service, no matter how temporary, due to server failure or other problems?
- **Responsiveness**—What is required in terms of responsiveness to queries? How much latency is acceptable in data synchronization? If you are controlling critical real-time security applications, for example, you have a substantially lower threshold for latency than if you are providing an e-mail address book.
- **Bandwidth**—Consider the amount of bandwidth available for directory traffic, both in terms of queries and replication. Do you have critical links that are already congested? Are there intermittent (dial-up) connections that must be accounted for in the directory design?

Considering Information Control Factors

A number of critical information management factors are involved in implementing a directory service. One issue that you must deal with is particularly difficult: the politics of information. Key political factors center on issues of information management, control, and privacy.

Consider the information ownership factors discussed in Chapter 2, in relation to your network and a distributed directory service. You must determine who is responsible for managing and controlling access to directory information. Information control policies must also be determined, for business security as well as protection of personal information. Consider questions such as the following:

- **Who owns which portions of the data?**—To the network administrator, it may seem natural that all information contained in the directory should be "owned" by the IT department. You can be sure, however, that not everyone will be in agreement. Consider that information about employees is often one of the most significant portions of directory information. Accordingly, the Human Resources department might feel that *they* should own some staff information. Likewise, if your directory manages customer accounts, your sales department might want control over the information. There is no single (or simple) answer, but you must ensure that your administrative approach takes these issues into account, perhaps by delegating management of sensitive information.

- **Who is responsible for accuracy of data?**—This might not be the same group that "owns" the information. You might want to make employees responsible for keeping their personal information updated, for example, and provide them with a simple Web form to do so. The ultimate ownership of the information would not rest with the individual staff member, but the duty of keeping it accurate would.
- **Who is responsible for initially providing the directory information?**—The initial gathering of information for population of the directory can be tedious, particularly if the information is dispersed across the enterprise. It is likely that much of the information you want for the directory is in a NOS or e-mail database, application database, or human resources management tool. Information from external databases such as these can frequently be imported into the directory via scripting or tools provided by the vendor. For the information that cannot be imported, however, you may want to consider distributing the responsibility for providing *small amounts* of information to individuals.
- **Information Privacy**—Corporations require access to a substantial amount of information about each employee and customer. Consequently, businesses are faced with the task of providing controlled access to the data where required, while protecting the information from unauthorized access. Regulations add another layer of requirements for data protection and accountability. This is true not only for personal information but also for sensitive corporate data.

With a clear sense of your enterprise requirements and objectives, you are ready to move on to evaluating your current environment.

Directory Services and Privacy

Consider how moving from a simple directory to a directory service can reframe the whole issue of privacy. When phone directories were the usual printed white pages, you could look up a telephone number only if you knew the name of the person or business. Next, reverse directories enabled looking up a person by his or her phone number, providing more (but still fairly limited) capabilities.

With the Internet, online white pages can provide significant advantages—the information is more likely to be current, you can access directories from any geographic area, and anyone can do a reverse lookup. People and businesses can now be located based on their addresses, and a map with directions to the listed address can be printed with a single click.

This is great for businesses—customers can find you and get directions to your business at the same time. But (on the personal side), do you want just anyone to get a map to *your house*?

This increased capability can be used for either good or bad. In whatever use, however, it has serious legal and organizational implications for your directory. Because your directory will contain sensitive information, you *must* consider the implications of access to that data. With identity theft on the rise, and many people rightfully objecting to their personal data being made publicly available, an "opt-in" policy for controlling exposure of any personal data seems useful. Clear policies should be written and consent obtained before *any* personal information is exposed to anyone other than the few people who *need* to know. Keep in mind that for international organizations, the regulations and legalities of protecting confidential information may be different for every country.

Assess Your Environment

After you have completed a detailed assessment of your needs and goals, you are prepared to take the next step: determining the current state of your business and network environment. You'll need to carefully assess your IT infrastructure and operations with regard to the effects and implications of implementing any directory service. If you are familiar with the current state of your enterprise, you will be better able to determine what is desired from the directory service and, ultimately, how to achieve your goals.

Evaluate Business Aspects

Although implementing a directory service is an IT operation, it is clearly also a business process, affecting the entire company. Business considerations should also be taken into account while planning the directory deployment and implementation. Aspects to consider include

- **Corporate organization**—You should collect information on critical business subdivisions and collaborative efforts so that related business requirements can be accommodated in the directory design. Are there multiple points of public presence, or business names, that must be accounted for in the directory design? Because it is probable that at least some portions of your directory tree will be modeled on your business organization, you should be sure that you have a current company organizational chart.
- **Impact of implementation on your business**—Consider the impact that any networkwide change will have on your business operations. What is planned for the business in the near future? Times of major business flux usually are not a good time to overhaul the corporate network.
- **Degree of business flexibility**—Assess the flexibility of your business operations. Does your business embrace change or strongly resist it? Is your business organization static or dynamic? Does your company often buy other companies? Are there frequent departmental shuffles? Consider the impact of these things when designing your directory tree. If you design your DIT around a corporate organizational chart that changes every 18 months, you will spend a lot of time reorganizing your directory (in this case, geographical divisions might be useful). Likewise, if staff changes that affect the use of network resources are common, you need to take this into account in your directory design to streamline user management.

- **Relationships with business partners**—Evaluate the impact of the directory service implementation on the relationships with your business partners. Do you share information with business partners, vendors, or others either electronically or otherwise? Do you have outsourced partners (such as Web hosting services) that will be impacted by the planned directory service? Although discontinuing certain outside services may be one goal of the directory implementation, management should be aware of the impact on important business relationships.

Analyze Current Information Organization

One of the common reasons for moving to an enterprisewide directory service is the desire to consolidate existing information management and network resource information. This frequently means subsuming existing directories and the associated information as part of the integration/ migration path. Existing management processes should be reviewed, as much of the information currently managed by various entities in your business will eventually be contained in and managed by the directory service. Look at the following information management factors:

- **Namespace organization**—An enterprise commonly has multiple directories, each with a different namespace. The primary directory in your current network is probably the one associated with your NOS. Can you integrate your existing namespace design? Does it need to be restructured? If so, is there a migration path from your current namespace to your proposed directory structure?
- **Current naming schemes**—You'll want to identify the naming schemes in use in your enterprise environment; there are likely to be several. What naming schemes (such as those used in your e-mail or network operating system) are currently in use in your environment? Does the directory provide support for these naming schemes (or does it replace them)? For example, Active Directory uses the DNS naming convention for its core naming scheme but provides backward compatibility to the NT NetBIOS-based services. Consider the impact of changing a primary naming scheme, perhaps in such a way that everyone's network logon name *changes*; how many users will you have to inform, and how smoothly will all these users migrate to their new usernames?
- **Resource location**—Determine how network resources are currently located. Do network users commonly browse to locate printers and file shares, or are static mappings done when users log on to the network? As an example of one approach—when a user logs on to an eDirectory server, needed network and application directories are mapped to logical drives via login scripts.
- **Existing directories**—You probably already have a number of directories and directory-like products in your organization, either as standalone applications or integrated into another piece of software. Determine exactly what information current directories are managing, and what is relying on their services. Assess the different management products in use and determine whether their functionality can be consolidated via the directory service.

Assessing the Network Infrastructure

The capabilities of the underlying network components can substantially affect the overall performance of any network service. This is particularly true for a directory service, because it concentrates traffic on particular network segments, and on the directory servers. Ascertain the state of your core network components by evaluating the following:

- **Network topology**—Start your assessment by looking at the physical topology of the network. You need to know the bandwidth of the local segments as well as each WAN connection. These values are useful in assessing the impact of replication traffic for local and remote partitions. Does the directory need to be exposed inside the firewall, outside the firewall, or both?
- **Network hardware**—Identify hardware that is part of the network infrastructure, such as routers and bridges. These devices may be manageable via a directory service. For instance, there is an initiative called Directory Enabled Networking (DEN) that is focused on developing the technology to allow directory services to manage network devices.
- **Servers**—Determine the quantity, distribution, and nature of your servers—how many servers, where are they physically located, and what services are they providing to your network? How many logon servers, application servers, print servers, and file servers do you have on your network? Determine which network operating systems are in use on your network—do you have more than one core NOS, and if so, how are the different NOS types connected, and what kinds of data or services are shared?
- **Workstations**—You will need similar information about the clients on your network—how many and what operating systems are they using, which servers do they access? You will want to pay particular attention to where clients are in relationship to critical servers, such as e-mail. Do people log on or access resources across dial-up or WAN connections?
- **External Clients**—If your directory service is going to be accessed via public channels, such as the Internet, you need to consider the numbers and types of clients that will be used. Will external access be done primarily from businesses, where you can count on relatively new computers and reasonable bandwidth, not to mention on-site tech support; or from home users with highly variant systems and dial-up connections?
- **Other network factors**—Is your network more static or dynamic? Do you have test environments that need to be isolated from the production environment? What else is planned for the network? How does this impact your directory service plans? Do you have outsourced services (such as Web hosting or call-center management) that will be affected?

Identifying Network Services

Many network services are required for core operations and applications. Accordingly, you need to identify all the critical services used by your network and applications. Examine how the various services are being managed, paying particular attention to duplicated tasks. Services you should gather information about include

- **Network services**—Evaluate the network services used in your network environment; what are they used for, and what depends on the service. Make a list of the network services (DNS, DHCP, WINS, and so on) so that you can determine whether services will be supported, ignored, or rendered obsolete by the new directory service product.
- **Security services**—Your network probably uses multiple security methods and protocols, requiring you to determine the degree to which a directory service supports or replaces them. Be sure that you evaluate the use of Web security services such as Public Key Infrastructure (PKI) certificate management, Secure Sockets Layer (SSL), and others. Do you use security identifiers, such as SmartCards, photos, or biometrics that the directory must support?
- **Application services**—Identify the key applications used in your business. Do you have critical applications that rely on a specific NOS or directory service? Custom applications should also be carefully assessed. These applications are frequently among the most important, and yet, because they are custom written, may have integration issues.

Important Dimensions to Consider

Determine your overall approach to particular aspects of a directory service because this can make a difference in your evaluation. Every directory situation differs—different approaches are desirable for different environments, depending on how the directory is going to be used. Consider basic factors such as the following:

- **DIT design**—For internal directory services, this generally comes down to a decision between designing the top of the directory tree along geographic boundaries or business divisions. Lower portions of the DIT may be divided along business functional lines or perhaps used to organize directory objects into OUs by class (users, groups, and so on)

Having a Map Can Be Useful

If you don't already have one, you should create a network map, including bandwidth, WAN links, and national (language) boundaries. You can then add the number and location of important components and management functionality to the map as a means of drawing a complete picture of your network environment. This will prove helpful when it is time to plan your directory because you will be able to sketch both needed services and proposed configurations on the network map.

for management purposes. If the directory service is going to be used on the Internet, the directory tree needs to be designed to support the required operations and users.

- **Naming**—The naming model can make a substantial difference in how easy it is for people to determine and remember object names. Your naming standards should provide a clear and simple method of naming objects in a way that facilitates their identification and location.
- **Administration**—How is the directory going to be managed? Are you planning on centralized or delegated administration? Be sure that responsibility for backups of the directory and maintenance of directory servers are clearly assigned (with redundancy) because reliable directory operations will likely be crucial.
- **Education**—Decide whether administrators and users will be formally trained in classes, expected to self-study through commonly available resources (and allocated time), or some combination of the two. Remember that external users, such as those who access your Web site, are not going to be trained at all and therefore your implementation *must* be intuitive.

Key Factors in Directory Services

Now that you have reviewed your network environment and determined your requirements and goals, you can move on to evaluating the available directory service products. It is important at this point to keep your specific purpose in focus, because the operational requirements will depend on size and distribution of your information resources, as well as security, administration, and integration demands. You should also thoroughly analyze the information repositories, ownership, and management factors, and consider necessary migration processes prior to committing to a specific directory service implementation.

Key factors you will likely want to consider regarding the planning and implementation of a directory include the core functionality, administration, performance, security, and other directory design factors.

An Architectural Touchstone

As the archetype of directory service designs, X.500 provides a structure that all directory designs can be compared against, so that the degree of directory functionality can be assessed. Understanding the similarities and differences between a particular directory service implementation and the X.500 standards also brings architectural elements into focus. A directory service does not necessarily need to comply exactly with X.500, but it will be helpful if you understand how it does *not*.

Core Directory Functionality

To evaluate a directory service, begin by examining the core functionality needed in your environment. By this time, it is probably clear which aspects of your desired directory service are considered critical—either a given product supports them or you find a product that does. Other aspects are less make-or-break, but are important nonetheless. Look at whether the products you are considering meet your needs regarding the following:

- **Scope of directory**—Investigate the product's management scope. Determine the range of information the directory integrates and manages, including how down-level directories and external resources are handled. Most critically, be sure that whatever is *essential* to you is within the capabilities of the directory service. Extensibility is an important aspect to consider because it provides you with the mechanism to expand the directory scope as needed.
- **Supported platforms**—A core issue when selecting a directory service product is the platforms on which it can operate. To a large extent, the question of supported platforms comes down to this: Does it run on what you are currently using, and can it integrate with your current NOS and server platforms?
- **Server requirements**—Of course you need to consider the vendor's recommendations for minimum server hardware, including processor, RAM, and storage space requirements. However, you also need to realistically assess the type of load that will be handled by your directory servers. Dedicated servers are usually recommended for adequately responsive directory service operations. Be sure to account for the expected number of clients and queries, as well as the amount of data handled by the typical directory server. Don't merely accept the vendors' metrics at face value—test the product on your lab servers and monitor the performance under varying loads. Benchmarks for server metrics may be available from a number of industry sources. Be sure you consider how replica placement affects the number of needed servers-——Active Directory's limitation of one replica per server is very different from eDirectory's limit of 250!
- **Client support**—Whether your current network clients are supported is another thing you need to determine. You are likely to have a mix of client platforms and the functionality provided to some clients might be limited. (*Limited* commonly means operating as if the server were a previous version.) You might find that some client machines require hardware or software upgrades to fully utilize the directory service. If so, verify that functionality will be adequate in the interim. Don't forget external clients, where you cannot control the installed software.
- **Dependencies**—Does the directory service require supporting services and, if so, are those services currently being provided on your network? Will existing services require substantial reconfiguration or replacement? You should be sure your directory administrators group includes people who are familiar with all the ancillary services required by

the directory. Active Directory requires DNS, for example, and, although it is not required that you run Windows 2000 DNS, it is highly recommended. Because of the interrelationship between DNS and Active Directory, a notable number of reported Active Directory problems can be traced to incorrect DNS configuration.

Logical Organization of Information

The tree design used by a directory service has major implications concerning the degree to which the product can meet your requirements. When evaluating a directory service product, pay close attention to product constraints and inherent functional limitations. Things to consider include the following:

- **Logical organization**—The logical organization allowed by a directory service product can play a critical role in tree design, naming, and Directory Information Base (DIB) partitioning and replication. The directory may provide a classic X.500-style tree (such as eDirectory) or integrate other models in the tree design (such as Active Directory). Directory trees may be logically subdivided for some reason, or perhaps multiple trees are linked for management purposes.
- **Desired tree design**—How do you want to design your tree? Do you need to account for WANs, international borders, or the business organization in your DIT design? What other directories or namespaces exist in your enterprise, and do you want to use one of them as the basis for your directory tree?
- **Tree design constraints**—Are there constraints on directory design or operations because of some aspect of the overall design? A salient example of this is Active

Vendor Responsiveness

Once, in the course of writing a book, we sent e-mail to two large vendors requesting information about their respective products.

In the first case, we selected an employee of the company who was publicly providing contact with the group controlling the product in question. The response was delayed and then merely routed us to another employee, who directed us to another (wrong) department. No follow-up occurred to determine whether we received the information.

In the second case, we sent e-mail to an employee of the company about 7 p.m. We had a response the same night and e-mail waiting from an employee in the product group the next morning offering to help. Over the next few days, we received a number of follow-up contacts with useful data about their product.

Although you probably aren't going to need data to write a book, you may want to seriously gauge some of the less-tangible aspects of a vendor's approach to their customers, such as whether they actually respond to your technical and information needs.

Directory. The Active Directory namespace integrates NT domains (complete with domain security boundary), and then uses the domain boundary to define the DIB partition. As described in Chapter 10, "Active Directory," this has some interesting implications. In light of the organization allowed by the directory, does your preferred DIT design work? If not, are the needed compromises ones you are willing to make?

- **Flexibility**—Will the directory be flexible enough to support your business as it grows in both size and complexity? What if your Internet user base doubles in size in the next six months? Does the directory provide the capability to easily reorganize to reflect company changes? Is there support for key tree functionality such as freely pruning, grafting, and moving objects within the tree?

Directory Data Management

You should also examine what sort of data repository is used, and how the DIB is managed. Key factors in DIB management revolve around the nature of the distribution and replications methods that are used, such as the following:

- **Partition flexibility**—Examine the degree of flexibility in partition management. Do you have the capability to subdivide or combine existing partitions? Does partition management require an inordinate amount of time or effort? Manual configuration of a small directory is a minor hassle, but the same lack of automation in a massive directory can be highly problematic.
- **Degree of control over replication**—Consider replication factors such as the replication granularity, latency, and degree of control over the scheduling, protocols, and routing of replication traffic. Are there restrictions on where replicas can be placed, protocols that can be used, number of replicas per server, and so on?
- **Effect of synchronization**—Synchronization methods and costs must also be considered, especially across WAN links. You are primarily able to control the impact of synchronization traffic via how you partition your directory, and using routing and scheduling. The method of synchronization used may have its own implications. eDirectory relies on time services, for example, requiring you to monitor an additional service to ensure data integrity.

From the Vendor's Perspective

Look at directory service products from the perspective of the vendor. Note how the vendor intended the directory to be organized and used. What directory models, preferred technologies, and overall approach was it using in its design? If you look at how the vendor views its directory, you can get a feel for how its product will work in your environment.

Scalability of the Directory

Examining DIB management in general is useful and gives you an idea of how the directory will impact your network. You will also want to determine specific limitations on the amount of information the directory stores, because it directly impacts the scalability of the directory service.

The question of scalability is frequently framed as "does the directory service work well in a large distributed implementation?" But, the *relevant* question is "does it scale sufficiently for *your* environment?"

You need to assess your expected tree size—keeping in mind that you will likely have objects for users, groups, computers, services, printers, other managed hardware, volumes, file shares, services, and application information. Remember to factor in the likely future growth and partnership needs of your business.

Each directory service has metrics concerning the data it stores that place fundamental constraints on directory scalability. These factors include

- **Objects per partition**—There are functional limits on the number of objects a partition can hold. This may vary widely, even from one version of a product to the next. For example, Novell redesigned the storage mechanisms for eDirectory v.8 and now states that eDirectory can hold millions of objects per partition, although prior versions only handled a few thousand.
- **Partitions per server**—There may also be restrictions on the number of partitions a server can hold. For example, Active Directory allows a domain controller to manage only a single partition. The total number of partitions in the DIT may also be limited based on operational factors.
- **Storage limitations**—There are probably also physical file storage limitations, which can be particularly significant for large networks. If you have lots of large objects in your directory, DIB partitions could exceed file or storage limits. The partition size may also be a consideration when implementing backup routines and when replicating to new DSAs.
- **Objects per tree**—One critical limitation occurs at the directory tree level rather than the partition. You should ensure that the directory supports an adequate number of objects to meet your needs in a single tree. With just about every directory, however, this number is theoretically well over a million. (Novell says an eDirectory tree can hold a billion objects, as just one example.) Therefore, it might seem that most enterprise networks are unlikely to run into this limitation, after all, there are only about a quarter of a billion people using the Internet. But, remember it was once said that "640KB should be enough RAM for anyone," so be sure that your selected directory can manage considerably more data than you think it will have to.

Security Standards and Integration

A critical factor in a directory service is how the product implements security for directory objects and information, as well as for applications that rely on its security services. Most directory service products on the market support a mix of proprietary security schemes and open standards. You should investigate a number of aspects of the security provided for the directory, applications, and the network platform on which it will be running. You can start by looking at the following:

- **Security design considerations**—Fundamental security design should be examined for compatibility with your current (and desired) approach to security. Different directory implementations approach the application of directory security from somewhat different tangents, as discussed in previous chapters.
- **Authentication methods**—Factors involved in the authentication method employed to identify users on your network include availability of strong authentication and the encryption technologies used. You may also need the directory to perform pass-through authentication to applications or other directories. Does the directory service need to support employee photographs, SmartCards, biometrics, or other authentication methods? If so, you may want to investigate the size of the associated information to assess the impact on data management factors such as DIB size and amount of traffic.
- **Access control**—You need to consider how the directory service handles access control. Are permissions attached to the structural DIT objects, for example, managed via groups and policies, or by some combination? What forms of permission inheritance and inheritance-blocking are provided?
- **Supported security standards**—You will want to know the degree to which a directory provides support for existing security standards, such as Kerberos, SSL/PCT, X.509

Scalability Is About More than Big Numbers!

Scalability is an important factor to consider when looking at directory service products, but there is more to scalability than sheer numbers. Some vendors loudly proclaim that their directory service can manage many millions of objects while remaining relatively quiet as to what's behind the numbers. It is critical to remember, however, that a directory service is much more than just a database that can handle a large number of entries.

A directory service requires tools that streamline management, DSAs which provide availability and responsiveness for large numbers of concurrent users, a client interface that is easy for the consumers of the directory information to use, and perhaps most importantly, directory-enabled applications that leverage the directory. Without all these, a directory service may become another isolated island of information to manage without ever delivering the potential benefits of a well thought out directory deployment.

certificates, and SASL. If you are going to deploy secondary security services (such as an X.509 certificate server), check the degree to which they are integrated with the directory. Verify that vendor's claims to support security standards (such as Kerberos or PKI) are verifiable in the directory's operations.

- **NOS integration**—The degree to which the directory service security integrates with the security of the various platforms used on your network is another important consideration. Seamless integration of directory security with the NOS security subsystem is fundamental for networkwide user authentication.

Directory Administration

One key area in evaluating directory services is the degree of difficulty in conducting administrative tasks. From the perspective that effective administration is essential in a directory service, the ease of administrative task performance is a baseline consideration. Administrative aspects of a directory service to assess include the following:

- **Degree of complexity**—An important aspect of directory administration is the degree of complexity—how easy is it to perform management tasks? Complexity can take many forms: perhaps numerous tools are required to effectively manage the entire directory; it may be difficult to ascertain effective access permissions; or some functions may be hidden entirely. Although complexity is not inherently bad (and it's pretty much unavoidable), it does require the vendor to pay particular attention to supplying powerful and flexible tools that streamline administration.
- **Support for delegation**—The capability to securely delegate management tasks is a significant advantage to a directory service, particularly for administrators of large or distributed directories. Assess how the directory service supports delegation and which subsets of rights or tasks can be delegated. Are tools designed to simplify delegation, perhaps by offering templates of permissions to support specific tasks, or via security equivalence to existing administrators or roles?
- **Effectiveness of management tools**—Another concern is the availability and capability of the tools used to manage the directory. Are the tools unified or distributed throughout multiple applications? Can they be extended to support custom capabilities? Are tools available to administer the directory across the Web or from other remote locations? Do administrative tools run on the necessary platforms?
- **Scope of management capabilities**—Does the directory integrate with other management tools to provide enhanced management capabilities? Is there integration of desktop management software for remote deployment and management of clients? Does it support the Simple Network Management Protocol (SNMP), that is, can it interface with intermediate network hardware and report on network traffic issues?

Education and Support

Any change in your network operations requires you to train your staff to some degree, and especially your IT group. The change to a directory-centric network can entail substantial training requirements. This is also true, to a lesser degree, of people who use the directory service as a client.

Educating people about new technology is always costly—in terms of both time and money. Books are purchased, classes are held (and paid for), people spend days away from their usual jobs—it's an involved and expensive process. Whatever this costs, failing to provide education is likely to cost more in long-term support costs and lost productivity.

Clearly one of the goals of IT management is to encourage staff members to train themselves. By providing people with the capability to conveniently explore a new technology—in small pieces and at their own pace—you can provide them with the knowledge they need to do their job, although not overwhelming them with tertiary details. Even with all the self-study, however, some more traditional educational expenses are unavoidable, including the following:

- **Administrator training**—Determine how much and what kind of training is going to be required for administrators to effectively manage the new directory service? Will classroom training be required or are there adequate resources available for self-teaching or online learning? Is there a substantial community of others working with the product active in newsgroups or on a mailing list?
- **User education resources**—Educated users require less technical assistance to do their jobs, reducing support costs. Additionally, the materials used frequently overlap enough that you can provide a trimmed down version of the IT staff's educational materials to the rest of your staff. One advantage to the explosion in Internet usage is the increased comfort many people feel when accessing information via a Web page. You can leverage this familiarity by providing Web-based interfaces for clients to access educational resources.
- **Availability and utility of documentation**—Although good documentation is always important, it is of special concern when you are planning something as complex as running a distributed network, or an entire business, with new software. Consider to what degree documentation concerning technical and operational aspects of the directory service is available. Does the available documentation provide a useful and sufficiently detailed explanation of the needed information?

Your Directory Is Valuable

When the directory contains your business information, and provides the underlying infrastructure for the core of your business operations, you cannot afford to let it become nonoperational (or even problematic). Compare such problems to the cost of redundant servers (as well as switches, routers, and backup devices)—hardware is cheap when compared to what network downtime can cost your business.

- **Availability, usefulness, and cost of technical support**—Professional-quality technical support is also important and rapidly becoming a scarce commodity. Cost-effective technical support for your directory service will likely be necessary at various times. Carefully check the vendor's support policy; it is likely to be somewhat limited (perhaps only covering installation issues for a brief period of time). Is additional support available in your area, either in the form of local consultants, or via engineers providing services from a remote location?

Support for Industry Standards and Initiatives

Another useful perspective can be gained by viewing the degree to which a directory service vendor supports widely accepted industry standards and, correspondingly, the degree to which a proprietary scheme is implemented. Many firms rely on industry-approved solutions for multiyear stability of network operations and are less inclined to use products that support proprietary technologies only. Commonly supported standards and initiatives include

- **LDAP**—The LDAP protocol is rapidly becoming the de facto standard for client access to most directory service products. As LDAP is being used more for interoperability purposes, and many applications and tools are being written to support LDAP, clearly

How Easy Is It?

Evaluate with particular care the question of "how easy is this directory service product for *people* to use?" Consider how many times per hour (per day, per week) people using your directory are going to attempt to carry out specific operations to fulfill some job-related task. To illustrate this point, imagine what would happen to productivity if looking up an e-mail address became *difficult* or *time consuming*.

Many corporations envision the directory service becoming the central point of access to all information on the enterprise network, certainly an admirable goal. If the directory is going to become the main method of accessing the information related to your enterprise, however, it had better be *very* easy to use.

Directory Training and Certifications

Just as networks did years ago, directory services are becoming an area of specialization for information technology professionals. For example, Novell has started to train Directory Engineers (with periodic recertification requirements)—essentially a CNE, MCSE, or CCIE with additional focus on directory service technologies. The Directory Engineer certification requires both a written test and a hands-on style exam, with the candidate performing a set of tasks on a live system. More information on the Novell Directory Engineer certification is available at `www.novell.com/education/cde/`.

LDAP support is useful or needed in most directory services. Particularly if clients will be primarily accessing directory information via the Internet, you will likely want to select a directory service solution with robust LDAP support.

- **DNS**—DNS is widely deployed on the Internet and, increasingly, on corporate networks. Dynamic DNS (DDNS) is also beginning to be employed (and even relied on) by some directory service products. Consider the degree to which the directory integrates DNS management functionality and replication processes into the directory. Integrated DNS is particularly important to companies with distributed networks and substantial investments in DNS name server deployment. There is also the question of whether you want congruence between your DNS namespace and your directory tree. If you are doing e-commerce (or any Internet presence), you should also examine the correlation between DNS namespaces used internally (intranet) and externally (Internet) and the related security implications.
- **Directory Interoperability Forum (DIF)**—DIF is a significant directory forum that was founded in 1999 by a group of directory vendors as a means of advancing directories based on open standards such as LDAP. Vendors participating in DIF include Novell, IBM, Isocor, Oracle, Lotus, Data Connection, and more than 25 others. The DIF Web site is `www.opengroup.org/directory`.
- **Directory-Enabled Networking (DEN)**—Cisco and Microsoft are leading the DEN initiative to promote enhanced management of network hardware and services via directory services. This capability provides a means of controlling use of the network infrastructure, routing, bandwidth, encryption, and other functionality via policies enforced by the directory. Other partners in DEN include Intel, 3Com and Hewlett-Packard. The DEN Web site is `www.cisco.com/warp/public/cc/techno/network/dirserv/den/index.shtml`.
- **Internet Engineering Task Force (IETF) working groups**—The IETF is an organization of internetworking engineers, vendors, researchers, and others who form *working groups* to focus on a particular area of Internet development. For example, IETF has three LDAP-related working groups: LDAPBIS (LDAP (v3) Revision), LDUP (LDAP Duplication/Replication/Update Protocols) and LDAPExt (LDAP Extensions). Information on these groups is available at: `www.ietf.org`.
- **eXtensible Markup Language (XML)** —The eXtensible Markup Language is employed in accessing and representing directory service content. Bowstreet Software, in an alliance with IBM, Microsoft, Novell, Oracle, Sun, and Netscape, lead the effort to develop an XML-based method of accessing, managing, and manipulating directory information called *Directory Services Markup Language* (DSML). XML is the underlying abstraction language used to create DSML. DSML enables vendors to create applications that can use and share information from multiple distributed directories operating on different platforms. DSML enables applications to use directory information without knowledge of the specific format used by any particular directory. DSML is being developed as an IETF open standard. The DSML web site is `www.dsml.org`. Novell is also developing its own version of an XML-based directory markup language, called DirXML.

Application and Programming Support

Because your business operations rely on your applications, the application support provided by the directory service product is clearly a key element. In addition to concerns about basic application compatibility issues, consider the following:

- **Compatibility with key applications**—Is the directory service compatible with all the currently deployed applications that are important to your business? Will critical proprietary applications continue to work, or can they be easily upgraded or replaced?
- **Supported APIs**—Look at the degree of support the directory service provides for programming languages and APIs commonly in use in systems and application development. The support provided by a directory service for application development can substantially influence the availability of directory-enabled applications. API support is also important if you plan to write in-house applications that use the directory.
- **Directory-enabled applications**—Earlier in this chapter, you were asked to identify the applications in use in your environment and decide which of them are important to integrate into the directory. You should verify the availability of directory-enabled versions of those products for your preferred directory platform.
- **Scripting languages**—Directory services that provide support for scripting languages as a means of accessing and manipulating directory information are convenient from the administrative perspective. Simple, yet powerful scripts can be quickly written to automate many directory management tasks. Scripting support also means that directory information is available via languages commonly used on the Web, such as JavaScript and VBScript.

Vendors for Open Standards

The Directory Interoperability Forum (DIF) is a particularly interesting group as it is largely made up of vendors of proprietary directory services. It is probably a good sign that these industry players have embraced open standards. The DIF has the following stated objectives:

- Fostering the widespread adoption of open standards for directories by working with major standards bodies such as IETF, Desktop Management Task Force (DMTF), and the Open Group.
- Expanding the market for application vendors supporting open directory standards.
- Increasing customer confidence concerning directories based on open standards.

The DIF has working teams on varied aspects of directory interoperability, including security, LDAP-DCE, mobile and directory, certification, e-business requirements, standards co-ordination, and others. To find more information on each working group, go to the DIF working group Web site at: `www.opengroup.org/directory/workprog.htm`.

Directory Service Performance

The performance capabilities and fault tolerance of the directory service must be evaluated in the context of your intended usage. To assess the performance available from a directory service product, you have to use the baseline requirements you established earlier and apply them to the technologies and methods used by the specific directory service.

First, consider the capabilities required in your application. Examine the requirements you defined earlier, and contrast that with the directory service capabilities. By applying the directory service product constraints to your required directory capabilities, you can determine baseline feasibility and approach with a given directory service product.

When you are evaluating your requirements and the capabilities of the directory service, there are many detailed questions you will need to ask.

Be sure to consider:

- **How well can the product handle your information base?**—Assess your expected directory size. When you are estimating the size of your directory, keep in mind that you will likely have objects for users, groups, computers, services, printers, other managed hardware, volumes, file shares, services, as well as application information. Keep the future growth of your business and network in mind.
- **How well can it handle your peak service demands?**—This is a combination of availability and responsiveness (as described earlier). Given the number of connections (all entities accessing the directory) that will be used on your network and the amount of bandwidth required, what kind of capability does the product DSA have to handle the load? How many queries will need to be processed (at peak loads, and minimal loads)? Factor in all users, applications, other network services—anything that requires services from the directory requires a connection. Will the DSA supply more than one network service to clients, and can it handle the load of all services combined?
- **Does it have effective fault tolerance?**—If a DSA fails, is there redundancy or failover support? Do discrete sections of the DIB become unavailable, or do alternative DSAs automatically handle the queries? Does all directory functionality still work, or do some things stop working—updates in a single-master directory, for example.

Next, factor in the product constraints. Every directory product has constraints on a variety of aspects of operation, such as the following:

- Metrics concerning the DIT and DIB (discussed earlier in this chapter)
- Number of directory servers required for adequate responsiveness
- Client/query load limits per DSA

Review the product constraints and assess the limitations with regard to your operational and business requirements.

Then, keeping both your required capabilities and the product constraints in mind, establish the baseline feasibility and "fit" of the directory service product for your environment. When you evaluate your goals and requirements, and factor in the constraints of the product, you are left with the set of information needed to assess baseline considerations for deployment:

- Determine the number of DSAs required per client (responsiveness) and the impact of replication on network traffic (bandwidth): Will you need more servers, faster servers, or more bandwidth? Excessive server load is generally dealt with by deploying more DSAs.
- Carefully assess the placement of DSAs and replicas in your network topology to provide adequate service to clients. You can restrict lookup traffic by ensuring that DSAs are placed in the correct locations—close to the people who use those partition resources.
- Examine how catalogs and indexes are used because they typically provide faster access to the directory contents and frequently play an important role in the overall responsiveness of your directory service. If the directory provides catalogs and indexes, you should examine whether you can customize them, how catalogs handle access control, and how effectively they facilitate resource location.
- Consider the impact of expected directory usage and replication traffic on the effective bandwidth of the infrastructure connecting these clients and servers. Partitioning and replication of the DIB are factors of particular concern, because the performance impact of replicating the directory information can be a significant factor, both within the LAN and across slower WAN links.

When evaluating the bandwidth usage of a directory service, assess the effect of the directory service methods used. Take a look at the following:

- How the directory partition information is replicated, the size of the unit of replication, the frequency of replication, and the effective bandwidth utilization.
- Overall percentage of network utilization for client logon, directory access, and directory replication.
- Does the directory service support QoS bandwidth metering?

Directory Interoperability

Because most enterprises have multiple directories in use (including NOS variants), the capability to link different directory services has become increasingly important. You'll want to evaluate the directory service's capability to share and synchronize information with other directories, and to assess issues in directory migration, such as the following:

- **Approach to Interoperability**—Start by determining the style of interoperability you need—are you planning on long-term coexistence of multiple directory services or migration to a single directory? Is support for the level of directory integration required for your environment provided? If you are planning on long-term coexistence, are directory synchronization or metadirectory tools available?

- **Support for managing the resources of other NOSs**—If you use multiple NOSs, you may decide to use each NOS directory service, and then synchronize data (if possible). Alternatively, you might deploy a directory service on one NOS to manage the resources of both. For instance, eDirectory is notable in that it provides directory service functionality not only on the NetWare platform, but other leading NOS platforms as well (Windows NT, Sun Solaris, and Linux), providing a means of smoothly integrating a broad range of NOS resources.
- **Migration factors**—Because migration to a new directory service is a substantial expense and business interruption for most firms, migration factors should be seriously evaluated in your review of each directory service product. You will want to examine which of your current directories can be replaced by the new directory service. Examine what it will take to migrate *your* network to the new directory service. Pay particular attention to the availability of migration tools and mechanisms such as LDIF bulk import/export capability. Consolidating directory information manually can be costly in terms of time and effort.
- **Metadirectory integration**—Some enterprise networks are using metadirectory products to facilitate interoperability among the disparate directories on their network. A meta-directory product can provide support for the transition from multiple application-specific directories to a unified directory environment.

Assessing the Costs

After you have determined a directory service approach that effectively supplies the needed solution, you need to look carefully at what it will cost. You also want to look at the benefits to be derived from the directory deployment. Keep in mind that enterprise management (and thus you) must find a balance between the cost and the benefit of every new tool and technology used in the corporate network environment.

One of the central concerns in TCO (Total Cost of Ownership)enterprise computing today it is *Total Cost of Ownership* (TCO). Determining TCO is an analytical process that attempts to precisely quantify the cumulative "cost" of owning and operating all IT components (directories, networks, computers, applications, and so on) within the corporation. It is important to remember, however, that in addition to costs of ownership, there are also benefits of ownership. Every model of evaluating TCO is based on a set of assumptions, which may (or may not) accurately or adequately reflect the cost or benefit factors in *your* enterprise environment.

Although many methods of cost assessment of networks and directory services exist, they are essentially beyond the scope of this book (see the sidebar); they are described here in summary only.

...At What Cost?

The direct costs of a directory service implementation are at least partially knowable. With close evaluation, what you will pay for the software and hardware components is comparatively clear. The initial costs for a directory service include the following:

- **Software (per server/client)**—Pay close attention to the license cost structure—is it per server, per client? Are client licenses required for Internet access to the directory? Do you need to purchase other products that are required to support directory functionality?
- **New or upgraded hardware**—Do you need to upgrade existing servers or purchase new ones? Will other network components require hardware upgrades for adequate performance of the directory?
- **Documentation, training, and support**—What will adequate documentation cost? What will training and support cost?

Obviously, this is not the total expense for a directory service; there are additional deployment costs and ongoing maintenance expenses. The preceding list does, however, represent much of the immediately knowable aspects of the initial expense.

TCO is a much-less-direct financial measure, because it includes less directly tangible costs such as deployment, administration, maintenance, and programming. Significant industry vendors and analysts have used various TCO criteria, but these assessment criteria are often affected by technology or vendor bias, selective focus, or (our favorite) numbers fabricated from a single event and generalized from there.

Clearly, the numbers used to assess your cost of ownership should be based on your real financial and networking information, not an arbitrary set of values proposed by others. From your information, you can more closely determine the *actual* costs as they apply to *your* network and environment.

The Technology Is Affordable

Whatever the numbers, most companies that want to use directory services can afford to slowly integrate the technology into their network and business operations. Deliberative integration provides time for business to assess the impact of the change and to minimize the disruption of normal business operations.

Costing Methods Vary

Directory and network metrics are the subject of much debate, as vendors and industry analysts discuss various strategies for assessing information technology infrastructure costs. When you look at the different approaches to cost analysis, the specifics of how costs and savings are calculated vary substantially between models. Numerous TCO models point to a common core set of issues and factors in analyzing cost of ownership, including administration, capital investment, technical support, and end-user operations. Some sources for in-depth enterprise costing formulas are

- Forrester Research at www.forrester.com
- The Burton Group at www.tbg.com
- The Gartner Group at www.gartner.com

...For What Gain?

You are implementing a directory service for a reason, right? So, setting all the directory theory aside for a moment, just how is implementing this directory service going to benefit the company? Many people think of benefits in terms of money; they plan to save money by consolidating directories, streamlining network management, increasing productivity, and so on. Of course, you probably will see some of those benefits (...eventually).

However, buying and implementing a directory service is not likely to *make* you money in the near term—and it surely will *cost* you money in the near term. Although in the long term the implementation of a directory service can save enterprise businesses substantial amounts of money, directory deployment will be initially expensive in terms of software, hardware, network infrastructure, training, and administration costs.

A common measure, called Return on Investment (ROI), is used to describe the return (over time) of the value invested in such infrastructure costs. Like TCO, the ROI for a directory service implementation is highly variable. Vendors will proclaim substantial benefits that (should) result in a positive ROI. For the enterprise, however, a directory service implementation is an actual expense over an extended period of time, and returns (via productivity and so forth) are much more speculative.

Theoretical savings and other monetary benefits from the use of a directory service typically include the following:

- **Less administration required**—Reduction of duplicated management tasks is frequently stated as a means by which a directory service will save you money. However, those administrators will probably be busy learning how to make the new directory service work. Therefore, although they will be doing fewer repetitive tasks, they will also be doing more *different* ones.
- **Reduced user-support costs**—One commonly mentioned savings is lowered support costs from a network that is centralized, easier to use, and that supports remote desktop management. Using the directory as a common storage point for configuration information means fewer misconfigured applications, faster recovery from system crashes, and perhaps a centralized means of application deployment.

- **Elimination of paper directories**—Your business may be able to reduce or cease production of hard copies of information. This proves especially useful for information that is widely distributed, commonly misplaced, and contains information that changes frequently and is, therefore, outdated quickly (such as employee telephone listings).
- **Other possible savings**—Some less easily measured sources of savings may apply to your situation, such as lowered exposure to security risks, reduction in process delays, or a more efficient use of the network resources.

As you can see, ROI estimations can help and they can provide focus, guidelines, and direction. The degree of ROI really depends on what you do with the directory service, however—how you use it and the context in which it is implemented. The directory can become a powerful management tool, enabling you to assess and control your business as well as your network. A directory service could also be applied in a variety of valuable e-commerce implementations (and depending on the success of the site, could substantially improve your ROI).

For most networks, however, ROI will be a more subtle set of factors that reduce costs over time and improve user productivity via simplified information management.

The Upgrade Domino Effect

It starts slowly—you just want to upgrade a specific capability of a few servers—just a little thing really. And then you decide that just a little more RAM would really help performance and enable you to add more concurrent users. Then you discover that *now* you have enough RAM for that application you've been wanting, but the application requires more storage space (on each of the servers)....

Directory services are by no means immune to "the upgrade domino effect." In fact, they are a likely cause of it (new hardware, new versions of applications, more administrative time, user training, and so on). After all, one of the primary reasons people implement a networkwide directory service is to take advantage of applications that support it; and new applications may require additional resources.

Is It Going to Make You Money?

Are you planning to make money from the directory service? If so, be specific about how, and verify your details carefully. Unless your business is actually implementing the directory service in a for-profit operation (such as an e-commerce site, or selling the data contained in your directory), you will probably not directly make money from deploying a directory service

References

APPENDIX

A

There are references available on many of the technologies and products discussed in this book. The following sections list resources, broken down by major topic (such as X.500 or LDAP) and grouped by type (books, RFCs, and so on).

X.500

Books

Chadwick, David. 1996. *Understanding X.500: The Directory.* International Thomson Computer Press. This title is out of print, but portions of the text are available at `www.isi.salford.ac.uk/staff/dwc/Version.Web/Contents.htm`.

Radicati, Sara. 1994. *X.500 Directory Services.* International Thomson Computer Press. ISBN: 1-850-32879-x.

Standards

X.500 Information Technology—Open Systems Interconnection—The Directory: Overview of Concepts, Models, and Services, first published in 1988.

X.501 Information Technology—Open Systems Interconnection—The Directory: Models, first published in 1988.

X.509 Information Technology—Open Systems Interconnection—The Directory: Authentication Framework, first published in 1988.

X.511 Information Technology—Open Systems Interconnection—The Directory: Abstract Service Definition, first published in 1988.

X.518 Information Technology—Open Systems Interconnection—The Directory: Procedures for Distributed Operation, first published in 1988.

X.519 Information Technology—Open Systems Interconnection—The Directory: Protocol Specifications, first published in 1988.

X.520 Information Technology—Open Systems Interconnection—The Directory: Selected Attribute Types, first published in 1988.

X.521 Information Technology—Open Systems Interconnection—The Directory: Selected Object Classes, first published in 1988.

X.525 Information Technology—Open Systems Interconnection—The Directory: Replication, first published in 1993.

X.530 Information Technology—Open Systems Interconnection—The Directory: Use of Systems Management for Administration of the Directory, first published in 1997.

RFCs

Note: For any RFC, use the RFC# as `www.ietf.org/rfc/rfc####.txt` to get to the RFC.

For example `www.ietf.org/rfc/rfc1035.txt`

1249—"DIXIE Protocol Specification." T. Howes, M. Smith, and B. Beecher, (August 1991, Informational).

1274—"The COSINE and Internet X.500." Schema P. Barker and S. Kille, (November 1991, Proposed standard).

1275—"Replication Requirements to Provide an Internet Directory Using X.500." S.E. Hardcastle-Kille, (November 1991, Informational).

1276—"Replication and Distributed Operations Extensions to Provide an Internet Directory Using X.500." S.E. Hardcastle-Kille, (November 1991, Proposed standard).

1279—"X.500 and Domains." S.E. Hardcastle-Kille, (November 1991, Experimental).

1308—"Executive Introduction to Directory Services Using the X.500 Protocol." C. Weider, J. Reynolds, (March 1992, Informational).

1309—"Technical Overview of Directory Services Using the X.500 Protocol." C. Weider, J. Reynolds, and S. Heker, (March 1992, Informational).

1330—"Recommendations for the Phase I Deployment of OSI Directory Services (X.500) and OSI Message Handling Services (X.400) Within the ESNET Community." ESCC X.500/X.400 Task Force, ESnet Site Coordinating Committee (ESCC), (May 1992, Informational).

1373—"Portable DUAs." T. Tignor, (October 1992, Informational).

1430—"A Strategic Plan for Deploying an Internet X.500 Directory Service." S. Hardcastle-Kille, E. Huizer, V. Cerf, R. Hobby, and S. Kent, (February 1993, Informational).

1431—"DUA Metrics (OSI-DS 33 [v2])." P. Barker, (February 1993, Informational).

LDAP

Books

Howes, Timothy A., Mark C. Smith, and Gordon S. Good. 1999. *Understanding and Deploying LDAP Services*. Macmillan Technical Publishing. ISBN: 1-57870-070-1.

Howes, Timothy A., and Mark C. Smith. 1997. *LDAP: Programming Directory-Enabled Applications with Lightweight Directory Access-Protocol*. Macmillan Technical Publishing. ISBN: 1-57870-000-0.

RFCs

As with DNS, quite a few RFCs concern LDAP. You can search for any RFC by number or keyword at `www.rfceditor.org/rfcsearch.html`.

In addition to the RFCs listed here, you may want to consult the IETF postings regarding the current status of working groups at: `www.ietf.org/html.charters/wg-dir.html`.

The LDAP RFCs are listed in numeric order:

1778—"The String Representation of Standard Attribute Syntaxes." T. Howes, S. Kille, W. Yeong, and C. Robbins, (March 1995, [obsoletes 1488, updated by 2559] Draft standard).

1823—"The LDAP Application Program Interface." T. Howes and M. Smith, (August 1995, Informational).

1959—"An LDAP URL Format." T. Howes and M. Smith, (June 1996, Proposed standard).

2164—"Use of an X.500/LDAP Directory to Support MIXER Address Mapping." S. Kille, (January 1998 [obsoletes 1838], Proposed standard).

2247—"Using Domains in LDAP/X.500 Distinguished Names." S. Kille, M. Wahl, A. Grimstad, R. Huber, and S. Sataluri, (January 1998, Proposed standard).

2251—"Lightweight Directory Access Protocol (v3)." M. Wahl, T. Howes, and S. Kille. (December 1997, Proposed standard).

2252—"Lightweight Directory Access Protocol (v3)." M. Wahl, A. Coulbeck, T. Howes, and S. Kille, (December 1997, Proposed standard).

2253—"Lightweight Directory Access Protocol (v3)." M. Wahl, S. Kille, and T. Howes. (December 1997, Proposed standard).

2254—"The String Representation of LDAP Search Filters." T. Howes, (December 1997 [obsoletes 1960], Proposed standard).

2255—"The LDAP URL Format." T. Howes and M. Smith, (December 1997, Proposed standard).

2256—"A Summary of the X.500(96) User Schema for Use with LDAPv3." M. Wahl, (December 1997, Proposed standard).

2307—"An Approach for Using LDAP as a Network Information Service." L.Howard, (March 1998, Experimental).

2559—"Internet X.509 Public Key Infrastructure Operational Protocols - LDAPv2." S. Boeyen, T. Howes, and P. Richard, (April 1999 [updates 1778], Proposed standard).

2587—"Internet X.509 Public Key Infrastructure LDAPv2 Schema." S. Boeyen, T. Howes, and P. Richard, (June 1999, Proposed standard).

2589—"Lightweight Directory Access Protocol (v3): Extensions for Dynamic-Directory Services." Y. Yaacovi, M. Wahl, and T. Genovese, (May 1999, Proposed standard).

2596—"Use of Language Codes in LDAP." M. Wahl and T. Howes, (May 1999, Proposed standard).

2649—"An LDAP Control and Schema for Holding Operation Signatures." B. Greenblatt and P. Richard, (August 1999, Experimental).

2657—"LDAPv2 Client versus the Index Mesh." R. Hedberg, (August 1999, Experimental).

Online Resources

LDAP (v3) Revision (ldapbis)

`www.ietf.org/html.charters/ldapbis-charter.html`

LDAP Extension (ldapext)

`www.ietf.org/html.charters/ldapext-charter.html`

LDAP Duplication/Replication/Update Protocols (ldup)

`www.ietf.org/html.charters/ldup-charter.html`

DNS

Books

Albitz, Paul, and Cricket Liu. 1998. *DNS and BIND (Third Edition).* O'Reilly & Associates. ISBN: 1-56592-512-2.

Masterson, Michael, Herman Knief, Scott Vinick, and Eric Roul. 1998. *Windows NT DNS.* New Riders. ISBN: 1-56205-943-2.

RFCs

Many RFCs collectively make up the DNS standards. You can search for any RFC by number or keyword at `www.rfc-editor.org/rfcsearch.html`.

The DNS RFCs are listed here in numeric order:

805—"Computer Mail Meeting Notes." J. Postel, (February 1982).

811—"Hostnames Server." K. Harrenstien, V. White, and E. Feinler, (March 1982).

819—"The Domain Naming Convention for Internet User Applications." Z. Su and J. Postel, (August 1982).

881—"The Domain Names Plan and Schedule." J. Postel, (November 1983 [updated by 897, 921]).

897—"Domain Name System Implementation Schedule." J. Postel, (February 1984 [updates 881; updated by 921]).

920—"Domain Requirements." J. Postel and J. Reynolds, (October 1984).

921—"Domain Name System Implementation Schedule." Revised by J. Postel, (October 1984 [updates 897, 881]).

952—"DoD Internet Host Table Specification." K. Harrenstien, M. Stahl, E. Feinler, (October 1985).

974—"Mail Routing and the Domain System." Craig Partridge, (January 1986, Standard).

1032—"Domain Administrator's Guide." M. Stahl, (November 1987).

1033—"Domain Administrators Operations Guide." M. Lottor, (November 1987 [updated by 1912]).

1034—"Domain Names—Concepts and Facilities." P. Mockapetris, (November 1987 [obsoletes 882, 883, 973; updated by 1101, 1122, 1183, 1706, 1876, 1982, 2181, 2308 2535], Standard).

1035—"Domain Names—Implementation and Specification." P. Mockapetris, (November 1987 [obsoletes 882, 883, 973; updated by 1101, 1122, 1183, 1706, 1876, 1982, 1995, 1996, 2052, 2136, 2137, 2181, 2308, 2535], Standard).

1101—"DNS Encoding of Network Names and Other Types." P. Mockapetris, (April 1989 [updates 1034, 1035], Proposed standard).

1122—"Requirements for Internet Hosts—Communication Layers." Edited by R. Braden, (October 1989 [updates 1034, 1035], Standard).

1123—"Requirements for Internet Hosts—Application and Support." Edited by R. Braden, (October 1989 [updated by 2181], Standard).

1178—"Choosing a Name for Your Computer." D. Libes, (August 1990, Informational).

1183—"New DNS RR Definitions." C. Everhart, L. Mamakos, and R. Ullmann, and edited by P. Mockapetris, (October 1990 [updates 1034, 1035; updated by 2052], Experimental).

1464—"Using the Domain Name System to Store Arbitrary String Attributes." R. Rosenbaum, (May 1993, Experimental).

1480—"The US Domain." A. Cooper and J. Postel, (June 1993 [obsoletes 1386], Informational).

1535—"A Security Problem and Proposed Correction with Widely Deployed DNS Software." E. Gavron, (October 1993, Informational).

1536—"Common DNS Implementation Errors and Suggested Fixes." A. Kumar, J. Postel, C. Neuman, P. Danzig, and S. Miller, (October 1993, Informational).

1591—"Domain Name System Structure and Delegation." J. Postel, (March 1994, Informational).

1611—"DNS Server MIB Extensions." R. Austein and J. Saperia, (May 1994, Proposed standard)

1612—"DNS Resolver MIB Extensions." R. Austein and J. Saperia, (May 1994, Proposed standard).

1706—"DNS NSAP Resource Records." B. Manning and R. Colella, (October 1994 [obsoletes 1348, 1637; updates 1034, 1035], Informational).

1713—"Tools for DNS Debugging." A. Romao, (November 1994, Informational).

1794—"DNS Support for Load Balancing." T. Brisco, (April 1995, Informational).

1876—"A Means for Expressing Location Information in the Domain Name System." C. Davis, P. Vixie, T. Goodwin, and I. Dickinson, (January 1996 [obsoletes 1712; updates 1034, 1035], Experimental).

1884—"IP Version 6 Addressing Architecture." Edited by R. Hinden and S. Deering, (December 1995, Proposed standard).

1886—"DNS Extensions to Support IP Version 6." S. Thomson and C. Huitema, (December 1995, Proposed standard).

1912—"Common DNS Operational and Configuration Errors." D. Barr, (February 1996 [obsoletes 1537], Informational).

1956—"Registration in the MIL Domain." D. Engebretson and R. Plzak, (June 1996, Informational).

1982—"Serial Number Arithmetic." R. Elz and R. Bush, (August 1996 [updates 1034, 1035], Proposed standard).

1995—"Incremental Zone Transfer in DNS." M. Ohta, (August 1996 [updates 1035], Proposed standard).

1996—"Notify: A Mechanism for Prompt Notification of Authority Zone Changes." P. Vixie, (August 1996 [updates 1035], Proposed standard).

2010—"Operational Criteria for Root Name Servers." B. Manning and P. Vixie, (October 1996, Informational).

2052—"A DNS RR for Specifying the Location of Services (DNS SRV)." A. Gulbrandsen and P. Vixie, (October 1996 [updates 1035 1183], Experimental).

2053—"The AM (Armenia) Domain." E. Der-Danieliantz, (October 1996, Informational).

2136—"Dynamic Updates in the Domain Name System (DNS UPDATE)." P. Vixie (editor), S. Thomson, Y. Rekhter, and J. Bound, (April 1997 [updates 1035], Proposed standard).

2137—"Secure Domain Name System Dynamic Update." D. Eastlake III (April 1997 [updates 1035], Proposed standard).

2146—"U.S. Government Internet Domain Names." Federal Networking Council, (May 1997 [obsoletes 1816], Informational).

2163—"Using the Internet DNS to Distribute MIXER Conformant Global Address Mapping (MCGAM)." C. Allocchio, (January 1998 [obsoletes 1664], Proposed standard).

2168—"Resolution of Uniform Resource Identifiers Using the Domain Name System." R. Daniel and M. Mealling, (June 1997, Experimental).

2181—"Clarifications to the DNS Specification." R. Elz and R. Bush, (July 1997 [updates 1034, 1035 1123; updated by 2535], Proposed standard).

2182—"Selection and Operation of Secondary DNS Servers." R. Elz, R. Bush, S. Bradner, and M. Patton, (July 1997).

2219—"Use of DNS Aliases for Network Services." M. Hamilton and R. Wright, (October 1997).

2230—"Key Exchange Delegation Record for the DNS." R. Atkinson, (November 1997, Informational).

2240—"A Legal Basis for Domain Name Allocation." O. Vaughan, (November 1997, Informational).

2247—"Using Domains in LDAP/X.500 Distinguished Names." S. Kille, M. Wahl, A. Grimstad, R. Huber, and S. Sataluri, (January 1998, Proposed standard).

2307—"An Approach for Using LDAP as a Network Information Service." L. Howard, (March 1998, Experimental).

2308—"Negative Caching of DNS Queries (DNS NCACHE)." M. Andrews, (March 1998 [updates 1034, 1035]).

2317—"Classless IN-ADDR.ARPA Delegation." H. Eidnes, G. de Groot, and P. Vixie, (March 1998).

2345—"Domain Names and Company Name Retrieval." J. Klensin, T. Wolf, and G. Oglesby, (May 1998, Experimental).

2377—"Naming Plan for Internet Directory-Enabled Applications." A. Grimstad, R. Huber, S. Sataluri, and M. Wahl, (September 1998, Informational).

2517—"Building Directories from DNS: Experiences from WWWSeeker." R. Moats and R. Huber, (February 1999, Informational).

2535—"Domain Name System Security Extensions." D. Eastlake, (March 1999 [obsoletes 2065; updates 2181, 1035, 1034], Proposed standard).

2536—"DSA KEYs and SIGs in the Domain Name System (DNS)." D. Eastlake, (March 1999, Proposed standard).

2537—"RSA/MD5 KEYs and SIGs in the Domain Name System (DNS)." D. Eastlake, (March 1999, Proposed standard).

2538—"Storing Certificates in the Domain Name System (DNS)." D. Eastlake and O. Gudmundsson, (March 1999, Proposed standard).

2539—"Storage of Diffie-Hellman Keys in the Domain Name System (DNS)." D. Eastlake, (March 1999, Proposed standard).

2540—"Detached Domain Name System (DNS) Information." D. Eastlake, (March 1999, Experimental).

2541—"DNS Security Operational Considerations." D. Eastlake, (March 1999, Informational).

2782—"A DNS RR for specifying the location of services (DNS SRV)." A. Gulbrandsen, P. Vixie, L. Esibov, (February 2000 obsoletes RFC 2052 Proposed standard).

2373—"IP Version 6 Addressing Architecture." R. Hinden, S. Deering (July 1998 obsoletes RFC 1884 Proposed standard).

2874—"DNS Extensions to Support IPv6 Address Aggregation and Renumbering." M. Crawford, C. Huitema, (July 2000 Proposed standard).

Online Resources

www.dns. net/dnsrd/

www.ietf.org/rfc.html

www.rfc-editor.org/rfcsearch.html

ftpeng.cisco.com/fred/rfc-index/rfc.html

www.acmebw.com/askmr.htm

Novell Directory Services

Books

Kearns, David, and Brian Iverson. 1998. *The Complete Guide to Novell Directory Services.* Sybex Network Press. ISBN: 0-7821-1823-2.

Kearns, David. 2000. *Mastering Novell Directory Services*. Sybex Network Press. ISBN: 0-7821-2632-4

Hughes, Jeffrey F., and Blair W. Thomas. 1999. *Novell's Guide to NetWare 5 Networks.* IDG Books Worldwide. ISBN: 0-7645-4544-2.

Hughes, Jeffrey F., and Blair W. Thomas. 1998. *NDS for NT.* IDG Books Worldwide. ISBN: 0-7645-4551-5.

Hughes, Jeffrey F., and Blair W. Thomas. 1996. *Novell's Guide to IntranetWare Networks.* IDG Books Worldwide. ISBN: 0-7645-4516-7.

Hughes, Jeffrey F., and Blair W. Thomas. 1996. *Novell's Four Principles of NDS Design.* IDG Books Worldwide. ISBN: 0-7645-4522-1.

Marymee, J. D., and Sandy Stephens. 1998. *Novell's Guide to Integrating IntraNetware and NT.* IDG Books Worldwide. ISBN: 0-7645-4523-x.

Henderson, Jim, and Kuo, Peter. Novell's Guide to Troubleshooting NDS. 1999. Novell Press. ISBN: 0-7645-4579-5.

Kuo, Peter. 2000. *Novell's NDS Basics*. Novell Press. ISBN: 0-7645-4726-7.

RFCs

1634—"Novell IPX Over Various WAN Media (IPXWAN)." M. Allen, (May 1994, [Obsoletes RFC1551, RFC1362], Informational).

2165—"Service Location Protocol." J. Veizades, E. Guttman, C. Perkins, and S. Kaplan, (June 1997, Standards track).

2608—"Service Location Protocol, Version 2." J. Veizades, E. Guttman, C. Perkins, and M. Day, (June 1999, [Updates 2165], Standards track).

2609—"Service Templates and Service: Schemes." E. Guttman, C. Perkins, and J. Kempf, (June 1999, [Updates 2165], Standards track).

2241—"DHCP Options for Novell Directory Services." D. Provan, (November 1997, Standards track).

Online Resources

Novell eDirectory

`www.novell.com/products/nds`

Online eDirectory documentation:

`www.novell.com/documentation/lg/ndsedir/docui/index.html`

NDS eDirectory glossary:

`developer.novell.com/research/devnotes/1999/septembe/02/d990902.pdf`

digitalme:

`www.digitalme.com`

Single Sign-on:

`www.novell.com/products/sso/`

ZENworks:

`www.novell.com/products/ZENworks/index.html`

NDS development:

`www.developer.novell.com/nds/`

DirXML:

`www.novell.com/products/nds/DirXML/`

Novell Connection:

`www.nwconnection.com`

Active Directory

Books

Cone, Eric K., Jon Boggs, and Sergio Perez. 1999. *Planning for Windows 2000.* New Riders. ISBN: 0-7357-0048-6.

Microsoft Corporation. 1999. *Microsoft Windows 2000 Server Resource Kit*. Microsoft Press, ISBN: 1572318058.

Lowe-Norris, Alistair. 2000. *Windows 2000 Active Directory*. O'Reilly and Associates. ISBN: 1565926382.

Olsen, Gary L., and Ty Loren Carlson. 2000. *Windows 2000 Active Directory Design and Deployment*. New Riders Publishing ISBN: 1578702429.

Masterson, Michael, Herman Knief, Scott Vinick, and Eric Roul. 1998. *Windows NT DNS.* New Riders. ISBN: 1-56205-943-2.

Online Resources

Microsoft Directory Services

`www.microsoft.com/windows2000/technologies/directory/default.asp`

Active Directory

`www.microsoft.com/windows2000/technologies/directory/AD/default.asp`

AD technical documentation:

`www.microsoft.com/windows2000/techinfo/default.asp`

Deploying AD:

`www.microsoft.com/windows2000/techinfo/planning/default.asp`

ADSI:

`www.microsoft.com/windows2000/techinfo/howitworks/activedirectory/`
`adsilinks.asp`

AD glossary:

www.microsoft.com/windows2000/techinfo/howitworks/activedirectory/glossary.asp

Windows 2000:

www.microsoft. com/windows2000/

Other Resources

Standards

ISO 3166—Codes for the Representation of Countries. The International Organization for Standardization, 1988 (Third Edition).

RFCs

1760—"The S/KEY One-Time Password System." N. Haller, (February 1995, Informational).

2743—"Generic Security Service Application Program Interface, Version 2, Update 1." J. Linn, (January 2000 [obsoletes 2078], Proposed standard).

2222—"Simple Authentication and Security Layer (SASL)." J. Myers, (October 1997, Standards track).

2289—"A One-Time Password System." N. Haller, C. Metz, and P. Nesser, (February 1998 [obsoletes 1938], Standards track).

Online Resources

Directory Interoperability forum:

www.opengroup.org/directory

Directory-Enabled networking:

www.cisco.com/warp/public/cc/techno/network/dirserv/den/index.shtml

NWFusion Newsletter on directories

www.nwfusion.com/newsletters/dir/

Glossary

APPENDIX

B

[root] The traditional eDirectory reference for the root of the directory tree.

abstract classes Used as templates to define other classes.

Abstract Syntax Notation One (ASN.1) An OSI standard defining the syntax used for storing information that will be exchanged between different systems, storing data in a series of type-value pairs.

access control Access control mechanisms provide differential levels of access to directory objects. The specifics of access control mechanisms vary between directory service implementations.

Access Control Decision Function (ACDF) An algorithm defined in the X.500 standards to determine access control permissions by examining the contents of the ACI items of both the object and DUA.

Access Control Entry (ACE) A single security-related directory entry linked to a specific object. An ACE can grant or deny a particular user (or group) a specific set of access rights to directory object.

Access Control Information (ACI) ACI is stored with each protected item in the directory and is used to determine which users are granted access, and what kind of access is granted.

Access Control Inner Administrative Area (ACIA) A permeable security boundary used by X.500 to allow delegation of access control administration.

Access Control Lists (ACL) An ACL contains security information concerning a directory object, such as who can access the object and what operations they can perform.

Access Control Service Element (ACSE) X.500 uses ACSE to create and tear down associations between directory agents, essentially managing the bind (connection) and unbind (disconnect) processes.

Access Control Specific Administrative Area (ACSA) An ACSA defines an autonomous area of security in X.500.

Access Control Specific Point (ACSP) The administrative point of an ACSA.

ACI items Access Control Information (ACI) items are the operational attributes that control access to protected items in the directory.

Active Directory Microsoft's network directory service, first released as part of Windows 2000. Active Directory blends support for the NetBIOS namespace, DNS location service, LDAP for directory access, and Windows domain security.

Active Directory Services Interface (ADSI) Microsoft's proprietary API, which is used for Active Directory, as well as to support accessing directory objects residing in multiple namespaces.

Address (A) record An Address (A) resource record is used in DNS zone files to specify the linkage between a host (computer) name and its corresponding IP address (also commonly called a host record).

Administrative and Operational Information Model This X.500 model describes the directory from the perspective of the network administrator, viewing all the directory information in a unified DIT.

administrative point The administrative point is the root node of an X.500 administrative area. There are two major categories of administrative points: Specific (SAP) and Inner (IAP), which correspond to the root nodes of SAAs and IAAs.

alias A secondary logical representation of an existing object that functions as a pointer to the original object.

ASN1 ID A globally unique number assigned by Novell when schema extensions are registered with them (similar to the X.500 OID).

asymmetric cryptography Asymmetric cryptography uses pairs of keys (public/private) to encrypt information (also called public key).

asynchronous Asynchronous communications allow multiple client requests to be sent to a DSA without requiring prior return of results from earlier requests.

attribute An individual value of a directory object, such as `name` or `password`. Attributes hold the information associated with directory objects.

attribute access Attribute access refers to when a user or application attempts to access information held within an object (such as a telephone number), as opposed to the object itself (browsing the directory tree).

attribute access permissions The sets of permissions that can be set on attribute access. These permissions commonly include actions such as read, compare, add, and remove.

attribute definition The schema definition of an attribute, which includes the attribute syntax and any constraints placed on the attribute.

attribute syntax The attribute syntax defines the acceptable data structure of an attribute.

attributed name The X.500 style where a naming attribute (`cn`) and a name (`shelly`) combine to form the object name. (`cn=shelly`).

authentication The mechanism that verifies that the individual user is who they claim to be, usually by association with a shared-secret password or public key.

Authentication Server (AS) An Authentication Server (AS) provides the user authentication portion of Kerberos security.

authoritative In general, authoritative is used to describe the controlling source of the information.

authoritative name server An authoritative name server (as defined in DNS) contains current resource records for a specified zone and is designated via a SOA record.

Autonomous Administrative Areas (AAA) In the X.500 model, an AAA denotes a directory subtree that is managed by an independent organization. Each organization is completely responsible for its portion of the global DIT.

auxiliary class An auxiliary class is like an abstract class in that it defines a set of attributes and object characteristics. Auxiliary classes are used to support an additional derivation of an existing object.

backlink eDirectory uses backlinks to keep track of external references to an object.

Backup Domain Controller (BDC) A Windows NT domain controller that holds a read-only copy of the SAM database.

Basic Access Control (BAC) The X.500 security model that defines entry access and attribute access permissions, and the use of these permissions to control categories of directory operations (such as add, read, and so on). Application of permissions is segregated via access control administrative areas.

Berkeley Internet Name Domain (BIND) A Unix-based vendor-specific version of DNS that (among other distinctions) notably specifies the use of a boot file for startup functionality.

bindery A single server directory used by NetWare 2.x-3.x. The bindery is a flat namespace, with entries corresponding to users and physical network resources.

bindery context A collection of eDirectory container objects that are represented as a flat namespace for NetWare bindery clients.

bindery services eDirectory's bindery service supports down-level clients and provides them with a bindery style view of a subset of the directory contents.

boot file A text file used by DNS to specify configuration commands to be executed at startup of the DNS services.

bridgehead server A bridgehead server is used to manage Active Directory replication between sites and across slower communications links, such as WAN connections.

cache file A DNS file containing host address resource records for the root DNS name servers.

caching only name server A DNS name server that is not linked to any specific zones, and does not contain its own zone files.

canonical name In general, a canonical name is an alias to a directory object. In DNS, a canonical name is an alias to a hostname and is specified in a CNAME resource record.

catalog Catalogs contain a subset or an index of the directory contents to provide a fast method of locating network resources.

centralized directory A centralized directory holds the entire directory namespace on a single server. Copies of the directory information may be stored on additional servers.

certificate An X.509 certificate is a collection of data that associates the public keys of network users with their DN in the directory, and is stored within the directory as user object attributes.

Certificate Authority (CA) A Certificate Authority creates and manages X.509 certificates for the users, servers, and other CAs.

chaining Chaining is defined by X.500 as a process where a DSA passes a query to other DSAs, collects results, and compiles them before they are returned to the client.

changelog A changelog contains a record of all the changes that have been made to the directory. Using this method, when a replication process is initiated, the supplier "replays" the changelog to the consumer.

class A schematic definition of a type of object allowed within the directory. A class is a possible object, not an actual object, that is, the User object for Brynna (`CN=Brynna`) is an instance of the User class definition.

class definition An object class definition specifies the information that is required to create an instance of a particular type of object. Class definitions also determine how objects work in relationship to other objects in the directory.

CN (common name) The most frequently used naming attribute for leaf objects.

CNAME record A Canonical NAME (CNAME) resource record is used within a DNS zone file to specify an alias for a hostname (similar to an X.500 alias).

collective attribute An attribute that is stored in a single location and referred to by multiple objects; used for data that is common to many objects (such as a fax number).

collective attribute specific area An X.500 administrative area that has collective attributes assigned to it.

complete replication Complete replication sends a copy of the entire directory database to each server with every directory update.

Connectionless LDAP (CLDAP) CLDAP provides the functionality of LDAP over a connectionless protocol (UDP).

ConsoleOne A Java-based administrative console for eDirectory. It is available in both Windows and Web versions.

consumer In replication, a consumer is the replica receiving the update.

consumer reference An X.500 DSA uses a consumer reference to identify a replication consumer (that is, a shadow). This information is the reciprocal of that in the Supplier Reference.

container object Container objects are used to provide structure and organization for the directory tree and hold other objects.

Content Rule Content rules define what attributes each object class contains.

context An object's place in the directory tree is its context, which is referenced by the string of object names between it and the tree root. Also called context prefix.

controls Controls specify extended handling information used for a LDAP single query (analogous to X.500 service controls).

convergence When all replicas of a partition contain the same data.

country code A two-letter designator for each country, such as UK, DE, or US, assigned by the ISO 3166 Maintenance Agency.

create-time inheritance Create-time inheritance (used by Active Directory) is where effective permissions are determined and written (to the object's ACL) at the point of creation or change.

cross references Cross references are used to point to a naming context that is neither superior nor subordinate to the current naming context.

database layer The database layer in Active Directory that abstracts the DIB management operations, isolating the DSA from the storage subsystem (the ESE).

delegation In directory services, delegation is the assignment of administrative control over directory subtrees or objects.

dereferencing The process where the directory determines the underlying object to which an alias is referring.

DIB fragment The portion of the DIB that is held by a single DSA.

digital signature A summary of the data produced by a one-way hash function encrypted with the sender's public key.

digitalme An eDirectory-based technology that acts as a personal information management system for individuals to use in managing their online identity.

directory Provides a way to securely store, organize, and access information. Operates within a network to facilitate user access to information and resources and to ease network administration.

Directory Access Control Domain (DACD) A DACD is a filtered subset of an X.500-defined access control area (ACSA or ACIA).

Directory Access Markup Language (DAML) A directory markup language that uses a set of XML elements and attributes to represent LDAP directory operations in XML documents.

Directory Access Protocol (DAP) The X.500 protocol that provides client access to the directory.

Directory Administrative and Operational Information Model In X.500, this model describes the directory as the administrator sees it—with the operational attributes that contain information used internally by the directory to keep track of modifications and subtree properties.

Directory Administrative Authority Model This X.500 model assumes different people or organizations will administer different parts of the DIT, and provides a way for the DIT to be divided into subtrees that can be delegated as needed.

Directory Distribution Model The X.500 Directory Distribution Model defines how directory information is shared by multiple DSAs.

Directory Enabled Networking (DEN) A collaboration between network infrastructure device vendors and directory service vendors seeking to enable directory-based control over infrastructure devices (such as routers and switches).

Directory Functional Model The X.500 Directory Functional Model defines the directory as one or more DSAs that collectively provide DUAs with access to directory information.

Directory Information Base (DIB) The DIB (an X.500 term) contains all the information in the directory, and is commonly distributed, partitioned, and replicated to enhance availability and responsiveness.

Directory Information Model The original 1988 X.500 specification defined only the Directory Information Model, which deals with the most basic view of directory—the one which a typical directory user sees.

Directory Information Shadowing Protocol (DISP) The X.500 DISP is used by a DSA to replicate a partition to another DSA, and to transmit information during replica update operations.

Directory Information Tree (DIT) A directory tree is a hierarchical arrangement of container objects within a contiguous namespace. The directory tree is used to represent a logical hierarchy, as well as to visually display the arrangement of objects within the tree.

Directory Interoperability Forum (DIF) DIF is a group of vendors who have joined efforts to support the development of directory-enabled application development and open directory standards.

Directory Management Domain (DMD) A X.500 DMD consists of a set of DSAs and DUAs administered by a specific organization. DMD policies apply to DSA operations and can be used to limit the operations and services provided by one or more DSAs.

directory object An instance of the underlying class definition.

directory operational attribute Directory operational attributes are used for operational parameters that apply to every DSA, such as access control.

Directory Operational Binding Management Protocol (DOP) An X.500 protocol used by a pair of DSAs to establish a binding agreement for use in distributed operations.

directory service In its most general definition, a directory service provides the means to hierarchically organize and manage information, and to retrieve the information by name association. Directory services provide an information management technology that can be applied to a wide range of business operations.

Directory Service Markup Language (DSML) An XML language representing directory information in a standard format to facilitate data exchange.

Directory System Agent (DSA) The X.500 term for the server component of a directory service. Each DSA handles a portion of the DIT and multiple DSAs interoperate as a system to provide transparent access to the distributed directory.

Directory System Protocol (DSP) An X.500 protocol that supports the interaction between DSAs necessary for distributed directory operations.

Directory User Agent (DUA) The client application of an X.500 defined directory service.

DirX An X.500 directory product by Siemens.

DirXmetahub A metadirectory solution from Siemens.

DirXML A Novell metadirectory technology integrating eDirectory with other directories or datastores via an XML-based directory markup language.

Distinguished Name (DN) A fully qualified X.500 object name that unambiguously identifies and positions an object within the directory tree.

distributed directory A distributed directory subdivides the directory namespace it holds, and multiple copies of the subsets of directory information are spread throughout the network, but are logically linked into one directory. X.500 directory services are designed to extend this distribution to the entire world.

Distributed Reference Link (DRL) A DRL contains a list of all the external references created for an eDirectory object.

DIT Domain In X.500 a DIT Domain is the section of the global DIT managed by a specific Domain Management Organization (DMO). A DIT Domain consists of one or more Autonomous Administrative Area (AAAs), which may be disjointed (that is, unconnected).

DNS domain namespace DNS domain namespace defines a hierarchical tree of domains.

domain A DNS domain is a logical organizing structure for naming and location services. Windows NT 4 organizes resources into NT domains that enforce security boundaries, and usually represent a subdivision of the company.

domain component (dc) LDAP domain components are used to map to DNS domains, providing for integration of the DNS and LDAP namespaces.

Domain Controller (DC) The Active Directory DSA.

domain directory partition In Active Directory, a domain directory partition contains all objects within the domain, and is only replicated to DCs for a specific domain.

Domain Local Groups Domain Local Groups are new in Active Directory, and are used to grant access to resources within a single domain, to any user or group in the forest.

Domain Management Organization (DMO) A specific administrative authority that manages a portion of the global X.500 DIT.

Domain Name System (DNS) The service used to locate network servers on the Internet and many corporate networks. A DNS server translates the "friendly name" of a network server (for example, `www.mythical.org`) into its corresponding IP address (for example, `192.168.111.90`).

Domain Naming Master The Domain Naming Master controls the additions and deletions of domains within an Active Directory forest, ensuring the uniqueness of the domain names.

domain subtree The contiguous directory subtree contained with a single Active Directory domain.

domain tree Active Directory uses a tree of domains, which collectively comprise a contiguous DNS namespace.

domain trust A process where a relationship is formed between domains to support an exchange of security credentials, allowing users in one domain to gain access to resources in the trusting domain. Active Directory uses automatic two-way transitive trusts between domains.

DSA Information Model The information contained in this X.500 model locates a DSA in relationship to other DSAs and describes how various DSAs interact to control shared directory information.

DSA Information Tree A DSA Information Tree is comprised of the complete set of names (and associated DSEs) known by a specific DSA.

DSA Specific Entry (DSE) An entry in the DIT as held by a specific DSA.

DSAPI The traditional method of programming eDirectory, providing all the functionality of the XDS APIs from X.500.

DSA-shared operational attribute The information used between DSAs to perform replication, containing information that applies to a single DSA, such as the time of the last replica update.

dynamic directory entry Nonpersistent directory objects that disappear from the directory after a designated length of time if not refreshed.

Dynamic DNS (DDNS) DDNS provides a mechanism for DNS resource records to be dynamically updated to reflect changing server and client availability and IP addresses.

Dynamic Host Configuration Protocol (DHCP) DHCP is commonly used to manage a pool of IP addresses and dynamically supply those addresses to network clients.

eDirectory Novell's eDirectory, originally named NDS, was first designed to manage distributed NetWare networks, and is now a general-purpose, cross-platform directory service. eDirectory is based in X.500 architecture, using both proprietary protocols and native LDAP.

effective class The class of object that can be instanced (created) in the directory tree.

effective rights The set of access rights that result when all security factors are combined and assessed; effective rights denote which operations can actually be performed.

entry Another term for an object.

entry access When a user accesses an object as a named entity in the directory (browsing the directory tree), rather than information held within an object (such as a telephone number).

entry access permissions Entry access permissions are the set of permissions that can be granted or denied when accessing named objects. These permissions typically include read, browse, add, remove, modify, and rename.

eTrust Directory An X.500 directory service from Computer Associates (the product was formerly Open Directory).

extensibility The ability to extend the directory in some way; commonly extended areas include schema, operations, and interconnectivity.

eXtensible Directory Access Protocol (XDAP) A markup language designed as a transport neutral framework to support search and retrieval operations on directories.

eXtensible Markup Language (XML) A generic markup language supporting the creation of custom vocabularies for manipulating information, transforming data from one format to another, and representing information in a generic form accessible by a wide range of applications and services.

Extensible Storage Engine (ESE) Active Directory uses the ESE as its data storage layer. The ESE works with the database layer to provide the DIB functionality for Active Directory. The ESE is an enhanced version of Jet, an indexed database engine used by Exchange.

eXtensible Stylesheet Language (XSL) A stylesheet technology for formatting data, providing flexible control over the presentation of the data.

extension Extensions allow the use of arguments to support new directory operations and enhanced functionality. Extensions rely on a pre-arranged agreement between the communicating directory components on the set of new operations, along with the methods used to invoke the functionality.

external reference A temporary pointer to an object created by eDirectory when a server needs to reference an object that it is not contained in a local replica.

federated naming The ability to perform name resolution across different namespaces (also called federation), a process that is at the core of the interoperability between directories.

filter A constraint applied to a directory query that restricts the information returned.

flat namespace A namespace in which all objects are held below a single superior object, as if in a common container.

floating master A server that has been temporarily assigned the role of a master for a particular directory operation, such as replication or schema modifications.

Floating Single Master Operation (FSMO) An operation that requires the election of a single master. Microsoft calls this a flexible single master operation.

forest An Active Directory namespace containing one or more disjoint (noncontiguous) domain trees.

forest root In Active Directory, the first domain of the first tree in the forest defines the forest root.

forwarder A list of DNS name servers that are to be contacted prior to forwarding queries to the root name servers, used to control traffic.

full replica In Active Directory, a replica containing the information for a single domain.

Fully Distinguished Name (FDN) A FDN is an eDirectory name that is treated as complete and resolved from the tree root. A FDN is a DN preceded by a period "." (for example, `.meggan.mythical.org`).

Fully Qualified Domain Name (FQDN) A FQDN is a DNS domain name specified with the complete set of required values and with the terminating root delimiter "." as the rightmost value (for example, `host.domain.tld.`).

Generic Security Service API (GSSAPI) GSSAPI defines an interoperable security system for use on the Internet. GSSAPI provides a protocol and mechanism independent interface to underlying security methods.

Global Catalog (GC) A Global Catalog (GC) server contains an index to all Active Directory objects in the forest, providing an efficient means for applications and users to query the directory for objects based on one or more known attributes.

global group Active Directory global groups are equivalent to NT 4 global groups, and can be used to grant access to any resources in the forest to members of its domain and other global groups.

Globally Unique IDentifier (GUID) A unique 128-bit number generated for each Active Directory object at the point that it is created.

granularity Granularity refers to the ability to control operations such as replication and access control to a fine degree, usually meaning down to the attribute level. This provides extremely flexible security and minimizes replication traffic.

group policy A set of policies enforced on a group of computers or users within the Active Directory.

hierarchy A hierarchy in a directory service refers to the parent-child structure of the nodes of the directory tree. A parent object is immediately above its child object in the directory hierarchy.

host The DNS term for a server.

`in.addr.arpa` A reserved domain name suffix used for DNS reverse lookups.

incremental replication Incremental replication sends only a subset of the DIB, containing only the data that has been changed.

incremental zone transfer An incremental zone transfer allows the master name server to send only the resource record information that has changed since the last zone transfer with that secondary server.

Infrastructure Master In Active Directory, a single Infrastructure Master role enforces object consistency for operations that span domains, and synchronizes group-to-user references.

inheritance The mechanism by which permissions that are granted to objects high in the tree flow to objects below them.

inherited ACL Each eDirectory partition root has an inherited ACL, which contains the effective rights for that partition.

inherited rights Rights that are granted to an object and flow down to objects beneath in the tree.

Inherited Rights Filter (IRF) An IRF blocks the inheritance of access rights from higher in the tree.

Inner Administrative Areas (IAA) X.500 defines IAAs as a type of administrative division within a directory designating an area with delegated administrative tasks or collective attributes.

Inner Administrative Point (IAP) An administrative point for the IAA. See *administrative point*.

instance A specific occurrence of an object based on a class definition.

International Standards Organization (ISO) As its name suggests, an international standards body which manages standards processes for communications and networking technologies.

International Telecommunications Union (ITU) An international telecommunications standards body that developed the X.500 specifications (and many others).

Internet Assigned Numbers Authority (IANA) An Internet standards body responsible for the assignment of IP addresses.

Internet Corporation for Assigned Names and Numbers (ICANN) ICANN is a non-profit corporation formed to manage critical Internet infrastructure administration functions formerly performed by the IANA. ICANN is responsible for IP address allocation and DNS system management, including control of the root DNS name servers.

Internet Engineering Task Force (IETF) An organization of internetworking engineers, vendors, researchers, and others who form working groups to work on an area of Internet development. IETF has two LDAP related working group—LDUP (LDAP Duplication/Replication/Update Protocols) and LDAPExt (LDAP Extension).

Internetwork Packet eXchange (IPX) The network protocol used for NetWare, and thus earlier versions of NDS.

iPlanet Directory Server LDAP directory service from the Sun|Netscape alliance, commonly deployed in Internet and intranet environments.

iPlanet Directory Server Integration Edition A Sun|Netscape meta-directory product leveraging its iPlanet Directory Server.

iterative name resolution Iterative name resolution is a DNS process (similar to the X.500 referral process) where the name server receiving the name query either answers the query authoritatively or refers the client to another name server.

Java Naming and Directory Interface (JNDI) Sun's proprietary API that provides access to LDAP, NIS+, eDirectory, and other directory services.

Kerberos Kerberos is a security protocol developed for secure communication across an unsecure network, and operates by authenticating clients and issuing tickets for authentication of the client to a network service. The client and service then encrypt all communications, providing a means to operate securely over a public medium.

Key Distribution Center (KDC) The collective reference to an Authentication Server (AS) and a Ticket Granting Server (TGS), used by Kerberos security.

Knowledge Consistency Checker (KCC) Active Directory uses the KCC process to create the replication topology, and determines replication routes between DCs in a site based on the quality of available connections.

knowledge references References to remote DIB partitions maintained by DSAs as a means of piecing together the DIT for searches and replication.

lame delegation This is when a DNS name server is delegated as authoritative for a specific DNS zone, yet does not respond to name queries with authoritative results.

latency The delay between a directory query and the DSA response is referred to as latency (or query latency). Latency is also used to refer to the delay in updates between all directory replicas, described as update latency.

LDAP C API The LDAP C API is a low-level programming interface supporting all DAP operations, and used in the development of directory applications written in C.

LDAP Data Interchange Format (LDIF) LDIF has been defined as a means of describing LDAP entries in a standardized text format to facilitate the exchange of directory information.

LDAP URL (Uniform Resource Locator) An LDAP URL provides a means of locating directory servers using DNS and then completing the query via LDAP.

leaf object A leaf object in a directory represents a manageable object—in network directories leaf objects commonly represent network entities (users, servers, and so on), applications, and services.

Lightweight Directory Access Protocol (LDAP) A dedicated client access protocol for communicating with a directory and viewing or manipulating the objects contained within it. LDAP was designed as a simplified subset of the X.500 Directory Access Protocol (DAP) to provide basic access to X.500-based directories.

location service A network service providing name to address resolution for clients. Also called lookup services.

location-independence Refers to forms of naming in which the name of a network object is not dependent on its location in the network.

logical naming model A logical naming model uses symbolic names that are transparently mapped to physical device names.

loosely-consistent replication With loosely-consistent replication, the data on all directory servers does not have to be exactly the same at any given time. Changes to the DIB are replicated more slowly and network servers gradually "catch up" to the changes made on other directory servers.

mandatory attribute Attributes that must have values at all times during an object's lifetime.

master A writeable replica that is responsible for supplying data updates to other replicas; sometimes refers to the DSA holding that replica.

master DSA In X.500, a master DSA is the DSA that holds the master copy of each directory entry—the copy of the object that is writeable.

master name server A master name server is the source of the DNS zone resource records during a zone transfer.

master replica Master replicas are fully functional, allowing all directory operations on everything in the directory, objects, tree design, the schema, and so on. At least one master replica must exist per partition.

matching rules The rules that determine if a directory entry meets the criteria for a search.

metadirectory A metadirectory does some form of integration or integrated management of multiple directory services. This may take the form of a top-layer directory, synchronization tools, or a transitional management tool during a long migration process.

Microsoft Management Console (MMC) A console interface that provides the framework for the Active Directory administration tools, hosting programs constructed as snap-ins. The MMC provides the mechanism to add, remove, and manipulate modular snap-in programs.

Microsoft Metadirectory Services A meta-directory solution from Microsoft.

mixed environment In Active Directory, a mixed environment refers to having Active Directory in native mode (that is, all DCs are running Windows 2000) yet still having network servers and clients that are not Active Directory-aware.

mixed mode Mixed mode is the Active Directory default operating mode, and provides the maximum compatibility with down-level servers and clients. Mixed mode supports NT 4 replication methods as well as Active Directory domain replication.

multicasting Multicasting occurs when a DUA sends a request to multiple DSAs simultaneously.

multimaster replication Multimaster replication is where more than one replica can accept changes. Use of multimaster replication ensures that nonavailability of a given replica will not impede the use or administration of the network.

multivalued RDN A multivalued RDN is where an object has more than one naming attribute designated.

name form Defines the allowable RDN values for a structural object class, and contains at least one attribute whose value is used to form the entry's RDN.

name query A query sent by the client to a name server requesting the IP address of a particular DNS hostname.

name resolution The process by which name queries are resolved (varies between directory service implementations).

name server In DNS, name servers resolve host and domain names to corresponding IP addresses.

namespace A collection of objects that reside within a common logical container and follow the same naming convention.

naming attribute The attribute designated within a class definition to name instances of that class.

naming context In X.500, a naming context is a subdivision of the directory information that is stored on a specific DSA and managed by a common administrative authority. Analogous to a partition.

naming model The structure that determines how objects within a directory are named. Also called naming format, or naming convention.

native mode Native mode provides operational enhancements to Active Directory, including new types of groups, nested groups, and multimaster replication between DCs, thus removing support for NT 4 BDCs.

NetBIOS Stands for Network Basic Input Output System, and is a network technology that early Windows networks were based on (later versions have shifted to TCP/IP).

NetSync NetSync is used by eDirectory to administer a mixed NetWare 3.x–4.x environment.

NetWare Administrator NetWare Administrator is the legacy NDS/eDirectory management tool.

NetWare Name Services (NNS) NNS was as an add-on to NetWare 3 designed to synchronize the binderies of a group of NetWare servers.

Nexor Directory An X.500 directory product by Nexor focused on secure messaging.

noneffective class A class of objects that cannot be instanced in the directory.

Nonspecific Subordinate Reference (NSSR) A special type of subordinate reference containing the name of a DSA holding a child naming context but not the RDN of that context.

non-writeable replica A replica that cannot accept changes; it may be read-only or catalog.

Novell Directory Services Earlier name for eDirectory, see *eDirectory*.

Novell LDAP (NLDAP) eDirectory's version of LDAP.

object A data structure with a specified set of attributes and syntax, and which represents a network entity or other information set.

Object IDentifier (OID) The OID uniquely identifies each schema element and is assigned by ANSI, IETF, or a similar organization.

Open Systems Interconnect (OSI) A standard defining a related hierarchy of networking protocols.

OpenLDAP An open source LDAP directory product from the Open Foundation.

operational attributes Operational attributes contain information that is used internally by the directory to keep track of directory modifications and subtree properties. Used to manage the directory, these attributes are not usually visible to users.

operational extensions Operational extensions allow the use of predefined syntaxes and methods to support operations not included in the basic LDAP specifications.

operations master An Active Directory domain controller that has been assigned a flexible single master operations role (that is, Domain Naming, Schema, Relative ID, Infrastructure, and PDC Emulator).

optional attributes Optional attributes do not require values for object creation.

originating write A successful write updating a property on the DC performing the update is called an originating write. Replication updates are not considered originating writes.

partial replica A copy of a directory partition that contains only a subset of the contents of that partition.

partition A subdivision of the DIB or directory information. A copy of a partition is called a replica (master or shadow).

partition root The container object at the root of the directory partition which usually names the partition.

Passport A Microsoft Web service that provides single sign-on to Web sites belonging to Microsoft and selected partners.

PDC Emulator In Active Directory, the PDC Emulator supplies compatibility with down-level clients and NT 4 BDCs, handling NT 4 client authentication and replication. Only one DC in each domain can be used to perform the PDC Emulator role.

permissions In general, permissions are a security mechanism to enforce access control. In X.500, security models define entry access and attribute access permissions, and the use of these permissions to control directory operations.

permutability A property of some asymmetric encryption methods, where either key in the pair can be used to encrypt the message contents, and the other key can be used to decrypt the contents.

physical naming model A physical naming model uses actual network device names to locate attached resources.

P rimary Domain Controller (PDC) The Primary Domain Controller is a Windows NT server that contains the master copy of the user accounts database.

primary name server In DNS, the primary name server for a given zone holds the master copy of the DNS data.

primary shadowing In X.500, primary shadowing is where the shadow consumer gets data directly from the Master DSA.

Private Communications Technology (PCT) A channel security protocol used on the Internet and supported in many directory services.

propagation The process where a server sends directory updates to other servers containing partition replicas.

property Another term for directory attribute.

Property Version Numbers (PVN) Property-based replication values directly associated with an object property, which Active Directory uses to manage replication collisions.

Public Key Infrastructure (PKI) PKI refers to the security infrastructure using the public-key cryptographic technologies.

Quality of Service (QoS) QoS allows the provision of guaranteed bandwidth on network devices such as routers.

RadiantOne VDS A virtual directory service from Radiant Logic.

read/write replica A replica that allows directory updates, yet lacks some functionality of a master replica, such as the ability to modify the schema.

recursive query A DNS recursive query is similar to the X.500 chaining process, in which query resolution is pursued on the server-side and only complete results are returned to the client.

referral The process by which a DSA sends a DUA the names of other DSAs to contact to fulfill a submitted query.

Relative Distinguished Name (RDN) The term RDN is used to refer to two different names: In X.500, an RDN is the name of an object paired with the appropriate name type attribute, such as `CN=Brynna`. In eDirectory, a RDN is a DN relative to the location of the object that is referencing it.

relative domain names DNS domain names not ending in a trailing "." referred to as relative domain names such as `www.mythical.org`.

Relative ID (RID) Master In Active Directory, a RID Master is responsible for supplying the RID sequences to all DCs within the forest.

Relative Identifier (RID) An identifier used with an Active Directory domain identifier to construct the SIDs for security principals within domains, and is assigned by a single DC in the forest.

Remote Operation Service Element (ROSE) ROSE provides support (on an application sublayer of the OSI model) for the request/reply style of interaction between X.500 protocols.

replica A copy of a single partition of the DIB; replicas vary in functionality with some types allowing writes and others being read-only.

replica ring The collection of eDirectory servers holding replicas of a particular partition.

replica server eDirectory's term for a DSA—a server that is running eDirectory is described as a replica server.

replication The process of copying the contents of a DIB partition to another DSA.

replication agreement A replication agreement specifies the parameters that will govern the replication process. This includes factors such as role of each server, dataset to be replicated, and scheduling.

replication consumer The DSA receiving updates to the directory.

replication supplier The DSA sending the directory updates.

Request For Comments (RFC) A technical document published as a proposed standard at the end of the public review process managed by the IETF.

resolver Analogous to an X.500 DUA, the client-side software component in DNS is referred to as a DNS resolver.

resource record (RR) A single entry in the DNS database, roughly analogous to a directory object. A resource record consists of a series of fields identifying the record type and network host associated with the record.

reverse lookup The DNS process of finding a hostname based on IP address.

reverse lookup file A special zone file referenced when a DNS name server is searching the `in-addr.arpa` domain to perform a reverse lookup.

root context A logical construct referring to the entries immediately subordinate to the root of the directory tree.

root domain The theoretical root of the DNS namespace, delimited by the terminating period.

root DSE The directory entry that effectively represents the root of the directory tree, the root DSE stores information on the capabilities of the DSA.

root knowledge reference The root knowledge references are the partitions at the root of the Directory Information Tree (DIT), used to locate the tree root.

root name server The root name servers in DNS are the authoritative servers for top-level domains.

runtime inheritance When using runtime inheritance, the directory dynamically gathers the relevant ACLs and calculates permissions at the time of access.

S/KEY The S/KEY One-Time Password system was designed to prevent intruders from obtaining user passwords via packet sniffers, and so on, and is designed to counter a replay attack.

Security Accounts Manager (SAM) The Windows NT subsystem responsible for handling of security principals.

schema The directory schema is the core information structure that defines the directory objects and their properties.

Schema Master Used by Active Directory to control all changes to the schema for the entire forest.

secondary name server A backup server for a DNS zone providing redundancy for load balancing and fault tolerance.

secondary shadowing In X.500 replication, secondary shadowing is where a shadow consumer becomes a shadow supplier for other shadow consumers.

second-level domain In DNS, a second-level domain is a domain immediately subordinate to the top-level domains, which are assigned to specific organizations or people.

Secure Sockets Layer (SSL) The authentication process of Secure Sockets Layer (SSL) combines the simple password authentication method with a secure connection.

SecureWay Directory An LDAP directory product from IBM.

Security Authority X.500 defines the Security Authority as the specific administrative authority for an ACSA.

security context In Active Directory, a security context for access control is comprised of the user account data (including SID, groups, and privileges), and is assessed when a user attempts to access a protected object.

security descriptor In Active Directory, an ACL is stored in a binary form called a security descriptor.

security equivalence eDirectory allows the assignment of security permissions based on the security status of another user or another directory object.

Security IDentifier (SID) An area SID is defined by the NT security subsystem, and is used to identify security principals.

security model A conceptual model that combines a set of security technologies and operations to control access to directory information.

security policy A security policy is a group of ACI items that are implemented as a set.

security principal A network entity (such as a user or group) that can be granted permissions to access resources.

Security Support Provider Interface (SSPI) Active Directory's interface for security providers, supporting Kerberos, SSL/PCT, and X.509 security technologies.

Service Advertising Protocol (SAP) SAP may be used by eDirectory to support advertising and discovery of directory servers on IPX networks.

service control LDAP service controls are used to specify preferred modes of functionality or restrictions on how the DSA handles a particular request and provides a method of specifying constraining information for a single query.

Service Location Protocol (SLP) SLP is used for advertising and location services by eDirectory running on TCP/IP networks.

Service Principal Name (SPN) A SPN is a unique name used to identify and register a specific instance of a service in Active Directory.

shadow In X.500, a nonmaster replica of a partition is described as a shadow.

shadow DSA An X.500 DSA holding a shadow copy of an object is considered the shadow DSA for that object.

Simple Authentication and Security Layer (SASL) SASL allows for the use of different security providers by supplying a way for connection-oriented protocols to specify an authentication method and optional security layer.

Simple Mail Transport Protocol (SMTP) An industry standard protocol for e-mail services delivered over TCP/IP.

Simplified Access Control Functionally a subset of the X.500 basic access control scheme, simplified access control does not support ACIAs.

single master replication In single master replication, data can only be modified on one server—although there are usually copies of the DIB on other servers. The directory server holding the master replica is also responsible for updating all other replicas whenever there is a change to the directory.

Single Sign-On (SSO) A technology providing a method for securely storing and retrieving passwords used by applications other than the directory.

site A site is an Active Directory term denoting a set of TCP/IP subnets with good connectivity, that is subnets that are interconnected at 10mbs or more.

site link Site links represent the connections between networks. Site links contain the information Active Directory uses to manage the network connections for replication, defining frequency, cost, and availability for each site link.

site link bridge Combined sets of overlapping Active Directory site links.

slave A mode of DNS name server operations, where it is configured to send DNS queries only to name servers specified in the `forwarders` entry.

slave name server A DNS name server operating in slave mode.

Specific Administrative Areas (SAA) SAA are defined by X.500 as subtrees of autonomous administrative areas in which entries are viewed from a specific administrative perspective.

Specific Administrative Point (SAP) The node at the root of a specific administrative area. By attaching subentries to the specific administrative point, different types of administrative control may be defined.

SRV record The Service Resource Record (SRV) is a DNS record type used to specify the location of named services. The SRV record maps the name of a network service to the IP address of the server providing the service (such as LDAP).

Standalone LDAP Daemon (SLAPD) The first LDAP server, developed by a group at the University of Michigan.

Standalone LDAP Update Replication Daemon (SLURPD) SLURPD provides synchronization for SLAPD servers by writing a changelog file and replaying it to shadow servers.

Start Of Authority (SOA) The SOA record is the first entry within a DNS zone file, and refers to the DNS name server that is authoritative for the specified DNS domain.

store Active Directory defines the physical storage of the directory replica as the directory store.

strong authentication Strong authentication uses public key cryptography to produce security credentials, providing controlled access to the directory, and is considered far more secure for transmission of sensitive data.

structural class In a directory schema, structural (or effective) classes are those that are used to form the directory tree.

structure rules In a directory schema, structure rules define the logical tree structure of the directory and determine where objects can reside and how they are named.

stub resolver A DNS resolver component that provides a minimum functionality and relies on recursive operations for name resolution and address translation.

subclass An object is a subclass of all the objects from which it is derived. In X.500, a subclass attribute in the schema is used to denote an object's superclasses.

subdomain Used within DNS to specify organizational subdivisions and are prepended to the second level domain name.

subentry Used to select a sub-portion of the directory and to define specific properties that should be applied to that portion of the DIT.

subordinate knowledge reference Subordinate knowledge references indicate a DIB partition directly below the current partition, and are used to walk down the tree.

subschema A schema that applies to only a portion of the directory, usually a subtree.

subschema specific area This defines the particular directory subtree associated with a subschema.

subtree A directory subtree starts at a container object and extends downward until another subtree definition is encountered. The subtree description can also be filtered by object type so that, for example, a subtree could consist of only the user objects within a directory subtree.

superclass Those classes from which a class definition inherits some attributes and characteristics.

superior knowledge reference A superior knowledge reference is information used by a DSA holding a naming context to locate the naming context immediately above it to form the complete directory namespace.

superior rules In a directory schema, superior rules are used in an object class definition to delimit which container objects can hold a particular object class.

supplier The DSA that provides the data during the synchronization process.

supplier reference A supplier reference contains information used in replication to identify the DSA that will be providing the update.

symmetric cryptography With symmetric (also called shared-secret or private key) cryptography, the sender and receiver share the same user-provided key.

synchronization Directory synchronization is the process by which changes made to one replica of a partition are propagated to other replicas of that partition.

synchronous operations Directory operations that return the actual results of the operation to the client (as opposed to asynchronous operations that return the operation's message ID).

syntax The attribute syntax determines syntactical constraints of the attribute and matching rules, defining the range of acceptable content.

target object The object to which an alias points, that is, the aliased object.

ticket A ticket is a Kerberos security token.

Ticket Granting Server (TGS) A TGS is part of the Key Distribution Center functionality provided by Kerberos, and supplies the tickets used in authentication processes.

tightly consistent Directories whose data is kept fully synchronized are considered tightly consistent.

time server Time servers provide standardized network time to directory servers and clients that rely on time stamps for data integrity.

Time-To-Live (TTL) The length of time a dynamic object or attribute should exist. If the information is not refreshed before the TTL expires, it is deleted.

tombstone When a directory object is deleted, a tombstone is created in its place in case the object needs to be re-created. If the object is not re-created after a designated time the tombstone is automatically deleted.

top-level domain (tld) In DNS, a top-level domain is one of the reserved domain names (`.com`, `.org`, `.net`, and others) used to group domains by type of organization.

transitive synchronization Used by eDirectory to synchronize replicas on servers using different protocols, by employing an intermediary eDirectory server that supports both protocols.

transitive trust Active Directory defines a transitive trust as where a trust relationship with one domain is extended automatically to any other domain trusted by the trusted domain. (If C trusts B, and B trusts A, then C trusts A.)

transitive vector Used by eDirectory to store information relating to current synchronization status of a replica server.

Transport Control Protocol/Internet Protocol (TCP/IP) The network protocol used for communication on the Internet and also employed in most corporate networks.

Transport Layer Security (TLS) A secure authentication process that uses password authentication over a secure connection, and requires that both the client and server have public key certificates.

tree-walking The process of following a series of knowledge references from partition to partition to locate a directory object.

trust In Windows NT, a trust relationship defines a common security framework between domains. In Active Directory, trust relationships are transitive (automatic) for all domains with the domain tree.

trust link In Active Directory, a trust link is a relationship established between DCs to pass authentication information between domains.

trust path A trust path is defined in Active Directory as the set of trust links between domains, used for passing authentication requests—essentially the route between the DC for a server receiving a request and the DC in the domain of the requesting user.

trustee An entity that has been granted access to an eDirectory resource is considered a trustee of that resource.

typed names If the abbreviation corresponding to the object's naming attribute is used when forming its name, it is considered typed (for example, `cn=jody`). This style of naming is also known as attributed.

typeless naming Typeless naming does not use the naming attribute abbreviation in the object name (for example, `jody`).

Uniform Resource Locator (URL) The common method of referencing Web sites, such as `www.mythical.org`.

unit of replication The information set that is sent with a directory update.

Universal Group In Active Directory, Universal groups can be used to provide users within the forest access to any resources in the forest.

Universal Naming Convention (UNC) The naming convention used on Windows networks, UNC names take the form of `\\server\share` or `\\merlin\docs`.

Update Sequence Number (USN) A USN is a unique 64-bit value used by Active Directory synchronization. When an object (or property) is updated, the version number is incremented and stored in the object with a new USN. USNs are compared during replication to ensure data consistency.

up-to-date vector A set of server-USN pairs maintained by every replica server in Active Directory listing all other replicas for that site, and containing the highest USN received from each. During replication, a server sends its up-to-date vector to the initiating server, which uses it to filter propagated changes.

useful attribute sets In X.500, useful attribute sets provide a way of quickly adding a logical collection of attributes to support a specific functionality, such as postal addressing.

user attributes X.500 defines user attributes as those that represent the information a directory client would normally see; names, telephone numbers, and so on. User attributes do not include administrative data.

User Information Model The X.500 User Information Model describes the directory as a typical directory user would see it. The entire directory appears as one large tree with no boundaries and contains only user attributes.

User Principal Name (UPN) A UPN is an attribute of the Active Directory user object, and must be unique across the tree. UPNs have two parts: the UPN prefix which is the user logon name, and the UPN suffix which is the DNS name of the domain containing the user object.

Virtual Directory Service (VDS) A meta-directory service that does not store any data but rather acts as a front end that redirects queries to the connected directories.

Windows 2000 The first version of Microsoft's Windows network operating system that includes Active Directory.

Windows Internet Naming Service (WINS) WINS supplies NetBIOS name to IP address translation services for Windows NT networks.

writeable replica A replica that accepts updates, usually a master or a read/write.

X.500 A set of ISO/ITU specifications that define a distributed, network-independent directory service for the messaging systems described in the X.400 specification. Information, administrative, and security models as well as distributed operation methods, client and server protocols, and APIs are described in detail.

XDS XDS (open Directory Service) was initially developed by X/Open (now the Open Software Foundation) and the XAPI Association as a programmatic interface to X.500 DSAs, providing DAP functionality.

XMLDAP The iPlanet XMLDAP Directory Gateway's XML schema defines the XMLDAP markup language.

XSL Transformations (XSLT) An XML vocabulary designed to support the transformation of XML documents between different formats.

zone A single contiguous portion of the DNS tree, represented by a series of resource records stored in a zone file.

zone delegation Process by which a DNS name server is given authority for a particular zone.

zone file A zone file contains all data regarding a specific portion of the DNS directory—the specific set of resource records defining hosts, services, and so on, within that zone.

zone transfer The process whereby a secondary receives a complete copy of the zone information from an authoritative name server. A zone transfer transmits a copy of the resource records of a specific zone to the receiving (secondary) server.

INDEX

A

B

C

E

G

H

I

M

O

P

T

U

X-Y-Z